Annesley William Streane

The Book of the Prophet Jeremiah, Together with the Lamentations

With map, notes and introduction

Annesley William Streane

The Book of the Prophet Jeremiah, Together with the Lamentations
With map, notes and introduction

ISBN/EAN: 9783337037413

Printed in Europe, USA, Canada, Australia, Japan

Cover: Foto ©Lupo / pixelio.de

More available books at **www.hansebooks.com**

The Cambridge Bible for Schools.

GENERAL EDITOR :—J. J. S. PEROWNE, D.D.,
DEAN OF PETERBOROUGH.

THE BOOK OF THE PROPHET

JEREMIAH,

TOGETHER WITH THE

LAMENTATIONS,

WITH MAP NOTES AND INTRODUCTION

BY

THE REV. A. W. STREANE, M.A.

FELLOW OF CORPUS CHRISTI COLLEGE, CAMBRIDGE.

EDITED FOR THE SYNDICS OF THE UNIVERSITY PRESS

Cambridge:
AT THE UNIVERSITY PRESS.

London: CAMBRIDGE WAREHOUSE, 17, PATERNOSTER ROW.
Cambridge: DEIGHTON, BELL, AND CO.

1881

[All Rights reserved.]

Cambridge:
PRINTED BY C. J. CLAY, M.A.
AT THE UNIVERSITY PRESS.

PREFACE
BY THE GENERAL EDITOR.

THE General Editor of *The Cambridge Bible for Schools* thinks it right to say that he does not hold himself responsible either for the interpretation of particular passages which the Editors of the several Books have adopted, or for any opinion on points of doctrine that they may have expressed. In the New Testament more especially questions arise of the deepest theological import, on which the ablest and most conscientious interpreters have differed and always will differ. His aim has been in all such cases to leave each Contributor to the unfettered exercise of his own judgment, only taking care that mere controversy should as far as possible be avoided. He has contented himself chiefly with a careful revision of the notes, with pointing out omissions, with

PREFACE.

suggesting occasionally a reconsideration of some question, or a fuller treatment of difficult passages, and the like.

Beyond this he has not attempted to interfere, feeling it better that each Commentary should have its own individual character, and being convinced that freshness and variety of treatment are more than a compensation for any lack of uniformity in the Series.

DEANERY, PETERBOROUGH.

CONTENTS.

JEREMIAH.

		PAGES
I. INTRODUCTION.		
	Chapter I. Life and Times of Jeremiah	ix—xxv
	Chapter II. Character and Style of the Book...	xxv—xxx
	Chapter III. Contents and Arrangement	xxx—xxxviii
II. TEXT AND NOTES		1—352

LAMENTATIONS.

I. INTRODUCTION.
    Chapter I. Name, Position, Date and Structure of the Book .... 353—355
    Chapter II. Authorship of the Book .... 355—358
    Chapter III. Subject-matter and Purpose of the Book 359, 360

II. TEXT AND NOTES .... 361—391

APPENDIX.
    Note I. Traditions relating to Jeremiah .... 393—395
    Note II. Other Prophecies ascribed to Jeremiah.. 395, 396
    Note III. Jeremiah as a Type of Christ 396
    Note IV. Approximation to a chronological Arrangement of the Contents of the Book 396

INDEX... 397—404

MAP OF JERUSALEM.

_{*} The Text adopted in this Edition is that of Dr Scrivener's *Cambridge Paragraph Bible*. A few variations from the ordinary Text, chiefly in the spelling of certain words, and in the use of italics, will be noticed. For the principles adopted by Dr Scrivener as regards the printing of the Text see his Introduction to the *Paragraph Bible*, published by the Cambridge University Press.

"It is difficult to conceive any situation more painful than that of a great man, condemned to watch the lingering agony of an exhausted country, to tend it during the alternate fits of stupefaction and raving which precede its dissolution, and to see the symptoms of vitality disappear one by one, till nothing is left but coldness, darkness, and corruption."

LORD MACAULAY.

INTRODUCTION.

CHAPTER I.

LIFE AND TIMES OF JEREMIAH.

1. THE public life of Jeremiah, author of the Book which bears his name, embraces a period marked by political and social changes of no ordinary character, and the Book itself displays to us the circumstances and relations of the people of the time to a degree which the writings of none of the other prophets can approach. The events, of which the detailed narrative is here given, affected both the Jewish people, to whom it was his lot to declare the will of God, and the neighbouring nations, on whose relative strength and disposition, favourable or the reverse, then depended the prosperity and even the existence of Judaea as a nation. We shall therefore take in order

> The few notices which we possess of Jeremiah anterior to his call to public office as a prophet;
> The political condition of neighbouring nations, so far as it affected Judaea;
> The social condition of Judaea at the time of the prophet's call;
> His call and subsequent history.

2. *Notices of Jeremiah before his call to prophetic office.*

Chap. i. 1 gives us (*a*) his name, (*b*) his parentage, (*c*) his descent, and family dwelling-place.

(*a*) In the Hebrew his name takes the form Yirmyahu, or (shortened) Yirmya. Its meaning has not been reached with any certainty. Conjectures are,

i. that of Gesenius[1], 'appointed of Jehovah.'

ii. that of Hengstenberg[2], 'Jehovah throws,' thus tracing the origin of the word as a Jewish name to the opening of Moses' song of triumph (Exodus xv.) on the occasion of the overthrow of the Egyptians, 'the horse and his rider hath he *thrown* into the sea,' and further making the individual application in the prophet's case to be the work which (chap. i. 10) was specially given into his charge. "See, I have this day set thee over the nations, and over the kingdoms, to root out, and to pull down, and to destroy, and to throw down, to build, and to plant[3]."

iii. That of Simonis[4], 'exalted of the LORD;' i.e. (i) the LORD'S exalted one, 'Jehovah shall exalt,' or (ii) the LORD'S (i.e. the greatest) exaltation, compare Moses 'exceeding fair,' *marg.* fair to God (Acts vii. 20). This is at least as good as either of the former.

We have the name several times in the enumeration of David's mighty men.

(*b*) We are told (chap. i. 1) that Jeremiah was the son of Hilkiah. The same is the name of the high-priest, who in the eighteenth year of Josiah's reign, and therefore five years subsequently to Jeremiah's call (chap. i. 2), discovered the Book of the Law in the house of the Lord (2 Kings xxii. 8). Were we sure that these two notices refer to one and the same person, we could with more certainty picture to ourselves the character of Jeremiah's bringing up, and the nature of the influences which would be brought to bear upon him from the fact of his father's holding not only the chief position in religious matters but also the foremost place in the reforms instituted by Josiah. And although Hilkiah seems to have been not an uncommon name

---

[1] 'Jecit; id est, collocavit, constituit.' He refers it to a Chaldee root, occurring Dan. vii. 9, 'I beheld till the thrones were (cast down, A. V. or) *set*' (*Thesaurus*, sub v.).
[2] *Christologie des a. B.* (Clarke's Library), II. 361. "He who bore it (the name) was consecrated to that God who with an Almighty hand throws to the ground all His enemies."
[3] But see note on chap. i. 1.
[4] *Onomasticon*, p. 535.

at the time¹, there is some amount of probability in this conjecture. The respect with which the prophet was as a rule treated by the princes and by the successive kings of Judah (chaps. xxxvi. 19, 25, xxxviii. 8—10), as shewn in particular by the contrast between the treatment with which he met and that which fell to the lot of Urijah (chap. xxvi. 23, 24), accords with this view, as does the fact that Baruch, a man of good birth² and brother of Seraiah, who held high office in Zedekiah's court (chap. li. 29), was willing to be in his employ as scribe. The remaining part of the opening sentence of the Book of Jeremiah has indeed been adduced as an objection. For

(c) it is there stated that Jeremiah was (not only a priest, but) of the priestly city of *Anathoth*. The priests were not distributed over the country, but lived together in certain cities which with the lands in their neighbourhood had been assigned to their use. From thence they went up by turns to minister in the Temple at Jerusalem. Thus the religious instruction of the people in the country generally was left to the heads of families, until the establishment of synagogues, an event which did not take place till the return from the captivity, and which was the main source of the freedom from idolatry that became as marked a feature of the Jewish people thenceforward as its practice had been hitherto their great national sin.

Anathoth is mentioned as a city of the priests in Joshua xxi. 18. At the end of David's life also we read that Abiathar the highpriest, after the failure of Adonijah's attempt to obtain the throne of Israel, retired to Anathoth³. Now Abiathar's descent from Aaron was through Ithamar (this younger branch of Aaron's descendants seem to have possessed the office from the time of Eli to that of Abiathar only), while Hilkiah, the high-priest of Josiah's time, traced his lineage through Phinehas, son of Eleazar, the elder son of Aaron (1 Chron. vi. 4—13). Hence it has been inferred that Hilkiah would not be connected with

---

¹ Comp. chap. xxix. 3. Hilkiah, father of Gemariah an envoy sent by Zedekiah to Nebuchadnezzar.
² According to Josephus 'one of a very eminent family,' *Ant.*, x. 9 § 1 (Whiston's Edition, 1864).
³ 1 Kings ii. 26.

Anathoth. In reply, however, it has been pointed out that there is nothing to shew the impossibility or even improbability that descendants of *both* sons of Aaron should dwell in the same priestly town, and that it is even likely that the dominant family would secure for its high-priest a dwelling in a place so conveniently adjacent to Jerusalem[1]. And further we may notice that Hilkiah is not the only name which is common to the historical and to the prophetic record of these times. Shallum is uncle of Jeremiah (chap. xxxii. 7), and Shallum is also husband to Huldah the prophetess (2 Kings xxii. 14); and again, Ahikam the son of Shaphan, joined with Hilkiah the high-priest and others as one of Josiah's chief supporters in his work of external reformation, can scarcely be any other than Ahikam son of Shaphan, who in the reign of Jehoiakim protected Jeremiah, when the elders of the land were compassing his death.

Jeremiah speaks of himself at the time of his call as a child (chap. i. 6), and although the expression might be taken merely to signify a sense of incompetence for the work to which he was being summoned, yet it was probably not without a literal fitness, as we find him apparently in full vigour of manhood for the space of forty years from that date.

3. *The political condition of neighbouring nations so far as it affected Judaea.*

The position of Judaea exposed it to attack from Egypt on the one side, from the eastern empire of Nineveh on the other. It was not strong enough to cope with either of these without the countenance, if not active support, of the other kingdom, and therefore the problem which it had to solve was, with which of these it should throw in its lot. In the time of Isaiah,

---

[1] 'Anata,' on a broad ridge 1¼ hours N.N.E. from Jerusalem. The cultivation of the priests survives in tilled fields of grain with figs and olives. There are the remains of walls and strong foundations, and the quarries still supply Jerusalem with building stone. Grove, Art. in Smith's *Bibl. Dict.* It was discovered by Dr Robinson who tells us (*Researches*, 1. p. 437, 3rd edition) that it seems to have been a walled town and a place of strength, but is apparently not directly mentioned by any writer since the days of Jerome. His party found the fragments of a column or two among the ruins.

whose prophecies terminated in the reign of Hezekiah, that prophet had earnestly dissuaded his countrymen from an Egyptian alliance. "Woe to the rebellious children, saith the Lord...that walk to go down into Egypt and have not asked at my mouth; to strengthen themselves in the strength of Pharaoh, and to trust in the shadow of Egypt. Therefore shall the strength of Pharaoh be your shame, and the trust in the shadow of Egypt your confusion... For the Egyptians shall help in vain, and to no purpose" (Is. xxx. 1—7). The same in substance was said by Sennacherib, king of Assyria, to Hezekiah through his messenger Rabshakeh (Is. xxxvi. 5, 6). Hezekiah's reliance on God and his prayerful spirit were presently rewarded by the miraculous overthrow of Sennacherib's host (Is. xxxvii. 36) and the violent death, thirteen years later, of their leader, who was succeeded by his son Esarhaddon. This destruction of Sennacherib's army in the 14th year of Hezekiah (B.C. 693)[1] secured Judaea against the fate which had befallen the Northern kingdom at the hands of Shalmanezer. There was no important expedition made against Palestine during Esarhaddon's reign (B.C. 679—666) except that which he early undertook against Jerusalem in vengeance for his father's overthrow. This resulted in the removal of Manasseh, Hezekiah's son and successor, as a captive to Babylon[2]; but Manasseh was soon allowed to return, and seems to have been left in peace during the rest of his reign, Esarhaddon finding troubles nearer home quite sufficient to occupy his attention. His son Assurbanipal made expeditions into Egypt, which he divided into twelve small principalities, thus delivering Judaea from all present fear from that quarter. He is thought to have been 'the great and noble Asnapper' (Ezra iv. 10) who brought over various tribes and settled them in the cities of Samaria, but, although the king of Judah is mentioned in the recently-discovered Assyrian inscriptions, yet

---

[1] So Neteler in examination of Schrader's 'Die Keilinschriften und das Alte Testament' as quoted in the Introduction to the Book of Jeremiah in the *Speaker's Commentary*.

[2] Esarhaddon was the only king of Nineveh who lived at Babylon. This shews the accuracy of the sacred record. He dwelt there for the last eleven years of his life, and there died.

the Ninevite king would appear to have left Judaea undisturbed. Meanwhile Psammetichus reunited Egypt under his sovereignty, and during his long reign (B.C. 658—605) succeeded in making his country extremely formidable to its Jewish neighbour. In his time Manasseh died, Amon his son followed for two years, and was succeeded by his son Josiah, whose reign was marked by an outward reformation of morals and renewal of religious rites long in abeyance. In the 6th year of his reign the Scythians, who had marched into Palestine, were checked by Psammetichus and induced to return. Thus the Scythian incursion had made no real difference in the political position. Judaea was still wavering between the old established power of Egypt, whose prestige had been fully restored under Psammetichus, and the rapidly growing Eastern power, at present lodged at Nineveh, but soon to be transferred to Babylon.

The manner in which external nations affected Judaea in times subsequent to Jeremiah's call to be a prophet we shall trace later.

4. *The social condition of Judaea at the time of the prophet's call.* The religious reform of Hezekiah's time had been followed by a terrible reaction in the reign of Manasseh. "He built altars for all the host of heaven in the two courts of the house of the Lord" (2 Chron. xxxiii. 5), he set up an idol in the Temple itself and dedicated his sons to Moloch by making them pass through the fire in the valley of the son of Hinnom (ibid. ver. 6). His subsequent repentance, of which the Books of Chronicles tell us, seems to have come too late to have much permanent effect upon the ordering of the kingdom, and no improvement was likely under such a man as his son Amon shewed himself to be during his brief reign. This was the state of affairs when Josiah came to the throne. The land was now recovering from the effects of the frequent and destructive attacks of the Assyrian monarchs, and its continued rest in the earlier years of Josiah was in itself favourable to the plans of that king for his country's moral and spiritual welfare. With good advisers in Ahikam, Hilkiah and others, and with a nation probably more than half weary of idolatry

and its attendant evils, even before the alarm was sounded by the discovery of the lost Book of the Law, it was an opportunity not to be neglected for an attempt at the revival of religion such as Josiah undertook. And yet the reformation, as in the time of Hezekiah, seems not to have penetrated much below the surface. The picture which Jeremiah draws of the condition of the people, of the prevalence of dishonesty, of open licentiousness, of murder, adultery, false swearing, is such that never does there appear to have been more need than then of one who should convict men of their sins, and stir them to a sense of the requirements of the Divine Law.

5. *Jeremiah's call and subsequent history.* We cannot say whether Jeremiah at any period of his life received a formal training in the schools of the prophets instituted by Samuel and existing at Ramah, Bethel, Jericho, Gilgal, and elsewhere. They answered in some respects to our Theological Colleges, and the chief subjects of study were the Law, music and sacred poetry. The sacred narrative itself would suggest that Jeremiah, so far as human means went, was prepared for his work rather by the instruction and associations which he would have in Anathoth, and was thence called direct to the task of declaring the will of the Almighty to His disobedient people. In particular the discovery of the Book of the Law by Hilkiah, made a few years after Jeremiah's call, but apparently before he had entered upon his life's work, must have made much stir at his native town, as we know that it did in Jerusalem. Whatever portion of the five Books of Moses, as we now possess them, it may have contained, it must, we are sure, have included those graphic pictures which stand in Deut. xxviii. of the punishments which were to follow neglect of God and lapse into idolatry. That Book made upon Jeremiah a profound impression, of which we see the fruit in the references to and quotations from it which abound in his prophecies[1]. The

---

[1] Compare ii. 6 with Deut. xxxii. 10; v. 15 with Deut. xxviii. 49, etc.; vii. 33 with Deut. xxviii. 26; xi. 3 with Deut. xxvii. 26; xi. 4 with Deut. iv. 20; xi. 5 with Deut. vii. 12, 13; xv. 4, xxiv. 9, xxix. 18, xxxiv. 17 with Deut. xxviii. 25; xxii. 8, 9 with Deut. xxix. 24—26; xxiii. 17 with Deut. xxix. 18, etc.; xxxiv. 13, 14 with Deut. xv. 12.

solemn covenant entered into by the nation (2 Kings xxiii. 3) must have fixed itself deeply in his mind and heart. "The king went up into the house of the Lord... and all the people, both small and great; and he read in their ears all the words of the book of the covenant that was found in the house of the Lord. And the king stood by a pillar and made a covenant before the Lord, to walk after the Lord, and to keep his commandments... with all their heart and with all their soul... and all the people stood to the covenant." These solemn words and the no less significant acts that followed, contrasted as they were with the state of wickedness which existed around the prophet, wrought upon his mind that effect, which God employed as the means of calling forth his declarations of impending woe, and thus making him the typical prophet of sorrow, and a derivative from his name (jeremiad) a synonym for lamentation.

6. It was under such circumstances as these that the actual *call* occurred, and in a form evidently altogether unlooked for. It does not come to him in the shape of a vision of the Divine Majesty as to Isaiah (chap. vi.), or of the mysterious living creatures and wheels within wheels such as was given to Ezekiel (chap. i.), but without startling symbol or ecstatic trance the command is received. He shrinks from the prospect, not from fear of the innocent blood which the Jews, following the example of their late king Manasseh (2 Kings xxi. 16), "shed very much," but from honest distrust of his own power to take the lead and deal boldly and successfully with the evils of the day, gaining a hearing and producing an impression by the power of his language joined to the solemn import of his message. The Lord reassures him, touches his mouth, and sends him forth as His prophet to the nations. The visions, by which He strengthens his hands and suggests the burden of his prophecy, we shall treat in their place in chap. i.

7. Jeremiah now addresses himself to the impurity and crime which he sees around him. The worship of Baal and Astarte, and the unholy pleasures to which that worship ministered, were the subjects at once of bitter mourning and of stern rebuke.

The example of the Gentiles around stimulated the Jews to break through all restraint, and the sacrifice of their children to Moloch was but the attempt of an alarmed conscience to atone for other crimes. The restoration of the Temple and celebration of the Passover Jeremiah tells them are of no avail so long as their hearts are as foul as they were before. Nothing short of a complete amendment can avert the calamities of which they read in the newly discovered Book (vii. 4—7). Such was Jeremiah's teaching during the eighteen years which lay between his call and the death of Josiah. There is but little of incident to record during this period. He presented himself from time to time "rising early and speaking" (xxv. 3), and was exposed to "reproach and derision daily" (xx. 7). The men of Anathoth itself sought his life (xi. 21), and his brethren "dealt treacherously" with him (xii. 6). He is sometimes inclined to be silent and leave the world to take its course, seeing that he was but "a man of strife and a man of contention to the whole earth" (xv. 10). Towards the end of Josiah's reign the question arose whether he should side with the new Chaldaean power or with Egypt. Jeremiah declared for the former, and Josiah going forth in obedience probably to this decision of the prophet to arrest the progress of Pharaoh-nechoh, son of Psammetichus, who was marching against Chaldaea, was slain in battle at Megiddo.

8. Jehoahaz (the Shallum of chap. xxii. 11), Josiah's son and successor, reigned but three months. He was the second son of Josiah, and probably on account of his personal qualifications was raised to the throne in preference to the eldest son Jehoiakim. In accordance with the custom of all kings whose title was disputed, he was anointed with the holy oil, as though he were the founder of a new dynasty, and adopting what appears to have been another custom of that period (a custom which has been adopted also by the Popes) he assumed a new name (Jehoahaz = the Lord possesses), which was probably intended to serve as a charm or happy omen[1]. If so, it grievously failed of its object. In spite of the consequences of his father's opposition to Egypt he maintained

---

[1] Stanley's *Jewish Church*, II. 447.

the same policy, as is shewn by his being presently carried off by Pharaoh-nechoh to Riblah, while the land was put under tribute (2 Kings xxiii. 33). Although he did that which was evil in the sight of the Lord (ver. 32), Jeremiah speaks of him, as of his father, with kindness and sorrow. "Weep sore for him that goeth away, for he shall return no more, nor see his native country" (chap. xxii. 10).

9. Jehoiakim, another and elder (2 Chron. xxxvi. 2, 5) brother, was placed on the throne by the king of Egypt and reigned eleven years (according to the received chronology B.C. 609—597), during which period Jeremiah occupies a most important position. The favour of the court was no longer, as in the days of Josiah, and probably in those of Jehoahaz, on the side of the godly. Jehoiakim "did evil in the sight of the Lord" (2 Kings xxiii. 37). He laid exorbitant tribute upon the people of the land, already impoverished by war, and desired apparently to surpass even the palmy days of his predecessor Solomon in the magnificence of the palaces which should mark his reign and minister to his comfort. Forced labour, the exaction of which had produced much discontent even in Solomon's time (1 Kings xii. 4), excited still more indignation in the present condition of the people. Their new king's desire for his own glorification and neglect of the worship of God is the subject of a striking portion of Jeremiah's writings, viz. chap. xxvi., and also chap. xxii., "Woe to him that buildeth his house by unrighteousness, and his chambers by wrong; that useth his neighbour's service without wages, and giveth him not for his work: that saith, I will build me a wide house and large chambers, and cutteth him out windows; and it is ceiled with cedar and painted with vermilion" (xxii. 13, 14). The disregard of religion on the part of the king was thus the means of effecting a speedy separation between the true servants of God and the empty professors. The latter fall back into idolatry and wickedness; the former are refined by the adversity, and their faithfulness shines the more brightly.

10. Real and not pretended service is the lesson which Jeremiah in the above chapters enforces, and in so doing he

exasperates priests and false prophets alike by the very truth of the charges which he brings. They accuse him before the princes and people of disloyalty and demand his death; while he replies that the message does not consist of his own words, "*The Lord sent me* to prophesy against this house, and against this city, all the words that ye have heard" (xxvi. 11, 12). The judges, probably appointed in the days of Josiah, at any rate persons willing to deliver a righteous decision, gave the lie direct to the accusation, saying, 'this man is *not* worthy to die.' In so doing they followed the precedent adduced to them of Hezekiah's conduct towards the prophet Micah in a similar case, rather than conform to the arbitrary and cruel procedure of the present king in the murder of Urijah the prophet (xxvi. 17—24).

11. During the two years which followed, Jeremiah continued to declare the signs of the times, and to maintain in opposition to those who still advocated alliance with Egypt against Babylon, that the latter kingdom would assuredly prevail. He affirmed, as did Ezekiel later (Ezek. xxix. 18—20), that "all these lands are given into the hand of Nebuchadnezzar," the "servant" of God. He illustrated his words by the symbols of the moulding and remoulding of the potter's clay, and by the solemn breaking of an earthen vessel in the valley of Hinnom in presence of the chief of the priests and people (chaps. xviii. xix.). This excited the wrath of Pashur, son of Immer (to be distinguished from the son of Melchiah of chap. xxi.), who appears to have been like Jeremiah both priest and prophet, but who prophesied lies in the name of the Lord (chap. xx. 6). At his hands Jeremiah underwent ignominious treatment (chap. xx. 2), including apparently imprisonment for a time.

12. About this period occurred the first and partial fulfilment of his prophecies concerning the supremacy to be asserted by Babylon. In the 4th year of Jehoiakim's reign Nebuchadnezzar smote the army of Pharaoh-nechoh in Carchemish, an ancient fortress which commanded the passage of the river Euphrates (see note on chap. xlvi. 2)[1]. He then advanced into Palestine,

---
[1] Stanley's *Jewish Church*, II. 451.

driving many of its inhabitants to seek refuge within the walls of Jerusalem. Among others who thus came within reach of Jeremiah's words were the Rechabites, and this was accordingly the occasion of the interview which the prophet had with them, and from which he pointed a moral for his countrymen (chap. xxxv.). Nebuchadnezzar advanced to Jerusalem, and carried away Daniel and others as well as vessels from the Temple to Babylon (2 Chron. xxxvi. 6, 7; Dan. i. 1). Nebuchadnezzar's father Nabopolassar, joined with Cyaxares the Mede, as leader of the insurrection at Babylon, had just succeeded in overthrowing the ancient Empire of Nineveh, of which Assurbanipal, mentioned above (§ 3), was the last monarch. Nebuchadnezzar was in command of the army, and would doubtless have taken more effectual measures for the subjugation of Judaea, but for the report of his father's illness, which caused him to return hastily in order to secure his succession to the throne.

13. The Jews failed to profit by the warning which God thus granted them. In the course of the year following the withdrawal of Nebuchadnezzar, Jeremiah, himself hidden in some retreat from the wrath of the king which he knew would be excited by what he was about to do, sent Baruch his follower with a roll to be read in the Temple on a solemn feast day in the ears of all the people. The substance of it was reported to the king; the roll was fetched by his order, read before him, and in spite of the intercession of certain of the princes who were present, was burned piece by piece in the fire that was upon the hearth. Whereupon there was written by Baruch at the prophet's dictation and communicated to the king another roll containing in addition to the contents of the former a rebuke to him for his impious act and further announcements of God's coming vengeance. These words, though received by the king with a mixture of anger and contempt, had no doubt the effect which God designed in preserving the salt of the people during those evil times, and supporting them through the captivity which was approaching in the reign of Jehoiakim's two successors. So when Luther's books were publicly burned by order of the Papal Nuncio, the remark made to the Emperor Charles's ministers

was 'Do you imagine that Luther's doctrines are found only in those books that you are throwing into the fire? They are written where you cannot reach them, in the hearts of the nation[1].' To this time are most naturally to be referred Jeremiah's absence from Jerusalem, and the symbol of the linen girdle which he was commanded (chap. xiii.) to take to the river Euphrates and hide in a hole of the rock[2]. Jeremiah and Baruch would probably find it unsafe to return to Jerusalem for some years, in fact until towards the close of Jehoiakim's reign. The king received no more warnings. It would appear from the indignation and dismay with which Jeremiah's words were greeted, that up to that date the Chaldaeans had not actually come to Jerusalem. The time of judgment however at length arrived, and from the brief notices we have of this period, we can but gather that Jehoiakim after three years of unwilling payment as tribute of the money which he yearned to spend upon his own luxurious indulgences, rebelled against Babylon (2 Kings xxiv. 1), was attacked (Nebuchadnezzar being too much occupied to come in person) by numerous bands of Chaldaeans, Ammonites, Moabites, and Syrians, the subjects of Babylon (2 Kings xxiv. 2), and, probably in an engagement with some of these, came to a violent end and a dishonoured burial. His body was cast out and exposed ignominiously, dragged away and in accordance with Jeremiah's prophecy (xxii. 18, 19, where see notes; compare xxxvi. 30) buried with the burial of an ass beyond the gates of Jerusalem.

14. Jehoiachin (=Jeconiah, chaps. xxiv. 1, xxvii. 20, xxviii. 4, xxix. 2, and=Coniah, chaps. xxii. 24, 28, xxxvii. 1), son and successor of Jehoiakim, and set up by Nebuchadnezzar, reigned like Jehoahaz but three months (B.C. 597). At the end of that time, the city being besieged by Nebuchadnezzar, he yielded himself up. The king himself, the people of the land, except the poorest, the treasures of the Temple and of the king's house,

---

[1] D'Aubigné, Bk. VI. chap. XI. (White's Translation, Vol. II. p. 216).
[2] See further in the notes.

were taken to Babylon, where Jehoiachin was detained in prison for thirty-six years, till Evil-Merodach, son and successor of Nebuchadnezzar, released him. Of Jeremiah's prophecies undoubtedly belonging to this reign we have but a few sentences (xxii. 24—30).

15. Zedekiah (B.C. 597—586), who received this name in place of Mattaniah from Nebuchadnezzar (2 Kings xxiv. 17), differed much from Jehoiakim. He was well-meaning, but weak. As Nebuchadnezzar's nominee he was more inclined than his predecessors had been to listen to that doctrine of submission to the Babylonian power which Jeremiah preached. But on the other hand he had no real zeal for the service of God, and he was essentially vacillating in disposition, yielding now to the suggestions of the prophet, now to those of the princes of the people, who advocated resistance single-handed or in alliance with Egypt. It was as in the days described in Isaiah i. 21—23. Through the overthrow of lawful authority in the Chaldaean invasions, certain of the most energetic spirits got the rule of the city virtually into their own hands. Zedekiah did what he could for the preservation of Jeremiah, but was practically powerless against the stronger wills and more vigorous leaders opposed to him. To this time belongs the vision of the good and evil figs (chap. xxiv., where see notes). All the best and worthiest part of the nation had been carried captive. Those left were like the "naughty figs, which could not be eaten, they were so bad," and they also, the prophet announced, were shortly to be consumed from off the land. To this time belongs also chap. xxix., containing his letter of advice to the exiles, viz. to submit to their captivity and await restoration to their land. There was a false prophet at Babylon at this time, Shemaiah, who sought to stir up the priests and people at Jerusalem against Jeremiah as a madman. In another letter written at the same time Jeremiah foretells this man's punishment (xxix. 32).

16. At the beginning of the ninth year of Zedekiah a Chaldaean army approached Jerusalem. The wealthiest of the people, who had taken advantage of the prevailing distress to

make slaves of their brethren, consented under this pressure to release them. But on the departure of the besieging army to meet that of Pharaoh-Hophra, which was thought to be about to attempt to raise the siege, the princes withdrew this boon from those lately manumitted. To this withdrawal Zedekiah was opposed, but was, or considered himself to be, powerless to prevent it, while Jeremiah denounced in the strongest terms the act and those concerned in it, including the king (xxxiv. 17—22). The prophet had already several years previously appeared in the streets with a yoke upon his neck to symbolize the impending servitude of the nation; and when Hananiah, who prophesied deliverance, had broken the yoke, he received the sentence of speedy death at the mouth of Jeremiah, because he had "spoken rebellion against the Lord." It was natural for self-reliant irreligious men to be highly displeased with such acts and words as these, and now Jeremiah's attempt during the temporary absence of the Chaldaeans to go forth to Anathoth in order to obtain provisions[1] gave his enemies the opportunity they desired to seize and imprison him as a deserter. From this after "many days" he was delivered by Zedekiah, who gave him liberty and a daily supply of food (xxxvii. 21). Although still declaring the speedy overthrow of Jerusalem, he now also prophesied plainly of the future restoration, and like the Roman, the report of whose having purchased at full value the ground on which Hannibal's army was encamped, carried dismay to that general's heart (Livy, XXVI. 11), he gave practical proof of his belief in the brighter days in store for his countrymen[2]. But the captains, unmoved by the distant visions of hope, again seized him, Zedekiah shewing once more his weakness (chap. xxxviii. 5). Each house in Jerusalem had a cistern for storing up water to be used in the dry season. Into one of these, damp and miry as it was, they let down the prophet, who was

[1] See the note on chap. xxxvii. 12.
[2] His purchase of a portion of a field for seventeen shekels (about £2. 2s. 6d. but representing a much larger amount according to the present value of money) shews that Jeremiah could not even then have been in needy circumstances.

rescued by Ebedmelech an Ethiopian eunuch. Another interview, first with the feeble-minded king, and then with Pashur (not the one mentioned chap. xx.) and with Zephaniah, effects no change in the position of affairs, and in the 11th year of Zedekiah the city is sacked, the Temple burnt, and he and his attendants taken prisoners while in the act of flight. Zedekiah is taken to Riblah on the northern frontier of Palestine, his sons are slain in his presence, and his eyes being then put out, he is immured in a dismal dungeon.

17. As for Jeremiah, Nebuzar-adan, captain of the guard, receives a special charge concerning his welfare (chap. xxxix. 11, 12), and having been recognised among the prisoners of war at Ramah a village about five miles from Jerusalem, he is offered his choice of remaining under the new governor of Judaea, Gedaliah, or living in an honourable captivity at Babylon. Gedaliah was of a family friendly to Jeremiah. He was son of Ahikam, and grandson of Shaphan, the friend of Hilkiah the highpriest, and perhaps identical with Hilkiah the father of the prophet[1]. Within two months however Gedaliah was murdered by Ishmael a prince of the blood royal. Many were slain. Jeremiah was probably among the prisoners, who while being carried off by Ishmael were rescued by Johanan. This last was one of those warlike captains who, as we saw, had sprung up during the later years of the kingdom. The prophet in vain warned the people against going down into Egypt, and foretold the want and misery which would ensue, if they disobeyed. The expectation of security from war and famine (chap. xlii. 14) prevailed; they forced Jeremiah to accompany them, and from Tahpanhes, a town near the eastern border of Lower (= Northern) Egypt, we draw the last certain notices that we possess of his life. He declares that Nebuchadnezzar's throne shall be set up there at the entry of Pharaoh's house (chap. xliii. 10), and (chap. xliv.) makes a dying protest against the idolatry of his countrymen, and their wanton worship of the moon ("the queen of heaven"). We have no notice in Scripture of his death.

---

[1] See above, § 2.

'The noble form of Jeremiah, the greatest of all the historical and literary prophets, fades from our sight together with the monarchy. In misery and continual peril of death he witnessed the fall of the State and the destruction of Jerusalem;—he survived it, but in the silent tomb of an alien land[1].'

For traditions, &c., concerning Jeremiah and for the prophet considered as a type of Christ, see Appendix.

CHAPTER II.

CHARACTER AND STYLE OF THE BOOK.

1. Jeremiah is personally the most interesting to us of all the prophets, because, unlike the others, he shews us the inmost recesses of his mind. The various qualities which made up the man are quickly and easily gathered from his own lips. There is hardly a clearer illustration of the Providence of God in raising up men for special sorts of work than is afforded by Jeremiah. We have just seen that they were no ordinary times in which he lived. 'The snake' of idolatry had been 'scotched not killed' by Hezekiah and Josiah. The spirit of disobedience and rebellion, which had been so long working in his countrymen, was now past remedy by all common means. Nothing but the nation's total overthrow, at least for a time, could effect a radical cure.

2. Glowing appeals, such as had been made by an Isaiah, a Hosea, a Micah in former days, would now have been of no avail. Those prophets had fulfilled their task, and the Holy Spirit had employed their special gifts for the work which belonged to their age. Jeremiah's office on the other hand was to utter and reiterate the warning, though sensible all the while that the sentence of condemnation was passed and would speedily be put into execution. It was not for him as for those who had preceded him to proclaim the certainty of God's protection, to urge resistance to the foe, to present scarce any but bright pictures of the future. Hopes like these, bestowed through

---

[1] Bunsen's *God in History* (Winkworth and Stanley), Vol. I. p. 67.

Isaiah, had since been forfeited, and now hardly anything remains save to mourn the downfall of the kingdom, to point again and yet again to the canker that had eaten out the vitals of the nation.

3. Such a task as this demanded one who, however weak in body, should be a man of rare courage, unterrified by popular clamour or princely disfavour, fixed in resolve, and thoroughly devoted to the ascertained will of God. He needed not natural gifts of oratory. His work was not to persuade, but rather to testify, to express the thoughts of the few remaining pious ones of the nation, not to gain the ear or influence the hearts of the abandoned crowd. The wearing effect of constant failure, the intense pain of seeing his nation advance step by step on the road to its overthrow, his powerlessness to avert the evils which he saw impending, the hostility and abuse which it was his daily lot to bear from those whom he sought to warn, a solitary life and prohibition of marriage[1]—these required as a counterpoise a heroic spirit that should not shrink from the encounter, as well as ceaseless devotion to Him whose commission he had borne even from the womb[2].

4. And yet he was naturally of a shy and timid disposition, shrinking from public life, deprecating all possibility of prophesying in God's name[3]. And after he had entered upon his work, his naturally desponding mind would suggest not only that the message he bore was a sad one, but that he had not had afforded him the proofs—the credentials which marked a true prophet—such as were granted to his predecessors. No miracle was wrought to attest his words. No prediction was fulfilled with speed, so as to indicate the solidity of his claims. On the contrary "the word of the Lord was a reproach to him, and a derision daily[4]."

5. At times he seems to have well-nigh despaired not only of success but of life itself. "Woe is me, my mother, that thou hast borne me a man of strife and a man of contention to the

---

[1] Chap. xvi. 2. [2] Chap. i. 5.
[3] Chap. i. 6.   [4] Chap. xx. 7.

whole earth!...every one of them doth curse me[1]." Immediately afterwards he contrasts the joy in which, inspired no doubt by the promises given him[2], he had entered upon the prophetic office, with the disheartening reception that awaited him. "Thy words were found and I did eat them; and thy word was unto me the joy and rejoicing of my heart...Why is my pain perpetual and my wound incurable, which refuseth to be healed?" Such is the bitterness of his sufferings that on one occasion we find him relating his resolve to keep silence. "The word of the Lord was made a reproach unto me and a derision daily. Then I said, I will not make mention of him, nor speak any more in his name: but his word was in mine heart as a burning fire shut up in my bones, and I was weary with forbearing, and I could not stay[3]."

6. Belonging to the orders both of Priest and Prophet, and living at the very time when each had sunk to its lowest state of degradation, he was compelled to submit to the buffeting which they each bestowed upon a man who was by his every word and deed passing sentence upon themselves. He saw them permitted to vent their rage upon his person, he saw them held in esteem by the people, their way prospering, those that dealt treacherously happy. "For the greater part of his mission he 'had no man likeminded with him.' From the first moment of his call he was alone, amidst a hostile world[4]." But through it all conscientious devotion to duty maintained its place within his heart. The promise that he should be as a brasen wall made at the time of his call[5] and renewed later[6] never failed him.

7. Jeremiah has been likened to several characters in profane history—to Cassandra, the Trojan prophetess, whose fate it was never to be believed, though prophesying nothing but the truth; to Phocion, the rival of Demosthenes in the last generation of Athenian greatness, who maintained the unpopular but sound doctrine that, if Athens were to escape worse evils, she must submit peaceably to the growing power of Macedon; to Dante,

---

[1] Chap. xv. 10.
[2] Chap. i. 10, 18.
[3] Chap. xx. 8, 9.
[4] Stanley's *Jewish Church*, II. 439.
[5] Chap. i. 18.
[6] Chap. xv. 20.

whose native state, Florence, was in relation to France and the Empire as Palestine was to Egypt and Babylon, while the poet like the prophet could only protest without effect against the thickening ills.

8. His style corresponds closely with what we should expect from his character. It displays

(*a*) Absence of ornament. This thoroughly befits his inartificial nature. He is not only pre-eminently the prophet of sorrow, but, as shrinking from anything like display of himself, and full of humility as of zeal for God's honour, he naturally was led to the simplest form of words to express the painful images which ever held possession of his thoughts. In him the glowing language and vivacity which characterize Isaiah's writings have no place, and while his style has a beauty of its own, it has at its best a shade of sadness, and its fervour, when it rises to such, is the fervour of expostulation or grief.

(*b*) Frequent repetition. This also is to be expected, inasmuch as the main subject, on which he is charged to deliver himself, is the same throughout. However manifold the images by which he illustrates the thought, however varied the intensity with which he regards it, the sins to be denounced and the penalties foretold are in the main identical[1].

[1] Chap. ii. 28 repeated in xi. 13.
,, v. 9, 29 ,, ix. 9.
,, vi. 13—15 ,, viii. 10—12.
,, vii. 14 ,, xxvi. 6.
,, x. 12—16 ,, li. 15—19.
,, xi. 20 ,, xx. 12.
,, xv. 2 ,, xliii. 11.
,, xvi. 14, 15 ,, xxiii. 7, 8.
,, xvii. 25 ,, xxii. 4.
,, xxiii. 19, 20 ,, xxx. 23, 24.
,, xxx. 11 ,, xlvi. 28.
,, xxxi. 35, 36 ,, xxxiii. 25, 26.

List of places in which the same thought or image is repeated—
The brasen wall, chap. i. 18, xv. 20.
The turned back, ii. 27, vii. 24, xxxii. 33.
Fury that burns like fire, iv. 4, xxi. 12.
The travailing woman, iv. 31, vi. 24, xiii. 21, xxii. 23, xxx. 6.

(c) Frequent cases of coincidence in language with earlier prophets, as well as especially with the Book of Deuteronomy. Of this also we may easily perceive the reason. It was natural that one daily exposed to so much obloquy for the nature of his predictions should be anxious to vindicate himself by shewing that there was no break, no want of harmony, between himself and the older prophets, that what he maintained was the same that they had ever maintained, viz. that idolatry and national crimes entailed national overthrow[1]. The newly-discovered Book of the Law would, we might well expect, supply him with many examples of this teaching.

(d) Numerous images used by way of illustration. But here we notice a peculiar mingling of the image and the thing signified by it. Jeremiah's vehemence and rapidity of thought are so great, that before he has done more than present us with a portion of the figure, he dismisses it, and falls back upon the subject itself. Thus e.g. (chap. i. 15) he speaks of the attack of hostile nations upon Jerusalem under the guise of judges sitting in the

Rising up early, vii. 13, 25, xi. 7, xxv. 3, 4, xxvi. 5, xxix. 19, xxxii. 33, xxxv. 14, 15, xliv. 4.
Water of gall, viii. 14, ix. 15, xxiii. 15.
The incurable wound, xv. 18, xxx. 12.
The figs too bad to be eaten, xxiv. 8, xxix. 17..

Phrases which often recur—
Walking in the stubbornness of the heart, chap. iii. 17, vii. 24, ix. 14, xi. 8, xiii. 10, xvi. 12, xxiii. 17.
The evil of men's doings, iv. 4, xxi. 12, xxiii. 2, 22, xxv. 5, xxvi. 3, xliv. 22.
The voice of mirth and the voice of gladness, the voice of the bridegroom and the voice of the bride, vii. 34, xvi. 9, xxv. 10, xxxiii. 11.
Men dying in the siege by the sword, by the pestilence, and by famine, xiv. 12, 15, 16, xv. 2, xviii. 21, xxi. 7, 9, xxiv. 10, xxvii. 13, xxix. 17, xxxii. 24, 36, xxxiv. 17, xxxviii. 2, xlii. 17, 22, xliii. 11, xliv. 13. (Taken with slight additions from the *Speaker's Commentary*.)

[1] Parallels between Jeremiah and older books, exclusive of those supplied by Deuteronomy, which have been already given (Introd. chap. i. § 5), are Is. iv. 2, xi. 1 with Jer. xxiii. 5, 6, xxxiii. 15; Is. xiii., xlvii. with Jer. l., li.; Is. xv. with Jer. xlviii.; Is. xl. 19, 20 with Jer. x. 3—5; Is. xlii. 16 with Jer. xxxi. 9; Hos. viii. 13 with Jer. xiv. 10; Ps. lxxix. 6 with Jer. x. 25; Ps. cxxxv. 7 with Jer. x. 13. (See Art. *Jeremiah* in Sm. *Bibl. Dict.*).

city gates for judgment. But no sooner has he indicated the simile, than he returns to language not of judgment but of war[1].

In regard to variations of style within the Book itself, the prophet shews more calmness and uniformity of tone in the earlier parts; the latter have more traces of individual suffering.

9. The Hebrew of Jeremiah displays a considerable number of words and grammatical forms, which do not belong to the language in its purer state. For his use of the species of cypher, or secret writing, called Atbash, see notes on chaps. xxv. 26, li. 1.

10. Jeremiah's style, however it may form a contrast with that of Isaiah and others, is yet truly poetical. 'If we compare Jeremiah's land with the fruitful Carmel and cedar-forest of Isaiah, it is a waste, but a poetic waste, and a true image of the melancholy state of things, which lay before his eyes[2].' 'He is certainly the greatest poet of desolation and sorrow, because he most deeply feels them[3].'

CHAPTER III.

CONTENTS AND ARRANGEMENT.

1. The prophecies of Jeremiah cover, as we have seen, a period of at least some thirty years. But when we proceed to read the Book in which they and the events which accompanied them are contained, we find that the order of arrangement is not that of time. Prophecies uttered in the reign of Zedekiah occur in the midst of those that relate to Jehoiakim. The Jewish captives carried to Babylon by Nebuchadnezzar are addressed in words of comfort, several chapters earlier than the announcement made to Jehoiakim that that event is imminent, while the prophecies which chiefly form the later portion of the Book and relate to foreign nations (chaps. xlvi.—li.), were most or all

---

[1] A similar characteristic is found chaps. iii. 1, vi. 3—5, 27—30, xxii. 6, xxv. 16, where see notes.
[2] Umbreit quoted in *Speaker's Commentary*.   [3] Ibid.

of them delivered before the final overthrow of the city and kingdom.

2. So far as any order is observable, it is an order not of time but of subject-matter. The following is a summary of the contents of the Book.

(i) Chaps. i.—xlv. Prophecies mainly relating to home events and history of the times.

(ii) Chaps. xlvi.—li. Prophecies relating to foreign nations.

(iii) Chap. lii. Supplementary and historical.

(i) may be subdivided thus:—

(*a*) Chaps. i.—xx. Prophecies mostly from the time of Jeremiah's call (13th year of Josiah) to the 4th year of Jehoiakim.

(*b*) Chaps. xxi.—xxv. 14. Prophecies directed at various times against the kings of Judah and against the false prophets.

(*c*) Chap. xxv. 15—38. A kind of summary of the fuller predictions against foreign nations which occur chaps. xlvi.—li.; perhaps placed here as suggested by the announcement of the approaching overthrow of Babylon, which ends (*b*).

(*d*) Chaps. xxvi.—xxviii. Prophecies concerning the fall of Jerusalem, with historical notices interspersed. These belong to different periods of Jeremiah's life, and seem grouped together here in accordance with the principle of arrangement mentioned above.

(*e*) Chap. xxix. Letter and message to the captives in Babylon.

(*f*) Chaps. xxx., xxxi. Prophecies mainly of comfort and hope.

(*g*) Chaps. xxxii.—xliv. History of the two years preceding the capture and destruction of Jerusalem by the Chaldaeans, and the prophecies of Jeremiah during that time. Chaps xxxv., xxxvi. break the chronological order here.

(*h*) Chap. xlv. A supplementary notice on the part of Baruch.

(ii) may be subdivided thus:—

(*a*) Chap. xlvi. 1. Superscription.

(*b*) Chap. xlvi. 2—28. Against Egypt.

(*c*) Chap. xlvii. Against the Philistines.

(*d*) Chap. xlviii. Against Moab.

(*e*) Chap. xlix. 1—6. Against Ammon.

(*f*) Chap. xlix. 7—22. Against Edom.
(*g*) Chap. xlix. 23—27. Against Damascus.
(*h*) Chap. xlix. 28—33. Against Kedar and Hazor.
(*i*) Chap. xlix. 34—39. Against Elam.
(*j*) Chaps. l., li. Against Babylon.

3. Such being the arrangement of the contents, we have now to enquire whether we have any clue which will guide us in an attempt to explain it. Such a clue is to be found in chap. xxxvi. We there read, as we have noticed already[1], that Baruch writes (ver. 2) in a roll Jeremiah's prophecies "against Israel and against Judah, and against all the nations" from the days of Josiah till the present (4th) year of Jehoiakim. When this roll was burned by the king, Baruch wrote another at the dictation of Jeremiah, as before, containing all the words of the previous one, while "there were added unto them many like words" (ver. 32). This therefore gives us the nucleus of the present Book, although the portion which precedes this part of the narrative, as we have it, cannot have been wholly contained in the roll which Baruch then wrote. Chap. xiii. (see notes there) belongs in all probability to the very end of Jehoiakim's reign or even to that of his successor. Chaps. xxi. and xxiv. also belong to the days of Zedekiah, as do chaps. xxvii.—xxxiv.

4. It appears then that Jeremiah, like other prophets, wrote or caused to be written by his scribe groups of prophecies either as he uttered them, or after some lapse of time. The title to the Book (chap. i. 1—3) next suggests to us by the peculiar form which it assumes, something of the way in which this was done. If we compare it with the Introduction to other prophecies, e.g. Isaiah or Hosea, we shall see not only that it differs from them in form, but that the difference is of a kind that implies repeated alteration from the original shape. Verses 1, 2 might very well be the heading of a prophecy including only the utterances of Josiah's reign. Verse 3 is evidently an addition

---

[1] Chap. i. § 13.

made when a further group was added, and even as it stands does not include that part of the history of the Book which belongs to the period after the overthrow of the Jewish kingdom. It is most probable therefore that at some earlier period than that treated of in chap. xxxvi. Jeremiah had written one or more groups of predictions, which would all no doubt be incorporated by him with the new matter contained in the roll of chap. xxxvi.

5. Again, by the close of Zedekiah's reign, much new matter was ready to be introduced into the Book. If we ask why this was not done in the chronological order that we might expect, the answer is to be found in the history of the period. At the very time that the collection of which the roll (chap. xxxvi.) consisted was made, Jeremiah was a prisoner, and presently had to fly for his life. He did not return to Jerusalem for some years. Secrecy had to be observed during this period, and in fact we have no prophecy of Jeremiah in the Book until the Chaldaeans' approach at the end of Jehoiakim's reign. Again, after the troubles and imprisonment which befel him during the reign of Zedekiah, on the capture of the city Jeremiah was taken in chains to Ramah, and though presently set free, yet by the death of Gedaliah and the forced flight into Egypt, followed probably by a speedy and violent death there, he would be hindered from an orderly arrangement of the whole Book of his prophecies. Accordingly the fulfilment of this duty, as we may suppose, fell to his trusty follower Baruch. Thus we find in the Book, as we now have it, certain portions of Jeremiah's later prophecies (e.g. chaps. xiii., xxi., etc.) inserted in the earlier roll; we find also the history connected with the last years of the kingdom, and the events which immediately followed, and the prophecy addressed by Jeremiah to Baruch himself (chap. xlv.).

6. We cannot, however, think Baruch to have been in any sense the author of the Book. The very words of that chapter, which is so strictly personal to himself (xlv., see especially ver. 5), shew what a gulf he felt to lie between him and his master. This feeling seems to be that which prevented him from venturing upon any thing like an *elaborate* arrangement of the

contents, much less upon an addition of any matter on his own responsibility[1]. Even if we grant (although it seems doubtful) that the 52nd chapter was added by Baruch, this does not constitute an exception to the statement made above, inasmuch as chapter 51 ends with words introduced specially to guard against any identification of the writer of the final one with the prophet. Lastly, if Baruch had felt himself empowered to add on his own authority to the words of Jeremiah, he would surely have given us an account of an event of such deep interest to himself and his readers as the prophet's death. 'Plainly there was a clearly defined distinction between the words of a prophet and those of the uninspired man[2].'

7. Thus then the very lack of order, if we may say so, which is displayed here, serves a valuable end in shewing that we possess the words of Jeremiah put together in those same troublous times in the course of which they were spoken, not arranged with the care and method which would have been afterwards employed to remodel and fit them to men's notions of propriety. It is not the Book of Jeremiah edited by a future generation, but his words, as they fell from the inspired lips themselves, that are thus in God's Providence preserved to us.

8. The question of which we have just treated, how far the Book of Jeremiah, as we now have it, gives us the *exact* words of the prophet himself, is closely connected with another, which we cannot omit to notice. It is well known that the earliest existing translation of the Old Testament is that made into Greek[3] for the use of the Jews and others, speaking that tongue, who lived at Alexandria in Lower Egypt (about B.C. 277). This translation for the most part adheres with tolerable fidelity to the Hebrew as we now possess it. But the Book of Jeremiah presents in places so startling an exception to this rule, that some

---

[1] The same is shewn by the style, which is so markedly the same throughout the Book.
[2] See *Speaker's Commentary*, p. 323, and for the explanation given above of the lack of order, p. 322.
[3] Commonly called the Septuagint, or LXX., from the number of translators said to have been employed for the purpose by Ptolemy Philadelphus.

INTRODUCTION. xxxv

have been induced to enquire, which is to be followed? Can it be that the Greek is in this case the more correct, and that the Hebrew represents a later edition of the writings of the prophet?

9. Looking first at the facts of the case we find

(*a*) that in the LXX., as compared with the Hebrew, there are very few additions, but an immense number of trifling omissions besides some of more importance. On the whole in the LXX. about one-eighth part of the text as it stands in the Hebrew is wanting. There is besides a certain amount of alteration of passages, affecting the sense.

(*b*) The arrangement of the prophecies against foreign nations differs in the two. In the LXX. instead of coming near the end of the Book (chaps. xlvi.—li.) they stand after chap. xxv. 13, and therefore before the section of kindred subject-matter which begins chap. xxv. 14. Also their order of sequence among themselves differs. See § 13 below.

10. This difference between the Hebrew and Greek forms of the Book existed in the time of Origen. In his Epistle to Africanus (p. 56, Migne Edition), he speaks of Jeremiah as a book 'in which we found much transposition and alteration of the words of the prophecies.' It is clear however (and this is an important point to notice) that it is not a case of two independent collections of Jeremiah's writings, since then the differences would extend over the whole work with tolerable evenness, instead of being confined in great measure to certain parts of it, and further (as a German commentator[1] remarks) we should not find the peculiar form of Introduction to the Book (noticed above) virtually the same, and chap. lii. added in both. Besides both forms of the Book must have existed very early, for, as soon as one authoritative form became known (a thing which would naturally take place in a very brief period with a prophet so illustrious and honoured as Jeremiah was in the eyes of his banished countrymen), no other differing to the extent that the

---

[1] Graf, *Einleitung*, lvi.

Greek form differs could venture to compete with it. Still there is sufficient difference to make it interesting to enquire, which text represents Jeremiah's own arrangement most truly.

11. Some[1] maintain the claims of the LXX., others[2] those of the Hebrew[3].

By the former is pleaded:

(*a*) That the earlier position of the prophecies directed against foreign nations is that which they are more likely to have occupied in Jeremiah's roll (compare the words of xxv. 13). To this it may be replied that Jeremiah himself or Baruch might well have deemed the end of the Book the fitting place for them, written as they may have been on separate parchments, and by this position leaving the prophecies which had to do with the Jews themselves distinct and preceding them. See further, however, in note on xxv. 13.

(*b*) That chaps. xxix. 16—20, xxxiii. 14—26, xxxix. 4—13, lii. 28—30 and some shorter passages do not occur in the LXX., and are not of a character to be accidentally omitted. For remarks on these see notes.

(*c*) That chap. xxix. 26 (last words of verse) introduces in Hebrew a Kabalistic mode of naming (omitted in LXX.) which Jeremiah would not have made use of. See note on verse for reply.

By the latter is pleaded:

Either (*a*) The arbitrary character of the renderings in the LXX. So Graf[4], "After the innumerable instances given above of the arbitrariness and capriciousness of the Alexandrian translator it is altogether impossible to give his new edition—for one can scarcely call it a translation—any critical authority, or to draw from it any conclusion as to the Hebrew text having ever

---

[1] e.g. Michaelis, Movers, Hitzig, Bleek.
[2] e.g. St Jerome, and many others in ancient times; among moderns, Ewald, Hävernick, Keil, and others.
[3] For further remarks on the respective claims of Heb. and LXX., see note on chap. xxv. 13.
[4] *Einleitung*, lvi., translated as above in *Speaker's Commentary*.

existed in a different form from that in which we have it at present."

Or (*b*) That, without bringing any such charge of arbitrariness against the Greek translator, the general nature of the omissions (about 2700 words in all) points to the conclusion that necessity for haste, not caprice, was the motive. The omissions here spoken of are such as do not curtail the sense, viz. the words 'the prophet' after 'Jeremiah,' the words 'saith the LORD,' or any such expression as 'the LORD of hosts, the God of Israel,' instead of simply 'the LORD.' On the death of Jeremiah, which seems to have occurred soon after Baruch had been forcibly conveyed to Egypt, the latter, both in deference to the opinion of his master and through dislike of the princes (chap. xliii. 3), who had brought him there, would desire to return. Several persons may then have been employed to transcribe in all haste, probably on more than one parchment roll, the original words which Baruch would undoubtedly wish to bring back to Palestine with himself. There occur in the course of the Book but few omissions which may not be explained on this hypothesis, which is that of Dean Payne Smith[1]. The LXX. is simply the Greek translation of this the authoritative form of the Book among the Egyptian exiles. Finally the frequency of intercourse between Egypt and Palestine caused the speedy addition of chap. lii. to the text possessed by the former.

12. Such a conjecture, in a matter which cannot but be obscure, is perhaps as good a one as can be offered. At any rate we find that Ezra and the men of the 'great Synagogue,' to whose labours we owe in so large a measure the determination of the Canon of the Old Testament, deliberately adopted the Hebrew form of the Book in preference to the Greek. That therefore is the form which had authority for the Jews of Palestine, and through them has now authority for us.

13. The following Table shews how, as has been said above in § 9 (*b*), the order of succession of the prophecies against foreign nations differs in the two.

[1] *Speaker's Commentary*, Vol. v. p. 324.

Hebrew.	Septuagint.
xlix. 34—39 (Elam).	xxv. 14—18.
xlvi. (Egypt).	xxvi.
l. (Babylon).	xxvii.
li. (Babylon).	xxviii.
xlvii. (Philistines).	xxix. 1—7.
xlix. 7—22 (Edom).	,, 7—23.
,, 1—6 (Ammon).	xxx. 1—5.
,, 28—33 (Kedar and Hazor).	,, 6—11.
,, 23—27 (Damascus).	,, 12—16.
xlviii. (Moab).	xxxi.

Thereupon the LXX. (chap. xxxii., etc.) takes up the Heb. chap. xxv. 15, etc.

THE BOOK OF THE PROPHET
JEREMIAH.

CHAP. I. 1—3. *Words of Introduction.*

THE words of Jeremiah the son of Hilkiah, of the priests 1
that *were* in Anathoth in the land of Benjamin: to 2

CHAP. I. 1—3. WORDS OF INTRODUCTION.

1. *The words of Jeremiah*]˙ A more common introduction to the prophetical books is "the word of the Lord." Certain Jewish commentators have suggested that a different phrase is used here because the words which follow are not confined to prophecies, but contain as well many notices of the personal history of Jeremiah. This reason would apply also to the opening words of the prophet Amos, where we find a phrase similar to that used here, and again to the opening of Ecclesiastes, in which book the Preacher gives various particulars of his life.

Jeremiah] For speculations on the meaning of the name, see Introduction chap. i. § 2. The derivation proposed by Hengstenberg "Jehovah throws" is unlikely inasmuch as the ill omen which it suggests is hardly in accordance with the fact that the name was far from uncommon. Some other Jeremiahs are mentioned in the Bible, viz.: (1) the father-in-law of Josiah (2 Kings xxiii. 31); (2) the head of a house in Manasseh (1 Chron. v. 24); (3, 4, 5) three mighty men in David's army (1 Chron. xii. 4, 10, 13); (6) the head of a priestly course (Neh. x. 2, xii. 1, 12); (7) the father of Jaazaniah, the Rechabite (Jer. xxxv. 3).

the son of Hilkiah] The small number of proper names among the Jews rendered it necessary to add the father's name for purposes of distinction. Compare the Welsh custom ap-Thomas, ap-Richard, etc. If we were to render by Ben-Hilkiah we should no longer be in danger of connecting the words that follow with Hilkiah rather than with the name of the prophet himself.

Anathoth] See Introduction, chap. i. § 2 (*c*).

Benjamin] The territory of this tribe was 26 miles in length by 12 in breadth, and was thus about the size of the county of Middlesex. It was bounded on the south by Judah, on the north by Ephraim, and was

whom the word of the LORD came in the days of Josiah the son of Amon king of Judah, in the thirteenth year of his reign. It came also in the days of Jehoiakim the son of Josiah king of Judah, unto the end of the eleventh year of Zedekiah the son of Josiah king of Judah, unto the carrying away of Jerusalem captive in the fifth month.

4—10. *Jeremiah's Call.*

Then the word of the LORD came unto me, saying,

---

for the most part hilly, being crossed by deep ravines which, mounting from the Philistine country on the west, descend precipitously into the valley of the Jordan on the east. The tribe of Benjamin is noteworthy as having supplied the first of the Jewish kings, as well as his namesake "Saul, who is also called Paul," the great Apostle of the Gentiles.

2. *came*] **was.** The Hebrew implies more than one Divine communication.

in the days of, etc.] For this and the following verse, as in all probability repeatedly altered from the original shape, see Introduction, chap. iii. § 4.

in the thirteenth year of his reign] According to the ordinary reckoning, B.C. 629, or perhaps two years later. Josiah had the year before (2 Chron. xxxiv. 3) commenced his reforms. These words, as forming part of the original heading of Jeremiah's prophecies, strictly speaking include only ch. i. 5—iii. 5, there being afterwards many prophecies which refer to other parts of Josiah's reign. Preserved, therefore, through the changes made in the title, they serve to illustrate the alterations which it has undergone. The period included in these two verses is one of 40½ years, viz. the latter part of Josiah's reign = 18 years; that of Jehoahaz = 3 months; that of Jehoiakim = 11 years; that of Jehoiachin = 3 months; that of Zedekiah = 11 years. The omission of the names of Jehoahaz and Jehoiachin is probably due to the shortness of their reigns.

3. *in the fifth month*] In this month took place the burning of the city by Nebuzaradan, Nebuchadnezzar's captain. The walls of the city also were then broken down. It had been captured in the preceding month (2 Kings xxv. 4, 8—10). The mourning appointed to take place in the fifth month in memory of the overthrow is mentioned in Zechariah (vii. 3).

4—10. JEREMIAH'S CALL.

4. *Then the word, etc.*] Here, in accordance with what has been said above, we revert from the title in its present form, adapted and re-adapted to the later prophecies, to the words which doubtless originally introduced the utterance of "the days of Josiah...in the thirteenth year of his reign" (*v.* 2). They are at once Jeremiah's plea and his support, the credentials of his mission to which he might refer the people when

Before I formed thee in the belly I knew thee; and before 5
thou camest forth out of the womb I sanctified thee, *and* I
ordained thee a prophet unto the nations. Then said I, 6

hostile and himself in seasons of despondency. They are words that
serve to place him from the outset in his true position before his countrymen, as one who spoke in virtue of God's commission, and not of
his own choice. We have in this section the declaration of God's purpose concerning him (*v.* 5); Jeremiah's protest (*v.* 6); God's reply
(*vv.* 7, 8); the act of divine consecration (*v.* 9); the nature of the
charge itself (*v.* 10).

5. *I knew thee*] meaning not mere acquaintance, but *approval* as a
consequence of this. The parallelism of contrast, frequent in the poetical books of the Bible, shews this to be the sense of the word in Ps. i. 6,
"The Lord *knoweth* the way of the *righteous*, but the way of the *ungodly* shall *perish*;" and when read in the light of that verse, two other
passages ("For I *know* him, that he will command his children and his
household after him, and they shall keep the way of the Lord,"
Gen. xviii. 19; and "The Lord is good, a strong hold in the day of
trouble; and he *knoweth* them that trust in him," Nahum i. 7) throw
light on the expression as used here.

before thou camest] Compare the promise of the angel to the father of
John the Baptist, "he shall be filled with the Holy Ghost, even from
his mother's womb" (Luke i. 15); and the yet more mysterious promise
made to the Virgin-mother of One greater than John, "The Holy Ghost
shall come upon thee, and the power of the Highest shall overshadow
thee" (Luke i. 35). Compare also Judges xiii. 5.

I sanctified thee] Solemn utterances like this have a tendency in
Hebrew to take the form of parallel clauses either of similarity of sense
as here ('knew—sanctified'), or of contrast, as in the first of the
instances above given.

and I ordained thee] **I have ordained thee.** The verb literally is
'have given.' The absence of '*and*' in the Hebrew points to this
change from the indefinite to the definite form of the perfect. Thus,
while the verbs 'knew,' 'sanctified,' refer to the time preceding the
prophet's birth, that which follows relates to the time of his call.

unto the nations] This points out a distinction between the work of
Jeremiah as a prophet, and that of many of his predecessors, such as
Elijah, or Elisha, whose predictions were concerned with the Jews only.
Those of Jeremiah on the other hand had to do with the heathen world
of that day as well as with the nations of subsequent ages. He unfolded
to them the order of Divine Providence, and foretold the blessings
coming on the earth through the Advent of the Messiah (xxiii. 5, xxxiii.
15). The Jewish interpretation limits the reference of the words to
judgments on the heathen nations, as contained in xxv. 8, etc. This is
proved to be wrong by ver. 10 (which see with notes).

6. Jeremiah shews that the prophetic office was not one of his own
seeking.

Ah, Lord GOD, behold, I cannot speak: for I *am* a child.
7 But the LORD said unto me, Say not, I *am* a child: for thou shalt go to all that I shall send thee, and whatsoever I com-
8 mand thee thou shalt speak. Be not afraid of their faces:
9 for I *am* with thee to deliver thee, saith the LORD. Then the LORD put forth his hand, and touched my mouth. And

Ah!] Rather, **Alas!** The same word in the Hebrew is used, e.g. Joshua vii. 7; 2 Kings iii. 10, and expresses not so much an entreaty that things should be arranged otherwise, as a lament that they are as they are. Jeremiah's position is thus different from that of Moses (Exod. iv. 10). The latter pleaded inability, "O my Lord, I am not eloquent," while the former acquiesces in the appointment, now announced to have been made so long before, pleads not inability but only youth and inexperience (compare Is. vi. 5; Ezek. iii. 15), and replies to the Almighty in the same spirit as Solomon at the beginning of his reign (1 Kings iii. 7), "I am but a little child: I know not how to go out or come in."

I cannot speak] meaning, I have not the powers of oratory necessary to win the attention and so sway the conduct of hostile numbers. For the prophet of those days eloquence, natural or acquired, was as necessary as for one who would be a popular preacher or prominent statesman in our own time.

I am a child] meaning, a very young man. The same word (*na-ar*) is used of Joshua (Exod. xxxiii. 11) at a time when we know him to have been forty-five years of age. In the case of Jeremiah, however, the length of his prophetic ministry shews that he must have been very youthful at its commencement. So Isaiah was probably not more than twenty years old when he began to prophesy.

7. Here again there is brought out the contrast between Moses and Jeremiah. The former had brought one excuse after another (Exod. iii. 11, 13; iv. 1, 10, 13), and consequently, as we read (iv. 14) "the anger of the Lord was kindled against Moses." But in Jeremiah's case encouragement alone was needed, and it is given at once in word and then in act.

8. *Be not afraid*] This is addressed not so much to the reason which Jeremiah had pleaded, viz. youth, but to that which, as the LORD saw, formed another cause for his shrinking from the task, viz. fear of those whom he was to address.

to deliver thee] Note the form of expression. The promise is not that the prophet in the exercise of his mission shall be preserved unhurt, although we are not without an instance of this sort of interposition (xxxvi. 26), but that he shall be delivered from destruction at the hands of his enemies.

9. *touched*] **caused it to touch.** An outward symbol of the gift of eloquence, which was being then and there bestowed. The same part of the verb (with a causative force) is used in the corresponding passage of Isaiah (vi. 7), where the solemn inauguration of his ministry is recorded. On the other hand, in Daniel (x. 16), where the object was

the LORD said unto me, Behold, I have put my words in thy mouth. See, I have this day set thee over the nations 10 and over the kingdoms, to root out, and to pull down, and to destroy, and to throw down, to build, and to plant.

11—19. *The Lord shews the Prophet the Vision of* (i) *the Almond Tree,* (ii) *the Boiling Caldron. He adds Words of Good Cheer.*

Moreover, the word of the LORD came unto me, saying, 11

merely to restore the power of articulate speech, the verb is "touched," not "caused to touch." The nature of God's dealing with Ezekiel was distinct from either of these (ii. 8).

10. *to root out*] The prophet is said to do in his own person that which he announces as about to be done by God. Compare xv. 1, "cast them out of my sight;" Is. vi. 10, "Make the heart of this people fat, &c.;" Ezek. xiii. 19, where the false prophets are spoken of as "slaying the souls that should not die" and "saving the souls alive that should not live;" Ezek. xliii. 3, where the prophet speaks of the vision that he saw when he "came to destroy the city." This last is softened off in the margin by the English translators, but quite unnecessarily. So in profane literature we find prophets spoken of as though they had a share in influencing the course of the future, which it was theirs only to predict.

> "And thou, O sacred maid, inspired to see
> The event of things in dark futurity,
> *Give* me what heaven has promised to my fate
> To conquer and command the Latian state."
> Aeneas to the Sibyl. Dryden's *Virgil,* VI. 100—103.

Three or four words are used to denote destruction, and two follow them implying restoration. This serves to shew that the earlier as well as the more important portion of the prophet's task was to consist in rebuke and in threatening; while nevertheless out of the ruins a better and more hopeful state of things should arise for Israel.

11—19. THE LORD SHEWS THE PROPHET THE VISION OF (i) THE ALMOND TREE, (ii) THE BOILING CALDRON. HE ADDS WORDS OF GOOD CHEER.

11. *the word of the Lord came unto me*] The prophets' "gift of prophesying was neither permanent, nor the result of their own volition, but wholly dependent on the divine pleasure." Archdeacon Lee, from whom the above quotation is made (*Inspiration of Holy Scripture* 4th ed. p. 170), instances 2 Kings iv. 27; Acts xx. 22, as proofs of this statement, and goes on to say that there are two classes of revelations, (i) when the action of the external senses is suspended; (ii) when the prophet is conscious of all that takes place around him. Under the former head come symbolic visions, such as

Jeremiah, what seest thou? And I said, I see a rod of an
12 almond tree. Then said the LORD unto me, Thou hast
13 well seen: for I will hasten my word to perform it. And
the word of the LORD came unto me the second time, saying,
What seest thou? And I said, I see a seething pot; and

the two that here follow. In them the things seen either surpass
the limits of human experience (e.g. Ezek. i. 4, etc.), or they appertain
to the world of sense in such measure that there is no difficulty
in describing them by means of human language (as in the present
instances). Further, it may be noticed that symbolic *visions* are thus
to be distinguished from symbolic *actions;* in the former the prophet
is but a spectator; in the latter (e.g. the symbol of the linen girdle,
Jer. xiii. 1—7) he takes an active part.

I see a rod of an almond tree] The almond tree in Palestine has
been compared to the snowdrop with us, as giving one of the first
signs of approaching spring. Dr Tristram (*Natural History of the
Bible*) tells us that at Bethany in the month of January he gathered
the blossoms in full bloom. They appear before the leaves open, like
those of the peach-tree in England. The Hebrew used here (*shâkêd*) is
not the ordinary word for an almond tree, but a poetical expression,
meaning *that which is awake*, and referring to the blossoming of
this tree as taking place while others are still in their winter sleep.
Accordingly the almond tree is made the subject of this vision—
an 'emblem of wakefulness and activity,' as is shewn by the interpretation given in ver. 12. The other mode of explanation, which
consists in rendering not "rod" but *staff*, such as is carried by travellers,
would quite change the character of the figure, which would then
exhibit the Almighty as about to set forth on a journey of vengeance.
This is unlikely and forced.

12. *I will hasten*] Rather, **I am wakeful** (keep watch, await my
opportunity) **for.** The point of the expression can only be perceived,
if we are aware that the Hebrew term is *shokêd*, a participle from
the same root as the word for almond tree in the former verse. Since
the punishment of captivity inflicted on Manasseh the Lord had not
visited upon His people their sins. That period of rest then was
like the winter, at the end of which the almond tree was the first
to wake. So now the Lord is rousing Himself. The period of trial
is rapidly approaching its end, and the punishment so long delayed
is about to be at last inflicted. At the same time there is a brighter
side too. The Lord is rousing Himself not only to punish but to
save. Through Jeremiah's ministry and Josiah's reforms religion is
to be kept alive in a remnant of those carried to Babylon, and so the
return from captivity shall at last be brought about.

13. *a seething pot*] The second vision is of a more uniform character than the first. It betokens nothing save disaster, and by it
the character of the future in store for the nation is more clearly brought

the face thereof *is* towards the north. Then the LORD said 14
unto me, Out of the north an evil shall break forth upon all
the inhabitants of the land. For lo, I will call all the 15
families of the kingdoms of the north, saith the LORD; and
they shall come, and they shall set every one his throne *at*

out. The word *sir*, here rendered pot, was a large vessel, as it was used in preparing pottage for a considerable number in 2 Kings iv. 38. It was also used for washing (Ps. lx. 8). Some render instead of "seething" (boiling) *blown upon;* i.e. a pot placed upon a fire made to burn brightly by blowing. A passage in Job (xli. 20) rather supports this view from the words which follow. "Out of his (leviathan's) nostrils goeth smoke, as out of a *seething* pot or caldron. *His breath kindleth coals.*" The figure of a pot boiling over is found also in Arabic poetry to express as here a war carried on with vehemence and ardour.

towards] **from the face of.** The pot is leaning away from the north. As the materials on which it is standing are consumed, it settles unevenly, and the southern side sinks. Thus it will presently be overturned, and send its scalding contents in that direction.

14. *Out of the north*] Interpretation of the second vision. It clearly points to the irruption of a hostile army into Judæa from a northerly direction. Some have taken this army to be the Scythian hordes. For reasons against this view see notes on iv. 6. The true explanation seems to be the following. The boiling pot is the region of Mesopotamia, where four great nations, Babylon, Nineveh, Elam, and Media are engaged in strife. The danger to Judæa had always depended on the fact that it lay on the direct road from the East to Egypt and thus was exposed to attacks by the way on the part of armies directed against the latter power. Esarhaddon, king of Assyria, had broken up Egypt into twelve small states, which had no thought of any foreign contest, and thus the Jews had had some relief from invasion. But besides this, the constant struggles of the four nations above mentioned with one another had the same effect. These constant struggles are the boiling caldron. The contest however gives signs of coming to an end. The caldron is settling down on one side. Victory is declaring for the Chaldæans of Babylon, and when they have established their superiority, that fury which has hitherto been put forth in strife within Mesopotamia will be directed against the Jews. The boiling contents of the caldron will be poured over Judæa.

an evil] **the evil,**—the evil which was to be expected, foretold by all the prophets as the result of national sin.

shall break forth] **shall be opened, shall disclose itself.**

15. *all the families of the kingdoms*] Each kingdom was composed of a mixture of races, here called families. The rendering however may be, *all the families, even the kingdoms,* in which case *kingdoms* would be only an explanation of the sense in which the word *families* is used.

they shall set every one his throne] The chiefs of the combined army, the rulers who are suggested by the word kingdoms, post themselves

the entering of the gates of Jerusalem, and against all the walls thereof round about, and against all the cities of
16 Judah. And I will utter my judgments against them touching all their wickedness, who have forsaken me, and have burnt incense unto other gods, and worshipped the works of

around the walls of the besieged city. Some take the sense to be that the blockade is thus made more sure. The generals take up their position at all the gates, that none may go out or come in. It is better however to take the word throne, to denote the seat from which judgment is delivered. The function of administering justice, which among us is delegated by the monarch to judges, was in the East exercised by the king in person, and the gate of the city, or rather a large space in its neighbourhood, was reserved free of buildings, and was the ordinary place at which trials were held and sentences declared. Cp. Deut. xvi. 18, xvii. 8; Ruth iv. 1. Here then the rulers of the invader's army, by a figure taken from the familiar proceedings of criminal justice, are said to be about to sit in judgment on the crimes of the people and inflict punishment on the guilty. For the word throne as used to denote the judgment-seat see Ps. ix. 4, cxxii. 5; Prov. xx. 8. The general sense of the verse is that it is not without reason, or as the blind act of ambitious and more powerful nations, that Jerusalem is to be overthrown. That overthrow will take place as a judicial act, as a consequence of wickedness, and after the case has been duly weighed in the balances.

and against all the walls thereof round about, and against all the cities of Judah] It is difficult to know whether we should connect this with 'shall come' or 'shall set.' The reason of the ambiguity lies in the fact that Jeremiah mingles the two thoughts of a besieging army and of a judicial sentence and its execution. It is in point of fact by the scaling of the walls of Jerusalem and the capture of the other cities of the country that the sentence is to be carried out, and Jeremiah here as elsewhere (see Introduction, chap. ii. § 8 (*d*) and note) breaks off his simile or metaphor with abruptness and takes up anew the literal statement.

16. *I will utter my judgments against them*] Literally, **I will speak my judgments with them.** An almost identical phrase in the Hebrew occurs again in this book, when Zedekiah is brought before Nebuchadnezzar at Riblah, and it is said that the latter "gave judgment upon him," marginal "spake with him judgments" (xxxix. 5); compare iv. 12.

touching all their wickedness] This is defined in the three clauses that follow, (i) the forsaking of the true God, (ii) the burning of incense to other gods, (iii) the worshipping of images.

other gods] The Greek (Septuagint) and Latin Vulgate translations seem to have felt a difficulty in this expression, since "there is none other God but one." Cp. St Paul "we know that an idol is nothing in the world" (1 Cor. viii. 4). Inasmuch then as the idols worshipped by

their own hands. Thou therefore gird up thy loins, and 17
arise, and speak unto them all that I command thee: be
not dismayed at their faces, lest I confound thee before them.
For behold, I have made thee *this* day a defenced city, and 18
an iron pillar, and brasen walls against the whole land,
against the kings of Judah, against the princes thereof,
against the priests thereof, and against the people of the
land. And they shall fight against thee; but they shall not 19
prevail against thee; for I *am* with thee, saith the LORD, to
deliver thee.

Gentiles represented things non-existent, beings of fancy only, the Greek and Latin render here *gods of foreign nations*.

17. Words of encouragement in this and the two next verses.

Thou therefore gird up thy loins] Gather up the lower part of the flowing Eastern robe. This was done in preparation for (i) a journey (Exod. xii. 11; 2 Kings iv. 29, ix. 1), (ii) a race (1 Kings xviii. 46), (iii) a conflict (Job xxxviii. 3, xl. 7). It implied (1) readiness for effort, (2) energy in action. As the sin of the people was great and manifold, and as the impending danger was not only near but terrible and destructive in its nature, so was it needful that without fear or favour the warning should be given, and that he to whom that warning was entrusted should 'deliver his soul,' and not by apathy or want of boldness involve himself in any way in the people's guilt.

be not dismayed...] The literal rendering would be, **be not broken down before them, lest I break thee down before them.** There is thus a play upon words in the Hebrew, which can hardly be reproduced in idiomatic English.

18. *a defenced city, and an iron pillar, and brasen walls*] Jeremiah was to be fortified by divine strength against the attacks which he should have to confront throughout his prophetic life. When all else was fluctuating and yielding to pressure from within and without, he alone was to represent resistance. The assaults would be severe, and hence the force of the three figures under which he is described. And as Jeremiah would need strength in a pre-eminent degree, so the figures under which it is described are more forcible than that used in the similar case of Ezekiel: "As an adamant harder than flint have I made thy forehead: fear them not" (Ezek. iii. 9).

against the kings of Judah] Josiah, Jehoahaz, Jehoiakim, Jehoiachin, Zedekiah. The use of the plural 'kings' shews him that his career is probably to be a long one.

the princes] the chief military and civil officers.

19. As fear on the part of the prophet was to forfeit all claim to God's protecting care of him in the fulfilment of his duty; so here there comes the promise, on the assumed condition of faithfulness to his trust, that his cause should be successful.

they shall not prevail against thee] When we compare portions of

CHAP. II. 1—13. *Under the Figure of Husband and Wife the Lord reminds the People of His Past Favours and charges them with Faithlessness to their First Love.*

2 Moreover the word of the LORD came to me, saying,

the subsequent history of Jeremiah, we find that in point of fact the prophet was from time to time thrust aside by his foes. The sense therefore here is *shall not finally prevail.* Before the prophet's death his cause should be vindicated, his predictions verified, and good seed sown. Compare the nature of the fulfilment of our Saviour's prayer for the Apostle Peter: "I have prayed for thee that thy faith fail not," Luke xxii. 32. This prayer did not prevent the Apostle from deserting and then denying Christ, although it was abundantly answered in his subsequent history. Even as our Lord's own prayer for His Father's help in the same chapter, "Father, if thou be willing, remove this cup from me," was answered not by its removal but by support from heaven; so Jeremiah was to hold his ground not in his own strength, but through the Almighty's constant presence.

CHAP. II. 1—13. UNDER THE FIGURE OF HUSBAND AND WIFE THE LORD REMINDS THE PEOPLE OF HIS PAST FAVOURS AND CHARGES THEM WITH FAITHLESSNESS TO THEIR FIRST LOVE.

1. *Moreover*] **And,** thus connecting with Jeremiah's Call the words which follow. They form the beginning of a long prophecy extending to the end of Chap. vi., and which has but one well-marked break, viz. at the end of Chap. iii. 5. More than one opinion has been held as to the time at which these prophecies were delivered. By far the most probable view however is that they form the substance of those which were given during the reign of Josiah. For

(*a*) The name of Josiah is expressly introduced in connexion with them (iii. 6), and accordingly any other view would require that this should be a later insertion in the text:

(*b*) The order of the prophecies, though far from chronological throughout the book, yet may be held to be so in any individual case in which there is no reason for the contrary belief, and this is specially probable at the beginning of the book, and where there is no apparent cause for deviation from the order of time:

(*c*) The character of the prophecies themselves falls in with this. In most cases of the later prophecies we find headings which tell us at what time they were uttered. In this portion we have but one such instance, and that somewhat vague (iii. 6 as referred to above). Again, these chapters seem to be not so much addresses or sermons delivered to the people on distinct and definite occasions as the later

Go and cry in the ears of Jerusalem, saying, Thus saith 2
the LORD; I remember thee, the kindness of thy youth, the
love of thine espousals, when thou wentest after me in the
wilderness, in a land *that was* not sown. Israel *was* holi- 3
ness unto the LORD, *and* the firstfruits of his increase: all

ones are, but rather given as the gist of the prophet's teaching during
all those early years of his ministry. Once more, in these chapters so
far from there being references to matters of later date than Josiah, such
as abound in the subsequent parts (e.g. invasion by the Babylonians, &c.),
there is no allusion to any contemporary events.

It has been held on the other hand that the mention of Egypt (ii. 16,
18, 36) compels us to consider these prophecies as spoken later. We
are reminded that Josiah was slain in fighting against the Egyptian
king. How then, it is asked, could the Jewish nation in his reign have
sought to ally themselves with that country? It does not however
follow that there may not have been then, as at other times, a large
and influential number who desired to connect themselves with Egypt,
and it was against them that Jeremiah directed his words of warning.
Another but an extremely improbable way of understanding the references
to Egypt in these chapters is a sort of compromise between the two
views, and consists in the supposition that Jeremiah, or Baruch at his
dictation, wrote down what was in substance at least his discourses to
the people in the days of Josiah, but modified them in accordance with
the more recent tenor of his words and of events.

The whole prophecy then (chaps. ii. 1—iii. 5) is the first recorded
utterance of Jeremiah after his Call, and consists of expostulation with
Israel for their idolatry.

2. *the kindness of thy youth, the love of thine espousals*] This has
been taken as meaning, the kindness and love *a*) of Israel towards God,
or *b*) of God towards Israel. In favour of *b*) is urged that Israel as a
matter of fact was ever in past time also straying from God. But on
the whole *a*) is more probable, (i) as being the more natural sense of
the words themselves, (ii) in that the 'kindness' and 'love' spoken of
evidently refer to the past, while God's attitude of grace towards
Israel is the same still that it has ever been, (iii) in that even in past
time Israel as a rule followed God. The exceptions from their very
nature would form the history and so fix themselves in the mind, just as
the brief reign of Queen Mary, and again the temporary overthrow of
the House of Stuart (1649—1660), in English History are more conspicuous than many long periods of tranquillity and peace.

3. *Israel was holiness unto the Lord, and the firstfruits of his increase*] Israel is as something set apart from ordinary uses, dedicated
to God. He is as the most precious part of the harvest, that part
which is consecrated as God's portion. The notion was familiar to the
people's minds through the yearly custom, prescribed Lev. xxiii. 10—14,
that a measure of the firstfruits should be waved by the priest before

that devour him shall offend; evil shall come upon them,
4 saith the LORD. Hear ye the word of the LORD, O house
5 of Jacob, and all the families of the house of Israel: Thus
saith the LORD, What iniquity have your fathers found in
me, that they are gone far from me, and have walked after
6 vanity, and are become vain? Neither said they, Where *is*
the LORD that brought us up out of the land of Egypt, that
led us through the wilderness, through a land of deserts

the Lord, and that none of the harvest should be enjoyed till this rite had been fulfilled.

all that devour him shall offend] The priest and his family alone were to eat of the firstfruits. No stranger was allowed to partake. See Lev. xxii. 10, 16. If any unhallowed person profaned the firstfruits by taking of them, he bore the iniquity of *trespass* in his eating. The word used there for trespass is from the same root as that which in this passage is rendered 'shall offend.' Thus the sense is that "Heathen, i.e. unconsecrated, nations, must not meddle with Israel, because it is the nation consecrated to God. If they do, they will bring such guilt upon themselves as those incur who eat the firstfruits." (*Speaker's Comm.*)

4. *all the families of the house of Israel*] addressed not to the ten tribes, but to the nation as a whole.

5. *have walked after vanity*] 'vanity' is here used in the same sense as in 1 Kings xvi. 13, "provoking the Lord God of Israel to anger with their vanities." The Jews regarded idols simply as unsubstantial, unreal, a breath. Hence vanity (emptiness) expresses their view. Compare "we know that an idol is nothing in the world" (1 Cor. viii. 4) and note on chap. i. 16. A further stage is reached in ver. 8, "things that do not profit" (compare ver. 11). Chap. x. 10 contrasts God as "the true God," "the living God;" while the notions of the unreal and the positively injurious are combined in xvi. 19, "Surely our fathers have inherited lies, vanity, and things wherein there is no profit."

and are become vain] a want of reality and of sense are the qualities which naturally become the marks of those who follow the empty and unprofitable. Compare Rom. i. 21—23, they "became vain in their imaginations...they became fools, and changed the glory of the incorruptible God into an image made like unto corruptible man, and to birds and fourfooted beasts and creeping things."

6. The prophet brings their thanklessness into bolder relief by depicting in the strongest colours the care lavished upon them of old. Utter forgetfulness is their return for the deliverance from Egyptian bondage, the preservation from the various dangers of the wilderness, and the bestowal of Canaan.

the wilderness] not in the sense which the word conveys to our ears. The expression in the original means merely the land not occupied

and of pits, through a land of drought, and of the shadow of death, through a land that no man passed through, and where no man dwelt? And I brought you into a plentiful 7 country, to eat the fruit thereof and the goodness thereof;

by any settled inhabitants. It by no means excludes the notion of abundant pasturage for cattle, just as it is described (xxiii. 10) as having its "pleasant places," but is yet liable as is there shewn to become a desert at any time through the drying up of the springs and rivers on which its vegetation was dependent.

deserts] really barren.

pits] one of the difficulties and dangers of travellers consisted in the rifts or clefts which had to be crossed or avoided by a circuitous route.

drought] hence perhaps the Rabbinic story that a rock followed the Israelites through the wilderness, to supply their thirst. St Paul, without in any way taking the story under his protection, applies it in the way of spiritual adaptation; "They drank of that spiritual Rock that followed them, and that Rock was Christ" (1 Cor. x. 4).

shadow of death] the Hebrew word may mean nothing beyond *darkness*, but the other rendering is the more probable one, and denotes the gloom which the traveller must feel in passing through a region, where the supply of the necessaries of life is so precarious.

that no man passed through, and where no man dwelt] the two words for 'man' differ in the original. The first means man in the strength, either of natural vigour, as here, or of rank or riches; the second denotes man as a member of the human race, and is equivalent to 'human being.' We have the same contrast elsewhere in the Hebrew, where however the English rendering differs; (Psalm xlix. 2), "High and low, *rich* and *poor*, one with another;" and (Is. ii. 9), "The *mean man* boweth down, and the *great man* humbleth himself." Compare St John vi. 10, where "men" on its first occurrence means simply persons.

7. *a plentiful country*] Literally, *a country of the Carmel*. The word Carmel properly means a piece of ground fertile and well cultivated, but was commonly used as the actual name of one such spot of Palestine, which, as the only promontory that the sea-board of the country possesses, juts out into the Mediterranean, and bounds the great plain of Esdraelon. It was the scene of the testing of the true God proposed by Elijah to the followers of Baal (1 Kings xviii.). This application of terms wholly or partly descriptive of natural features to denote an individual place which answers to such a description seems common in all languages. To it we owe in English such names as Newhaven, Newport, New Forest, Sandwich (=a sandy bay), Chelsea (=a shingle island) and Fairfield, the last being a good counterpart to the Hebrew name in the present case. Compare also as names for country houses 'The Woodlands,' 'The Plantations,' &c.

but when ye entered, ye defiled my land, and made mine
8 heritage an abomination. The priests said not, Where *is*
the LORD? and they that handle the law knew me not:

defiled] with (i) idolatry, (ii) sacrifices of their children; so Ps. cvi. 37, "they sacrificed their sons and their daughters unto devils." And as the land had been thus defiled by God's own people, the possessors of it, so now the heathen were about to obtain permission to do the like. Compare Ps. lxxix. 1, "O God, the heathen are come into thine inheritance; thy holy temple have they defiled."

mine heritage] Elsewhere it is generally Israel itself that goes by this name; e.g. "For the Lord's portion is his people; Jacob is the lot of his inheritance" (Deut. xxxii. 9). Compare 1 Sam. x. 1; 1 Kings viii. 51; Ps. xxviii. 9, lxxviii. 71; Is. xix. 25; Jer. x. 16.

8. The wickedness of the people is matched and encouraged by that of the chief men both in Church and State. Three classes of persons are spoken of.

(1) (this class is subdivided into two) *the priests*. The duty of the tribe of Levi was not only to minister at the altar, but to handle the law; i.e. to instruct the people in its precepts. Compare the words of "the blessing wherewith Moses the man of God blessed Israel before his death" (Deut. xxxiii.). He there says of Levi, "They shall teach Jacob thy judgments and Israel thy law" (ver. 10).

(2) *the pastors*, meaning, not ordained ministers according to the familiar application of the word in modern times, but, as elsewhere in the Old Testament, temporal rulers, kings, compare iii. 15. So in 1 Kings xxii. 17, when Micaiah the prophet desired to express to king Ahab his sense of his worthlessness as a ruler, he said, "I saw all Israel scattered upon the hills, as sheep that have not a shepherd." The same is the sense in Ezek. xxxiv. 2, "Woe be to the shepherds of Israel that do feed themselves! should not the shepherds feed the flocks?" So in Homer the kings are "shepherds of the people."

(3) *the prophets*, whose duty it was to declare the will of God from time to time, and urge upon the people reformation and a religious life. Jeremiah felt most keenly the wickedness of both priest and prophet, since in his own person he represented both orders, and "by a singularly tragical fate he lived precisely at that age at which both of those great institutions seemed to have reached the utmost point of degradation and corruption" (Stanley's *Jewish Church*, Vol. II. p. 439, 440). "He who by each of his callings was naturally led to sympathise with both, was the doomed antagonist of both, victim of one of the strongest of human passions, the hatred of Priests against a Priest who attacks his own order, the hatred of Prophets against a Prophet who ventures to have a voice and a will of his own" (*Ibid.*).

said not, Where is the Lord?] i.e. they were indifferent to God's will, and thought of nothing less than consulting Him.

they that handle the law] In addition to the remarks above made

the pastors also transgressed against me, and the prophets prophesied by Baal, and walked after *things that* do not profit. Wherefore I will yet plead with you, saith the LORD, 9 and with your children's children will I plead. For pass 10 over the isles of Chittim, and see; and send *unto* Kedar, and consider diligently, and see if there be such a *thing*.

on these words compare for the priest's share in the interpretation of the law chap. xviii. 18; Ezek. vii. 26.

Baal] The chief male object of worship on the part of the Phœnician nations. His worship prevailed at an early date among the Moabites (Numb. xxii. 41). Among the Jews that worship was celebrated with much pomp, and cruel rites frequently accompanied it, the priests cutting themselves with knives, and human sacrifices being sometimes offered. The word entered much into Phœnician (Carthaginian) proper names, Hannibal, Hasdrubal, Adherbal, etc. Some consider Baal to have been represented to his worshippers by the planet Jupiter, while others with more probability take him to be the sun-god, and so to be coupled with Ashtoreth, the moon-goddess, the chief female object of worship on the part of the same nations.

9. *with your children's children will I plead*] Even though it be necessary to continue the remonstrance to future generations, God will not fail to carry out His part, but will plead His cause still against those who desert Him.

10. *the isles of Chittim*] The Chittim ("Kittim") are mentioned as descendants of Javan in Gen. x. 4. Josephus identifies the original seat of the tribe with the town of Citium in Cyprus. Gradually the name seems to have been extended, so as to include not only the neighbouring islands, but even Macedonia (which word Ma-*ced*-onia may have been fancifully believed to be connected with Chittim) and Italy.

Kedar] As Chittim represented the parts of the world that lay to the westward of Palestine, so Kedar represented those which lay to the eastward. Kedar was the second son of Ishmael (Gen. xxv. 13) and seems from the many subsequent notices of his tribe in the Bible to have been destined to be in his posterity the most distinguished of the twelve brethren, princes, given in the genealogy. They dwelt on the north-west of Arabia, and extended to the borders of Palestine. Kedar occurs among the ancestry of Mohammed. In Psalm cxx. 5 ("Woe is me...that I dwell in the tents of Kedar") they are spoken of as a barbarous tribe, to dwell amongst whom was to be utterly cut off from the worship of the true God. Even they however, the Lord declares, do not furnish a parallel for the baseness which appertains to the Jews.

11 Hath a nation changed *their* gods, which *are* yet no gods?
but my people have changed their glory for *that which* doth
12 not profit. Be astonished, O ye heavens, at this, and be
13 horribly afraid, be ye very desolate, saith the Lord. For
my people have committed two evils; they have forsaken
me the fountain of living waters, and hewed them out
cisterns, broken cisterns, that can hold no water.

11. *a nation*] Not meaning any nation, for it was *true* of Israel that they had done this, but any heathen nation, according to the force of the Hebrew word.

which are yet no gods] Therefore it need not have occasioned surprise, if their worshippers had at some time deserted them.

their glory] Him, through Whom they had attained pre-eminence over all other nations, or better, Him to Whom all honour and glory were due. This latter accords more with the passage "Thus they changed *their glory* into the similitude of an ox that eateth grass" (Ps. cvi. 20).

12. *be ye very desolate*] Literally, **be ye dry**. By a figure common in all poetry nature is called upon to adapt herself, as though a living being, to the complexion of human affairs. So "He shall call to the heavens from above, and to the earth, that he may judge his people." "And the heavens shall declare his righteousness" (Ps. l. 4, 6). "Sing, O ye heavens...shout, ye lower parts of the earth; break forth into singing, ye mountains, O forest, and every tree therein: for the Lord hath redeemed Jacob and glorified himself in Israel" (Is. xliv. 23). "Sing, O heavens; and be joyful, O earth; and break forth into singing, O mountains; for the Lord hath comforted his people, and will have mercy upon his afflicted" (Is. xlix. 13). So here the heavens are bid to shrivel up in horror at the behaviour of the people.

13. *For my people have committed two evils*] The one sin of the heathen is idolatry, whereas this people have in addition renounced the service of God.

the fountain of living waters] More properly the reservoir (tank) into which living waters (those of wells and streams) are drawn and where they are stored. Isaiah (xliv. 3) had already spoken of God's blessing under this figure, "I will pour water upon him that is thirsty and floods upon the dry ground; I will pour my spirit upon thy seed and my blessing upon thine offspring," a passage to which our Lord perhaps alludes in John vii. 37—39.

cisterns] These were very familiar objects to those whom the prophet addressed. "There are thousands of these ancient cisterns in upper Galilee, where Josephus says there were two hundred and forty cities in his day, and the site of every one was pierced like a honeycomb with them" (Thomson, *The Land and the Book*, p. 287). It was no doubt into such a one that Joseph was cast by his brethren.

14—30. *Wickedness and obstinacy and consequent calamities of Israel.*

14 *Is* Israel a servant? *is* he a homeborn *slave?* why is he
15 spoiled? The young lions roared upon him, *and* yelled, and

broken cisterns, that can hold no water] "No comparison could more keenly rebuke the madness of a people who changed their glory for that which doth not profit. The best cisterns, even those in solid rock, are strangely liable to crack...and if by constant care they are made to hold, yet the water collected from clay roofs or from marly soil has the colour of weak soapsuds, the taste of the earth or the stable, is full of worms, and in the hour of greatest need it utterly fails...I have never been able to tolerate this cistern water except in Jerusalem, where they are kept with scrupulous care, and filled from roofs both clean and hard" (*ibid.*). The failure of the broken cistern, discovered at the moment of need, is the point of the comparison made by the prophet.

14—30. WICKEDNESS AND OBSTINACY AND CONSEQUENT CALAMITIES OF ISRAEL.

14. *Is Israel a servant? is he a homeborn slave?*] The relationship of master and servant, in our sense of the words, as a contract was unknown among the Jews. Domestic service was discharged by slaves, who might be roughly divided into two classes, (i) those captured in war or bought, (ii) those born and brought up in their master's house. For the latter there was more opportunity of escape from servitude than for the former. On the other hand the position of the latter was often preferable. In general the condition of the slave depended much on the character of his master, and from this consideration have sprung two different explanations of the passage. Some understand the questions as meaning, *Israel is the object of God's most careful protection. He is His most cherished possession, a member of His family. How is it then that he has been spoiled?* The answer is given in ver. 17. Others take it thus :—*Is Israel a slave, subject to all the miseries of such a lot, a prey to each whim of a cruel master? Far as this would seem from the truth, we are yet driven to suppose that his state is in no way superior to this, for he has been spoiled and carried captive.¹* This latter explanation falls in better with the form of the enquiries, as compared with the somewhat similar passages ver. 31, viii. 4, xiv. 19; and specially with xxii. 28, xlix. 1. The prophet no doubt has in particular before his view the captivity of the Ten Northern Tribes.

15. *The young lions roared upon him, and yelled*] This may be meant literally as what befell the land of Israel after the captivity of the Ten Tribes, and the introduction of the inhabitants of foreign cities in their room (2 Kings xvii. 25). It is more likely however to have reference to the cruelties practised upon the exiles by their captors, as well as to the frequent Assyrian invasions. Compare for this figure of speech words spoken by Isaiah (v. 29) of an attacking host, "Their roaring shall be like a lion, they shall roar like young lions; yea, they

they made his land waste: his cities are burnt without
16 inhabitant. Also the children of Noph and Tahapanes
17 have broken the crown of thy head. Hast thou not procured this unto thyself, in that thou hast forsaken the LORD
18 thy God, when he led thee by the way? And now what

shall roar and lay hold of the prey, and shall carry it away safe and
none shall deliver it." See also Mic. v. 8.

burnt] Many prefer to render the Hebrew, *are levelled to the ground*.

16. *Also*] **Even.** The sense is, *those in whom thou most trustedst*.

Noph] either a town in the South of Egypt, or, as it is more generally taken, Memphis the capital of Lower (i.e. Northern) Egypt, the word Noph representing some colloquial Shemitic or Egyptian pronunciation of the name.

Tahapanes] The Greek *Daphnae Pelusii*, which Herodotus mentions (Book II. 30) as a town in which a garrison was maintained against the Syrians and Arabians. It bears an important part in the history contained in the later chapters. Johanan and the other captains went there in disobedience to the words of the prophet (xliii. 7). We gather from this that it was one of the towns of Egypt nearest to the border of Palestine. Jeremiah here prophesies that Egypt shall be smitten by Nebuchadnezzar. The Jews continued during Jeremiah's time to dwell there. The towns of Noph and Tahapanes would both be well known to the Jews even in Josiah's day, the former as a capital city, the latter from its local position.

have broken] Or, if the present Heb. text is right, *shall feed upon*. The tense in the original makes it more likely that a prophecy is intended, while 'feed upon,' the proper sense of the verb, is illustrated by the mention of shepherds (captains of hostile armies) in vi. 3, xii. 10. It is possible, however, that a past event may be referred to, such as the attack upon Jerusalem by Shishak, king of Egypt, in the reign of Rehoboam, son of Solomon. In this case the sense will be, *Egypt has in past times shewn what she could do as a foe. Do not seek to ally yourselves with her now.*

the crown of thy head] Baldness was considered among the Jews a reproach. This is shewn in the history of Elisha (2 Kings ii. 23. See also Jer. xlviii. 45). Or the sense may be, *afflict thee, cause thee to mourn*, a shaven head being a sign of mourning (Is. iii. 24, xv. 2, xxii. 12).

17. Has not thy desertion of God in old time brought upon thee this trouble?

when he led thee by the way] Way is not here used in the secondary sense that it often bears as 'way of sinners,' 'way of the righteous,' 'way of the ungodly,' but, as is shewn by its meaning in the next two verses, in the sense of a literal path or journey, viz.—that through the wilderness. The worship of the golden calf and of Baal-peor was but the earliest exhibition of that same idolatrous spirit, which had broken out

hast thou to do in the way of Egypt, to drink the waters of
Sihor? or what hast thou to do in the way of Assyria, to
drink the waters of the river? Thine own wickedness shall 19
correct thee, and thy backslidings shall reprove thee: know

again and again, was now so terribly prevalent, and formed the cause
of the calamities which beset the kingdom.

18. *what hast thou to do in the way of Egypt*] The thought is the
same as that expressed by Isaiah (xxx. 1—3) "Woe to the rebellious
children...that walk to go down into Egypt, and have not asked at my
mouth...Therefore shall the strength of Pharaoh be your shame, and the
trust in the shadow of Egypt your confusion." Ever since the time
when Psammetichus king of Egypt reduced under his own sway the
twelve separate kingdoms into which that country had been formed, there
was a party of statesmen at Jerusalem who favoured an Egyptian alliance.
To this party Jeremiah ceased not to oppose himself.

to drink the waters of Sihor] to hold communication with Egypt,
and espouse its cause. The figure has been already suggested by the
mention of fountains and cisterns (ver. 13).

Sihor] The word, which properly means turbid, is shewn by the
context to be equivalent to the Nile, a word which itself denotes blue,
or dark. On the other hand the same name (though perhaps in each
case qualified by some explanatory addition) is sometimes at any rate
given apparently to a much smaller river, near the Egyptian frontier.

what hast thou to do in the way of Assyria] It has been objected
that Nineveh and with it the Assyrian empire had probably been some
time before overthrown, and that of Babylon established upon its ruins.
This however is far from certain, while, even granting it, the use of the
old name Assyria presents no difficulty, as we have a parallel more than
once in the case of this same empire. In 2 Kings (xxiii. 29) Pharaoh-
Nechoh (on the occasion of the battle of Megiddo) is spoken of as going
up "against the king of Assyria," meaning Nabopolassar; and again in
the Book of Ezra (vi. 22) Darius is spoken of under the same title. It
is very possible however that the mention of Assyria is to be quite
otherwise explained; that the prophet, as in ver. 16 (see notes there),
is speaking of past acts. Both Israel and Judah had vacillated for
many reigns between Egypt and Assyria. Menahem king of Israel
bribed Pul king of Assyria to support him, and to him also his successors
Pekahiah and Pekah seem to have looked, while Hoshea, who ended
the line of Israel, sought the aid of Egypt. Hezekiah looked towards
Egypt, Josiah met his death in fighting against it and on behalf of
the Eastern empire, Assyria's successor. Thus subservience now to
one now to the other quarter was a familiar thought to those whom
Jeremiah addressed.

to drink the waters of the river] Euphrates, the great river, on which
was built Babylon. Compare Is. viii. 7, "Now the Lord bringeth up
upon them the waters of the river, strong and many, even the king of
Assyria, and all his glory."

19. *Thine own wickedness shall correct thee*] Thy misdeeds shall

therefore and see that *it is* an evil *thing* and bitter, that thou hast forsaken the LORD thy God, and *that* my fear *is* not in thee, saith the Lord GOD of hosts. For of old time I have broken thy yoke, *and* burst thy bands; and thou saidst, I will not transgress; when upon every high hill and under every green tree thou wanderest, playing the harlot. Yet I had planted thee a noble vine, wholly a right

bear their own punishment with them. *Correct* in the sense (now growing obsolete) of *chastise*. So "Correct thy son and he shall give thee rest" (Prov. xxix. 17). The word occurs several times in Jeremiah in this sense (x. 24, xxx. 11, xlvi. 28).

and that my fear] depending on "it is an evil thing and bitter." In other words the evil and bitterness is twofold; (*a*) desertion, (*b*) indifference.

my fear] The fear of me.

20. *I have broken thy yoke, and burst thy bands*] A reference to the deliverance from slavery in Egypt. It is possible however to render the original as a continuance of the words of reproof contained in the previous verses; Thou didst *break thy yoke &c.*, i.e. thou didst cast off all allegiance to Me, thy Maker.

transgress] **serve.** *Transgress* is no doubt a later reading formed by a very slight change in one of the letters of the verb in the original.

when] **for.** The Hebrew word possesses both senses. The only reason however for its having that of *when* is removed by the correction of the preceding word.

wanderest] **bowest down.** The reference is to the rendering of idolatrous worship, renouncing of allegiance to the true God Who has espoused the people to Himself, and readiness to do homage to any and every object beside.

21. *a noble vine*] a Sorek vine, the word Sorek probably referring to the colour of the fruit, a vine bearing dark-purple grapes. It is the "choice vine" spoken of by Jacob in his blessing of his sons (Gen. xlix. 11).

vine] the first plant the cultivation of which is recorded in the Bible (Gen. ix. 20). The dream of Pharaoh's butler and the ancient Egyptian and Assyrian sculptures shew that it was cultivated early in Egypt and Assyria, while the same is proved for Palestine by the frequent mention of it in Scripture and the numerous remains of winepresses hewn out of the rock. In the Temple over the gates leading to the Holy Place was an extensive vine ornamentation "from which hung clusters of grapes the length of a man's stature." It was made from the gold offered from time to time in the temple and was the embodiment of a symbol often used by the prophets. "The charge made against the Jews, that they worshipped Bacchus, probably rose from this temple ornament; and it is not impossible that our Lord may have had a reference to it, when He spoke of Himself as the True Vine" (St John xv. 1). (See Geikie's *Life and Words of Christ*, I. 552.)

seed: how then art thou turned *into* the degenerate plant of a strange vine unto me? For though thou wash thee with nitre, and take thee much sope, *yet* thine iniquity *is* marked before me, saith the Lord God. How canst thou say, I am not polluted, I have not gone after Baalim? see thy way in the valley, know what thou hast done: *thou art* a swift

wholly a right seed] In a somewhat similar passage in Isaiah (v. 1—7) Israel is not as here the vine, but the vineyard in which it is planted.

how then art thou turned] That which had been sown, in other words the people, when first chosen to be God's, was uncorrupt. How is it then, He asks, that such 'right seed' can have produced such rotten boughs?

unto me] to my grief—a frequent use of the dative case.

22. *nitre*] not saltpetre, in which sense we now use the word, but carbonate of soda (*natron*). That this was the sense intended by our translators, is shewn by Holland, who in his translation of Pliny (XXXI. 10) distinguishes between saltpetre (called by Pliny, Aphro-natrum) and nitre. Pliny there describes the soda-lakes about 50 miles west of Cairo. "The natron occurs in whitish or yellowish efflorescent crusts, or in beds three or four feet thick and very hard, which in the winter are covered with water about two feet deep; during the other nine months of the year the lakes are dry, at which period the natron is procured" (the Rev. W. Houghton in *Sm. Bibl. Dict.*).

sope] As natron is a *mineral* so this is a *vegetable* alkali. The word is itself the Arabic name (*alkali*) for one of the plants *salsolakali* (saltwort) which are chiefly used in its production, and are found in abundance on the Mediterranean coast of Palestine, as well as on the shores of the Dead Sea. This and other plants on being burnt furnish ashes, the lye of which (formed by passing water through them) was used in Jeremiah's time for cleansing purposes. The immense heaps of rubbish frequently found in Palestine shew the extent of the manufacture. The admixture of oils or animal fat was much later than Jeremiah's time.

thine iniquity is marked] No mode of cleansing however diligently applied will suffice to remove the ingrained stain of sin.

marked] *stained*, according to the Old English use of the word, continued still in certain phrases, as to mark a sheep (with a brand), to mark a handkerchief.

23. *How canst thou say*] The people probably pleaded in their defence that the law of Moses was observed and the public worship of God revived by the king. "But," replies the prophet, "you still follow false gods, and that not only in secret, but in the public view."

Baalim] The Hebrew plural. Compare Cherubim, Seraphim. The word therefore is equivalent to the "other gods" of chap. i. 16.

the valley] In all probability this was the valley of Hinnom on the south side of Jerusalem. It was devoted under idolatrous kings to

24 dromedary traversing her ways; a wild ass used to the wilderness, *that* snuffeth up the wind at her pleasure; *in* her occasion who can turn her away? all they that seek her will not weary themselves; in her month they shall find her.
25 Withhold thy foot from being unshod, and thy throat from thirst: but thou saidst, There is no hope: no; for I have
26 loved strangers, and after them will I go. As the thief is ashamed when he is found, so is the house of Israel ashamed; they, their kings, their princes, and their priests,
27 and their prophets, saying to a stock, Thou *art* my father; and to a stone, Thou hast brought me forth: for they have turned *their* back unto me, and not *their* face: but in the time of their trouble they will say, Arise, and save us.
28 But where *are* thy gods that thou hast made thee? let them

impure sacrifices and human offerings to Moloch, who no doubt was one of the gods called collectively Baalim. (Compare vii. 31, 32, xix. 5, xxxii. 35.) The valley was defiled by Josiah in order that such sacrifices might cease, and here dead bodies of men and animals were cast. From the Hebrew word in a Greek dress (*Gehenna*) comes one of the names for the place of future punishment, of which this valley was considered by the later Jews a symbol, and which some of them believed to contain the entrance to hell. See note on chap. vii. 31.

dromedary] The Hebrew denotes a female that has not yet had a foal.

traversing] (literally, **entangling**) running quickly hither and thither in the eagerness of her passion, crossing and recrossing her own course. So Israel runs now here now there, ever in search of a fresh object of devotion, and forsaking her lawful spouse.

24. *a wild ass used to the wilderness*] casting off all trammels and revelling in uncontrolled licence.

snuffeth up the wind] looking out for every occasion that offers to sin. The false gods have no need of courting her favour. She is eager to enjoy them.

at her pleasure] or, *in her desire*.

25. *Withhold thy foot from being unshod, and thy throat from thirst*] This hardly refers to approaching captivity, to be averted on repentance, but rather means, Do not pursue thy shameless quest in recklessness and heat; and with this accord the words of the reply, which expresses the resolve to continue in sin, while yet the next verse intimates that the people are not altogether insensible to the disgrace of continuing in such a course.

27. *saying*] *inasmuch as they say*. In this consists their disgrace. They attribute to their idols the honour due to the Creator alone.

in the time of their trouble they will say, Arise, and save us] Their idols are but fair-weather friends. When a crisis comes, they will recognise this, and appeal for help to Him Whom they have rejected.

arise, if they can save thee in the time of thy trouble: for *according* to the number of thy cities are thy gods, O Judah. Wherefore will ye plead with me? ye all have transgressed against me, saith the LORD. In vain have I smitten your children; they received no correction: your own sword hath devoured your prophets, like a destroying lion.

31—37. *Israel is an unfaithful spouse, and shall be punished as such.*

O generation, see ye the word of the LORD. Have I been a wilderness unto Israel? a land of darkness? wherefore say my people, We are lords; we will come no more unto thee? Can a maid forget her ornaments, *or* a bride

28. *gods that thou hast made thee*] There is a savour of irony throughout this verse. The sarcasm here lies in the people's belief that the gods which their own hands had made were worth invoking.

for according to the number of thy cities are thy gods] The irony is continued. *It cannot be through any scarcity in number that the gods whom thou hast chosen come not to thine aid. Each several city has its own favourite object of worship. Surely one at least of all these might be found to hear and help.*

O Judah] A change in the mode of address from 'House of Israel.' Judah, though not yet afflicted with the evils which have fallen to the lot of the Ten Tribes, is solemnly warned that she is deeply involved in the sin for which they are already suffering.

29. *plead with me*] remonstrate against my wrath.

all] all the families of Israel.

30. *your prophets*] referring perhaps to Isaiah and Zechariah, perhaps to those whom Manasseh slew (2 Kings xxi. 16. Compare Nehem. ix. 26; Matt. xxiii. 35), or possibly to those slain by Jezebel (1 Kings xviii. 4, 13).

31—37. ISRAEL IS AN UNFAITHFUL SPOUSE, AND SHALL BE PUNISHED AS SUCH.

31. *O generation, see ye*] **O generation that ye are, see.**

a wilderness] Have I been like a place where ye lacked sustenance? It is not the word which denotes absolutely barren, evil ground. (See note on ver. 6.)

a land of darkness] *a land of intense darkness*. Have I been to you as a place, whose dangers were magnified to your imagination by the very fact of its deep gloom?

We are lords] **We wander free.** The same Hebrew verb occurs Gen. xxvii. 40, rendered in the English Version "thou shalt have the dominion." The notion of being master, of having power to carry out one's own will, is at the bottom in each case.

24   JEREMIAH, II.   [vv. 33—36.

her attire? yet my people have forgotten me days without
33 number. Why trimmest thou thy way to seek love? there-
34 fore hast thou also taught the wicked ones thy ways. Also
in thy skirts is found the blood of the souls of the poor
innocents: I have not found it by secret search, but upon
35 all these. Yet thou sayest, Because I am innocent, surely
his anger shall turn from me. Behold, I *will* plead with
36 thee, because thou sayest, I have not sinned. Why gaddest
thou about *so* much to change thy way? thou also shalt be

    32. *attire*] a band or girdle worn round the waist. The same word is translated head-bands in Is. iii. 20. It was an ornament which the bride assumed upon her wedding-day, and thus it marked a married woman. A matron would cherish this token of married life. Not so Israel, which has now for a long time forgotten her Husband.

    33. *Why trimmest thou thy way*] Literally, *Why makest thou thy way good?* The same phrase is used later (vii. 3, 5) but in a somewhat different sense. There it means, to amend the life, but here, to shew care, to devote oneself (to the worship of false gods).

    the wicked ones thy ways] **thy ways to wickednesses**; i.e. thou hast accustomed thy ways to the sight and practice of evil, trained thy ways in the wickedness which characterizes them.

    34. *blood of the souls*] souls used simply in the sense of persons, as is found in the New Testament also (Rev. xviii. 13) "souls of men."

    I have not found it by secret search] **not at house-breaking didst thou catch them.** The allusion, which is completely obscured in the English Version, is to the law (Ex. xxii. 2) by which it was permitted to slay a thief caught in the act of breaking into a house. The persons whom Israel had thus treated were in no such position, but such was nevertheless their fate. Those spoken of are probably, in part at any rate, the victims of the cruelty of Manasseh, of whom we read (2 Kings xxi. 16) that he "shed innocent blood very much, till he had filled Jerusalem from one end to another."

    but upon all these] The words are obscure. The sense may be (i) it was (not because those prophets were caught in any crime, but rather) *because they exposed and denounced all thy crimes* that thou hast thus shed their innocent blood; or, perhaps better, (ii) it was *because of this thy lust* for idolatry, that thou could'st not abide them.

    35. *Because*] **But,** a protest against the whole of the preceding accusation.

    surely his anger shall turn from me] because of the reformation since Manasseh's days. For 'shall turn' we should rather render *hath turned*, hath not fallen, and thus I am proved innocent.

    I will plead with thee] a different word from that used earlier in the chapter, and meaning rather, I will act the judge towards thee.

    36. *to change thy way*] See ver. 18 for some detail of the vacillation

ashamed of Egypt, as thou wast ashamed of Assyria. Yea, 37
thou shalt go forth from him, and thine hands upon thine
head: for the LORD hath rejected thy confidences, and thou
shalt not prosper in them.

CHAP. III. 1—5. *Israel has forfeited her privileges.*

They say, If a man put away his wife, and she go from 3
him, and become another man's, shall he return unto her

of Israel's policy. Manasseh and Amon also may have made a league with Egypt.

thou also shalt be ashamed of Egypt] This was literally fulfilled, when the Egyptians were expected to raise the siege of Jerusalem in the reign of Zedekiah, but failed to do so (Jer. xxxvii. 5).

thou wast ashamed of Assyria] One conspicuous instance of this was in the reign of Ahaz, when in spite of his presents to the king of Assyria, that monarch helped him not (2 Chron. xxviii. 21. See also Is. vii., viii). From this verse as from ver. 8 above it has been inferred by some that these chapters must have been, if not written, at any rate recast in the days of Jehoiakim; since in the days of Josiah, when Assyria was declining, there could have been no reason, it is thought, for seeking an alliance with Egypt. There is however nothing to prevent one supposing that the Jews looked with suspicion on the Eastern Empire, and that an influential party at any rate were willing to make overtures to Egypt, until Josiah finally committed himself to hostilities with that power by the act which led to his death at Megiddo. Further the whole tone of the discourse implies that the kingdom of Judah was still politically independent, a state in which it certainly was not during the reign of Jehoiakim.

37. *thou shalt go forth from him*] Egypt shall repulse thy advances, and thou shall return mourning.

thine hands upon thine head] Compare Tamar, who after the wrong put upon her by Amnon, "laid her hand on her head, and went on crying." (2 Sam. xiii. 19.)

thy confidences] those in whom thou confidest, Egypt and Assyria.

CHAP. III. 1—5. ISRAEL HAS FORFEITED HER PRIVILEGES.

1. *They say*] The Hebrew is simply *saying*. It probably is to be connected with the words 'hath rejected' (ii. 37) and to be rendered, *saying*, or, *for he saith*. The connexion of thought is: the Lord refuses to recognise either Egypt or Assyria as the lawful spouse of his people, at the same time saying that as they have chosen to forsake Him for them, He will act in accordance with the law of divorce and will refuse to receive Israel again.

shall he return unto her again?] When a woman left her husband in accordance with a bill of divorce and was married to another, even a bill of divorce given her by her new husband did not set her free to

again? shall not that land be greatly polluted? but thou hast played the harlot with many lovers; yet return again 2 to me, saith the LORD. Lift up thine eyes unto the high places, and see where thou hast not been lien with. In the ways hast thou sat for them, as the Arabian in the wilderness; and thou hast polluted the land with thy whoredoms 3 and with thy wickedness. Therefore the showers have been withholden, and there hath been no latter rain; and thou 4 hadst a whore's forehead, thou refusedst to be ashamed. Wilt thou not from this time cry unto me, My father, thou *art* 5 the guide of my youth? Will he reserve *his anger* for ever?

be reunited to the former one. See Deut xxiv. 1—4 for the words of the law on the subject.

yet return] **and thinkest thou to return.** This is by far the most probable sense. There is no invitation to the people, such as the English Version would suggest, to come back to God, but an expression of surprise that those who must be familiar with the teaching of the law on the subject of earthly marriage and divorce should fail to see the impossibility of playing fast and loose with God in such a matter—a thing forbidden even in human affairs. This explanation also accords better with ver. 2.

2. Israel is shameless and wholly given up to idolatrous excesses.

high places] **bare heights**, without trees.

the Arabian in the wilderness] the Bedaween freebooters, such as even at the present day make descents upon parties in that country for purposes of plunder. As is their eagerness to despoil a passing caravan or other company of travellers, so is that of Israel for the worship of false gods.

3. *latter rain*] that which fell in March and April, the second of the rainy seasons, the "early rain" (James v. 7) occurring in October and November. See chap. v. 24.

4. *Wilt thou not...cry*] **Hast thou not cried.**

from this time] from the time of Josiah's reforms. These were begun in the twelfth year of his reign and completed six years later on the occasion of his great celebration of the Passover feast (2 Chron. xxxiv. 3, xxxv. 19). This period of reforms is shewn by the expression 'this time' to be not long past, and so confirms the general view given above as to the date of this portion of the prophecy.

guide] The word may be rendered 'husband,' a sense which the original bears also in Prov. ii. 17.

5. The first part of the verse is a continuation of the words of Israel, expressing her confidence that the anger of her Divine Spouse will pass in spite of her faithlessness.

reserve] the sense of *keep back*, *restrain* in which we so often use this word might for a moment mislead the English reader. The context shews that the sense is *retain*, keep in exercise.

will he keep *it* to the end? Behold, thou hast spoken and done evil *things* as thou couldest.

6—20. *Grievously as both Israel and Judah have sinned, yet forgiveness awaits both, but conditionally on their repentance.*

6 The LORD said also unto me in the days of Josiah the king, Hast thou seen *that* which backsliding Israel hath done? she is gone up upon every high mountain and under every green tree, and there hath played the harlot. And 7 I said after she had done all these *things*, Turn thou unto me. But she returned not. And her treacherous sister

thou hast spoken and done evil things as thou couldest] **thou hast spoken thus but hast done evil things and carried them through.** The English Version makes the words and deeds of Israel to have been alike evil, whereas there is a contrast drawn between her specious words and her idolatrous ways. The last verb of the sentence, literally 'thou couldest,' expresses the power which Israel had not omitted to exercise for evil.

6—20. GRIEVOUSLY AS BOTH ISRAEL AND JUDAH HAVE SINNED, YET FORGIVENESS AWAITS BOTH, BUT CONDITIONALLY ON THEIR REPENTANCE.

6. *The Lord said also unto me in the days of Josiah the king*] It is clear that this prophecy like the last is a summary or condensation of Jeremiah's teaching at the time, and does not represent any one discourse. It is also clear that we are to take this and the preceding part together. Not only are the two alike in subject, but the very phrases used are to a great extent identical. One marked distinction however between the two lies in this, that while in the former no hope of forgiveness was held out (it being there assumed that there was no genuine repentance), we have here the distinct assurance of pardon on the appearance of contrition. It is possible that the mention of the days of Josiah may imply that this part of the prophecy is more immediately connected with the time of his reforms. Judah has not taken warning by the example of Israel's sin and punishment. Nay, she has added to apostasy treachery. Nevertheless an acknowledgment of sin from either portion of the nation will bring pardon.

backsliding Israel] The Hebrew is stronger. *Israel, the backsliding one*, literally '(which is) *apostasy* (itself).' So too in ver. 7 'treacherous' is literally *faithlessness*.

7. *I said*] to myself; I thought.

after she had done all these things, Turn thou unto me] better, *after she* has *done all these things*, she will return *unto me*.

treacherous] See ver. 6, above.

8 Judah saw *it*. And I saw, when for all the causes whereby backsliding Israel committed adultery I had put her away, and given her a bill of divorce; yet her treacherous sister
9 Judah feared not, but went and played the harlot also. And it came to pass through the lightness of her whoredom, that she defiled the land, and committed adultery with stones
10 and with stocks. And yet for all this her treacherous sister Judah hath not turned unto me with her whole heart, but
11 feignedly, saith the Lord. And the Lord said unto me, The backsliding Israel hath justified herself more than
12 treacherous Judah. Go and proclaim these words toward the north, and say, Return, thou backsliding Israel, saith

8. This and the seventh ver. correspond in the order of their thoughts and in the thoughts themselves. 'I said' (ver. 7) corresponds to 'I saw' (ver. 8). Israel's conduct is the subject of the first part in each sentence, and Judah's imitation of it that of the second part.

for all the causes whereby] *On account of all the causes for which*, was perhaps the actual legal phraseology with which the bill of divorce commenced.

9. *stones and with stocks*] idols of stone and of wood.

10. *for all this*] In spite of the warning thus afforded in the sin and consequent downfall of the sister-kingdom, Judah has put on a mere semblance of reformation, thereby aggravating her guilt. The surface only and not the core of the nation was affected by king Josiah's reforms.

11. Having thus thrice declared the part which 'her treacherous sister Judah' had played in forsaking the Lord for idols, He pronounces the sentence of condemnation, once more giving each kingdom the epithet appropriate to its sin, and charging Judah with hypocrisy as well as desertion. In spite of
 (i) greater privileges,
  (*a*) succession of kings of the same family, (*b*) Temple, (*c*) Levites;
 (ii) the warning example of Israel;
Judah has proved faithless.

"The verse is further important, *first* as accounting for the destruction of Jerusalem so soon after the pious reign of Josiah. Manasseh's crimes had defiled the land, but it was by rejecting the reforms of Josiah that they profaned it, and sealed their doom; *secondly*, as shewing that it is not by the acts of its government that a nation stands or falls. Ahaz and Manasseh lent the weight of their influence to the cause of idolatry: Hezekiah and Josiah to the cause of truth. But the nation had to determine which should prevail." (*Speaker's Comm.*)

12. *toward the north*] towards Assyria and Media, whither the Ten Tribes had been carried captive by Shalmaneser, king of the former country.

the LORD; *and* I will not cause mine anger to fall upon you: for I *am* merciful, saith the LORD, *and* I will not keep *anger* for ever. Only acknowledge thine iniquity, that thou hast 13 transgressed against the LORD thy God, and hast scattered thy ways to the strangers under every green tree, and ye have not obeyed my voice, saith the LORD. Turn, O backsliding 14 children, saith the LORD; for I am married unto you: and I will take you one of a city, and two of a family, and I will bring you *to* Zion: and I will give you pastors accord- 15

mine anger] **my face**. The sense is, I will not look severely upon you. Compare for the same phrase Gen. iv. 5, "Cain was very wroth and *his countenance fell*."

The offer in this verse is plainly conditional upon the repentance of Israel, and as in point of fact they were not restored, we may gather with certainty that the condition was not fulfilled.

13. Repentance and acknowledgment of definite sin alone are necessary to ensure pardon.

hast scattered thy ways] hast wandered hither and thither. Comp. ii. 23.

strangers] strange gods. Compare ii. 25.

14. *children*] **sons**. Although they have wandered and are now in "a far country" and "in want" (Luke xv. 13, 14) they can count on a Father's welcome, if they return in a filial spirit. By this rendering the mixture of metaphors is made more prominent. The people are at once sons that have left their Father's house, and a wife that has been divorced. "I am married unto you."

one of a city, and two of a family] One or two shall be converted to a sense of their guilt. Both 'family' and 'city' refer still to Jews, not to their Gentile captors. *Family* to the Jewish ear suggested a larger number than *city*. A mere village might bear the name of a city, while a family denoted the larger subdivisions of the tribes, admitted of many ramifications, and contained persons whose connexion with one another would according to our notions be but very slender. In this verse then the offer is, so to speak, individualised. The exiles are told that, even though there be no national repentance, yet as it is open to each one to return, so each shall be dealt with on his merits. At the return from the captivity in Babylon certain of the Ten Tribes may have accepted the invitation here given, and thus been the means of the partial fulfilment of the promise. In a fuller sense it has been in course of being carried out ever since, first in the conversion of Jews in the time of our Lord and the Apostles, and secondarily in the Christian Church. In the former period there were still dwelling within Palestine those who traced their descent from one or other of the Ten Tribes (Luke ii. 36), while the thought of the original unity of those descended from Israel's twelve sons appears elsewhere in the New Testament (Acts xxvi. 7; James i. 1).

15. *pastors*] For the sense see chap. ii. 8, and for the different sort of rulers which Israel had had compare Hosea viii.

ing to mine heart, which shall feed you with knowledge and
16 understanding. And it shall come to pass, when ye be
multiplied and increased in the land, in those days, saith
the LORD, they shall say no more, The ark of the covenant
of the LORD: neither shall it come to mind: neither shall
they remember it; neither shall they visit *it*; neither shall
17 *that* be done any more. At that time they shall call Jerusalem the throne of the LORD; and all the nations shall be
gathered unto it, to the name of the LORD, to Jerusalem:
neither shall they walk any more after the imagination of

16. A brief sketch of the exceeding blessings that shall follow, if Israel hearken. The ark, hitherto the seat of the special manifestation of God's glory, shall be forgotten, because He will shew Himself throughout Jerusalem, and the whole city shall be filled with His presence.

in those days] an ordinary phrase with the prophets to denote the time of the Messiah. Compare v. 18; xxxiii. 16.

they shall say no more, The ark of the covenant of the Lord] It shall be forgotten by those who have God Himself walking in the midst of their city. The ark with its top forming the mercy-seat, on which the visible brightness marking God's presence, the Shekinah, rested, was the centre of reverence, although hidden by the veil of the Temple which parted the Holy of Holies from the rest of the building. For the thought of the ark with the figures of the Cherubim upon it as God's throne, compare Ps. lxxx. 1, xcix. 1; also Exod. xxv. 22; Numb. vii. 89. As a matter of fact the ark of Mosaic times perished no doubt in the destruction of Jerusalem by the Chaldeans.

come to mind] The marginal reading 'come upon the heart illustrates the custom of speaking of the heart as the abode of the intelligence.

visit] or, possibly, miss, feel the want of.

neither shall that be done any more] The words might also be rendered *neither shall it (the ark) be made any more;* that is, no repairs shall be done to it.

17. *they shall call Jerusalem the throne of the Lord*] God's glory and visible presence shall be manifested, not as heretofore on the covering of the ark alone, but throughout the holy city. He will thus shew that His presence is not necessarily confined to the ark or temple, and therefore that the possession of these, on which the people were relying so much, by no means ensures protection from the foe or spiritual blessing.

all the nations] Gentile peoples shall be gathered into the Church of God, which shall thus become Universal.

neither shall they] the Jews and Gentiles thus united.

imagination] **stubbornness.** So the word doubtless means on its first occurrence in the Bible, Deut. xxix. 19 (of which this is apparently a citation), Ps. lxxxi. 12 ("lust"), and seven other times in Jeremiah.

their evil heart. In those days the house of Judah shall 18
walk with the house of Israel, and they shall come together
out of the land of the north to the land that I have given
for an inheritance unto your fathers. But I said, How shall 19
I put thee among the children, and give thee a pleasant
land, a goodly heritage of the hosts of nations? and I said,
Thou shalt call me, My father; and shalt not turn away
from me. Surely *as* a wife treacherously departeth from her 20

18. *with*] 'To,' the marginal rendering, is nearest the usual sense of the Hebrew word. If this be its proper rendering here, the clause will imply that the Ten Tribes will be the first to repent, and that then Judah, seeing this, will join them, that all may return together out of captivity. The prophet thus implies the subordinate position which Judah shall take in the future in comparison with the other Tribes, and that because of her greater iniquity, as already set forth. The word rendered 'with' in the Text need not however denote anything further than the coupling together of Israel and Judah. In Exod. xxxv. 22 we have the Hebrew word in this sense 'both men *and* women.'

The whole verse may be compared with Isaiah xi. 12, 13, he "shall assemble the outcasts of Israel, and gather together the dispersed of Judah from the four corners of the earth...Ephraim shall not envy Judah, and Judah shall not vex Ephraim." The unity there pictured as existing between the formerly rival kingdoms is the same idea as that of Jeremiah.

19, 20. The prophet is about to describe the thoughts of Israel. These verses form the transition. In them he introduces the LORD as telling of His own affection for Israel, and of the ingratitude with which that affection had been repaid. His manner of expressing the former of these thoughts is no doubt suggested by the language of the previous verse. The mention there of the land of promise leads Him to speak of the 'pleasant land,' the 'goodly heritage' that He was ready to bestow.

19. *But*] **And.** No opposition is intended.

I said] The pronoun should be emphatic. Whatever Israel's conduct may be, God's purposes and love are sure. The time referred to is the Exodus from Egypt.

How] Not a question as in the English Version, but How gloriously! How honourably!

among the children] the nations, which, as created all of them by God, are all of them His children, while Israel, unless it forfeits the right, may claim to be His first-born. Compare Exod. iv. 22, "Thus saith the Lord, Israel is my son, even my firstborn."

goodly heritage of the hosts] **heritage of the chief splendour**, or, **goodliest heritage.** The sense is that Israel shall have a more glorious land than any other nation. Compare a "land...flowing with milk and honey, which is the glory of all lands." (Ezek. xx. 6, 15.)

Thou shalt...and shalt not...] Better, *Ye shall...and shall not....*

husband, so have you dealt treacherously with me, O house of Israel, saith the LORD.

21—25. *Confession of sin on the part of Israel.*

²¹ A voice was heard upon the high places, weeping *and* supplications of the children of Israel: for they have perverted their way, *and* they have forgotten the LORD their ²² God. Return, ye backsliding children, *and* I will heal your backslidings. Behold, we come unto thee; for thou *art* the ²³ LORD our God. Truly in vain *is salvation hoped for* from the hills, *and from* the multitude of mountains: truly in the ²⁴ LORD our God *is* the salvation of Israel. For shame hath

20. *O house of Israel*] Israel here used of the Ten Tribes, but yet with a reference to Judah, as the latter would see her own misdeeds reflected in Israel.

21—25. CONFESSION OF SIN ON THE PART OF ISRAEL.

21. *high places*] See note on ver. 2 above. The voice comes from them not only as having been the places where idolatry had been practised, but in accordance with Eastern custom to choose some lofty or prominent place on which to make public lamentation. Compare chap. vii. 29; also Moab's overthrow lamented by that nation upon its "high places" (Is. xv. 2), and Jephthah's daughter bewailing her virginity "up and down upon the mountains" (Judg. xi. 37).

22. God's reply to the lamentation and expressions of repentance. The Hebrew is striking in its play on the word *turn*, *Turn*, ye *turned* children; I will heal your *turnings*.

Behold, we come] The offer of pardon is accepted. The picture is an impressive one; the cries of repentance on the part of a nation—their wandering on the hills in sorrow—the utterance of forgiveness—their return into favour.

23. *Truly in vain is salvation hoped for from the hills, and from the multitude of mountains*] **Truly in vain is it from the hills, in vain is revelry on the mountains.** The construction is obscure in the original. The returning Israelites contrast the orgies that belong to idol worship with the security and spiritual blessing which the Lord imparts.

24. Vain was the boisterous service spoken of in ver. 23. It is not merely without profit, but most hurtful.

shame] Bosheth = Baal, the god of shame, the god who brings disgrace, whose worship is an opprobrium to the worshipper. The Hebrew word is often elsewhere used as an equivalent for Baal. Compare xi. 13, where the two are identified, also Hos. ix. 10; so too as parts of compound proper names Baal and Bosheth are identified; Jerubbaal (Judg. vi. 32) = Jerubbesheth (2 Sam. xi. 21); Eshbaal (1 Chron. viii. 33) = Ishbosheth (2 Sam. ii. 8).

devoured the labour of our fathers from our youth; their flocks and their herds, their sons and their daughters. We lie down in our shame, and our confusion covereth us: for we have sinned against the LORD our God, we and our fathers, from our youth even unto this day, and have not obeyed the voice of the LORD our God.

CHAP. IV. 1—11. *Summing up of the message to Israel and Judah. Announcement of impending destruction to Jerusalem.*

If thou wilt return, O Israel, saith the LORD, return unto me: and if thou wilt put away thine abominations out of my sight, then shalt thou not remove. And thou shalt

hath devoured the labour] hath consumed the possessions (as enumerated immediately afterwards). Labour is here used for the fruits of toil. The verse seems to refer simply to the sacrifices offered to Baal, which were sometimes even human. Although flocks and herds yielded sacrifices to the LORD also, yet there could be no real similarity between such offerings and those which were exacted by a god like Baal. Others however take the *devouring* to consist in the temporal misfortunes resulting from estrangement from the true God, so that it is equivalent to saying, We have been ruined as a nation by our wickedness and idolatry.

25. *We lie down*] *We will lie down*, or, *Let us lie down*. Repentance for the misdeeds of the past shall be so strong that we shall be overwhelmed with emotion and shall lie prostrate under its influence. Compare for such a custom when under very painful feelings 2 Sam. xii. 16, xiii. 31; 1 Kings xxi. 4.

covereth] *shall cover*, or, *let* (our confusion) *cover*. For the thought compare Ps. cix. 29.

CHAP. IV. 1—11. SUMMING UP OF THE MESSAGE TO ISRAEL AND JUDAH. ANNOUNCEMENT OF IMPENDING DESTRUCTION TO JERUSALEM.

In verses 1—4 a severer mode of address is used towards Judah (3, 4) than towards Israel (1, 2).

1. *If thou wilt return*] both in the sense of a change of mind, and of a literal return from captivity, as its consequence.

return unto me] **unto me thou shalt return.**

abominations] false gods. Compare 1 Kings xi. 5, 7 where the two are shown to be identical; compare also 2 Kings xxiii. 13, and many passages in Jeremiah.

then shalt thou not remove] **and not stray.** This clause is not the completion of the sentence, as the English Version makes it to be, but merely expresses the thought of the previous clause in different

swear, The LORD liveth, in truth, in judgment, and in righteousness; and the nations shall bless themselves in him,
3 and in him shall they glory. For thus saith the LORD to the men of Judah and Jerusalem, Break up your fallow

language; verse 2 (the *apodosis* to the preceding *protasis*) expresses the consequence, in case the previous conditions are fulfilled. "Stray" refers to the restless search after one or another unreal object of worship, as described already (ii. 23, iii. 13).

2. *And thou shalt*] **Then thou shalt.**

The Lord liveth] *As the Lord liveth*. From the Eng. Version we might suppose that this is itself the subject, and not simply the form, of the oath. The Living God is "not the thing sworn to, but the thing sworn by" (*Speaker's Commentary*). Oaths by other gods are to be dismissed from their mouths. The people, while yet in the wilderness, are commanded by Moses to "cleave" to the Lord "and swear by His name, He is thy praise and He is thy God" (Deut. x. 20, 21). So now if they will give the same proof that in their minds He is supreme, there shall follow their own restoration, and through them a blessing to all nations of the world.

and the nations] **then the nations.**

shall bless themselves in him] in the LORD, not in Israel, as is shewn by the last clause, where in that case the verb to glory would be inappropriate. Jeremiah however doubtless alludes here, as is his wont, to the earlier Scriptures, such as "In thee shall all families of the earth be blessed" (Gen. xii. 3), etc. Compare Ps. lxiii. 11, "Every one that sweareth by him (God) shall glory." On the assumption that Israel repents, it will be through her that the Gentile nations shall obtain the blessing of God. This Jeremiah implies by his undoubted reference to the covenant made with Abraham, as quoted above. Thus then the end of the former part of ver. 1, and of the latter part of ver. 2, are the consequences of the conditions (single and threefold respectively), which precede them.

3. *For*] This with the following verse contains a direct application of the foregoing words to Judah. They were after all the part of the nation in which the prophet was most directly interested, and he thus naturally seeks to bring them within the compass of his prophecy, and to rouse them to do that which he had urged upon Israel.

Break up] **Make fallow for yourselves.** The contrast is not between uncultivated ground and that which bears a crop, but between that which receives much and that which receives but little attention. The figure is accordingly drawn from land allowed to lie fallow, in order that it might thereby be presently made the fitter for cultivation. Land in this condition would be overgrown by thorns, and it was that there might be the opportunity to free the soil from these that the cultivator permitted it to be at rest from time to time for a short period. The point of the command then is this:—as the farmer is careful to clear the soil of weeds, before sowing his seed, so do you use care in the

ground, and sow not among thorns. Circumcise yourselves 4 to the LORD, and take away the foreskins of your heart, ye men of Judah and inhabitants of Jerusalem: lest my fury come forth like fire, and burn that none can quench *it*, because of the evil of your doings. Declare ye in Judah, 5 and publish in Jerusalem; and say, Blow ye the trumpet in the land: cry, gather together, and say, Assemble yourselves,

work of repentance. No hasty or scanty sowing in this case will bear fruit that I can accept. It must be done thoughtfully and with sustained diligence in order to prove effectual.

4. *Circumcise yourselves to the Lord*] The addition of the last three words mark that the verb is used in a spiritual sense, as is further shewn by the mention of the 'heart' in the same connexion. The nature of the injunction then is that all impurity, and especially idolatry as the crying sin of the nation, should be put away.

like fire] consuming all that opposes itself to its progress.

5. With this verse begins a group of addresses here given in substance, and reaching to the end of chap. x. The general subject is the same throughout, a declaration of the coming evil. The words as we have them, in all probability, formed a part of the roll as read in the ears of Jehoiakim, or afterwards enlarged, and represent the gist of Jeremiah's preaching during the latter part of Josiah's reign, that of Jehoahaz, and the beginning of that of Jehoiakim. During the greater part of this time it was still possible for the people to avert calamity by repentance and amendment of life. After Jehoiakim's reign had fairly begun and he had shewn that even the check which Josiah's personal character and influence had put upon idolatry was now removed, the condition of the nation became desperate. The near approach or actual arrival of that condition therefore was present to Jeremiah's mind throughout this section and coloured all his utterances. He speaks of the hostile army and of the destruction which it is about to deal. Judgment comes from the north, like the hot blast of the tempest not to be warded off by any human devices. At the beginning of chap. vii. there is a break caused by a new heading, and that with the three chapters that follow probably give us the exact words spoken by Jeremiah on a special occasion during this period. See notes there.

This and the subsequent verses are connected with the preceding as being an expanded description of the punishment there threatened. They give us a graphic picture of the excitement and dismay caused throughout the defenceless portions of the land by the approach of the enemy, and the hasty retreat to walled towns on the part of the country people.

Blow ye] addressed either to those whose duty it was so to do, or to those who should first become aware of the danger.

cry, gather together] **cry aloud.**

Assemble yourselves] The inhabitants of the villages meet at a rendezvous and seek refuge in a body in the nearest fortified towns. So we

6 and let us go into the defenced cities. Set up the standard toward Zion: retire, stay not: for I will bring evil from the 7 north, and a great destruction. The lion is come up from his thicket, and the destroyer of the Gentiles is on his way; he is gone forth from his place to make thy land desolate; *and* thy cities shall be laid waste, without an inhabitant.

find e.g. that the Rechabites have done (chap. xxxv.) Compare the crowding of the inhabitants of Attica within the walls of Athens on the occasion of a Spartan invasion (Thuc. ii. 52).

6. *Set up the standard*] This was to be done not so much as affording a place of comparative security on a height, as to mark out the safest route to those who were seeking to attain the shelter of the walls of Jerusalem. The erection of lofty poles with banners waving from them would be a signal reaching further and therefore more expeditious than even the trumpet blast.

standard] Our Authorized English Version, as first published (in 1611), has by mistake *standards*. The mistake was not corrected till the first careful revision of that Version, made at Cambridge, 1629.

retire] **save your goods by flight.** The same Hebrew word is used and in the same sense in Exod. ix. 19; Is. x. 31 (English Vers. "gather").

evil from the north] Some have taken the reference to be to the Scythians. It is true that they made a descent *in the direction of* Judaea during the reign of Josiah (see Introduction, chap. i. § 3), and were checked by Psammetichus, king of Egypt. Even granting however that their invasion was made as late as or later than the time of this prophecy, there are two reasons fatal to the supposition that it has to do with them:

(i) There is nothing to shew that they ever invaded Judaea.
(ii) The description of the invading force does not suit them. We have no knowledge that they used chariots. On the contrary, the description exactly fits in with what we know otherwise of the armies of Chaldaea, who are therefore no doubt here meant.

7. *The lion*] **A lion.**

thicket] the usual lurking place of such.

the destroyer of the Gentiles] **a destroyer of nations.** He is not like an ordinary lion a destroyer of individuals, but of whole nations.

he is gone forth from his place] literally, *he has struck his tents*, as does an army. After Jeremiah's usual manner, he suddenly drops his metaphor, and begins to express his meaning directly and without figure.

without an inhabitant] fulfilled, as related chap. xliii. 5—7, "Johanan the son of Kareah...took all the remnant of Judah...So they came into the land of Egypt."

For this gird you with sackcloth, lament and howl: for the 8
fierce anger of the LORD is not turned back from us. And 9
it shall come to pass at that day, saith the LORD, *that*
the heart of the king shall perish, and the heart of the
princes; and the priests shall be astonished, and the prophets shall wonder. (Then said I, Ah, Lord GOD! surely 10
thou hast greatly deceived this people and Jerusalem, saying,
Ye shall have peace; whereas the sword reacheth unto the

8. *is not turned back from us*] The wickedness of the days of Manasseh has not been repented of. Any reformation has been merely on the surface, and those who imagine that it has been sufficient to recover God's favour towards His people will find their mistake.

9. *heart*] *understanding.* Their intellect shall be paralyzed.

the priests shall be astonished] because of the punishment which has followed upon their idolatries.

the prophets shall wonder] because of the non-fulfilment of their prophecies.

10. This verse has caused some perplexity to commentators. The difficulty consists in the fact that in it God is spoken of as employing deceit. The chief modes in which the difficulty has been met are

(i) Jeremiah is not speaking his own words but those of the false prophets, on finding that their predictions of peace are not coming to pass.

(ii) The words are those of Jeremiah himself, but used against the false prophets, whom he thus ironically assumes to have been inspired by God to utter vain predictions of prosperity.

(iii) God is said to have done Himself that evil which in point of fact He has only permitted to occur.

(i) and (ii) are harsh and far fetched, while (iii) was a mode of thought and speech familiar to the Jew (compare 1 Kings xxii. 21—23), who accordingly would not feel that there was any irreverence in this mode of expressing his difficulty. For the emotion which must have possessed Jeremiah at the time and drawn from him this startling exclamation, we may compare Elijah's case in 1 Kings xix. 10, 14. The prophet "broke into a wild cry, in which he gave expression to his pain, and, relieved, he felt the fire of duty burn bright again, and took up again the work of life." *Christ in Modern Life* (Rev. S. Brooke), p. 155.

"To me alone there came a thought of grief,
A timely utterance gave that thought relief,
And I again am strong."
                                            Wordsworth.

That the prophets were very eager to understand what was obscure in the predictions they uttered, we gather from 1 Pet. i. 10, 11. In this particular case the fulfilment, though sure, was in the yet distant future.

11 soul). At that time shall it be said to this people and to Jerusalem,

11—18. *Description of the enemy's attack.*

A dry wind of the high places in the wilderness toward
    the daughter of my people,
Not to fan, nor to cleanse,
12 *Even* a full wind from those *places* shall come unto me :
Now also will I give sentence against them.
13 Behold, he shall come up as clouds,
And his chariots *shall be* as a whirlwind :

soul] life.
11. Having given vent to the wail characteristic of his disposition he resumes his prophetic utterance.
At that time shall it be said] When the invader is advancing, the tidings shall be borne by messengers and fugitives as follows:

11—18. DESCRIPTION OF THE ENEMY'S ATTACK.

A dry wind] *A hot wind.* A wind from the east, such as is prevalent in that country, accompanied by a cloudless sky. As it comes down from the hills and across the barren wastes it withers up all vegetation, besides producing the utmost discomfort. "The air becomes loaded with fine dust, which it whirls in rainless clouds hither and thither at its own wild will...... The eyes inflame, the lips blister and the moisture of the body evaporates, under the ceaseless application of this persecuting wind" (Thomson, *The Land and the Book*, p. 295). "We have two kinds of sirocco, one accompanied with vehement wind, which fills the air with dust and fine sand" (*ibid.* p. 536).
high places] **bare heights.** Compare note on iii. 2.
not to fan, nor to cleanse] alluding to the Eastern mode of winnowing. By the vehemence of this wind wheat and chaff alike shall be swept away.
12. *a full wind from those places*] rather, *fuller than those* (winds) that are used to winnow and cleanse. Such a storm is meant as that described forcibly in Joel (ii. 30, 31), where the sun, as seen through columns of sand and dust, is the colour of blood, while those columns themselves are likened to "pillars of smoke."
unto] **for**; at My command.
now also will I] The pronoun is emphatic. I, in reply to their attack on me in the way of idol-worship, will, etc.
13. *as clouds*] So in Ezekiel (xxxviii. 16) the enemy Gog is said to be coming up against Israel "as a cloud to cover the land;" and in the prophecy of Joel (ii. 2) the invading army is extended over the land like "clouds and thick darkness, as the morning spread upon the mountains."
his chariots shall be as a whirlwind] The same comparison is used twice by the prophet Isaiah (v. 28, lxvi. 15).

His horses are swifter than eagles.
Woe unto us! for we are spoiled.
O Jerusalem, wash thine heart from wickedness, that thou 14
  mayest be saved.
How long shall thy vain thoughts lodge within thee?
For a voice declareth from Dan, 15
And publisheth affliction from mount Ephraim.
Make ye mention to the nations; behold, publish against 16
  Jerusalem,
That watchers come from a far country,

swifter than eagles] Compare chap. xlviii. 40; 2 Sam. i. 23; Lam. iv. 19; Hab. i. 8.

Woe unto us! for we are spoiled] This represents either the cry of the people on finding themselves hopelessly in the hands of the invading force, or the lament of the prophet himself as he realizes the state of things that he has just depicted. The former view is the more likely one. Compare ver. 19, etc.

14. *thine heart*] as opposed to mere surface-reform. Compare "hath not turned unto me with her whole heart but feignedly," (iii. 10).

How long] Thou hast wearied me with thy prolonged faithlessness.

vain] sinful, idolatrous. The Hebrew word, properly denoting sin of any kind, is used specially of the worship of idols. Thus Beth-el (house of God) is called (Hos. iv. 15, etc.) in consequence of the worship there practised, Beth-aven (house of iniquity, house of an idol). At the same time there is a play on the word which we cannot reproduce in English. This appears in the original of ver. 15 where the same word is used in another of its senses *affliction*, thus enforcing the truth that idolatry and disaster are necessarily conjoined.

15. The connexion is, It is high time to amend, for, etc.

Dan] on the northern border of Palestine, see Deut. xxxiv. 1. It is mentioned frequently in conjunction with Beersheba, the other limit; e.g. Judges xx. 1; 1 Sam. iii. 20, etc. It was a conspicuous seat of idolatry, sharing as it did with Bethel the distinction of being selected by Jeroboam as the seat of a golden calf (1 Kings xii. 29).

affliction] See ver. 14.

mount Ephraim] the range dividing Ephraim from Judah, eight or ten miles at most from Jerusalem itself. The language thus intimates the rapid approach of the enemy. It was but now they were at Dan, and already they are crossing the hills in the very neighbourhood of the Assyrians, as described in Is. x., and of the capital of the southern kingdom. Compare the rapid advance of the Etruscans as described in Macaulay's "Horatius," (*Lays of Ancient Rome*,) "Now from the rock Tarpeian," etc.

16. *Make ye mention*] The nations are summoned to witness the vengeance about to be taken even on the chosen people. The event is itself of the utmost importance, and the lesson will be a most impressive one.

watchers] besiegers, the Chaldaeans.

And give out their voice against the cities of Judah.
17 As keepers of a field, are they against her round about;
Because she hath been rebellious against me, saith the Lord.

18 Thy way and thy doings have procured these *things* unto thee;
This *is* thy wickedness, because *it is* bitter,
Because it reacheth unto thine heart.

> 19—26. *Picture of the horror and desolation that are at hand.*

19 My bowels, my bowels! I am pained *at* my very heart;
My heart maketh a noise in me; I cannot hold my peace,
Because thou hast heard, O my soul, the sound of the trumpet, the alarm of war.

20 Destruction upon destruction is cried; for the whole land is spoiled:

17. *keepers of a field*] "In the time of our translators it may be doubted whether the term *field* was ever used of enclosed plots of ground. Such enclosures were called parks, while the field was the open country. (Lev. xiv. 7, xvii. 5, etc.). In it not only was it necessary to watch the cattle (Luke ii. 8), but also the crops (Job xxvii. 18). Jeremiah therefore compares the tents of the besiegers on guard round Jerusalem to the booths erected by shepherds or husbandmen for the protection of their flocks or produce." (*Speaker's Comm.*)

18. *wickedness*] The Hebrew word means either wickedness, or its result, viz. *calamity*. The latter is the sense here, as the succeeding words shew.

bitter] Owing to the remembrance that it is virtually self-inflicted.

reacheth unto thine heart] inflicteth deadly wounds. Compare ver. 10.

19—26. PICTURE OF THE HORROR AND DESOLATION THAT ARE AT HAND.

19. *at my very heart*] **O the walls of my heart!** a separate exclamation. These brief utterances well represent the pangs to which the speaker is being subjected. That speaker is not Jeremiah only, but the people as a whole. This appears from the next verse, and from chap. x. 20.

maketh a noise] The word in the Hebrew denotes tumultuous movement, pain, and the expression of it in sound.

20. *Destruction upon destruction*] the tidings of one calamity after another, as in the case of the successive announcements to Job. So Macaulay's "Horatius" as referred to above:

"Every hour some horseman came
With tidings of dismay."

Suddenly are my tents spoiled, *and* my curtains in a moment.
How long shall I see the standard, *and* hear the sound 21
of the trumpet?
For my people *is* foolish, they have not known me; 22
They *are* sottish children, and they have none understanding:
They *are* wise to do evil, but to do good they have no
knowledge.
I beheld the earth, and lo, *it was* without form, and void; 23
And the heavens, and they *had* no light.
I beheld the mountains, and lo, they trembled, 24
And all the hills moved lightly.
I beheld, and lo, *there was* no man, 25
And all the birds of the heavens were fled.
I beheld, and lo, the fruitful place *was* a wilderness, 26

is spoiled] assuming that this had already taken place; so certain was it.
tents] This seems not merely a name for dwellings, retained from nomadic times, but a representation of the real state of things with much of the pastoral and agricultural part of the nation even then. Compare for the expression 2 Sam. xviii. 17, xx. 1; 1 Kings viii. 66, xii. 16.
curtains] another way of saying tents; so x. 20; Cant. i. 5;· Is. liv. 2.
21. *standard*] as above in ver. 6.
trumpet] not as summoning hosts to battle, but admonishing fugitives to hasten their flight. Those who have not yet fled for refuge to the cities are constantly warned of fresh reason for so doing. The term is prolonged, and the end of it is not in sight. How long shall this state of things last?
22. *For*] The last verse contained an appeal addressed to God to know the cause why this invasion was permitted. This verse contains God's reply. It is not without cause, *for*, etc.
known] had regard to.
23. The prophet sees in vision the vastness of the desolation that is coming upon the land. It is a return to the state of things described in the History of the Creation. Matter is as yet lying "without form and void." Wildness, solitude, and general disorder are indicated. All is chaotic.
24. *moved lightly*] In spite of their vast size they were shaken to and fro as though they were "a very little thing."
25. *all the birds of the heavens were fled*] as expecting some dread convulsion of nature.
26. *the fruitful place*] Heb. Carmel, (see ii. 7), probably taken

And all the cities thereof were broken down
At the presence of the LORD, *and* by his fierce anger.

27—31. *The suffering and dismay that shall attend upon the overthrow of the kingdom cannot by any devices be averted.*

27 For thus hath the LORD said,
    The whole land shall be desolate;
    Yet will I not make a full end.

28 For this shall the earth mourn, and the heavens above be black:
    Because I have spoken *it*, I have purposed *it*,
    And will not repent, neither will I turn back from it.

29 The whole city shall flee for the noise of the horsemen and bowmen;

however here as representing the most fruitful portions of the land in general.

a wilderness] literally, *the wilderness*, i.e. "changed into the wilderness with all its attributes" (Hitzig, as quoted by Keil). There is a complete reversal of the natural features of the soil.

"In no country is the contrast between the glorious past and the miserable present so startling and sad...The whole land is a venerable ruin." (*Through Bible Lands*, p. 387, P. Schaff., D.D., New York, 1878).

27—31. THE SUFFERING AND DISMAY THAT SHALL ATTEND UPON THE OVERTHROW OF THE KINGDOM CANNOT BY ANY DEVICES BE AVERTED.

27. This is no mere picture or flight of fancy, but a tremendous reality, *For*, etc.

yet will I not make a full end] The overthrow shall not be such as that which sooner or later befalls all other kingdoms. The contrast between the chosen people and the rest of the nations is thus very remarkable, as is also the frequency and consistency with which the promise of final deliverance appears even in the midst of the severest threatenings. This feature of prophecy is found as early as Lev. xxvi. 44. Compare chap. v. 10; also Is. vi. 13, xi. 11, 16; Ezek. xx. 34; Amos ix. 8: Mic. ii. 12.

28. *For this*] because of the desolation of the whole land.

shall the earth mourn] as deprived of her products.

be black] be in mourning from sympathy. Observe in the latter part of the verse the emphatic assurance of the certainty of the coming woe.

29. This verse is in point of fact the resumed description of the desolating effect of the invasion, verses 27, 28 being almost a parenthesis.

The whole city] **Every city.** That this is the right rendering is shewn by the last word of the verse, which is literally in *them* (not, in *it*).

They shall go into thickets, and climb up upon the rocks:
Every city *shall be* forsaken, and not a man dwell therein.
And when thou art spoiled, what wilt thou do? 30
Though thou clothest thyself with crimson, though thou
  deckest thee with ornaments of gold,
Though thou rentest thy face with painting, in vain shalt
  thou make thyself fair;

A new feature is thus introduced into the description. Not only shall the country people flee to Jerusalem, but the inhabitants of the various towns as well. The whole city would mean Jerusalem only. 'City' is here used for its inhabitants, as in 1 Sam. iv. 13 ("all the city cried out").

bowmen] These formed the chief feature in the armies of the Assyrians. See Layard's *Monuments of Nineveh*.

thickets] The word in the original according to the pure Hebrew use means clouds, but in local dialects it came to be used in the sense in which Jeremiah here employs it.

rocks] These, and the caves which they contained, were often used as places of refuge in the course of Jewish history. See chap. xvi. 16, also Judges vi. 2; 1 Sam. xiii. 6; and compare Is. ii. 19, 21.

30. *And when thou art spoiled*] **And thou, plundered one.** The singular is put collectively for the plural. Compare ver. 31 'the daughter of Zion;' so also Ps. xlv. 12 ("the daughter of Tyre," meaning Tyrian maidens).

rentest thy face with painting] This is illustrated by an Egyptian "practice universal among the females of the higher and middle classes and very common among those of the lower orders, which is that of blackening the edge of the eyelids both above and below the eye with a black powder called *kohl*. This is a collyrium commonly composed of the smoke black, which is produced by burning a kind of *liban*, an aromatic resin, a species of frankincense....*Kohl* is also prepared of the smoke black produced by burning the shells of almonds....*Antimony, it is said, was formerly used for painting the edges of the eyelids.* The *kohl* is applied with a small probe of wood, ivory, or silver, tapering towards the end, but blunt: this is moistened, sometimes with rose-water, then dipped in the powder and drawn along the edges of the eyelids....The custom of thus ornamenting the eyes prevailed among both sexes in Egypt in very ancient times: this is shewn by the sculptures and paintings in the temples and tombs of this country, and *kohl*-vessels with the probes and even with remains of the black powder have often been found in the ancient tombs" (Lane's *Modern Egyptians*, vol. i. pages 45, 46).

rentest thy face] **dividest thine eyes**, forcibly partest thine eyelids, i.e. by the process above described. *Rent* is the older form of *rend* and is the present not the past tense. It now occurs here only, but in older editions of the Bible is found in eleven other passages. As instances of its use in Shakespeare, compare

Thy lovers will despise thee, they will seek thy life.
31 For I have heard a voice as of a woman in travail, *and* the anguish as of her that bringeth forth her first child, The voice of the daughter of Zion, *that* bewaileth herself, *that* spreadeth her hands,
Saying, Woe *is* me now! for my soul is wearied because of murderers.

Chap. V. 1—9. *Is the punishment too severe? Nay; God cannot but punish the wickedness that prevails among high and low alike.*

5 Run ye to and fro through the streets of Jerusalem, and

"And will you *rent* our ancient love asunder."
Mids. Night's Dr. iii. 2. 215.
"Where sighes and groanes, and shrieks that *rent* the ayre
Are made, not mark'd."
Macbeth, iv. 3 (Ed. 1623).
(*The Bible-Word Book*, by Eastwood and Wright.)

thy lovers] those whom thou wouldest have as paramours, those for whose support thou carriest on intrigues (ii. 33, 36) are the very ones, O Jerusalem, who seek thy hurt.

31. Thy wiles shall have no effect; for already I hear thy cries of agony and dismay.

that bewaileth herself] **she sigheth.**

that spreadeth her hands] **she stretcheth out her hands** (in the attitude of a suppliant).

is wearied] **sinketh exhausted.**

Chap. V. 1—9. Is the punishment too severe? Nay; God cannot but punish the wickedness that prevails among high and low alike.

1. *Run ye to and fro*] Instead of saying simply that good men were difficult or impossible to find in Jerusalem, the prophet seeks to arrest the attention by challenging his hearers to find one by a thorough and extensive search. The last words of the verse are evidently an allusion to the history contained in Gen. xviii. 23—33. As Abraham obtained by a series of requests that ten righteous found within Sodom should procure its safety, so here one godly man is to do the like for Jerusalem. The statement, as seeming to imply that there was not even an individual exception to the universal depravity that reigned there, has caused to some a difficulty which they have sought to evade by saying that the righteous would be afraid to walk abroad, and so would remain shut up, as did Jeremiah and Baruch after the publication of the contents of the roll in the time of Jehoiakim. Others have taken

see now, and know, and seek in the broad places thereof, if ye can find a man, if there be *any* that executeth judgment, that seeketh the truth; and I will pardon it. And though 2 they say, The LORD liveth; surely they swear falsely. O 3 LORD, *are* not thine eyes upon the truth? thou hast stricken them, but they have not grieved; thou hast consumed them, *but* they have refused to receive correction: they have made their faces harder than a rock; they have refused to return. Therefore I said, Surely these *are* poor; they are foolish: 4 for they know not the way of the LORD, *nor* the judgment of their God. I will get me unto the great men, and will 5

this verse as proof that the prophecy must be later than Josiah. There is however no need of adopting either of these views. The words were never meant to be taken literally. They are but an emphatic and lively way of stating what was doubtless the case even towards the end of Josiah's reign, viz.—that the little good that was left in the land was driven out of sight by the prevailing wickedness, and exercised no appreciable effect upon it. Some righteous were then left, even as later in the time of Zedekiah the last king of Judah (xxiv. 5).

broad places] the market-places and other chief places of resort.

executeth] **doeth.** *Execute* has acquired a more contracted and formal sense since the time when the Eng. Version was made.

truth] *sincerity, good faith;* by no means confined to truth in *words*.

2. Though they take the most solemn form of oath, as opposed to those by heaven, by the earth, by Jerusalem, by the head, (Matt. v. 34, 35,) which were all held to be less binding, they yet use it to give weight to a lie. See note on iv. 2.

3. The reply of the messengers as to the result of their search.

the truth] *sincerity.* See ver. 1. They have thought to please Thee by outward blandishments and the appearance of reverence, but Thou hast seen their heart.

they have made their faces harder than a rock] Compare Ezek. iii. 7—9.

4. *Therefore*] **And.**

The prophet thinks, surely it is poverty and ignorance that misleads them.

foolish] The same word is rendered "dote" in chap. l. 36. It seems however if not to include at least to be nearly akin to the sense of sinful. See Numb. xii. 11.

the way of the Lord] the way prescribed by God to man that he should walk in it.

the judgment of their God] that which God judges or decrees to be right and lawful. The rendering of the word in 2 Kings xvii. 26 well illustrates its meaning here. The Samaritan immigrants "knew not *the manner* of the God of the land."

speak unto them; for they have known the way of the Lord, *and* the judgment of their God: but these have altogether 6 broken the yoke, *and* burst the bonds. Wherefore a lion out of the forest shall slay them, *and* a wolf of the evenings shall spoil them, a leopard shall watch over their cities: every one that goeth out thence shall be torn in pieces: because their transgressions are many, *and* their backslidings 7 are increased. How shall I pardon thee for this? thy children have forsaken me, and sworn by *them that are* no gods: when I had fed them to the full, they then committed adul-

5. *they have known*] They have had leisure to study the Law, and to learn therefrom the will of God.
broken the yoke, and burst the bonds] of the Law and of obedience. The bonds are the fastenings of the yoke upon the neck of the beasts that bear it.
This verse suggested to Dante the images in the opening Canto of his *Inferno:*
"A lion's aspect, which appeared to me,
He seemed as if against me he were coming
With head uplifted, and with ravenous hunger,
So that it seemed the air was afraid of him;
And a she-wolf, that with all hungerings
Seemed to be laden in her meagreness,
And many folk has caused to live forlorn!"
Canto I. ll. 45—51. Longfellow's Trans.

6. The beasts here mentioned are literally meant, and are not figurative of the enemy. This is shewn by the different sorts which are enumerated. Compare for this form of punishment Lev. xxvi. 22; 2 Kings xvii. 25; and so Ezek. xiv. 15.
evenings] **deserts.** The mistake arose from the similarity of the two words in Hebrew. That *deserts* (as opposed to a word, meaning time) is the right rendering is farther shown by the parallelism with "a lion out of *the forest.*"
leopard] **panther.**
watch over] lie in wait for, about to spring, as is the custom of these animals. Compare Hos. xiii. 7.

7. *How*] **Why.**
this] thy faithlessness.
thy children] the people of Jerusalem at large.
I had fed them to the full] or, according to another reading, *I had bound them to me by oath.* This reading, which differs to the slightest possible extent in the Hebrew from that rendered in the English Version, is on the whole the more probable one.
The last part of the verse is best understood in the sense of faithlessness to their Divine Spouse, but perhaps with at least an allusion to the impure rites which accompanied idolatry.

tery, and assembled themselves by troops *in* the harlots' houses. They were *as* fed horses in the morning: every one neighed after his neighbour's wife. Shall I not visit for these *things?* saith the LORD: and shall not my soul be avenged on such a nation as this?

10—18. *In spite of the feeling of security which prevails, the Lord will speedily bring a desolating foe.*

Go ye up upon her walls, and destroy; but make not a full end: take away her battlements; for they *are* not the LORD'S. For the house of Israel and the house of Judah have dealt very treacherously against me, saith the LORD. They have belied the LORD, and said, *It is* not he; neither shall evil come upon us; neither shall we see sword nor famine: and the prophets shall become wind, and the word *is* not in them: thus shall it be done unto them. Wherefore thus

8. *in the morning*] **roving about.**

10—18. IN SPITE OF THE FEELING OF SECURITY WHICH PREVAILS, THE LORD WILL SPEEDILY BRING A DESOLATING FOE.

10. *upon*] rather, *into.*

her walls] probably the thought in the prophet's mind is that of a vineyard walled in. Hence the use of the preposition *into* above. He had already likened Jerusalem to a *vine* (ii. 21). Compare for the figure Is. v. 1, etc.

make not a full end] For the characteristic of prophecy here shewn see iv. 27 above, with the remark and references there.

battlements] *tendrils*, so as to keep up the figure of the vine. Compare for the thought Is. xviii. 5. Observe that it is the tendrils only, not the vine itself, that must be removed. The degenerate members of the nation, whose connexion with the central stalk has virtually ceased, and who no longer draw sap from the root, are to be pruned away by adversity.

12. *It is not he*] When a prophet bears to them God's message of warning, their reply is: The prophet is preaching his own inventions; it is not God who speaks by him. Another view is that their reply is equivalent to that of the fool (Ps. xiv. 1). "There is no God:" but this is less likely.

13. *and the prophets shall become wind*] still the words of the rebellious.

the word] *He who speaks*, the LORD.

thus] In accordance with the prophet's own threats may it happen to them. "The Lord do so to you and more also" is the reply of the unbelieving Jews.

saith the LORD God of hosts, Because ye speak this word, behold, I will make my words in thy mouth fire, and this
15 people wood, and it shall devour them. Lo, I will bring a nation upon you from far, O house of Israel, saith the LORD: it *is* a mighty nation, it *is* an ancient nation, a nation whose language thou knowest not, neither understandest what they
16 say. Their quiver *is* as an open sepulchre, they *are* all
17 mighty *men*. And they shall eat up thine harvest, and thy bread, *which* thy sons and thy daughters should eat: they shall eat up thy flocks and thine herds: they shall eat up thy vines and thy fig trees: they shall impoverish thy
18 fenced cities, wherein thou trustedst, with the sword. Nevertheless in those days, saith the LORD, I will not make a full end with you.

14. Because ye (the people) deny that the word is from me, I will make thy (Jeremiah's) words to come to pass and their fulfilment to devour the people as fire devours wood.

15. *O house of Israel*] This address includes of course Judah and is even made to her principally, but only as representative of the whole nation, both the captive part and that which still remained in Palestine and which contained members of all the tribes.

mighty] *enduring, not to be got rid of* is rather the sense of the Hebrew.

ancient] Compare Genesis xi. 31. Even at the time of Terah's migration from Ur, it was a city of the *Chaldees*.

whose language thou knowest not] This was one of the terrors foretold in Deut. (xxviii. 49) as a consequence of disobedience. Appeals for mercy would be fruitless when made in a tongue not understood by the stranger.

16. *Their quiver is as an open sepulchre*] The figure of speech here differs somewhat from that in Psalm v. 9, "Their throat is an open sepulchre." There the sense is that it snatches down whatever comes within reach. Here the point of comparison is that "as an open grave is filled with dead men, so the quiver of this enemy is filled with deadly missiles." (Keil.)

Their quiver] For the mention of the enemy as bowmen compare iv. 29.

17. *which thy sons and thy daughters should eat*] or, *They shall eat thy sons and thy daughters.*

they shall impoverish] **it shall break down.** This is the most likely sense of the Hebrew verb, which is also in the singular, as are the earlier verbs in the verse with the exception of the second.

sword] meaning weapons of war generally, as in chap. xxxiii. 4; Ezek. xxvi. 9 ("axes").

18. A renewal of the promise at the beginning of the section (v. 10).

19—29. *The cause of this is Judah's rebellious spirit, and her devotion to unjust and deceitful gains.*

And it shall come to pass, when ye shall say, Wherefore doth the LORD our God all these *things* unto us? then shalt thou answer them, Like as ye have forsaken me, and served strange gods in your land, so shall ye serve strangers in a land *that is* not yours.   Declare this in the house of Jacob, and publish it in Judah, saying, Hear now this, O foolish people, and without understanding; which have eyes, and see not; which have ears, and hear not: fear ye not me? saith the LORD: will ye not tremble at my presence, which have placed the sand *for* the bound of the sea *by* a perpetual decree, that it cannot pass it: and though the waves thereof toss themselves, yet can they not prevail; though they roar, yet can they not pass over it?   But this people hath a revolting and a rebellious heart; they are revolted and gone.   Neither say they in their heart, Let us now fear

19—29. THE CAUSE OF THIS IS JUDAH'S REBELLIOUS SPIRIT, AND HER DEVOTION TO UNJUST AND DECEITFUL GAINS.

19. The connexion of thought with the last section is that while the punishment was to be severe, the wickedness which had called it forth was gross. Notice also the adaptation of the punishment to the nature of the offence.

in a land that is not yours] Such an expression as this would by no means have been suitable, if the enemy threatened by the prophet were the Scythians, who were a roving people, having no fixed habitation.

20. Addressed to all bystanders, who will share in the prophet's sorrow and zeal for reformation. The two great divisions of the people are here mentioned distinctly in order to give greater universality and consequent solemnity to the appeal which Jeremiah makes.

21. For the severe language employed compare chap. iv. 22; Hos. vii. 11.

22. *which have placed the sand*] God's *power* as shewn in nature illustrated. The sand appears but a feeble means of resisting blows administered by tons of water, yet He has ordained by the laws of nature that it shall be sufficient for the purpose. Is not such a God to be feared?

23. The people are not obedient as even inanimate nature is.

a revolting and a rebellious heart] They are not content with revolt, i.e. drawing back from the true God, quitting His service; but actually take up the position of foes.

24. God's *grace* as shewn in nature illustrated. As the people refused to fear Him in consideration of His power (ver. 22), so now they fail to fear Him who bestows the weather which shall bring to

the LORD our God, that giveth rain, both the former and the latter, in his season: he reserveth unto us the appointed ²⁵ weeks of the harvest. Your iniquities have turned away these *things*, and your sins have withholden good *things* ²⁶ from you. For among my people are found wicked *men:* they lay wait, as he that setteth snares; they set a trap, they ²⁷ catch men. As a cage *is* full *of* birds, so *are* their houses full *of* deceit: therefore they are become great, and waxen

maturity the produce of the field. The prophet thus makes a second appeal on somewhat different grounds from the former one. As this proof addresses itself chiefly to the thoughtful he says *"in their heart."* Any one can perceive that God is a Being possessed of *power*. It is necessary to consider and reflect upon His actions in the world of nature before we perceive that He is also a God who uses that power for loving purposes towards man.

rain, both the former and the latter]. The former (=early) rain was between October and December, the latter fell in March and April. The former marked the period of growth and nourishment of the corn, as that which followed preceded its ingathering.

the appointed weeks of the harvest] the seven weeks which intervened between the Feast of the Passover, and that of Weeks. At the former Feast on the day after the Sabbath the priest waved a sheaf of the first-fruits before the LORD (Lev. xxiii. 10), and again at the Feast of Weeks, bread of the first-fruits was offered (ver. 17). On the earlier occasion barley was the offering, on the latter wheat, the two harvests thus having a considerable interval between them.

25. The most natural sense of the verse is, not that these blessings are continued, while only the rich reap the benefit from them (so that the prophet would be addressing the poverty-stricken mass only), but that on account of the sins of the nation, there has been a real failure in the amount of rain and consequently in harvest.

26. *are found wicked men*] men of such great wickedness as to infect all.

they lay wait] In the Hebrew this verb is in the singular, in order to express the individual, solitary, stealthy action of these wicked men.

as he that setteth snares] **as fowlers stoop.** "Birdcatchers hide behind the extended nets till the birds have gone in, so as then to draw them tight" (Keil). Thus these men attack the poor and honest. Compare Is. xxix. 21; Mic. vii. 2.

trap] literally, *destroyer.*

they catch men] They by their wiles do as Nimrod is supposed by ancient commentators to have done by force. The Chaldee paraphrase on Gen. x. 9 speaks of him as "a hunter of the sons of men."

27. *cage*] a wicker basket, in which the birds, as they were caught, were placed. It was closed with a lid. It is identical with that mentioned in Amos (viii. 1), "a *basket* of summer fruit."

deceit] riches gained by deceit.

rich. They are waxen fat, they shine: yea, they overpass 28 the deeds of the wicked: they judge not the cause, the cause of the fatherless, yet they prosper; and the right of the needy do they not judge. Shall I not visit for these 29 *things?* saith the LORD: shall not my soul be avenged on such a nation as this?

30, 31. *Prophets, priests and people share the guilt.*

A wonderful and horrible thing is committed in the land; 30 the prophets prophesy falsely, and the priests bear rule by 31 their means; and my people love *to have it* so: and what will ye do in the end thereof?

28. *waxen fat*] Fatness was looked on as a mark of prosperity. Compare Deut. xxxii. 15 ("Jeshurun waxed fat and kicked"); Ps. xcii. 14 ("They shall be fat and flourishing"); Prov. xxviii. 25 ("He that putteth his trust in the LORD shall be made fat").

shine] referring to their sleekness of skin.

overpass the deeds of the wicked] **go beyond bound in wickedness.**

yet they prosper] **that they may prosper,** i.e. that the orphans by their help may receive succour.

29. The refrain taken up again from ver. 9.

30, 31. PROPHETS, PRIESTS AND PEOPLE SHARE THE GUILT.

30. This verse and the following contain a summing up of the charge against the people. Leaders and people unite in disaffection.

wonderful] **terrible.** The word properly means desolation, destruction.

31. "When Amos and Isaiah attacked the priesthood of Judah, they still felt that there remained the Prophets on whom the nation could fall back. But when Jeremiah mourned for Israel, he felt that there was no reserve in Judah. And when the Priesthood closed in hostile array around him, he felt that, as far as Jerusalem was concerned, the Prophets were no supporters." (Stanley's *Jewish Church*, II. 441.)

by their means] **at their hands.**

and my people love to have it so] The subject class are only too willing to be misled by their rulers. Love of idolatry has led the whole nation to turn their backs upon Him who chose them as His own.

CHAP. VI. 1—8. THE FOREIGN ARMY APPROACHES AND PREPARES TO BESIEGE JERUSALEM. A BRIEF INVITATION TO LEARN WISDOM EVEN NOW.

In this chapter Jeremiah furnishes the people with a lively representation of the troubles that were at hand. The chapter may be divided into four sections, each, after the first, beginning with the words, "Thus saith the Lord." The first (1—8) depicts the approach of the army and the preparations for a siege; the second (9—15) describes the capture of

CHAP. VI. 1—8. *The Foreign Army approaches and prepares to besiege Jerusalem. A brief invitation to learn wisdom even now.*

6   O ye children of Benjamin, gather yourselves to flee out of the midst of Jerusalem, and blow the trumpet in Tekoa, and set up a sign of fire in Beth-haccerem: for evil appeareth
2 out of the north, and great destruction. I have likened the

the city; the third (16—21) declares that the formal offerings made to God shall not help them in the day of their trouble; the fourth (22—30) sets out the cruelty with which the enemy shall treat them.

Calvin considers the lively description of the invasion and siege as a last attempt to reach ears, which had shewn themselves too dull to attend to the simple announcement of impending disaster.

1. *O ye children of Benjamin*] (*a*) Jeremiah was himself a Benjamite (chap. i. 1), (*b*) Jerusalem was in Benjamin, the boundary between that tribe and Judah lying in the valley of Hinnom, to the south of the city.

Tekoa] A village on an elevated and spreading hill about eleven miles south of Jerusalem forming part of the range which stretches from Hebron towards the Dead Sea. St Jerome writing in Palestine speaks of it as daily before his eyes. The name, derived from a Hebrew root meaning *to strike*, doubtless refers to the fastening of tent-pegs into the ground, and thus denotes the pastoral character of the inhabitants. From Tekoa came Joab's "wise woman" (2 Sam. xiv. 2). It was the birthplace of Amos (Am. i. 1), and it or its inhabitants are mentioned on several other occasions. It is still known by the same name (Tekû'a). The ruins which are found there however are probably all of Christian times. There is a play on words in the original, depending on the close similarity between the proper name and the Hebrew for "blow the trumpet." Doubtless therefore it is partly for this reason that Tekoa is mentioned, although it is also thoroughly appropriate as a town far south in Judea, and thus in the direction which would be taken by the inhabitants in the event of flight before an invading host from the north.

a sign of fire] Although the Hebrew word denotes properly a signal, and has no necessary reference to fire, the English is probably correct, as a word closely connected with this one is used in later Hebrew to denote the fire lighted to give notice of the appearance of the new moon. The same word as that used here is found (Judges xx. 38, 40), to denote a pillar of smoke agreed upon as a signal.

Beth-haccerem] (House of the vineyard) mentioned elsewhere only in Neh. iii. 14. St Jerome speaks of a village Beth-acharma on a hill between Jerusalem and Tekoa. This position corresponds to a conical-shaped hill called the Frank mountain, conspicuous from Bethlehem, and would be a very suitable spot for a beacon station.

appeareth] **is looking forth**, implying eagerness. Compare Judges v. 28 ("looked out").

2. *I have likened*] **I have destroyed.** The Hebrew verbs are identical in form, but the sense here requires the latter.

daughter of Zion *to* a comely and delicate *woman*. The 3
shepherds with their flocks shall come unto her; they shall
pitch *their* tents against her round about; they shall feed
every one *in* his place. Prepare ye war against her; arise, 4
and let us go up at noon. Woe unto us! for the day goeth
away, for the shadows of the evening are stretched out.
Arise, and let us go by night, and let us destroy her pa- 5
laces. For thus hath the LORD of hosts said, Hew ye down 6
trees, and cast a mount against Jerusalem: this is the city

to a comely and delicate woman] **comely and delicate (as she is).**
This is probably right, the verse constituting a tender lament over the
ill-fated city, and the feminine singular being used in accordance with
Hebrew idiom to denote the inhabitants collectively. Another rendering which is quite possible is "*to a pasturage, yea, a luxurious pasturage* have I likened the daughter of Zion."

3. The devastation produced by the enemy is spoken of under the
figure of shepherds, whose flocks eat up the herbage on every side. For
shepherds in the sense of persons in authority, compare chap. iii. 15.
There is, as elsewhere, a mixing of metaphor and fact. See Introd.
chap. ii. § 8 d.

every one in his place] The Hebrew is literally, *each his hand*. They
shall not need to encroach upon one another. They will each be able
abundantly to satisfy themselves in their own portion.

4. *Prepare*] **Sanctify.** Compare Is. xiii. 3, "my sanctified ones,"
said of the armies summoned to destroy Babylon. See also Jer. li.
27, 28. The entering upon war was looked upon as a solemn religious
act, and was accompanied by corresponding ceremonies. For those used
by the Jews in accordance with the Mosaic Law see Deut. xx. 2, etc.
For the employment of rites on such an occasion by the Babylonians,
compare Ezek. xxi. 21—23.

at noon] At this time an army would generally be resting after the
morning march, and awaiting the cooler time of the day to resume
active operations. Such is the eagerness of the enemy in this case
however that they will brave the full power of the sun's rays. Noon
also would be an unlikely time to be attacked, and so would be in
favour of the besiegers. Compare xx. 16.

5. The impatience of the soldiers at the delay takes the form of a
demand for a night assault.

6. *Hew ye down trees*] It is true that the Jews cut down trees for
the purpose of using the wood in making their approaches to a city.
Compare "Thou shalt build bulwarks (with trees not being fruit trees)
against the city that maketh war with thee," Deut. xx. 20. It cannot
however be discovered from the Assyrian monuments that such was
the custom of that nation. We must therefore suppose the command to
imply simply a clearing away of all obstacles to the approach of the enemy.

trees] probably **her (the city's) trees.**

cast a mount] Earth was carried in baskets, and poured in a heap,

to be visited; she *is* wholly oppression in the midst of her.
7 As a fountain casteth out her waters, so she casteth out her wickedness: violence and spoil is heard in her; before me
8 continually *is* grief and wounds. Be thou instructed, O Jerusalem, lest my soul depart from thee; lest I make thee desolate, a land not inhabited.

9—30. *Sin, hardness of heart, and the absence of any save formal service are bringing this punishment on the people.*

9 Thus saith the LORD of hosts, They shall throughly glean the remnant of Israel as a vine: turn back thine hand as a

until it was on a level with the walls. The assault was then made. Compare for this method, 2 Kings xix. 32; Is. xxix. 3. Herodotus speaks of it thus, in describing the campaign of Harpagus, general of Cyrus in Ionia: "Forcing the enemy to shut themselves up within their defences, he heaped mounds of earth against their walls, and thus carried the towns" (I. 162, Rawlinson's Trans.).

to be visited] literally, **visited** (with punishment).

7. This verse expands the thought of the last clause of ver. 6.

As a fountain casteth out] The Hebrew verb here used occurs very rarely elsewhere, and then in the sense of digging for water. A substantive however derived from the root, and bearing the undoubted sense of spring or well, seems to make the interpretation of Hebrew commentators the more likely, viz.—as the Eng. Version renders. The other translation proposed is *as a cistern cooleth*, referring to the store of rain water preserved fresh and cool in the cistern of a Jewish house for many months at a time. This however would be rather forced when applied to the next clause, where the verb recurs.

grief and wounds] *sickness and smiting,* i.e. disease produced by want, and deeds of violence.

8. *instructed*] The word is elsewhere translated *reformed,* or *corrected,* which illustrates its meaning here; e.g. Lev. xxvi. 23; Prov. xxix. 19.

lest my soul depart] The verb in the original is much stronger than *depart.* **lest my soul be parted.**

9—30. SIN, HARDNESS OF HEART, AND THE ABSENCE OF ANY SAVE FORMAL SERVICE ARE BRINGING THIS PUNISHMENT ON THE PEOPLE.

9. The beginning of the second of the four sections. See ver. 1. The spoiling shall be thorough. The gleaners shall go over and over again. Calamity shall not visit the land once only, but many times.

remnant of Israel] "Not the kingdom of Judah at large, but Judah already reduced by judgments" (Keil).

turn back thine hand] addressed to Nebuchadnezzar, or in general to the leader of the attack upon the land.

grapegatherer into the baskets. To whom shall I speak, 10
and give warning, that they may hear? behold, their ear *is*
uncircumcised, and they cannot hearken: behold, the word
of the LORD is unto them a reproach; they have no delight
in it. Therefore I am full *of* the fury of the LORD; I am 11
weary with holding in: I *will* pour *it* out upon the children
abroad, and upon the assembly of young men together: for
even the husband with the wife shall be taken, the aged
with *him that is* full of days. And their houses shall be 12

baskets] **tendrils.** The Hebrew word occurs only in this place. It bears a certain resemblance to the word used for *basket*, Gen. xl. 16—18, and comes from a root meaning *to twine*. It is still more like however to another word, whose meaning of vine-shoots is undoubted.

10. The thought of the indifference of the people suddenly lays hold on Jeremiah, and causes him to despair of finding any one to heed his warnings.

give warning] **testify.**

their ear is uncircumcised] not hallowed or dedicated to God's service, but devoted to profane uses only. This epithet is applied to the ear but once elsewhere (Acts vii. 51), and there it is used of the ear in conjunction with the heart, of which it is frequently spoken. It is applied in the Bible to the lips also.

a reproach] They treat it with contempt, and utterly fail to recognise its solemn importance.

11. *Therefore*] **But.**

the fury of the Lord] not, I am inspired with ardour for His cause, but, The wrath which He feels has been infused into me His prophet, that I may make it known to men.

I will pour it out] **pour it out** (imperative). This command is addressed by the prophet to himself, rather than by God to the prophet. The declaration is made without distinction of age, because the approaching punishment includes all alike. Five periods of life are mentioned.

abroad] **in the street,** at play. Compare Zech. viii. 5.

taken] detected, overtaken by punishment, not necessarily, taken captive. Compare viii. 9; Josh. vii. 15; 1 Sam. xiv. 41.

full of days] more than merely aged, one who has filled up the measure of life and is in the last stage of existence. See 1 Chron. xxix. 28.

12. These verses are almost identical with chap. viii. 10—12. All that they hold most dear shall be taken from them and given to others. The possessions thus to be transferred are enumerated as those which will be considered most desirable by their new possessors, for they stand at the beginning of the list in that form of the tenth commandment which appears in Deut. (v. 21).

turned unto others, *with their* fields and wives together: for I will stretch out my hand upon the inhabitants of the land, 13 saith the LORD. For from the least of them even unto the greatest of them every one *is* given to covetousness; and from the prophet even unto the priest every one dealeth 14 falsely. They have healed also the hurt of *the daughter of* my people slightly, saying, Peace, peace; when *there is* no 15 peace. Were they ashamed when they had committed abomination? nay, they were not at all ashamed, neither could they blush: therefore they shall fall among them that fall: at the time *that* I visit them they shall be cast down,

I will stretch out my hand] Compare for this phrase "He hath stretched forth his hand against them and hath smitten them," Is. v. 25.

13. That the calamity will come from the LORD is declared in the latter part of ver. 12. The cause of it is here given.

from the least of them even unto the greatest of them] Already in chap. v. 5 Jeremiah had gone from the poor to the rich with the vain hope that in the latter he should find the good which the former lacked.

is given to covetousness] **is greedy of gain,** not necessarily implying the hankering after that which is one's neighbour's, although this would naturally accompany an inordinate love of gain, as well as be suggested by the previous verse.

14. *They*] the leaders, prophets and priests.

the hurt] the shortcomings and sins of the nation.

of the daughter of my people] of my people collectively; see ver. 2 above.

slightly] *making nothing of it* is the literal rendering of the earliest Greek version (the Septuagint). These leaders are like worthless surgeons. They refuse to examine or probe the wounds of those who are under their charge, and for the sake of their own ease assure their patients that all is well.

15. *Were they ashamed when they had committed abomination?*] **They are brought to shame, because they have committed abomination.** This part of the verse is made interrogative in the English in order to avoid the difficulty which the seeming contradiction contained in the following words produces. Others have rendered *They ought to have been ashamed*. The sense of the whole however is simply, the shamefulness which really belonged to their acts they were too hardened to feel.

nay, they were not at all ashamed] **yet they take not shame to themselves.**

among them that fall] They shall not escape, when their countrymen whom they have led astray suffer.

visit] Compare for this expression ver. 6.

be cast down] **stumble.**

saith the LORD. Thus saith the LORD, Stand ye in the 16 ways, and see, and ask for the old paths, where *is* the good way, and walk therein, and ye shall find rest for your souls. But they said, We will not walk *therein*. Also I 17 set watchmen over you, *saying*, Hearken to the sound of the trumpet. But they said, We will not hearken. Therefore 18 hear, ye nations, and know, O congregation, what *is* among

16. The beginning of the third section, see ver. 1.
Take up your position on the public roads, and enquire which of the branching paths is the old established one. It will prove the good path, and that which alone ye may follow with divine sanction. Under this figure Jeremiah urges upon the people to enquire how their fathers walked, and what their course of conduct was, and thus to convince themselves that the precepts and threatenings which God put forth now were no new truths.

the good way] literally, *the way of the good*. Good is in the Hebrew a substantive. The sense is not that there are many old ways, amongst which by enquiry ye may find the best; but that the search for old paths will ensure their finding that one path which God approves. "Look enquiringly backwards to ancient history (Deut. xxxii. 7) and see how success and enduring prosperity forsook your fathers when they left the way prescribed to them by God, to walk in the ways of the heathen (Jer. xviii. 15); learn that there is but one way, the way of the fear of the LORD, in which blessing and salvation are to be found" (Jer. xxxii. 39, 40). (Graf as quoted by Keil.)

17. *watchmen*] sentinels (2 Sam. xiii. 34, xviii. 24—27), and thence used figuratively for the prophets (e.g. Ezek. iii. 17, xxxiii. 7).

over you] If we have regard to the 3rd person which follows ("they said") this *you* should be *them*. The 2nd person is accounted for by the fact that the address on the part of God to the people was still in the prophet's mind.

the sound of the trumpet] the mode of announcing the approach of danger. (Compare ver. 1; Amos iii. 6.) As sentinels are posted on the walls of a city to warn the inhabitants of the enemy's approach, so have the true prophets of the nation warned them of the consequences of their ways.

18. The Gentiles are summoned to bear witness to the justice of the punishment.

O congregation] This has been understood to refer to (i) righteous Jews, (ii) Gentiles, (iii) both together. (iii) appears the least likely of these, and (ii) on the whole the best, from the parallelism of the clauses. If we make the reference to be to the Jews, we have the awkwardness of thus diminishing the width of the appeal, while at once in ver. 19 it is again extended to the whole 'earth.'

what is among them] This again is obscure. Does it refer to (i) their wickedness, or (ii) its penalty? Probably the latter, from the

19 them. Hear, O earth: behold, I will bring evil upon this people, *even* the fruit of their thoughts, because they have not hearkened unto my words, nor *to* my law, but rejected
20 it. To what purpose cometh there to me incense from Sheba, and the sweet cane from a far country? your burnt offerings *are* not acceptable, nor your sacrifices sweet unto
21 me. Therefore thus saith the LORD, Behold, I will lay stumblingblocks before this people, and the fathers and the

words of the next verse, and thus the Latin Vulgate renders. The sense therefore is, *know what great things I will do to them.*

19. The conclusion of the threefold appeal. Thus God pledges Himself as it were in the sight of the whole world, that He will no longer forbear.

I] Emphatic in the Hebrew. They are to take notice that it is God who speaks.

fruit of their thoughts] Compare "fruit of their *doings*" (spoken however of the righteous), Is. iii. 10, and "the reward of the wicked's hands" in ver. 11. Here things are traced further towards their source.

20. "To obey is better than sacrifice" (1 Sam. xv. 22). The uselessness of ceremonial, if the heart be cold, is set forth elsewhere by Isaiah (i. 11); Hosea (vi. 6); Amos (v. 21, &c.); Mic. (vi. 6); and in the Psalms (l. 8).

incense from Sheba] Compare Virgil's mention of the honour paid to Venus at Paphos, "Centumque Sabaeo Ture calent arae" (*Aen.* I. 416—7). Incense (frankincense) was the resin of coniferous trees, and the true sort was obtained from the south of Arabia (Sheba=Yemen =Arabia Felix) or the opposite coast of Africa. Theophrastus and others attest this. Ecclus. i. 8 (Apocrypha) however speaks of a tree growing in Palestine and known as the frankincense tree. The Israelites a year after leaving Egypt were commanded (Exod. xxx. 34) to use frankincense, and as there was no tree in Egypt which would produce it, they must have either used the gum or resin of some tree in the wilderness, or somehow procured a supply from a greater distance. See J. Smith's *History of Bible Plants*, pp. 173—6.

the sweet cane] Compare Is. xliii. 24, and ("*sweet calamus*") Exod. xxx. 23, and ("*calamus*") Cant. iv. 14; Ezek. xxvii. 19. "It was probably what is now known in India as the Lemon Grass (*Andropogon Schoenanthus*). Aromatic reeds were known to the ancients as the produce of India and the region of the Euphrates" (*Sp. Comm.* Exod. *l. c.*). J. Smith (see above) on the other hand takes the sweet cane to be the sugar cane. "Although the art of making sugar from them was probably then unknown to the Jews, the canes would nevertheless be highly valued for sweetening food or drink" (pp. 33—4).

21. *stumblingblocks*] the invasion of the enemy, which shall as it were trip them up in their easy-going ways.

sons together shall fall upon them; the neighbour and his friend shall perish. Thus saith the LORD, Behold, a people 22 cometh from the north country, and a great nation shall be raised from the sides of the earth. They shall lay hold on 23 bow and spear; they *are* cruel, and have no mercy; their voice roareth like the sea; and they ride upon horses, set in array as men for war against thee, O daughter of Zion. We 24 have heard the fame thereof: our hands wax feeble: anguish hath taken hold of us, *and* pain, as of a woman in travail. Go not forth *into* the field, nor walk by the way; for the 25 sword of the enemy *and* fear *is* on every side. O daughter 26

the fathers and the sons together] There shall be a general and promiscuous destruction.

22. The last of the four sections.
from the north country] See note on i. 14.
shall be raised] **shall rouse itself.**
the sides of the earth] an expression for the far distance, the extremity of the earth. Compare xxv. 32 ("the coasts of the earth"); Ps. xlviii. 2; Is. xiv. 13. It has been supposed from the terms of this verse that the Scythians must be the enemy spoken of. Chap xxxi. 8 however, which gives these very epithets to the country whither Israel was carried captive, shews that we may quite as fairly interpret them of Chaldaea.

23. *cruel*] "The word means *ruthless, inhuman*. In the Assyrian monuments we constantly see warriors putting the vanquished to death; in others, rows of impaled victims hang round the walls of the besieged towns; and in others, men are collecting in heaps hands cut from the vanquished. Sennacherib even boasts that he salted the heads of slaughtered Edomites, and sent them in wicker baskets to Nineveh." (*Sp. Comm.*)

they ride upon horses] Compare iv. 13, viii. 16.
set in array as men for war] **equipped as a man for war.** This should begin a new sentence. The verb is in the singular in the Hebrew, and thus means not the horsemen, but the whole army.

24. Jeremiah places himself in the position of his fellow-countrymen on the arrival of the news.

fame] *report*. Compare Gen. xlv. 16, "And the fame thereof was heard in Pharaoh's house," &c.

25. *the sword of the enemy*] literally, (there is) **a sword to the enemy,** i.e. the enemy is armed. Elsewhere the enemy is himself spoken of as the instrument in God's hands, e.g. Isaiah x. 5, "O Assyrian, *the rod* of mine anger, and the staff in their hand is mine indignation." Ps. xvii. 13 is an instance only if the rendering of the English Version be accurate, which is at the least doubtful.

and fear is on every side] The *and* should be omitted. The remaining words are a favourite expression with Jeremiah. Borrowing from

of my people, gird *thee* with sackcloth, and wallow thyself in ashes: make thee mourning, *as* for an only *son*, most bitter lamentation: for the spoiler shall suddenly come upon us.
27 I have set thee *for* a tower *and* a fortress among my people, that thou mayest know and try their way. They *are* all grievous revolters, walking with slanders: *they are* brass and iron; they *are* all corrupters. The bellows are burnt, the

Ps. xxxi. 13, he uses them chap. xx. 3, 10, xlvi. 5, xlix. 29. See especially notes on the first-named chapter.

26. *daughter of my people*] collective, as in chap. iv. 11. Compare vi. 2.

wallow thyself in] This is probably right, as also in chap. xxv. 34; Ezek. xxvii. 30; Mic. i. 10. The earlier rendering was *sprinkle thyself with*. The Hebrew word is thought by Gesenius to be actually connected etymologically with the German *wälzen* (our *wallow*).

as for an only son] The importance attributed by the Jews to the possession of children involved extreme grief, if posterity were thus cut off. Compare xxii. 30, and Amos viii. 10; Zech. xii. 10.

27—30. In these verses the LORD reassures Jeremiah of his divine commission. He appears under the figure of one testing metal, while after Jeremiah's manner the figure and the thing signified by it are intermingled in expression (see for other cases Introd. chap. ii. § 8 d). The result of the testing process is that no precious metal is found. All is dross.

27. *a tower*] **a tester** (*trier*). It was owing to a difficulty presented by the following substantives that this was rendered *tower*.

a fortress] probably the right rendering. Compare i. 18. Jeremiah is promised that he shall receive protection while carrying out the duty which so exasperates the people against him. The brief, parenthetical character of the assurance has caused difficulty. Other proposed renderings are (i) gold and silver ore, (ii) a cutter of ore, (iii) a separator. Beyond the fact however that the Hebrew root signifies to cut, much support cannot be had for these conjectures, while *fortress* is the ordinary sense which the word bears elsewhere.

28. *grievous revolters*] Heb. *revolters of revolters*, one of the ways of expressing the superlative in that language. Compare Gen. ix. 25. So Ezek. xxxii. 21, "The strong among (literally, of) the mighty."

walking with slanders] going about with slanderous intent. The same thought is expressed chap. ix. 4.

they are brass and iron] a recurrence to the metaphor, which is however again immediately deserted. They have none of the precious metal in them.

brass] **copper.**

29. The best rendering probably is **The bellows glow; by reason of the fire the lead is used up; in vain hath the smelter smelted, and the wicked have not been separated.**

are burnt] This is by no means an impossible rendering, denoting

lead is consumed of the fire; the founder melteth in vain: for the wicked are not plucked away. Reprobate silver shall 30 men call them, because the LORD hath rejected them.

CHAPS. VII.—X. *Address delivered by Jeremiah at the gate of the Temple.*

CHAP. VII. 1—7. *Safety lies not in ceremonial excellence, but in moral uprightness.*

The word that came to Jeremiah from the LORD, saying, 7

that through the long continued effort to find something not dross in the nation, not only the lead but also the bellows were consumed.

the lead is consumed of the fire] There is an alternative rendering arising from various readings in the Hebrew, viz.;—*from their fire lead only;* i.e. no trace of anything more valuable appears to reward the long assay.

30. *Reprobate...rejected*] There is a play on the words in the Hebrew. *Refuse—refused.*

CHAPS. VII.—X. ADDRESS DELIVERED BY JEREMIAH AT THE GATE OF THE TEMPLE.

CHAP. VII. 1—7. SAFETY LIES NOT IN CEREMONIAL EXCELLENCE, BUT IN MORAL UPRIGHTNESS.

The chief question to be answered in regard to these chapters as a whole is the date to which they are to be referred, whether to the reign of (i) Josiah or (ii) Jehoiakim. In seeking to determine this, we must at once take into consideration chap. xxvi., whose opening verses have a marked resemblance to these, and which is expressly stated (ver. 1) to have been delivered in the beginning of the reign of Jehoiakim. If the prophecy of that chapter therefore be merely a summarised form of that which is contained in these, no more is to be said. In favour of that later date also is urged that (*a*) Jeremiah seems to be now dwelling not at Anathoth but at Jerusalem, since he is told not as in (ii. 2) to "Go and cry," &c. but simply (vii. 2) to "stand in the gate of the Lord's house," &c.; (*b*) idolatry is represented as practised openly in the streets of Jerusalem (vii. 17) and in the Temple itself (vii. 30); (*c*) children are burned in the valley of Tophet in honour of Moloch (vii. 31). In favour of the earlier date it may be said that (*a*) these chapters are closely connected with those which precede them and which confessedly belong to the time of Josiah; (*b*) the agreement of chap. vii. and chap. xxvi. is by no means such as to warrant us in the belief that they are merely a full and an abbreviated report respectively of the same discourse, especially when we remember the frequency with which Jeremiah is wont to repeat himself; (*c*) the circumstances which immediately followed upon the threat that Jerusalem should become as Shiloh (given in chap. xxvi. 8, &c.) by no means accord with the long prophecy

2 Stand in the gate of the Lord's house, and proclaim there this word, and say, Hear the word of the Lord, all *ye of Judah*, that enter in at these gates to worship the Lord. 3 Thus saith the Lord of hosts, the God of Israel, Amend your ways and your doings, and I will cause you to dwell in 4 this place. Trust ye not in lying words, saying, The temple

contained in the remainder of these chapters. The last argument seems of considerable weight. Perhaps the best conjecture on a subject which must always involve some uncertainty is that the discourse (which may well be the summary of several) belongs to the *later* period of Josiah's reign. Thirteen years intervened between the completion of his measures of reformation and his death. Probably towards the end of this period matters were changing rapidly for the worse, and the enmity of individuals against Jeremiah (a marked feature of the time of Jehoiakim and Zedekiah) was becoming already prominent.

The discourse has three natural divisions: (*a*) vii. 1—viii. 3, Rebuke for shameless idolatry and pollution of the very Temple; (*b*) viii. 4—ix. 22, Announcement of punishment that shall come on the people for their sin; (*c*) ix. 23—x. 25, Reasoning with the people on the folly of idolatry and exhortation to follow the true and only God.

2. *the gate of the Lord's house*] The scantiness of our knowledge as to the details of the Temple courts hinders us from going beyond a conjecture as to Jeremiah's exact position. In Herod's Temple there were seven gates connecting the inner with the outer court, viz. three on the north, three on the south, and one on the east. If this represented the state of things in Solomon's Temple, Jeremiah would probably have stood at one of these looking down upon the people who were assembled in the outer court prepared to pass in. It may have been "the new gate," that at the entry of which Baruch read the roll (xxxvi. 10) in the adjoining chamber of Gemariah in the inner (Eng. Version, "higher") court.

all ye of Judah] **all Judah**. The occasion was in all probability one of the three great annual feasts or other solemn gatherings. If this discourse were spoken on such an occasion towards the end of Josiah's reign, we can easily understand how a repetition of the first part of it (chap. xxvi.) on a recurrence of the circumstances at the beginning of the reign of Jehoiakim might provoke the attack upon the prophet which immediately followed.

3. The thought is the same as that of Deut. vii. 12—15, one of the many passages of that book which influenced the language of Jeremiah.

your ways and your doings] a favourite combination with Jeremiah (compare ver. 5, iv. 18, xviii. 11, xxvi. 13, xxxv. 15), and in a less degree with Ezekiel (xiv. 22, 23, xx. 43, xxxvi. 17), see also Zech. i. 4, 6. *Ways* will mean rather the settled habits, *doings* the separate acts which go to form them.

4. *lying words*] those of the false prophets, who maintained that

of the LORD, The temple of the LORD, The temple of the LORD, *are* these. For if you throughly amend your ways and your doings; if you throughly execute judgment between a man and his neighbour; *if* ye oppress not the stranger, the fatherless, and the widow, and shed not innocent blood in this place, neither walk after other gods to your hurt: then will I cause you to dwell in this place, in the land that I gave to your fathers, for ever and ever.

8—20. *Shiloh's sanctity was no protection to it, neither shall Jerusalem or its Temple save those who openly disown their God.*

Behold, ye trust in lying words, *that* cannot profit. Will the possession of the Temple was enough. God would never suffer it to be overthrown, and thus its presence would be a kind of charm that would protect Jerusalem and its inhabitants.

The temple of the Lord] The threefold repetition is for the sake of emphasis. Compare xxii. 29; Is. vi. 3. In this particular case however it further suggests "the energy of iteration that only belongs to Eastern fanatics" (Stanley's *Jewish Church*, II. 438), and may be compared with the cry of the priests of Baal on Carmel, who "called on the name of Baal from morning even until noon, saying, O Baal, hear us" (1 Kings xviii. 26), "as the Mussulman Dervishes work themselves into a frenzy by the invocation of 'Allah, Allah!' until the words themselves are lost in inarticulate gasps" (Stanley, II. 254).

these] the buildings of the Temple, to which Jeremiah would doubtless point his finger, as he spoke.

6. *If ye oppress not the stranger, the fatherless, and the widow*] The Mosaic Law was strong in its denunciation of such conduct; Exod. xxii. 21, &c.; Deut. xxiv. 17, &c.

shed not innocent blood] by oppression, by judicial murders, e.g. that of Urijah by Jehoiakim (chap. xxvi. 23), which may be among those here referred to, although it had probably not yet taken place.

in this place] in Jerusalem, as shewn in ver. 7.

to your hurt] These words belong to the whole of the verse.

7. The land was given them, conditionally on their observing their part of the covenant, as "an everlasting possession" (Gen. xvii. 8). The last words of the verse however, if we follow the arrangement of the Hebrew stops, belong, not to "gave," but to "dwell in."

8—20. SHILOH'S SANCTITY WAS NO PROTECTION TO IT, NEITHER SHALL JERUSALEM OR ITS TEMPLE SAVE THOSE WHO OPENLY DISOWN THEIR GOD.

8. *that cannot profit*] Or perhaps, *so that ye profit not*.

ye steal, murder, and commit adultery, and swear falsely, and burn incense unto Baal, and walk after other gods 10 whom ye know not; and come and stand before me in this house, which is called by my name, and say, We are de- 11 livered to do all these abominations? Is this house, which is called by my name, become a den of robbers in your 12 eyes? Behold, even I have seen *it*, saith the Lord. But go ye now unto my place which *was* in Shiloh, where I set my name at the first, and see what I did to it for the wicked- 13 ness of my people Israel. And now, because ye have done all these works, saith the Lord, and I spake unto you,

9. *Will ye steal*] **Stealing**, &c. All the verbs are in the infinitive in the original, a mood which is used when the object is to present the action itself in the strongest light. See the like usage in xxxii. 33; Is. xxi. 5. The prophet follows an order almost the exact converse of that in the Decalogue, to "walk after other gods" being a breach of the first commandment, and the words "whom ye know not" an allusion to the words introductory to the whole in Exodus xx., "I am the Lord thy God, which brought thee out of the land of Egypt, out of the house of bondage."

10. *We are delivered*] We are by the discharge of this religious formality set free for a return to wickedness. That this is the sense of the Hebrew words, according to Jeremiah's use of them, is abundantly shewn by Graf in his notes on this passage.

11. *den of robbers*] a place of retreat in the intervals between acts of violence. This verse is alluded to (in connexion with Is. lvi. 7) in Matt. xxi. 13, and the parallel passages (Mark xi. 17 and Luke xix. 46).

12. *Shiloh*] A town of Ephraim and in a central position in the land. For this reason doubtless among others it was chosen by Joshua as the resting place of the ark and tabernacle. It was a considerable town in the time of the judges (Judg. xx. 47 compared with xxi. 12, 19, 23). It fell into grievous idolatry (Ps. lxxviii. 58, &c.), and hence its fate, viz. loss of the ark in the last days of Eli (1 Sam. iv.) and capture with attendant cruelties on the part of the Philistines. It thenceforward was a place of utter insignificance. Jeroboam passed it by when setting up calves for his worship. In Jeremiah's time it existed as a small village (chap. xli. 5). St Jerome (*Comm. on Zeph.* i. 14) remarks, "At Silo, where once was the tabernacle and ark of the Lord, there can scarcely be pointed out the foundation of an altar." It is the modern village of Scilun, about half way between Jerusalem and Nablous. "A Tell, or moderate hill, rises from an uneven plain, surrounded by other higher hills, except a narrow valley on the south, which hill would naturally be chosen as the principal site of the town. The tabernacle may have been pitched on this eminence, where it would be a conspicuous object on every side. The ruins found there at present are very inconsiderable." Sm. *Bibl. Dict.* Art. *Shiloh.*

rising up early and speaking, but ye heard not; and I
called you, but ye answered not; therefore will I do unto 14
this house, which is called by my name, wherein ye trust,
and unto the place which I gave to you and to your fathers,
as I have done to Shiloh. And I will cast you out of my 15
sight, as I have cast out all your brethren, *even* the whole
seed of Ephraim. Therefore pray not thou for this people, 16
neither lift up cry nor prayer for them, neither make intercession to me: for I *will* not hear thee. Seest thou not 17
what they do in the cities of Judah and in the streets of
Jerusalem? The children gather wood, and the fathers 18
kindle the fire, and the women knead *their* dough, to make
cakes to the queen of heaven, and to pour out drink offer-

13. *rising up early and speaking*] This phrase either as here or
with slight variations is frequent with Jeremiah (ver. 25, xi. 7, xxv. 3,
4, xxvi. 5, xxix. 19, xxxii. 33, xxxv. 14, 15, xliv. 4), while not occurring
elsewhere.

14. *unto this house*] to the Temple and its precincts where Jeremiah and his hearers were standing. This had been the fate not of the
Tabernacle only but of the buildings adjacent. That there were such
we see from the history in 1 Sam. i—iii.

15. *all your brethren*] Not only Shiloh, but the whole northern kingdom was an illustration of the consequences of unfaithfulness.

Ephraim] stands for the whole of the northern tribes, as being the
leading one amongst them: so in Is. vii. 2, and often elsewhere.

16. *pray not thou*] Another way of shewing the people to what a
pitch their wickedness had come. So in chap. xiv. 7, &c. when Jeremiah does intercede, the prayer is refused (ver. 11), and in chap. xv. 1
even the intercession of Moses and Samuel it is declared would be of
no avail, although earlier in the history, and therefore before they had
become utterly depraved, Moses had more than once interceded with
success (Numb. xi. 2, xiv. 19, xvi. 22).

17. The Lord reminds the prophet of facts, which prevent prayer
from being any longer listened to on behalf of the people.

18. Both sexes and all ages unite in the public dishonouring of God's
name by shameless idolatries.

cakes] The Hebrew word has a foreign appearance, as though the
things signified were introduced from without, like the form of idolatry
of which they made a part. Bread mixed with oil or roasted herbs
(Suidas), cakes containing pine-seeds and raisins (Theodoret), malted
grain, a species of confection called in Egypt *Neideh* (De Sacy), are
three of the opinions as to their nature. "These cakes were probably
like those which were offered in Athens at the full moon in the middle
of the month Munychion to Artemis as the moon goddess; they were
shaped like the full moon and had lights stuck in them." Graf.

the queen of heaven] If we take the Heb. reading from which the

ings unto other gods, that *they* may provoke me to anger.
19 Do they provoke me to anger? saith the LORD: *do they* not *provoke* themselves to the confusion of their own faces?
20 Therefore thus saith the Lord GOD; Behold, mine anger and my fury *shall be* poured out upon this place, upon man, and upon beast, and upon the trees of the field, and upon the fruit of the ground; and it shall burn, and shall not be quenched.

21—28. *The fact that the moral has always taken precedence of the ceremonial law in God's sight has never been acknowledged by Israel.*

21 Thus saith the LORD of hosts, the God of Israel; Put your burnt offerings unto your sacrifices, and eat flesh.
22 For I spake not unto your fathers, nor commanded them

marginal translation (*frame*, or *workmanship*) is drawn, we should rather render *service of heaven*. This however is unnecessary. The "queen of heaven" is the moon, worshipped by the Assyrians as the receptive power in nature, and contrasted with the sun, Baal, the fertilising power. Her worship is to be distinguished from that of Astarte, a star, viz. Venus. They were similar however in so far as they were both accompanied by impure rites. The foreign form of the Heb. for *queen*, as in the case of the word *cakes* above, is probably meant as a hit at the foreign origin of the worship.

19. Will they not bring about their own vexation and shame?

21—28. THE FACT THAT THE MORAL HAS ALWAYS TAKEN PRECEDENCE OF THE CEREMONIAL LAW IN GOD'S SIGHT HAS NEVER BEEN ACKNOWLEDGED BY ISRAEL.

21. *Put your burnt offerings unto your sacrifices*] Burnt offerings (holocausts) were consumed whole, while of sacrifices certain portions were reserved to be eaten by the priest and the offerer. Accordingly the sense here is *either* (i) reserve, if you like, of the offerings of which ye now consume the whole: I care not, for in either case ye are breaking a higher law; *or* (ii) add one sacrifice to another. Multiply your victims *ad libitum*, it will avail you nought. The latter of these explanations avoids the objection that the Jews would abhor the idea of failing rigidly to consume those animals which were offered in burnt offering.

22. Some have seen a difficulty in reconciling this verse with the institution of sacrifices through Moses. They accordingly consider that such passages of the Pentateuch as enjoin them did not exist in its original form, that the Book of Deuteronomy as a whole is the composition of Jeremiah, and that the entire notion of laws concerning sacrifice, &c. came in in the time of Ezra. To this we may reply that (i) regu-

in the day that I brought them out of the land of Egypt, concerning burnt offerings or sacrifices: but this thing com- 23 manded I them, saying, Obey my voice, and I will be your God, and ye shall be my people: and walk ye in all the ways that I have commanded you, that it may be well unto you. But they hearkened not, nor inclined their ear, but 24 walked in the counsels *and* in the imagination of their evil heart, and went backward, and not forward. Since the day 25 that your fathers came forth out of the land of Egypt unto this day, I have even sent unto you all my servants the prophets, daily rising up early and sending *them:* yet they 26 hearkened not unto me, nor inclined their ear, but hardened their neck: they did worse than their fathers. Therefore 27 thou shalt speak all these words unto them; but they will

larly instituted sacrifices are expressly mentioned in chap. xxxiii. 18, as well as referred to in vi. 20, vii. 21, xiv. 12, xvii. 26; (ii) Hosea and Amos, prophets prior in date to Jeremiah, testify the same; (iii) the frequent censure of sacrifice offered as a perfunctory task shews that it was a powerful institution to the supposed efficacy of which men could thus trust; (iv) the discovery of the Book of the Law in Josiah's reign in all probability before this prophecy was uttered, (whether that Book were the Pentateuch or Deuteronomy) as well as the feeling which it produced, precludes such a supposition. The sense of the verse is sufficiently clear. The phraseology of Jeremiah (see below) proves that he had in his mind the promulgation of the Ten Commandments on Sinai. Now among these we find no direction concerning sacrifice, and they were the only precepts which had the honour of being treasured up in the Ark. Thus they from the first received the chief place. The Jews, it may be added, in their public service read this portion of the prophets along with Lev. vi—viii., thus shewing their belief that the sacrifices are but secondary. Compare for the sentiment of the verse 1 Sam. xv. 22.

23. From the fact that obedience to the moral Law always ranked first, it follows (and this is Jeremiah's special point) that sacrifices were wholly worthless when offered by the immoral.

Obey my voice] not an exact quotation; the nearest approach is Exod. xix. 5.

in all the ways] Only once elsewhere does this precise phrase occur, viz. Deut. v. 33, immediately after the repetition of the Ten Commandments.

24. *imagination*] **stubbornness.** Compare iii. 17.

went] literally *were.* That has been their condition ever since the exodus from Egypt.

26. *hardened their neck*] Compare for the phrase chap. xix. 15; 2 Kings xvii. 14; Neh. ix. 16, 17, 29; Prov. xxix. 1.

27. *Therefore thou shalt*] The Hebrew is *And thou shalt...and*

not hearken to thee: thou shalt also call unto them; but
28 they will not answer thee. But thou shalt say unto them,
This *is* a nation that obeyeth not the voice of the LORD
their God, nor receiveth correction: truth is perished, and
is cut off from their mouth.

29—34. *The Scene of their Wickedness shall be also that of their Punishment.*

29 Cut off thine hair, *O Jerusalem*, and cast *it* away, and
take up a lamentation on high places; for the LORD hath
30 rejected and forsaken the generation of his wrath. For the
children of Judah have done evil in my sight, saith the
LORD: they have set their abominations in the house which

they will not...and thou shalt...and they will not. It is not a command so much as a statement that the rule on which the people have acted still holds good. We might render "*Speak...and they will not hearken to thee: call unto them, and,*" &c.
 28. *But*] Yet. Although they have been, and will be, consistent in iniquity, yet Jeremiah must fulfil his part as prophet.
 a nation] the nation. They stand out prominent, as *the* disobedient people, a disobedience the guilt of which is enhanced by their privileges, by the Lord's being "their God."
 truth] *faithfulness*. Compare chap. v. 3.

29—34. THE SCENE OF THEIR WICKEDNESS SHALL BE ALSO THAT OF THEIR PUNISHMENT.

 29. *Cut off thine hair*] The verb is feminine in the original, thus shewing that the English Version is right in the inserted words, the inhabitants collectively being spoken of as elsewhere in the fem. sing. *Hair* is literally *crown*. The word from its use of the Nazarite's hair as a crown or consecrated diadem (Numb. vi. 7), comes to have the sense it bears here. So the anointing-oil on the head of the high-priest is called his *diadem* (Lev. xxi. 12). When the Nazarite was defiled by contact with a dead body, he was obliged to shave his head. So now must Jerusalem act, as about to be contaminated thus, as well as because she is faithless to her vows as a virgin consecrated to the LORD.
 cast it away] Those who understand *crown* or *diadem* literally, make these words to refer to the overthrow of the monarchy at the Babylonian conquest now approaching. This however is quite unnecessary.
 high places] bare heights. Compare chap. iii. 2.
 30. *they have set their abominations*] See 2 Kings xxi. 5, which relates that Manasseh profaned the Temple itself in the manner here mentioned.

is called by my name, to pollute it. And they have built 31 the high places of Tophet, which *is* in the valley of the son of Hinnom, to burn their sons and their daughters in the fire; which I commanded *them* not, neither came it into my heart. Therefore, behold, the days come, saith the LORD, 32 that it shall no more be called Tophet, nor the valley of the son of Hinnom, but the valley of slaughter: for they shall

31. *high places*] A different word from that in ver. 29, and meaning *altars*.

Tophet] A place near the eastern extremity of the southern reach of the valley of Hinnom. Three explanations have been given of the name. (i) *A drum*, on account of the noise made to drown the cries of the children being sacrificed to Moloch—

> "for the noise of drums and timbrels loud
> Their children's cries unheard that passed through fire
> To his grim idol."
> Milton, *P. L.* I. 394—6.

(ii) *A burning*, compare τέφ-ρα, *tep-idus*. (iii) *A spitting*. This is shewn to be the most likely by a comparison of chaps. xix. 5, xxxii. 35, which scarcely differ from the present passage except in having *Baal* not *Tophet*. The substitution then of Tophet for Baal in the present passage is merely a parallel for that of *Bosheth* (shame) for the same word. Compare chap. iii. 24 and note. The word is almost peculiar to Jeremiah (that of Is. xxx. 33 is somewhat different), its occurrence in 2 Kings xxiii. 10 being possibly in some way due to him.

valley of the son of Hinnom] Nothing is known of Hinnom. The view that it is not a proper name, but means "wailers" (alluding to the human sacrifices) is disproved by its occurrence as early as Josh. xv. 8. The valley had long an evil name, (*a*) as the place of impure offerings, (*b*) as defiled by Josiah, (*c*) as the receptacle for the offal and filth of the city. Hence it became with the Rabbis the visible sign of the place of future punishment, Gehenna (γέεννα, Matt. v. 22). The valley, narrow, with steep and rugged rocks on either hand, formed a natural defence to the city on the western and southern sides, joining the eastern valley of the Kedron.

to burn their sons and their daughters in the fire] in honour of Moloch the fire-god, who is often identified with Baal, the sun-god. Two questions have been asked concerning the nature of this worship. (i) Were the children destroyed or merely passed through the fire as a sort of purification? The present passage shews that the former was the case. (ii) Granting that they perished, were they slain previously? This we gather with *probability* from Ezek. xvi. 21.

Whether this part belong to the time of Josiah or Jehoiakim, the reference is evidently not to the present but to the sin of the past unrepented of.

33 bury in Tophet, till there be no place. And the carcases of this people shall be meat for the fowls of the heaven, and for the beasts of the earth; and none shall fray *them* away.

34 Then will I cause to cease from the cities of Judah, and from the streets of Jerusalem, the voice of mirth, and the voice of gladness, the voice of the bridegroom, and the voice of the bride: for the land shall be desolate.

CHAP. VIII. 1—3. *The dead bodies shall meet with indignities worse than death.*

8 At that time, saith the LORD, they shall bring out the bones of the kings of Judah, and the bones of his princes, and the bones of the priests, and the bones of the prophets, and the bones of the inhabitants of Jerusalem, out of their

32. *till there be no place*] Two appalling features connected with the bloodshed that is coming are set forth—(*a*) The valley defiled by bloody sacrifices shall now be defiled by the carnage of war. (*b*) This carnage shall extend far beyond the valley, 'They shall bury in Tophet **for want of room** elsewhere.' Such is the more approved as well as the oldest rendering.

33. Burial, owing to the multitude of corpses and fewness of survivors, shall be impossible, and birds and beasts shall have their way unmolested. The passage is taken almost word for word from Deut. xxviii. 26.

fray] The word is obsolete, except as a provincialism. It is the root of *affray* (participle, *afraid*), "he thought hir to affraye" (Chaucer's *Clerk's Tale*). Wedgwood derives it from the root *fray* (Latin, *frango, fragor*) while *fray* in the sense of rub is connected with the Latin *frico*. (*Bible Word-Book*.)

34. *the voice of the bridegroom, and the voice of the bride*] a frequent expression with this prophet. See chaps. xvi. 9, xxv. 10, xxxiii. 11. "The marriage feast ... continued usually for seven days, with the greatest mirth. ... Singing, music, and dancing, merry riddles, and the play of wit, amused the house night after night, while the feast was prolonged." Geikie's *Life and Words of Christ*, 1. 474.

desolate] Properly, a place which has *become desolate*.

CHAP. VIII. 1—3. THE DEAD BODIES SHALL MEET WITH INDIGNITIES WORSE THAN DEATH.

1. *they shall bring out*] Four causes are suggested by Michaelis: (*a*) The hope of finding spoil, treasures and ornaments of value being often buried with the dead, (compare Darius's fruitless visit to the tomb of Nitocris, Herod. I. 187); (*b*) accident, in digging a hole in order to light a fire; (*c*) wantonness; (*d*) the erection of earthworks for the siege.

graves: and they shall spread them before the sun, and the 2 moon, and all the host of heaven, whom they have loved, and whom they have served, and after whom they have walked, and whom they have sought, and whom they have worshipped: they shall not be gathered, nor be buried; they shall be for dung upon the face of the earth. And 3 death shall be chosen rather than life by all the residue of them that remain of this evil family, which remain in all the places whither I have driven them, saith the LORD of hosts.

4—17. *The people have been hardened and unblushing in their iniquity.*

Moreover thou shalt say unto them, Thus saith the LORD; 4 Shall they fall, and not arise? shall he turn away, and not return? Why *then* is this people of Jerusalem slidden back 5

2. *spread*] *scatter*, carelessly, not of any fixed purpose.

before the sun] heavenly bodies will not be prevented by all the offerings and devotion they received from using their influence to hasten the rotting of the carcases of their sometime worshippers.

whom they have loved] The gradual progress in idolatry expressed by this and the succeeding verbs is worthy of notice: fondness, submission, adaptation of conduct, frequency of service, treasonable acceptance in the place of God.

be gathered] for burial.

3. The thought and much of the language corresponds with Lev. xxvi. 36—39; Deut. xxviii. 65—67.

family] used of the whole nation. Compare chap. iii. 14 with note; also xxv. 9.

which remain] This probably did not stand in the text originally, but represents an inadvertent repetition by the copyist of the same Hebrew word in the previous line.

places] the lands outside Palestine.

4—17. THE PEOPLE HAVE BEEN HARDENED AND UNBLUSHING IN THEIR INIQUITY.

4. We have had (chaps. vii. 28—viii. 3) a kind of parenthesis, setting forth the nature of the coming punishment. Jeremiah now returns to the subject of the conduct which has procured it.

they] **one**, impersonal. If a man stumble, he will naturally regain his footing; if he lose his way, he will return to it. But this people doth not so. In the Hebrew '*turn away*' and '*return*' are the same verb. Compare for the repetition of the word '*return*' chap. iv. 1, where however there is no play on the word.

5. *slidden back...backsliding...return*] All three expressions are

by a perpetual backsliding? they hold fast deceit, they
6 refuse to return. I hearkened and heard, *but* they spake
not aright: no man repented him of his wickedness, saying,
What have I done? every one turned to his course, as the
7 horse rusheth into the battle. Yea, the stork in the heaven
knoweth her appointed times; and the turtle and the crane
and the swallow observe the time of their coming; but my

from the same root in the original. "*Why do* they *turn away with
a perpetual turning?*"

deceit] either (i) their own treachery towards God, or, better, (ii) their idols, as being a denial of God, and deluding those who confide in them.

refuse] *scorn, loathe.*

6. *I*] God is still the speaker.

hearkened and heard] implying an anxiety to give every chance of amendment.

not aright] virtually one word in the Hebrew, *not right* = *wrong.* See note on chap. ii. 8. The same expression occurs chaps. xxiii. 10, xlviii. 30.

repented] **repents.**

What have I done?] shewing reflection and contrition.

course] implying rapid motion, an eager plunge into wrong-doing. A more probable reading is the pl. *courses,* thus expressing that each follows his individual bent.

rusheth] literally, *overfloweth.* Thus two metaphors (a fiery steed, and a torrent) are combined.

7. Even migratory birds are punctual to their seasons.

stork] There are two species found in Palestine, the white and the black, the former dispersed generally in pairs over the whole country, the latter living in the marshes and in large flocks. They have been observed to reach Palestine on March 22. After a few weeks they proceed to Northern Europe.

in the heaven] which makes its nest on high (compare Ps. civ. 17), alluding to its custom of selecting the loftiest situation—a pillar, a ruin, a tall tree; or, better, which takes flight by day at a great height, unlike other migratory birds. (Tristram, *Nat. Hist. of Bible,* 246, quoted in *Sp. Comm.*)

turtle] The turtle dove was very abundant in Palestine from early time (Gen. xv. 9). A pair of these formed the alternative offering instead of pigeons for the poor. "One of the first birds to migrate northwards, the turtle...immediately on its arrival pours forth from every garden, grove and wooded hill its melancholy yet soothing ditty." (Tristram in *Sm. Bibl. Dict.*)

crane] **swift** (*Cypselus*). Several species of it are found in Palestine, from which country the swallow does not migrate.

swallow] **crane.**

people know not the judgment of the LORD. How do ye 8 say, We *are* wise, and the law of the LORD *is* with us? Lo, certainly in vain made he *it;* the pen of the scribes *is* in vain. The wise *men* are ashamed, they are dismayed and 9 taken: lo, they have rejected the word of the LORD; and what wisdom *is* in them? Therefore will I give their wives 10 unto others, *and* their fields to them that *shall* inherit *them:* for every one from the least even unto the greatest is given to covetousness, from the prophet even unto the priest every one dealeth falsely. For they have healed the hurt of 11 the daughter of my people slightly, saying, Peace, peace; when *there is* no peace. Were they ashamed when they 12

judgment] ordinance, law, which is thus recognised by the lower animals.

8. *the law*] The reply of the priests and false prophets was, We have the written Law, and are learned in its language and precepts. Such men were the two Pashurs (chaps. xx. 1, xxi. 1) and Shemaiah (chap. xxix. 24, &c.) who boasted of the Law newly discovered in the Temple. Some take the Hebrew for *wise*, here, and in chap. xviii. 18 to denote a special class of persons.

Lo, certainly...] **In truth lo! the lying pen of the scribes hath made it** (the Law) **a lie.** The English marginal rendering is thus fairly correct ('The false pen of the scribes worketh for falsehood'). They have used their knowledge of the Law to deceive others, in assuring them that they may sin with impunity.

scribes] First found as a *class* in Josiah's time (2 Chron. xxxiv. 13). This class probably arose in Hezekiah's day (compare Prov. xxv. 1). Hence the preservation of so many prophecies of his time, while most of the words of earlier prophets have been lost. The schools of the prophets (1 Sam. xix. 20, &c.) no doubt helped much towards the same result. We gather that the Law must have existed in writing before the class of scribes could have grown up, and therefore the modern view that the "Books of Moses" were a late fabrication may be disproved even from this verse alone.

9. *what wisdom*] literally, *wisdom of* (=*in*) *what matter*.

10—12. Almost identical with chap. vi. 12—15 above. See notes there. There is no valid ground however for supposing it to be a later insertion here. Jeremiah frequently repeats himself. Compare ver. 15 with xiv. 19, v. 9 with 29 and ix. 9, vii. 31—33 with xix. 5—7 and xxxii. 35, x. 12—16 with li. 15—19, xv. 13, 14 with xvii. 3, 4, xvi. 14, 15 with xxiii. 7, 8, xxiii. 5, 6 with xxxiii. 14—16, xxiii. 19, 20 with xxx. 23, 24.

Therefore] Because '*my people know not*,' &c. (end of ver. 7).

that shall inherit] **that shall take possession of.** The idea is that of forcible seizure on the part of the invader.

had committed abomination? nay, they were not at all ashamed, neither could they blush: therefore shall they fall among them that fall: in the time of their visitation they ¹³ shall be cast down, saith the LORD. I will surely consume them, saith the LORD: *there shall be* no grapes on the vine, nor figs on the fig tree, and the leaf shall fade; and *the things that* I have given them shall pass away from them. ¹⁴ Why do we sit still? assemble yourselves, and let us enter into the defenced cities, and let us be silent there: for the LORD our God hath put us to silence, and given us water of gall to drink, because we have sinned against the LORD. ¹⁵ *We* looked for peace, but no good *came; and* for a time ¹⁶ of health, and behold trouble. The snorting of his horses was heard from Dan: the whole land trembled at the sound of the neighing of his strong ones; for they are come, and

13. *I will surely consume them*] **I will gather and sweep them away.** There is a play on the two verbs in the Hebrew which is untranslateable.

there shall be] These words had best be omitted. The description concerns the *present* state of the people, who are the vine and fig tree spoken of.

shall fade] **fadeth.** A contrast to the righteous man, who is like the tree with leaves ever green, chap. xvii. 8; Ps. i. 1—3.

the things that I have given them shall pass away from them] **I appoint unto them those that shall pass over them**, viz. the destroying foe, which shall inundate them as a flood. The same figure is used Is. viii. 8, xxviii. 15. For this somewhat difficult clause in the original other renderings have been proposed, but they are rather forced, (i) *I deliver them up to those who pass over them*, (ii) *I gave to them that* (viz. *my Law*) *which they trangress*.

14. The people address one another and urge the best course that remains under the circumstances announced in the previous verse.

be silent] better, *perish*. Compare 1 Sam. ii. 9.

hath put us to silence] The original is even stronger, *has decreed our ruin*.

gall] the margin reads 'poison.' It was a bitter plant. There have been suggested (i) *poppy*, hence 'water of gall' (also chaps. ix. 15, xxiii. 15) = opium (see Matt. xxvii. 34), but this its grape-like berries (Deut. xxxii. 32) forbid, (ii) *hemlock*, (iii) *colocynth* (a kind of cucumber), (iv) *tares*, (v) *night-shade* (*belladonna*). The last seems the most probable meaning.

16. *Dan*] As the northernmost boundary, probably with no reference to its having been one of the great seats of idolatry.

land] or, *earth*.

strong ones] *war-horses*. The same epithet is used as a substitute

have devoured the land, and all that is in it; the city, and those that dwell therein. For behold, I will send serpents, 17 cockatrices, among you, which *will* not *be* charmed, and they shall bite you, saith the LORD.

18—22. *A bitter Lament for the people.*

When I would comfort myself against sorrow, my heart *is* 18 faint in me. Behold the voice of the cry of the daughter of 19 my people because of them that dwell in a far country: *Is* not the LORD in Zion? *is* not her king in her? Why have they provoked me to anger with their graven images, *and* with strange vanities? The harvest is past, the summer is 20 ended, and we are not saved. For the hurt of the daughter 21

for the noun, chaps. xlvii. 3, l. 11 (Eng. Version "bulls"). The horse is the embodiment of strength in Scripture. See Job xxxix. 19; Ps. xxxiii. 17, cxlvii. 10.

17. *cockatrices*] **vipers.** There are several Hebrew words for serpent. The kind mentioned here probably is that called in Latin *regulus*. We gather from Isaiah (xi. 8) that it burrowed underground, and (lix. 5) that it produced eggs. The serpent to which Dan is compared (Gen. xlix. 17) *may* be the same.

which will not be charmed] Compare Eccles. x. 11. The serpent-charming art is still kept up in the East. It is supposed that the sharp shrill sounds which the charmers produce by their voice or an instrument are the means by which the desired result is reached. They also "repeatedly breathe strongly into the face of the serpent and occasionally blow spittle, or some medicated composition upon them." *The Land and the Book*, p. 154.

18—22. A BITTER LAMENT FOR THE PEOPLE.

18. *When I would comfort myself against*] literally, *O my comfort in*, i.e. *O that I could comfort myself in.*

in me] *on me*, as an oppressive burden.

19. *because of them that dwell in*] **from.** Jeremiah is in thought anticipating the captivity, and the distressful cries of the exiles in the direction of their home.

Why have they...] This is the LORD's reply.

strange] **foreign.**

20. *summer*] *vintage, ingathering of fruits.* As when the harvest was bad, there remained yet hopes from the yield of grapes, figs, olives, &c., and till these hopes had failed to be realized, men did not despair; so the people had lost one chance after another, and were now without any hope. Accordingly it is again the people who speak here, and use what is obviously a proverbial saying.

21. *the hurt*] literally, *the breaking, the breach,* and so the verb that follows.

of my people am I hurt; I am black; astonishment hath
taken hold on me. *Is there* no balm in Gilead; *is there* no
physician there? why then is not the health of the daughter
of my people recovered?

CHAP. IX. 1—9. *Lament continued.*

9 O that my head were waters, and mine eyes a fountain of
tears,
That I might weep day and night for the slain of the
daughter of my people!

2 O that I had in the wilderness a lodging place of way-
faring men;
That I might leave my people, and go from them!
For they *be* all adulterers, an assembly of treacherous *men*.

3 And they bend their tongues *like* their bow *for* lies:

I am black] Either (i) I am diseased, for which is quoted Job xxx. 28
(compare Ps. xxxviii. 7); or better (ii) I am in mourning garb,
Ps. xxxv. 14.

22. *balm*] Red balsam from Mecca was grown in Roman times in
the gardens of Jericho. That meant here however was gum from (i) the
terebinth or mastic tree or (ii) the opobalsamum. It is mentioned as
early as Gen. xxxvii. 25.

Gilead] a mountainous part of Palestine, east of the Jordan, south
of Bashan, and north of Moab.

is there no physician there?] Is there no priest or prophet, who can
heal the sin of Israel or apply a remedy?

why then is not...?] better, *why is no healing gone up upon the
daughter of my people?*

CHAP. IX. 1—9. LAMENT CONTINUED.

1. *fountain*] **reservoir.** See chap. ii. 13 and note.
2. *a lodging place*] a caravanserai, hospice, (khan), such as were
found in lonely places. They differed from the inn in not having any
resident host, or supplying food to the traveller. Shelter was all that
they afforded. The most desolate spot, if it but sufficed to cover him,
is to the prophet an object of yearning, that so he may escape the sights
which thrust themselves upon him in Jerusalem.

adulterers] See note on last words of chap. ii. 20.

treacherous] *faithless* (towards God, chap. v. 11, but here) towards
each other, as shewn by what follows.

3. *tongues*] **tongue.**
like] **which is.**
for lies] **with lying.** In the figure the bow represents the tongue
and lying the arrow which fills it. The bow was strung by pressure
from the foot, while the string was pushed up to the notch.

> But they are not valiant for the truth upon the earth;
> For they proceed from evil to evil,
> And they know not me, saith the LORD.
> Take ye heed every one of his neighbour, 4
> And trust ye not in any brother:
> For every brother will utterly supplant,
> And every neighbour will walk *with* slanders.
> And they will deceive every one his neighbour, 5
> And will not speak the truth:
> They have taught their tongue to speak lies,
> *And* weary themselves to commit iniquity.
> Thine habitation *is* in the midst of deceit; 6
> Through deceit they refuse to know me, saith the LORD.
> Therefore thus saith the LORD of hosts, 7
> Behold, I will melt them, and try them;

But they are not valiant for the truth] **And not according to faithfulness do they rule**, i.e. those who in positions of power do not observe fidelity in their dealings with their fellow men.

know] acknowledge.

4. Compare for the general sense Mic. vii. 5, 6. "The violence which had in the earlier period of the divided kingdom characterized the northern dynasty, in the reigns of Manasseh and Josiah penetrated the fortunes of Jerusalem also. It had become a mortal battle between two fierce parties. The persecution of the prophets by Manasseh had provoked the persecution of the idolatrous priests by Josiah. The mutual distrust, which had already in the time of Hezekiah broken up families and divided the nearest friends, and made a man's worst enemies those of his own household, had now reached the highest degree of intensity; 'Every man had to take heed of his neighbour and suspect his brother'" (Stanley, *J. Ch.* II. 437).

will utterly supplant] "It might be rendered, *Every brother is a thorough Jacob*" (*Sp. Comm.*) Gen. xxvii. 36.

will walk with slanders] *slandereth.* The present tense is best. Compare chaps. vi. 28 and xii. 6.

5. Here, as in the previous verse, the verbs had best be rendered in English by present tenses.

weary themselves] Their will to do evil outstrips their power.

6. *Thine*] The people are still addressed, the sense being a repetition of the thought of ver. 4. Others make these words to be from God to the prophet, pointing out to him his danger; but this is not so good.

Through deceit they refuse to know me] Their evil disposition towards one another leads to rejection of God. Compare 1 John iv. 20.

7. *melt them, and try them*] by the essay of affliction. Compare Is. xlviii. 10. The two operations, *melting* to remove the dross, *trying,*

For how shall I do for the daughter of my people?
8 Their tongue *is as* an arrow shot out; it speaketh deceit:
One speaketh peaceably to his neighbour with his mouth,
But in heart he layeth his wait.
9 Shall I not visit them for these *things*? saith the LORD:
Shall not my soul be avenged on such a nation as this?

10—22. *The calamity set forth in further detail.*

10 For the mountains will I take up a weeping and wailing,
And for the habitations of the wilderness a lamentation,
Because they are burnt up, so that none can pass through them;
Neither can *men* hear the voice of the cattle;
Both the fowl of the heavens and the beast
Are fled; they are gone.
11 And I will make Jerusalem heaps, *and* a den of dragons;

in order to ascertain whether the metal is now pure, are brought together again in Zech. xiii. 9.

how shall I do for] **how should I deal in regard to.** The LORD justifies His course of action in bringing correction upon the nation.

8. *an arrow shot out*] better, **a murderous arrow.**

9. Repeated from chap. v. 9.

10—22. THE CALAMITY SET FORTH IN FURTHER DETAIL.

10. This and the following verses describe the desolation of the land, the exile of its inhabitants and the slaughter of children and young men in the cities.

For] On account of, not upon. Although the latter is the primary sense of the Hebrew word, yet that it is not its meaning as used in this particular phrase, is shewn 2 Sam. i. 17, and elsewhere.

habitations] better, **pastures.**

wilderness] a sort of land which would not bear tillage, but was productive of grass.

burnt up] through lack of any cultivation, which might have counteracted the scorching effect of the sun's rays.

men] **they.**

11. *dragons*] **jackals.** There are two very similar Hebrew words, which have been confused in the English Version, but which have apparently quite distinct meanings. (i) Tannim, the word found here (also in chaps. x. 22, xiv. 6, xlix. 33, li. 37). It can hardly have the sense of serpent (dragon), for (*a*) it is often connected with the word for ostrich; (*b*) the animal is compared (xiv. 6) to the wild asses snuffing

And I will make the cities of Judah desolate, without an inhabitant.
Who *is* the wise man, that may understand this? 12
And *who is he* to whom the mouth of the LORD hath spoken, that he may declare it,
For what the land perisheth
And is burnt up like a wilderness, that none passeth through?
And the LORD saith, Because they have forsaken my law 13 which I set before them,
And have not obeyed my voice, neither walked therein;
But have walked after the imagination of their own heart, 14
And after Baalim, which their fathers taught them:
Therefore thus saith the LORD of hosts, the God of 15 Israel;
Behold, I *will* feed them, *even* this people, with wormwood,

up the wind; (*c*) its *wailing* is referred to Mic. i. 8, and probably Job xxx. 29. For this last reason specially it is identified with the jackal. (ii) Tannin, occurring chap. li. 34, where compare note. See Sm. *Bibl. Dict.* Art. *Dragon*.

12. *Who is the wise man*] meaning that there are none such found, with a hint at the would-be wise, the false prophets.

For what the land perisheth] It is better to make this a new question, itself the explanation of "this." That which the truly wise and taught of God can alone understand and declare is the cause on account of which the ruin comes. Compare Hos. xiv. 9. **Wherefore hath the land perished?**

13. *I set before them*] Not referring so much to the first giving of the Law as to the constant enforcing of it by the prophets. We may (with Kimchi a Jewish commentator) compare Deut. xxx. 11—14, (quoted Rom. x. 6, &c.).

therein] The gender in the Hebrew shews that *law*, not *voice*, is the thing referred to.

14. *imagination*] **stubbornness.** See note on chap. iii. 17.

Baalim] See note on chap. ii. 8, 23.

which their fathers taught them] The evil was not the growth of one generation.

15. The people shall be subjected to the bitterest woes, here likened to wormwood and water of gall.

will feed] **am feeding.** It had already begun.

wormwood] (*absinthium*) from a Hebrew root signifying to abuse, to curse. See note on xxiii. 15.

And give them water of gall to drink.
16 I will scatter them also among the heathen, whom neither they nor their fathers have known:
And I will send a sword after them, till I have consumed them.
17 Thus saith the Lord of hosts,
Consider ye, and call for the mourning *women*, that they may come;
And send for cunning *women*, that they may come:
18 And let them make haste, and take up a wailing for us,
That our eyes may run down *with* tears,
And our eyelids gush out with waters.
19 For a voice of wailing is heard out of Zion, How are we spoiled!
We are greatly confounded, because we have forsaken the land,

water of gall] See note on chap. viii. 14.

16. "I will scatter you among the heathen, and will draw out a sword after you" is found in Lev. xxvi. 33. This prophecy of long standing was now to be fulfilled, because the condition of its fulfilment, viz. the iniquity of the nation, was full. For the sword which was to pursue them in Egypt the land of their exile see the still more definite threatenings in chaps. xlii. 16, xliv. 27.

till I have consumed them] not implying that every individual of the people should perish, for this would be contrary both to the fact and to such passages as chap. iv. 27. It is the dross, the impurity, that shall be wholly consumed on a foreign soil.

17, 18. Many are the dead, slain in battle and through the other horrors of war. Let the survivors bestir themselves and have the usual honours paid to the memory of the loved ones departed. "This custom continues to the present day in Judea, that women with dishevelled locks and bared breasts in musical utterance invite all to weeping." St Jerome. "There are in every city and community women exceedingly cunning in this business.... When a fresh company of sympathisers comes in, these women 'make haste' to 'take up a wailing' that the newly come may the more easily unite their tears with the mourners. They know the domestic history of each person, and immediately strike up an impromptu lamentation, in which they introduce the names of their relations who have recently died, touching some tender chord in every heart." *The Land and the Book*, p. 103.

cunning] *skilful*. Compare Esau, a cunning hunter (Gen. xxv. 27); David, a cunning player on the harp (1 Sam. xvi. 18); Uzziah's engines, invented by cunning men (2 Chron. xxvi. 15).

19. *forsaken*] **left**. It was not a voluntary departure.

Because our dwellings have cast *us* out.
Yet hear the word of the LORD, O ye women, 20
And let your ear receive the word of his mouth,
And teach your daughters wailing,
And every one her neighbour lamentation.
For death is come up into our windows, *and* is entered 21
into our palaces,
To cut off the children from without, *and* the young men
from the streets.
Speak, Thus saith the LORD, 22
Even the carcases of men shall fall as dung upon the open
field,
And as the handful after the harvestman, and none shall
gather *them.*

23—26. *The knowledge of God and of His judgments is after all the principal thing.*

Thus saith the LORD, 23

our dwellings have cast us out] more probably, **they (the enemy) have cast down our dwellings.** That the Hebrew verb can be used in this sense is shewn by Dan. viii. 11 "the place of his sanctuary *was cast down.*" The occurrence to which the prophet refers is recorded 2 Kings xxv. 9.

20. Rosenmüller thinks that the women in particular are called upon to lament, because it was they who were the leaders in the idolatry that had brought about this ruin. He compares chap. xliv. 15—19. It seems more probable that they are addressed thus, as those who should naturally in accordance with custom lead the lament. Compare 2 Sam. i. 24. Such will be the mortality, that the ordinary mourners will by no means suffice.

Yet] **For**, connected in thought with "let them make haste," etc. (ver. 18). There is a further reason for assembling, besides lamentation. Ye must impart to your daughters and neighbours your own skill.

21. Death works in a twofold manner, viz.—within and without. In the shape of famine and sickness he steals in at the windows as a thief (compare Joel ii. 9) and the greatest houses are not exempted from his visit: he also cuts off the young and vigorous in the open (Compare Zech. viii. 5).

22. *Speak, Thus saith the Lord*] The very abruptness of this break gives it force and point.

the handful after the harvestman] either (i) that which should be bound up with others into sheaves by one following the actual wielder of the sickle, or, perhaps better, (ii) the handful forgotten by the reaper, and left in the field. The neglect, and not the scanty amount, of the leavings will thus be the point of the comparison.

and none shall gather them] perhaps, *which (handful) none gathers.*

Let not the wise *man* glory in his wisdom,
Neither let the mighty *man* glory in his might,
Let not the rich *man* glory in his riches:

24 But let him that glorieth glory in this,
That *he* understandeth and knoweth me,
That I *am* the LORD which exercise lovingkindness, judgment, and righteousness, in the earth:
For in these *things* I delight, saith the LORD.

25 Behold, the days come, saith the LORD,
That I will punish all *them which are* circumcised with the uncircumcised;

26 Egypt, and Judah, and Edom, and the children of Ammon, and Moab,
And all *that are* in the utmost corners, that dwell in the wilderness:

23—26. THE KNOWLEDGE OF GOD AND OF HIS JUDGMENTS IS AFTER ALL THE PRINCIPAL THING.

23. From this verse to the end of the whole prophecy (x. 25) Jeremiah sets forth the folly of trusting to man's devices, and specially to the idols, the works of his hands. As examples of men who trusted severally in wisdom, might, riches, an ancient Jewish Commentary gives Solomon, Samson (deceived by a woman and hence meeting his death), Ahab.

24. The first part of the verse is quoted in the form "he that glorieth, let him glory in the Lord" (1 Cor. i. 31; 2 Cor. x. 17).

understandeth and knoweth] The former relates rather to the intellect, the latter to the emotions, the heart.

lovingkindness, judgment, and righteousness] He who understands and knows God as shewing forth these qualities, will himself be conformed to His image. Israel as a nation had utterly failed in this respect.

25. They shall therefore share the fate of all other nations that recognise not God.

all them which are circumcised with the uncircumcised] **all** (that are) **circumcised in** (their) **uncircumcision**, all who, even though possessors of the outward pledge of God's favour, are without purity of heart.

26. *Egypt, and Judah, and Edom*] The position of Judah between Egypt and Edom is a mark of degradation.

that are in the utmost corners] **that have the corners of their hair polled**, Herodotus (Book iii. 8) ascribes this custom to the Arabs, viz.:—cutting off the hair from the edges of the beard, and from the temples. The practice was forbidden to the Israelites (Lev. xix. 27). See chap. xlix. 28, and 32 with note, shewing that *there* at least the tribes referred to are those of Kedar.

the wilderness] the desert of Arabia, eastward of Palestine.

For all *these* nations *are* uncircumcised,
And all the house of Israel *are* uncircumcised in the heart.

CHAP. X. 1—16. *The folly of idolatry.*

Hear ye the word which the LORD speaketh unto you, O 10
house of Israel:
Thus saith the LORD, 2
Learn not the way of the heathen,

all these nations are uncircumcised] Herodotus indeed seems to make the Egyptians to have practised this rite (Book ii. 36, 37, 104), but he probably means to refer only to their princes and priests.

uncircumcised in the heart] and thus virtually on a par with the nations, to whom in outward rite they were superior.

CHAP. X. 1—16. THE FOLLY OF IDOLATRY.

Exception has been taken to this section, as a later insertion, and three arguments are brought against it. (i) It introduces a break in the sense, the passage not cohering with that which has gone before. (ii) It must from its subject matter be addressed to a people already in exile. (iii) Its language differs much from that of Jeremiah. It has accordingly been referred to the writer of Isaiah xl.—lxvi, who is thought by many on account of difference of style not to be the author of the earlier part of that Book. We reply to (i) that there is a natural connexion between this section and chap. ix. 24, "I am the LORD which exercise lovingkindness, judgment, and righteousness in the earth;" to (ii) that there was as much need of warning the people against that idolatry which was daily increasing in strength among them while still at home, as there was afterwards, when suffering the consequences of it as captives; to (iii) that in several verses Jeremiah's peculiar expressions are found, e.g. vain, vanity, applied to idols (verses 3, 15), and that at any rate the language is by no means that of the later portion of Isaiah (see specially chaps. xl. xli. xliv. xlv, where the same subject is dealt with). The author of the spurious letter from Jeremiah to the exiles of Babylon, which forms chap. vi. in the Apocryphal Book of Baruch, seems to have drawn its matter and language to a large extent from this section together with chap. xxix. 1—23. There is undoubtedly in this whole chapter less smoothness and connexion between the parts than we generally find in Jeremiah. This however is no proof whatever that such smoothness and connexion did not exist in the sermon of which this forms the conclusion, since it is quite likely that that conclusion has been preserved to us only in a fragmentary form.

It is strongly in favour of the genuineness of the section that it is found in the earliest Greek (Septuagint) Version in spite of the frequent omissions which there occur.

And be not dismayed at the signs of heaven;
For the heathen are dismayed at them.
3 For the customs of the people *are* vain:·
For *one* cutteth a tree out of the forest,
The work of the hands of the workman, with the axe.
4 They deck it with silver and with gold;
They fasten it with nails and with hammers, that it move not.
5 They *are* upright as the palm tree, but speak not:
They must needs be borne, because they cannot go.
Be not afraid of them; for they cannot do evil,
Neither also *is it* in them to do good.
6 Forasmuch as *there is* none like unto thee, O Lord;

2. *the signs of heaven*] not the sun, moon and stars (which should be for signs, etc. Gen. i. 14), nor the signs of the Zodiac, but heavenly portents, comets, meteors and the like.
For the heathen are dismayed at them] This is given not as the reason why the Israelites were likely to fall into this sin (through force of example), but as the reason why it was sinful and forbidden.
3. *customs*] **ordinances.**
people] **nations.**
vain] **vanity,** Jeremiah's word for an idol.
For one cutteth a tree] **For it is wood, that one hath cut.**
4. The idol is covered with plates of silver and gold, and secured to its place.
It is clear in spite of certain distinctions of language noticed above, that Is. xl—xliv. is closely connected with these verses. Either then (*a*) Jeremiah borrowed from Isaiah, in which case the whole of Isaiah in accordance with the traditional belief was written before the Babylonian captivity; or (*b*) the writer of those chapters borrowed from Jeremiah, which is refuted by the differences of style; or (*c*) the section is an insertion in Jeremiah by a later author; but then it would hardly appear in the Septuagint (see above). *Sp. Comm.*
(Other instances of possible quotation from the later portion of Isaiah on the part of Jeremiah are v. 25—Is. lix. 2; xii. 1—Is. lvii. 1; xii. 9—Is. lvi. 9; xiii. 16—Is. lix. 9; xiv. 7—Is. lix. 12; xlviii. 18—Is. xlvii. 1. Dean Payne Smith, *The Authenticity, etc. of Isaiah Vindicated*, p. 107.)
5. *upright as the palm tree*] **as a pillar of turned work,** a pillar resembling a palm tree. These idols are stiff and lifeless as such. Others render "*like pillars in a garden of cucumbers,*" in which sense the Hebrew word is found in Is. i. 8. That this was the sense in which the Jews themselves understood it at the time when the book of Baruch was written appears from the verse (Baruch vi. 70) evidently based on this, "as a scarecrow in a garden of cucumbers."
6. *Forasmuch as there is none*] **None at all is.** The Hebrew has a

Thou *art* great, and thy name *is* great in might.
Who would not fear thee, O King of nations? for to thee doth it appertain: 7
Forasmuch as among all the wise *men* of the nations, and in all their kingdoms, *there is* none like unto thee.
But they are altogether brutish and foolish: 8
The stock *is* a doctrine of vanities.
Silver spread into plates is brought from Tarshish, 9
And gold from Uphaz, the work of the workman, and of the hands of the founder:

double negative, thus emphasizing the denial. The English Version has misunderstood one of the negatives, and so rendered it *forasmuch as*.

7. *doth it appertain*] *it is fitting.* "Thine is the kingdom" is the comment of the Chaldee paraphrase, which exactly hits the sense.

wise men] *wise ones,* gods included.
kingdoms] **royal estate.**
there is none] **none at all is.**
kingdoms] **royal estate.**

8. *altogether*] The Hebrew is *in one* and had therefore best be rendered by the two words *all together* rather than simply by a word equivalent to *wholly.*

The stock is a doctrine of vanities] **The teaching of idols is (a piece of) wood.** The sense is not that the block of wood teaches foolishness, but that it can never in the instruction which it gives go beyond itself. As water cannot rise above its source, so the idol is wood and can never get beyond it.

9. The grammatical construction of the two verses is closer than would appear from the Eng. Version, "a piece of wood, silver beaten into plates, from Tarshish it is brought, etc."

Tarshish] either (i) Tarsus in Cilicia (Josephus); or (ii) Carthage (the Septuagint); or (iii) Tartessus in Spain. This last is the generally received opinion now. The mineral products supplied by Tarshish to Tyre, silver, iron, tin and lead (Ezek. xxvii. 12), were exactly those in which Spain was rich. In Strabo's time the port had ceased to exist; hence the confusion as to the locality.

Uphaz] "Probably Uphaz was a place in the neighbourhood of the river Hyphasis (now the *Gharra,* the S.E. limit of the Punjab), the Sanscrit name for which is Vipâçâ." *Sp. Comm.* Many however identify it with Ophir (there being a considerable similarity in the Hebrew words), about whose position there are very wide differences of opinion, the chief views being (i) India (Josephus); (ii) India or the east coast of Arabia, at any rate some place where Sanscrit was the language spoken, (Max Müller, *Sc. of Lang.* Ed. vi. vol. I. 230); (iii) Africa, so Milton,

"Mombasa, and Quiloa and Melind
 And Sofala, thought Ophir, to the realm
 Of Congo and Angola furthest South." *P. L.* XI. 399—401.

Blue and purple *is* their clothing:
They *are* all the work of cunning *men*.
10 But the Lord *is* the true God,
He *is* the living God, and an everlasting king:
At his wrath the earth shall tremble,
And the nations shall not be able to abide his indignation.
11 Thus shall ye say unto them, The gods that have not made the heavens and the earth, *even* they shall perish from the earth, and from under these heavens.
12 He hath made the earth by his power,
He hath established the world by his wisdom,
And hath stretched out the heavens by his discretion.
13 When he uttereth his voice, *there is* a multitude of waters in the heavens,
And he causeth the vapours to ascend from the ends of the earth;
He maketh lightnings with rain,

founder] **goldsmith**.
blue and purple] The former probably was a bluish purple, while the latter had a strong tinge of red.
cunning] See note on ix. 17.
10. *the true God*] literally, *a God who is truth*.
11. The verse appears in Chaldee. Hence some suppose it to be an interpolation. But (i) no one would call attention to his interpolation by writing it in a different language from the text; and (ii) it harmonizes completely with the context. The object therefore is either (*a*) that the Jews might thus have put into their mouths the very words in which they should while in exile address their Chaldee conquerors, which is somewhat improbable; or (*b*) because it is a proverb and thus given in the language of the common people (Aramaic).
from under these heavens] more probably, *from under the heavens—these Gods*.
12. "The splendour of this glory appeareth unto us in and through the works of his hands," Bp. Pearson on the Creed, Art. 1. Some see the doctrine of the Trinity foreshadowed here—Power, Wisdom, Understanding or Skill ('*discretion*'). Verses 12—16 are repeated li. 15—19.
13. *When he uttereth his voice, there is a multitude of waters in the heavens, and he causeth*] *When he thundering giveth the roar of waters in the heavens, he causeth*. This is probably the best rendering. The literal translation is *At the voice of his giving etc*. The ascent of the vapours is spoken of poetically as though it were the consequence of the thunder, because it is seen to follow it.
vapours] *clouds*, literally, *ascended ones*.

And bringeth forth the wind out of his treasures.
Every man is brutish in *his* knowledge: 14
Every founder is confounded by the graven image:
For his molten image *is* falsehood, and *there is* no breath
    in them.
They *are* vanity, *and* the work of errors: 15
In the time of their visitation they shall perish.
The portion of Jacob *is* not like them: 16
For he *is* the former of all *things;*
And Israel *is* the rod of his inheritance:
The LORD of hosts *is* his name.

17—22. *The prophet returns to the subject of the coming woe.*

Gather up thy wares out of the land, 17

with rain] **for the rain,** i.e. *to accompany the rain.*
14. *in his knowledge*] either (i) *without knowledge*, i.e. bereft of it; or perhaps better, (ii) *from* (in) *that very thing in which he thinks he has shewn skill*, viz.:—the idol. The latter seems more in accordance with the parallelism evidently intended between this and the next clause, *knowledge* in the one corresponding to *graven image* in the other. We may compare Rom. i. 22.
founder] **goldsmith,** as in ver. 9.
confounded] *brought to shame.*
15. *work of errors*] a work which misleads, deceives. Others however understand the Hebrew in the sense of mockery, a thing to be ridiculed.
visitation] See vi. 6.
16. *The portion of Jacob*] The true God, upon whom Israel has a claim.
former] maker, fashioner.
all things] the whole, the universe.
the rod of his inheritance] The Hebrew word rendered rod sometimes means a sceptre. Hence the meaning has been taken to be, Israel is the people over whom God specially rules. But the sceptre is rather the sign than the object of kingly power. Therefore it seems better to refer the word to its other common sense of a measuring rod, so that the import will be, Israel is the people whom God has marked out for Himself as His peculiar possession.

17—22. THE PROPHET RETURNS TO THE SUBJECT OF THE
COMING WOE.

17. Some would take this and the following section, which ends the chapter, as composed either (*a*) in the times of Jehoiakim, when on account of his revolt against Nebuchadnezzar Syrians, Chaldaeans, etc.

O inhabitant of the fortress.
18 For thus saith the LORD,
Behold, I will sling out the inhabitants of the land at this once,
And will distress them, that they may find *it so*.
19 Woe is me for my hurt! my wound *is* grievous:
But I said, Truly this *is* a grief, and I must bear it.
20 My tabernacle is spoiled, and all my cords are broken:
My children are gone forth *of* me, and they *are* not:
There is none to stretch forth my tent any more,
And to set up my curtains.

were sent against him (2 Kings xxiv. 1, 2) or, inasmuch as we do not read of the city as besieged on that occasion, (*b*) in the days of Jehoiachin, when this event did occur (2 Kings xxiv. 10). Both views however are put aside by recollecting that this is a prophecy, not a statement of that which was actually occurring.

thy wares] **thy bundle**. The Hebrew word occurs here only. It seems to mean a few articles gathered together, rather than any considerable amount or burden. Hence it suggests hasty flight.

O inhabitant of the fortress] *O thou that sittest in the siege*, i.e. thou who art in a besieged city. Others less well have suggested (*a*) *in a fortified city*, (*b*) *in distress*.

18. *sling out*] For this strong figure of speech compare 1 Sam. xxv. 29; and for a somewhat similar one Is. xxii. 18.

at this once] **at this time**, as opposed to former occasions, when plunder and a tribute imposed formed the utmost punishment.

they may find it so] In the absence of any expressed object to the verb, interpreters have suggested many, e.g. (i) *the distress*, (ii) *God*, (iii) *God's fulfilment of His threat*, (iv) *the besieged*. If, as seems best, we take this last as the object to be supplied, the sense of the whole will be, I will drive them, as a hunter would do, into a small space (the city), so that the besiegers may find them out.

19. The prophet now begins a lament in the person of the nation.

hurt] literally, *breaking*, the same word which is rendered *destruction* in chap. iv. 6.

a grief] (my) **grief**. The literal sense of the word is *sickness, suffering*.

20. The spoiling and exile are represented under the figure of one whose tent had been captured and children carried away, so that she is at once impoverished and bereaved.

tabernacle] Tents seem frequently to have been used in the country parts. Phrases which imply this are often found, e.g. chap. xxxv. 7; 1 Kings xii. 16, etc. See chap. iv. 20 with note.

cords] of the tent.

are not] Compare Gen. xlii. 36.

curtains] which hung round it.

For the pastors are become brutish, 21
And have not sought the LORD:
Therefore they shall not prosper;
And all their flocks shall be scattered.
Behold, the noise of the bruit is come, 22
And a great commotion out of the north country,
To make the cities of Judah desolate,
And a den of dragons.

23—25. *Jeremiah in the Name of the People deprecates God's Wrath.*

O LORD, I know that the way of man *is* not in himself: 23
It is not in man that walketh to direct his steps.
O LORD, correct me, but with judgment; 24
Not in thine anger, lest thou bring me to nothing.

21. *pastors*] See note on chaps. ii. 8, and xvii. 16.
they shall not prosper] **they have not prospered**, or, better, **they have not acted prudently.** The Hebrew word occurs in both senses.
shall be scattered] **are scattered.**

22. *Behold, the noise of the bruit is come*] Literally, *The voice of a rumour; behold it comes.* Thus, while in point of grammar = the voice or the rumour, it is in sense that which *is rumoured* by the approaching army.
bruit] only once elsewhere in the Bible, viz. Nah. iii. 19.
great commotion] Compare chaps. vi. 23, viii. 16.
the north country] Compare chap. i. 14, etc.
dragons] See note on chap. ix. 11.

23—25. JEREMIAH IN THE NAME OF THE PEOPLE DEPRECATES GOD'S WRATH.

23. *the way of man is not in himself*] Man cannot determine what course he shall take; he is in God's hands throughout.
man that walketh] The word for *man* here differs from the former, and implies *strong man, man at his best.* The same word is rendered "*high*" Psalm xlix. 2; and "*great man*" Is. ii. 9. See above, chap. ii. 6 with note.
to direct his steps] to ensure success. The same word occurs Ps. xxxvii. 23 ("The steps of a good man *are ordered* by the LORD"), and its sense there seems to determine that in which it occurs here. All prosperity, as well as the converse, comes from God.

24. *with judgment*] Compare chap. xlvi. 28 "*I will...correct thee in measure*," where the word is the same. See note on ii. 19. Vindictive punishment, as opposed to that which has for its object the reformation of the offender, is the kind here deprecated.
bring me to nothing] *render me insignificant*, not, *wholly destroy me.* They had been already assured that this should not happen.

25   Pour out thy fury upon the heathen that know thee not,
And upon the families that call not on thy name:
For they have eaten up Jacob, and devoured him, and consumed him,
And have made his habitation desolate.

CHAP. XI. 1—14. *Judah has been false to the Covenant, and meet punishment must ensue.*

11 The word that came to Jeremiah from the LORD, saying,
2   Hear ye the words of this covenant, and speak unto the

25. This verse occurs almost word for word in Ps. lxxix. 6, 7, probably one of the Psalms written after the captivity. "Its language would apply almost equally well either to the time of Nebuchadnezzar or to that of Antiochus Epiphanes." Dean Perowne, *Introduction to the Psalm*. Hence, if it be granted that this passage is certainly of Jeremiah's authorship and prior to the exile, this passage must be the original, and that in the Psalm the derived.

The moral of the whole sermon contained chaps. vii.—x. is well summed up thus. It "has just one lesson from beginning to end, and that is the lesson of reality. You cannot be and are not religious, says the prophet, unless you lead religious lives. If you go to the temple, and take part in its services, and on your return home say, We are now delivered to do these bad things in our daily lives, that is, we are now free to do them, have compounded with God by going to His temple and being very devout there, and may now go on in our usual wicked ways; if thus you confess your sins only to repeat them, then you are the worse for your pretence of devotion and not the better. Instead of honouring God by going to church, you have made His house a den of robbers." Dean Payne Smith, *Expositor*, vol. VII. p. 461.

Chaps. xi., xii. form a connected prophecy, either as having been uttered at one definite time in the prophet's life, or as embodying the substance of his teaching during a particular epoch of his ministry. That epoch has been placed by some in the reign of Jehoiakim, while one commentator (Graf), who connects the prophecy of chap. xiii. with that contained in these chapters, makes the whole to be as late as Jehoiachin's time (see note on xi. 18). Chaps. xi., xii. however belong in all probability to the reign of Josiah, for (*a*) "the words of this covenant" (xi. 3) evidently have reference to that made by Josiah and his subjects before the LORD (2 Kings xxiii. 3), and (*b*) Jeremiah had not yet removed his residence to Jerusalem, but was still apparently dwelling at Anathoth (xi. 21). See further in introductory remarks to chap. xii.

CHAP. XI. 1—14. JUDAH HAS BEEN FALSE TO THE COVENANT, AND MEET PUNISHMENT MUST ENSUE.

2. *Hear ye*] The plural verb has been thought to refer to (*a*) the people (viz. the 'men of Judah and inhabitants of Jerusalem') who are

men of Judah, and to the inhabitants of Jerusalem; and 3
say thou unto them, Thus saith the LORD God of Israel;
Cursed *be* the man that obeyeth not the words of this cove- 4
nant, which I commanded your fathers in the day that I
brought them forth out of the land of Egypt, from the iron
furnace, saying, Obey my voice, and do them, according to
all which I command you: so shall ye be my people, and I
will be your God: that *I* may perform the oath which I 5
have sworn unto your fathers, to give them a land flowing

thus exhorted to report to each other the message from the LORD;
(*b*) the priests and elders; (*c*) the prophets. The last is the best, for it
is natural, inasmuch as the words are directly addressed to one of their
number, that the whole body should be included simply under the pronoun 'ye.' This verse therefore contains the general injunction laid
upon the prophets as a class, and is followed by the special command to
Jeremiah.

3. This and the following verses contain several references to the
Book of Deuteronomy. The prophet is commanded to remind the people
of those terms of the covenant under which alone they held the land.

Cursed be the man that obeyeth not] The words are an adaptation of
the last of the solemn warnings (Deut. xxvii. 15—26) to be pronounced
against those who failed to observe the enactments of the Law, "Cursed
be he that *confirmeth* not all the words of this law to do them." The
observance of this ceremony on their arrival in the land was enjoined
by Moses, and was accordingly carried out (Josh. viii. 30—35). For
confirm of the passage in Deuteronomy is substituted *obey* by Jeremiah,
because in the former case the acknowledgment of the obligation at the
outset was the point of importance, while now a life of actual obedience
to it is that which is needed.

the words of this covenant] Compare for the expression Deut. xxix.
1, 9.

4. *in the day that I brought them forth*] at the time of their leaving
Egypt. The covenant enjoined in Deuteronomy was the same in essence
as that which was made on Sinai and which was confirmed by solemn
ceremonies (Exod. xxiv. 5—8), and thus its enactment followed the
exodus from Egypt at but a short interval.

the iron furnace] another point of connexion with Deuteronomy, where
this same expression occurs, meaning Egypt (iv. 20). It is found also in
Solomon's prayer at the dedication of his Temple (1 Kings viii. 51). Compare Isaiah xlviii. 10 ("I have chosen thee in the *furnace of affliction*").

do them] namely, the words of this covenant (ver. 3).

5. *that I may perform*] Some would make the quotation of the
substance of the Mosaic precept to end with ver. 4, so that the opening
words of ver. 5 should be the direct address of God to Jeremiah, and
refer accordingly to the present time. It seems better however to take
them as the quotation continued from the Pentateuch, their substance
being found in Deut. vii. 12, 13.

with milk and honey, as *it is* this day. Then answered I, and said, So be it, O Lord. Then the Lord said unto me, Proclaim all these words in the cities of Judah, and in the streets of Jerusalem, saying, Hear ye the words of this covenant, and do them. For I earnestly protested unto your fathers in the day that I brought them up out of the land of Egypt, *even* unto this day, rising early and protesting, saying, Obey my voice. Yet they obeyed not, nor inclined their ear, but walked every one in the imagination of their evil heart: therefore I will bring upon them all the words of this covenant, which I commanded *them* to do; but they

your fathers] Abraham, Isaac and Jacob, as ancestors of those who entered upon the enjoyment of the land.

flowing with milk and honey] Comp. chap. xxxii. 22; Exod. iii. 8, 17, xiii. 5, xxxiii. 3; Ezek. xx. 6, 15.

as it is this day] *this day* omitting *as it is* will be the rendering, if we take the whole sentence as proposed above. The phrase in the Hebrew seems often, or even generally, to have this sense (compare Deut. viii. 18; 1 Kings iii. 6 and specially viii. 61), although its more literal rendering is that which is adopted by the English Version.

So be it] **Amen.** As the words of the Lord were in effect those of the curses to be pronounced as directed (Deut. xxvii.), so the prophet's reply is that assigned to the people on the same occasion. Thus it testifies to the prophet's sense of the justice of the divine announcement, and further expresses his readiness to aid in the carrying out of God's will in the matter.

6. After the exhortation to the prophetic class generally (ver. 2), and the warning of the consequences which had always attended upon disobedience to the precepts of the Law, Jeremiah is commanded to make a direct appeal to the people to conform to the agreement to which they had from old time given their consent.

the cities of Judah] Jeremiah may very probably have accompanied Josiah in the journeys which he made to Bethel and to the cities of Samaria for the overthrow of idolatry. Compare 2 Kings xxiii. 15, 19.

7. *rising early*] See chap. vii. 13.

8. The first part of this verse is almost word for word the same with chap. vii. 24.

imagination] **stubbornness.** See chap. iii. 17.

I will bring] rather, *I have brought*, not meaning that the result of the people's disobedience had as yet displayed itself in its full terrors, but that, as instances in their past history were not wanting (e.g. the captivity of the Ten Tribes and the events recorded 2 Chron. xxxiii. 11) to prove that temporal calamity followed upon neglect of God's Law, so the glaring disobedience which now existed had already involved the certainty that the provisions of the covenant in the way of penalties should be carried out to the full.

did *them* not. And the LORD said unto me, A conspiracy 9
is found among the men of Judah, and among the inhabitants of Jerusalem. They are turned back to the iniquities 10
of their forefathers, which refused to hear my words; and
they went after other gods to serve them: the house of
Israel and the house of Judah have broken my covenant
which I made with their fathers. Therefore thus saith the 11
LORD, Behold, I *will* bring evil upon them, which they shall
not be able to escape; and though they shall cry unto me,
I will not hearken unto them. Then shall the cities of Judah 12
and inhabitants of Jerusalem go, and cry unto the gods unto
whom they offer incense: but they shall not save them at
all in the time of their trouble. For *according to* the number 13
of thy cities were thy gods, O Judah; and *according to* the
number of the streets of Jerusalem have ye set up altars to
that shameful thing, *even* altars to burn incense unto Baal.
Therefore pray not thou for this people, neither lift up a cry 14

9. *A conspiracy*] Possibly this may mean that there were actual measures taken in secret against Josiah on account of his reforms. At any rate the expression denotes a considerable amount of agreement in the pursuance of idolatry, and in all probability further points to a secresy of combination.

10. *their forefathers*] The Hebrew is *their fathers, the first ones*, thus bringing us back to the wilderness times, and pointing to the idolatry committed there.

and they went after] **yea, they are gone after.** In the Hebrew the word 'they' is emphatic, and therefore refers to the Jews of the prophet's day as contrasted with their forefathers of the time of Moses. Israel and Judah are placed on a par as regards crime, that it may be inferred that no less punishment than had been already meted out to the former was in store for the latter.

11. *will bring*] **am bringing,** or, as the Heb. participle is often a future, **am about to bring.**

12, 13. Compare the almost identical language used in chap. ii. 27, 28.

13. *streets*] *open places*. So in chap. vii. 17.

that shameful thing] See note on chap. iii. 24. The verse has been taken to imply that altars, such as are here mentioned, were actually set up in most if not all of the streets of Jerusalem, and hence it has been said that this portion of the prophecy cannot be as early as the reign of Josiah. The verse however need mean no more than that a strong though secret opposition existed to the reforming work of that king and that the worship of Baal was practised, though not openly, in all parts of the country and city.

14. *Therefore pray not thou*] The people's wickedness had gone beyond the limits at which intercession would avail. Their own cry,

or prayer for them: for I will not hear *them* in the time that they cry unto me for their trouble.

15—20. *The People resent the Prophet's faithful rebuke.*

15 What hath my beloved to do in mine house, *seeing* she hath wrought lewdness *with* many, and the holy flesh is passed from thee? when thou doest evil, then thou rejoicest.
16 The Lord called thy name, A green olive tree, fair, *and* of goodly fruit: with the noise of a great tumult

when it should be uttered, would be a sign, not of penitence, but merely of suffering. The whole verse closely resembles chap. vii. 16.

15—20. THE PEOPLE RESENT THE PROPHET'S FAITHFUL REBUKE.

15. *my beloved*] Judah; so chap. xii. 7.

to do in mine house] The people by their idolatry have made any entrance of the Temple on their part to be an intrusion. Having rejected their Father, they have no claim upon His house.

lewdness] the better rendering is *guile*. Her service of God has been but hypocrisy and deception.

with many] There is no authority for the word *with*. The Hebrew however is very difficult. If the reading in the original be retained, we may join the word either with the preceding or succeeding ones. Hence we have the renderings (i) She hath wrought lewdness *in crowds*, or (ii) *The chief men* and the holy flesh are, etc. Of these the former keeps closer to the sense of the original word, and is less rugged, but involves a violation of grammar in the following clause (unless, by a slight alteration of one Heb. word, we there read, *and they cause the holy flesh to pass, etc.*) Another reading has been followed by the Septuagint translators, who render the whole verse, *How has my beloved wrought abomination in my house? Shall vows and holy flesh remove from thee thy wickedness, or by these shalt thou escape?* i.e. Shall promises or sacrifices profit thee?

is passed] Possibly, *they cause* (the holy flesh) *to pass*.

when thou doest evil] There is no Hebrew for *thou doest*. It seems best however to understand the clause in that way, though some would translate the latter part of the verse thus, *Shall vows and holy flesh remove thy* calamity *from thee? then mayest thou exult*. This depends on the fact that the same word in Hebrew will stand for moral evil and the physical evil which is its consequence. The last part of this rendering however seems scarcely in Jeremiah's style.

16. *called thy name*] acknowledged thee to be worthy of comparison with.

A green olive tree] Compare for this figure as applied to the nation Hosea xiv. 6. It is taken from a tree which abounds in Palestine, being indeed in many parts the only one to be seen.

of goodly fruit] "Olive oil is obtained by expression from the pulp of the fruit, and is of great economical importance, not only in Pales-

he hath kindled fire upon it, and the branches of it are broken. For the LORD of hosts, that planted thee, hath 17 pronounced evil against thee, for the evil of the house of Israel and of the house of Judah, which they have done against themselves to provoke me to anger in offering incense unto Baal. And the LORD hath given me knowledge 18 *of it*, and I know *it*: then thou shewedst me their doings. But I *was* like a lamb *or* an ox *that* is brought to the 19

tine, but also in Southern Europe. It is extensively used in the preparation of food, and may be called the milk of these countries." (J. Smith's *History of Bible Plants*).

tumult] The word in the original is used but once elsewhere, Ezek. i. 24 (where Eng. Vers. has "speech"). It there occurs in reference to the noise made by an army on the march. This therefore *may be* its sole sense, which would quite agree with Jeremiah's custom of hasty assumption and dismissal of a metaphor noticed in Introduction chap. II. § 8 (*d*), where see instances. It is however very possible on the other hand that the word may denote here the noise of a storm of rain, or of crackling flames, either of which would be excellently adapted to the figure which the rest of the verse contains of a fair fruit tree struck and maimed by lightning.

17. The strong contrast which exists between the first and second parts of ver. 16 is renewed here in other words. The Planter of the Tree, who took delight in His work, now designs nothing but evil against it, and that because of its failure to bear the fruit which He had purposed.

the evil of the house of Israel and of the house of Judah] The branches of the tree are the whole nation. The one part has already had its branches broken by the storm, and the turn of the other will soon come.

18. This and the following verses have been placed by some as late as the time of Jehoiachin or even Zedekiah, because agreeing with what we read of the general feeling which then existed against Jeremiah. There seems however no sufficient cause for separating them from the words which precede. There is an easy connexion in thought between the two parts. The prophet proceeds from the general charge of wickedness against Israel to specify a particular attack upon himself as the messenger of the LORD. The men of Anathoth, his native city, among whom therefore he would seem still to be at this time resident (see remarks at the beginning of notes on this chapter), hoping either to put him out of the way, or at any rate to terrify him into silence, had secretly conspired against his life. The LORD however had shewn him their intentions.

hath given] **gave.**
know] **knew.**

19. *like a lamb or an ox*] **like a tame lamb.** The Hebrew rendered by the English Version *ox* is indeed found in Psalm cxliv. 14 in that sense but only as a poetical expression, *the domesticated ones*. It was common among the Arabs, and apparently the Jews also (2 Sam. xii. 3), to bring

slaughter; and I knew not that they had devised devices against me, *saying*, Let us destroy the tree with the fruit thereof, and let us cut him off from the land of the living,
20 that his name may be no more remembered. But, O LORD of hosts, that judgest righteously, that triest the reins and the heart, let me see thy vengeance on them: for unto thee have I revealed my cause.

21—23. The Punishment of Anathoth is therefore foretold.

21 Therefore thus saith the LORD of the men of Anathoth, that seek thy life, saying, Prophesy not in the name of the
22 LORD, that thou die not by our hand: therefore thus saith the LORD of hosts, Behold, I will punish them: the young men shall die by the sword; their sons and their daughters
23 shall die by famine: and there shall be no remnant of

up a pet lamb with the family. To such then Jeremiah likens himself, as he dwells among the men of his own town, and is ignorant of the death with which he was threatened at their hands.

the tree with the fruit thereof] This apparently has the force of a proverb. 'Fruit' (Heb. 'bread') may mean the words spoken by the prophet, of which the men of Anathoth desired to be rid. It seems better however to take the whole phrase in the sense of utter destruction. Not only is the existing tree to be destroyed, but the chance of reproduction by the sowing of its seed is to be prevented. Jeremiah's "own village of Anathoth, occupied by members of the sacred tribe, was for him a nest of conspirators against his life. Of him, first in the sacred history, was the saying literally fulfilled, 'a Prophet hath no honour in his own birth-place'" (Stanley's *Jewish Church*, ii. 440).

20. *that triest the reins and the heart*] to whom the inmost thoughts and purposes are known. Compare chap. xx. 12, also chap. xvii. 10.

unto thee have I revealed] *upon thee have I rolled* is the rendering proposed by some. That of the Eng. Vers. however keeps closer to the original.

21—23. THE PUNISHMENT OF ANATHOTH IS THEREFORE FORETOLD.

21. *saying, Prophesy not*] See also Amos ii. 12. It would appear, when we compare ver. 18, that the men of Anathoth first conspired against Jeremiah, and afterwards on discovering that he had become aware of their secret designs, substituted threats for plots.

22. When the siege of Jerusalem shall come and battles be fought outside its walls, those of military age and sex shall be slain in combat, while the children shall perish within the city.

23. *there shall be no remnant*] This need not include the whole of Anathoth, but may refer only to the families of the actual conspirators against Jeremiah's life. Among those who returned from the captivity are mentioned "The men of Anathoth, an hundred twenty and eight" (Ezra ii. 23).

them: for I will bring evil upon the men of Anathoth, *even the year of their visitation*.

CHAP. XII. 1—4. *The Prophet deprecates the Prosperity of the Wicked.*

Righteous *art* thou, O LORD, when I plead with thee: yet 12 let me talk with thee of *thy* judgments. Wherefore doth the way of the wicked prosper? *wherefore* are all they happy that deal very treacherously? Thou hast planted them, yea, 2

even the year] better, *in the year*. The time referred to is that of the siege and capture of Jerusalem. Anathoth, as lying in the neighbourhood of the besieging armies, would be exposed to the horrors of war even to a greater extent than the capital city.

CHAP. XII. 1—4. THE PROPHET DEPRECATES THE PROSPERITY OF THE WICKED.

This first paragraph is best understood as still having reference to the treachery of the prophet's fellow-townsmen, while the subsequent paragraphs dealing with the people at large and the approaching troubles succeed naturally. Others would make chap. xii. a separate discourse, while others again consider it to contain summaries or fragments of three distinct addresses (verses 1—6, 7—13, 14—17). Those who consider these chapters or parts of them to belong to a time later than Josiah's reign make the "evil neighbours" of ver. 14 to be bands of Syrians, Moabites and Ammonites who came up against Jehoiakim along with the Chaldaeans on his revolt against Nebuchadnezzar at the conclusion of the 3rd year of his reign. On the other hand the apparent allusion to a drought in ver. 4 accords with similar references in earlier chapters belonging to Josiah's reign (iii. 3, v. 24).

1. *Righteous art thou*] God's justice is established as the result of every enquiry into His ways. Jeremiah, while admitting this, yet asks how it can be reconciled with (i) the prosperity of the wicked, (ii) his own adversity.

talk with thee of thy judgments] **reason the case with thee** as the English margin reads.

the wicked] the men of Anathoth. The general question was one which much exercised the men of the old dispensation, who had no *clear* view of any but temporal rewards and punishments. See Psalms xxxvii., xxxix., xlix., lxxiii., and the book of Job, specially chap. xxi. 7, etc.

happy] **at peace.**

2. *planted*] The same metaphor is used of the whole nation, 2 Sam. vii. 10. The figure of a tree is worked out in the verse. They have been placed in security and have prospered throughout life. We may compare Isai. xl. 24 for the same figure applied in that case to the overthrow of those who are the subjects of Divine wrath.

they have taken root: they grow, yea, they bring forth fruit: thou *art* near in their mouth, and far from their reins.
3 But thou, O LORD, knowest me: thou hast seen me, and tried mine heart towards thee: pull them out like sheep for the slaughter, and prepare them for the day of slaughter.
4 How long shall the land mourn, and the herbs of every field wither, for the wickedness of them that dwell therein? the beasts are consumed, and the birds; because they said, He shall not see our last end.

5, 6. *Greater Trials yet are to come upon the Prophet.*

5 If thou hast run with the footmen, and they have wearied thee, then how canst thou contend with horses? and *if* in

near in their mouth, and far from their reins] They honour God with their lips, but their heart is far from Him. The *reins* are taken for the seat of the affections and desires as the heart for that of the will.

3. Thou knowest my devotion, why then am I thus in trouble? **Let thy justice be vindicated.**

hast seen] **seest.**
tried] **tryest.**
pull them out] a very strong expression in the Hebrew. The same verb is used (chap. x. 20, "are broken") of the rending of the cords which stretch a tent. The sense then is, Take thou speedy and forcible measures to requite mine enemies after their deserts.

4. The drought in the land, as arising from the wickedness of its inhabitants, seems opposed to the earlier verses, where the prophet declares his perplexity at finding that misfortunes do not follow upon the wickedness of the ungodly. This, however, is a contradiction only in appearance. The calamities of the land fall upon the innocent more than the guilty. The rich and powerful oppressor and evildoer escapes.

every] **the whole.**
the beasts are consumed, and the birds] The animate as well as the inanimate creation suffers.

they said, He shall not see our last end] 'They' are Jeremiah's enemies, but the sense of their words is not so clear, although they plainly express in some sort the cause of the calamities. Some make the word 'He' to refer to God, others to Jeremiah. In the former case the sense is, He will not trouble Himself to interfere; we may go on to the end unpunished: in the latter, He (the prophet), although he threatens us with speedy destruction, shall not himself outlive us.

5, 6. GREATER TRIALS YET ARE TO COME UPON THE PROPHET.

5. God replies to Jeremiah in this and the following verse. He intimates to him by means of two proverbial expressions that he must brace himself to endure even worse things than any that he has as yet been called upon to face. The attacks of the men of Anathoth may

the land of peace, *wherein* thou trustedst, *they wearied thee*, then how wilt thou do in the swelling of Jordan? For even thy brethren, and the house of thy father, even they have dealt treacherously with thee; yea, they have called a multitude after thee: believe them not, though they speak fair *words* unto thee.

7—13. *The devastation to be wrought in the land.*

I have forsaken mine house, I have left mine heritage; I have given the dearly beloved of my soul into the hand of her enemies. Mine heritage is unto me as a lion in the

have galled him, but the treachery set on foot against him includes men of his own family, and so is yet more wounding and bitter than he supposes. He must not therefore think of being impatient at anything that he may hitherto have been called upon to undergo, but feel that he has need of all his resolution to meet the trouble which shall presently be disclosed.

if in the land of peace, wherein thou trustedst, they wearied thee] rather, *in a land of peace thou art secure*, i.e. up to this time thou hast been in comparative safety.

the swelling] *the pride*. The reference is, not as in the English Version, to the overflowing of the river's banks, but to the danger which existed in the form of lions and other wild beasts, ranging amid the luxuriant vegetation produced by the moisture of the river and its tributaries. Compare for the same expression chaps. xlix. 19, l. 44; Zech. xi. 3.

6. *a multitude*] **aloud**. Compare note on iv. 5. Thine own immediate relations will raise a shout (*a hue and cry*, according to Luther's rendering) against thee, as though thou wert a criminal seeking to escape from justice, and this will be worse than anything that thou hast yet suffered. Compare for the general sense chap. ix. 4.

7—13. THE DEVASTATION TO BE WROUGHT IN THE LAND.

7. The LORD is still the speaker. There is no reason to consider this paragraph, or that which concludes the chapter, as distinct and later utterances (see opening remarks on the Chapter). The connexion is easy. The base and wicked state into which the land had fallen could but result in its overthrow and desolation, at least for a time.

mine house] shewn by the parallelism of the clauses to mean, not the Temple, but the nation itself.

hand] *palm*. Israel is placed, as it might be a cup, upon the hand of her conqueror, incapable of offering any resistance to his will. Compare Gen. xl. 11, which is literally "I set the cup upon Pharaoh's palm." (*Sp. Comm.*). Compare also note on chap. xv. 21.

8. *as a lion*] The open hostility of the people towards the LORD

forest; it crieth out against me: therefore have I hated it.
9 Mine heritage *is* unto me *as* a speckled bird, the birds round about *are* against her; come ye, assemble all the beasts of
10 the field, come to devour. Many pastors have destroyed my vineyard, they have trodden my portion under foot, they
11 have made my pleasant portion a desolate wilderness. They have made it desolate, *and being* desolate it mourneth unto me; the whole land is made desolate, because no man
12 layeth *it* to heart. The spoilers are come upon all high places through the wilderness: for the sword of the Lord

is likened by Him to the angry roar and fierce attack of a lion ranging the forest. He therefore withdraws and leaves it as some savage beast to the solitude that it has made for itself.

have I hated it] I have treated it as though I hated it. Compare Mal. i. 3. The tenses in this and the preceding verse are in the prophetic past.

9. *Mine heritage is*] *Is mine heritage* ... ? This is a preferable rendering, although the Hebrew admits of both. So the next clause, *Are the birds, etc.?*

bird] Some would render *hyaena*, but this does not supply so good a figure, which rather is that of birds assembling round one of their own kind, and maltreating it, because its plumage attracts their attention as unusual.

assemble] i.e. cause to assemble. This part of the verse seems taken from Is. lvi. 9.

come] bring them.

10. *pastors*] the same persons who in chap. vi. 3 are called *shepherds*, viz. the leaders of the invading host.

vineyard] For Israel spoken of under this figure compare Is. v. 1, etc.

have trodden my portion under foot] They have broken ruthlessly through the fence, and have trampled upon the carefully tilled soil and well-tended produce within.

11. *They have made*] In the Hebrew the verb is singular. This change of number is not unusual, and consequently the enemy may still be the real subject here, as in the former verse, while in strict grammar the verb will be impersonal (*one has made*). But it is better perhaps to make the prophet himself the speaker of this and the following verses of the paragraph, and understand the word God as the nominative to the verb.

unto me] If we take the prophet as the speaker, we shall better render the Hebrew preposition *round about*. Jeremiah looks forth in every direction upon the land as it will appear after its overthrow.

12. *high places*] See note on chap. iii. 2.

the wilderness] the pastures which, though fertile enough for cattle, contained no fixed human habitations. See note on ii. 6.

shall devour from the *one* end of the land even to the *other* end of the land: no flesh *shall* have peace. They have 13 sown wheat, but shall reap thorns: they have put themselves to pain, *but* shall not profit: and they shall be ashamed of your revenues because of the fierce anger of the LORD.

14—17. *The future of the enemies of Israel.*

Thus saith the LORD against all mine evil neighbours, 14 that touch the inheritance which I have caused my people Israel to inherit; Behold, I will pluck them out of their land, and pluck out the house of Judah from among them. And it shall come to pass, after that I have plucked them 15 out, I will return, and have compassion on them, and will

the sword of the Lord] these spoilers, as His representatives. Compare vi. 25 with note; also xxv. 29.
shall devour] devoureth.
no flesh shall have peace] None of this sinful nation shall enjoy health or prosperity.

13. *They have sown wheat, but shall reap thorns*] evidently a proverb, meaning, as the words that follow it shew, They have used their best endeavours to obtain pleasure, the object of their desire, and have been rewarded with the very opposite of that harvest which they sought.
shall reap] have reaped.
shall not profit] do not profit.
they shall be ashamed] be ye ashamed. The verb is imperative.
revenues] produce (of the fields). The word is used in a wider sense than that which it bears in the present day, when it is generally used either of large private incomes, or of public monies obtained by taxation, etc.

14—17. THE FUTURE OF THE ENEMIES OF ISRAEL.

14. See introductory note to the Chapter.
mine evil neighbours] no doubt Syrians and others, who would feel that Israel's time of difficulty was their opportunity. The promise in this and the following verses then is that, while they and Judah shall be punished, yet on the repentance of each, it will be pardoned, and from the evil past, present, and to come, there will finally result a widespread acknowledgment of God, and establishment of His position as a righteous Judge throughout all the world. This is the answer to Jeremiah's murmurings on the subject of the prosperity of the wicked.
pluck out] The verb must mean the same in the two clauses. Thus here it will refer to the removal of Judah into captivity, and not, as some have taken it, to their subsequent deliverance.

15. *I will return, and*] an ordinary Hebrew idiom meaning no

bring them again, every man to his heritage, and every man
16 to his land. And it shall come to pass, if they will diligently learn the ways of my people, to swear by my name, The LORD liveth; as they taught my people to swear by Baal; then shall they be built in the midst of my people.
17 But if they will not obey, I will utterly pluck up and destroy that nation, saith the LORD.

CHAP. XIII. 1—11. *The acted symbol of the linen girdle.*

13 Thus saith the LORD unto me, Go and get thee a linen

more than *I will again.* The return of the Moabites is specifically mentioned in chap. xlviii. 47; that of the Ammonites in chap. xlix. 6.

16. Not only shall they be restored respectively to their lands, but they shall be established therein, if they heartily adopt the worship of the true God.

to swear by my name] to give this outward sign that to them He is supreme. See note on chap. iv. 2.

as they taught my people to swear by Baal] The Jews are now to be the leaders in godliness, instead of in idolatry as beforetime.

built] securely established, and incorporated with the people of God. For the phrase see chaps. xxiv. 6, xlii. 10, xlv. 4.

The blessings promised to Abraham, as about to be imparted through his seed to all the nations of the earth, are here again foretold. Christianity is to spring out of Judaism, but unlike it to be world-wide.

CHAP. XIII. 1—11. THE ACTED SYMBOL OF THE LINEN GIRDLE.

1. *Thus saith the* LORD] The date of this prophecy is determined almost with certainty by ver. 18, where the word *queen* is in the original *queen mother.* She who is spoken of here has indeed been taken by some to be "Jedidah, the daughter of Adaiah of Boscath" (2 Kings xxii. 1) mother of Josiah. It is much better however to make the 'king' to be Jehoiachin, and his mother (carried captive with him to Babylon, chap. xxix. 2) Nehushta. The prophecy then would be uttered either within the three months during which Jehoiachin reigned, or at the close of the reign of Jehoiakim.

Go and get thee a linen girdle] Commentators differ on the question whether this and the subsequent acts of the prophet were real or done only in symbol. In support of the latter view it is urged (i) that we have in the narrative no reference to the length of the journey (250 miles each way) which would be involved in a literal carrying out of the command; (ii) that there could be no object gained by going so long a distance merely to prove that a girdle buried in the ground would become unfit for use. On behalf of the former view it is pointed out (i) that we have nothing in the shape in which the narrative is given us to support the view that the actions are not carried out in their literal sense; (ii) that in point of fact Jeremiah was absent from Jerusalem during the

girdle, and put it upon thy loins, and put it not in water.
So I got a girdle, according to the word of the Lord, and 2
put *it* on my loins. And the word of the Lord came unto 3
me the second time, saying, Take the girdle that thou hast 4
got, which *is* upon thy loins, and arise, go to Euphrates,
and hide it there in a hole of the rock. So I went, and hid 5
it by Euphrates, as the Lord commanded me. And it 6
came to pass after many days, that the Lord said unto me,
Arise, go to Euphrates, and take the girdle from thence,
which I commanded thee to hide there. Then I went to 7
Euphrates, and digged, and took the girdle from the place
where I had hid it: and behold, the girdle was marred, it

greater part of the later years of Jehoiakim's reign, that we have no account of him during that period, and that he therefore may well be supposed during part of the time to have been in or near Babylon. This view would agree with the kind feeling shewn towards him by Nebuchadnezzar at the taking of Jerusalem (chap. xxxix. 11) which seems to point to an earlier acquaintance. It has also been suggested, to escape the difficulty of the long journey from Jerusalem to the Euphrates, that we should understand the word for Euphrates (P'rath) either (i) = Ephrath = Bethlehem, or (ii) = an Arabic word, meaning a place near the water, a crevice opening from the water into the land. Neither of these last views however are tenable. See note on ver. 4.

a linen girdle] Linen, not woollen, garments were appointed for priestly wear, and consequently linen was felt to belong to sacred uses. It was thus the fittest material for that which should symbolize the people of God. The girdle symbolizes them, inasmuch as it was that article of dress which would be most closely bound about the person of the wearer, and thus it marked the special bond existing between the Lord and Israel.

put it not in water] probably that the soiled appearance which it would soon exhibit might represent the pollution of the people.

4. *go to Euphrates*] The river which runs through Babylon, about to be the city of exile, is naturally chosen as that on the banks of which the girdle should rot.

hide it there in a hole of the rock] The expression "*digged*" (ver. 7) has been thought to shew, that by *rock* is meant the rocky or stony soil on the bank, such as might be found on that part of the river which flows through Babylonia. It need not however mean more than that Jeremiah had filled up the clift with earth or small stones. In this case '*the rock*' would be on an upper portion of the river, before it reaches the plains of Babylonia.

6. *after many days*] the seventy years of the Captivity.

7. *the girdle was marred*] As the words "put it not in water" (ver. 1) probably refer to the moral pollution of the people, which brought about their exile, so this expression points to the effect of that event in

8 was profitable for nothing. Then the word of the LORD
9 came unto me, saying, Thus saith the LORD, After this
manner will I mar the pride of Judah, and the great pride
10 of Jerusalem. This evil people, which refuse to hear my
words, which walk in the imagination of their heart, and
walk after other gods, to serve them, and to worship them,
11 shall even be as this girdle, which is good for nothing. For
as the girdle cleaveth to the loins of a man, so have I caused
to cleave unto me the whole house of Israel and the whole
house of Judah, saith the LORD; that *they* might be unto
me for a people, and for a name, and for a praise, and for
a glory: but they would not hear.

12—14. *The spoken symbol of the bottles.*

12 Therefore thou shalt speak unto them this word; Thus
saith the LORD God of Israel, Every bottle shall be filled
with wine: and they shall say unto thee, Do we not cer-

---

the way of physical decay. This is limited however to the ungodly
by the words of ver. 10. Both verses doubtless are an echo of Lev.
xxvi. 39; "They that are left of you shall pine away in their iniquity
in your enemies' lands."

9. *mar the pride*] The greatness of the nation should be crushed by
the sufferings and humiliation of exile. The verse seems based upon
Lev. xxvi. 19, "I will break the *pride* of your power," where the Hebrew
word is the same as in this place.

10. *imagination*] **stubbornness.** See chap. iii. 17. The godly
portion of the people on the other hand were to be preserved and
brought again to their land. This is shewn under the symbol of the
baskets of figs, chap. xxiv.

11. The aptitude of the symbol is pointed out. As the girdle from
its very nature must cling closely to the person, so Israel was that
people whom God chose out to be most closely united with himself.

12—14. THE SPOKEN SYMBOL OF THE BOTTLES.

12. *bottle*] **jar.** These are not the skin bottles spoken of in the
New Testament (Matt. ix. 17, etc.) but earthenware.

shall be filled with wine] Under this figure is described the intoxication through which the people shall be rendered helpless to resist the
foreign foe, while they quarrel one with another. It was no doubt in
part owing to factious strife as well as to national idolatry that the
overthrow came. The figure of filling a person with wine in the sense
of bringing upon him Divine punishment for perverseness and head-
strong continuance in sin is found also chap. xxv. 15; Ps. lx. 3; Is. li.
17, while for Israel under the figure of a bottle or jar compare chap.
xviii. 1—6.

tainly know that every bottle shall be filled *with* wine? Then shalt thou say unto them, Thus saith the LORD, Behold, I *will* fill all the inhabitants of this land, even the kings that sit upon David's throne, and the priests, and the prophets, and all the inhabitants of Jerusalem, *with* drunkenness. And I will dash them one against another, even the fathers and the sons together, saith the LORD: I will not pity, nor spare, nor have mercy, but destroy them.

15—27. *Another appeal to Judah. Her wickedness however seems inveterate.*

Hear ye, and give ear; be not proud: for the LORD hath spoken. Give glory to the LORD your God, before he cause darkness, and before your feet stumble upon the dark mountains, and, while ye look for light, he turn it into the shadow

Do we not certainly know...] not, as some have taken the sense to be, Are we not certain of prosperity and an abundant vintage? but, What need is there of telling us such a truism? The people would shew in the plainest manner possible how their minds were out of tune with the Divine warnings, whose very form they would thus utterly fail to recognise.

14. *And I will dash them one against another*] Seized with the giddiness which accompanies intoxication, they shall be a source of mutual destruction.

even the fathers and the sons together] The overthrow shall be of the most harrowing description.

15—27. ANOTHER APPEAL TO JUDAH. HER WICKEDNESS HOWEVER SEEMS INVETERATE.

15. *be not proud*] Your boast that your privileges render you secure, is an idle one.

16. *Give glory*] This is a Hebrew idiom for *confess your sins*. So Joshua says to Achan "My son, give, I pray thee, glory to the Lord God of Israel, and make confession unto him." (Josh. vii. 19). Compare Mal. ii. 2, and the words of the Jews to the man blind from his birth, whom our Lord cured, "Give God the praise" (John ix. 24) i.e. acknowledge thyself an impostor.

before he cause darkness] Darkness in the Bible is a symbol of ignorance or of wickedness. Compare for this Is. viii. 22, ix. 2; Lam. iii. 6.

the dark mountains] **the mountains of twilight.** The comparison is to persons subject to a twofold difficulty, namely, (i) the unevenness of their road; (ii) the gathering gloom. The thought of mountains as hindrances is illustrated by the proverbial saying (applied in Luke iii. 5

17 of death, *and* make *it* gross darkness. But if ye will not hear it, my soul shall weep in secret places for *your* pride; and mine eye shall weep sore, and run down *with* tears, 18 because the LORD's flock is carried away captive. Say unto the king and to the queen, Humble yourselves, sit down: for your principalities shall come down, *even* the crown of 19 your glory. The cities of the south shall be shut up, and none shall open *them:* Judah shall be carried away

by St John the Baptist to the coming of Christ), "Every mountain and hill shall be made low" (Is. xl. 4).

and make] yea make. There is no conjunction in the original, and the clause is merely added to intensify.

gross] thick. The Hebrew for 'gross darkness' is one word, literally *cloudy darkness*.

17. *in secret places*] Inasmuch as the time for warning and rebuke will then have passed, the prophet will retire (as he did in the reign of Jehoiakim), and mourn apart.

the LORD'S flock] as the rulers are called elsewhere shepherds (pastors), so the ruled are the flock. Compare Zech. x. 3.

is carried away captive] The tense probably signifies in accordance with the prophetic style that the event is pictured so vividly to the mind that it seems to have already taken place. The prophecy however (see above) may have been uttered so late in the short reign of Jehoiachin, that the captivity (of 2 Kings xxiv. 12—16) had already begun.

18. *Say*] The LORD now addresses the prophet.

the queen] *the queen mother*, Nehushta (see note on ver. 1). The fact that the kings practised polygamy, and took wives from their subjects, was the cause of the high position which the king's *mother* assumed. Accordingly she is frequently mentioned in connexion with the accession of one and another, e.g. 1 Kings xv. 13; 2 Kings x. 13. Compare 1 Kings ii. 19. In Jehoiachin's case especially, as he was but eighteen (2 Kings xxiv. 8; *eight* only, according to 2 Chron. xxxvi. 9) years old, when he came to the throne, his mother would have a considerable share in the government.

Humble yourselves, sit down] Sit down humbly. The Hebrew language, being scantily supplied with adverbs, often expresses their sense by an additional verb.

principalities] head tires, viz. the 'crown' which follows.

19. *The cities of the south shall be shut up*] Some take this to mean that, as was done by Sennacherib (2 Kings xviii. 13), the enemy should invest the southern towns of Palestine before advancing to reduce the capital city to submission. It is better to take it, as the second part of the verse suggests, as in Isaiah xxiv. 10. Ruins block the entrance to the cities, and that because of the desolation. There is none to clear a passage to the deserted dwellings. The verbs in this verse are in the past tense, which is however very possibly the prophetic past. See ver. 17.

captive all of it, it shall be wholly carried away captive.
Lift up your eyes, and behold them that come from the 20
north: where *is* the flock *that* was given thee, thy beautiful
flock? What wilt thou say when he shall punish thee? for 21
thou hast taught them *to be* captains, *and* as chief over
thee: shall not sorrows take thee, as a woman in travail?
And if thou say in thine heart, Wherefore come these *things* 22
upon me? For the greatness of thine iniquity are thy skirts
discovered, *and* thy heels made bare. Can the Ethiopian 23
change his skin, or the leopard his spots? *then* may ye also
do good, that are accustomed to do evil. Therefore will I 24

20. *Lift up your eyes*] The Hebrew verb is fem. and sing., whereas the possessive pronoun is plural. This shews that the subject is a noun of multitude, viz. Jerusalem personified as the daughter of Zion. This thought harmonizes with the words 'the flock that was given thee,' the inhabitants of the land in general.
them that come from the north] See note on chap. i. 14.
21. *when he shall punish thee*...] **if He set over thee those whom thou hast accustomed to thee as familiar friends, for a head.** The reference is probably both to the Egyptians and to the Babylonians. Israel courted the friendship now of the one, now of the other, and was then made to taste their rule in turn.
22. *thy skirts discovered*] thy flowing robe pulled aside, so that thou shalt appear in the garb of servitude, bare-legged, doing the work of a slave.
thy heels made bare] barefoot and suffering from the roughness of the road, as thou art led captive. 'Made bare' is literally **treated with violence.**
23. *the Ethiopian*] the Cushite, meaning the African branch, and not that which seems in early times to have spread across Arabia to the Tigris and Euphrates. Ethiopia lay south of Egypt, bounded by the Libyan deserts on the West and by Abyssinia on the south. Through the Jews' intercourse with Egypt the Ethiopians were familiar to them. They were thus acquainted with the "merchandise of Ethiopia" (Is. xlv. 14), which consisted of gold, ebony and elephants' tusks (Herod. Bk. III. 97, 114) and jewels (Job xxviii. 19). The people were known as tall ("men of stature," Is. xlv. 14; compare Herod. III. 20, "The Ethiopians...are said to be the tallest...men in the whole world"). For this reason probably they were chosen as attendants upon kings; see chap. xxxviii. 7.
the leopard] See chap. v. 6. Cant. iv. 8 shews that this animal was found on the mountains of Palestine. "It is now not uncommonly seen in and about Lebanon, and the southern maritime mountains of Syria." (Kitto, quoted in *Sm. Bibl. Dict.*).
then may ye also do good] So incorrigible is Judah, that her conversion would be no less wonderful than a suspension of natural laws.

scatter them as the stubble that passeth away by the wind
25 of the wilderness. This *is* thy lot, the portion of thy measures from me, saith the LORD; because thou hast forgotten
26 me, and trusted in falsehood. Therefore will I discover
27 thy skirts upon thy face, that thy shame may appear. I have seen thine adulteries, and thy neighings, the lewdness of thy whoredom, *and* thine abominations on the hills in the fields. Woe unto thee, O Jerusalem! wilt thou not be made clean? when *shall it* once *be?*

CHAP. XIV. 1—6. *Description of the drought.*

14 The word of the LORD that came to Jeremiah concerning the dearth.

24. *stubble*] the broken straw, when the separation of the grain, which *we* effect by winnowing, had been attained through the trampling of the stalks by oxen.
the wind of the wilderness] the east wind which blew strong from the Arabian desert. Compare chap. iv. 11.
25. *the portion of thy measures*] *the portion measured.* The word translated *measure* may however very well mean, as it does elsewhere, *an upper garment.* Then the rendering will be, *that which is placed in thy lap*, which brings us in the end to the same thought.
falsehood] idolatry. Compare chaps. x. 14, xvi. 19.
26. *Therefore will I*] This is scarcely strong enough. The Hebrew implies a contrast and a retaliation. *Thou* hast had thy turn, and now I shall take mine, and shall requite thee. As thou didst give thyself up to disgraceful idolatries, so I will now cover thee with disgrace.
27. The people's zealous pursuit of false gods is put once more in the most forcible language.
and thine abominations] even *thine abominations.* This word is meant to sum up the previous expressions.
in the fields] *in the* open.
when shall it once be?] after how long yet? i.e. Although (ver. 23) there is no chance that this generation turn from sin, yet may we not look for a reformation at some time, even though distant?

CHAP. XIV. 1—6. DESCRIPTION OF THE DROUGHT.

1. *The word of the Lord that came*] This and the following chapter contain a succession of short utterances, which some have sought, but without success, to assign to particular crises of history (e.g. xiv. 17—19 and xv. 7, to Josiah's defeat and death at Megiddo, or xv. 8, etc., to Jehoiakim's subjugation by Nebuchadnezzar). These conjectures have but little probability. The famine, which seems the occasion of this part of the prophecy, is probably a later one than that which is spoken of earlier in the Book (chaps. iii. 3, xii. 4), because in this place it is associated with disaster in war (verses 17, 18). The probabilities

> Judah mourneth, and the gates thereof languish; 2
> They are black unto the ground;
> And the cry of Jerusalem is gone up.
> And their nobles have sent their little ones to the waters: 3
> They came to the pits, *and* found no water;
> They returned *with* their vessels empty;
> They were ashamed and confounded, and covered their heads.
> Because the ground is chapt, 4

therefore are that the section, like the greater portion of this division of the Book, was in substance included within the Roll read in the ears of Jehoiakim, and so represents the state of matters during the earlier part of that king's reign, when all hope of permanent reform, such as had been cherished in the days of Josiah, had well nigh disappeared. Some would continue this section to chap. xvii. 18. Chap. xvi. however clearly begins a new portion. We may subdivide as follows: (*a*) xiv. 2—6, description of the drought; (*b*) xiv. 7—xv. 9, the prophet's pleadings and excuses on behalf of the people, each followed by the Lord's reply; (*c*) xv. 10—21, Jeremiah complains of persecution. He receives comfort and assurance of protection.

dearth] **drought.** The original word is in the plural (*droughts*), which may imply a *series* of dry years.

2. City and country, high and low, man and beast alike suffer.

the gates] put, as often in Heb., for cities, i.e. for the inhabitants. The gate was the place in which justice was administered and also that of general resort. Hence it is often poetically substituted for the city of which it formed so important a part, or, as here, by a somewhat further stretch of the figure, for the inhabitants. For gate = city compare Deut. xvii. 2; and so too 1 Kings viii. 37, in which latter "cities" of Eng. Vers. should be literally *gates*.

they are black unto the ground] an abbreviated way of saying, they are black (= in mourning garb) and sit upon the ground. Compare for the sense chap. xiii. 18; also Ps. cxxxvii. 1 ("By the rivers of Babylon there *we sat down*") and Is. xlvii. 1 ("Come down, and *sit in the dust*").

3. *little ones*] **mean ones,** i.e. servants. The Heb. word is rare, occurring elsewhere only chap. xlviii. 4.

pits] cisterns, or tanks, where the water was kept till wanted for use. See note on chap. ii. 13.

covered their heads] as a sign of the greatest grief or confusion. Compare 2 Sam. xix. 4; Esth. vi. 12.

4. *Because the ground is chapt*] **Because of the ground, which is dismayed.** *Chapt* is indeed literal, and it is possible that nothing more may be meant than the cracks produced by drought. It is more likely however that the verb is used in the secondary sense which it bears, as above rendered. If this be so, *the ground* may well stand for *the tillers* of it, as "gates" (ver. 2) for the people who assembled there. It is only

110   JEREMIAH, XIV.   [vv. 5—8.

For there was no rain in the earth,
The plowmen were ashamed, they covered their heads.
5 Yea, the hind also calved in the field, and forsook *it*,
Because there was no grass.
6 And the wild asses did stand in the high places,
They snuffed up the wind like dragons;
Their eyes did fail, because *there was* no grass.

7—12. *The prophet's first intercession. God's answer.*

7 O LORD, though our iniquities testify against us, do thou
it for thy name's sake: for our backslidings are many; we
8 have sinned against thee. O the hope of Israel, the saviour

a less usual application of the principle on which the *Sublime Porte* stands for the Turkish Government, *England*, etc., for the inhabitants.

5. *Yea*] or, *For*. The dismay was increased by the sight of the hind, which was known to be tender in her care for her offspring, deserting it, and seeking merely the preservation of her own life. Compare Lam. i. 6. The care which the hind bestows upon its young is set forth by several ancient writers. Aristotle tells how they bring their young to a secure retreat which has but one approach; Pliny, that they teach them to run and to flee at the approach of danger; and Solinus, that they carefully hide their young ones, forcing them by blows with their feet to conceal themselves in the thickets (Bochart, P. I., Bk. III., ch. 17). Compare for this character borne by the hind Prov. v. 19.

6. *high places*] Compare chap. iii. 2.
snuffed up the wind] gasped for breath, as oppressed by heat and thirst.
dragons] **jackals.** See note on chap. ix. 11.
their eyes did fail] In place of the sharpness of sight, which they naturally enjoyed, their sufferings were depriving them wholly of the power of vision.
grass] more literally, plants, or herbage. It is the "herb" of Gen. i. 11, 12.

7—12. THE PROPHET'S FIRST INTERCESSION. GOD'S ANSWER.

7. *do thou it*] **deal.**
for thy name's sake] either (i) in accordance with the name, under which Thou hast revealed Thyself, The Lord God, merciful and gracious, etc. (Exod. xxxiv. 6); or (ii) for Thy honour, that the heathen may behold Thy might and faithfulness. This latter seems the more usual sense of the phrase, for which see Ps. lxxix. 9, cvi. 8; Is. xlviii. 9; Ezek. xx. 9, 14, 22; and for the thought Josh. vii. 7—9.
for our backslidings are many] The connexion is, The maintenance of Thine own honour is the only plea that we can urge, and no merits of ours, *for*, etc.

8. *hope of Israel*] a favourite expression with Jeremiah (See chaps.

thereof in time of trouble, why shouldest thou be as a stranger in the land, and as a wayfaring man *that* turneth aside to tarry for a night? Why shouldest thou be as a man astonied, as a mighty *man that* cannot save? yet thou, O LORD, *art* in the midst of us, and we are called by thy name; leave us not. Thus saith the LORD unto this people, Thus have they loved to wander, they have not refrained their feet, therefore the LORD doth not accept them; he will now remember their iniquity, and visit their sins. Then said the LORD unto me, Pray not for this people for their good. When they fast, I will not hear their cry; and when they offer burnt offering and an oblation, I will not accept them: but I will consume them by the sword, and by the famine, and by the pestilence.

13—17. *A second appeal and the reply.*

Then said I, Ah Lord GOD! behold, the prophets say

xvii. 7, 13, l. 7). Compare St Paul (Acts xxviii. 20) "the hope of Israel," a passage which serves as a link between the phrase as used in the Old Testament and the two occurrences of the word hope as applied directly to Christ (Col. i. 27; 1 Tim. i. 1).

as a stranger in the land, and as a wayfaring man] as one who has no interest in the country or in the people among whom he is sojourning.

turneth aside] literally, *stretcheth out (his tent)*; lives after the manner followed both then and now by travellers there.

9. *as a man astonied*] The illustration is the hesitation and inactivity of one whom some sudden occurrence has deprived of his usual presence of mind.

10. *Thus saith the Lord*] This and the next two verses contain God's reply to Jeremiah's prayer. The people have rejected Him, and He therefore now rejects them.

Thus have they loved] Some would explain 'thus,' with a firmness of purpose in idolatry equal to that which I shall shew in punishing them for their sin. But it seems better to take it as simply meaning *In the manner and to the degree already pointed out*, e.g. in chap. ii.

the Lord doth] not *I do*, which we might have expected as according better with the form of verses 11, 12. Here, on the contrary, Jeremiah gives in his own words God's answer. This part of the verse is a quotation from Hos. viii. 13.

12. Outward signs of repentance and submission shall be of no avail, either as being unreal, or too tardy.

by the sword, and by the famine, and by the pestilence] These three forms of punishment are united elsewhere. See Lev. xxvi. 25, 26.

13—17. A SECOND APPEAL AND THE REPLY.

13. *Ah*] **Alas.**

unto them, Ye shall not see the sword, neither shall ye have famine; but I will give you assured peace in this place. 14 Then the LORD said unto me, The prophets prophesy lies in my name: I sent them not, neither have I commanded them, neither spake unto them: they prophesy unto you a false vision and divination, and a thing of nought, and the 15 deceit of their heart. Therefore thus saith the LORD concerning the prophets that prophesy in my name, and I sent them not, yet they say, Sword and famine shall not be in this land; By sword and famine shall those prophets be 16 consumed. And the people to whom they prophesy shall be cast out in the streets of Jerusalem because of the famine and the sword; and they *shall* have none to bury them, them, their wives, nor their sons, nor their daughters: 17 for I will pour their wickedness upon them. Therefore thou shalt say this word unto them;

the prophets] The false prophets in Jeremiah's time had acquired paramount influence. He therefore pleads with God for the people as having been misled by them. The reply condemns the prophets, but does not in any way excuse those who have hearkened to them.
14. *divination*] *conjuring.*
a thing of nought] *a vanity* or *falsehood*. The Hebrew word is of uncertain origin, and may mean either the response of an idol-god, or as rendered above. Probably it is itself equivalent to idol, in accordance with the Jewish mode of regarding such. See note on chaps. i. 16 and ii. 5. There are thus enumerated three ways in which the false prophets practised 'the deceit of their heart' (i.e. which their heart had devised; compare chap. xxiii. 26), viz. a pretended vision, conjuring and the responses supposed to be given by idols.
15. *Therefore thus saith the Lord*] As in the last section, God is represented sometimes as speaking through the prophet, and sometimes in His own name.
16. *they shall have none to bury them*] It has been remarked that, contrary to what we might have expected, the punishment of the people is dwelt on and emphasized more than that of the prophets who misled them. The reason appears to be twofold: (i) the mention of the prophets' punishment is only incidental, as consequent upon the plea put forward by Jeremiah in ver. 13; (ii) God desires to shew that the deceit practised by the prophets affords no manner of excuse for the people. The latter could not have been deceived, except by their own consent.
their wickedness] This should be itself their punishment (compare chap. ii. 19), descending upon their head like a storm.
17. *Therefore thou shalt say this word*] The words that follow are Jeremiah's, whereas this formula should properly introduce an address from God. Compare chap. xiii. 12. The difficulty however is rather

17—22. *A lament and renewed appeal on behalf of the stricken city and people.*

Let mine eyes run down *with* tears night and day, and let them not cease:
For the virgin daughter of my people is broken *with* a great breach, *with* a very grievous blow.
If I go forth *into* the field, then behold the slain with the sword: 18
And if I enter *into* the city, then behold them that are sick with famine:
Yea, both the prophet and the priest go about into a land that they know not.
Hast thou utterly rejected Judah? hath thy soul lothed 19 Zion?
Why hast thou smitten us, and *there is* no healing for us?
We looked for peace, and *there is* no good;
And for the time of healing, and behold trouble.

apparent than real. The prophet's lamentation in the section that follows is equivalent to an announcement of terrible woes on the part of the Lord. The form in which the announcement is put serves the purpose of expressing it in a more striking and lively manner.

17—22. A LAMENT AND RENEWED APPEAL ON BEHALF OF THE STRICKEN CITY AND PEOPLE.

17. *run down with tears*] a frequent expression with the prophet (chap. ix. 18, xiii. 17. Compare Lam. ii. 18, iii. 48, 49).

the virgin daughter of my people] she who has been hitherto preserved from harm with care like that bestowed on an Eastern maiden.

18. *go about into a land that they know not*] There is some difficulty as to the precise sense, which is probably, journey into a land they know not (i.e. a land of exile). Other renderings suggested are, (i) go as beggars into a land which they know not, (ii) wander about in the land (Palestine) and know not what to do.

19. "The Lord had indeed distinctly refused the favour sought for Judah; yet the command to disclose to the people the sorrow of his own soul at their calamity (verses 17 and 18) gave the prophet courage to renew his application." Keil.

hath] or **hath**. It is a double question, just as in ver. 22.

we looked...] This passage has occurred already (chap. viii. 15).

20—22. In these verses three several pleas are urged on behalf of the people: (i) their contrition, (ii) God's honour, (iii) their hopelessness of any other aid.

20 We acknowledge, O Lord, our wickedness, *and* the iniquity of our fathers:
For we have sinned against thee.
21 Do not abhor *us*, for thy name's sake,
Do not disgrace the throne of thy glory:
Remember, break not thy covenant with us.
22 Are there *any* among the vanities of the Gentiles that can cause rain?
Or can the heavens give showers?
Art not thou he, O Lord our God? therefore we will wait upon thee:
For thou hast made all these *things*.

CHAP. XV. 1—9. *A more particular description of the impending woes.*

15 Then said the Lord unto me, Though Moses and Samuel stood before me, *yet* my mind *could* not *be* toward this people: cast *them* out of my sight, and let them go forth.

20. *and the iniquity*] There is no conjunction in the original, and thus is forcibly expressed the continuity through successive generations of the evil whose punishment they now deprecate.

21. *Do not abhor us*] Us is not in the Hebrew, and is best omitted.
do not disgrace] literally, *do not treat as foolish, contemptible.* The word is the same as that rendered "lightly esteemed" in Deut. xxxii. 15.
the throne of thy glory] Jerusalem, or more particularly the temple, where the visible glory rested above the ark.

22. *vanities*] idols.
art not thou he, O Lord] rather, **art not thou the Lord?** or, **is it not thou, O Lord?**
all these things] i.e. the heaven and the rain which it sends. The only hope of obtaining aid from them is to address their Maker.

CHAP. XV. 1—9. A MORE PARTICULAR DESCRIPTION OF THE IMPENDING WOES.

1. *Though Moses and Samuel stood before me*] For this expression as equivalent to intercession compare chap. xviii. 20. The sense of the whole clause is, Even though those who have had such weight in past times were now to seek to avert my wrath, they would fail. For Moses see Exod. xvii. 11, xxxii. 11—14; Numb. xiv. 13—20, and for Samuel 1 Sam. vii. 9, xii. 23; and for these two united in a similar connexion of thought see Ps. xcix. 6.
my mind could not be toward] I could not incline with favour towards.
let them go forth] The people are pictured as assembled before God

And it shall come to pass, if they say unto thee, Whither 2
shall we go forth? then thou shalt tell them, Thus saith
the LORD; Such as *are* for death, to death; and such as
are for the sword, to the sword; and such as *are* for the
famine, to the famine; and such as *are* for the captivity,
to the captivity. And I will appoint over them four 3
kinds, saith the LORD: the sword to slay, and the dogs to
tear, and the fowls of the heaven, and the beasts of the
earth, to devour and destroy. And I will cause them to be 4
removed into all kingdoms of the earth, because of Manasseh the son of Hezekiah king of Judah, for *that* which he
did in Jerusalem. For who shall have pity upon thee, O 5
Jerusalem? or who shall bemoan thee? or who shall go
aside to ask how thou doest? Thou hast forsaken me, 6
saith the LORD, thou art gone backward: therefore will I
stretch out my hand against thee, and destroy thee; I am
weary with repenting. And I will fan them with a fan in 7

with the prophet as their intercessor, when the announcement is made that intercession is in vain.

2. *Whither shall we go forth?*] If we are driven unpardoned from the presence of the Lord, to what shall we betake ourselves? The reply is a stern and even ironical one.

death] probably meaning death by pestilence. Compare chap. xiv. 12. Some take the four sorts of punishment here spoken of, as an ascending series, overthrow by the sword of the enemy being more of a disgrace than death by disease, and death by famine more painful as well as more prolonged than either, while captivity includes at any rate the possibility of all these three. It is however unlikely that any such climax is intended by the prophet.

3. *four kinds*] four sorts of destructive agencies. The first shall take effect on the living, the remainder upon the dead. Similar threats occur chaps. xix. 7, xxxiv. 20.

the dogs to tear] Compare the case of Jezebel (2 Kings ix. 35, 36).

4. *to be removed into*] rather, *to be tossed to and fro in*, or, *to be a terror unto*.

that which he did] Manasseh's wickedness is recounted in 2 Kings xxi. 3—7.

5. Such shall be the plight of the city, that none shall have either the care or the courage to approach her.

6. *gone backward*] The same figure, to express rejection of God's service, was used chap. vii. 24.

I am weary with repenting] In language adapted to the understanding of men God is spoken of as repenting, either as here, when punishment long delayed is at last to be inflicted (compare Gen. vi. 6); or when threatened evil has been averted by timely reformation, e.g. Jon. iii. 10.

8—2

the gates of the land; I will bereave *them* of children, I will destroy my people, *sith* they return not from their ways.
8 Their widows are increased to me above the sand of the seas: I have brought upon them against the mother of the young men a spoiler at noonday: I have caused *him* to fall

    7. *I will fan them with a fan*] This expression, as denoting not mere defeat but dispersion, renders it improbable that this and the two following verses refer, as some have thought (see above), to the overthrow and death of Josiah at Megiddo, deep as was the impression made upon the nation by that mournful occurrence (see Zech. xii. 11). We should rather read **I have fanned.**

    the gates of the land] The same phrase is used Nah. iii. 13. It means either the *borders* (the parts by which men enter and leave the country), or by the figure of speech called synecdoche (the part standing for the whole) *cities*, inasmuch as their gates, like our market places, were the chief resorts.

    I will bereave them] **I have bereaved them.**
    I will destroy] **I have destroyed.**
    sith they return not from their ways] better, *from their ways they return not*. The addition of the conjunction, which does not occur in the Hebrew, only weakens the force of the clause.

    sith] In ordinary editions of the Bible this word occurs only Ezek. xxxv. 6. Until the editions of 1762 (Dr Paris) and 1769 (Dr Blayney) however it occurred here and in the margin of Zech. iv. 10, while the later of those two editions was the first to exclude it from Jer. xxiii. 38. This points to the fact that *since* (a contraction of the Old English *sithence*) was then taking its place in ordinary speech. Both sith and sithence are found in Shakespeare.

> "Thou hast one son; for his sake pity me,
>   Lest in revenge thereof, *sith* God is just,
> He be as miserably slain as I."
> Hen. VI., Pt. 3, I. 3.

"*Sithence*, in the loss that may happen, it concerns you something to know it."
All's well that ends well, I. 3.

    8. *to me*] to my sorrow.
    the mother of the young men] Some have taken *the mother* to mean the mother city, Jerusalem, and *young man* (for the word in the original is singular) Nebuchadnezzar, rendering in that case, I have brought against Jerusalem a young and vigorous warrior. It is however more natural to consider that both substantives are used as nouns of multitude, just as 'she that hath borne' in the following verse. Thus the meaning will be that even the mothers of youths, warriors in the prime of their strength, shall not on that account escape.

    at noonday] probably not implying daring and a consciousness of overwhelming strength, that needed not secresy, but rather as in chap. vi. 4 (where see note) an unexpected attack.

upon it suddenly, and terrors *upon* the city. She that hath 9
borne seven languisheth: she hath given up the ghost; her
sun is gone down while *it was* yet day: she hath been
ashamed and confounded: and the residue of them will I
deliver to the sword before their enemies, saith the LORD.

10—14. *The Prophet's personal lament. God's reply.*

Woe is me, my mother, that thou hast borne me a man 10
of strife and a man of contention to the whole earth! I
have neither lent on usury, nor *men* have lent to me on

I have caused......] I have brought suddenly upon her (the mother) anguish and terrors.

9. *She that hath borne seven*] and therefore, especially with the Jewish eagerness for offspring, might have thought herself secure and prosperous. Seven was the perfect number. Compare 1 Sam. ii. 5.

while it was yet day] before she had reached the evening of her life. Compare for a similar phrase in the same sense Amos viii. 9. If the passage refer to Megiddo (see note on ver. 7 above), there *may* be a reference to an eclipse of the sun (the date of which however is far from certain) mentioned by Herodotus (Book I. 74) as suddenly changing day to night and thereby putting a stop to a battle between the Medians and Lydians.

10—14. THE PROPHET'S PERSONAL LAMENT. GOD'S REPLY.

10. *Woe is me, my mother*] We may compare with this verse Job iii. 1, etc., which latter however is expressed in language of much greater bitterness.

Savonarola, the great Italian reformer (*died* 1498), while yet the ruling mind in Florence and in possession of full popularity, foresaw the troubles in which he, like the Old Testament prophet, would be involved by his fearless condemnation of vice, and in the midst of one of his striking sermons thus addressed the Almighty, "O Lord, whither hast thou led me? From my desire to save souls for Thee, I can no longer return to my rest. Why hast Thou made me 'a man of strife, and a man of contention to the whole earth?'" W. R. Clark's *Savonarola*, p. 230. See also note on xx. 7.

I have neither lent...] "Unto a stranger thou mayest lend upon usury; but unto thy brother thou shalt not lend upon usury." Deut. xxiii. 20. Compare Ps. xv. 5. Among the Jews the law of jubilee was a check upon mortgages, while commerce with other nations was also discouraged by Moses. In such a state, *necessity* being almost the sole motive for borrowing, the money lender would naturally be held in extreme disfavour. The same has been the view of other nations and ages. "Interest is money begotten of money; so that of the sources of gain this is the most unnatural" (Aristotle, *Politics*, Bk. I. chap. 3, end).

11 usury; *yet* every one of them doth curse me. The LORD said, Verily it shall be well with thy remnant; verily I will cause the enemy to entreat thee *well* in the time of evil, and in
12 the time of affliction. Shall iron break the northern iron
13 and the steel? Thy substance and thy treasures will I give to the spoil without price, and *that* for all thy sins, even in
14 all thy borders. And I will make *thee* to pass with thine enemies into a land *which* thou knowest not: for a fire is kindled in mine anger, *which* shall burn upon you.

"Sources of gain, which incur the hatred of mankind, as those of tax-gatherers, of *usurers*." Cicero, *de Officiis*, Bk. I. § 150. Compare

"When did friendship take
A breed for barren metal of his friend?"
Mer. of Venice, Act I. Sc. 3, ll. 134—5.

11. *it shall be well with thy remnant*] rather, *thy loosing shall be for good*, i.e. *in the troublous times that are coming thou shalt be delivered*. This seems better than either of two other renderings proposed, viz. (i) I have loosed thee for good, (ii) I have strengthened thee for good. Both these adopt a slightly different reading in the Heb.

to entreat thee well] **to supplicate thee.** Not only shall the prophet be freed from abuse and cursing, but those who have treated him thus shall come to invoke his aid. This actually occurred on several occasions. See chap. xxi. 1, 2, xxxvii. 3, xlii. 2.

12. *the northern iron and the steel*] This has been understood of Jeremiah, of the Jews, of Nebuchadnezzar, and of the Chaldaean empire. The last is by far the most probable import of the words. Compare chap. vi. 1, xiii. 20, where the Chaldees are spoken of as a power from the North. The connexion of thought in verses 11—13 therefore is, An evil time is approaching, a time in which the Jews will inevitably be vanquished by a superior foe, and the land spoiled by her enemies.

steel] **brass**, i.e. bronze, an alloy of copper and tin. Brass in the ordinary sense (an alloy of copper and zinc) was not known to the ancients.

13. This and the following ver. appear in a modified form in chap. xvii. 3, 4. The LORD addresses the prophet as representing the people, and thus the punishments spoken of are to be understood as having reference to the nation at large.

without price] either, *seized by violence*, as opposed to the obtaining by purchase, or, better, *unvalued*, treated by God as nothing worth.

14. *I will make thee to pass with thine enemies*] If we retain the reading which stands in the Heb. text, the sense will be as Eng. Vers., or the 'substance' and 'treasures' may be understood as the *object* of the verb ('*I will make them to pass*'). The slightest change in a Heb. letter would however give us the somewhat easier sense, *I will make thee to serve thine enemies*, as in xv. 4.

for a fire is kindled in mine anger] a quotation from Deut. xxxii. 22.

15—18. *A last appeal to God on the part of the prophet.*

O LORD, thou knowest: remember me, and visit me, and ¹⁵ revenge me of my persecutors; take me not away in thy longsuffering: know that for thy sake I have suffered rebuke. Thy words were found, and I did eat them; and thy word ¹⁶ was unto me the joy and rejoicing of mine heart: for I am called by thy name, O LORD God of hosts. I sat not in ¹⁷ the assembly of the mockers, nor rejoiced; I sat alone because of thy hand: for thou hast filled me *with* indigna-

The words there announce the punishment which shall come upon Israel for the idolatry into which it shall fall.

15—18. A LAST APPEAL TO GOD ON THE PART OF THE PROPHET.

15. This verse is connected in sense with ver. 10. The Lord's reply to Jeremiah's lament in that verse fails to satisfy him, inasmuch as coupled with it have been mentioned again the coming afflictions of his countrymen, while at the same time his own present condition remains unaltered.

thou knowest] viz. the persecutions to which I am exposed, and my own innocence, and earnestness in Thy work. These thoughts he expands in the next two verses.

take me not away in thy longsuffering] Deprive me not of all joy or of life itself through mercy towards my enemies.

16. He describes the joy with which he first received the divine commission.

were found] This verb occurs in the same connexion in Ezek. iii. 1, as implying in the most general sense the *obtaining* without particularising the manner.

I did eat them] This remarkable expression seems intended to convey two notions: (i) joyful acceptance, (ii) close union. So in Ezek. ii. 8, iii. 1—3.

am called] rather, *was called*. The prophet is still speaking of the original summons to preach. Literally the clause would run, *for thy name was called upon me.*

17. *mockers*] **laughers.** Jeremiah is not taking credit to himself for having never joined with the enemies of God, although the Eng. Vers. might seem to imply this. The word simply means those engaged in festivity. It is the word used e.g. of the women who went out to meet Saul and David after the slaughter of Goliath (1 Sam. xviii. 7), and of the procession accompanying the ark (2 Sam. vi. 5).

because of thy hand] For this expression, as betokening a solemn charge in the name of God, compare Is. viii. 11; Ezek. i. 3, and still more distinctly Ezek. xxxvii. 1. Compare the case of David, 1 Chron. xxviii. 19; also the statement of the Apostle, that "men of God spake as they were moved (literally, borne along) by the Holy Ghost" (2 Pet. i. 21).

18 tion. Why is my pain perpetual, and my wound incurable, *which* refuseth to be healed? wilt thou be altogether unto me as a liar, *and as* waters *that* fail?

19—21. *God's reply. Faithful discharge of duty shall bring with it deliverance.*

19 Therefore thus saith the Lord, If thou return, then will I bring thee again, *and* thou shalt stand before me: and if thou take forth the precious from the vile, thou shalt be as my mouth: let them return unto thee; but return not thou 20 unto them. And I will make thee unto this people a fenced brasen wall: and they shall fight against thee, but they shall not prevail against thee: for I *am* with thee to

indignation] The sins of the people had thenceforward been only too manifest to him.

18. Why dost Thou grant me no relief from persecution?

a liar] literally, *a lie*. The words which follow shew that the prophet is thinking of a watercourse, which as being dry belies the anticipations of the thirsty traveller. So Jeremiah's hopes of joy and success in his work have not been hitherto realized. The same figure, so natural in a hot country, occurs Job vi. 15.

19—21. God's reply. Faithful discharge of duty shall bring with it deliverance.

19. *If thou return*] If thou wilt dismiss thy doubts and thy tone of reproach and distrust.

shalt stand before me] shalt be my minister. The phrase is a common one in this sense. (See note on xxxv. 19). It is used of Elijah (e.g. 1 Kings xviii. 15), of Elisha (2 Kings iii. 14): so also in Prov. xxii. 29.

if thou take forth the precious from the vile] The figure is that of the refining of metals, in which by the process of melting there is a separation made of the earthy and other matters that constitute the dross. As to the application of the metaphor various views have been taken:

(i) that the prophet is not to mix with the words which God puts in his mouth any of his own opinions or comments.

(ii) that he is to convert to righteousness certain of the general mass of his ungodly countrymen.

(iii) that he is to cleanse his own heart from the unworthy suspicions as to God's faithfulness, which though mixed with better thoughts he had just shewn to be there entertained. This last view seems the one most in accord with the context.

my mouth] my mouth-piece, spokesman. The same expression is used of Aaron Exod. iv. 16, and compare vii. 1.

let them return...] Do not surrender anything of the truth in order by smooth speeches to win over the people. Stand thou firm, and let *them* repent and amend.

save thee and to deliver thee, saith the LORD. And I will 21 deliver thee out of the hand of the wicked, and I will redeem thee out of the hand of the terrible.

CHAP. XVI. 1—13. *The prophet is to enforce his warnings by self-denial and an ascetic life.*

The word of the LORD came also unto me, saying, Thou 16 shalt not take thee a wife, neither shalt thou have sons nor 2 daughters in this place. For thus saith the LORD concerning 3 the sons and concerning the daughters that are born in this place, and concerning their mothers that bare them, and concerning their fathers that begat them in this land; they 4 shall die of grievous deaths; they shall not be lamented; neither shall they be buried; *but* they shall be as dung upon the face of the earth: and they shall be consumed by the sword, and by famine; and their carcases shall be meat for the fowls of heaven, and for the beasts of the earth. For 5 thus said the LORD, Enter not *into* the house of mourning,

20, 21. These verses are substantially a repetition of chap. i. 18, 19.

21. *the hand of the terrible*] *the palm of the terrible.* See note on chap. xii. 7.

the terrible] those who combine power with tyrannical violence.

CHAP. XVI. 1—13. THE PROPHET IS TO ENFORCE HIS WARNINGS BY SELF-DENIAL AND AN ASCETIC LIFE.

2. *Thou shalt not take thee a wife*] Marriage was a state of life in special favour with the Jews, as connected with the hope which each parent cherished that the Messiah might be born of his or her line. By his act of self-denial therefore Jeremiah was to shew his "return" (chap. xv. 19) and full submission to the will of God, while it would at the same time be a forcible mode of conveying the message of coming woes which he was charged to deliver to the people.

this place] *this land*, as shewn by ver. 3.

4. *grievous deaths*] deaths by wasting diseases or famine. The same Hebrew word is used of this last visitation in chap. xiv. 18.

they shall not be lamented; neither shall they be buried] We may compare the condition of things in the plague at Athens B.C. 430: "Such was the state of dismay and sorrow, that even the nearest relatives neglected the sepulchral duties...the dead and dying lay piled upon one another not merely in the public roads, but even in the temples...Those bodies which escaped entire neglect were burnt or buried without the customary mourning and with unseemly carelessness." Grote's *Hist. of Greece*, Chap. XLIX.

5. *Enter not...*] The prophet's abstinence from the accustomed marks of respect to the dead and sympathy with the relatives is to be a

neither go to lament nor bemoan them: for I have taken away my peace from this people, saith the LORD, *even lov-* 6 *ingkindness and mercies.* Both the great and the small shall die in this land: they shall not be buried, neither shall *men* lament for them, nor cut themselves, nor make 7 themselves bald for them: neither shall *men* tear *themselves* for them in mourning, to comfort them for the dead; neither shall *men* give them the cup of consolation to drink for 8 their father or for their mother. Thou shalt not also go *into* the house of feasting, to sit with them to eat and to 9 drink. For thus saith the LORD of hosts, the God of Israel; Behold, I will cause to cease out of this place in your eyes,

forecast of the time when such abstinence shall become general on account of the universal prevalence of suffering and death.

mourning] The word thus rendered here occurs but once elsewhere (Amos vi. 7), and is there translated *banquet*. In this place it probably means *mourning feast*. A loud noise, as produced either by pleasurable or painful emotions, is its primary sense.

bemoan] not an infinitive mood coupled with 'to lament,' as might at first sight appear, but imperative, as the preceding 'go.'

my peace] that which ensured them prosperity.

6. *nor cut themselves, nor make themselves bald*] It was strictly forbidden in the Mosaic Law (Lev. xix. 28, xxi. 5; Deut. xiv. 1) to practise either of these *for the dead*. We gather however from this, and yet more clearly from other passages (chap. vii. 29, xli. 5; Ezek. vii. 18; Amos viii. 10; Mic. i. 16; and specially Is. xxii. 12), that the rule had either been relaxed, or was directed only to those cases in which such practices might be resorted to as propitiatory offerings for the deceased, and not as mere signs of mourning. The former of these practices, as representing, though in a modified form, the heathen custom of human sacrifices as a propitiation to the spirit of the departed, would naturally be forbidden. Herodotus (Bk. IV. 71) describes the funeral rites of a Scythian King as requiring no less than six human victims. (See further in Art. 'Cuttings in the flesh,' *Sm. Bibl. Dict.*)

7. *tear themselves*] **break** (**bread**). The Hebrew word is the same (with a slight difference in the spelling) as that used Lam. iv. 4. The reference is to the custom that the friends of those who were in mourning should urge them to eat. See in illustration of this usage 2 Sam. iii. 35, xii. 16, 17. Bread also was distributed to mourners and to the poor at funerals, "Pour out thy bread on the burial of the just," Tobit iv. 14. Compare Is. lviii. 7 (where the Heb. is the same) "to *deal* thy bread" etc.

the cup of consolation] wine similarly administered as a refreshment by the friends. 'Give...strong drink unto those that be of heavy hearts' (Prov. xxxi. 6) expresses the principle on which this was done.

8. Jeremiah should stand aloof from social joys no less than sorrows, because of the evil that was so near.

and in your days, the voice of mirth, and the voice of gladness, the voice of the bridegroom, and the voice of the bride. And it shall come to pass, when thou shalt shew 10 this people all these words, and they shall say unto thee, Wherefore hath the LORD pronounced all this great evil against us? or what *is* our iniquity? or what *is* our sin that we have committed against the LORD our God? Then shalt 11 thou say unto them, Because your fathers have forsaken me, saith the LORD, and have walked after other gods, and have served them, and have worshipped them, and have forsaken me, and have not kept my law; and ye have done worse 12 than your fathers; for behold, ye walk every one after the imagination of his evil heart, that *they* may not hearken unto me: therefore will I cast you out of this land into a 13 land that ye know not, *neither* ye nor your fathers; and there shall ye serve other gods day and night; where I will not shew you favour.

14—21. *The punishment shall be the most severe and therefore the deliverance the most signal and blessed yet known.*

Therefore behold, the days come, saith the LORD, that it 14

9. *in your eyes, and in your days*] an emphatic caution against their assuming that the present state of things would last their own time, and overthrow be reserved for their posterity.

the voice of mirth...] See note on chap. vii. 34.

10. Compare chap. v. 19, of which this passage is in substance a repetition. Here however there are virtually three charges brought against the people: (i) hypocrisy, (ii) idolatry, (iii) a baseness exceeding that of former generations. This last charge has been already (chap. vii. 26) brought.

12. *imagination*] **stubbornness**. Compare chap. iii. 17.

that they may not] If we substitute *so as not to*, a rendering which is quite as faithful to the original, we avoid the somewhat awkward change from the second to the third person.

13. *a land*] **the** *land*. The definite article, which stands in the Hebrew, has its proper force. The country to which they were presently going as captives was one which they were not ignorant of, geographically speaking, although they had no practical experience of it. This last is often the sense of *know* in the Bible.

shall ye serve] rather, **ye may** *serve*, an ironical permission. There should be nothing to interfere with that idolatry to which they were already so devoted.

where] **because**.

shall no more be said, The LORD liveth, that brought up the
15 children of Israel out of the land of Egypt; but, The LORD
liveth, that brought up the children of Israel from the land
of the north, and from all the lands whither he had driven
them: and I will bring them again into their land that I gave
16 unto their fathers. Behold, I will send for many fishers,
saith the LORD, and they shall fish them; and after will I
send for many hunters, and they shall hunt them from every
mountain, and from every hill, and out of the holes of the
17 rocks. For mine eyes *are* upon all their ways: they are not
hid from my face, neither is their iniquity hid from mine
18 eyes. And first I will recompense their iniquity and their sin
double; because they have defiled my land, they have filled

14—21. THE PUNISHMENT SHALL BE THE MOST SEVERE AND THEREFORE THE DELIVERANCE THE MOST SIGNAL AND BLESSED YET KNOWN.

14. *the days come*] The deliverance from Egypt shall pale before the new and still more marvellous rescue of the people from their Babylonian masters. Verses 14 and 15, as asserting the blessing in store for the people in the future, form a striking contrast to the gloomy character of the remainder of the passage. Some have accordingly supposed that these verses are interpolated from chap. xxiii. 7, 8. There is however no reason to believe that they are not genuine. The greatness of the deliverance is the strongest proof of the greatness of the calamity which shall have preceded, and this last it is the main object with Jeremiah throughout to prove. Besides, it is but customary with the prophet to throw in a bright thought like this among gloomy ones. See chaps. iii. 14, iv. 27, v. 10, 18, xxvii. 22, xxx. 3, xxxii. 37.

16. The people shall be hunted down and captured, wherever they may be found. To express this vividly the prophet makes use of the figures of hunting and fishing. As a net was extended under and around the place where a shoal of fish was collected, so some of the enemy should surround and seize those who are collected together in the towns. Others again, who had fled into the country for refuge, should be overtaken by the light-armed who went in pursuit like hunters in quest of game. The lack of compassion on the part of the foe, and the certainty of capture, are brought out with equal force by the figures employed. The people were sufficiently acquainted with the history of their country to feel the significance of the description. See note on chap. iv. 29, with references there given.

18. *first*] before I restore them to their land.

double] because their sin is twofold. See note on chap. ii. 13.

because they have defiled] The latter part of this verse is best arranged somewhat differently, viz.: *Because they defiled my land with the carcases*

mine inheritance with the carcases of their detestable and abominable things. O Lord, my strength, and my fortress, 19 and my refuge in the day of affliction, the Gentiles shall come unto thee from the ends of the earth, and shall say, Surely our fathers have inherited lies, vanity, and *things wherein there is* no profit. Shall a man make gods unto 20 himself, and they *are* no gods? Therefore behold, I *will* 21 this once cause them to know, I will cause them to know mine hand and my might; and they shall know that my name *is* The Lord.

Chap. XVII. 1—4. *The sin is indelible. Hence the necessary severity of the coming chastisement.*

The sin of Judah *is* written with a pen of iron, *and* with 17 the point of a diamond: *it is* graven upon the table of their

of their detestable things, and with their abominations they filled mine inheritance.

the carcases of their detestable and abominable things] either, unclean animals (or animals of any kind) offered to idols, or the idols themselves, called carcases, as being in their nature polluting to the touch like a dead body (Numb. xix. 11).

19—21. The connexion of thought seems to be: Woeful as is the idolatry of the Jews, their punishment, repentance and consequent restoration to favour, being witnessed by heathen nations, shall lead even the most distant of these last to acknowledge the Lord. But is it not all but incredible that a man should consider the work of his own hands to be a god? Yet because of this sin (and also perhaps in order to impress the nations of the earth) God's power shall be shewn forth for evil and afterwards for good.

19. *my strength, and my fortress*] *my strength and my stronghold.* The two Hebrew substantives, being derivatives of the same root, give an effect which we can hardly reproduce in the English.

21. *this once*] **at this time.** The punishment now impending is to stand out distinct, not to be compared for its severity with any other. See note on chap. x. 18.

Chap. XVII. 1—4. The sin is indelible. Hence the necessary severity of the coming chastisement.

1. *a pen of iron*] used for making permanent marks on a hard surface, e.g. on rocks (Job xix. 24).

point] literally, the *finger nail*, in which sense the word is used in Deut. xxi. 12. Here however it means the tip of the stylus or pencil used by gravers.

a diamond] The Hebrew word, which likewise means *a thorn*, occurs in the sense of diamond also in Ezek. iii. 9; Zech. vii. 12 ("adamant").

2 heart, and upon the horns of your altars; whilst their children remember their altars and their groves by the green trees 3 upon the high hills. O my mountain in the field, I will give thy substance *and* all thy treasures to the spoil, *and* 4 thy high places for sin, throughout all thy borders. And thou, even thyself, shalt discontinue from thine heritage

"Pliny tells us (*Hist. Nat.* XXXVII. 15) that the ancients were well acquainted with its cutting powers, and used to set it in iron, as is now done for the use of glaziers." *Sp. Comm.* Gesenius is disposed to connect the Hebrew with a Greek word, meaning emery powder (for polishing). This however is very doubtful, in spite of a similarity in sound which exists between the two.

the table of their heart] their inward nature. Compare Prov. iii. 3, vii. 3.
horns] probably metal projections from the corners (Exod. xxvii. 2).
altars] either, (*a*) the two altars (of burnt-offering and of incense respectively) employed in the Temple worship, or, (*b*) which is more probable from the context, altars set up to the Baals throughout Jerusalem and Judah.

2. *Whilst their children remember*...] In the Heb. it is not quite clear whether the word 'children' is the subject or object of the verb 'remember.' With the former, which seems the somewhat preferable rendering, the meaning will be (i) their children's minds will be profoundly impressed by the horrors that they are called on to witness, or, more generally, (ii) the children will be so well taught in idolatry by their parents that the tendency towards it will on the very smallest provocation rise up in the mind. With the latter rendering the sense will be, As they remember their children, so they remember their altars, etc., i.e. (i) their love for their idolatry will be as great as that which they feel as parents for their children, or (ii) the thought of the one is inseparably connected with that of the other on account of their sacrifice of human victims to their idols.

groves] Ashêrim: not *groves* (for see 1 Kings xiv. 23; 2 Kings xvii. 10), but wooden pillars or monuments set up in honour of Ashtoreth (Astarte).

by the green trees] literally, *upon each green tree.* The preposition is difficult to explain. It may be an early error of a copyist in the Heb. At any rate the sense seems to be that given in the Eng. Vers.

3. *O my mountain in the field*] This is generally acknowledged to mean Jerusalem or Zion. Some would make it the accusative, governed by 'give,' 'thy' referring then to the people, while 'substance' and 'treasures' will be in apposition with 'mountain.' Jerusalem is called *the mountain in the field*, not because the height on which it is built is not surrounded by still loftier mountains, but because of its position as the head and centre of the nation. 'My mountain' will in any case suggest the whole country. This is shewn by the concluding words of the verse.

for sin] *because of* (thy) *sin*. So in chap. xv. 13, which almost coincides in expression with this verse.

4. *even thyself*] The original probably means, *through thine own fault.*

that I gave thee; and I will cause thee to serve thine enemies in the land which thou knowest not: for ye have kindled a fire in mine anger, *which* shall burn for ever.

5—8. *Faith in man leads to destruction, faith in God to security.*

Thus saith the LORD; Cursed *be* the man that trusteth in 5 man, and maketh flesh his arm, and whose heart departeth from the LORD. For he shall be like the heath in the 6 desert, and shall not see when good cometh; but shall inhabit the parched places in the wilderness, *in* a salt land and not inhabited. Blessed *is* the man that trusteth in the 7 LORD, and whose hope the LORD is. For he shall be as a 8

discontinue] There seems a reference to such passages as Exod. xxiii. 11, where the same verb is used of the rest given to the land every seventh year, and Deut. xv. 2, where the reference is to the setting free of creditors in the seventh year. Judah, having disregarded the sabbatical rest in times past, will be forced to recognise it now by being carried away from her land into captivity. See 2 Chron. xxxvi. 21.

For notes on the rest of the verse see chap. xv. 14, which closely resembles it.

5—8. FAITH IN MAN LEADS TO DESTRUCTION, FAITH IN GOD TO SECURITY.

5—8. The antithesis in these verses is sharply defined, the two courses of human conduct making the men who practise them respectively to fade and to flourish.

5. *Cursed be the man...*] This is supposed to have direct reference to Jehoiakim, who revolted from Nebuchadnezzar and looked for aid from Egypt (2 Kings xxiv. 1).

his arm] that on which he depends in order to attain his wants.

6. *the heath*] rather **the destitute man.** A similar word is rendered *heath* in chap. xlviii. 6, where the same correction should accordingly be made. The only other occurrence of this word is Ps. cii. 17, where the sense is not doubtful. Here it is probable that the rendering of the word by the name of a plant (a rendering which has found favour from very early times) arose from the supposed necessity of making it harmonize closely with verse 8, especially as the Arabic word for *juniper* is of similar sound. Two species only of heath grow in Palestine, the one (Erica vagans) on the coast plains (but not in large quantities), the other (Erica orientalis) on Lebanon. Therefore in any case the Eng. Vers. is inaccurate.

shall not see when good cometh] shall have no experience of good fortune.

8. *he shall be as a tree*] The image of Ps. i. 3 is here more elaborately developed.

tree planted by the waters, and *that* spreadeth out her roots by the river, and shall not see when heat cometh, but her leaf shall be green; and shall not be careful in the year of drought, neither shall cease from yielding fruit.

9—11. *All wicked devices God will detect and punish.*

9 The heart *is* deceitful above all *things*, and desperately 10 wicked: who can know it? I the LORD search the heart, *I* try the reins, even to give every man according to his ways, 11 *and* according to the fruit of his doings. *As* the partridge sitteth *on eggs*, and hatcheth *them* not; *so* he that getteth riches, and not by right, shall leave them in the midst of his days, and at his end shall be a fool.

shall not see] *shall not* **fear.** Both readings, differing only by a letter, occur in the Hebrew. That adopted by our Version is probably the later one, and arises from a desire to make it answer still more closely to ver. 6.

9—11. ALL WICKED DEVICES GOD WILL DETECT AND PUNISH.

9. When prosperity and adversity are thus meted out respectively to the two great classes of mankind, the God-fearing and the wicked, how is it that all do not for the sake of their own interests pass from the latter to the former? It is because of the innate depravity of the human heart.

desperately wicked] **desperately sick.** The same word is translated *incurable* in chap. xv. 18, xxx. 12.

10. *I the Lord search the heart, I try the reins*] Compare xi. 20 and xx. 12.

ways] **way.**

11. *As the partridge*...] *As the partridge pileth up eggs which she laid not.* This is probably the closer rendering. The Heb. rendered in the Eng. Vers. *sitteth on* occurs only once elsewhere (Is. xxxiv. 15) "of the snake (A. V. great owl) gathering her young to keep them warm, but the root is found frequently in the Chaldee in the sense of laying in a heap, with especial reference to birds." *Sp. Comm.* We need not take the statement to indicate more than a popular belief of that day, of which the prophet availed himself by way of an illustration. A less probable explanation of the sense of the passage is that which makes the illustration to consist in this, viz. that the partridge calls the young of other birds under her wings, but that they forsake her when they hear the cry of the true parent. In any case the application is plain. Riches unlawfully gotten are as precarious and shortlived a possession as the young that have not been hatched by the bird that would pass for their parent.

shall leave them in the midst of his days] Here again some have seen an allusion to the fate of Jehoiakim, who died at the age of thirty-six years. But the doubt on the part of the prophet expressed in ver. 15 as

12—18. *Throughout all the Prophet looks to God as the Saviour of those who prove faithful.*

A glorious high throne from the beginning *is* the place of our sanctuary. O LORD, the hope of Israel, all that forsake thee shall be ashamed, and they that depart from me shall be written in the earth, because they have forsaken the LORD, the fountain of living waters. Heal me, O LORD, and I shall be healed; save me, and I shall be saved: for thou *art* my praise. Behold, they say unto me, Where *is* the word of the LORD? let it come now. As for me, I have not hastened from *being* a pastor to follow thee: neither

to the fulfilment of Jeremiah's words, makes it unlikely that so remarkable a proof of his truth-speaking had been already afforded.

12—18. THROUGHOUT ALL THE PROPHET LOOKS TO GOD AS THE SAVIOUR OF THOSE WHO PROVE FAITHFUL.

12, 13. These verses are probably to be taken as one sentence, the whole of ver. 12 being in form an invocation of the temple as the scene of God's visible glory, but in reality an address to Himself. *A throne of glory, exalted from the beginning, the place of our sanctuary, hope of Israel, the Lord, all that forsake thee, etc.* Such an address to the temple is by no means in conflict with chap. vii. 4, where idolaters are warned that their feeling of security in being the possessors of the House of God is ill-founded. Here the temple is spoken of in its relation to true believers, whose joy in it rested on their faith in Him who was revealed through the glory that abode on the mercy-seat.

13. *shall be written in the earth*] shall disappear, like writing on any soft substance. The simile would naturally suggest itself to the prophet. "From the scarcity of writing materials a board covered with sand is used to this day in schools for giving lessons in writing; and the Arabs have a method of fortune-telling, the invention of which is ascribed by them to the patriarch Enoch...effected by certain signs drawn upon d." *Sp. Comm.*

the fountain] See chap. ii. 13 with note, also ix. 1.

14. Jeremiah prays that God's character for faithfulness may be vindicated in his own case.

15. This verse shews that the time is before the capture of Jerusalem the end of Jehoiakim's reign. If that event had occurred, the people could not, as here, challenge the prophet to point out a fulfilment of his prophecies of woe.

now] not denoting time, but in the sense of *I pray thee*.

16. *pastor*] This word is generally applied elsewhere to kings or other rulers (see chap. ii. 8, with note). There is no real difficulty however in understanding it here of Jeremiah (and similarly of others in xxii. 22) in his capacity of leader, authoritatively guiding the thoughts and acts of the people. Compare "shepherd" in Eccles. xii. 11.

to follow thee] **after** *thee*. The sense, which is obscured in the Eng.

have I desired the woeful day; thou knowest: that which
17 came out of my lips was right before thee. Be not a terror
18 unto me: thou *art* my hope in the day of evil. Let them
be confounded that persecute me, but let not me be confounded: let them be dismayed, but let not me be dismayed:
bring upon them the day of evil, and destroy them *with*
double destruction.

19—27. *Conformity to the Law will yet ensure prosperity.*

19 Thus said the LORD unto me; Go and stand in the gate
of the children of the people, whereby the kings of Judah

Vers., is closely connected with the succeeding clause. Jeremiah had
neither sought to resign the office of being as it were an assistant-shepherd, directing the steps of the people in the path which God had
marked out for them, nor were his forecasts of sorrow to be understood
as meaning that he hoped for that which he thus predicted.
the woeful day] the overthrow of Jerusalem. The word here rendered 'woeful' is the same as the "desperately wicked" of ver. 9,
where see note.
thou knowest] He appeals to God to confirm his protest.
was right] **was**. The insertion of the word *right* is misleading.
What Jeremiah really says is that his words were not his own, but were
all spoken as in God's sight and in compliance with His will.
  17. *terror*] a cause of *dismay*. See chap. i. 17, with note. The
same word (*dismayed*) occurs twice in the succeeding verse.
  thou art my hope] in accordance with the promise of chap. xv. 11.
  18. *destroy them with double destruction*] **break them with a double
breaking**. This may mean a literally twofold punishment, the one part
for their apostacy as a nation, the other for their treatment of Jeremiah.
It seems more likely however that *double* is merely equivalent to *utter,
complete*.

19—27. CONFORMITY TO THE LAW WILL YET ENSURE
PROSPERITY.

It is a question whether this prophecy be a continuation of the preceding, or a short separate prophecy placed here but having no immediate connexion with any other. On the whole it has the air of being
the latter, whether we consider the mode of its introduction, its subject-matter, or its general tone. The depravity of the people does not seem
of such long standing or so hopeless as in the former prophecies. The
similar language in chap. xxii. 1—5 gives some probability to the belief
that the two were composed about the same time.
  19. *the children of the people*] This expression may mean either *the
common people* as opposed to the rich (so in chap. xxvi. 23 and 2 Kings
xxiii. 6) or *the laity* as distinct from the priests (so in 2 Chron. xxxv. 5,

come in, and by the which they go out, and in all the gates of Jerusalem; and say unto them, Hear ye the word of the 20 LORD, ye kings of Judah, and all Judah, and all the inhabitants of Jerusalem, that enter in by these gates: Thus 21 saith the LORD; Take heed to yourselves, and bear no burden on the sabbath day, nor bring *it* in by the gates of Jerusalem; neither carry forth a burden out of your houses 22 on the sabbath day, neither do ye any work, but hallow ye the sabbath day, as I commanded your fathers. But they 23 obeyed not, neither inclined their ear, but made their neck stiff, that *they* might not hear, nor receive instruction. And 24 it shall come to pass, if ye diligently hearken unto me, saith the LORD, to bring in no burden through the gates of this city on the sabbath day, but hallow the sabbath day, to do no work therein; then shall there enter into the gates of this 25 city kings and princes sitting upon the throne of David,

margin). The latter is the more probable of the two, as there would not be a gate called after the common people but used also for the passage of the kings. It is thus most likely that the gate in question was one of those leading to the temple, perhaps the main entrance to the outer court, while the priests would pass in by side entrances. If we suppose further that, as in our Lord's time, there was traffic carried on in the Temple court, or at the entrance to it, this whole passage will receive additional significance.

21. *to*] in. This is both more literal and more forcible than the Eng. Vers. The closest rendering would be *in your souls;* as we should say, *Lay it to heart.*

21, 22. *bear no burden......neither carry forth a burden*] It appears that the inhabitants both of town and country habitually broke the fourth commandment by engaging in traffic on the Sabbath. The latter brought in their produce for sale in Jerusalem, while the former would bring from their houses commodities to be offered in exchange. We may compare Neh. xiii. 15—22.

22. *neither do ye any work*] The prohibition of manual labour on the Sabbath was in after times carried to an absurd extreme by the stricter expounders of the Law. Thus it was forbidden by them to a woman to wear on that day a ribbon that was only fastened and not stitched on her dress, for thus, they said, she was carrying a burden on the Sabbath day!

23. Substantially the same as chap. vii. 26.

25. *then shall there enter*] Prosperity, permanence, and religious devotion shall be the three characteristic features of the Jewish State, if only they will hallow the Sabbath.

kings and princes] In the parallel verse, chap. xxii. 4, kings alone are mentioned. There however the address is to the king, here directly

riding in chariots and on horses, they, and their princes, the men of Judah, and the inhabitants of Jerusalem: and this
26 city shall remain for ever. And they shall come from the cities of Judah, and from the places about Jerusalem, and from the land of Benjamin, and from the plain, and from the mountains, and from the south, bringing burnt offerings, and sacrifices, and meat offerings, and incense, and bringing
27 *sacrifices of* praise, *unto* the house of the LORD. But if you will not hearken unto me to hallow the sabbath day, and not to bear a burden, even entering in at the gates of Jerusalem on the sabbath day; then will I kindle a fire in the gates thereof, and it shall devour the palaces of Jerusalem, and it shall not be quenched.

CHAP. XVIII. 1—17. *The figure of the Potter's Clay and its meaning.*

18 The word which came to Jeremiah from the LORD, saying,

to the people, and the effect is increased by the picture of a grand procession of the royal house and their followers, all attending upon the person of the king. In strictness, the princes (see note on chap. i. 18) not "sitting upon the throne of David," "they" will refer to the kings only.

26. We have here enumerated the sections of the country still left in the possession of the Israelites, i.e. of the tribes of Judah and Benjamin.
the land of Benjamin] lying north of Judah.
the plain] stretching from the hill-country to the Mediterranean.
the mountains] the central part, including the wilderness of Judah which lay to the westward, and reaching to the Dead Sea.
burnt offerings, and sacrifices, and meat offerings, and incense] Three sorts of offerings are here mentioned, two bloody and one unbloody. Meat offerings (a name whose sound is rather misleading to our ears now) consisted of flour and oil, and had (Lev. ii. 1) frankincense (the 'incense' of this verse) strewn upon them. The incense offering (Exod. xxx. 7) is expressed by a different word in the Hebrew, although frankincense was one of the ingredients which entered with sweet spices into its composition (Exod. xxx. 34).
sacrifices of praise] **praise.** It is not meant that any special kind of sacrifices are called by this name, but that the offering of all the sacrifices just mentioned is an expression of praise. So in chap. xxxiii. 11.

27. Disobedience in this matter shall be followed by an exhibition of God's wrath, which shall take the form of a general conflagration (2 Kings xxv. 9).

CHAP. XVIII. **1—17.** THE FIGURE OF THE POTTER'S CLAY AND ITS MEANING.

1. *The word which came...*] The words and events of chapters

Arise, and go down *to* the potter's house, and there I will 2
cause thee to hear my words. Then I went down *to* the 3
potter's house, and behold, he wrought a work on the wheels.
And the vessel that he made of clay was marred in the hand 4

xviii.—xx. may all be considered as having this for their heading.
Chap. xviii. gives and explains the figure of the potter's clay, and adds
the effect upon the people. Chap. xix. gives and applies the figure
of the potter's broken vessel, while chap. xx. describes the sufferings
of Jeremiah in consequence, and his complaints. The two symbolical
actions probably occurred within the first four years of Jehoiakim's reign.
For (i) there seems from the language used to be still a chance for the
people (the calamity threatened had not yet arrived), and (ii) the mention of Pashur (chap. xx. 1, 2) as the person who puts the prophet in
the stocks, leads us to the same conclusion. "In Zedekiah's reign
Pashur's office was held by Zephaniah (chap. xxix. 25, 26), so that after
Jehoiakim's death Pashur must have been carried into captivity with
Jeconiah. But as such an outrage upon a prophet as that committed
by Pashur upon Jeremiah would certainly not have been allowed in
Josiah's time: and as after the first four years of Jehoiakim Jeremiah
was in hiding, and dared not shew himself till just at last, when the
Chaldeans were marching upon Jerusalem, no other date for this prophecy is probable except that given above." *Sp. Comm.*

3. *I went down*] probably from the Temple, where his prophecies
would naturally be delivered, as the place of resort, and one that was
solemn and impressive in its associations. This was in the upper part
of the city. The potters were probably south of the valley of Hinnom.

the potter's house] The comparison (as in ver. 6) of man to the clay
and God to the potter was a familiar one. Compare with this passage Job x. 9, xxxiii. 6; Is. xxix. 16, xlv. 9, lxiv. 8. The trade was a
very early one. The Hebrews had themselves been concerned in it
while yet in Egypt (Ps. lxxxi. 6). Dr Thomson (*The Land and the
Book*, p. 520) thus describes what he saw at Jaffa (Joppa): "There was
the potter sitting at his 'frame,' and turning the 'wheel' with his foot.
He had a heap of the prepared clay near him, and a pan of water by his
side. Taking a lump in his hand, he placed it on the top of the wheel
(which revolves horizontally) and smoothed it into a low cone, like the
upper end of a sugar-loaf, then thrusting his thumb into the top of it, he
opened a hole down through the centre, and this he constantly widened
by pressing the edges of the revolving cone between his hands. As it
enlarged and became thinner, he gave it whatever shape he pleased with
the utmost ease and expedition."

the wheels] literally, probably, *the two stones*, not however that they
were really of that material. "How early the wheel came into use in
Palestine, we know not, but it seems likely that it was adopted from
Egypt. It consisted of a wooden disc placed on another larger one, and
turned by the hand by an attendant, or worked by a treadle." Sm.
Bibl. Dict., Art. 'Pottery.'

4. *And the vessel......was marred*] "From some defect in the clay,

of the potter: so he made it again another vessel, as seemed
5 good to the potter to make *it*. Then the word of the LORD
6 came to me, saying, O house of Israel, cannot I do with
you as this potter? saith the LORD. Behold, as the clay *is*
in the potter's hand, so *are* ye in mine hand, O house of
7 Israel. *At what* instant I shall speak concerning a nation
and concerning a kingdom, to pluck up, and to pull down,
8 and to destroy *it;* if that nation, against whom I have
pronounced, turn from their evil, I will repent of the evil
9 that I thought to do unto them. And *at what* instant I
shall speak concerning a nation, and concerning a kingdom,
10 to build and to plant *it;* if it do evil in my sight, that *it*
obey not my voice, then I will repent of the good, where-
11 with I said *I* would benefit them. Now therefore go to,
speak to the men of Judah, and to the inhabitants of Jerusalem, saying, Thus saith the LORD; Behold, I frame evil
against you, and devise a device against you: return ye

or because he had taken too little, the potter suddenly changed his mind, crushed his growing jar instantly into a shapeless mass of mud, and beginning anew, fashioned it into a totally different vessel." (Thomson, *ibid.*)

 6. *cannot I do with you as this potter?*] The comparison is between the absolute power of God over Israel and that of the potter over the material on which he works. At any moment he can crush it up or alter its shape. Verses 7—10 go on to shew however that God is not arbitrary in the matter. It is still the conduct of the people that determines their ultimate fate.

 "First of the prophets, Jeremiah proclaims distinctly what had been more or less implied throughout, that predictions were subject to no overruling necessity, but depended for their fulfilment on the moral state of those to whom they were addressed; that the most confident assurance of blessing could be frustrated by sin; that the most awful warnings of calamity could be averted by repentance." Stanley's *Jewish Church*, II. 445.

 7. *At what instant*] literally, **Suddenly**. The same word occurs at the beginning of ver. 9. The rendering in the two cases probably is *At one time—at another*. The verbs (*pluck up*, etc.) in this and in ver. 9 remind us of chap. i. 10.

 8. *I will repent*] speaking after the manner of men. The sense is, *I will alter my treatment*, for among men change of conduct implies change of purpose.

 11. The direct application of the figure to the people here begins.

 frame] The Heb. word is the same as that for *potter*, and so is specially appropriate.

now every one from his evil way, and make your ways and your doings good. And they said, There is no hope: but we will walk after our own devices, and we will every one do the imagination of his evil heart. Therefore thus saith the LORD; Ask ye now among the heathen, who hath heard such *things:* the virgin of Israel hath done a very horrible thing. Will *a man* leave the snow of Lebanon *which cometh* from the rock of the field? *or* shall the cold flowing waters that come from another place be forsaken? Because my people hath forgotten me, they have burnt incense to vanity,

make your ways and your doings good] See note on chap. vii. 3.

12. *There is no hope*] We have gone too far to turn back now. The same expression both in the Hebrew and English occurred chap. ii. 25.

imagination] **stubbornness.** Compare chap. iii. 17.

13. *Ask ye now among the heathen*] An appeal is made of a similar kind to that in chap. ii. 10, 11.

the virgin of Israel] She who was tended with the utmost care by the Almighty has in spite of it all broken through the sanctity which hedged her around. The expression stands of course, as in chap. xiv. 17, for the people collectively.

14. *Will a man leave...*] **Doth the snow of Lebanon cease from the rock of the field?** This is much to be preferred as the reading of the Hebrew. Lebanon (= the white mountain) is so called from the perpetual snow which rests on its highest points. Tacitus (*Histories*, Bk. v. chap. 6) speaks of it as a secure retreat for snows. So Thomson (*The Land and the Book*, p. 20), "the higher half of Lebanon looked like a huge snow bank drifted up against the sky."

the rock of the field] Some understand this to be Jerusalem, on account of somewhat similar expressions applied to it (chap. xvii. 3), *my mountain in the field*, and (chap. xxi. 13) *rock of the plain*. The difficulty however of connecting the snows of Lebanon with any water supply to Jerusalem is too great. Hence *the rock* will be most naturally understood of Lebanon, and *the field* of the country at large.

shall the cold flowing waters...] **do strange cold trickling waters dry up?** Does the water that percolates through the rocks, coming from some unknown (*strange*) regions and cold (thus free from much evaporation), disappear? The reference may very possibly be to the waters of Siloam or some other familiar supply coming in the way thus described. It is difficult to understand the epithet *strange*, if it refer merely to the water flowing down the sides of Lebanon, and produced by the melting of the snows. The general sense at any rate is clear. Nature is constant in her operations, but God, the Rock of Israel, is forsaken by those who used to follow Him.

15. *Because*] **For.** This continues the thought of the 13th verse, ver. 14 being parenthetic.

vanity] idols.

136 JEREMIAH, XVIII. [vv. 16—18.

and they have caused them to stumble in their ways *from* the ancient paths, to walk *in* paths, *in* a way not cast up;
16 to make their land desolate, *and* a perpetual hissing; every one that passeth thereby shall be astonished, and wag his
17 head. I will scatter them as *with* an east wind before the enemy; I will shew them the back, and not the face, in the day of their calamity.

18—23. *The Prophet desires retribution for his enemies.*

18 Then said they, Come, and let us devise devices against Jeremiah; for the law shall not perish from the priest, nor counsel from the wise, nor the word from the prophet. Come, and let us smite him with the tongue, and let us not

they have caused] The pronoun refers either to false prophets and priests, or, which is better, to the idols (see the case of Ahaz, 2 Chron. xxviii. 23).
from the ancient paths] These mean the godly lives which their forefathers led, but in which their children have now stumbled. Compare for the figure chap. vi. 16, with notes.
in paths] *in* by-*paths*.
not cast up] not raised above the inequalities and obstructions of the adjoining fields.
16. *desolate*] The word is cognate to that presently rendered *shall be astonished*. We may therefore render respectively *a dismay...shall be dismayed*. See note on *wonderful* in chap. v. 30.
hissing] not in contempt or anger, but in amazement at so appalling a spectacle.
17. *as with an east wind*] better perhaps, *as an east wind*.
I will shew them the back, and not the face] in answer to the people's own behaviour towards Him. See chap. ii. 27.

18—23. THE PROPHET DESIRES RETRIBUTION FOR HIS ENEMIES.

18. *Then said they*] the leaders among those whom Jeremiah had addressed.
the law shall not perish...] See note on chap. viii. 8. There were certain classes of persons in the state, viz. the priests, the wise and the prophets, who were thought infallible, as being in undoubted possession of the truth. The appeal therefore is made to them against Jeremiah. *The law* is not doctrine in general, but the Mosaic Law, as the basis of all the teaching of the prophets, and under the special guardianship of the priests.
smite him with the tongue] report his words to the king. Compare for another case Amos vii. 10, 11.

give heed to any of his words. Give heed to me, O LORD, 19
and hearken to the voice of them that contend with me.
Shall evil be recompensed for good? for they have digged 20
a pit for my soul. Remember that I stood before thee
to speak good for them, *and* to turn away thy wrath from
them. Therefore deliver up their children to the famine, 21
and pour out their *blood* by the force of the sword; and let
their wives be bereaved of their children, and *be* widows;
and let their men be put to death; *let* their young men *be*
slain by the sword in battle. Let a cry be heard from their 22
houses, when thou shalt bring a troop suddenly upon them:
for they have digged a pit to take me, and hid snares for
my feet. Yet, LORD, thou knowest all their counsel against 23
me to slay *me:* forgive not their iniquity, neither blot out
their sin from thy sight, but let them be overthrown before
thee; deal *thus* with them in the time of thine anger.

19. *Give heed to me, O Lord*] He prays God to give him that hearing, which his enemies refused him.
20. *Shall evil be recompensed for good?*] Jeremiah had interceded for the people in times past, e. g. chap. xiv. 7, 21.
21. *pour out their blood by the force of the sword*] literally, *pour them out upon the hands of the sword:* a forcible expression, meaning, Cast them upon the sword, so that their blood may be thereby shed. It will help us to understand the severity of the punishment here invoked, if we remember that in the attack on God's prophet these were the leaders, who incurred therefore the responsibility of directing the attacks of the multitude.
22. The last verse has painted the havoc wrought in battle outside the walls. This one goes on to the next stage of the coming calamity, the sacking of the houses of the city, and the cruelties attendant upon it.
they have digged a pit] For this and the following figure we may compare Ps. lvii. 6.
23. *Yet*] But. The sense is, Although they conceal their devices, yet there is no concealment from Thee.
deal thus with them in the time of thine anger] rather, *deal with them* (as Thou art wont to act) *in time of wrath.*
The imprecations in these verses may be compared with those found in certain Psalms, notably Pss. lxix. and cix. In them we see a feature which has caused much difficulty to some, but which is to a large extent explained, when we remember that (i) those thus spoken of were the enemies of God and His Church, not merely the personal foes of the writer; (ii) the general spirit of the Old Dispensation was sterner than that of the New; (iii) the comparative darkness in which a future existence was then

CHAP. XIX. 1—13. *The figure of the Broken Vessel and its meaning.*

19 Thus saith the LORD, Go and get a potter's earthen bottle, and *take* of the ancients of the people, and of the ² ancients of the priests; and go forth unto the valley of the son of Hinnom, which *is by* the entry of the east gate, and ³ proclaim there the words that I shall tell thee, and say, Hear ye the word of the LORD, O kings of Judah, and inhabitants of Jerusalem; Thus saith the LORD of hosts, the God of Israel; Behold, I *will* bring evil upon this place, the which whosoever heareth, his ears shall tingle. ⁴ Because they have forsaken me, and have estranged this place, and have burnt incense in it unto other gods, whom

shrouded would naturally make righteous men the more eager that God's glory should be vindicated and His people avenged in the present life.

CHAP. XIX. 1—13. THE FIGURE OF THE BROKEN VESSEL AND ITS MEANING.

1. *get a potter's earthen bottle*] In the figure of chap. xviii. (the potter's clay) the distinguishing feature was the power of God to alter the destinies of a people at any moment, just as the potter's work (ver. 4) was made "again another vessel." The special lesson *here* is that there may come a time in the history of a nation when its persistent obduracy shall demand that the only alteration in its destiny shall take the form of breaking, destruction.

ancients] the same word which is elsewhere rendered *elders*. Those who from position, or it might be age, were the leading men of the State and of the Church.

2. *the valley of the son of Hinnom*] See note on chap. vii. 31, which explains how well the place was adapted to the message that Jeremiah had to deliver.

the east gate] rather, *the sherd-gate*. The Hebrew name, which does not occur elsewhere, seems to have been given it from the fragments of broken pottery cast here as refuse. It may probably have been identical with one of the two gates mentioned in Nehemiah (iii. 14, 15) as leading from the city into this valley.

3. *kings*] The plural is used, as not only the reigning king is addressed, but the whole dynasty, whose accumulated transgressions with those of their people are now about to be punished.

his ears shall tingle] The same expression was used by the prophets of Manasseh's time (2 Kings xxi. 12) in reference to the evil in which his doings would result, and earlier still, of the consequences of the sins of Eli's house (1 Sam. iii. 11).

4. *have estranged*] have treated it as a place of whose sanctity they are not aware.

neither they nor their fathers have known, nor the kings of
Judah, and have filled this place *with* the blood of innocents; they have built also the high places of Baal, to burn 5
their sons with fire *for* burnt offerings unto Baal, which I
commanded not, nor spake *it*, neither came *it* into my
mind: therefore behold, the days come, saith the LORD, 6
that this place shall no more be called Tophet, nor The
valley of the son of Hinnom, but The valley of slaughter.
And I will make void the counsel of Judah and Jerusalem 7
in this place; and I will cause them to fall by the sword
before their enemies, and by the hands of them that seek
their lives: and their carcases will I give to be meat for the
fowls of the heaven, and for the beasts of the earth. And 8
I will make this city desolate, and a hissing; every one
that passeth thereby shall be astonished and hiss because
of all the plagues thereof. And I will cause them to eat 9

whom neither they...] The right construction is probably somewhat
different from that given in the Eng. Vers. *They, their fathers and the
kings of Judah*, are in strictness nominatives to the first verb, *have forsaken*. Thus the rendering will be, *They have forsaken, etc., whom
they knew not, they and their fathers and the kings of Judah*,

innocents] not children, the sacrifice of whom is first mentioned in
the next verse, but in general innocent persons. Compare 2 Kings
xxi. 16.

5, 6. These verses have occurred already in substance, chap. vii. 31,
32. See notes there and on ii. 23.

6. *The valley of slaughter*] The valley of Hinnom, as possessing
water, was a natural place for an attacking army to take up its position.
Some have thought that the name 'valley of slaughter' refers in particular
to successful assaults made by the enemy upon the Jews when these were
attempting with an armed force to hold possession of the water supply,
so necessary for the maintenance of life within the city.

7. *I will make void*] The Heb. verb is that from which is derived the
original word for 'vessel' in ver. 1. Hence it is evidently intended as
a play on the word, and means literally, *I will pour out*. It has been
thought that Jeremiah here suited the action to the word, and having
previously filled with water the vessel which he bore, now poured out
the contents on the ground, as he spoke. For the latter part of the verse
compare vii. 33.

8. *desolate, and a hissing*] See note on chap. xviii. 16.

plagues] *blows, wounds.* The word plague is generally used only of
pestilences, although in point of derivation (Greek) it should mean
simply *blows*.

9. The verse is taken from the opening words of Deut. xxviii. 53—
57, in which passage are described at length the unnatural straits to

the flesh of their sons and the flesh of their daughters, and they shall eat every one the flesh of his friend in the siege and straitness, wherewith their enemies, and they that seek their lives, shall straiten them. Then shalt thou break the bottle in the sight of the men that go with thee. And shalt say unto them, Thus saith the Lord of hosts; Even so will I break this people and this city, as *one* breaketh a potter's vessel, that cannot be made whole again: and they shall bury *them* in Tophet, till *there be* no place to bury. Thus will I do unto this place, saith the Lord, and to the inhabitants thereof, and *even* make this city as Tophet: And the houses of Jerusalem, and the houses of the kings of Judah, shall be defiled as the place of Tophet, because of all the houses upon whose roofs they have burnt incense

which hunger shall drive the besieged. Compare a briefer expression of the same, Levit. xxvi. 29. This had already been the state of things in the siege of Samaria by the Syrians (2 Kings vi. 28, 29), and that it actually occurred in fulfilment of this prophecy, when the Chaldeans besieged Jerusalem, we learn from Lam. iv. 10.

10. The first of the two thoughts to be connected with the pitcher, the pouring out of the people as water spilt on the ground, has been made sufficiently plain by the prophet (verses 7—9). He now proceeds to the second sign, viz. the breaking of the pitcher.

"The people...have the same custom of breaking a jar, when they wish to express their utmost detestation of any one. They come behind or near him, and smash the jar to atoms, thus imprecating upon him and his a like hopeless ruin." Thomson, *The Land and the Book*, p. 641.

11. *that cannot be made whole again*] In this lies the special point of the figure here used. See above, note on ver. 1.

and they shall bury them...] The Septuagint omits the last part of this verse. The apparent arbitrariness, however, which is so often displayed by that Version in this Book, prevents us from attributing very much weight to such an omission when unsupported by good evidence. The words seem to have a natural connexion both with what precedes and with what follows. The overthrow of Jerusalem shall be so sudden and complete, that there shall not be room for burial, unless by using even the unclean place of Tophet for that purpose.

12. As Tophet had been made an unclean place by the practice of idolatry, so shall all the houses of Jerusalem be made unclean by corpses, because of the idolatries which have been practised upon their roofs.

13. *because of all*] better, **even** *all*.

upon whose roofs they have burnt incense] "The flat roofs of oriental buildings were used for gatherings at festivals (Judg. xvi. 27), for exercise (2 Sam. xi. 2), for the erection of booths at the feast of tabernacles (Neh. viii. 16), and for public meetings (Matt. x. 27). They seem also to have been the favourite places for star-worship (Zeph. i. 5)."

unto all the host of heaven, and have poured out drink offerings unto other gods.

CHAP. XIX. 14—XX. 6. *Pashur's vengeance and the Prophet's rejoinder.*

Then came Jeremiah from Tophet, whither the LORD had 14 sent him to prophesy; and he stood in the court of the LORD's house; and said to all the people, Thus saith the 15 LORD of hosts, the God of Israel; Behold, I will bring upon this city and upon all her towns all the evil that I have pronounced against it, because they have hardened their necks, that *they* might not hear my words. Now 20 Pashur the son of Immer the priest, who *was* also chief governor in the house of the LORD, heard *that* Jeremiah

Sp. Comm. To this list we may add that they were used as places of retirement for conversation (1 Sam. ix. 25, 26), or prayer (Acts x. 9).

CHAP. XIX. 14—XX. 6. PASHUR'S VENGEANCE AND THE PROPHET'S REJOINDER.

14. This, as introducing another address of Jeremiah, given us in the brief summary of ver. 15, is the opening of a new paragraph. It is unfortunate therefore that the division of chapters does not here correspond more closely with the sense. This address, as delivered in the Temple precincts, would be heard by a larger number than those who had just formed his audience in the valley.

15. *all her towns*] all the other cities belonging to Judah. Compare xxxiv. 1. The prophecy in the valley of Hinnom spoke of Jerusalem only. We may thus gather that the addition of the words 'and upon all her towns' is but a slight indication of the fact that this address was in reality even fuller and more explicit in its threatenings than the former.

hardened their necks] See note on vii. 26.

XX. **1.** *Now Pashur the son of Immer*] possibly the father of Gedaliah of chap. xxxviii. 1, while "Pashur the son of Malchiah" of that verse is probably identical with the Pashur of chap. xxi. 1. Both this last and the Pashur of the present verse belonged to one of the twenty-four priestly courses formed by David, he who is here mentioned being head of the sixteenth course (1 Chron. xxiv. 14), whose ancestor was Immer (perhaps the Amariah of Neh. x. 3, xii. 2). The other belonged to the fifth course, that of which Melchiah (=Malchijah of 1 Chron. xxiv. 9) was head. For him see notes on *Zephaniah*, xxi. 1. Of the priestly courses the houses represented by the two Pashurs were the strongest amongst the few which returned from Babylon (Ezra ii. 36—39).

chief governor] The Hebrew expression, *Pakîd Nāgîd*, is peculiar, and the exact sense is not quite clear. Either (i) the former word defines more closely the somewhat general sense of overseer which be-

2 prophesied these things. Then Pashur smote Jeremiah the prophet, and put him in the stocks that *were* in the high gate of Benjamin, which *was* by the house of the Lord. 3 And it came to pass on the morrow, that Pashur brought forth Jeremiah out of the stocks. Then said Jeremiah unto him, The Lord hath not called thy name Pashur, but 4 Magor-missabib. For thus saith the Lord, Behold, I will

longs to the latter, or (ii) the former word expresses that the dignity denoted by the latter was held by him only as *deputy* for another. In favour of (ii) is the occurrence of the word *Pakîd* in xxix. 26 ("officers"), where the general sense suggests such a meaning. Zephaniah, the person there spoken of, is called "the second priest" in chap. lii. 24; 2 Kings xxv. 18.

2. *Then Pashur smote*] The utterance of these warnings and threats in the very Temple was too much for the authorities of that place. They proceeded to inflict punishment in its ordinary forms, viz. stripes (no doubt the *forty save one* which kept safely within the limits permitted in Deut. xxv. 3; compare 2 Cor. xi. 24) followed by confinement in the stocks.

the prophet] As this title is here for the first time given to Jeremiah, while it occurs with frequency afterwards, it has been thought by some to indicate that all subsequent to chaps. i.—xix. was written after the prophet's death. We can however see clear reasons for the use of this official title here as well as later in the Book without having recourse to any such hypothesis. It is in almost every case obviously inserted to mark out Jeremiah's official character and position where these are questioned or liable to question from one quarter or another. Here, e.g., the intention is to suggest a protest against Pashur's conduct. In like manner St Paul styles himself ἀπόστολος, when his authority is likely to be questioned.

the stocks] The Hebrew word is from a root meaning *to twist*. It therefore expresses the cramped position which the body of the person confined was forced to occupy. The punishment seems thus to answer rather to that denoted by our word **pillory**, the neck and arms being confined while the legs and the body are kept in a bent position. It seems to have been somewhat common at this time. See xxix. 26. The passage 2 Chron. xvi. 10 (where Eng. Vers. has "prison-house") speaks of a special chamber for the purpose. In Job xiii. 27, xxxiii. 11 the Heb. word is different, and there the Eng. Vers. ("stocks") is probably strictly accurate, as it is also Acts xvi. 24. (See Sm., *Bibl. Dict.*, Art. 'Stocks.')

high gate of Benjamin, which was by] rather, **upper gate of Benjamin, which was in**, the northern gate of the upper (inner) court of the Temple, and to be distinguished from the *city* gate of the same name (xxxvii. 13, xxxviii. 7). The one here meant had been built by Jotham (2 Kings xv. 35).

3. *hath not called thy name Pashur, but Magor-missabib*] For the

make thee a terror to thyself, and to all thy friends: and they shall fall by the sword of their enemies, and thine eyes *shall* behold *it;* and I will give all Judah into the hand of the king of Babylon, and he shall carry them captive into Babylon, and shall slay them with the sword. Moreover I will deliver all the strength of this city, and all the labours thereof, and all the precious things thereof, and all the treasures of the kings of Judah will I give into the hand of their enemies, which shall spoil them, and take them, and carry them to Babylon. And thou, Pashur, and all that dwell in thine house shall go into captivity: and thou shalt come *to* Babylon, and there thou shalt die, and shalt be buried there, thou, and all thy friends, to whom thou hast prophesied lies.

last word see note on vi. 25. The original of "fear is on every side" here appears as a proper name, and as it is obviously expressive of the fate announced by the prophet as coming on Pashur, much ingenuity has been applied by commentators to the name which he already bore, in order to make a forcible contrast between the two. No satisfactory basis however has been obtained for their conjectures *joy around, joy on every side, abundance of brightness,* and the like, and it is not of course *necessary* that the name Pashur should have had any such significance.

4. *a terror to thyself, and to all thy friends*] the interpretation of the new name. The nature of Pashur's punishment may be gathered from the fact that it was not, as far as we know, a violent death, of which indeed there is no trace in the language here. He was to be carried to Babylon, and there die. We know (see note on ver. 1) that his house was one of the most flourishing in numbers at the end of the captivity. Accordingly the punishment here pointed to probably consisted in remorse at the ruin which he had brought upon his country by opposing the counsels of Jeremiah. He "belonged to the warlike party, whose creed it was that Judaea by a close alliance with Egypt might resist the arms of Assyria. Apparently he had been led away by his zeal to give himself out as invested with prophetic powers, in order to gain greater credence for his views. This would help to account for the extreme violence with which he treated Jeremiah, and would also increase the bitterness of his anguish when he saw to what a result his counsels and false predictions had led his 'friends,' i.e. his partizans." *Sp. Comm.*

5. *strength*] **stores.**
labours] **gains,** results of labour.

6. *prophesied lies*] thus shewing that Pashur was not only a priest but also had assumed to himself without warrant the functions of a prophet, and had insisted that the warnings of Jeremiah were absurd. See xiv. 13—15.

7—13. *The Prophet's cry unto God for help in his trouble.*

7 O Lord, thou hast deceived me, and I was deceived:
Thou art stronger than I, and hast prevailed:
I am in derision daily,
Every one mocketh me.

8 For since I spake, I cried out,
I cried violence and spoil;
Because the word of the Lord was made a reproach unto me,
And a derision, daily.

9 Then I said, I will not make mention of him,
Nor speak any more in his name.
But *his word* was in mine heart as a burning fire shut up in my bones,

7—13. The Prophet's cry unto God for help in his trouble.

7. *deceived*] *enticed, persuaded.*
art stronger than I] *hast taken hold of me.* This and ver. 9 shew us that the prophets did not speak of their own will. It was an influence which they could not resist that urged them forward, in spite of the certain ills that should follow to themselves. Compare xxiii. 29; so Amos iii. 8 ("The Lord God hath spoken; who can but prophesy?"), and 1 Cor. ix. 16 ("Necessity is laid upon me").

8. *since I spake, I cried out*] rather, *as often as I speak, I must call out*. The verbs rendered *cried out* and *cried* have no connexion in the original. The former means to complain loudly, the latter simply to *call aloud*.

violence and spoil] not so much, or at any rate not solely, that of which Jeremiah himself was the victim, but that directed by the upper classes generally against those weaker than themselves. Compare v. 26—28, vii. 9, ix. 4 with notes.

a reproach unto me, and a derision] Words applied to his own case by the great Florentine, Savonarola, in one of his many sermons from the Cathedral pulpit during the last years of the fifteenth century, when the fortunes of his State, owing to the misdeeds of rulers and people, were reduced to a very low ebb. "Thy sins, O Florence......are the cause of these stripes. And now repent, give alms, offer prayers, become united. O people, I have been a father to thee; I have wearied myself all the days of my life to make known to thee the truths of the faith and of holy living, and *I have had nothing but tribulations, derision, and reproach.*" Clark's *Savonarola*, p. 169.

daily] **the whole day.**

9. *his word was*] better, *there was*. In the Heb. *was* and *shut up* are masculine, while *burning* is feminine, agreeing with *fire*. But the

And I was weary with forebearing, and I could not stay.
For I heard the defaming of many, fear on every side. 10
Report, *say they*, and we will report it.
All my familiars watched for my halting, *saying*,
Peradventure he will be enticed, and we shall prevail against him,
And we shall take our revenge on him.
But the LORD *is* with me as a mighty terrible one: 11
Therefore my persecutors shall stumble, and they shall not prevail:
They shall be greatly ashamed: for they shall not prosper:
Their everlasting confusion shall never be forgotten.

idiom of the language by no means forbids us to consider all these words as alike referring to the substantive.

I was weary with forbearing] Compare vi. 11, where the Heb. is almost the same.

and I could not stay] or, perhaps, *and I* (consequently) *prevail not;* but the Heb. may mean, *I cannot endure it* (cannot refrain myself). There is a change of tense in the original, which serves to mark this as the lasting result of the whole.

10. *defaming*] talk. Jeremiah gives us snatches as it were of the conversation which he heard going on around him among his enemies.

fear on every side] expressing the perilous case in which he stood.

Report, say they, and we will report it] probably the words of two individuals or groups of his foes, the first urging upon the second to bring his language under the notice of the authorities, the second assenting to the suggestion.

familiars] literally, *men of my peace*, i.e. acquaintances, those to whom I should give the ordinary salutation, Peace be with you.

watched for my halting] This is probably right and suggested by the language of Ps. xxxv. 15, xxxviii. 17. It has also however been explained as a further definition of 'familiars,' meaning therefore men who should stand at my side to protect me. The literal translation is *those who watch my side.*

enticed] into some act, which will lay him open to attack.

11. In this and the two following verses the prophet's courage is renewed. His faith brightens the prospect before him, and through it he sees that all will yet be well with the righteous.

terrible one] *warrior.*

ashamed] *put to shame.*

they shall not prosper] This would be unnecessary to say after the assertion made already, that they should be put to shame. The sense is rather, **they have not acted prudently.** See note on x. 21.

their everlasting confusion shall] *with everlasting disgrace that shall.* The words probably refer to *put to shame,* although they may also

12   But, O LORD of hosts, that triest the righteous,
     And seest the reins and the heart,
     Let me see thy vengeance on them:
     For unto thee have I opened my cause.
13   Sing unto the LORD, praise ye the LORD:
     For he hath delivered the soul of the poor from the hand of evildoers.

14—18. *A renewed outburst of passionate grief.*

14   Cursed *be* the day wherein I was born:
     Let not the day wherein my mother bare me be blessed.
15   Cursed *be* the man who brought tidings to my father, saying,
     A man child is born unto thee;
     Making him very glad.
16   And let that man be as the cities which the LORD overthrew, and repented not:

---

belong to the verb immediately preceding them (*they have acted foolishly with an everlasting*, etc.).

12. Virtually the same as xi. 20.

13. This exclamation of praise may be compared with those which break out from time to time in the course or at the conclusion of many even among the most mournful and despondent of the Psalms.

14—18. A RENEWED OUTBURST OF PASSIONATE GRIEF.

14. *Cursed be the day*] These words may be compared with those which Job (iii. 3; compare x. 18) first uttered after his seven days of silent grief, although those passages are even more violent than this. The words however are sufficiently intense in their tone to cause some difficulty, especially when we compare them with those which have gone immediately before. Hence it has been sought to explain them as (i) words put by Jeremiah in the mouth of Pashur, (ii) words misplaced by copyists, (iii) words placed here by Jeremiah, although really uttered by him at a different time, and only introduced now by way of contrast to the happier feelings to which he had just given expression, and to remind him of the passionate trouble from which he had been delivered. These explanations are all rather desperate remedies. We are probably nearer the true explanation, if we say that the words express in the intense language of Eastern emotions the bitterness of the pangs which ever and again seized upon the prophet's mind and heart, as he contemplated his position and that of his country. Compare David's imprecation on Gilboa, as the scene of the death of Saul and Jonathan (2 Sam. i. 21).

15. *making him*] *he made him*, added in a tone of bitter reflection.

And let him hear the cry in the morning, and the shouting at noontide;
Because he slew me not from the womb;   17
Or that my mother might have been my grave,
And her womb *to be* always great *with me*.
Wherefore came I forth out of the womb   18
To see labour and sorrow,
That my days should be consumed with shame?

CHAP. XXI. 1—7. *Zedekiah's appeal to the Prophet. His reply, announcing the approaching capture of the city.*

The word which came unto Jeremiah from the LORD, 21

16. *cry*] *lamentation*, of cities suffering the horrors of war. *shouting*] *war-cry*.
17. *or that*] Probably *so that* is the sense. The prophet is not thinking of the possibility of that which he wishes, but simply of the blessing which he would have felt it not to have lived, and so to have escaped his present anguish. This is further explained in ver. 18.

In Jeremiah's conduct here and in the support given him now and throughout the rest of his life "we should see the greatness of God's grace, which raises again those who are stumbling to their fall, and does not let God's true servants succumb under the temptation... And that Jeremiah did indeed victoriously struggle against this temptation we may gather from remembering that hereafter, when, especially during the siege of Jerusalem under Zedekiah, he had still sorer afflictions to endure, he no longer trembles or bewails the sufferings connected with his calling." Keil.

CHAP. XXI. 1—7. ZEDEKIAH'S APPEAL TO THE PROPHET. HIS REPLY, ANNOUNCING THE APPROACHING CAPTURE OF THE CITY.

1. *The word which came*] This commences a new division of the whole book. The substance of the roll of chap. xxxvi. has been given in the preceding chapters, while fragments of the same are doubtless included in this portion. We here pass at once from the time of Jehoiakim to that of Zedekiah the last king of Judah, and the occasion on which (ver. 4) the city was attacked by the Chaldaeans (see Introd. chap. i. § 16). Zedekiah under these circumstances follows the example set by Hezekiah towards Isaiah the great prophet of *his* time (2 Kings xix. 2) and sends Pashur and Zephaniah to Jeremiah to ask for a declaration of the future. The prophet replies in this and the three following chapters to the effect that the successive crimes of kings, prophets and priests, which he speaks of in detail, have secured for Judah the unenviable fate now visibly at hand, while there appear however from time to time gleams of brighter things. Chaps. xxi, xxii. describe the sins of the successive kings, xxiii. 1—8 gives expression to Messianic

when king Zedekiah sent unto him Pashur the son of Melchiah, and Zephaniah the son of Maaseiah the priest, say-
2 ing, Inquire, I pray thee, of the LORD for us; for Nebuchadrezzar king of Babylon maketh war against us; if so be that the LORD will deal with us according to all his wondrous
3 works, that he may go up from us. Then said Jeremiah
4 unto them, Thus shall ye say to Zedekiah: Thus saith the LORD God of Israel; Behold, *I will* turn back the weapons of war that *are* in your hands, wherewith ye fight against the king of Babylon, and against the Chaldeans, which besiege you without the walls, and I will assemble them into
5 the midst of this city. And I myself will fight against you

hopes, xxiii. 9—40 sharply rebukes prophets and priests, xxiv. shews under the similitude of baskets of figs the rottenness to which the State has now under Zedekiah been reduced.

Pashur the son of Melchiah] See note on xx. 1.

Zephaniah] (see also note on xx. 1) mentioned again xxix. 25, xxxvii. 3, lii. 24. In this last place he is spoken of as "the second priest," meaning, next to the high-priest in rank. He was one of those slain by Nebuchadnezzar at Riblah. Both he (as we may gather from that fact) and Pashur (chap. xxxviii. 1, 4) belonged to the party who were for refusing to recognize and submit to Nebuchadnezzar's overwhelming power, and thus were politically hostile to Jeremiah.

the priest] These words belong to Zephaniah not Maaseiah, as (chap. i. 1) "of the priests" to Jeremiah not Hilkiah. Compare xxii. 11.

2. *Inquire, I pray thee, of the Lord*] not, Ask for His help, but, Seek a revelation of the future. Compare the case of Josiah (2 Kings xxii. 13).

Nebuchadrezzar] This is a nearer approach than Nebuchadnezzar to the correct spelling of the word. Nabo-kudurri-uzur presents perhaps the nearest sound in English writing. The meaning is very doubtful, but it probably includes the name of the God Nebo.

his wondrous works] Zedekiah may have been induced by the somewhat similar circumstances above referred to in Hezekiah's reign, when Isaiah was thus appealed to, to hope for a promise of miraculous deliverance (2 Kings xix. 6, 7, 35, 36).

4. *turn back*] Those who are engaged outside the walls in trying to baffle the Chaldaeans as they take up their positions for the siege, are to be driven back by the foe into the city.

without the walls] These words are probably to be connected, not with 'besiege,' but with 'fight.'

assemble them] gather the weapons together.

5. *I myself*] Not only shall the sword of the enemy devour you, but also the pestilence. This was a visitation considered as coming most direct from the hand of God. Compare 2 Sam. xxiv. 14.

with an outstretched hand and with a strong arm, even in anger, and in fury, and in great wrath. And I will smite 6 the inhabitants of this city, both man and beast: they shall die of a great pestilence. And afterward, saith the LORD, 7 I will deliver Zedekiah king of Judah, and his servants, and the people, and such as are left in this city from the pestilence, from the sword, and from the famine, into the hand of Nebuchadrezzar king of Babylon, and into the hand of their enemies, and into the hand of those that seek their life: and he shall smite them with the edge of the sword; he shall not spare them, neither have pity, nor have mercy.

8—14. *Counsel to the people and the king.*

And unto this people thou shalt say, Thus saith the 8 LORD; Behold, I set before you the way of life, and the way of death. He that abideth in this city shall die by the 9 sword, and by the famine, and by the pestilence: but he that goeth out, and falleth to the Chaldeans that besiege you, he shall live, and his life shall be unto him for a prey. For I have set my face against this city for evil, and not for 10 good, saith the LORD: it shall be given into the hand of the king of Babylon, and he shall burn it with fire. And touch- 11

with an outstretched hand and with a strong arm] The phrase is suggested by Deut. where it occurs several times (iv. 34, v. 15, xxvi. 8).
7. *and such*] **even** *such*. The whole verse is as explicit as possible in its assurance that none shall escape either the sword or submission to the conqueror's pleasure.

8—14. COUNSEL TO THE PEOPLE AND THE KING.

8. *the way of life, and the way of death*] A somewhat similar expression in Deut. (xxx. 19) may probably have suggested these words to Jeremiah. 'Life,' however, here does not mean prosperity, but the mere avoidance of death.
9. *falleth to the Chaldeans*] giveth himself up, not as an act of treachery against his own countrymen (see xxxvii. 13, 14) but simply as a means of saving his life.
for a prey] something snatched up hurriedly and borne away with him rather than his secure possession.
10. *I have set my face against this city*] Compare xliv. 11, also Amos ix. 4, where we have a similar phrase—*to look closely at, to direct the attention to*. Hence, as the phrase itself is ambiguous, the words are added, 'for evil and not for good.'
11. The counsel here given to the royal house seems not to have

ing the house of the king of Judah, *say*, Hear ye the word
12 of the LORD. O house of David, thus saith the LORD;
Execute judgment in the morning, and deliver *him that is*
spoiled out of the hand of the oppressor, lest my fury go
out like fire, and burn that none can quench *it*, because of
13 the evil of your doings. Behold, I *am* against thee, O inhabitant of the valley, *and* rock of the plain, saith the
LORD; which say, Who shall come down against us? or
14 who shall enter into our habitations? But I will punish you
according to the fruit of your doings, saith the LORD: and
I will kindle a fire in the forest thereof, and it shall devour
all things round about it.

CHAP. XXII. 1—9. *A further exhortation to amend.*

22 Thus saith the LORD; Go down *to* the house of the king

formed part of Jeremiah's reply to the king's messengers at this time, but to be the first section of that series of prophecies which, altered probably at different dates, are thus placed in a historical connexion by Jeremiah himself or Baruch. This particular section (verses 11—14) belongs to a time when there was still a possibility of escape by amendment of life.

touching] **as to.** The word *say*, which follows, should be omitted. It is a direct address from the prophet to the royal house of Judah.

12. *Execute judgment in the morning*] An important part of the king's duties was personally to hear and adjudicate upon cases in the open space at the city gate. Compare 2 Sam. xv. 2—4.

in the morning] probably, *every morning*, as the same Heb. expression means Amos iv. 4, and a similar one Ps. ci. 8 ("early" in Eng. Vers.). It was the ordinary time for business, while it was still cool.

him that is spoiled] See chap. xx. 8 with note.

13. *inhabitant*] The Heb. is *inhabitress*, i.e. the feminine used collectively for the body of the inhabitants. See iv. 31, vi. 2, vii. 29, xiv. 17.

and rock] **rock.** The 'and' should be omitted. Jerusalem is called both 'valley' and 'rock' (compare xvii. 3 with note) because, although it is lower than the surrounding mountains, yet the hills on which it is built rise high above the plain.

14. *the forest thereof*] *her forest*, i.e. of Jerusalem. The expression does not mean literal trees, of which there was nothing like a forest in the neighbourhood of the city, but denotes either the houses clustering together like a forest, or more generally, the beauty and grandeur of the place. Compare for the general sense note on *Gilead*, etc. chap. xxii. 6; also Is. x. 34, where Sennacherib, king of Assyria, is likened to "the thickets of the forests," and to "Lebanon."

CHAP. XXII. 1—9. A FURTHER EXHORTATION TO AMEND.

1. *Thus saith the Lord*] This section is of the same general cha-

of Judah, and speak there this word, and say, Hear the 2
word of the LORD, O king of Judah, that sittest upon the
throne of David, thou, and thy servants, and thy people
that enter in by these gates: Thus saith the LORD; Execute 3
ye judgment and righteousness, and deliver the spoiled out
of the hand of the oppressor; and do no wrong, do no
violence, to the stranger, the fatherless, nor the widow, neither shed innocent blood in this place. For if ye do this 4
thing indeed, then shall there enter in by the gates of this
house kings sitting upon the throne of David, riding in
chariots and on horses, he, and his servants, and his people.
But if ye will not hear these words, I swear by myself, saith 5
the LORD, that this house shall become a desolation. For 6
thus saith the LORD unto the king's house of Judah; Thou
art Gilead unto me, *and* the head of Lebanon: *yet* surely I

racter as the four verses preceding it—exhortation mingled with threats
and promises. It is followed by remarks on Jehoahaz (10—12), Jehoiakim (13—19), and Jehoiachin (24—30). Chaps. xxii—xxiv. were probably sent by Jeremiah in writing to king Zedekiah. They consist of
prophecies uttered from time to time, possibly now modified somewhat
in language, as they were thus re-issued, to suit the needs of the present
occasion. That they were not the utterance of the moment, e.g. that
when the words were originally uttered the siege was not yet in progress,
we gather from such notices as that of ver. 2, 'thou, thy servants, and
thy people that *enter in by these gates.*'

Go down] from the temple towards the king's house, which was on
lower ground. Compare xxxvi. 10—12.

2. *these gates*] The prophet was probably to address the king surrounded by his retinue in this place of public resort. See note on xxi. 12.

3. This evidently refers to the special crimes of Jehoiakim more fully
stated elsewhere.

do no wrong] applying equally with 'do no violence' to the words
which follow. The reference is to the king's oppression of his own
people in order to build himself sumptuous palaces and at the same
time pay tribute to Pharaoh Nechoh. See verses 13—17; 2 Kings
xxiii. 35.

neither shed innocent blood] For the significance of this prohibition
as applied to Jehoiakim see xxvi. 20—23; 2 Kings xxiv. 4.

4. See notes on xvii. 25.

people] subjects.

5. *shall become a desolation*] *A fire* is what is threatened in the
parallel passage xvii. 27.

6. *unto*] or, *concerning*.

Gilead unto me, and the head of Lebanon] 'And' should be omitted.

will make thee a wilderness *and* cities *which* are not inhabi-
7 ted. And I will prepare destroyers against thee, every one
with his weapons: and they shall cut down thy choice
8 cedars, and cast *them* into the fire. And many nations shall
pass by this city, and they shall say every man to his neighbour, Wherefore hath the LORD done thus unto this great
9 city? Then they shall answer, Because they have forsaken
the covenant of the LORD their God, and worshipped other
gods, and served them.

10. *Lament for Jehoahaz.*

10   Weep ye not for the dead, neither bemoan him:

The comparison is to the things that are most precious. Gilead was remarkable for its balm (see notes on viii. 22), and for its flocks of goats
(Cant. iv. 1, vi. 5). Here however from the union of the word with
Lebanon the reference probably is to the woods of its hill country on
either side of the river Jabbok, which flowed through the midst of it.
The head of Lebanon will denote the forests (Ps. lxxii. 16; Is.
xxxvii. 24) which crowned its highest parts. To these the king's palace
might well be likened (compare ver. 23). "It lay on the north-east-
ern eminence of Mount Zion, and contained the so-called forest-house
of Lebanon (1 Kings vii. 2, etc.)." Keil.

I will make thee a wilderness] Jeremiah goes suddenly back from
figurative language to matter of fact. For this as one of his characteristics see note on chap. vi. 3.

and cities] **cities.** We should have expected *city*. The plural is
probably used because the palace of the king represented, and is therefore treated as equivalent to, the dwellings of the whole people throughout the land. The desolating of the one involved that of the others.

7. *prepare*] **sanctify.** See note on vi. 4, and compare Is. xiii. 3
("sanctified ones"), in both of which passages the Heb. word is the same
as here.

thy choice cedars] either the forest-house of Lebanon (see note on
ver. 6) or, better, the chief men of the state.

8, 9. The same language is used elsewhere of the land (Deut. xxix.
24—26) and of Solomon's Temple (1 Kings ix. 8, 9).

8. *every man to his neighbour*] *to one another.* The text is a literal
rendering of a common Heb. idiom.

10. LAMENT FOR JEHOAHAZ.

10. This is the first of the sections which treat consecutively of the
three immediate predecessors of Zedekiah. The sense of the verse
is that even the fate of Josiah, who was slain in battle at Megiddo
(2 Kings xxiii. 29), was preferable to that of his son and successor, who

But weep sore for him that goeth away:
For he shall return no more,
Nor see his native country.

11, 12. *The fate of Jehoahaz is determined.*

For thus saith the LORD touching Shallum the son of 11 Josiah king of Judah, which reigned instead of Josiah his father, which went forth out of this place; He shall not return thither any more: but he shall die in the place 12 whither they have led him captive, and shall see this land no more.

was carried captive to Egypt only to die in that strange land (2 Kings xxiii. 34).

Weep ye not for the dead] We know (2 Chron. xxxv. 25) that the lamentations for Josiah came to be a fixed custom.

weep sore for him...no more] This expression is applied also by the Jews to one who dies childless, who cannot 'return' (live again) in his posterity, and thus has no hope of having the Messiah among his direct descendants. See Edersheim's *Sketches of Jewish Social Life*, p. 98.

11, 12. THE FATE OF JEHOAHAZ IS DETERMINED.

11. *Shallum*] The only other place where this name is given to a son of Josiah is the genealogical list of 1 Chron. iii. 15. But there Shallum appears as the fourth son, whereas we gather from the narrative in the Kings that Jehoahaz, although younger than Jehoiakim, was about fourteen years older than Zedekiah (2 Kings xxiii. 31, 36, xxiv. 18). Thus we conclude that the Shallum mentioned in 1 Chron. is quite a distinct person, not elsewhere spoken of, and there is some ground for believing that the Johanan of that list=Shallum of this verse. Thus the name Shallum would be that which he originally bore, Jehoahaz (*the Lord shall help*) that which he assumed when made king, and Johanan (if indeed this be the same person) a name (*the Lord is gracious*) assumed by or given him on some other occasion. According to this last supposition the title "first-born" given to Johanan in the list in Chronicles would express not the literal fact but the legal position which was given him, and which may have been either the cause or the consequence of his having precedence of his elder brother Jehoiakim as regards the throne. Other hypotheses to account for the name Shallum here are unlikely, e.g. (i) that it had reference to the shortness of his reign, as alluding to Shallum king of Israel, who was king for one month (2 Kings xv. 13), or (ii) that it means the requited one (from the sense of the Heb. root), him whom God had marked out for punishment.

king of Judah] referring to Shallum. See note on *the priest* xxi. 1.

Jehoahaz had represented the anti-Egyptian policy, which Jeremiah had always urged. (Hence his deposition by Pharaoh Nechoh.) "This

13—23. *Censure of Jehoiakim, of whose crimes captivity was the result.*

13 Woe unto him that buildeth his house by unrighteousness,
And his chambers by wrong;
That useth his neighbour's service without wages,
And giveth him not *for* his work;
14 That saith, I will build me a wide house, and large chambers,
And cutteth him out windows;
And *it is* cieled with cedar, and painted with vermilion.
15 Shalt thou reign, because thou closest *thyself* in cedar?

may account for the tenderness and pity with which Jeremiah speaks of him in his Egyptian exile." *Sm. Bibl. Dict.* I. 967 *b*.

13—23. CENSURE OF JEHOIAKIM, OF WHOSE CRIMES CAPTIVITY WAS THE RESULT.

13. *that buildeth his house by unrighteousness*] Jehoiakim, as though it were not enough to involve the land in a heavy tribute to the king of Egypt, exacted forced labour from his own subjects that he might have a sumptuous palace built for himself.

chambers] **upper chambers.** The construction of these without such aid as is afforded by modern appliances would naturally cause most difficulty and so give rise to most dissatisfaction.

for his work] **his hire.** The Heb. word occurs in the same sense Job vii. 2 ("work"), and another form of it Lev. xix. 13 ("wages").

14. *large*] This, and not the marginal *through-aired*, is the right rendering.

chambers] **upper chambers.**

cutteth him out] The word in the Hebrew is the same as that translated "rentest" in iv. 30. As there it was used of the eyes of the body, so here of those of the house, *maketh wide*.

windows] The Heb. word is unusual in its form, and it has been also explained as *my windows*, or *his windows*, or *windowy* (i.e. an adjective, *house* being understood).

it is cieled] or, *roofing it*, by a slight change of one letter in the original.

vermilion] the red sulphuret of mercury, or *cinnabar*.

15. *Shalt thou reign*] Dost thou expect that such a course will prolong thy reign? or, perhaps better, Dost thou think that to be a king merely means self-indulgence?

closest thyself] **viest in cedar (palaces),** or, according to others, **viest with the cedar,** the same word as that rendered "contend" in xii. 5, which is its natural sense. The context sufficiently suggests his ancestor Solomon with his cedar-palaces as the person whom he sought to rival.

Did not thy father eat and drink,
And do judgment and justice,
And then *it was* well with him?
He judged the cause of the poor and needy; then *it was* well *with him:* 16
Was not this to know me? saith the Lord.
But thine eyes and thine heart *are* not but for thy covetousness, 17
And for to shed innocent blood,
And for oppression, and for violence, to do *it.*
Therefore thus saith the Lord concerning Jehoiakim the son of Josiah king of Judah; 18
They shall not lament for him, *saying,* Ah my brother! or, Ah sister!
They shall not lament for him, *saying,* Ah lord! or, Ah his glory.
He shall be buried *with* the burial of an ass, 19

My father] Josiah.
16. *Was not this to know me*] In choosing what was righteous he shewed himself acquainted with the character of Him whose pleasure he was doing.
17. *covetousness*] gain. This was sought (i) by oppression and forced labour, (ii) by putting to death on false charges and seizing upon the possessions of the victims.
innocent blood] See note on ver. 3. Jehoiakim "remained fixed in the recollections of his countrymen, as the last example of those cruel, selfish, luxurious princes, the natural product of Oriental monarchies, the disgrace of the monarchy of David." (Stanley's *Jewish Church,* II. 448).
18. *Jehoiakim*] now at last mentioned by name.
Ah my brother!] the lamentation of relations shall be wanting.
Ah sister!] a general expression denoting the sorrow felt for the loss of a near relation, and introduced here probably for the sake of the parallelism.
Ah lord! or, Ah his glory] the lamentations of subjects and friends, those outside his family.
19. *buried with the burial of an ass*] i.e. as the succeeding words explain, *cast forth dishonoured.* The fulfilment of this is not recorded. The accounts of the time are very brief both in the Kings and Chronicles. For the probable circumstances of the case see Introduction chap. i. § 13. The assertion that Jehoiakim "slept with his fathers" (2 Kings xxiv. 6) does not in any way clash with this passage or with the parallel one which occurs later in this book (xxxvi. 30). The same is said of Ahab, although dying in battle (1 Kings xxii. 40); besides which the fact that Baruch

Drawn and cast forth beyond the gates of Jerusalem.
20 Go up *to* Lebanon, and cry; and lift up thy voice in Bashan,
And cry from the passages:
For all thy lovers are destroyed.
21 I spake unto thee in thy prosperity;
But thou saidst, I will not hear.
This *hath been* thy manner from thy youth,
That thou obeyedst not my voice.
22 The wind shall eat up all thy pastors,
And thy lovers shall go into captivity:
Surely then shalt thou be ashamed and confounded for all thy wickedness.
23 O inhabitant of Lebanon, that makest thy nest in the cedars,
How gracious shalt thou be when pangs come upon thee,
The pain as of a woman in travail.

included this among Jeremiah's prophecies at a date subsequent to Jehoiakim's death shews that no difficulty as to the fulfilment was felt then, when all the circumstances, whatever they may have been, were still fresh in men's memories.

20. The prophet now, as an introduction to his lamentation over the next king Jehoiachin (Coniah) bewails the consequences of the policy of that king's father Jehoiakim. The people, under the figure of a woman as on former occasions (see xxi. 13), is called upon to ascend the heights which the Chaldaean hosts would successively pass in their advance southwards upon Jerusalem, viz. Lebanon in the north, the hills of Bashan (Ps. lxviii. 15, 16) in the north-east, and Abarim in the south-east.

passages] **Abarim**, a range of mountains to the south-east of Palestine. One of them was Nebo, from which Moses viewed the land (Deut. xxxii. 49).

thy lovers] Egypt and the other nations, with whom many of the people were disposed to unite against the Chaldaean power. They are enumerated in xxvii. 3.

21. *prosperity*] times of prosperity (literally, *prosperities*).

22. *eat up*] *depasture.* There is a play intended on the word *pastors* which follows.

pastors] See notes on ii. 8, and xvii. 16. Thy leaders, in whom thou hast confidence, shall be borne away into exile by the wind of adversity.

23. *inhabitant of Lebanon*] in reference to the cedar palaces of the king and his nobles. See ver. 6.

how gracious shalt thou be] **how shalt thou groan**, or perhaps better, **how pitiable shalt thou be.** A difficult expression in the Hebrew.

24—30. *The judgment upon Jehoiachin.*

As I live, saith the LORD, though Coniah the son of Je- 24 hoiakim king of Judah were the signet upon my right hand, yet would I pluck thee thence; and I will give thee into the 25 hand of them that seek thy life, and into the hand *of them* whose face thou fearest, even into the hand of Nebuchadrezzar king of Babylon, and into the hand of the Chaldeans. And I will cast thee out, and thy mother that bare thee, 26 into another country, where ye were not born; and there shall ye die. But to the land whereunto they desire to 27 return, thither shall they not return. *Is* this man Coniah a 28 despised broken idol? *is he* a vessel wherein *is* no pleasure? wherefore are they cast out, he and his seed, and are cast

24—30. THE JUDGMENT UPON JEHOIACHIN.

24. *Coniah*] called also *Jeconiah* xxiv. 1, xxvii. 20, xxviii. 4, xxix. 2; 1 Chron. iii. 16; Esth. ii. 6, and *Jehoiachin* lii. 31; 2 Kings xxiv. 6, etc.; 2 Chron. xxxvi. 8, 9. All three names have the same sense, *The Lord will establish.* The change to Jehoiachin, as in the case of his uncle Jehoahaz (the Shallum of ver. 11), was probably made on his accession to the throne. Here therefore Jeremiah calls him by his former name.

king of Judah] shewing that it was during his reign that this section of the prophecy was delivered.

signet] even though he were as dear as a precious stone, set by way of seal in a signet ring, is to the owner. Jehoiachin's conduct, though not directly mentioned here, is marked with sufficient clearness in 2 Kings xxiv. 9, and Ezek. xix. 5—9, where he is likened to a young lion that "devoured men" and "laid waste their cities."

26. *thy mother*] See note on xiii. 18.

and there shall ye die] He was detained in prison at Babylon for thirty-six years, until released by Evil-Merodach, son and successor of Nebuchadnezzar, who nevertheless retained him in a sort of honourable captivity for the rest of his days (chap. lii. 31—34), which were probably not very many. At the end of two years Evil-Merodach himself was slain.

27. *desire*] literally, *are lifting up their soul.*

28. *idol*] **vessel**, a piece of earthenware cast out as useless.

and his seed] He was eighteen years of age, when he came to the throne (2 Kings xxiv. 8). The number "eight" which stands in 2 Chron. xxxvi. 9 is probably an error in transcription. Hence he may have had at least one son at this time. The expression 'and his seed' may however be quite a general one, implying merely that he is driven into exile, so as not to have a son who shall rule after him. The bewailing of the fate of Coniah seems from the following verse to be due rather to the fact that thus the line of kings was cut off, than to any personal excellence of his own.

₂₉ into a land which they know not? O earth, earth, earth,
₃₀ hear the word of the LORD. Thus saith the LORD, Write ye this man childless, a man *that* shall not prosper in his days: for no man of his seed shall prosper, sitting upon the throne of David, and ruling any more in Judah.

CHAP. XXIII. 1—4. *A remnant shall return and unrighteous be replaced by righteous rulers.*

23 Woe be unto *the* pastors that destroy and scatter the
2 sheep of my pasture! saith the LORD. Therefore thus saith the LORD God of Israel against the pastors that feed my people; Ye have scattered my flock, and driven them away, and have not visited them: behold, I will visit upon you
3 the evil of your doings, saith the LORD. And I will gather the remnant of my flock out of all countries whither I have

29. *O earth, earth, earth*] Compare for the repetition chap. vii. 4. Here probably *land* would better give the sense. His country is to have a lasting lesson impressed upon it.

30. *Write ye*] addressed to those who kept a record of such things in the family registers.

childless] In 1 Chron. iii. 17, etc. he appears to have had children, and Salathiel (Matt. i. 12) is reckoned as his son. Salathiel was however descended from David through his son Nathan (Lk. iii. 27—31) and not through the line of the kings (Solomon, Rehoboam, etc.), and thus was only counted to Jehoiachin (Jeconias of Matt. i. 12) according to the *legal* not the *natural* line. It was thus at any rate true that no child of Jehoiachin succeeded to the throne.

CHAP. XXIII. 1—4. A REMNANT SHALL RETURN AND UNRIGHTEOUS BE REPLACED BY RIGHTEOUS RULERS.

1. *Woe be unto the pastors*] To the rebukes directed against individual kings the prophet adds a few words in condemnation of those in high places generally.

the pastors] **shepherds** (omitting *the*), rulers of the state as a whole. See notes on ii. 8 and xvii. 16.

pasture] *pasturing*.

2. *against*] better, *concerning*.

scattered] by leading them into idolatry, as well as by literal scattering of them by exile, voluntary or forced, in Egypt or Babylon.

driven them away] the very opposite of that which is an Eastern shepherd's duty, viz. to go before his flock, leading them to pasture or fold (Is. xl. 11; John x. 3, 4).

visited...visit upon] The twofold sense of the Hebrew word is kept up in the English. Because the shepherds have not visited their flock for good, they shall themselves be visited with punishment.

driven them, and will bring them again to their folds; and they shall be fruitful and increase. And I will set up shep- 4 herds over them which shall feed them: and they shall fear no more, nor be dismayed, neither shall they be lacking, saith the LORD.

5—8. *Promise of the Messiah.*

Behold, the days come, saith the LORD, that I will raise 5 unto David a righteous Branch, and a King shall reign and prosper, and shall execute judgment and justice in the

3. *I have driven*] The deed with which the pastors were charged in ver. 2 is here attributed to God. It was by His act that the people were driven out, although it was brought about through the sins of their rulers.

folds] *pastures* (but no connexion in the original with the word *pasture* of ver. 1); the same word as that rendered *pasturage* in a note on chap. vi. 2. Properly speaking it combines the sense of habitation and pasture, and thus is specially suitable in a passage like this, where the people are spoken of under the figure of a flock. See also note on xxv. 30.

4. *lacking*] missing, like sheep which in the absence of the shepherd have become the prey of wild beasts.

5—8. PROMISE OF THE MESSIAH.

5. The mention of good shepherds serves as the introduction to one of the few clear Messianic prophecies of Jeremiah. Besides this we have xxxiii. 15—18, and less plainly xxx. 9, where see note.

the days come] The phrase, according to Jeremiah's employment of it (compare ver. 7, xxx. 3, xxxi. 27, 31, 38, xxxiii. 14), implies a special call to note the announcement thus introduced. In spite of the troubles which are now gathering round them there are none the less surely days of deliverance coming.

Branch] *Germ, Sprout.* The word (*tsemach*) is the same as that used chap. xxxiii. 15, and in Zech. iii. 8 and vi. 12, and means rather that which is immediately connected with the root, and contains as it were the spring of life, which passes out from it downwards through the root and upwards through the stem and branches. The word used in Is. xi. 1 on the other hand (*netzer*) denotes *branch* properly so called. Some have sought to explain the word found in this place as used in a collective sense (posterity generally). But although the word is often used collectively of literal plants, yet in this passage it plainly points to an individual Messiah, on whom the nation's hopes should rest. This is proved by the words immediately following in this verse, as well as by the passages in Zechariah just now adduced, where it is explicitly said to have reference to an individual.

a King shall reign] or, *he shall reign as King.*

and prosper] *and do wisely* is a better rendering here. See notes on x. 21 and xx. 11.

6 earth. In his days Judah shall be saved, and Israel shall dwell safely: and this *is* his name whereby he shall be called, 7 THE LORD OUR RIGHTEOUSNESS. Therefore behold, the days come, saith the LORD, that they shall no more say, The LORD liveth, which brought up the children 8 of Israel out of the land of Egypt; but, The LORD liveth, which brought up and which led the seed of the house of Israel out of the north country, and from all countries whither I had driven them; and they shall dwell in their own land.

9—14. *Rebuke of Prophets and Priests.*

9 Mine heart within me is broken because of the prophets;

execute judgment and justice] Exactly the same expression is used of David, the ancestor of the Messiah, in 2 Sam. viii. 15.

6. *Israel shall dwell safely*] a reminiscence of Deut. xxxiii. 28.

safely] securely.

he shall be called] Because the name that follows is in xxxiii. 16 given to Jerusalem, some few commentators have tried to make it refer to 'Israel' here. But the general sense of the passage is quite opposed to such a view. The Messiah's work shall be indicated by the name that He is to bear.

The Lord our Righteousness] *Jehovah Tsidkenu* is the Heb. If we render as the Eng. Vers., we may assign either of two senses to the name; (i) the Messiah is called Lord and also our righteousness, because through His merits and death we are justified from sin; (ii) *He by Whom the Lord grants us righteousness*, just as in xxxiii. 16 Jerusalem, as representing the repentant and restored Church, is called by the same name, as being that through which the Lord will work righteousness. In either case the Messiah is spoken of as Mediator between God and man, and therefore as joining in Himself the natures of both. A preferable rendering however is that proposed by Bp. Thirlwall (*Remains*, III. p. 471), on the analogy of Jehovah-Shammah (marginal for "The Lord is there," Ezek. xlviii. 35), **The Lord is our Righteousness**. In this way either, as here, the Messiah, or, as there, Jerusalem is called by a name implying "that in the Messianic times Jehovah is to be the righteousness of Jerusalem, to bestow righteousness upon her with all its attendant blessings." Compare Ps. xlvi. 5; Is. xlv. 24; Rev. xxi. 3, 4.

7, 8. These verses have already occurred with but slight differences as xvi. 14, 15. There they served to throw a gleam upon the dark prospect of captivity, here they seem to have been introduced by the prophet in order to connect the national restoration with Messianic hopes.

9—14. REBUKE OF PROPHETS AND PRIESTS.

9. *because of the prophets*] This should rather come as the introduc-

All my bones shake;
I am like a drunken man,
And like a man whom wine hath overcome,
Because of the LORD, and because of the words of his holiness.
For the land is full *of* adulterers; · 10
For because of swearing the land mourneth;
The pleasant places of the wilderness are dried up,
And their course is evil, and their force *is* not right.
For both prophet and priest are profane; 11
Yea, in my house have I found their wickedness, saith the LORD.
Wherefore their way shall be unto them as slippery *ways* 12 in the darkness:
They shall be driven on, and fall therein:
For I will bring evil upon them, *even* the year of their visitation, saith the LORD.
And I have seen folly in the prophets of Samaria; 13

tion to the section, *Concerning* the prophets. The Hebrew would indeed bear the sense which the Eng. Vers. gives, but the other is the preferable rendering, as the prophet's reason for being heart-broken is given elsewhere in the verse ('because of the Lord,' etc.).

the words of his holiness] the words which He in the holiness of His nature had put forth concerning the wicked doings of the false prophets.

10. *adulterers*] viz.:—the false prophets. The word may be employed here in the secondary sense of idolatry which it often bears in Jeremiah, as even those who professed to be prophets of the true God may have been guilty in this manner.

swearing] violation of the third Commandment in any form.

mourneth] referring very possibly to the drought of Josiah's days, and thus determining approximately the date of the first utterance of this section of the prophecy.

not right] See note on chap. viii. 6.

11. *in my house have I found their wickedness*] Here again it is uncertain whether the wickedness was like that of Eli's sons, or such idolatry as we know was practised in Manasseh's time and later within the Temple precincts (2 Kings xxi. 5, xxiii. 12).

12. *ways*] or, *places*. Ps. xxxv. 6 was probably in the prophet's mind here.

driven on] *thrust down.*

even the year of their visitation] See note on xi. 23.

13. *folly*] literally, that which is tasteless, hence irrational, an

They prophesied in Baal,
And caused my people Israel to err.
14 I have seen also in the prophets of Jerusalem a horrible thing:
They commit adultery, and walk in lies:
They strengthen also the hands of evildoers,
That none doth return from his wickedness:
They are all of them unto me as Sodom,
And the inhabitants thereof as Gomorrah.

15—32. *Rebuke of the Prophets continued.*

15 Therefore thus saith the LORD of hosts concerning the prophets; Behold, I will feed them with wormwood, and make them drink the water of gall: for from the prophets of Jerusalem is profaneness gone forth into all the land.
16 Thus saith the LORD of hosts, Hearken not unto the words of the prophets that prophesy unto you: they make you

epithet naturally applied to idolatry, an idol being "nothing in the world" (1 Cor. viii. 4). See notes on i. 16, ii. 5.
prophets of Samaria] They were simply idolaters, who made no secret of their belief or practice. The prophets of Jerusalem on the other hand were thoroughly immoral besides.
in Baal] i.e. in his name. For Baal see note on ii. 8.
14. *I have seen also*] **But I have seen.** There is a contrast intended between the prophets of the two places.
They commit adultery, and walk in lies] more literally, *committing adultery and walking in falsehood*.
They strengthen] by their indifference to good as well as by their direct encouragement of evil.
are] *are become*.
all of them] all the inhabitants of Jerusalem.
thereof] of Jerusalem.

15—32. REBUKE OF THE PROPHETS CONTINUED.

15. *Behold, I will......*] The language is identical with that of ix. 15, where however the reference is to the people as a whole.
will feed] am feeding.
wormwood] Compare Deut. xxix. 18; Prov. v. 4; Lam. iii. 15. Wormwood "belongs to the genus Artemisia, a genus of the Composite family, of which there are many species... They are generally of a hoary aspect and of a strong aromatic odour, and all have a strong bitter taste." J. Smith's *History of Bible Plants*, pp. 66, 67.
water of gall] See note on chap. viii. 14.

vain: they speak a vision of their own heart, *and* not out of the mouth of the LORD. They say still unto them 17 that despise me, The LORD hath said, Ye shall have peace; and they say *unto* every one that walketh after the imagination of his own heart, No evil shall come upon you. For 18 who hath stood in the counsel of the LORD, and hath perceived and heard his word? who hath marked his word, and heard *it*? Behold, a whirlwind of the LORD is gone 19 forth *in* fury, even a grievous whirlwind: it shall fall grievously upon the head of the wicked. The anger of 20

16. *make you vain*] deceive you with vain hopes, speak peace to those who are going on still in wicked courses. Compare next verse. This is a test whereby the false may be distinguished from the true prophet.

of their own heart] devised by themselves, the heart being considered as the seat of the *intellect*. Hence the expression does not mean, in accordance with their own *wishes*, however true that was.

17. *still*] *continually.*

The Lord hath said] The Heb. is an expression which does not elsewhere introduce the words of the Lord. It therefore seems to be here used by Jeremiah as characteristic of the false prophets.

unto every one] more literally, *as to every one.*

imagination] **stubbornness.** See iii. 17.

18. *who hath stood*] meaning, that at any rate these *false* prophets had not done so.

counsel] *familiar intercourse.*

and hath perceived and heard] rather, *that he should perceive and hear.*

who hath marked his word] *who hath marked* **my word?** The Heb. has both readings, but the latter, as being less likely to be substituted by a copyist for the former, is preferable. The sudden change of person ('heard *his* word...marked *my* word') in such cases is far from rare in the prophets. Their personality was, so to speak, identified for the time with Him who spoke through them.

19. *a whirlwind*] **a tempest.**

in fury] rather, *even fury*, an explanation of *tempest.*

a grievous whirlwind] *a whirling tempest.* The last word is virtually the same in the Heb. (differing only in gender) with that rendered 'tempest' above. There is no authority for inserting the word 'grievous' in the Eng. Vers.

shall fall grievously] literally, *shall whirl*, the same word in the Heb. as 'whirling' above.

Dreams were of course actually sent from time to time from God (i.e. Gen. xx. 3, xxxi. 24; Numb. xii. 6; 1 Kings iii. 5, etc.). Another kind of test therefore, by which to recognise the true prophet, was required, and this and the next verse give us the sort of message which the false

the Lord shall not return, until he have executed, and till he have performed the thoughts of his heart: in the
21 latter days ye shall consider it perfectly. I have not sent *these* prophets, yet they ran: I have not spoken to them, yet
22 they prophesied. But if they had stood in my counsel, and had caused my people to hear my words, then they should have turned them from their evil way, and from the evil of
23 their doings. *Am* I a God at hand, saith the Lord, and
24 not a God afar off? Can any hide himself in secret places that I shall not see him? saith the Lord. Do not I fill
25 heaven and earth? saith the Lord. I have heard what the prophets said, that prophesy lies in my name, saying, I
26 have dreamed, I have dreamed. How long shall *this* be in the heart of the prophets that prophesy lies? yea, *they are*
27 prophets of the deceit of their own heart; which think to cause my people to forget my name by their dreams which

prophets never thought of bearing, and by which therefore a true prophet might be known. The two verses occur again with slight changes chap. xxx. 23, 24.

20. *the latter days*] in after time, when punishment shall have given you spiritual insight, probably not, as the phrase sometimes means, in the days of the Messiah.

consider] **understand.**

21. *ran*] were eager to act as though in my name, thrust themselves into an office to which they have not been called.

22. *my counsel*] See ver. 18.

and had caused] **then they would have caused.**

then they should have turned] **and would have turned.**

23. *a God at hand*] Do ye think that my knowledge is subject to human limitations, so that false prophets may escape my sight?

24. *Can any*] **Or can any.**

25. *I have dreamed, I have dreamed*] These were the words with which they caught the ear of the crowd, and so gained a sure hearing for their pretended revelations.

26. *How long shall this be...*] This and the following verse consist rather of two questions, the first being broken off short and the second undergoing in the middle a change of construction. *How long* (shall this state of things continue)? *Is it in the mind of the prophets that prophesy falsehood and the prophets of the deceit of their heart—do they think to make my people forget my name by their dreams which they declare every man to his neighbour, as their fathers forgot my name by (reason of) Baal?*

How long] For a question thus broken off compare xiii. 27; Ps. vi. 3, xc. 13; Is. vi. 11.

they tell every man to his neighbour, as their fathers have forgotten my name for Baal. The prophet that hath a 28 dream, let him tell a dream; and he that hath my word, let him speak my word faithfully. What *is* the chaff to the wheat? saith the LORD. *Is* not my word like as a fire? 29 saith the LORD; and like a hammer *that* breaketh the rock in pieces? Therefore behold, I *am* against the prophets, 30 saith the LORD, that steal my words every one from his neighbour. Behold, I *am* against the prophets, saith the 31 LORD, that use their tongues, and say, He saith. Behold, I 32

27. *every man to his neighbour*] *one to another*, each prophet to those who will listen.

for Baal] *by (reason of) Baal*, as above. As idolatry of that form had led earlier generations astray, so pretended revelations were doing the same work now.

28. Mere dreams and the truth of God are to be kept asunder.

faithfully] *in truth*.

What is the chaff to the wheat?] God's word contains nourishment and life. Other words are but as chaff, or rather **straw**.

29. This verse, while adding other characteristics of God's word, viz. penetration and power, forms at the same time a suitable introduction to the threatenings against the false prophets that follow.

like as a fire] literally, *thus—like a fire*. *Thus* is to call attention to the figure that follows. The true word of God consumes all that cannot abide the test, and breaks down the most stony resistance. For this last characteristic of it, though from a somewhat different point of view, compare xx. 8, 9.

30. Imitation of the phrases of the true prophets, and the unauthorised use or even fabrication of dreams to suit their purpose, are the two features of the false prophets' teaching brought out in these three verses.

I am against] *I am upon*, I am even now descending upon them with punishment (and so in next verse).

steal my words] They have themselves no revelation to impart, and therefore proclaim as their own that which has been said by others. Inasmuch as the words which they thus steal are God's, those others from whom they thus steal will include the prophets of God, in whose mouths those words formed a coherent and true testimony, as well as other false prophets, who had previously appropriated and marred these fragments of actual revelation.

31. *use*] literally, *take*. The tongue is the only weapon which they have to use.

He saith] This phrase, borrowed from the true prophets, will, they expect, help their sayings to pass as genuine.

By the side of the Party of the Nobles "perhaps opposed to them, perhaps allied with them, in that strange combination which often

am against them that prophesy false dreams, saith the LORD, and do tell them, and cause my people to err by their lies, and by their lightness; yet I sent them not, nor commanded them: therefore they shall not profit this people at all, saith the LORD.

33—40. *The eternal disgrace of false Prophets and Priests.*

33 And when this people, or the prophet, or a priest, shall ask thee, saying, What *is* the burden of the LORD? thou shalt then say unto them, What burden? I will even forsake you, saith 34 the LORD. And *as for* the prophet, and the priest, and the people, that shall say, The burden of the LORD, I will even 35 punish that man and his house. Thus shall ye say every one to his neighbour, and every one to his brother, What hath the LORD answered? and, What hath the LORD 36 spoken? And the burden of the LORD shall ye mention no

brings together, for purposes of political or religious animosity, parties themselves most alien to each other, was the great body of the Sacerdotal, and even of the Prophetic order. There were those who directly lent themselves to magical rites...who recited the old prophetic phrases, often careless of what they meant." Stanley's *J. Ch.* II. 438.

32. *therefore*] or simply *and*.

33—40. THE ETERNAL DISGRACE OF FALSE PROPHETS AND PRIESTS.

33. *What is the burden*] The word burden, meaning in the prophets a saying of weight concerning some approaching trouble, would be used jestingly by such persons as are here described. "What new prophecy hast thou for us to hear? At any rate we will warrant it to be a mournful one."

What burden?] If the Heb. reading of which this is a translation be the right one, these two words are repeated by the prophet from the question, in order that he may reply in the words that follow (keeping up the thought of *burden*), "I will even forsake you, or rather, **I will even cast you away** (*disburthen* myself of you)." It is very possible however that we should read *Ye are the burden*, in which case the words that follow have even more point. This reading is obtained merely by a different division of the words in the Heb., and does not involve any change of letters.

35. For the future the actual utterances of the Lord are alone to be sought.

answered] when the people have sought counsel.

spoken] without such enquiries.

36. *the burden of the Lord shall ye mention no more*] "The very name of the 'burden of the Lord,' which had summed up the burning

more: for every man's word shall be his burden; for ye have perverted the words of the living God, of the LORD of hosts our God. Thus shalt thou say to the prophet, What ₃₇ hath the LORD answered thee? and, What hath the LORD spoken? But sith ye say, The burden of the LORD; there- ₃₈ fore thus saith the LORD; Because you say this word, The burden of the LORD, and I have sent unto you, saying, Ye shall not say, The burden of the LORD; therefore behold, ₃₉ I, even I, will utterly forget you, and I will forsake you, and the city that I gave you and your fathers, *and cast you* out of my presence: and I will bring an everlasting reproach ₄₀ upon you, and a perpetual shame, which shall not be forgotten.

CHAP. XXIV. 1—10. *The two baskets of Figs.*

The LORD shewed me, and behold, two baskets of figs 24

thoughts of Amos and Isaiah, was to be discontinued altogether." Stanley's *J. Ch.* II. 445.

every man's word shall be his burden] **every man's burden shall be his** (use of the) **word**. He who has jokingly enquired after the 'burden of the Lord' shall find that those lightly spoken words of his are in very deed the heaviest load to bear.

perverted] used jestingly, twisted from their solemn purpose.

38. *sith*] if. See also note on xv. 7.

39. *will utterly forget you*] The Heb. may also be rendered, *will assuredly take you up* (make you a *burden*). In either case there is certainly a play on the word for burden, which cannot be reproduced in English.

forsake] **cast away**. This saves us from the necessity of supplying with the Eng. Vers. 'and cast you' in the clause that follows.

and cast you out of] **from**.

CHAP. XXIV. 1—10. THE TWO BASKETS OF FIGS.

1. *The Lord shewed me*] This section of the message sent to Zedekiah (see notes on xxi. 1) is limited in its reference to the circumstances of that king's own reign.

two baskets of figs] The meaning of the vision is given with sufficient clearness in the subsequent verses. It was probably directed against a feeling which somewhat naturally arose in the minds of the people who had not been carried away in Jehoiakim's captivity, and who might contrast themselves favourably with those who had been thus removed. To them God here says that the real contrast is exactly the reverse of that which they suppose. Of the good and evil figs, the latter represent such as have failed to draw any improvement from the fate which has overtaken their brethren, while those who have been carried off to Babylon

were set before the temple of the LORD, after that Nebuchadrezzar king of Babylon had carried away captive Jeconiah the son of Jehoiakim king of Judah, and the princes of Judah, with the carpenters and smiths, from Jerusalem, and had brought them *to* Babylon. One basket *had* very good figs, *even* like the figs *that are* first ripe: and the other basket *had* very naughty figs, which could not be eaten, they were so bad. Then said the LORD unto me, What seest thou, Jeremiah? And I said, Figs; the good figs, very good; and the evil, very evil, that cannot be eaten, they are so evil. Again the word of the LORD came unto me, saying, Thus saith the LORD, the God of Israel; Like these good figs, so will I acknowledge them that are carried away captive of Judah, whom I have sent out of this place

shall yet be the subjects of God's love and grace. "With the exiles there are indeed some of the choicest spirits of the nation; Ezekiel, and Daniel (Dan. i. 1) with his three companions." Stanley's *J. Ch.* II. 459. Both the baskets contained fruit that had been gathered, and whose ripening time was therefore over, but here their likeness ceased. So both classes of the people, the exiles and those who for the time remained, had had their period of probation, but with results that on the whole differed essentially.

were set] **set**.
Nebuchadrezzar] See note on xxi. 2.
Jeconiah] See note on xxii. 24.
carpenters] **workmen**.

2. *the figs that are first ripe*] The proper time for gathering figs in Palestine is in August. Certain kinds of trees, however, bear twice in the year, in which case the first crop, ripening in June, are esteemed a special delicacy. See Hos. ix. 10; Mic. vii. 1; Nah. iii. 12.

naughty] The word "in modern usage is almost confined to the nursery, but in its original sense it is frequent in old writers.

'A *naughty* fellow, a seditious fellow; he maketh trouble and rebellion in the realm; he lacketh discretion.' Latimer, *Sermons*, p. 240.

'So shines a good deed in a *naughty* world.'
SHAKESPEARE, *Merch. of Ven.* V. 1."
Eastwood and Wright's *Bible Word-Book*.

"The bad figs may have been such either from having decayed and thus been reduced to a rotten condition, or as being the fruit of the sycamore, which contains a bitter juice." See Tristram's *Nat. Hist. of the Bible*, p. 399.

5. *so will I acknowledge*] As one looks with pleasure on good fruit, so will I **look upon**.

into the land of the Chaldeans for *their* good. For I will 6 set mine eyes upon them for good, and I will bring them again to this land: and I will build them, and not pull *them* down; and I will plant them, and not pluck *them* up. And I will give them a heart to know me, that I *am* the 7 LORD: and they shall be my people, and I will be their God: for they shall return unto me with their whole heart. And as the evil figs, which cannot be eaten, they are so 8 evil; surely thus saith the LORD, So will I give Zedekiah the king of Judah, and his princes, and the residue of Jerusalem, that remain in this land, and them that dwell in the land of Egypt: and I will deliver them to be removed into all 9 the kingdoms of the earth for *their* hurt, to be a reproach and a proverb, a taunt and a curse, in all places whither I shall drive them. And I will send the sword, the famine, 10 and the pestilence, among them, till they be consumed from off the land that I gave unto them and to their fathers.

for their good] belongs to 'acknowledge,' not to 'have sent.' This is shewn by such passages as ver. 6, chap. xxi. 10; Neh. v. 19; Amos ix. 4.

6. *eyes*] **eye.**

7. *a heart to know me*] The last verse announced their restoration to their land. The building and planting there spoken of are shewn to mean more than such a restoration. They shall be restored in a spiritual sense also, purified in heart by their adversity.

for] or, *when*.

8. *them that dwell in the land of Egypt*] This may have reference only to Jews who accompanied Jehoahaz when he was carried off by Pharaoh-nechoh (2 Kings xxiii. 34), or may indicate to us that others during the subsequent reigns also took refuge there, as being a kingdom opposed to the Babylonian power.

9. *to be removed*] **for dismay.** See note on xv. 4, where the same Heb. word is rendered *a terror*. The verse is the substance of Deut. xxviii. 25, 37.

10. The fresh captivity shall be preceded by the same horrors as before. Those who are represented by the evil figs were thus, still dwelling in the land, to be wasted by famine, pestilence and sword, while, notwithstanding the return of many from Babylon, the nation should thenceforward have its representatives living in exile throughout 'the kingdoms,' to be 'a reproach and a proverb, a taunt and a curse.'

CHAP. XXV. 1—7. *The long-continued Disobedience of the People.*

25 The word that came to Jeremiah concerning all the people of Judah in the fourth year of Jehoiakim the son of Josiah king of Judah, that *was* the first year of Nebuchad- 2 rezzar king of Babylon; the which Jeremiah the prophet spake unto all the people of Judah, and to all the inhabi- 3 tants of Jerusalem, saying, From the thirteenth year of Josiah the son of Amon king of Judah, even unto this day, that *is* the three and twentieth year, the word of the LORD

CHAP. XXV. 1—7. THE LONG-CONTINUED DISOBEDIENCE OF THE PEOPLE.

1. *The word that came*] The reply of the prophet to Zedekiah's message, comprised in the last four chapters, has come to an end. Accordingly we here return to a prophecy delivered during the time of Jehoiakim. It extends throughout the chapter. The latter part of ver. 13 however ("even all that...all the nations") is obviously an addition made on the occasion of its being added, perhaps by the prophet himself, perhaps by Baruch, to the collection of his prophecies. The object of this prophecy is to point out (i) the cause of the coming overthrow of Judah (verses 1—7), (ii) Babylon's victory and subsequent ruin (8—14), (iii) the wine-cup of God's fury to be drunk by all nations from Egypt to the Eastern kingdoms [Elam, Media and Babylon (15—29)], (iv) the judgment to come upon all peoples of the earth (30—38).

in the fourth year] Up to this period of Jeremiah's life we have not any prophecy so closely dated as the present. Compare chap. iii. 6 and xxvi. 1 ("In the beginning of the reign of Jehoiakim"). The addition of the year of Nebuchadrezzar serves to mark still more forcibly the fact that it was a turning-point in history (see Introduction, chap. I. § 12). The prophecy seems to have been delivered about 605 B.C., between the news of the victory of Nebuchadrezzar at Carchemish and the arrival of the Chaldaean army under the walls of Jerusalem. The main objects of the prophet were to point out the sins of the past, and to give advice for the future. That advice was to accept the result of the battle of Carchemish, to yield to Babylon as the power which God had appointed to bear rule over Palestine and the other kingdoms for the next seventy years, and to seek comfort at the same time from the knowledge that the enemy, whose authority the king and many of his people were so reluctant to recognise, would have his day and then in his turn perish, while brighter fortunes should dawn upon the people of God.

2. *spake unto all the people*] Thus we see that the time had not yet arrived, when Jeremiah was unable through fears for his life to go into any public place. See chap. xxxvi. 1, 5, 26.

3. *the three and twentieth year*] Josiah reigned thirty-one years, and it was in the thirteenth year of that king (chap. i. 2) that Jeremiah was

hath come unto me, and I have spoken unto you, rising early and speaking; but ye have not hearkened. And the 4 LORD hath sent unto you all his servants the prophets, rising early and sending *them;* but ye have not hearkened, nor inclined your ear to hear. *They* said, Turn ye again now 5 every one from his evil way, and from the evil of your doings, and dwell in the land that the LORD hath given unto you and to your fathers for ever and ever: and go not after 6 other gods to serve them, and to worship them, and provoke me not to anger with the works of your hands; and I will do you no hurt. Yet ye have not hearkened unto me, saith 7 the LORD; that *ye* might provoke me to anger with the works of your hands to your own hurt.

8—14. *Babylon's Victory and subsequent Ruin.*

Therefore thus saith the LORD of hosts; Because ye 8 have not heard my words, Behold, I will send and take 9 all the families of the north, saith the LORD, and Nebuchadrezzar the king of Babylon, my servant, and will bring them

called. He therefore prophesied for eighteen or nineteen years in that reign. To this we are to add the reign of Jehoahaz (three months), and more than three years of Jehoiakim.

rising early and speaking] See note on vii. 13.

4. *all his servants the prophets*] The people's wickedness was aggravated yet further by the fact that the call to repentance and amendment had come not from Jeremiah only, but from many other accredited messengers of God. Compare vii. 13, 25, xxxv. 15.

5. *They said*] more literally, *Saying.*

for ever and ever] literally, *from everlasting to everlasting.* The otherwise absolutely permanent character of that which they are forfeiting by their iniquity is strongly brought out by the expression.

7. *works of your hands*] idols. Described thus in contempt also xxxii. 30 (where see note). The expression is probably taken from Deut. xxxi. 29. In each case 'works' is literally *work*, and here only is it made plural in Eng. Vers.

8—14. BABYLON'S VICTORY AND SUBSEQUENT RUIN.

9. *the families of the north*] For these see chap. i. 14, 15.

families] races ascribing their descent to the same ancestor. Of these there would be many in the Babylonish empire. For this use of the word, as wider than that in which it is more familiar to us, see notes on iii. 14, and compare viii. 3.

and Nebuchadrezzar] *and* **to** *Nebuchadrezzar*, thus depending not on *take* but on *I will send.*

my servant] so called also in xxvii. 6 and xliii. 10. Compare Ezek. xxix. 19, 20 ("because *they wrought for me*, saith the Lord God").

against this land, and against the inhabitants thereof, and against all these nations round about, and will utterly destroy them, and make them an astonishment, and a ¹⁰hissing, and perpetual desolations. Moreover I will take from them the voice of mirth, and the voice of gladness, the voice of the bridegroom, and the voice of the bride, the sound of the millstones, and the light of the candle. ¹¹And this whole land shall be a desolation, *and* an astonishment; and these nations shall serve the king of Babylon ¹²seventy years. And it shall come to pass, when seventy years are accomplished, *that* I will punish the king of Babylon, and that nation, saith the LORD, for their iniquity,

an astonishment] *a destruction.* Compare v. 30 with note.
a hissing, and perpetual desolations] See note on xviii. 16, and compare xix. 8.
10. *the voice of mirth...*] Compare vii. 34 with note. Here mention of the millstones and of the candle (lamp) is added, to increase the force of the warning. Not only all sign of mirth, but also of domestic labour and social cheer, should vanish. See the same description somewhat amplified in Rev. xviii. 22, 23.
11. *a desolation, and an astonishment*] See ver. 9.
seventy years] This may mean (i) the duration of the Babylonish empire, or (ii) the length of the Jewish captivity in Babylon: (ii) is clearly the sense in xxix. 10. Here however (i) is rather suggested by the words 'these *nations*.' Either period can easily be shewn to have been *about* 70 years.

(i) The successive Sovereigns and the lengths of their reigns were Nebuchadnezzar 44 years, Evil-Merodach 2 years, Neriglissor 4 years, Nabonedus 17 years, in all 67 years. To this is to be prefixed the year that intervened between the capture of Jerusalem by Nebuchadnezzar and the death of his father Nabopolassar.

(ii) In this case the captivity will have to be reckoned, not from the deportation of Jehoiachin's time (2 Kings xxiv. 14—16), but from (605 B.C.) the 4th year of Jehoiakim ("the third year" Dan. i. 1—3) to (536 B.C.) the liberation under Cyrus.

In either case it is quite sufficient to make an approximation to the number seventy. The Jewish love for round numbers and especially for one so significant in symbolism, as having for its elements seven and ten, would cause the number seventy to their ears when used in such a connexion to stand for any number not differing by much from that amount. This must accordingly have been a deeply marked occasion for Jeremiah, when he learnt, as we may suppose for the first time, that there was no hope for those who like himself had come to anything like mature years, that they would see the end of the exile that was now at hand.

and the land of the Chaldeans, and will make it. perpetual desolations. And I will bring upon that land all my words which I have pronounced against it, *even* all that is written in this book, which Jeremiah hath prophesied against all the nations. For many nations and great kings shall serve themselves of them also: and I will recompense them according to their deeds, and according to the works of their own hands.

15—30. *The Wine-cup of God's fury is to be drunk by all the nations.*

For thus saith the LORD God of Israel unto me; Take

13. *even all that is written in this book, which Jeremiah hath prophesied against all the nations*] At this point there presents itself one of the most marked discrepancies between the Septuagint Version of Jeremiah and the Hebrew. (See Introduction, chap. III. §§ 8—12.) The Greek Version ends the sentence with "in this book," and for the rest reads "What Jeremiah prophesied against the nations. Elam." Upon which follows what with us appears as chap. xlix. 35—39, and then the other prophecies against foreign nations including Babylon, which in the Heb. text (and Eng. Vers.) come at the end of the whole Book (chaps. xlvi.—li.). This fact, coupled with the expression *which Jeremiah hath prophesied*, an expression hardly likely to have been used by Jeremiah himself, has suggested to some that the arrangement in the Septuagint may be closer to the form in which Jeremiah at first at any rate arranged his writings. One or two other omissions in the Greek, as compared with the Heb. of these verses ("and to Nebuchadrezzar," see note on ver. 9, "the king of Babylon...and the land of the Chaldeans," ver. 12), have been thought to point in the same direction. According to this view then the words 'which (what) Jeremiah hath prophesied against all the nations' will stand as the immediate introduction to those prophecies, that still follow upon this passage in the Septuagint; while ver. 14, not occurring in that Version, will be a marginal note or gloss, afterwards inserted as such notes often were by a copyist in the text, and intended to account for the preceding words, now that the detailed prophecies which they originally introduced had been withdrawn.

14. *shall serve themselves of them also*] The pronoun *them* in the Heb. is repeated for the sake of emphasis, and refers to the Chaldaeans. Their punishment shall be severe. As they have done to the people of God, so shall He requite them. The same sentiment is expressed in the prophecy specially directed against Babylon, but written some years later, chap. l. 29, li. 24.

15—30. THE WINE-CUP OF GOD'S FURY IS TO BE DRUNK BY ALL THE NATIONS.

15. *For thus saith*] In this section we have the rapid enumeration

the wine cup of this fury at mine hand, and cause all the
16 nations, to whom I send thee, to drink it. And they shall drink,
and be moved, and be mad, because of the sword that I will
17 send among them. Then took I the cup at the Lord's hand,
and made all the nations to drink, unto whom the Lord
18 had sent me: *to wit*, Jerusalem, and the cities of Judah,
and the kings thereof, *and* the princes thereof, to make
them a desolation, an astonishment, a hissing, and a curse;
19 as *it is* this day; Pharaoh king of Egypt, and his servants,

of those kingdoms which should be involved with the Jews in the overthrow.

the wine cup of this fury] more literally, *this wine-cup, namely fury*. The likening of disaster to a bitter draught is frequent in the Bible. See chaps. xlix. 12, li. 7; Job xxi. 20; Ps. lx. 3, lxxv. 8; Is. li. 17, 22; Ezek. xxiii. 31; Hab. ii. 15; Rev. xiv. 8, xvii. 4, xviii. 3.

16. *be moved*] **reel.**

be mad] The words mean, behave as madmen. Their dismay at the horrors of war shall be so great, that they will have the bearing of men drunken or insane.

the sword] Here Jeremiah, as so often, returns suddenly from figure to fact. See for other instances Introd. chap. II. 8 (*d*).

17. *Then took I the cup*] not however in any literal sense, just as the cup was not a literal cup, but along with its contents a figurative expression for the wrath of God as manifested in a national subjugation. Hence the view, which has been maintained, that Jeremiah presented a cup of actual wine to the ambassadors of these various powers, assembled, according to this hypothesis, for counsel in Jerusalem, may be dismissed, as utterly improbable. The figure was sufficiently carried out by the proclamation of God's message in Jerusalem, whence it might be conveyed to the other nations united by a common danger.

18. We may perceive a certain system (south to north) in the enumeration. After Jerusalem and Judah the prophet takes in order the furthest south (Egypt), south-east (Uz), south-west (Philistines), east (Edom, etc.), west (Tyre, etc.), east and northwards (Dedan, etc. to the Medes), and finally the north far and near (ver. 26).

kings] For the use of the plural see note on xix. 3.

a desolation...] See notes on v. 30 and xviii. 16.

as it is this day] may well be an insertion of Jeremiah's after the fulfilment of the prophecy.

19. *Pharaoh*] a name belonging not to an individual but (compare *Cesar* and *Czar*) to the monarch as such. The word is no doubt Coptic, more or less altered in shape by its transmission to us through Hebrew. According to the latest view it = great house (compare *Sublime Porte*), while others have thought it to be either (i) from PI = the definite article and OURO = king, or (ii) PI RA = sun-god, whom the king of Egypt represented. (For authorities see Schaff's *Through Bible Lands*, p. 91.)

and his princes, and all his people; and all the mingled 20
people, and all the kings of the land of Uz, and all the
kings of the land of the Philistines, and Ashkelon, and
Azzah, and Ekron, and the remnant of Ashdod: Edom, 21
and Moab, and the children of Ammon, and all the kings 22
of Tyrus, and all the kings of Zidon, and the kings of the
isles which *are* beyond the sea, Dedan, and Tema, and Buz, 23

20. *the mingled people*] This phrase, which occurs also ver. 24, seems to mean in general those who without being connected by blood with the nation had for one reason or other attached themselves to it (compare l. 37). Some have thought that here there is a particular reference to mercenary troops from Ionia and Caria, whom Psammetichus, father of Pharaohnechoh, had hired. This however is probably too limited a reference.

and all the kings of the land of Uz] The Septuagint Version omits these words, and it has been supposed that it did so, as knowing that Uz lay much too far north to be introduced at this part of the enumeration. On the contrary however Uz appears (Lam. iv. 21) to have been in the neighbourhood of Idumaea, and therefore not far from Egypt.

and Ashkelon] **even** Ashkelon.

Azzah] Gaza, which is the ordinary spelling, although that adopted here (and in Deut. ii. 23; 1 Kings iv. 24) is perhaps nearer the Heb.

the remnant of Ashdod] For twenty-nine years Psammetichus pressed the siege of Azotus without intermission, till finally he took the place (Rawl. *Herod.* II. 157). The coincidence is very remarkable between what we might have gathered as the likely result of such a protracted siege followed by capture and the expression here 'the remnant of Ashdod.' If we compare this list of Philistine towns with earlier ones (Josh. xiii. 3; 1 Sam. vi. 17) we notice that Gath is here wanting, as it is also Amos i. 7, 8; Zeph. ii. 4; and Zech. ix. 5, 6. It is not apparently as belonging to Judah that it is omitted in these places, for though taken by David (1 Chron. xviii. 1) it recovered independence afterwards (1 Kings ii. 39). The reason therefore probably is that it was no longer a separate kingdom.

22. *Tyrus*] This form in place of Tyre is found in the Eng. Vers. of Jeremiah, Ezekiel, Hosea, Amos, Zechariah, besides the Apocryphal Books of Esdras, Judith and Maccabees.

Zidon] the ordinary form of the name in the O. T. Compare xxvii. 3, xlvii. 4. Sidon however, which as the Greek form is that which occurs in the N. T., we find also in Gen. x. 15, 19. The similar usage in the name Zion (Sion) may be compared.

isles] more literally, *inhabited places.* The word is used however most commonly of the places which were, roughly speaking, west of Palestine, and thus it had special reference to the islands of the Grecian Archipelago.

23. *Dedan*] a tribe descended from Abraham by his wife Keturah (Gen. xxv. 3) and dwelling S.E. of Edom. Their caravans maintained a trade between Tyre and Arabia (Ezek. xxvii. 15, 20).

24 and all *that are* in the utmost corners, and all the kings
of Arabia, and all the kings of the mingled people that
25 dwell in the desert, and all the kings of Zimri, and all the
26 kings of Elam, and all the kings of the Medes, and all the
kings of the north, far and near, one with another, and all
the kingdoms of the world, which *are* upon the face of the
earth: and the king of Sheshach shall drink after them.

Tema] descendants of Ishmael (Gen. xxv. 15).
Buz] See Gen. xxii. 21. Elihu was a Buzite (Job xxxii. 2).
all that are in the utmost corners] For a more correct rendering see note on ix. 26, and for the persons referred to here xlix. 28, 32.
24. *Arabia*] the part near Palestine.
the mingled people] See note on ver. 20.
25. *Zimri*] This name as that of a people occurs here only. It is commonly connected with Zimran, son of Abraham by Keturah (Gen. xxv. 2). A people of similar name are said to have occupied a territory between Arabia and Persia. This would agree with the context here.
Elam] Persia.
26. *all the kings of the north*] put thus vaguely, as dwelling beyond the ken of the Israelitish nation.
which are upon the face of the earth] This would not suggest to the Jewish ear, as it does to us, the thought of absolutely universal dominion on the part of Babylon. This we see from such passages as Dan. ii. 38, iv. 22, where the sense intended to be conveyed cannot be in accordance with the sound of the words taken literally.
king of Sheshach] *Sheshach* has been taken by some as equivalent to *Hur* (*Ur*), a city containing a very celebrated temple of the moon-god, whose name, as it can be shewn, was, or might have been, read in one of the ancient dialects of Babylon as Shishaki (Rawl. *Herod.* I. p. 505, 506). This is however improbable. *Sheshach* is rather = *Babel* (Babylon) in accordance with a secret (Kabalistic) system of writing dating from an unknown antiquity among the Jews. This system took different forms, of which this (called *Atbash*) consists in substituting the last letter of the Heb. alphabet for the first, the last but one for the second and so on. Sh Sh Ch will on this principle take the places of B B L. This is confirmed by li. 41, where Sheshach and Babylon occur in parallel clauses. Another instance of this is seen in li. 1, where the Heb. (Le B Ka Ma Y) for "the midst of them that rise up against me" becomes, when thus transmuted, CaSDIM = Chaldaeans, which is the actual rendering of the Septuagint. They however omit the whole clause in the present passage and the word Sheshach in li. 41. If that word be intended to be significant in itself as well and not to be merely a transmutation of Babel, it will mean either (i) a mass of people or buildings, or (ii) a sinking, downfall, in which case li. 64 will contain an allusion to this name.

Therefore thou shalt say unto them, Thus saith the LORD of 27
hosts, the God of Israel; Drink ye, and be drunken, and
spue, and fall, and rise no more, because of the sword
which I will send among you. And it shall be, if they 28
refuse to take the cup at thine hand to drink, then shalt
thou say unto them, Thus saith the LORD of hosts; Ye
shall certainly drink. For lo, I begin to bring evil on the 29
city which is called by my name, and should ye be utterly
unpunished? Ye shall not be unpunished: for I *will* call
for a sword upon all the inhabitants of the earth, saith the
LORD of hosts. Therefore prophesy thou against them all 30
these words, and say unto them,

30—38. *The judgment to come upon all the peoples of the earth.*

The LORD shall roar from on high,
And utter his voice from his holy habitation;
He shall mightily roar upon his habitation;
He shall give a shout, as they that tread *the grapes*,
Against all the inhabitants of the earth.
A noise shall come *even* to the ends of the earth; 31

shall drink after them] The turn of Babylon shall itself come to perish.
28, 29. Resistance is vain. If God's own people suffer, much more the heathen.

30—38. THE JUDGMENT TO COME UPON ALL THE PEOPLES OF THE EARTH.

30. *The Lord shall roar*] The figure in this section is that of a lion coming forth from his covert, and terrifying by his approach the shepherds and their flocks. There is no escape and the slain cover the earth.

upon his habitation] **against** *his* **pasture.** The word in the Heb. is the same as in xxiii. 3, where see note. It is important that it should not be rendered *habitation* here with the Eng. Vers., as it is contrasted in sense with the 'holy habitation,' heaven, of the previous clause, and means the land of the chosen people.

a shout] literally, *a vintage shout*, derived from a root meaning to tramp, and alluding to the cry with which the treaders of the grapes used to animate their toil. We see however that the word might also mean a battle shout. Compare li. 14 for its use as against Babylon.

31. *A noise*] The word denotes a sound like the trampling of a multitude such as an army. It is variously rendered in the Eng. Vers.

For the LORD hath a controversy with the nations,
He *will* plead with all flesh;
He will give them *that are* wicked to the sword, saith the LORD.

32 Thus saith the LORD of hosts,
Behold, evil *shall* go forth from nation to nation,
And a great whirlwind shall be raised up from the coasts of the earth.

33 And the slain of the LORD shall be at that day
From *one* end of the earth even unto the *other* end of the earth:
They shall not be lamented, neither gathered, nor buried;
They shall be dung upon the ground.

34 Howl, ye shepherds, and cry;
And wallow yourselves *in the ashes*, ye principal of the flock:
For the days of your slaughter and of your dispersions are accomplished.
And ye shall fall like a pleasant vessel.

Is. xiii. 4, "a *tumultuous* noise;" Is. xvii. 12, "the *rushing* of nations... like the *rushing* of mighty waters;" Hosea x. 14, "Therefore shall a *tumult* arise;" Amos ii. 2, "Moab shall die with *tumult*."

hath a controversy...will plead with] See note on ii. 9, 35. We have here the same two Heb. verbs and in the same order. In the former clause therefore God is as it were the prosecutor and in the latter the judge, **will give judgment.**

he will give them that are wicked] literally, (as for) *the wicked he will give them*. Thus the object of the verb is made more emphatic.

32. *whirlwind*] **tempest**, as in xxiii. 19.

33. *the slain of the Lord*] For the phrase compare Is. lxvi. 16.

34. *wallow yourselves in the ashes*] See note on vi. 26. *Roll* (*upon the ground*) is the probable meaning here, the words 'in the ashes' being added apparently only because they occur in the Heb. of the other passage.

principal of the flock] not equivalent with 'shepherds,' although parallel to it in the construction, but rather, chief among the sheep, wealthy ones of the people, whose rank and riches avail nothing now.

and of your dispersions] The Heb. is difficult in point of grammar. The best rendering seems to be, *And I will disperse you.* Accordingly the words 'are accomplished' will refer to 'the days of your slaughter' only.

like a pleasant vessel] In order not to change the figure so abruptly, which however is quite in keeping with Jeremiah's style, it has been proposed to alter the Heb. reading slightly for the purpose of rendering

And the shepherds shall have no way to flee,   35
Nor the principal of the flock to escape.
A voice of the cry of the shepherds,   36
And a howling of the principal of the flock, *shall be heard:*
For the LORD *hath* spoiled their pasture.
And the peaceable habitations are cut down   37
Because of the fierce anger of the LORD.
He hath forsaken his covert, as the lion: 38
For their land is desolate
Because of the fierceness of the oppressor,
And because of his fierce anger.

CHAP. XXVI. 1—6. *A few words of solemn warning, addressed to the people collectively.*

In the beginning of the reign of Jehoiakim the son of 26

like chosen rams. Even with the new reading however there is a difficulty in translating thus, and to this we may add that the figure of a *vessel* in such a connexion has been already used by Jeremiah (chap. xxii. 28). Here a vessel of fragile material by a fall and consequent fracture suddenly ceases to be of any value.

36. *shall be heard*] These words are best omitted. Thus we shall better get the force of the prophet's exclamation, which is in fact the cry which he has called upon them (ver. 34) to make and which he already hears.

hath spoiled] **spoileth.**

37. *habitations*] better, *pastures.* The Heb. word is not however exactly the same as in ver. 30.

cut down] better, *put to silence.* See notes on viii. 14, where the Heb. verb is the same. These pastures so lately abounding in flocks are now silent; in other words the country is denuded of its inhabitants.

38. *He hath forsaken his covert*] a repetition of the figure with which the section opened. The Lord is gone forth in wrath to lay waste.

the fierceness of the oppressor] Owing to the word rendered 'oppressor' being scarcely found elsewhere except as an adjective in the expression "oppressing sword" (xlvi. 16 and l. 16), a reading which by a slight alteration of the Heb. text we may obtain here, that reading has been adopted by some. The (Latin) Vulgate renders the Heb. word above referred to in its more ordinary sense of *a dove,* and it has accordingly been supposed that the Babylonian army bore such a device on their standards. This however is little more than conjectural. On the whole there seems no necessity to alter the reading of the Heb. text.

CHAP. XXVI. 1—6. A FEW WORDS OF SOLEMN WARNING,
    ADDRESSED TO THE PEOPLE COLLECTIVELY.

1. *In the beginning of the reign of Jehoiakim*] For a discussion of the

Josiah king of Judah came this word from the LORD, saying,
2 Thus saith the LORD; Stand in the court of the LORD's house, and speak unto all the cities of Judah, which come to worship *in* the LORD's house, all the words that I com-
3 mand thee to speak unto them; diminish not a word: if so be they will hearken, and turn every man from his evil way, that I may repent me of the evil, which I purpose to do
4 unto them because of the evil of their doings. And thou shalt say unto them, Thus saith the LORD; If ye will not hearken to me, to walk in my law, which I have set before
5 you, to hearken to the words of my servants the prophets, whom I sent unto you, both rising up early, and sending
6 *them*, but ye have not hearkened; then will I make this house like Shiloh, and will make this city a curse to all the nations of the earth.

question, whether these verses are a summary of chaps. vii.—x., see note at the beginning of chap. vii. This chapter as a whole gives us a rapid sketch of the circumstances under which Jeremiah had delivered himself of the prophecies that went before. The more definite he had become in his warnings, the more he excited the wrath of the false prophets and of those who sided with them; and now that he had explicitly announced (xxv. 11) a seventy years' captivity, their indignation boiled over, and they sought to compass his death. From the contents of this chap. then we can realize better under what conditions and with what courage the prophet continued his forecastings of definite calamity in the chapters which follow. 'The beginning' will naturally denote some date earlier than the fourth year of Jehoiakim's reign, when the crisis came about, and Jeremiah was no longer listened to nor tolerated (chap. xxxvi.).

2. *the court of the Lord's house*] probably the outer court, as that in which the people would assemble; so chap. xix. 14. The spot may have been the same as that occupied by Baruch when he read the roll (xxxvi. 10).

diminish not a word] "Ye shall not add unto the word which I command you, neither shall you diminish ought from it," was the command given through Moses to Israel (Deut. iv. 2; compare xii. 32). Here of course the temptation was only in the way of suppression, through natural shrinking from the danger involved in honest discharge of duty.

5. *rising up early, and sending*] For this phrase see note on vii. 13.

6. *Shiloh*] See note on vii. 12.

will make this city a curse to] will subject it to the curses, will make it vile in the sight, of all nations. So in chap. xxiv. 9.

7—15. *Impeachment of Jeremiah by the priests and prophets before the princes and people. His defence.*

So the priests and the prophets and all the people heard ⁷ Jeremiah speaking these words in the house of the LORD. Now it came to pass, when Jeremiah had made an end ⁸ of speaking all that the LORD had commanded *him* to speak unto all the people, that the priests and the prophets and all the people took him, saying, Thou shalt surely die. Why hast thou prophesied in the name of the LORD, saying, ⁹ This house shall be like Shiloh, and this city shall be desolate without an inhabitant? And all the people were gathered against Jeremiah in the house of the LORD. When the princes of Judah heard these things, then they ¹⁰ came up from the king's house *unto* the house of the LORD,

7—15. IMPEACHMENT OF JEREMIAH BY THE PRIESTS AND PROPHETS BEFORE THE PRINCES AND PEOPLE. HIS DEFENCE.

7. *prophets*] The Septuagint, in order to make the sense clearer, renders the Heb. here, as in verses 8, 11 and 16, "*false* prophets."

8. The reverence in which the people held one who, as they had reason to believe (in spite of their desire to think the contrary), was a prophet of God, is here incidentally shewn. No one ventured to lay hands on him till he had finished his address.

Thou shalt surely die] That prophet, who spoke without God's command, was according to the Mosaic Law (Deut. xviii. 20) to be put to death. The charge against Jeremiah then was of this nature, and the alleged proof, that it was impossible in the nature of things that such a calamity could be allowed to happen to the people of God.

9. *all the people were gathered against*] *all the people were gathered unto*. The people were not universally against Jeremiah, and therefore the words *all the people* in ver. 8 are not to be taken as implying more than that a large following accompanied the priests and prophets. In ver. 16 on the other hand we find "all the people" on Jeremiah's side.

10. *the princes of Judah*] The position and powers of these persons are not quite clear. They have been thought to be the heads of prominent houses in the tribes, which had a sort of hereditary jurisdiction first from local influence in their country abodes, and afterwards, when on account of the dangers and disturbances incidental to a country life in these troublesome times, they had removed to Jerusalem. Their employment in high offices about the court and the constantly increasing weakness of the monarchy would help them to the further acquisition of such power as we find them here exercising. After the return from the captivity the Sanhedrin succeeded to their powers, and held them in a more precisely defined form.

came up] See xxii. 1 ("go down").

and sat down in the entry of the new gate of the LORD's
11 *house*. Then spake the priests and the prophets unto the
princes and to all the people, saying, This man *is* worthy to
die; for he hath prophesied against this city, as ye have
12 heard with your ears. Then spake Jeremiah unto all the
princes and to all the people, saying, The LORD sent me to
prophesy against this house and against this city all the
13 words that ye have heard. Therefore now amend your
ways and your doings, and obey the voice of the LORD your
God; and the LORD will repent him of the evil that he
14 hath pronounced against you. As for me, behold, I *am* in
your hand: do with me as seemeth good and meet unto
15 you. But know ye for certain, that if ye put me to death,
ye shall surely bring innocent blood upon yourselves, and
upon this city, and upon the inhabitants thereof: for of
a truth the LORD hath sent me unto you to speak all these
words in your ears.

16—24. *Result of the trial. Cases of Micah and Urijah.*

16 Then said the princes and all the people unto the priests

the entry of the new gate of the Lord's house] literally, *the door of the new gate of the Lord.* Such a place as this was the ordinary one for trials. This particular gate was in all probability that built by Jotham (2 Kings xv. 35).

11. *This man is worthy to die*] literally, *A sentence of death is due to this man.*

hath prophesied against this city] Compare for the scene and thought Acts vi. 12, 13.

as ye have heard with your ears] This is addressed to the people only, as they (ver. 7) and not the princes had been actually present at Jeremiah's address.

12. Jeremiah's defence is that the message is from God and therefore true. Let his accusers beware, lest in putting him to death they be really fighting against God. Compare Gamaliel's language as to the Apostles (Acts v. 39).

13. *your ways and your doings*] See note on vii. 3.

15. *of a truth*] St Thomas Aquinas (*Summ. Theol.*) points to Jeremiah's words here as an illustration of the firmness of conviction which in the main sustained the prophets in their trying and dangerous calling.

16—24. RESULT OF THE TRIAL. CASES OF MICAH AND URIJAH.

16. The princes and people, not being prejudiced as were Jeremiah's accusers, gave a fair decision. "The nobles, reckless and worldly

and to the prophets; This man *is* not worthy to die: for he hath spoken to us in the name of the LORD our God. Then rose up certain of the elders of the land, and spake to all the assembly of the people, saying, Micah the Morasthite prophesied in the days of Hezekiah king of Judah, and spake to all the people of Judah, saying, Thus saith the LORD of hosts;

Zion shall be plowed *like* a field,
And Jerusalem shall become heaps,
And the mountain of the house as the high places of a forest.

Did Hezekiah king of Judah and all Judah put him at all to death? did he not fear the LORD, and besought the LORD, and the LORD repented him of the evil which he had

as they were, with a deeper sense of justice than his fanatical assailants, solemnly acquitted him." Stanley, *J. Ch.* They perceived from his words and manner that he was, as he gave himself out to be, a prophet of God, counselling reformation, and warning of its necessity.

This man is not worthy to die] literally (compare ver. 11), *No sentence of death is due to this man.*

17. *the elders of the land*] "The elders of Israel" appear as early as Exod. iii. 16. Their action in civil procedure we gather from Ruth iv. 2, etc. The involuntary homicide had to make out his case to the satisfaction of the elders of the city of refuge, before being admitted. The institution of elders was continued among the Ten Tribes in their separation (1 Kings xx. 7). It has been conjectured that as the princes represented the king in judgment, so the elders represented the people, adding their assent to the previously expressed decision.

18. *Micah* (better, **Micaiah**) *the Morasthite*] one of the Minor Prophets, who prophesied in the days of Jotham, Ahaz and Hezekiah. The passage here quoted as uttered in the days of the last-named king agrees *verbatim* with Mic. iii. 12.

Morasthite] native of Moresheth, a place by Eusebius and St Jerome identified with Morasthi, a small village east of Eleutheropolis, where the prophet's tomb had once been shewn. This however had disappeared in St Jerome's time.

19. *Did Hezekiah...put him at all to death?*] The words of Micah had been to the full as harsh-sounding as any that had been uttered by Jeremiah. The precedent supplied by the case of the former prophet therefore, the elders argue, is in favour of him who is now attacked.

besought] The Heb. is literally *stroked the face of*; and so in Exod. xxxii. 11; 1 Sam. xiii. 12. We are not elsewhere told that Hezekiah's prayers were in direct connexion with the prophecy of Micah. There is however no difficulty in the way of our accepting the testimony of these elders, that it was so.

pronounced against them? Thus *might* we procure great
20 evil against our souls. And there was also a man that
prophesied in the name of the LORD, Urijah the son of
Shemaiah of Kirjath-jearim, who prophesied against this
city and against this land according to all the words of
21 Jeremiah: and when Jehoiakim the king, with all his mighty
men, and all the princes, heard his words, the king sought
to put him to death: but when Urijah heard *it*, he was
22 afraid, and fled, and went *into* Egypt; and Jehoiakim the
king sent men *into* Egypt, *namely*, Elnathan the son of
23 Achbor, and *certain* men with him into Egypt. And they
fet forth Urijah out of Egypt, and brought him unto Jehoiakim the king; who slew him with the sword, and cast
24 his dead body into the graves of the common people. Nevertheless the hand of Ahikam the son of Shaphan was with

Thus might we procure...] rather, *And we are* (thinking of) *committing* (what will prove) *a great evil against our souls*.
  20. *there was also a man*] This narrative was probably introduced later by Jeremiah to shew the danger in which he stood at the time, and does not form a portion of that which was said on the occasion by any of the parties present. It would have been a dangerous attack to make upon Jehoiakim, the reigning king. It is hardly likely also that there would have been time between the accession of Jehoiakim and the somewhat vague date assigned to this attack on Jeremiah (ver. 1) for all these events to have occurred in the case of Urijah.
  Kirjath-jearim] probably identical with the present *Kuriet-el-Enab*, a city on the borders of Judah and Benjamin (Josh. xv. 9, xviii. 14, 15), about ten miles N.W. of Jerusalem on the road to Joppa (Jaffa). It was the resting place of the ark for twenty years (see 1 Sam. vi. 20—vii. 2).
  21. *mighty men*] As the princes were the *civil*, so these were the *military* chiefs.
  22. *Elnathan the son of Achbor*] He is mentioned again xxxvi. 12, 25. He may have been the "Elnathan of Jerusalem," who is mentioned as Jehoiachin's maternal grandfather in 2 Kings xxiv. 8. Achbor was one of the deputation sent by Josiah to Huldah the prophetess (2 Kings xxii. 12) when the Law was found in the House of the Lord.
  23. *they fet forth Urijah out of Egypt*] "As Jehoiakim was a vassal of Egypt (2 Kings xxiii. 34), he would easily obtain the surrender of a man accused of treason. Jeroboam, on the contrary, and others had found a safe refuge there in the days of Solomon, 1 Kings xi. 17, 40" (*Sp. Comm.*). For *fet* compare *to fet* in xxxvi. 21, and
  "To see my tears and hear my deep-*fet* groans."
         SHAKESPEARE, *II Henry VI*. Act II. Sc. 4.
  into the graves of the common people] probably in the neighbourhood of the brook Kidron. See note on xvii. 19 and 2 Kings xxiii. 6.
  24. *Nevertheless*] **But.**

Jeremiah, that *they* should not give him into the hand of the people to put him to death.

CHAPS. XXVII.—XXIX. *The sway of Babylon over Judea and the neighbouring nations will be by no means brief.*

CHAP. XXVII. 1—11. *Warning to the neighbouring nations.*

In the beginning of the reign of Jehoiakim the son of 27

Ahikam the son of Shaphan] He was one of the five sent by Josiah (2 Kings xxii. 12) to consult Huldah. His son Gedaliah stood the prophet's friend subsequently, when the former was left by Nebuchadrezzar a governor of the land (xxxix. 14, xl. 5). It was in the chamber of another son of Shaphan, Gemariah, that Baruch read Jeremiah's roll in the ears of the people.

CHAP. XXVII.—XXIX. THE SWAY OF BABYLON OVER JUDEA AND THE NEIGHBOURING NATIONS WILL BE BY NO MEANS BRIEF.

These three chapters belong to the time of Zedekiah (see below). The power of Babylon had already been shewn forth upon Judah. Some of the people had been carried captive, and the present king existed as such only upon sufferance. Under these circumstances the neighbouring nations were willing to make common cause with the Jews against their foe, while in Palestine there were still many who would not believe that the danger from Babylon was anything more than a passing one. In these three chapters therefore Jeremiah sets himself to correct the most pressing evil, namely this notion of the possibility of getting rid of the power which had become paramount in the Eastern world. He addresses on the subject (in this chap. verses 1—11) the neighbouring nations, (12—15) Zedekiah, (16—22) the priests and prophets, (in chap. xxviii.) the false prophets, (in chap. xxix.) the exiles in Babylon.

CHAP. XXVII. 1—11. WARNING TO THE NEIGHBOURING NATIONS.

1. *In the beginning of the reign of Jehoiakim*] It is clear from verses 3, 12 and 20 that for *Jehoiakim* we must read *Zedekiah*. This is not without support among Heb. MSS., while the Syriac Version also reads the name of the latter king. The Septuagint omits the verse. It is therefore either a later insertion in the text, or a confusion between the opening verses of chaps. xxvi. and xxvii. led to the introduction of the wrong name here. In xxviii. 1, where the same words are further defined as "in the fourth year and in the fifth month," it has been supposed that "in the beginning...Judah" is a note first placed by a copyist in the margin as a comment on the date mentioned, and then by a subsequent hand inserted in the text. The difficulty however which is avoided by this explanation, viz. that the fourth year of a reign consisting of but

Josiah king of Judah came this word unto Jeremiah from
the LORD, saying, Thus saith the LORD to me; Make thee
bonds and yokes, and put them upon thy neck, and send
them to the king of Edom, and to the king of Moab, and to
the king of the Ammonites, and to the king of Tyrus, and
to the king of Zidon, by the hand of the messengers which
come *to* Jerusalem unto Zedekiah king of Judah; and command them to say unto their masters, Thus saith the LORD
of hosts, the God of Israel; Thus shall ye say unto your
masters; I have made the earth, the man and the beast that
are upon the ground, by my great power and by my outstretched arm, and have given it unto whom it seemed meet
unto me. And now have I given all these lands into the
hand of Nebuchadnezzar the king of Babylon, my servant;
and the beasts of the field have I given him also to serve
him. And all nations shall serve him, and his son, and his

---

eleven years in all cannot properly be called its beginning is not a very
serious one. Any part of Zedekiah's reign which preceded his journey
to Babylon in the fourth year (chap. li. 59) might naturally be spoken of
in these terms.

2. *bonds and yokes*] The former were cords by which the wooden
beams composing the yoke proper were fastened together. The use of
the plural 'yokes' here seems to shew that Jeremiah did not merely
exhibit one yoke on his own neck (chap. xxviii. 10), and consider this
act as a figurative sending of yokes to the various kings (compare xxv.
17), but that he made one for each king and gave them to the ambassadors.

3. The five kings are enumerated in geographical order from south
to north, if we assume that the Ammonites were at any rate *not south*
of Moab. Their position, probably from the wandering character of the
nation (observe the expression *Ammonites*, not Ammon), is ill-defined in
any notices that we have.

the messengers] These, as we may gather from the import of
Jeremiah's message to them, had come for the purpose of bringing about
a defensive and offensive alliance against the Babylonian power.

5. The terms of the message are these:—God, as Creator of the
world and of all that is in it, has the right to give it to whomsoever He
will. He has therefore placed Nebuchadnezzar in power for such time
as it shall please Him, and none may resist His will.

6. *the king of Babylon, my servant*] So xxv. 9, where see note.
and the beasts of the field] Compare xxviii. 14; Dan. ii. 38.

7. *him, and his son, and his son's son*] If this prophecy be meant
to be taken literally, it will signify that the power of Babylon would last
for three generations of rulers. According to profane history however

son's son, until the very time of his land come: and *then* many nations and great kings shall serve themselves of him. And it shall come to pass, *that* the nation and kingdom 8 which will not serve the same Nebuchadnezzar the king of Babylon, and that will not put their neck under the yoke of the king of Babylon, that nation will I punish, saith the LORD, with the sword, and with the famine, and with the pestilence, until I have consumed them by his hand. There- 9 fore hearken not ye to your prophets, nor to your diviners, nor to your dreamers, nor to your enchanters, nor to your sorcerers, which speak unto you, saying, Ye shall not serve the king of Babylon: for they prophesy a lie unto you, to 10 remove you far from your land; and *that* I should drive you out, and ye should perish. But the nations that bring 11 their neck under the yoke of the king of Babylon, and serve him, those will I let remain still in their own land, saith the LORD; and they shall till it, and dwell therein.

it was somewhat more prolonged. For the successive rulers and their lengths of reign see note on chap. xxv. 11. In the seventeenth year of Nabonnedus Babylon was taken by Cyrus. We may thus conclude that the expression in the text merely means that for the Jews and the other nations there was to be no speedy riddance of Babylon, as the false prophets taught. Compare the use of the phrase in Deut. iv. 25, vi. 2. The Septuagint omit the verse, perhaps from the difficulty which they felt in harmonising its statements, when taken literally, with the facts of history.

the very time] the appointed end. Compare Is. xiii. 22, where a similar expression is used of Babylon.

many nations and great kings shall serve themselves of him] For the phrase see xxv. 14. Babylon should yield her dominions to the empires and kingdoms that should follow, viz. Persia, Greece, and the fragments of the latter empire.

8. *by his hand*] Death not only by the sword, but also by famine and pestilence might well be ascribed to Nebuchadnezzar's hand, as the two latter would closely attend upon war.

9. *dreamers*] **dreams**, either those which the diviners etc. professed to have had, or those which the people brought to them for interpretation.

enchanters] The exact sense of the Heb. word is disputed. According to some it means bringers of *clouds* (storms); others explain fascinators, bewitching with the *evil eye*.

11. *the nations...*] In the Heb. it is 'the *nation*' that brings *its* neck' etc.

12—22. *Warning to the king, priests and people.*

12 I spake also to Zedekiah king of Judah according to all these words, saying, Bring your necks under the yoke of the king of Babylon, and serve him and his people, and live. 13 Why will ye die, thou and thy people, by the sword, by the famine, and by the pestilence, as the LORD hath spoken against the nation that will not serve the king of Babylon? 14 Therefore hearken not unto the words of the prophets that speak unto you, saying, Ye shall not serve the king of 15 Babylon: for they prophesy a lie unto you. For I have not sent them, saith the LORD, yet they prophesy a lie in my name; that I might drive you out, and that ye might perish, 16 ye, and the prophets that prophesy unto you. Also I spake to the priests and to all this people, saying, Thus saith the LORD; Hearken not to the words of your prophets that prophesy unto you, saying, Behold, the vessels of the LORD'S house *shall* now shortly be brought again from Babylon: for 17 they prophesy a lie unto you. Hearken not unto them;

12—22. WARNING TO THE KING, PRIESTS AND PEOPLE.

12—15. These verses correspond in the main to the previous section, the warning against the false prophets in verses 14, 15, answering to that of 9, 10. Although Zedekiah is addressed, the plural is used throughout on account of his many sympathisers among all ranks.

16—22. The same message is addressed to the priests and to the people.

16. *the vessels of the Lord's house*] They had been made by Solomon (1 Kings vii. 15, 23, 27, 48—50). Some had been taken by Nebuchadnezzar in the time of Jehoiachin (ver. 20; 2 Kings xxiv. 13). The rest (ver. 22) should follow. See the fulfilment in 2 Kings xxv. 13. In the Septuagint these verses appear in a very much shortened form, viz.:—"For thus saith the Lord of the rest of the vessels, which the king of Babylon took not, when he carried away Jechonias from Jerusalem, they shall go to Babylon, saith the Lord." That the Septuagint have thus omitted the statement that the vessels should remain in Babylon till the end of the captivity ("until the day that I visit them," ver. 22), has been thought, as in ver. 7 above, to point to an historical difficulty, the vessels according to this view having in point of fact been sent back to Jerusalem soon after the commencement of the captivity. The passage of Baruch (i. 8) however, which alone is quoted in support of this view, besides sharing in the uncertainty which would belong to any unsupported statement in an Apocryphal Book, only asserts that there were returned "silver vessels, which Sedecias (Zedekiah) the son of Josias king of Juda had made."

serve the king of Babylon, and live : wherefore should this
city be laid waste? But if they *be* prophets, and if the word 18
of the LORD be with them, let them now make intercession
to the LORD of hosts, that the vessels which are left in the
house of the LORD, and *in* the house of the king of Judah,
and at Jerusalem, go not to Babylon. For thus saith the 19
LORD of hosts concerning the pillars, and concerning the
sea, and concerning the bases, and concerning the residue
of the vessels that remain in this city, which Nebuchadnezzar 20
king of Babylon took not, when he carried away Jeconiah
the son of Jehoiakim king of Judah from Jerusalem to
Babylon, and all the nobles of Judah and Jerusalem; yea, 21
thus saith the LORD of hosts, the God of Israel, concerning
the vessels that remain *in* the house of the LORD, and *in*
the house of the king of Judah and of Jerusalem; they shall 22
be carried to Babylon, and there shall they be until the day
that I visit them, saith the LORD; then will I bring them
up, and restore them to this place.

CHAP. XXVIII. 1—11. *Warning to the false prophets
through Hananiah. Hananiah's rejoinder.*

And it came to pass the same year, in the beginning of 28
the reign of Zedekiah king of Judah, in the fourth year, *and*
in the fifth month, *that* Hananiah the son of Azur the
prophet, which *was* of Gibeon, spake unto me in the house

18. *intercession*] This word had by no means once that limited
meaning of prayer *for others* which we now ascribe to it. See Ap.
Trench, *Synonymes*, 7th ed. p. 179. Compare chap. xxxvi. 25.
19. *the sea*] at which the priests washed their hands and feet
before offering sacrifice (1 Kings vii. 23—26).
the bases] the supports of the ten lavers at which the animals about
to be offered as burnt-offerings are washed (1 Kings vii. 27—37;
2 Chron. iv. 6).

CHAP. XXVIII. 1—11. WARNING TO THE FALSE PROPHETS
THROUGH HANANIAH. HANANIAH'S REJOINDER.

1. *in the beginning*] See note on xxvii. 1.
which was of Gibeon] Gibeon was one of the cities of the priests
(Josh. xxi. 17), and therefore Hananiah may well have been himself
a priest, as was Jeremiah.
The false prophets were among the severest trials to which Jeremiah
had to submit; see xxiii. 9, xxix. 8, 9, 31, 32. Compare Ezek. xiii.

of the LORD, in the presence of the priests and of all the
2 people, saying, Thus speaketh the LORD of hosts, the God
of Israel, saying, I have broken the yoke of the king of
3 Babylon. Within two full years *will* I bring again into this
place all the vessels of the LORD's house, that Nebuchadnezzar king of Babylon took away from this place, and
4 carried them *to* Babylon: and I *will* bring again to this
place Jeconiah the son of Jehoiakim king of Judah, with all
the captives of Judah, that went into Babylon, saith the
LORD: for I will break the yoke of the king of Babylon.
5 Then the prophet Jeremiah said unto the prophet Hananiah
in the presence of the priests, and in the presence of all the
6 people that stood in the house of the LORD, even the
prophet Jeremiah said, Amen: the LORD do so: the LORD
perform thy words which thou hast prophesied, to bring
again the vessels of the LORD's house, and all that is carried
7 away captive, from Babylon into this place. Nevertheless
hear thou now this word that I speak in thine ears, and in
8 the ears of all the people. The prophets that have been
before me and before thee of old prophesied both against
many countries, and against great kingdoms, of war, and of
9 evil, and of pestilence. The prophet which prophesieth of

2. *The Lord of hosts, the God of Israel*] Either this solemn form of introduction was a usual one with all who claimed the prophetic gift, or Hananiah assumed it as implying an equal claim to inspiration with Jeremiah, in whose mouth we so constantly find the formula, e.g. vii. 3, 21, xvi. 9, xix. 3, 15, xxv. 27, xxvii. 4, 21, ver. 14 of the present chapter and often subsequently (xxix. 4, 8, 21, 25, etc.).
4. Hananiah here contradicts Jeremiah's prophecy in chap. xxii. 26, 27. It is by no means necessary to assume that there is here involved an expression of personal hostility towards the present king Zedekiah, or that he was absent at this time on his visit to Babylon to take the oath of allegiance which he so soon afterwards violated, and hence might safely be alluded to as unpopular. The words of Hananiah need not mean more than that all the captives should return home within two years.
6. *Amen.*] *So be it.* Compare xi. 5 with note.
7, 9. The tenor of all preceding prophecies has been calamity and war. If then Hananiah's forecasts are in opposition to these, the presumption is against him, and he can only be proved a true prophet by the fulfilment of his predictions, an event which Jeremiah in spite of his wishes is assured will not take place.
8. *of war, and of evil, and of pestilence*] For 'evil' another reading

peace, when the word of the prophet shall come to pass, *then* shall the prophet be known, that the LORD hath truly sent him. Then Hananiah the prophet took the yoke from 10 off the prophet Jeremiah's neck, and brake it. And Hananiah 11 spake in the presence of all the people, saying, Thus saith the LORD; Even so will I break the yoke of Nebuchadnezzar king of Babylon from the neck of all nations within the space of two full years. And the prophet Jeremiah went his way.

12—17. *Rebuke and punishment of Hananiah.*

Then the word of the LORD came unto Jeremiah *the* 12 *prophet*, after that Hananiah the prophet had broken the yoke from off the neck of the prophet Jeremiah, saying, Go 13 and tell Hananiah, saying, Thus saith the LORD; Thou hast broken the yokes of wood; but thou shalt make for them yokes of iron. For thus saith the LORD of hosts, the God 14 of Israel; I have put a yoke of iron upon the neck of all these nations, that *they* may serve Nebuchadnezzar king of Babylon; and they shall serve him: and I have given him the beasts of the field also. Then said the prophet Jeremiah 15 unto Hananiah the prophet, Hear now, Hananiah; The

is *famine*. This however probably arose from the recollection of Jeremiah's frequent union of sword, famine and pestilence (xiv. 12, xxi. 9, xxiv. 10, xxvii. 8, 13, xxix. 17, 18). Here however war, not sword, is the introductory word.

9. *when the word of the prophet shall come to pass*] This was from the first the criterion of a true prophet (Deut. xviii. 22) unless he advocated idolatry, in which case he was not to be believed, even though his "sign or wonder" came to pass (Deut. xiii. 1—3).

10. Hananiah, instead of waiting the issue of events, as Jeremiah suggests that he should do, has recourse to an act of violence that shall impress the multitude.

12—17. REBUKE AND PUNISHMENT OF HANANIAH.

13. *Thou hast broken the yokes of wood*] Hananiah's act only served, by exciting the Jews to resistance, to render the servitude which they should undergo more harsh. Had Zedekiah not resisted further he and the remainder of the people might have been spared the horrors of a siege and their subsequent exile.

thou shalt make] perhaps, *thou hast made*, i.e. by this action of thine.

14. *I have given him the beasts of the field also*] See xxvii. 6 with note.

Lord hath not sent thee; but thou makest this people to
16 trust in a lie. Therefore thus saith the Lord; Behold, I
will cast thee from off the face of the earth: *this* year thou
shalt die, because thou hast taught rebellion against the
17 Lord. So Hananiah the prophet died the same year in the
seventh month.

CHAP. XXIX. 1—3. *Circumstances under which Jeremiah's letter to the exiles was written.*

29 Now these *are* the words of the letter that Jeremiah the
prophet sent from Jerusalem unto the residue of the elders
which were carried away captives, and to the priests, and to
the prophets, and to all the people whom Nebuchadnezzar
2 had carried away captive from Jerusalem to Babylon; (after
that Jeconiah the king, and the queen, and the eunuchs,

16. *I will cast thee*] literally, *I send thee away*. There is apparently a play on the word, which is the same as that rendered 'sent' in ver. 15. The Lord hath not *sent* thee here to prophesy, but is now *sending* thee away to die.

because thou hast taught rebellion against the Lord] For the law in such cases see Deut. xiii. 5, xviii. 20.

17. *in the seventh month*] two months after this time (see ver. 1).

CHAP. XXIX. 1—3. CIRCUMSTANCES UNDER WHICH JEREMIAH'S LETTER TO THE EXILES WAS WRITTEN.

1. *Now these are the words of the letter*] The exiles in Babylon were subjected to the same danger from false prophets as their fellowcountrymen, who remained at home. The former were however on the whole a better class (chap. xxiv. 5—7), and thus the prophet might hope that his words would have more effect. The assertion that the captivity would speedily come to an end, which was loudly made at Babylon as at Jerusalem by those who bid recklessly for their favour, would prevent the captivity from having the salutary effect which it was intended to have upon both those who went and those who remained. It was therefore Jeremiah's duty earnestly to deprecate such a belief, and insist in the plainest language that the punishment should last for seventy years.

the residue of the elders] This probably means those who had survived the journey, and the (perhaps two or three years') interval since then.

2. *After that Jeconiah...*] This gives us only an approximation to the date of the letter. It may have been as late as the fourth year of Zedekiah, when he went up himself with Seraiah (li. 59) to Babylon. It is more likely however on account of the different names mentioned in connexion with this journey (ver. 3) to have been sent on a somewhat

the princes of Judah and Jerusalem, and the carpenters, and the smiths, were departed from Jerusalem;) by the 3 hand of Elasah the son of Shaphan, and Gemariah the son of Hilkiah, whom Zedekiah king of Judah sent unto Babylon to Nebuchadnezzar king of Babylon, saying,

4—14. *Release shall come, but not till after seventy years.*

Thus saith the LORD of hosts, the God of Israel, unto all 4 that are carried away captives, whom I have caused to be carried away from Jerusalem unto Babylon; build ye houses, 5 and dwell *in them;* and plant gardens, and eat the fruit of them; take ye wives, and beget sons and daughters; and 6 take wives for your sons, and give your daughters to husbands, that they may bear sons and daughters; that ye may be increased there, and not diminished. And seek the 7 peace of the city whither I have caused you to be carried away captives, and pray unto the LORD for it: for in the peace thereof shall ye have peace. For thus saith the LORD 8 of hosts, the God of Israel; Let not your prophets and your diviners, that *be* in the midst of you, deceive you, neither hearken to your dreams which ye cause to be dreamed. For 9

earlier occasion not elsewhere mentioned. At any rate it appears to have been later than chap. xxiv., to which it plainly alludes more than once. Compare ver. 17 with xxiv. 2, 8, and ver. 18 with xxiv. 9.

the queen] See note on chap. xiii. 18.

the princes of Judah and Jerusalem, and the carpenters, and the smiths] Compare chap. xxiv. 1.

3. *Elasah*] As the son of Shaphan he may have been a brother of Ahikam (xxvi. 24) who, taking Jeremiah's side in political matters, would be well received at Babylon.

4—14. RELEASE SHALL COME, BUT NOT TILL AFTER SEVENTY YEARS.

4—7. Instead of looking for an immediate return to Palestine, which would cause the exiles to sit loose to the country where they found themselves, they were to be interested in its welfare and to make homes for themselves. Otherwise they would not only fail to obtain any influence, but would soon dwindle away.

7. *seek the peace of the city*] probably referring not to Babylon only, but to any city in which a body of exiles might be planted.

8. *your dreams which ye cause to be dreamed*] The dreams may be either (i) those of the people, induced by their restlessness and in turn intensifying that condition, or (ii) those announced by the false prophets, as portending a speedy return to Palestine. The form of the verb in

they prophesy falsely unto you in my name: I have not sent
10 them, saith the LORD. For thus saith the LORD, That after seventy years be accomplished at Babylon I will visit you, and perform my good word towards you, in causing you to
11 return to this place. For I know the thoughts that I think towards you, saith the LORD, thoughts of peace, and not of
12 evil, to give you an expected end. Then shall ye call upon me, and ye shall go and pray unto me, and I will hearken
13 unto you. And ye shall seek me, and find *me*, when ye
14 shall search for me with all your heart. And I will be found of you, saith the LORD: and I will turn away your captivity, and I will gather you from all the nations, and from all the places whither I have driven you, saith the LORD; and I will bring you again into the place whence I caused you to be carried away captive.

15—23. *The mouths of the False Prophets at Babylon shall soon be stopped.*

15 Because ye have said, The LORD hath raised us up pro-

the original is peculiar. On the whole the latter sense is perhaps the better of the two.

10. *after seventy years*] See note on xxv. 11.

at Babylon] **for** *Babylon*. The announcement has respect to the duration of the empire of Nebuchadnezzar and his successors, and only secondarily to the consequent limitation of the captivity.

my good word] my gracious promise. See xxvii. 22.

11. *For I know*] The pronoun is emphatic in the original. The suppressed contrast however is not, as some have taken it to be, between the false prophets' ignorance and God's knowledge, but rather between this latter and the suspicions and faithlessness of the people. Ye may think me regardless, but I know to the contrary.

an expected end] **a future** (literally, *something after*), **and an expectation.** Compare Prov. xxiii. 18, xxiv. 14, 20.

12. *Then shall ye call upon me*] Here comes the reason for the favourable change that God has announced as about to come when the punishment shall be completed.

15—23. THE MOUTHS OF THE FALSE PROPHETS AT BABYLON SHALL SOON BE STOPPED.

15, 16. A difficulty has been found in connecting these two verses. Hence it has been suggested that the former has got out of its place and should rightly stand before ver. 20. Others would wholly omit verses 16—19. These however are very unlike an interpolation, being much too long to be a marginal note which might in the hands of a copyist

phets in Babylon; *Know* that thus saith the LORD of the 16
king that sitteth upon the throne of David, and of all the
people that dwelleth in this city, *and of* your brethren that
are not gone forth with you into captivity; thus saith the 17
LORD of hosts; Behold, I will send upon them the sword,
the famine, and the pestilence, and will make them like vile
figs, that cannot be eaten, they are so evil. And I will per- 18
secute them with the sword, with the famine, and with the
pestilence, and will deliver them to be removed to all the
kingdoms of the earth, to be a curse, and an astonishment,
and a hissing, and a reproach, among all the nations whither
I have driven them: because they have not hearkened 19
to my words, saith the LORD, which I sent unto them by
my servants the prophets, rising up early and sending *them;*
but ye would not hear, saith the LORD. Hear ye there- 20

find its way into the text, and unlikely to have been inserted without
cause from the very difficulty which exists at first sight in discovering
the connexion of thought. The Septuagint it is true omits these verses,
but, as has been said before (notes on chap. xix. 11), this by itself forms
no sort of argument against them. The sense appears to be in fact this.
One of the difficulties raised by the exiles when the prospect of seventy
years' captivity was held out to them would be, We have prophets here
at Babylon who tell us just the reverse of all this. Which shall we
believe? To this the reply of Jeremiah is twofold. (i) These prophets'
teaching shall soon be disproved. The king and the remnants of the
kingdom, upon whose continued existence at Jerusalem they lay such
stress, will soon pass away. Ye shall not soon be restored to your
brethren, but they shall be exiles and scattered like to you. (ii) The
false prophets, who thus delude you, shall themselves miserably perish
and become a proverb and by-word.

15. *in Babylon*] literally, *as far as Babylon*, i.e. His prophets reach
even hither.

16. *Know that thus saith*] *Yea, thus saith*, is perhaps more literal,
but the Eng. Vers. expresses the sense with sufficient closeness.

of the king] *concerning the king.* See note on ver. 24.

17. *vile figs*] Compare xxiv. 2—8. The exiles would probably have
already heard of that prophecy, and if not, they would naturally learn it
now from the embassy who brought this letter. The word rendered *vile*
is derived from a root meaning *to shudder*, and hence is a word intended to express intense badness.

18. For the general sense and language of the verse compare xix. 8,
xxiv. 9, xxv. 18, xlii. 18.

to be removed to] See note on xv. 4.

19. *ye would not hear*] The sudden change of person is very natural,
and yet serves to shew us incidentally the scrupulous care with which

fore the word of the Lord, all *ye of* the captivity, whom
21 I have sent from Jerusalem to Babylon: thus saith the
Lord of hosts, the God of Israel, of Ahab the son of
Kolaiah, and of Zedekiah, the son of Maaseiah, which
prophesy a lie unto you in my name; Behold, I will deliver
them into the hand of Nebuchadrezzar king of Babylon;
22 and he shall slay them before your eyes; and of them shall
be taken up a curse by all the captivity of Judah which *are*
in Babylon, saying, The Lord make thee like Zedekiah and
like Ahab, whom the king of Babylon roasted in the fire;
23 because they have committed villany in Israel, and have
committed adultery with their neighbours' wives, and have
spoken lying words in my name, which I have not commanded them; even I know, and *am* a witness, saith the
Lord.

the Jews have handed down from one to another the letter of the Scriptures. An obvious alteration would have been to turn this second person into the third, but it was retained. Jeremiah desires to shew that it was not merely *other* persons who had behaved wickedly, and by thus including the very people whom he was addressing, he prepared the way for the opening words of ver. 20.

20. This begins the second part of Jeremiah's answer to the objection supposed to be raised on the part of the exiles in ver. 15. The prophets, of whom they there speak, shall perish, and that by a cruel death.

21. Of these two prophets nothing further is known.

22. *Kolaiah, curse* (kelâlâh) and *roasted* (kâlâh) are three such similar words that a play on them as used in these verses seems intended. The son of *Kolaiah* was to be called Kelâlâh (a curse) because the king of Babylon kâlâh (roasted) him in the fire. That this form of punishment was not too cruel to be uncommon we learn as well from the Moloch rites so often spoken of, and the passing "through the brick kiln" (2 Sam. xii. 31), as from the case of Shadrach and his companions (Dan. iii. 20) and various references to the subject in Assyrian inscriptions deciphered in modern times.

23. *I know*] The Heb. is rather difficult. Probably the best literal rendering of it is *I am one who knows*.

24—32. Shemaiah the Nehelamite rebuked and threatened.

On the arrival at Babylon of Jeremiah's letter, which ends with ver. 23, there is much indignation on the part of the false prophets, and one of them, Shemaiah by name, writes to Zephaniah the acting high-priest, urging upon him that he should take severe measures to silence Jeremiah as a madman. This suggestion however Zephaniah is so far from following that he shews the letter to the prophet, who writes again to

24—32. *Shemaiah the Nehelamite rebuked and threatened.*

Thus shalt thou also speak to Shemaiah the Nehelamite, 24 saying, Thus speaketh the LORD of hosts, the God of Israel, 25 saying, Because thou hast sent letters in thy name unto all the people that *are* at Jerusalem, and to Zephaniah the son of Maaseiah the priest, and to all the priests, saying, The 26 LORD hath made thee priest in the stead of Jehoiada the priest, that *ye* should be officers in the house of the LORD, for every man *that is* mad, and maketh himself a prophet, that thou shouldest put him in prison, and in the stocks. Now therefore why hast thou not reproved Jeremiah of Ana- 27 thoth, which maketh himself a prophet to you? For there- 28

Babylon, this time for the purpose of condemning Shemaiah's conduct in the severest terms, and announcing its penalty.

24. *to*] or, *concerning*, as the same preposition in the original is rendered in ver. 31. See also ver. 16.

the Nehelamite] named thus no doubt after a village not otherwise known. The alternative rendering *dreamer* suggested in the margin of the Eng. Vers. is very improbable.

25. *letters*] The Heb. might mean a single letter, but the plural is probably right.

in thy name] The "thy" is probably to be emphasized. Shemaiah spoke in his own name, not as Jeremiah in the name of the Lord.

Zephaniah] mentioned xxi. 1 (which however belongs to a somewhat later time than this) as having been sent with Pashur by Zedekiah to Jeremiah. He is also mentioned chap. lii. 24, 2 Kings xxv. 18 as "second priest" or the high-priest's deputy. He seems to have been put to death when the city was finally taken by the Chaldaeans.

26. This and the two following verses give us the words of Shemaiah's letter to Zephaniah, as quoted in Jeremiah's reply.

thee] Zephaniah.

in the stead of Jehoiada] Some have referred this to Jehoiada the high-priest of the days of king Joash (2 Kings xi. 4, etc.). Against this view however are the words that follow, viz.:—that ye should be officers = *pākîds* = deputies. This shews that the Jehoiada here mentioned was himself but a deputy. He may well have come in between Pashur (xx. 1) and Zephaniah. There were doubtless many changes of this kind in such troublous times.

that is mad] Madness was looked on in the East as a sort of gift of prophecy perverted.

prison] **the pillory.** See note on chap. xx. 2, where the same word is rendered "stocks."

the stocks] rather, **the collar.** Another meaning suggested is *a close prison house*. The word however occurs in the former sense in the kindred Arabic, and may well denote that which confined the neck.

fore he sent unto us *in* Babylon, saying, This *captivity is
long*: build ye houses, and dwell *in them;* and plant gardens,
29 and eat the fruit of them. And Zephaniah the priest read
30 this letter in the ears of Jeremiah the prophet. Then came
31 the word of the LORD unto Jeremiah, saying, Send to all
them of the captivity, saying, Thus saith the LORD concerning Shemaiah the Nehelamite; Because that Shemaiah hath
prophesied unto you, and I sent him not, and he caused
32 you to trust in a lie: therefore thus saith the LORD; Behold,
I will punish Shemaiah the Nehelamite, and his seed: he
shall not have a man to dwell among this people; neither
shall he behold the good that I will do for my people, saith
the LORD; because he hath taught rebellion against the
LORD.

28. *For therefore he sent*] Because ye have allowed him to do as he likes at home, he has taken the same liberty with us. We may however render simply, *Forasmuch as he hath sent*, etc.

32. *therefore thus saith the Lord*] These and the following words come at length as the part of the sentence answering to "because thou hast sent," etc. of ver. 25. The intervening break has resulted from the long explanation and detail which was necessary. The punishment to be inflicted on Shemaiah was twofold, First, he was to leave no children behind him, and secondly, he should see no good come upon his people, either in the way of the speedy return which he had been promising them, or in the way of peace and comparative prosperity in exile.

CHAPS. XXX.—XXXIII.

Hitherto the general tone of Jeremiah's prophecies has been gloomy. Any gleams of brightness that have from time to time appeared (e. g. iii. 14, xvi. 14, 15, xxiii. 3) have borne but a very small proportion to the long stretches of melancholy foreboding and stern declaration of coming punishment, which have formed the gist of his prophecies. In chaps. xxx.—xxxiii. we have a marked change in this respect, and the whole tone here is that of hope. This is the more remarkable, as chaps. xxxii., xxxiii. were written in the tenth year of Zedekiah, and in the midst of the siege (xxxii. 1, compare xxxiii. 1), while it seems probable from the internal evidence that the two earlier chapters, connected so closely with these in subject-matter, were composed and committed to writing somewhere about the same date. The prophet was in prison, famine and pestilence held possession of the city, and the prospects of the nation were such as to create despair in every mind. It was at such a time as this, when humanly speaking the people most needed the comfort of hope, and yet the prophet, had he been speaking his own words, was least likely to be able or willing to afford it them, that it was announced

Chap. XXX. 1—5. *Introduction.*

The word that came to Jeremiah from the Lord, saying, 30
Thus speaketh the Lord God of Israel, saying, Write thee 2
all the words that I have spoken unto thee in a book. For 3
lo, the days come, saith the Lord, that I will bring again
the captivity of my people Israel and Judah, saith the Lord:
and I will cause them to return to the land that I gave to
their fathers, and they shall possess it. And these *are* the 4
words that the Lord spake concerning Israel and concerning Judah. For thus saith the Lord, 5

through Jeremiah that the people of God should not perish, that through them the Gentile nations should be led to a knowledge of the truth, and that the Righteous Branch should yet arise from the house of David and Zion's name be *The Lord our Righteousness*. We may divide the whole prophecy into three parts : (i) "The triumphal hymn of Israel's salvation" (Hengst.) xxx., xxxi.; (ii) The purchase by Jeremiah of a field in Anathoth with an explanation of the significance of this act; (iii) Promise of restoration of the nation with renewed glory conferred on the house of David and the Levitical priesthood.

Chap. XXX. 1—5. Introduction.

2. *Write thee all the words*] Jeremiah had already in the fourth year of Jehoiakim's reign adopted this method of securing that his words should have permanent effect upon the minds of his countrymen. It was now still more necessary that they should be committed to writing, as many had meanwhile been removed to Babylon and a second deportation of captives was imminent. Besides we are not sure how far he may at this time have possessed personal freedom. See chap. xxxiii. 1.

that I have spoken unto thee] From a certain amount of similarity between these chaps. and iii.—vi. (especially iii. 17—25) it has been thought that the former are contemporary with the latter, i. e. that both are to be referred to the days of Josiah. This however is quite unsustained by the opinion of commentators generally or by the probabilities of the case.

3. *For......I will bring again the captivity*] This verse shews that "all the words" (ver. 2) are not to be taken as meaning all the revelations that God had ever made to Jeremiah, but that which He had declared to him upon the special subject of the restoration of the people.

4. *concerning Israel and concerning Judah*] Both divisions of the kingdom of David are thus mentioned, as they are to be spoken of separately in the prophecy which follows in chap. xxxi. (Israel 1—22, Judah 23—26).

5—9. *When all is darkest, deliverance shall come.*

We have heard a voice of trembling,
Of fear, and not of peace.

6 Ask ye now, and see whether a man doth travail with child?
Wherefore do I see every man *with* his hands on his loins, as a woman in travail,
And all faces are turned into paleness?

7 Alas! for that day *is* great, so that none *is* like it:
It *is* even the time of Jacob's trouble;
But he shall be saved out of it.

8 For it shall come to pass in that day, saith the LORD of hosts,
That I will break his yoke from off thy neck,
And will burst thy bonds,
And strangers shall no more serve themselves of him:

5—9. WHEN ALL IS DARKEST, DELIVERANCE SHALL COME.

5. *We have heard a voice of trembling*] The prophet begins the prophecy which is to contain the promise of deliverance with a description which shall intensify the contrast that is coming. The restoration can only be effected by the overthrow of their oppressors in war, which of necessity involves 'trembling.'

Of fear, and not of peace] **Fear and no peace.** It is best to take the words thus, as those of the exiles themselves. The approaching capture of Babylon does not bring them unmixed joy. They must in common with their masters submit to the horrors and uncertainties of war and siege.

7. *that day is great, so that none is like it*] the day of the overthrow of Babylon. It is even greater than that of Nineveh, as described by Nahum (ii. 10—12, iii. 8, 10). The language here seems to be suggested by Joel ii. 2, 11.

he shall be saved out of it] Here we have the transition to the joyous note which dominates the rest of the prophecy.

8. *his yoke*] Does this mean (i) the yoke imposed by him (the king of Babylon) or (ii) borne by him (Israel)? To take it in the second sense might have seemed an intolerably harsh construction in the face of the instantaneous change of person 'from off thy neck' but for the frequency with which such a change occurs in Jeremiah, another instance presenting itself in the latter part of this same verse. If (ii) be right however, the change from 'his (yoke)' to 'thy (neck),' as occurring in the very same clause, is even harsher than from 'thy (bonds)' to '(of) him.'

bonds] The Heb. is the word rendered as here in the text of xxvii. 2, where however see note.

serve themselves of him] This phrase has been already used, in xxv. 14, xxvii. 7.

But they shall serve the LORD their God, 9
And David their king, whom I will raise up unto them.

10—17. *Israel shall not be as now forgotten and afflicted.*

Therefore fear thou not, O my servant Jacob, saith the 10
LORD;
Neither be dismayed, O Israel:
For lo, I *will* save thee from afar,
And thy seed from the land of their captivity;
And Jacob shall return,
And shall be in rest, and be quiet,
And none shall make *him* afraid.
For I *am* with thee, saith the LORD, to save thee: 11
Though I make a full end of all nations whither I have scattered thee,
Yet will I not make a full end of thee:
But I will correct thee in measure,
And will not leave thee altogether unpunished.
For thus saith the LORD, 12
Thy bruise *is* incurable,
And thy wound *is* grievous.

9. *the Lord their God, and David their king*] For the whole expression as uniting the Lord and the Messiah compare Hos. iii. 5, and for the Messiah spoken of elsewhere also under the name David, Ezek. xxxiv. 23, 24, xxxvii. 24.

Bp Jer. Taylor (Epistle Dedicatory to his *Ductor Dubitantium*) applies verses 7 and 9 to the English Commonwealth under Oliver Cromwell and the Restoration of the House of Stuart. "We have been sorely smitten and for a long time; for (that I may use the words of the prophet) 'Alas, for that day was great, so that none was like it, it was even the time of Jacob's trouble....But since God hath left off to smite us with an iron rod, and hath once more said unto these nations, They shall serve the Lord their God, and David their king, whom I have raised up unto them;' now our duty stands on the sunny side," etc.

10—17. ISRAEL SHALL NOT BE AS NOW FORGOTTEN AND AFFLICTED.

10. *from afar*] from thy distant land of exile.
11. *Yet will I not make a full end of thee*] See note on iv. 27.
I will correct thee in measure] See note on ii. 19, and on x. 24.
12. *Thy bruise is incurable*] more literally, *It is ill with thy bruise. incurable*] See note on xvii. 9.
The pronouns in the verse are fem. as referring to the *nation*, as in xxii. 20 and often elsewhere. For the whole verse compare Lam. ii. 13.

13 *There is* none to plead thy cause, that thou mayest be
bound up:
Thou hast no healing medicines.
14 All thy lovers have forgotten thee;
They seek thee not;
For I have wounded thee *with* the wound of an enemy,
with the chastisement of a cruel one,
For the multitude of thine iniquity;
Because thy sins were increased.

13. It has been already pointed out (Introd. chap. II. 8) that Jeremiah frequently mixes together an image or figure of speech and the thing which it represents. Here we have a case of the rapid interchange of two images or figures. In the same verse the people of God appears as defendant in a suit at law, and as one suffering from a wound which cannot be staunched.

There is none to plead thy cause] Thine enemies at present are having it all their own way, as they arraign thee for thy sins before the bar of God's Justice.

that thou mayest be bound up] This, which obviously has no connexion with the earlier metaphor, should be joined with the words that follow. For (the pressing together of) **thy wound (there is no healing, no plaister).** The Heb. thus rendered *wound* comes from a root signifying to press together (the sides of a wound). It occurs but seldom (Hos. v. 13 twice; Obad. 7) but in each other case the sense is clear.

medicines] **plaister**, literally, *that which goes up* (on the wound).

14. *thy lovers*] the nations which sought to ally themselves with thee. See xxvii. 3.

For the multitude...] This had best be rendered **because of** *the multitude*, or, **the greatness**, etc. Thus the whole verse will form three divisions, each subdivided into two parallel clauses:

All thy lovers have forgotten thee,
They seek thee not;
For I have wounded thee with the wound of an enemy,
With the chastisement of a cruel one;
Because of the multitude of thine iniquity,
Because thy sins were increased.

were increased] literally, *are strong*.

15. Here again we get a parallelism of clauses, and we must further amend the punctuation of the Eng. Vers.

Why criest thou for thine affliction?
(Because) thy sorrow is incurable?
Because of the multitude of thine iniquity,
Because thy sins are increased,
I have done these things unto thee.

Why criest thou for thine affliction? 15
Thy sorrow *is* incurable for the multitude of thine iniquity:
Because thy sins were increased, I have done these things unto thee.
Therefore all they that devour thee shall be devoured; 16
And all thine adversaries, every one of them, shall go into captivity;
And they that spoil thee shall be a spoil,
And all that prey upon thee will I give for a prey.
For I will restore health unto thee, 17
And I will heal thee of thy wounds, saith the LORD;
Because they called thee an Outcast, *saying*,
This *is* Zion, whom no man seeketh after.

18—24. *Jerusalem shall be prosperous and in favour with God.*

Thus saith the LORD: 18
Behold, I *will* bring again the captivity of Jacob's tents,
And have mercy on his dwelling places;

Why criest thou, &c.] Why dost thou complain of that which is the natural consequence of thy sins?
sorrow] properly **pain of body**, or **hurt**.
incurable] See note on xvii. 9.
for the multitude] This we alter as in the previous verse.
16. *Therefore*] Because thou hast undergone thy portion of suffering and it is plain that none other than myself can deliver thee.
all they that devour thee] See chap. ii. 3 with note.
17. *I will restore health unto thee*] better, *I will place* a healing plaister *upon thee*. See viii. 22, also note on xxxiii. 6, where the word is translated *cure* in the Eng. Vers. *Healing plaister* is a preferable rendering to that which represents more closely the sense of the corresponding Arabic word, viz. the new skin which forms over a wound in healing. In this latter way however some would translate the Heb. here.
Zion] The Septuagint have "a spoil," shewing that they followed a reading in the original, not now found in any Heb. authorities, but differing only slightly from the other which is beyond doubt correct.

18—24. JERUSALEM SHALL BE PROSPEROUS AND IN FAVOUR WITH GOD.

18. *the captivity of Jacob's tents*] For the word *tents* see note on chap. iv. 20. The sense here is in general, *The Jews who have been taken captive shall dwell again in their land as aforetime.*

And the city shall be builded upon her own heap,
And the palace shall remain after the manner thereof.
19 And out of them shall proceed thanksgiving and the voice of them that make merry:
And I will multiply them, and they shall not be few;
I will also glorify them, and they shall not be small.
20 Their children also shall be as aforetime,
And their congregation shall be established before me,
And I will punish all that oppress them.
21 And their nobles shall be of themselves,
And their governor shall proceed from the midst of them;
And I will cause him to draw near, and he shall approach unto me:
For who *is* this that engaged his heart to approach unto me? saith the LORD.

upon her own heap] meaning, not heap of ruins, but the hill on which she had previously stood, on her old site. A 'hill' was the usual position of the eastern cities (Matt. v. 14), as helping to protect them alike from sudden attack and from inundation. Hence the frequency with which the word Tel (which is the Heb. here translated *heap*) forms part of the name of a city; Telassar (Thelassar) (2 Kings xix. 12; Is. xxxvii. 12); Tel-Haresha = Tel-Harsa and Tel-Melah (Ezra ii. 59; Neh. vii. 61); Tel-Abib (Ezek. iii. 15).

shall remain after the manner thereof] **shall be inhabited after its fashion**, i.e. it shall be occupied by a king and shall be kept up with all the appliances and state suitable for such a place.

19. *And out of them*] both city and palace.

shall proceed thanksgiving] Compare xxxiii. 11.

20. *Their children*] The Heb. is *His* (Jacob's) children, and so for the other pronouns of the verse.

as aforetime] as in the times of David and Solomon, the golden age of the Jewish kingdom.

congregation] the people collectively.

21. A Messianic prophecy. As the Jews were now coming under foreign rule, so the promise is that in the end they shall again be placed under a Prince of their own. This Prince shall draw near to God without a go-between, in other words he shall be Priest as well as King. Thus he shall be greater than even David or Solomon.

their nobles] Both pronoun and substantive are singular, *his* (Jacob's) *mighty one*.

of themselves] This expression *may* mean something more than Jewish, opposed to foreign, as explained above. It may further imply that the new Ruler shall spring from a lowly family, one as yet unknown to fame. This sense however we cannot press.

that engaged his heart to approach] **that hath staked his life** *to*

And ye shall be my people, and I will be your God. 22
Behold, the whirlwind of the Lord goeth forth *with* 23 fury,
A continuing whirlwind:
It shall fall with pain upon the head of the wicked.
The fierce anger of the Lord shall not return, until he 24 have done *it*,
And until he have performed the intents of his heart:
In the latter days ye shall consider it.

CHAP. XXXI. 1—9. *Peace, plenty and the blessing of God shall yet abide with Israel.*

At the same time, saith the Lord, 31
Will I be the God of all the families of Israel,

approach. None but the priests were permitted to enter the Lord's presence, and the Holy of Holies was open but once a year to the high-priest himself. To all others this was a profanity to be punished with death. For Messiah as being God the Son the approach to the Father was open. This is the thought concealed in the verse till Christian times should bring it to light. Even to Jewish ears however the expressions betokened the Messiah.

23. This and the following verse are nearly identical with xxiii. 19, 20 (see notes there), where judgment is pronounced upon the false prophets. The reference in this place is not quite clear, although there is every reason to believe that the verses are genuine. If they are connected with the foregoing section, the connexion will be, Although these blessings are in store for the nation, yet the wicked, those who continue impenitent, shall reap none of the benefit nor have their punishment in any wise abated. If on the other hand, as seems more probable, they should be joined with the following section, the sense will be, Babylon (and all other nations as well as individuals who oppose themselves to the Lord) shall suffer for it, while the repentant Israel shall be accepted and blessed.

A continuing whirlwind] The rendering of the participle has caused some difficulty. Probably *sweeping* or *rushing* is the meaning intended, as the senses in which the original word is found elsewhere, viz. *sojourning* (1 Kings xvii. 20) and *assembling* (Hos. vii. 14) are here unsuitable.

24. *consider*] **understand.**

CHAP. XXXI. 1—9. PEACE, PLENTY AND THE BLESSING OF GOD SHALL YET ABIDE WITH ISRAEL.

1. *At the same time*] *In the latter days* spoken of at the end of chap. xxx.

all the families of Israel] the twelve tribes. Afterwards the Northern kingdom is dealt with (2—22), then the Southern (23—26), and then again both together (27—40).

And they shall be my people.
2 Thus saith the LORD,
The people which were left of the sword found grace in the wilderness;
Even Israel when *I* went to cause him to rest.
3 The LORD hath appeared of old unto me, *saying*,
Yea, I have loved thee *with* an everlasting love;
Therefore *with* lovingkindness have I drawn thee.
4 Again I will build thee, and thou shalt be built, O virgin of Israel:
Thou shalt again be adorned *with* thy tabrets,

2. Interpretations which have been offered of this verse are to refer it (i) to the Exodus from Egypt, (ii) to the return from exile. According to (i) the sense will be, The escaped from Pharaoh's oppression were supported in the desert that lay between Egypt and Canaan; according to (ii) Those who survive the sufferings of the Assyrian captivity are promised a safe journey through the desert home. On the other hand in li. 50 the Jews delivered from Babylon are spoken of as escaped from the sword, and are told to remember the Lord *afar off* (see note on verse 3). If we accept (ii), the verb will of course be in the *prophetic* past. The expression "left of the sword" hardly suits the circumstances of the Egyptian bondage or the deliverance from that servitude. On the other hand even if in the case of these words we adopt (ii), it is open to us to understand those that follow as relating to the wilderness of Sinai, which therefore will make a third possible interpretation. Perhaps on the whole (ii) is best, understanding however the expression "found grace in the wilderness" to be chosen as having a distinct allusion to the wilderness journey of old time. The grace then shewn God has now determined to repeat.

Even Israel when I went to cause him to rest] **Let me go to give him rest** (or, **when he (the Lord) went to find him rest**), **even Israel**.

3. *The Lord hath appeared of old unto me*] It is best to take this as put in the mouth of the people themselves.

of old] **from afar**, as the same Heb. word is rendered chap. xxx. 10. The people from their distant exile in Assyria think upon God as dwelling upon His accustomed seat, Mount Zion.

with lovingkindness have I drawn thee] rather, **I have prolonged** loving-kindness **to thee**. So the Heb. word is rightly rendered in Ps. xxxvi. 10, cix. 12.

4. *I will build thee, and thou shalt be built*] For build=make to prosper, see note on xii. 16.

O virgin of Israel] The nation is addressed under the figure of a woman, as so often.

tabrets] The margin has *timbrels*. Both words are used in the Eng. Vers. to translate the Heb. *tôph*, the *duff* or *diff* of the Arabs, a hoop on

And shalt go forth in the dances of them that make merry.

Thou shalt yet plant vines upon the mountains of Samaria: 5

The planters shall plant, and shall eat *them* as common things.

For there shall be a day, 6

That the watchmen upon the mount Ephraim shall cry,

Arise ye, and let us go up *to* Zion unto the LORD our God.

For thus saith the LORD; 7

Sing with gladness for Jacob,

which pieces of brass are often fixed, and over which parchment is extended. It is thus played with the fingers like our tambourine. The whole group of words (compare French *tambour, tabouret*, Provençal *tabor*, Eng. *tabor*, Span. *tambor*, Ital. *tamburo*) were probably introduced into Europe by the Crusaders, who learned the name and use of the instrument from the Saracens. *Taber* is used as a verb (to beat as a tabor or tabret) in Nah. ii. 7. The name *tōph* is probably derived either from the sound or from a root meaning to strike (Gk. τύπ-τω, τύμπ-ανον, Eng. *thump, tap*). The tabret was used in early times by the Syrians of Padan-aram (Gen. xxxi. 27), played principally by women (Ex. xv. 20; Jud. xi. 34; 1 Sam. xviii. 6; Ps. lxviii. 25), but also by prophets (1 Sam. x. 5) and by others (2 Sam. vi. 5; 1 Chron. xiii. 8). See Sm., *Bibl. Dict.*, Art. 'Timbrel.'

5. *shall eat them as common things*] Our version here quite misses the sense, which is *shall eat* **the fruit**. The fruit borne by a tree for the first three years was not to be gathered, that of the fourth year was to be consecrated to God, while that of the fifth year the owner might eat. See Lev. xix. 23—25; Deut. xx. 6, xxviii. 30. The word which in those passages expresses the handing over of the fruit to God or to the owner's use, as the case may be, is that used in this passage also.

6. *watchmen*] According to a Jewish tradition, which is by them referred back to Moses himself, watchers were placed seven times a year on the 30th day of the month on heights round Jerusalem to await the appearance of the new moon and thus determine the beginning of the month, which with them coincided with its phases. When they made the announcement, the news was conveyed from the Mount of Olives by beacon fires upon the hills. These watchmen are posted in the present case in order that members of the Northern kingdom may go up to keep the Feasts in Jerusalem, thus betokening the end of the schism which had so long kept the two kingdoms apart.

7. *Sing*] The imperatives throughout are in the plural, and that not Israel only is meant, but in general all who are acquainted with the circumstances of the nation before and after this joyful change in its fortunes, is rendered probable by ver. 10 ("O ye nations").

And shout among the chief of the nations:
Publish ye, praise ye, and say,
O Lord, save thy people, the remnant of Israel.
8 Behold, I *will* bring them from the north country,
And gather them from the coasts of the earth,
And with them the blind and the lame,
The woman with child and her that travaileth with child together:
A great company shall return thither.
9 They shall come with weeping,
And with supplications will I lead them:
I will cause them to walk by the rivers of waters
In a straight way, wherein they shall not stumble:
For I am a father to Israel,
And Ephraim *is* my firstborn.

10—14. *Similar promises renewed.*

10 Hear the word of the Lord,
O ye nations,

among the chief of the nations] either, *at the head of the nations*, or *on account of the chosen people*, now restored to their rightful position.

O Lord, save] *Hosannah*, the expression of a joyful wish, or congratulation, rather than strictly speaking a prayer. Compare Ps. cxviii. 25; Matt. xxi. 9.

8. The Lord's reply to the joyous acclamation.
north country] See note on chap. iii. 12.
coasts of the earth] See note on vi. 22.
the blind and the lame...] None shall be omitted, even those who would naturally have most difficulty in travelling shall return.
thither] **hither**, to Palestine, where the prophet is now writing.

9. *with weeping*] tears at once of contrition for their rebellion and of joy at their return.
supplications] not *favours*, as the Eng. margin reads.
by the rivers] **to** *the rivers*.
Ephraim is my firstborn] These words may merely express the choice of Israel as against all other nations of the world. It is also however very possible that Ephraim may here mean the Northern kingdom (of which this was the principal tribe), and then the sense will be, Although its punishment came earlier than that of the Southern kingdom, yet if it repent, it shall be forgiven first. Compare for this sense chap. iii. 18 with note.

10—14. Similar promises renewed.

10. *O ye nations*] See note on ver. 9.

And declare *it* in the isles afar off, and say,
He that scattered Israel will gather him,
And keep him as a shepherd *doth* his flock.
For the Lord hath redeemed Jacob, 11
And ransomed him from the hand of *him that was* stronger than he.
Therefore they shall come and sing in the height of Zion, 12
And shall flow *together* to the goodness of the Lord,
For wheat, and for wine, and for oil,
And for the young of the flock and of the herd:
And their soul shall be as a watered garden;
And they shall not sorrow any more at all.
Then shall the virgin rejoice in the dance, 13
Both young men and old together:
For I will turn their mourning into joy,
And will comfort them, and make them rejoice from their sorrow.
And I will satiate the soul of the priests with fatness, 14

the isles] See note on xxv. 22.

He that scattered Israel will gather him] The nations are instructed that as it was not their doing but God's, that His people had been subject to a foreign yoke, so now their restoration was His work alone.

12. *shall flow together*] **shall flow.** The exact sense however is not quite plain. Does it continue the picture which the first clause gives us of the returned tribes assembling in joyful worship on the holy mountain, that they may receive the blessings of a fruitful land, or are they likened to a river which pours down from Zion, so that, their religious service over, they go forth to their several abodes to reap the produce of the field, vineyard and oliveyard? There is good authority for the latter of these, but the use of the word in the parallel passages (chap. li. 44; Is. ii. 2; Mic. iv. 1) makes the former to be perhaps on the whole the better of the two.

for wheat...] or, **to the corn, to the wine** etc., as an explanation of that in which "the goodness of the Lord" shall consist.

wheat] **corn.**

sorrow] **pine,** waste away through listlessness and inactivity, such as they had felt when exiles. Compare ver. 25 and note.

13. *both young men*] **and** young men, etc. This rendering will save us from imagining, as the Eng. Vers. suggests, that any but the virgins shew their rejoicing by the special means of the dance. With the others we have merely to understand *rejoice*.

14. *satiate*] literally, *water*.

the soul of the priests with fatness] The sacrifices shall be so numerous that the priests and their families shall have more than enough for their share. The priest's portion was the wave-breast and heave-shoulder (Lev. vii. 31—34).

And my people shall be satisfied with my goodness, saith the LORD.

15—26. *Ephraim's weeping and remorse shall disappear. Judah also shall be brought back.*

15 Thus saith the LORD;
A voice was heard in Ramah,
Lamentation, *and* bitter weeping;
Rahel weeping for her children
Refused to be comforted for her children, because they *were* not.

15—26. EPHRAIM'S WEEPING AND REMORSE SHALL DISAPPEAR. JUDAH ALSO SHALL BE BROUGHT BACK.

15. This verse is specially familiar to our ears, though the use made of it by St Matt. (ii. 17, 18), who, having related the slaughter of the Innocents at Bethlehem, adds, "Then was fulfilled that which was spoken by Jeremy the prophet, saying, In Rama was there a voice heard, lamentation," etc. It is possible that there may have been a place of this name near Bethlehem which has since disappeared (and in favour of this may be advanced the meaning of the name, which is simply *high-place*), but this is by no means necessary in order to understand the Apostle's use of the verse. It is quoted by him as an illustration, or type. The mourning at Ramah is a forecast of that bitter wailing which shall be raised by the mothers of the slaughtered babes, while Rachel's name (Rahel), used in the prophecy, is naturally associated with Bethlehem by the fact that her tomb was in its neighbourhood (Gen. xxxv. 16—19, xlviii. 7). The two best known Ramahs in the O.T. history are (*a*) a city mentioned first in Josh. xviii. 25, between Gibeon and Beeroth, five miles north of Jerusalem; and (*b*) the birth-place, home, and place of burial of Samuel (1 Sam. i. 19, xxv. 1). The latter was in Mount Ephraim, the limits of which are however rather vague, and was probably about four miles north-west of Jerusalem. Both of these are much too far from Bethlehem to be in any way *immediately* connected with the subject in illustration of which St Matt. quotes the passages. One or other of them was doubtless the Ramah at which the exiles were assembled before departing for Babylon, as described chap. xl. 1. The appropriateness of calling upon Rachel to weep in Ramah consists in this, that she, the one of Jacob's wives who had so ardently longed for children (Gen. xxx. 1), and mother of Ephraim, Manasseh, and Benjamin, should in a conspicuous border town of the two kingdoms, with both of which she was thus immediately connected, lament the overthrow of her offspring. The fitness of the figure is unaltered, whether we take the reference to be to some special butchery on the part of the Assyrian captors, of which Ramah was remembered in Jeremiah's day as the scene, or only to their general cruelty.

Thus saith the LORD, 16
Refrain thy voice from weeping,
And thine eyes from tears:
For thy work shall be rewarded, saith the LORD;
And they shall come again from the land of the enemy.
And there is hope in thine end, saith the LORD, 17
That *thy* children shall come again to their own border.
I have surely heard Ephraim bemoaning himself *thus;* 18
Thou hast chastised me, and I was chastised,
As a bullock unaccustomed *to the yoke;*
Turn thou me, and I shall be turned;
For thou *art* the LORD my God.
Surely after that I was turned, I repented; 19
And after that I was instructed, I smote upon *my* thigh:
I was ashamed, yea, even confounded,
Because I did bear the reproach of my youth.
Is Ephraim my dear son? *is he* a pleasant child? 20

16. *thy work shall be rewarded*] As children have been in thy life and thy death a subject of pain and grief to thee, and as these thy descendants again have grievously perished, so the recompense for all this trouble now arrives, and thou shalt witness the return of the captives.

18. The Lord declares that He has heard Ephraim confessing that his punishment was the just consequence of his sin, and praying for acceptance.

as a bullock unaccustomed to the yoke] as a calf that has not been tamed.

19. *after that I was turned*] The word 'turn,' as we have already seen (chap. iii. 22, viii. 4), is ambiguous, meaning either turning *from* or *to* God. Here the parallel clause which follows ('after that I was instructed,' etc.) would rather suggest the latter of these senses. Repentance, however, comes *after* this turning, and thus it is shewn to mean turning away from God, seeing that turning towards Him would come not after, but before or with, repentance.

instructed] by punishment. Compare the use of the word "taught" (the same verb in the Heb.), Judg. viii. 16.

I smote upon my thigh] in token of contrition.

the reproach of my youth] the disgrace brought upon me by the sins of my earlier life as a nation.

20. God is represented as the speaker. He asks Himself whether Ephraim is still beloved by Him. The answer is contained in the words that follow. As often as He makes mention of him, His affection towards him is stirred. The picture is of course adapted to human modes of thought and feeling, and represents God as acting in the same

> For since I spake against him, I do earnestly remember him still:
> Therefore my bowels are troubled for him;
> I will surely have mercy upon him, saith the Lord.
> 21 Set thee up waymarks, make thee high heaps:
> Set thine heart toward the highway,
> *Even* the way *which* thou wentest:
> Turn again, O virgin of Israel,
> Turn again to these thy cities,
> 22 How long wilt thou go about, O thou backsliding daughter?
> For the Lord hath created a new *thing* in the earth,
> A woman shall compass a man.

way in which a man would, when thinking upon the ingratitude and rebellion of a son, whom he nevertheless cannot but continue to love.

pleasant child] literally, *a child of delights, a beloved child.*

since I spake against him] rather, *as often as I speak of him.*

my bowels are troubled] They were the supposed seat of the emotions. *My affection is stirred within me.*

21. *waymarks*] stones either as *sepulchral* (2 Kings xxiii. 17, "title;" Ezek. xxxix. 15, "sign"), or, as here, to mark the road.

high heaps] pillars, **sign-posts**. The verse is a lively way of calling upon the people to make all speed to return.

set thine heart] The heart in Heb. denotes the seat of the intellect. Hence the sense is, *turn thy attention* to the way by which thou wentest into exile, that thou mayest retrace thy steps.

22. *How long wilt thou go about*] How long wilt thou hesitate to return? A sign follows, in order to induce Israel to complete her reconciliation with her offended God.

the Lord hath created...] Much difficulty has been felt in the explanation of the last part of the verse. Any rendering which will not present 'a new thing,' a complete exception to the established order of things, will plainly not satisfy the requirements of the context. This disposes at once of such as *the woman will become manly in spirit, the woman will keep close to the man, the woman will seek protection from the man*, all of which have been proposed. The only help we seem to get for the (Heb.) verb of the clause, which primarily means, as in the Eng. Vers., to 'compass,' surround, comes from Deut. xxxii. 10, "He (the Lord) *led* him (Israel) *about*, he instructed him, he kept him as the apple of his eye;" and Ps. xxxii. 10, "He that trusteth in the Lord, mercy shall *compass* him *about*," where the verb is that used here. The same notion then of cherishing and protecting will here signify that such is the Lord's condescension towards Israel, that He will for her glory allow the natural order to be reversed, and deign to accept protection (of His Temple, services, honour, etc.) at her hands. This thought is really Messianic, for it attains completion only in the Incarnation of the Divine Son of

Thus saith the LORD of hosts, the God of Israel; 23
As yet they shall use this speech in the land of Judah and
   in the cities thereof,
When I shall bring again their captivity;
The LORD bless thee, O habitation of justice, *and* moun-
   tain of holiness.
And there shall dwell in Judah itself, 24
And *in* all the cities thereof together,
Husbandmen, and they *that* go forth with flocks.
For I have satiated the weary soul, 25
And I have replenished every sorrowful soul.
Upon this I awaked, and beheld; 26
And my sleep was sweet unto me.

27—34. Israel and Judah together shall serve God and prosper.

Behold, the days come, saith the LORD, 27
That I will sow the house of Israel and the house of Judah

God, growing up and in youth at any rate cherished (Luke ii. 52) by the Jewish nation, of which in His human nature He was a child. Accordingly many interpreters in all ages have understood the passage of the miraculous conception of Christ. It can hardly, however, be limited to this.

The Septuagint ("men shall walk about in safety"), departing from the words of the original, and seeking to render the sense only, have missed the meaning.

23. The Lord now turns from Israel (Ephraim) to Judah, and in this and the next two verses promises her like blessing.

23. *As yet*] rather, **Again**, as was the use in former time.
mountain of holiness] The expression seems to be used indifferently of the Temple Mountain and of Jerusalem as a whole. See Ps. ii. 6; Is. xi. 9, xxvii. 13, and especially for Jerusalem the following: Is. lxvi. 20; Dan. ix. 16; Zech. viii. 3.

24. *they that go forth*] *they that go* **about**, opposed to dwellers in fixed habitations, such as the inhabitants of the towns and husbandmen.

25. *sorrowful*] **pining**, practically the same word as that rendered "sorrow" in ver. 12, where see note.

26. The words of the prophet himself, as they are not suitable either to God or to the exiles. The ecstatic state under which Jeremiah had received the foregoing communications he here calls 'sleep,' and as the prophecy had been of so unusually cheering a character, that sleep might well be called sweet.

27—34. ISRAEL AND JUDAH TOGETHER SHALL SERVE GOD AND
                        PROSPER.

27. *I will sow...with the seed of man, and with the seed of beast*] I

214   JEREMIAH, XXXI.   [vv. 28—31.

With the seed of man, and *with* the seed of beast.

28 And it shall come to pass, *that* like as I have watched over them,
To pluck up, and to break down, and to throw down,
And to destroy, and to afflict;
So will I watch over them, to build, and to plant, saith the LORD.

29 In those days they shall say no more,
The fathers have eaten a sour grape,
And the children's teeth are set on edge.

30 But every one shall die for his own iniquity:
Every man that eateth the sour grape,
His teeth shall be set on edge.

31 Behold, the days come, saith the LORD,
That I will make a new covenant

will make the people and their cattle to prosper and multiply so fast, that the offspring of both shall seem almost to spring from the ground after the manner of seed sown.

28. *I have watched over them*] The Heb. verb is the same as that rendered "I will hasten" in the Eng. Vers. of chap. i. 12, where see note.

to pluck up, &c.] Compare chap. i. 10, xviii. 7, 9. Thus the later and more cheering part of the message for which Jeremiah was ordained is now being delivered by him.

29, 30. The words 'The fathers have eaten,' &c. (quoted also Ezek. xviii. 2) was a common proverb among the Jews, suggested probably, though not (in the sense in which they used it) supported, by the words of the Second Commandment (Exod. xx. 5, 6). The punishment which succeeded to the accumulated iniquities of "the third and fourth generation" could be averted by repentance ("shewing mercy unto thousands of them that love me and keep my commandments"). The commandment, therefore, is in no way opposed to the words 'every one shall die for his own iniquity,' words which express that juster view of the sins of *each* generation, younger as well as older, which was to succeed the complaining tone adopted by those blind to their own disobedience, and convinced that they, though innocent, were suffering only for their fathers' faults. We should read the plural **sour grapes** in both verses, the Heb. being a noun of multitude.

31—34. We have here the announcement of a new covenant which should supersede that made at the time of the Exodus from Egypt, differing from it (i) in permanence, (ii) in the principle by which it should be maintained unbroken. The Mosaic Law consisted of duties imposed upon the people from without; the spring of action which should produce willing conformity to the new covenant was to be wholly within. Moses indeed (Deut. xxx. 6) speaks of the people's hearts being circumcised to love

With the house of Israel, and with the house of Judah:

32 Not according to the covenant that I made with their fathers
In the day *that* I took them by the hand,
To bring them out of the land of Egypt;
Which my covenant they break,
Although I was a husband unto them, saith the LORD:

33 But this *shall be* the covenant that I will make with the house of Israel;
After those days, saith the LORD,
I will put my law in their inward parts,
And write it in their hearts;
And will be their God,
And they shall be my people.

34 And they shall teach no more every man his neighbour, and every man his brother, saying, Know the LORD:
For they shall all know me,

the Lord with all their heart and soul, but now the motive power that belongs to the new dispensation is for the first time made plain. The sense of forgiveness (ver. 34) through God's grace shall call out such a spirit of gratitude as shall ensure a willing service, depending on inward not outward motives, based on love, not fear. The new covenant therefore is at once to replace the old (see Heb. viii. 8—12), and yet, new in form, to be still the same in substance. 'I will be their God, and they shall be my people,' was the central object of the old (Exod. xxix. 45; Lev. xxvi. 12), even as it is now of the new.

32. *in the day that*] referring not to the single night of their departure from Egypt, but to the whole exodus time, whose culminating point was when the Law was given at Sinai.

although I was a husband unto them] The only important difference in the form of the passage as quoted in the Epistle to the Hebrews (see above) is that this clause, following the Septuagint rendering, appears in the form "and I regarded them not." The Eng. Vers. here is undoubtedly a more faithful rendering of the Heb. The argument of the writer of the Epistle however in no way depended upon the sense of this clause, and there was therefore no reason why he should not give it as it stood in the Authorised Version of his day (Septuagint).

34. The sense is not that there shall be no longer any need of instruction in religion, but that there shall be a directness of access to God, both for Jew and Gentile, which did not exist under the old covenant. (See note on the word *know*, chap. xvi. 13.) A distinctive feature of the

> From the least of them unto the greatest of them,
> saith the LORD:
> For I will forgive their iniquity,
> And I will remember their sin no more.

35—40. *The restoration of Israel to favour is as certain as the ordinances of nature.*

35 > Thus saith the LORD, which giveth the sun for a light by day,
> *And* the ordinances of the moon and of the stars for a light by night,
> Which divideth the sea when the waves thereof roar;
> The LORD of hosts *is* his name:

36 > If those ordinances depart from before me, saith the LORD,
> *Then* the seed of Israel also shall cease
> From being a nation before me for ever.

37 > Thus saith the LORD;
> If heaven above can be measured,
> And the foundations of the earth searched out beneath,
> I will also cast off all the seed of Israel
> For all that they have done, saith the LORD.

old covenant was *awe* (Exod. xx. 19. "And they said unto Moses, Speak thou with us and we will hear: but let not God speak with us, lest we die"). Human mediation was necessary. But in future, while the knowledge of forgiveness and the quickening graces of the Spirit shall inspire men with a more lively desire to know God as He has revealed Himself to man, the barrier is broken down and there is an immediate approach to Him through the great High Priest, Christ Jesus. Such is the full sense of the words in their application to the Christian dispensation, though from the nature of the case it is a sense only disclosed by the event. See Eph. iii. 12; Heb. iv. 16, x. 19—22.

35—40. THE RESTORATION OF ISRAEL TO FAVOUR IS AS CERTAIN AS THE ORDINANCES OF NATURE.

35. *divideth the sea when...*] **stirreth up** *the sea* **so that** *its waves roar*.

36. *a nation*] **a people.** The word *nation* implies fixity of habitation, government, etc.

37. If men can find, by measuring, a limit to the height of heaven, or probe the earth through and through, then and not otherwise will God utterly reject the whole of his people, whatever He may meanwhile do to individuals among them.

Behold, the days come, saith the LORD, 38
That the city shall be built to the LORD
From the tower of Hananeel unto the gate of the corner.
And the measuring line shall yet go forth over against it 39
Upon the hill Gareb, and shall compass about to Goath.
And the whole valley of the dead bodies, and of the 40
  ashes,
And all the fields unto the brook of Kidron,
Unto the corner of the horse gate towards the east,
Shall be holy unto the LORD;
It shall not be plucked up, nor thrown down any more
  for ever.

38. *Behold, the days come*] The word *come* is omitted in the earliest form of the Heb. text, but probably by an error in copying, as the phrase is a favourite one with Jeremiah. See note on xxiii. 5.

that the city shall be built] The words which follow no doubt express an enlarging of the bounds of the city, but from our ignorance of the exact position of the places named, we cannot see precisely how it was so. From the mention made of "the tower of Hananeel" in Neh. iii. 1, xii. 39; and of "the corner-gate" in 2 Kings xiv. 13 (compare Zech. xiv. 10 for both places) it appears likely that the former was at or near the north-east and the latter the north-west corner of the city wall.

to the Lord] **for** *the Lord*, for His honour.

39. This verse, continuing the description from the north-west corner, takes the western side of Jerusalem and promises an extension in that direction also towards the valley of Hinnom southwards.

Gareb] a word meaning *itch*. Hence it is thought the name here may denote the hill of lepers, and thus mark a spot naturally outside the boundaries of the existing city. Nothing further is known of this name.

Goath] **Goah.** To this place also we have no clue beyond what this verse supplies.

40. *valley of the dead bodies*] the valley of Hinnom, into which carcases of criminals and of animals were cast.

and of the ashes] Although this valley was as a whole unclean, yet a part of it would seem to have been reserved for the ashes which (Lev. vi. 11) were ordered to be carried out after a sacrifice "without the camp into a clean place." The word for ashes denotes properly fat and ashes mixed, such as would be left from a sacrifice.

all the fields] The right reading and the more difficult one seems that which the Septuagint have preserved, although they did not venture to do more than transcribe the Heb. word Sademoth. It probably means either *quarries* or *clefts, rugged rocks.*

the horse gate] mentioned Neh. iii. 28.

This verse makes the same announcement as to the south side of Jerusalem as the earlier ones had done for the north and west sides, viz., that it should in the future enclose spaces now considered unclean.

CHAP. XXXII. 1—5. *Commencement of the history of the two years preceding the destruction of Jerusalem.*

32 The word that came to Jeremiah from the LORD in the tenth year of Zedekiah king of Judah, which *was* the 2 eighteenth year of Nebuchadrezzar. For then the king of Babylon's army besieged Jerusalem: and Jeremiah the prophet was shut up in the court of the prison, which *was* 3 *in* the king of Judah's house. For Zedekiah king of Judah had shut him up, saying, Wherefore dost thou prophesy, and say, Thus saith the LORD, Behold, I *will* give this city

Nothing is said of the east side, or of the rebuilding of the Temple, although Jeremiah had foretold its destruction, as well as that of the city. Hence we may gather that he is speaking not so much of the literal city as of the spiritual Jerusalem, the Church of the "new covenant," which shall include nations hitherto considered profane, and at once extend the salvation which it offers and banish impurity.

CHAP. XXXII. 1—5. COMMENCEMENT OF THE HISTORY OF THE TWO YEARS PRECEDING THE DESTRUCTION OF JERUSALEM.

1. *The word that came*] This is the introduction to a long section of the Book more continuously historical than any of the preceding portions. It gives the incidents of the two years preceding the capture of Jerusalem, the capture itself, and the events which immediately followed, with prophecies interspersed. The first incident related is Jeremiah's purchase of the field from Hanameel, an act intended to encourage the people to hope for a return from captivity, and in order that it may be brought out that it is in spite of the gloomiest appearances that Jeremiah's faith in the future is thus firm, his own circumstances and those of the state are given with great particularity in these five introductory verses.

the tenth year of Zedekiah] The siege had commenced in his ninth year (xxxix. 1), but the Chaldaeans, hearing that an Egyptian army was approaching, had departed for a time (xxxvii. 5). Jeremiah, about the same time, was found leaving Jerusalem, and charged with falling away to the Chaldaeans, and in spite of his denial he was imprisoned. He seems however after a while to have had the stringency with which he was at first treated relaxed (xxxii. 12, xxxviii. 1). We find nevertheless that he was still 'shut up in the court of the prison' (ver. 2). This part of the narrative therefore is somewhat subsequent in date to those incidents above referred to which are recounted later.

the eighteenth year of Nebuchadrezzar] This agrees with the other two occasions on which his reign is compared directly in date with those of kings of Judah (xxv. 1, lii. 12).

2. *the court of the prison*] rather, *the court of the* **guard**, the quarters of the sentries who guarded the palace.

into the hand of the king of Babylon, and he shall take it; and Zedekiah king of Judah shall not escape out of the hand of the Chaldeans, but shall surely be delivered into the hand of the king of Babylon, and shall speak with him mouth to mouth, and his eyes shall behold his eyes: and 5 he shall lead Zedekiah *to* Babylon, and there shall he be until I visit him, saith the LORD: though ye fight with the Chaldeans, ye shall not prosper.

6—15. *Jeremiah's purchase and its meaning.*

And Jeremiah said, The word of the LORD came unto 6 me, saying, Behold, Hanameel the son of Shallum thine 7 uncle *shall* come unto thee, saying, Buy thee my field that *is* in Anathoth: for the right of redemption *is* thine to buy *it*. So Hanameel mine uncle's son came to 8

4. This verse occurs again in almost the same words at chap. xxxiv. 3, where see note.

5. *until I visit him*] The words are in themselves ambiguous. It was not necessary for Zedekiah to know exactly what was to happen to him. See chap. xxxix. 6, 7. For *visit* in a good sense see chaps. xxvii. 22, xxix. 10; in a bad sense vi. 15, xlix. 8; Numb. xvi. 29. And after all Zedekiah's fate contained good as well as evil. See chap. xxxiv. 4, 5.

6—15. JEREMIAH'S PURCHASE AND ITS MEANING.

7. *Hanameel the son of Shallum thine uncle*] The last two words according to Heb. usage (see note on "the son of Hilkiah," chap. i. 1) should rather belong to the first of the proper names, and this agrees with the Heb. text of ver. 12. The distinct statement in verses 8 and 9 however that Hanameel was Jeremiah's first cousin makes it necessary either to refer the word *uncle* of this verse to Shallum, and consider the word *son* in the Eng. Vers. of ver. 12 to have been accidentally omitted by a Heb. copyist, or, as Heb. names of relationship are used much more loosely than with us, to take the word which we render uncle, as including either relationship.

my field] The question arises how any member of a Levitical family such as Jeremiah's was (chap. i. 1) could sell land in spite of the law in Lev. xxv. 34. It may have been that the law did not apply to property in land which came to a Levite through the female line and in accordance with the law of inheritance mentioned Numb. xxvii. 8.

Anathoth] See Introd. chap. I. § 2 (*c*).

the right of redemption is thine to buy it] If land was, or was about to be, sold, the nearest of kin was bound to purchase or re-purchase it as the case might be (see Lev. xxv. 24, 25; Ruth iv. 6), so that land should not pass from one family to another. The land in question must

me in the court of the prison according to the word of the LORD, and said unto me, Buy my field, I pray thee, that *is* in Anathoth, which *is* in the country of Benjamin: for the right of inheritance *is* thine, and the redemption *is* thine; buy *it* for thyself. Then I knew that this *was* the
9 word of the LORD. And I bought the field of Hanameel my uncle's son, that *was* in Anathoth, and weighed him the
10 money, *even* seventeen shekels of silver. And I subscribed

have been within 2000 cubits (the cubit=about 18 or 19 inches) of the city. See Numb. xxxv. 5.

8. *the right of inheritance is thine*] Jeremiah being the next heir, we infer that Hanameel had no children.

Then I knew...] as falling in with what had been announced to him beforehand (ver. 6, 7).

9. *my uncle's son*] See note on ver. 7.

weighed him the money, even seventeen shekels of silver] The shekel weighed about 220 of our grains. The Heb. is literally, as the margin renders it, *seven shekels and ten pieces of silver*. Hence since the amount, as it stands, may appear small (about £2. 2s. 6d.), it has been suggested that the *seven* were *golden* shekels. This however is improbable, and it is by no means certain that the sum was really a small one. At any rate it would appear from the aim of the whole transaction, that it was the fair price of the field. We do not of course know its size, but it is likely that it was but a small one, the property of the Levites being of limited extent in accordance with what has been mentioned above. We must remember also that in those days silver was of much more value than in our own. Araunah's threshing floor, oxen and implements were bought at a time of great prosperity for fifty shekels (2 Sam. xxiv. 24. See *Sp. Comm.* for other instances bearing the same way). We are also to remember that as Jeremiah had no children, the land would at the year of jubilee, which may not have been far off, revert to the next heirs of Hanameel, and Jeremiah's interest in it under any circumstances extended only to that date.

10. *And I subscribed the evidence*] **And I wrote the particulars in the deed.** If we replace 'evidence' by *deed* all through, we shall see the sense more clearly. It appears that Jeremiah made out and signed in the presence of witnesses, whose signatures also were added, two copies of the deed of purchase, specifying the particulars of the land, and the conditions under which he bought it (viz. that it should be restored at the jubilee, etc.). He then caused one of these deeds to be sealed up and the other left open, the former to be referred to, in case at any time it were suspected that the latter had been tampered with. Both deeds were delivered solemnly to Baruch in the presence of the seller, the witnesses and all the Jews who happened to be present, that he might preserve them secure against damp in an earthen vessel, and that thus a proof of a transaction so important in its bearing on the prospects of the nation should be permanent.

the evidence, and sealed *it*, and took witnesses, and weighed *him* the money in the balances. So I took the evidence of 11 the purchase, *both* that which was sealed *according to* the law and custom, and that which was open: and I gave the 12 evidence of the purchase unto Baruch the son of Neriah, the son of Maaseiah, in the sight of Hanameel mine uncle's *son*, and in the presence of the witnesses that subscribed the book of the purchase, before all the Jews that sat in the court of the prison. And I charged Baruch before them, 13 saying, Thus saith the LORD of hosts, the God of Israel; 14 Take these evidences, this evidence of the purchase, both which is sealed, and this evidence which is open; and put them in an earthen vessel, that they may continue many days. For thus saith the LORD of hosts, the God of Israel; 15 Houses and fields and vineyards shall be possessed again in this land.

16—25. *The prophet asks the Lord how his recent action could be consistent with coming events.*

Now when I had delivered the evidence of the purchase 16

sealed it] not in our sense of adding a seal to a signature ("under one's hand and seal") but sealed up, closed securely.

11. *the evidence of the purchase*] **the deed of purchase.** See note above.

according to the law and custom] rather, **the offer and the conditions**, literally, *the thing fixed and the statutes*, the two parts of which the deed consisted, as explained above, viz. the description of the property and the conditions under which it was sold.

12. *the evidence of the purchase...the book of the purchase*] **the purchase deed** in each case, and so in ver. 14. See former notes.

in the court of the prison] See note on ver. 2.

15. *shall be possessed*] *shall be* **bought.**

"It is not the only time in the history of States and Churches that he who has been denounced as a deserter and traitor [see note on *the tenth year of Zedekiah* ver. 1] becomes in the last extremity the best comforter and counsellor. Demosthenes, who had warned his fellow country-men in his earlier days against their excessive confidence, in his later days was the only man who could reassure their excessive despondency." Stanley's *Jewish Church*, II. 465.

For an illustration of the above transaction from Roman history see Introd. chap. I. § 16.

16—25. THE PROPHET ASKS THE LORD HOW HIS RECENT ACTION COULD BE CONSISTENT WITH COMING EVENTS.

16. *I prayed unto the Lord*] Jeremiah still felt a difficulty in reconciling the obvious sense of the transaction which he had just carried

unto Baruch the son of Neriah, I prayed unto the LORD,
17 saying, Ah Lord GOD! behold, thou hast made the heaven and the earth by thy great power and stretched out arm,
18 and there is nothing too hard for thee: thou shewest lovingkindness unto thousands, and recompensest the iniquity of the fathers into the bosom of their children after them: the Great, the Mighty God, the LORD of hosts, *is* his name,
19 great in counsel, and mighty in work: for thine eyes *are* open upon all the ways of the sons of men: to give every one according to his ways, and according to the fruit of
20 his doings: which hast set signs and wonders in the land of Egypt, *even* unto this day, and in Israel, and amongst *other*
21 men; and hast made thee a name, as *at* this day; and hast brought forth thy people Israel out of the land of Egypt with signs, and with wonders, and with a strong hand, and with a stretched out arm, and with great terror;
22 and hast given them this land, which thou didst swear to their fathers to give them, a land flowing with milk and
23 honey; and they came in, and possessed it; but they obeyed

out at the Lord's command with that overthrow which at the command of the same Lord he had so frequently announced to the guilty city. This difficulty he expresses towards the end of this section, the earlier part being introductory and setting forth the goodness of God as repeatedly shewn in the history of the people and on the other hand their ingratitude.

17. *Ah*] **Alas.** See note on chap. i. 6.
too hard for thee] literally, *too* wonderful *for thee.*
18. *recompensest the iniquity of the fathers*] See note on xxxi. 29.
into the bosom] The Eastern garment formed at the bosom numerous folds, which served as a pocket. Compare Ruth iii. 15; Prov. xvii. 23.
20. *which hast set*] *who wroughtest.*
even unto this day] The construction is elliptical. We must understand before these words, *and hast continued them* (signs and wonders).
and in Israel] **both** *in Israel.*
and amongst other men] In illustration of *men,* thus used of heathen nations in opposition to Israel, compare Is. xliii. 4.
21. Almost the same as Deut. xxvi. 8. For the terror caused to neighbouring nations by the miracles attendant upon the Exodus compare Exod. xv. 14; Deut. iv. 34.
22. *a land flowing with milk and honey*] See note on xi. 5.
23. *possessed it*] The verb in the Heb. is the same as that rendered "shall inherit" in chap viii. 10, where see note.
law] Another reading in the Heb. is *laws,* but that which our version follows is the better one.

not thy voice, neither walked in thy law; they have done nothing of all that thou commandedst them to do: therefore thou hast caused all this evil to come upon them: behold the mounts, they are come *unto* the city to take it; and the city is given into the hand of the Chaldeans, that fight against it, because of the sword, and *of* the famine, and *of* the pestilence: and what thou hast spoken is come to pass; and behold, thou seest *it*. And thou hast said unto me, O Lord God, Buy thee the field for money, and take witnesses; for the city is given into the hand of the Chaldeans.

26—35. *The first part of the Lord's reply; Judgment.*

Then came the word of the LORD unto Jeremiah, saying, Behold, I *am* the LORD, the God of all flesh: is there any thing too hard for me? Therefore thus saith the LORD; Behold, I *will* give this city into the hand of the Chaldeans, and into the hand of Nebuchadrezzar king of Babylon, and he shall take it: and the Chaldeans, that fight against this city, shall come and set fire on this city, and burn it with the houses, upon whose roofs they have offered incense unto Baal, and poured out drink offerings unto other gods, to provoke me to anger. For the children of Israel and the children of Judah have only done evil before me from their youth: for the children of Israel have only provoked me to anger with the work of their hands, saith the LORD. For

24. *the mounts*] See note on chap. vi. 6.
are come unto the city] The enemy have pushed them forward so that they already reach to the walls.
is given] The thing is virtually done, there being a complete blockade, and no hope of rescue for the starving population within.
25. The two things, the state of the city and God's command, are placed side by side that their apparent inconsistency may be most strikingly shewn.

26—35. THE FIRST PART OF THE LORD'S REPLY; JUDGMENT.

27. *too hard for me*] See ver. 17 and note.
29. *and burn it*] This would in fact have been the duty of the Jews themselves according to Deut. xiii. 12—16.
with the houses] literally, *and the houses*.
30. *from their youth*] from the earliest times of the nation. In chap. ii. 2 the Exodus is spoken of as the youth of Israel.
the work of their hands] This may mean their wicked deeds gene-

this city hath been to me *as* a provocation of mine anger and of my fury from the day that they built it even unto this day; that *I* should remove it from before my face, 32 because of all the evil of the children of Israel and of the children of Judah, which they have done to provoke me to anger, they, their kings, their princes, their priests, and their prophets, and the men of Judah, and the inhabitants of Jerusalem. 33 And they have turned unto me the back, and not the face: though *I* taught them, rising up early and teaching *them*, 34 yet they have not hearkened to receive instruction. But they set their abominations in the house, which is called by 35 my name, to defile it. And they built the high places of Baal, which *are* in the valley of the son of Hinnom, to cause their sons and their daughters to pass through *the fire* unto Molech; which I commanded them not, neither came it into my mind, that *they* should do this abomination, to cause Judah to sin.

36—44. *Second part of the Lord's reply; Mercy.*

36 And now therefore thus saith the LORD, the God of

rally, but it seems better to take it as referring to their idols in regard to which similar expressions are often used (chap. x. 3, 9; Deut. iv. 28; 2 Kings xix. 18, etc.).

31. *as a provocation of*] literally, *upon*. The preposition which Jeremiah uses is often employed by him in a vaguer sense than is usual elsewhere in the Bible. Here the meaning seems to be that the city constitutes a burden which rests on God's wrath, so to speak, and makes it incumbent upon Him to display it in the shape of punishment.

from the day that they built it] from the earliest times of the occupation of it by Israel (from David's days; 2 Sam. v. 6, 7).

33. *though I taught them...*] This and the two participles following are infinitives (as in chap. vii. 9 where see note), *and there was a teaching of them*, &c.

35. See notes on vii. 30, 31 where this and ver. 34 have already occurred in the main. In addition it is to be remarked that here Baal and Molech are identified. "Molech the *king* and Baal the *lord* are simply different names of the sun god, but in altered relations. Molech is the sun as the mighty fire, which in passing through the signs of the Zodiac burns up its own children." *Sp. Comm.* Compare with these last words the classical legend of Kronos who devoured his children as they were born.

36—44. SECOND PART OF THE LORD'S REPLY; MERCY.

36. *And now therefore*] These words resume the thought of ver. 27

Israel, concerning this city, whereof ye say, it shall be delivered into the hand of the king of Babylon by the sword, and by the famine, and by the pestilence; behold, I ³⁷ *will* gather them out of all countries, whither I have driven them in mine anger, and in my fury, and in great wrath; and I will bring them again unto this place, and I will cause them to dwell safely: and they shall be my people, and I ³⁸ will be their God: and I will give them one heart, and one ³⁹ way, that *they* may fear me for ever, for the good of them, and of their children after them: and I will make an ever- ⁴⁰ lasting covenant with them, that I will not turn away from them, to do them good; but I will put my fear in their hearts, that *they* shall not depart from me. Yea, I will ⁴¹ rejoice over them to do them good, and I will plant them in this land assuredly with my whole heart and with my whole soul. For thus saith the LORD; Like as I have ⁴² brought all this great evil upon this people, so will I bring upon them all the good that I have promised them. And ⁴³ fields shall be bought in this land, whereof ye say, *It is* desolate without man or beast; it is given into the hand of the Chaldeans. *Men* shall buy fields for money, and sub- ⁴⁴

"is there any thing too hard for me?" In spite of the richly deserved ruin which has been dwelt on in the intermediate verses, deliverance and restoration to the land shall assuredly come.

39. *and one way*] See note on chap. vi. 16.

that they may fear me for ever] The words seem suggested by those of Deut. iv. 10, as the next words are also taken from that Book (vi. 24).

for ever] literally, *all the days*. Compare Matt. xxviii. 20, where our Saviour says to His disciples, "I am with you *alway*," literally, *all the days*.

40. The sense would be made clearer by the omission of the comma after *turn away from them*. God's side of the covenant is that He will not turn away (cease) from doing his people good; their side, that His fear shall be in their hearts, so that they shall not depart from Him.

41. *assuredly*] *in truth*, referring to God's purpose. The other rendering (Eng. margin), *in stability*, is less correct, as referring to the condition of the people.

43. *fields*] literally, *the field*. As opposed to 'fields' at the beginning of ver. 44, the sense here is *the open country*. See note on chap. iv. 17. We are therefore pointed to a large increase in the population generally.

44. *fields*] individual properties, as in that case of which the particulars have been given.

scribe evidences, and seal *them*, and take witnesses in the land of Benjamin, and in the places about Jerusalem, and in the cities of Judah, and in the cities of the mountains, and in the cities of the valley, and in the cities of the south: for I will cause their captivity to return, saith the LORD.

CHAP. XXXIII. 1—13. *Renewed promise of return and of honour among the nations.*

33 Moreover the word of the LORD came unto Jeremiah the second time, while he was yet shut up in the court of the 2 prison, saying, Thus saith the LORD the maker thereof, the LORD that formed it, to establish it; the LORD *is* his name; 3 call unto me, and I will answer thee, and shew thee great 4 and mighty *things*, which thou knowest not. For thus saith

subscribe evidences] **write the particulars of the purchase in the deed.**

in the land of Benjamin...] The several parts of the land are specified in order to make the promise more distinct that it should be possessed again in its entirety. See note on chap. xvii. 26, where the word "plain" is the same in the Heb. as that here rendered *valley* (and in xxxiii. 13 "vale").

I will cause their captivity to return] probably not, I will bring back the captives, but rather, I will remove their captive condition and restore them to their former estate.

CHAP. XXXIII. 1—13. RENEWED PROMISE OF RETURN AND OF HONOUR AMONG THE NATIONS.

1. *the second time*] From the tenor of the communication as well as from the words which follow in this verse we gather that it was not much subsequent to the former.

in the court of the prison] *in the court of the* **guard.** See chap. xxxii. 2 with note.

2. *the maker thereof*] *who does* it (viz. that which he has purposed).

the Lord is his name] He is God and not man, and so is unchangeable and omnipotent. Compare xxxi. 35.

3. *great and mighty things*] The only other cases where the Heb. occurs have reference to the cities of the Amorites (Deut. i. 28, ix. 1, and once or twice elsewhere). It is there rendered in the Eng. Vers. *fenced*, or *walled*, and hence the notion of *mighty*, as in the text. But the Heb. for 'mighty things' becomes by the easy change of one letter the original expression in Is. xlviii. 6, there rightly rendered "hidden things." Some have supposed accordingly that, as the Isaiah passage is obviously not taken from this, this has been taken from it either by Jeremiah himself or by some one subsequent to him, and that the right

the LORD, the God of Israel, concerning the houses of this city, and concerning the houses of the kings of Judah, which are thrown down by the mounts, and by the sword; they come to fight with the Chaldeans, but *it is* to fill them with the dead bodies of men, whom I have slain in mine anger and in my fury, and for all whose wickedness I have hid my face from this city. Behold, I *will* bring it health and cure, and I will cure them, and will reveal unto them the abundance of peace and truth. And I will cause the captivity of Judah and the captivity of Israel to return, and will build them, as at the first. And I will cleanse them from all their iniquity, whereby they have sinned against me, and I will pardon all their iniquities, whereby they have

reading here is that found in Isaiah. This assumption is improbable, although we may fitly say that this whole passage is more in the style of Isaiah than of Jeremiah.

4. *by the mounts, and by the sword*] rather, **against** *the mounts and* **against** *the sword*. These houses of the city and of the kings were not thrown down by the besiegers, as our Version suggests, but by the besieged, in order to make room for defensive works to be raised against these forms of attack. See chap. v. 17 with note, and Is. xxii. 10; also Ezek. xxvi. 9 where for "axes" we should read *swords*.

5. *they come*] As far as grammar is concerned 'they' should refer to 'houses.' As the sense precludes this, the verse becomes extremely difficult. The Septuagint cuts the knot by the omission of the word. Among the expedients proposed the most satisfactory seems to be that we should understand the besieged Jews to be meant, who, although not directly mentioned, can be readily understood from the sense of the earlier part of the passage: *While they come to fight with the Chaldaeans and to fill them* (the houses) *with*, &c. The sudden change from the *buildings* to the *people* is illustrated immediately in ver. 6.

have hid my face] a phrase used elsewhere also (e.g. Deut. xxxi. 17) to express displeasure.

6. *I will bring it health and cure*] *I will* **lay upon** *it a bandage and a remedy*, i.e. **a healing bandage**. See notes on chaps. viii. 23, xxx. 17.

I will bring it...I will cure them] For the change from city (*it*) to inhabitants (*them*) see note on ver. 5.

and will reveal unto them] *and will roll down* (pour out) *upon them*, is another possible translation, but (as in xi. 20, where see note) our Version's rendering is better.

truth] (God's) faithfulness.

8. *And I will cleanse them*] This distinctive feature of the new covenant has been already brought out strongly in xxxi. 34. We shall have it again, l. 20.

sinned, and whereby they have transgressed against me.
9 And it shall be to me a name of joy, a praise and an honour before all the nations of the earth, which shall hear all the good that I do unto them: and they shall fear and tremble for all the goodness and for all the prosperity that I procure
10 unto it. Thus saith the LORD; Again there shall be heard in this place, which ye say *shall be* desolate without man and without beast, *even* in the cities of Judah, and in the streets of Jerusalem, that are desolate, without man, and
11 without inhabitant, and without beast, the voice of joy, and the voice of gladness, the voice of the bridegroom, and the voice of the bride, the voice of them that shall say, Praise the LORD of hosts: for the LORD *is* good; for his mercy *endureth* for ever: *and* of them that shall bring the sacrifice of praise *into* the house of the LORD. For I will cause to return the captivity of the land as at the first, saith
12 the LORD. Thus saith the LORD of hosts, Again in this place, *which is* desolate without man and without beast, and in all the cities thereof, shall be a habitation of shep-
13 herds causing *their* flocks to lie down. In the cities of the mountains, in the cities of the vale, and in the cities of the south, and in the land of Benjamin, and in the places about Jerusalem, and in the cities of Judah, shall the flocks pass again under the hands of him that telleth *them*, saith the LORD.

9. *they shall fear and tremble*] as inferring, and rightly, that the God who so honours those who seek Him will punish with equal emphasis those who disregard Him.

10. *which ye say shall be desolate*] **of which ye say, It is desolate.**

11. *the voice of joy..*] See note on vii. 34.

Praise the Lord of hosts: for the Lord is good; for his mercy endureth for ever] These clauses seem to have been liturgical forms used in the Temple services. This we gather from such passages as 2 Chron. v. 13, vii. 3, 6; Ezra iii. 11; Ps. cvi. 1.

and of them that shall bring] rather, (**and**) **that bring**, or, *as they bring*, to be joined with *them that shall say*, etc. above.

the sacrifice of praise] For the probable sense see note on xvii. 26.

I will cause to return the captivity of the land] See note on xxxii. 44.

12. *a habitation of shepherds*] See note on ix. 10, also vi. 2.

13. *In the cities...*] See note on xxxii. 44.

under the hands of him that telleth them] *Tell* is used, as often in

14—18. *The Kingly and Priestly Offices shall be re-established.*

Behold, the days come, saith the LORD, that I will perform that good thing which I have promised unto the house of Israel and to the house of Judah. In those days, and at that time, will I cause the Branch of righteousness to grow up unto David; and he shall execute judgment and righteousness in the land. In those days shall Judah be saved, and Jerusalem shall dwell safely: and this *is the name* wherewith she shall be called, The LORD our righteousness. For thus saith the LORD; David shall never want a man to sit upon the throne of the house of Israel; neither shall the priests the Levites want a man before me to offer burnt offerings, and to kindle meat offerings, and to do sacrifice continually.

old English, in the sense of *count*. Other instances in the Bible are Gen. xv. 5; Ps. xxii. 17, xlviii. 12. Compare Shakespeare,
 "While one with moderate haste might *tell* a hundred."
                                   Hamlet, Act. I, Sc. 2.
so Milton,
 "And every shepherd *tells* his *tale* (counts the number of his sheep)
  Under the hawthorn in the dale."
                                   L'Allegro, 67.
For *tale* in the Bible in the sense of *number* see Exod. v. 8, 18; 1 Sam. xviii. 27; 1 Chron. ix. 28.—*Bible Word Book*.

14—18. THE KINGLY AND PRIESTLY OFFICES SHALL BE RE-ESTABLISHED.

The Septuagint omit from ver. 14 to the end of the chapter.
15, 16. See notes on xxiii. 5, 6.
17, 18. The permanence of the kingly and priestly line is here emphatically declared. But elsewhere Jeremiah no less plainly announces the cutting off of both, of the former in xxii. 30, xxx. 21, of the latter in iii. 16, xxxi. 33. We must therefore take the passage as one of the prophet's pictures of the Christian dispensation, clothed in a Jewish dress, the only form in which it could present any meaning to those to whom it was delivered. It is no doubt to such passages as this that St Peter refers (1 Pet. i. 10, 11), when he speaks of the prophets as "enquiring and searching diligently... what or what manner of time the Spirit of Christ which was in them did signify, when it testified beforehand the sufferings of Christ, *and the glory that should follow*." Christ uniting the offices of King and Priest should make the spiritual Israel more glorious than ever.

19—22. *God's Covenant is as certain as the ordinances of nature.*

19 And the word of the Lord came unto Jeremiah, saying,
20 Thus saith the Lord; If you can break my covenant of the day, and my covenant of the night, and that there should
21 not be day and night in their season; *then* may also my covenant be broken with David my servant, that he should not have a son to reign upon his throne; and with the
22 Levites the priests, my ministers. As the host of heaven cannot be numbered, neither the sand of the sea measured: so will I multiply the seed of David my servant, and the Levites that minister unto me.

23—26. *Renewal of the assurance to the people as a whole, with the same illustration.*

23 Moreover the word of the Lord came to Jeremiah, saying,
24 Considerest thou not what this people have spoken, saying,

19—22. God's Covenant is as certain as the ordinances of nature.

20. The argument of this section is the same as that of chap. xxxi. 35—37. The only distinction is that while there the fixity of God's work in nature is appealed to as an illustration of the fixity with which he will retain Israel as His people, here the same natural laws are appealed to as illustrating the certainty with which the particular blessings of the monarchy and priesthood are secured to the people.

21. The covenant with David's line is given 2 Sam. vii. 12—16, while that with the Levites (so far as it was not included in the general covenant to maintain Israel, of whom the Levites were an integral part) was made in the person of Phinehas (Numb. xxv. 13).

23—26. Renewal of the assurance to the people as a whole, with the same illustration.

24. *Considerest thou not...*] **Hast thou not seen,** etc.?

this people] Some understand these words of the heathen, in order to escape the difficulty of giving to them the same reference (viz. to the Jews), as the words 'my people' just after. In usage however, the two expressions differ exactly as is required here, the former being used frequently by Jeremiah (e.g. iv. 10, v. 14, 23, etc.) of the people in a state of estrangement from God, while the latter denotes the same people as viewed with affection by Him. The sense of this verse then is, that the people, seeing that both Israel and Judah ('the two families') are being apparently cast off, despise their own nation, despair of any better days, and consider their national existence to be a thing of the past.

The two families which the LORD hath chosen, he hath even cast them off? thus they have despised my people, that *they* should be no more a nation before them. Thus saith the 25 LORD; If my covenant *be* not with day and night, *and if* I have not appointed the ordinances of heaven and earth; then will I cast away the seed of Jacob, and David my 26 servant, *so* that *I* will not take *any* of his seed *to be* rulers over the seed of Abraham, Isaac, and Jacob: for I will cause their captivity to return, and have mercy on them.

CHAP. XXXIV. 1—7. *Prophecy of the burning of the city and the captivity of Zedekiah.*

The word which came unto Jeremiah from the LORD, 34 when Nebuchadnezzar king of Babylon, and all his army, and all the kingdoms of the earth of his dominion, and all the people, fought against Jerusalem, and against all the

thus they have] **and** *they have.*
that they should be] so that they are.
26. There shall yet be rulers and priests over Israel in its spiritual sense viz. the Christian Church, the natural successor and development of Judaism. For this thought one step further advanced, and pointing faintly to the means by which the issue was to be brought about, compare Is. lxvi. 19—21.

CHAP. XXXIV. 1—7. PROPHECY OF THE BURNING OF THE CITY AND THE CAPTIVITY OF ZEDEKIAH.

1. *The word which came*] The similarity between the earlier part (verses 2, 3) of this message to Zedekiah and that of xxxii. 3—5 suggests what is the ordinary view, that this prophecy is merely the fuller form of the same. Verses 4, 5 however are not sufficiently like anything in the former passage, and rather suggest a peaceful reign and death in Jerusalem, followed by kingly obsequies. Either therefore this is in fact their sense, and the verse is really a conditional promise, though here given in an abbreviated form with the condition omitted (see xxxviii. 17, where the condition is given), or the words mean only that Zedekiah should escape with his life in the destruction of the city, and should on the occasion of his death in Babylon receive from his fellow-exiles the honours here described.

Nebuchadnezzar...and all his army] The long enumeration of the hostile forces seems meant to refer to their number and perhaps unwieldiness, as composed of many different nations whose connecting links were of the slenderest. Compare Ezek. xxvi. 7, where the like description is given of Nebuchadnezzar's attack on Tyre.

and all the people] *and all the* **peoples,** separate nations.

2 cities thereof, saying, Thus saith the LORD, the God of Israel; Go and speak to Zedekiah king of Judah, and tell him, Thus saith the LORD; Behold, I *will* give this city into the hand of the king of Babylon, and he shall burn it with
3 fire: and thou shalt not escape out of his hand, but shalt surely be taken, and delivered into his hand; and thine eyes shall behold the eyes of the king of Babylon, and he shall speak with thee mouth to mouth, and thou shalt go *to*
4 Babylon. Yet hear the word of the LORD, O Zedekiah king of Judah; Thus saith the LORD of thee, Thou shalt
5 not die by the sword: *but* thou shalt die in peace: and with the burnings of thy fathers, the former kings which were before thee, so shall they burn *odours* for thee; and they will lament thee, *saying*, Ah lord! for I have pronounced
6 the word, saith the LORD. Then Jeremiah the prophet spake all these words unto Zedekiah king of Judah in Jeru-
7 salem, when the king of Babylon's army fought against Jerusalem, and against all the cities of Judah that were

---

all the cities thereof] including Lachish and Azekah of ver. 7. The fact that those cities were not taken, and that Jeremiah was still free ('go and speak' ver. 2) shews us that the date was early in this last campaign of Nebuchadnezzar, and probably in the ninth year of Zedekiah.

3. *thine eyes shall behold the eyes of the king of Babylon*] See xxxii. 4. "The fact of Zedekiah's interview with Nebuchadnezzar at Riblah, and his being carried blind to Babylon, [see chap. lii. 11], reconciles two predictions of Jeremiah and Ezekiel, which at the time of their delivery must have appeared conflicting, and which Josephus indeed particularly states that Zedekiah alleged as his reason for not giving more heed to Jeremiah. The former of these (Jer. xxxii. 4) states that Zedekiah shall 'speak with the king of Babylon mouth to mouth, and his eyes shall behold his eyes,' the latter (Ezek. xii. 13) that 'he shall be brought to Babylon and shall not see it, though he die there.'" Sm. *Bibl. Dict.* Art. *Zedekiah.*

5. *in peace*] in tranquillity. See note on xi. 12.

with the burnings of thy fathers] See 2 Chron. xvi. 14, xxi. 19.

shall they burn odours] Shall they **make a burning**. There is nothing in the Hebrew implying more than a burning, which might have been of wood, perhaps with some of the personal property of the deceased. Odours would probably have been difficult for the exiles to procure in Babylon, if the words here really have reference to the actual event. (See note on *The word which came*, ver. 1.)

Ah lord] See xxii. 18 with note.

left, against Lachish, and against Azekah: for these defenced cities remained of the cities of Judah.

8—11. *The treatment received by the Hebrew servants.*

This is the word that came unto Jeremiah from the LORD, 8 after that the king Zedekiah had made a covenant with all the people which *were* at Jerusalem, to proclaim liberty unto them; that every man should let his manservant, and 9

7. *against Lachish, and against Azekah*] Both these were in the low country of Judah near the borders of Egypt. Nebuchadnezzar would not venture to advance on his career of conquest into Egypt, leaving such important fortresses untaken.

8—11. THE TREATMENT RECEIVED BY THE HEBREW SERVANTS.

8. *had made a covenant*] This covenant was merely to the effect that the Law of Moses regarding Hebrew slaves should be carried out. There were two classes of rules on the subject in the Pentateuch, apparently but not really conflicting. According to Exod. xxi. 2 a Hebrew male slave was to be set free after six years' service, and by Deut. xv. 12, this was extended to female slaves. In Lev. xxv. 39—55 on the other hand we find that a Hebrew slave was to be treated not as a slave, but a hired servant, and to be set free at the jubilee (each fiftieth year; but see note on ver. 14 below). It is clear however, from the context of this last passage that it had regard to out-door service, tillage, etc., while the others are concerned with domestic slavery. This law seems to have fallen out of use among many Jews. In general the Mosaic Law would be more closely kept at Jerusalem than elsewhere, and it may well be that the coming in of many of the wealthier Jews from the country to avoid the invading army, made the laxity on their part more conspicuous by contrast. This, coupled with the conscience-quickening power of impending danger, in meeting which the slaves, if enfranchised, would be more ready to co-operate with their former masters, seems to have induced Zedekiah, naturally too weak-minded a man to have displayed much vigour in urging any such conduct upon his subjects, to make the agreement with them here spoken of. It probably has reference to all slaves who according to the above law had a claim to freedom either of shorter or longer standing. It is possible indeed that all Hebrew slaves, even those who had not completed their six years' servitude, were in the terror of the moment set free. It appears however that when the Babylonian army withdrew for a short time to meet the Egyptian force from which they imagined themselves in danger (xxxvii. 5), the Jews, fancying all danger passed, basely withdrew the gift of freedom from their newly emancipated compatriots of both sexes.

to proclaim liberty unto them] The same phrase is used of the proclamation made in the year of jubilee (Lev. xxv. 10).

every man his maidservant, *being* a Hebrew or a Hebrewess, go free; that none should serve himself of them, *to wit*, 10 of a Jew his brother. *Now* when all the princes, and all the people, which had entered into the covenant, heard that every one should let his manservant, and every one his maidservant, go free, that none should serve themselves of 11 them any more, then they obeyed, and let *them* go. But afterwards they turned, and caused the servants and the handmaids, whom they had let go free, to return, and brought them into subjection for servants and for handmaids.

12—22. *The punishment of their masters which is to ensue.*

12 Therefore the word of the LORD came to Jeremiah from 13 the LORD, saying, Thus saith the LORD, the God of Israel; I made a covenant with your fathers in the day that I brought them forth out of the land of Egypt, out of the house of 14 bondmen, saying, At the end of seven years let ye go every

9. *serve himself of them*] See note on xxx. 8.
10. *heard*] The Hebrew verb is the same as that rendered later in the verse 'obeyed.' In strictness therefore it should be rendered alike in both places. For the sake of the English idiom however, which does not repeat a verb in this way, it is better to vary. "It is part of the courtesy of oriental countries to represent obedience as the necessary result of hearing another's wishes."—*Sp. Comm.*
11. *they turned, and caused...to return*] they **again brought back.** For the Hebrew idiom, which our version has literally translated, see note on chap. xii. 15.

12—22. THE PUNISHMENT OF THEIR MASTERS WHICH IS TO ENSUE.

12. *Therefore the word of the Lord came to Jeremiah*] The prophet reminds the people of the covenant which God made with their fathers, of the circumstances under which it was made, of their shortlived obedience to it, and then announces the penalty.
13. *the house of bondmen*] The phrase occurs Deut. vii. 8, and the phrase 'house of bondage' frequently in Exod. and Deut. The point of its use here is to remind Israel that their position, as recently delivered from slavery when this covenant was made, should have taught them to be specially tender of others.
14. *At the end of seven years*] As *we* should say *of six years*. In Hebrew counting of this kind both the first and the last items were reckoned in. So the jubilee was in strictness the forty-ninth (the seventh Sabbatical) not the fiftieth year. Compare the rite of circumcision administered on the eighth (seventh) day after birth, and our Lord's Resurrection on "the third (second) day."

man his brother a Hebrew, which hath been sold unto thee; and when he hath served thee six years, thou shalt let him go free from thee: but your fathers hearkened not unto me, neither inclined their ear. And ye were now turned, and 15 had done right in my sight, in proclaiming liberty every man to his neighbour; and ye had made a covenant before me in the house which is called by my name. But ye turned 16 and polluted my name, and caused every man his servant, and every man his handmaid, whom ye had set at liberty at their pleasure, to return, and brought them into subjection, to be unto you for servants and for handmaids. Therefore 17 thus saith the LORD; Ye have not hearkened unto me, in proclaiming liberty, every one to his brother, and every man to his neighbour: behold, I proclaim a liberty for you, saith the LORD, to the sword, to the pestilence, and to the famine; and I will make you to be removed into all the kingdoms of the earth. And I will give the men that have transgressed 18 my covenant, which have not performed the words of the covenant which they had made before me, when they cut the calf in twain, and passed between the parts thereof, the 19 princes of Judah, and the princes of Jerusalem, the eunuchs, and the priests, and all the people of the land, which passed between the parts of the calf; I will even give them into 20 the hand of their enemies, and into the hand of them that

hearkened] the same verb as in ver. 10, where see note.

15. *And ye*] The pronoun is emphatic, as contrasting them with the former generations. *At last* men were found to obey.

in proclaiming liberty] See note on ver. 8.

17. *I proclaim a liberty for you*] The people, hitherto God's servants, and secure in that service, shall be cast off by Him, and shall accordingly, being no longer under His protection as their Owner, be exposed to the perils which follow.

to be removed] See notes on xv. 4, and xxiv. 9.

18. The construing of this verse presents a difficulty. 'When they cut the calf in twain' is literally *the calf which they cut in twain*. 'Calf' then is most probably either a second accusative after 'I will give,' or, better, in apposition to 'the covenant.' In the former case the rendering will be, '*I will make the men...the calf*' i.e. I will cut them in pieces as they have done to the calf of sacrifice, in the latter, *I will give*...(resuming this at ver. 20 *I will even give*) *the men...which have not performed the words of the covenant...even the calf which they cut*, &c. See Gen xv. 10 for ceremonies of this kind as attendant upon a covenant.

seek their life: and their dead bodies shall be for meat unto the fowls of the heaven, and to the beasts of the earth. ²¹ And Zedekiah king of Judah and his princes will I give into the hand of their enemies, and into the hand of them that seek their life, and into the hand of the king of Babylon's ²² army, which are gone up from you. Behold, I *will* command, saith the LORD, and cause them to return to this city; and they shall fight against it, and take it, and burn it with fire: and I will make the cities of Judah a desolation without an inhabitant.

CHAP. XXXV. 1—11. *The incident of the Rechabites.*

35 The word which came unto Jeremiah from the LORD in the days of Jehoiakim the son of Josiah king of Judah, ² saying, Go unto the house of the Rechabites, and speak unto them, and bring them *into* the house of the LORD, into ³ one of the chambers, and give them wine to drink. Then I took Jaazaniah the son of Jeremiah, the son of Habazi-

21. *which are gone up*] The same verb is also used of raising the siege in xxxvii. 5 ("departed,") 11 ("was broken up").

CHAP. XXXV. 1—11. THE INCIDENT OF THE RECHABITES.

1. *The word which came...in the days of Jehoiakim*] This and the following chapter form a remarkable break in the narrative of chaps. xxxii—xliv. They at once bring us back seventeen years, viz. from the tenth year of the reign of Zedekiah to the fourth year of Jehoiakim, when the Babylonian army had entered Palestine and compelled many of its inhabitants to take refuge within Jerusalem. Among these were the Rechabites, and the unwonted presence of a nomadic tribe like theirs must have produced quite a sufficient interest and stir to cause Jeremiah's act and subsequent address to make a deep impression upon the people.

2. *Go unto the house*] The families (compare Gen. vii. 1, &c.) are meant, not the dwelling-houses. See ver. 7.

of the Rechabites] They were a wandering tribe of Kenite descent and thus connected with Moses' father-in-law (Jud. i. 16). Some of that family had settled in the south of Judah (ibid.) others near Kedesh in Naphtali (Jud. iv. 11). This branch however as we see were nomadic.

chambers] used as store-houses (1 Chron. xxviii. 12) or places of meeting for those whose duties lay about the Temple. It is the same word in the original as that which occurs three times in ver. 4.

3. *Jaazaniah*] apparently the leader of the tribe or of that part of it which had taken refuge in Jerusalem.

niah, and his brethren, and all his sons, and the whole house of the Rechabites; and I brought them *into* the 4 house of the LORD, into the chamber of the sons of Hanan, the son of Igdaliah, a man of God, which *was* by the chamber of the princes, which *was* above the chamber of Maaseiah the son of Shallum, the keeper of the door: and 5 I set before the sons of the house of the Rechabites pots full *of* wine, and cups, and I said unto them, Drink ye wine. But they said, We will drink no wine: for Jonadab 6 he son of Rechab our father commanded us, saying, Ye

4. *and I brought them into the house of the Lord*] that so what was to follow might be made most prominent and be most widely known.

the sons of Hanan] meaning probably not the actual sons but the disciples, Hanan being the name of a prophet or teacher, who like many others founded a school of 'sons.' Of him however we know nothing further.

Igdaliah] the longer form of Gedaliah, a name which we meet so frequently in the later chapters of this historical portion as belonging to the son of Ahikam.

a man of God] i.e. a prophet, viz. Hanan, not Igdaliah. See note on chap. i. 1.

Maaseiah] probably father of the Zephaniah (xxi. 1, xxix. 25, xxxvii. 3) who is mentioned as second priest in lii. 24.

keeper of the door] literally, *keeper of the threshold*. There were three of these officers (lii. 24; 2 Kings xxv. 18). They may have had charge respectively of the outer and inner courts of the Temple and of the entrance door itself. They seem to have stood next in rank after the high-priest and his deputy (ibid.), and were charged with the care of the money contributed for the restoration of the Temple (2 Kings xii. 9).

5. *pots*] **bowls**, large vessels, from which drinking cups were filled.

6. *We will drink no wine: for Jonadab...commanded us*] Jonadab is the same who assisted Jehu (2 Kings x. 15—28) in the overthrow of the worship of Baal, and for two or three hundred years his descendants had been faithful to the command which he had imposed on them. The reason for the command doubtless was the corruption and excess which he saw to be engendered and fostered by city-life. Thus the customs of towns were to be avoided, and an ascetic life to be followed, strongly resembling that practised within the limits of Israel by the Nazarites (Numb. vi.).

the son of Rechab] father or more likely perhaps an ancestor of Jonadab. The word means Rider, and hence it has been conjectured that it is rather an epithet (*the bold Rider*) than a proper name. If this be so, which however is but doubtful, it has been remarked as a strange coincidence that his son Jonadab should have been so closely allied (see ref. to 2 Kings x. above) with one who is noted as driving his chariot furiously (2 Kings ix. 20).

shall drink no wine, *neither* ye, nor your sons for ever:
7 neither shall ye build house, nor sow seed, nor plant vineyard, nor have *any*: but all your days ye shall dwell in tents; that ye may live many days in the land where ye *be*
8 strangers. Thus have we obeyed the voice of Jonadab the son of Rechab our father in all that he hath charged us, to drink no wine all our days, we, our wives, our sons, nor our
9 daughters; nor to build houses for us to dwell in: neither
10 have we vineyard, nor field, nor seed: but we have dwelt in tents, and have obeyed, and done according to all that
11 Jonadab our father commanded us. But it came to pass, when Nebuchadrezzar king of Babylon came up into the land, that we said, Come, and let us go *to* Jerusalem for fear of the army of the Chaldeans, and for fear of the army of the Syrians: so we dwell at Jerusalem.

12—17. *Application of this incident to the Jews.*

12   Then came the word of the LORD unto Jeremiah, saying,
13 Thus saith the LORD of hosts, the God of Israel; Go and tell the men of Judah and the inhabitants of Jerusalem, Will ye not receive instruction to hearken to my words?

---

7. *neither shall ye build house...*] A noteworthy instance of a body of persons in the same country but in later times, the description of whom coincides almost verbally with that of the Rechabites, is the case of the Nabathaeans of whom Diodorus Siculus (XIX. 94) says that they neither sow seed, nor plant fruit-tree, nor use wine, nor build a house, and if any one is found transgressing these rules, death is the penalty. "We find however nomads using wine, Gen. xxvii. 25, and even sowing corn, ib. xxvi. 12, as it was possible to buy the one, and to break up the encampment after reaping the other." *Sp. Comm.*

11. *for fear of the army of the Chaldeans*] It was necessary that they should justify themselves for thus taking up their quarters in a town in spite of the strictness of their nomadic rules. It was only for the sake of self-preservation.

Syrians] These were allies of the Chaldaeans at this period, as we learn also from 2 Kings xxiv. 2.

12—17. APPLICATION OF THIS INCIDENT TO THE JEWS.

12. *Then came the word*] Jeremiah is told to go and apply the lesson which the Rechabites taught. For this purpose he is to go forth from the chamber where his interview with them was held, and address the people we must suppose in the adjacent Temple court.

saith the LORD. The words of Jonadab the son of Rechab, 14 that he commanded his sons not to drink wine, are performed; for unto this day they drink none, but obey their father's commandment: notwithstanding I have spoken unto you, rising early and speaking; but ye hearkened not unto me. I have sent also unto you all my servants the 15 prophets, rising up early and sending *them*, saying, Return ye now every man from his evil way, and amend your doings, and go not after other gods to serve them, and ye shall dwell in the land which I have given to you and to your fathers: but ye have not inclined your ear, nor hearkened unto me. Because the sons of Jonadab the son of Rechab 16 have performed the commandment of their father, which he commanded them; but this people hath not hearkened unto me: therefore thus saith the LORD God of hosts, the 17 God of Israel; Behold, I will bring upon Judah and upon all the inhabitants of Jerusalem all the evil that I have pronounced against them: because I have spoken unto them, but they have not heard; and I have called unto them, but they have not answered.

18, 19. *The Rechabites' reward.*

And Jeremiah said unto the house of the Rechabites, 18 Thus saith the LORD of hosts, the God of Israel; Because ye have obeyed the commandment of Jonadab your father, and kept all his precepts, and done according unto all that he hath commanded you: therefore thus saith the LORD of 19 hosts, the God of Israel; Jonadab the son of Rechab shall not want a man to stand before me for ever.

14. *are performed*] *are* established, they not only are carried out but are secure in their hold upon the minds of those who practise them.
unto this day] for *about* three hundred years.
16. *Because*] This conjunction really belongs rather to the latter part of the verse, as it was not the obedience of the Rechabites but the disobedience of the Jews that involved punishment. Its place however makes the contrast between the two parties more marked.

18, 19. THE RECHABITES' REWARD.

19. *shall not want a man to stand before me for ever*] Disobedience being followed by ruin, so shall obedience be by lasting prosperity, and that prosperity shall be of the purest kind, viz. ministering in the presence of God. Such seems to be the sense of the words *to stand before me*.

CHAP. XXXVI. 1—10. *Jeremiah's Roll dictated to Baruch and read before the people.*

36 And it came to pass in the fourth year of Jehoiakim the

See chaps. vii. 10, xv. 19, and in reference to the tribe of Levi Deut. x. 8, xviii. 5, 7. This also is the sense given to the words here in the Targum of Jonathan, a Hebrew commentary on the Prophets which reflects the views of pious Rabbis of our Lord's time. Traces of the fulfilment of this promise are (i) Ps. lxxi. (*possibly* however earlier than this time) the heading of which in the Septuagint makes it belong to "the sons of Jonadab and the first captives" and thus includes them among the Levites to whom it fell to conduct the sacred music and occasionally no doubt to compose the words to which it was set; (ii) omitting one or two other and more obscure references in the O. T., in the account of the martyrdom of James the Just (Eusebius, *Eccles. Hist.* II. 23) "priests of the sons of Rechab" are spoken of; (iii) Benjamin of Tudela, a Jewish traveller of the 12th century, mentions a body of Jews who were called Rechabites, and whose customs corresponded with those detailed in Jeremiah; (iv) Dr Wolff (*Journal*, 1829) describes a body of Rechabites near Mecca who claimed to be sons of Jonadab. See *Sm. Bibl. Dict.* Art. *Rechabites.*

CHAP. XXXVI. 1—10. JEREMIAH'S ROLL DICTATED TO BARUCH AND READ BEFORE THE PEOPLE.

1. *And it came to pass in the fourth year of Jehoiakim*] Here we have the particulars of Jeremiah's record in a permanent form of the substance of those prophecies which he had been uttering against Judah and Jerusalem. This chapter like the last (where see note on ver. 1) is a break in the historical section (chaps. xxxii.—xliv.), as they both go back to the fourth year of Jehoiakim. The attack on Jerusalem by Nebuchadnezzar's army, through fear of which the Rechabites had taken refuge, occurred in that year, and it is important to determine whether the command to prepare the Roll was prior or subsequent to this event. For the view that the attack had not yet taken place ver. 29 is quoted, where however see note. For the other view, which is much the more probable, we have the facts (*a*) that the first capture of Jerusalem by Nebuchadnezzar took place (see xxv. 1 with note) in the thirty-fourth month of Jehoiakim's reign, and probably therefore early in the fourth (calendar) year, and (*b*) that the Roll was not read till the ninth month of the fifth year of Jehoiakim (ver. 9), and even allowing for the slow rate of writing in those days, nine months would be almost or quite enough for the completion of such a work. It is important to notice the order of these events. In chap. xxv. we have the announcement plainly made that the captivity shall be no trifling or passing matter, but shall last seventy years. Thereupon comes at a distance of at most but a few months the capture of the city. The indignation with which that first distinct prophecy of captivity was received must now have been qualified by a fear that the threatened punishment was but too evidently coming upon the nation. This is the state of people's minds, when on a fast

son of Josiah king of Judah, *that* this word came unto Jeremiah from the LORD, saying, Take thee a roll of a book, ² and write therein all the words that I have spoken unto thee against Israel, and against Judah, and against all the nations, from the day I spake unto thee, from the days of Josiah, even unto this day. It may be that the house of Judah will ³ hear all the evil which I purpose to do unto them; that they may return every man from his evil way; that I may forgive their iniquity and their sin. Then Jeremiah called ⁴ Baruch the son of Neriah: and Baruch wrote from the mouth of Jeremiah all the words of the LORD, which he had spoken unto him, upon a roll of a book. And Jere- ⁵ miah commanded Baruch, saying, I *am* shut up; I cannot

day, specially appointed in connexion with the national danger, very possibly fixed for the first anniversary of the capture of the city, Jeremiah gives the king and people a summary of the warnings which he had for so many years sounded in their ears without avail.

2. *Take thee a roll of a book*] The command to Isaiah (viii. 1) was "Take thee a great roll." The word used in his case however, though bearing some resemblance to the Hebrew word here, meant rather a tablet of wood or metal, with a thin coating of wax. Here the substance on which the prophet was to write was parchment. Several skins were stitched together and attached to a roller of wood at one or both ends. The writing was arranged in columns parallel to the rollers, so that as the parchment was gradually unrolled from one end to the other, the successive columns could be read. Our word *volume* (that which is *rolled up*) points by its derivation to this older form of book.

write therein all the words] This would be done in part by transcribing from such comparatively fragmentary records as are spoken of in chaps xxii. 30, xxx. 2, and in part from the prophet's memory, which would supply him with the substance at any rate of the prophecies which he had uttered for the twenty-three years of his mission on the subjects indicated in ver. 3.

3. *It may be that the house of Judah*...] Compare for a similar expression of hopefulness chap. xxvi. 3. Meantime probably (see note on ver. 1, above) the capture of Jerusalem had added to the prophet's hope that this final warning might be effectual.

4. *Then Jeremiah called Baruch*] He has been mentioned already (xxxii. 12, 13) as the prophet's attendant.

5. *I am shut up*] The same verb in the original is used chaps. xxxiii. 1, xxxix. 15, where it means imprisoned. Here however, it cannot have that force, as we see by ver. 19, but simply means that he was hindered from addressing the people by some cause, probably danger to his life arising from the extreme unpopularity of his recent utterances.

6 go *into* the house of the LORD: therefore go thou, and read in the roll, which thou hast written from my mouth, the words of the LORD in the ears of the people *in* the LORD'S house upon the fasting day: and also thou shalt read them 7 in the ears of all Judah that come out of their cities. It may be they will present their supplication before the LORD, and will return every one from his evil way: for great *is* the anger and the fury that the LORD hath pronounced against 8 this people. And Baruch the son of Neriah did according to all that Jeremiah the prophet commanded him, reading in the book the words of the LORD *in* the LORD's house. 9 And it came to pass in the fifth year of Jehoiakim the son of Josiah king of Judah, in the ninth month, *that* they proclaimed a fast before the LORD *to* all the people in Jerusalem, and *to* all the people that came from the cities of 10 Judah unto Jerusalem. Then read Baruch in the book the words of Jeremiah *in* the house of the LORD, in the chamber of Gemariah the son of Shaphan the scribe, in the higher court *at* the entry of the new gate of the LORD's house, in the ears of all the people.

6. *the fasting day*] or, *a fast-day*. The original may bear either sense, as implying that the day was or was not already determined.

7. *they will present their supplication*] literally, *their supplication will fall*. The attitude of the petitioners is transferred in thought to the petition. We have the same phrase in several other places (xxxvii. 20, xxxviii. 26, etc.), and sometimes (xxxvii. 20, xlii. 2) with the further sense, which hardly belongs to it here, of acceptance.

8. *And Baruch...did according to all*] This concise statement that Baruch discharged the commands laid on him, is followed by the detailed account of the same in the subsequent verses.

9. *in the ninth month*] our December, see ver. 22. Thus the fast was not that annual one of the seventh month, the only stated fast of the Law (Lev. xvi. 29, xxiii. 27), but specially appointed probably, either in memory of the capture of the city by the Chaldaeans in the previous year, or on account of the blow given to the independence of the Jews by the battle of Carchemish, and the anticipation of a speedy attack from Nebuchadnezzar.

10. *in the chamber*] probably at the door of it, so as to be heard by the people.

Gemariah the son of Shaphan the scribe] Shaphan was himself scribe in the days of Josiah (2 Kings xxii. 3). We gather from xxvi. 24 that this Gemariah was brother of Ahikam, who was friendly to Jeremiah. He is, of course, distinct from the Gemariah mentioned xxix. 3.

11—19. *The Roll is read before the princes.*

When Michaiah the son of Gemariah, the son of Shaphan, 11 had heard out of the book all the words of the LORD, then 12 he went down *into* the king's house, into the scribe's chamber: and lo, all the princes sat there, *even* Elishama the scribe, and Delaiah the son of Shemaiah, and Elnathan the son of Achbor, and Gemariah the son of Shaphan, and Zedekiah the son of Hananiah, and all the princes. Then 13 Michaiah declared unto them all the words that he had heard, when Baruch read the book in the ears of the people. Therefore all the princes sent Jehudi the son of 14 Nethaniah, the son of Shelemiah, the son of Cushi, unto Baruch, saying, Take in thine hand the roll wherein thou hast read in the ears of the people, and come. So Baruch the son of Neriah took the roll in his hand, and came unto them. And they said unto him, Sit down now, and read 15 it in our ears. So Baruch read *it* in their ears. Now it 16 came to pass when they had heard all the words, they were afraid both one and other, and said unto Baruch, We will surely tell the king of all these words. And they asked 17 Baruch, saying, Tell us now, How didst thou write all these

11—19. THE ROLL IS READ BEFORE THE PRINCES.

11. *When Michaiah...had heard*] As it was in the chamber of Michaiah's father that Baruch had been allowed to read the roll, Gemariah, engaged at the moment at a council of the princes in another room, would naturally be desirous of learning as soon as might be the particulars of what had occurred.

12. *then he went down*] See notes on xxii. 1, xxvi. 10.

Elnathan the son of Achbor] mentioned chap. xxvi. 22.

14. *Jehudi...the son of Cushi*] Although the first of these names also means a Jew, and the second an Ethiopian, it is more probable that both are distinctly proper names here. There may however still be a reference to Ethiopian descent in the latter name.

15. *Sit down*] These words taken with ver. 19 shew that the princes were favourably disposed towards Baruch and Jeremiah. The same has been marked already in chap. xxvi. 16. Baruch took the position ordinarily assumed by an Eastern teacher. Compare Luke iv. 20.

16. *they were afraid both one and other*] literally, *they trembled every one to his neighbour*, i.e. they looked at each other and trembled.

We will surely tell] rather, **We must certainly tell**. It is in no wise a threat, but the expression of a solemn duty.

17. *How didst thou write*] They desired to know how far the words

18 words at his mouth? Then Baruch answered them, He pronounced all these words unto me with his mouth, and I
19 wrote *them* with ink in the book. Then said the princes unto Baruch, Go, hide thee, thou and Jeremiah; and let no man know where ye *be*.

20—26. *It is read before the King. Its fate.*

20 And they went in to the king into the court, but they laid up the roll in the chamber of Elishama the scribe, and
21 told all the words in the ears of the king. So the king sent Jehudi to fet the roll: and he took it out of Elishama the scribe's chamber. And Jehudi read it in the ears of the king, and in the ears of all the princes which stood beside
22 the king. Now the king sat *in* the winterhouse in the ninth month: and *there was a fire on* the hearth burning before
23 him. And it came to pass, *that* when Jehudi had read three or four leaves, he cut it with the penknife, and cast *it* into the fire that *was* on the hearth, until all the roll was

might be Baruch's own, that they might be able to state to the king the amount of responsibility for them which rested upon each.

19. *Go, hide thee, thou and Jeremiah*] See note on ver. 5.

20—26. IT IS READ BEFORE THE KING. ITS FATE.

20. *into the court*] into the inner court yard, where the king's apartments were.

they laid up] *they gave in charge*, committed to safe keeping.

21. *fet*] See note on xxvi. 23.

beside] literally, *above*, referring to the fact that the king was sitting and his attendants standing.

22. *in the winter-house in the ninth month*] See note on ver. 9 above. Amos (iii. 15) mentions both winter and summer houses. "Such language is easily understood by an Oriental. In common parlance the lower apartments are simply *el beit*—the house; the upper is the *allîyeh*, which is the summer house. Every respectable dwelling has both... If these are on the same storey, then the external and airy apartment is the summer *house*, and that for winter is the interior and more sheltered room. It is rare to meet a family which has an entirely separate dwelling for summer."—Thomson, *The Land and the Book*, p. 309.

there was a fire on the hearth burning] Hearths are unknown in the East. Braziers containing charcoal are placed in a depression in the middle of a room for purposes of warming. Render therefore here, **the fire-pan** *was burning*.

23. *leaves*] **pages**, literally, *folding doors*, referring to the ordinary arrangement of the writing as described above (see note on ver. 2).

penknife] literally, *scribe's knife*.

on the hearth] **in the fire-pan**.

consumed in the fire that *was* on the hearth. Yet they were 24 not afraid, nor rent their garments, *neither* the king, nor any of his servants that heard all these words. Neverthe- 25 less Elnathan and Delaiah and Gemariah had made intercession to the king that *he* would not burn the roll: but he would not hear them. But the king commanded Jerahmeel 26 the son of Hammelech, and Seraiah the son of Azriel, and Shelemiah the son of Abdeel, to take Baruch the scribe and Jeremiah the prophet: but the LORD hid them.

27—32. *Its contents re-written.*

Then the word of the LORD came to Jeremiah, after that 27 the king had burnt the roll, and the words which Baruch wrote at the mouth of Jeremiah, saying, Take thee again 28 another roll, and write in it all the former words that were in the first roll, which Jehoiakim the king of Judah hath burnt. And thou shalt say to Jehoiakim king of Judah, Thus 29 saith the LORD; Thou hast burnt this roll, saying, Why hast thou written therein, saying, The king of Babylon shall certainly come and destroy this land, and shall cause to

24. *Yet they were not afraid...neither the king*] Contrast with this the conduct of the king's father when the newly found Book of the Law was read in his ears (and compare 1 Kings xxi. 27). Josiah on that occasion in sorrowful dismay rent his garments (2 Kings xxii. 11) but his son now rends not his garments, but the Roll itself. And thus passed away "his last chance, his last offer of mercy: and as he threw the torn fragments of the roll on the fire he threw there in symbol his royal house, his doomed city, the temple, and all the people of the land."—*Sp. Comm.*

24. *nor any of his servants*] This cannot refer to the princes, who, as we have seen (ver. 16), were by no means of the king's mind.

25. *Elnathan...had made intercession*] See note on xxvi. 22; also on xxvii. 18. Elnathan seems to have changed his view of things, as we find him here so thoroughly on Jeremiah's side.

26. *the son of Hammelech*] As this name might be rendered *the king*, some would take it so here, understanding that Jerahmeel was Jehoiakim's son. It is however in all probability simply a proper name. See chap. xxxviii. 6.

27—32. ITS CONTENTS RE-WRITTEN.

29. *The king of Babylon shall certainly come*] See note on ver. 1. This expression by no means proves that the king of Babylon had not come already. It is probable that this prophecy was uttered after such a visitation, a much less severe disaster however than that

30 cease from thence man and beast? Therefore thus saith the LORD of Jehoiakim king of Judah; He shall have none to sit upon the throne of David: and his dead body shall be cast out in the day to the heat, and in the night to the 31 frost. And I will punish him and his seed and his servants for their iniquity; and I will bring upon them, and upon the inhabitants of Jerusalem, and upon the men of Judah, all the evil that I have pronounced against them; 32 but they hearkened not. Then took Jeremiah another roll, and gave it to Baruch the scribe, the son of Neriah; who wrote therein from the mouth of Jeremiah all the words of the book which Jehoiakim king of Judah had burnt in the fire: and there were added besides unto them many like words.

CHAP. XXXVII. 1—5. *Zedekiah's reign. The Siege of the city is temporarily raised.*

37 And king Zedekiah the son of Josiah reigned instead of Coniah the son of Jehoiakim, whom Nebuchadrezzar king 2 of Babylon made king in the land of Judah. But neither

which Jeremiah here threatens, and which in consequence of the impenitence of king and people did a few years later come to pass. The destruction was carried still further in the sacking of the city at the end of Zedekiah's reign. We gather from the verse that it was this threat that most stirred the passionate wrath of the king, whose spirit was probably already chafed by the humiliation which he and his city had lately undergone.

30. *He shall have none to sit upon the throne of David*] In point of fact he was succeeded by his son Jehoiachin, but he was immediately besieged by Nebuchadnezzar, and at the end of three months carried to Babylon. See further in note on xxii. 30.

his dead body shall be cast out] See note on xxii. 19.

32. *and there were added...many like words*] This second Roll therefore, still preserved to us in the earlier chapters of the Book, is fuller than that which was read in the ears of the people, and which contained briefer extracts from many years of prophecies.

CHAP. XXXVII. 1—5. ZEDEKIAH'S REIGN. THE SIEGE OF THE CITY IS TEMPORARILY RAISED.

1. *And king Zedekiah...reigned*] Here we return from the two parenthetical chapters which concerned the time of Jehoiakim to the last king of Judah, and the narrative (begun chap. xxxii.) of the last two years of that monarch's reign.

whom Nebuchadrezzar...made king] i.e. Zedekiah. See 2 Kings

he, nor his servants, nor the people of the land, did hearken unto the words of the LORD, which he spake by the prophet Jeremiah. And Zedekiah the king sent Jehucal the son of 3 Shelemiah and Zephaniah the son of Maaseiah the priest to the prophet Jeremiah, saying, Pray now unto the LORD our God for us. Now Jeremiah came in and went out among 4 the people: for they had not put him *into* prison. Then 5 Pharaoh's army was come forth out of Egypt: and when the Chaldeans that besieged Jerusalem heard tidings of them, they departed from Jerusalem.

6—10. *Jeremiah foretells the return of the Chaldaeans.*

Then came the word of the LORD unto the prophet Jere- 6 miah, saying, Thus saith the LORD, the God of Israel; Thus 7 shall ye say to the king of Judah, that sent you unto me to inquire of me; Behold, Pharaoh's army, which is come forth to help you, shall return *to* Egypt into their own land.

xxiv. 17. These first two verses are a sort of sketch of the position of affairs.

3. *And Zedekiah the king sent*] This mission took place later than that related in chap. xxi. 1, which was sent when Nebuchadnezzar's army was approaching Jerusalem. In this case on the contrary the siege had begun and been raised, and the hopes of the people were excited in consequence.

Jehucal] In chap. xxxviii. 4 he proposes that Jeremiah should be put to death.

Zephaniah] the deputy high-priest. See chaps. xxi. 1, xxix. 25, lii. 24, 26, 27. 2 Kings xxv. 18, 20, 21.

Pray now unto the Lord our God for us] There seemed to be a hope that as in the time of Sennacherib's invasion, when Hezekiah was king (2 Kings xix. 35), there might now be given in answer to prayer a miraculous overthrow of the invading host.

4. *came in and went out*] was still free, had not suffered arrest. That was immediately to follow.

5. *when the Chaldeans...heard tidings of them, they departed*] See notes on xxxiv. 8 and 21. We do not know whether the retreat on the part of the Egyptians which followed was due to a defeat from the Chaldaeans, or not. The latter seems the most natural construction of the words which end ver. 7. Pharaoh-Hophra (called Apries by Herodotus), although an ally of the king of Judah, yet would feel it a serious matter to come face to face with such a force as that which Nebuchadnezzar was able to bring into the field. For this Pharaoh's reign and overthrow see note on chap. xliv. 30.

8,9 And the Chaldeans shall come again, and fight against this city, and take it, and burn it with fire. Thus saith the LORD; Deceive not your selves, saying, The Chaldeans 10 shall surely depart from us: for they shall not depart. For though ye had smitten the whole army of the Chaldeans that fight against you, and there remained *but* wounded men among them, *yet* should they rise up every man in his tent, and burn this city with fire.

11—15. *Jeremiah is seized under a misunderstanding and imprisoned.*

11 And it came to pass, *that* when the army of the Chaldeans was broken up from Jerusalem for fear of Pharaoh's army, 12 then Jeremiah went forth out of Jerusalem to go *into* the land of Benjamin, to separate himself thence in the midst

6—10. JEREMIAH FORETELLS THE RETURN OF THE CHALDAEANS.

8. The prophet is careful to leave no ground whatever for hope.

10. *there remained but wounded men*] Our version fails to give the full force of the Hebrew, which is that even though but a few individuals remained, and those severely wounded (literally, transfixed), they would be more than a match for the Jews. So certainly was it God's purpose that Jerusalem should be overthrown.

wounded] The same Heb. word is, according to the common rendering, used in a secondary sense ("stricken through") of those dying of hunger in Lam. iv. 9. See however note there.

11—15. JEREMIAH IS SEIZED UNDER A MISUNDERSTANDING AND IMPRISONED.

11. *was broken up*] See note on xxxiv. 21.

12. *to separate himself*] rather, **to take his portion.** The Hebrew is difficult. The verb means literally *to cause to divide*, and hence the best explanation here seems to be to refer it to a portion of land in the neighbourhood of Anathoth belonging to him. He would naturally wish to take this opportunity of securing himself in the possession of it, so far as he might, particularly as the circumstances of the siege, and his knowledge that it was only raised for a time, would make it necessary for him to do his utmost to provide himself with the means of subsistence. Another rendering is that of the Eng. margin, *to slip away*.

in the midst of the people] There was naturally a rush to get out of the city not only on account of the close confinement which the people had suffered, but because of the past and prospective scarcity and consequent high price of provisions. It therefore behoved all to furnish themselves as far as they could with these or with money for their purchase. We cannot connect Jeremiah's action with the portion of land which he is described in chap xxxii. as purchasing, as that event had not yet occurred.

of the people. And when he was in the gate of Benjamin, 13 a captain of the ward *was* there, whose name *was* Irijah, the son of Shelemiah, the son of Hananiah; and he took Jeremiah the prophet, saying, Thou fallest away to the Chaldeans. Then said Jeremiah, *It is* false; I fall not away to 14 the Chaldeans. But he hearkened not to him: so Irijah took Jeremiah, and brought him to the princes. Wherefore 15 the princes were wroth with Jeremiah, and smote him, and put him *in* prison *in* the house of Jonathan the scribe: for they had made that the prison.

16—21. *Zedekiah takes compassion on the prophet.*

When Jeremiah was entered into the dungeon, and into 16 the cabins, and Jeremiah had remained there many days;

13. *the gate of Benjamin*] on the north side of the city, mentioned also by this name in xxxviii. 7; Zech. xiv. 10. It led through the territory of Benjamin to that of Ephraim, and hence appears also (2 Kings xiv. 13; Nehem. viii. 16, xii. 39) as "the gate of Ephraim."

a captain of the ward] literally, *a lord of the watch*, i.e. one charged with the duty of taking cognisance of those who passed the gate.

Thou fallest away] For the same Heb. verb, applied, in accordance with our own idiom, in this secondary sense of going over to the enemy compare 1 Sam. xxix. 3; 2 Kings xxv. 11. The views which Jeremiah was known to hold as to the propriety of yielding to the Chaldaeans (e.g. as expressed somewhat later in the words of chap. xxi. 9) would give some ground for suspicion under these circumstances.

15. *the princes were wroth with Jeremiah*] These were not the princes who had looked upon the prophet with favour in the reign of Jehoiakim (xxvi. 16, xxxvi. 19). Those were now no doubt exiles, and these their successors, as thoroughly opposed to the Chaldaean rule, and sympathizing with their compatriots of Babylon, had no favour to bestow upon Jeremiah. They would remember how he had likened them to evil figs (chap. xxiv.).

16—21. ZEDEKIAH TAKES COMPASSION ON THE PROPHET.

16. *dungeon*] literally, "house of the pit."

cabins] The marginal reading *cells* is better. In Heb. indeed the word is found here only, but in the Chaldee and Syriac dialects it is found in the sense of *shop*. Thus it probably means a vaulted recess off a passage or room. In Jerusalem at the present day "the whole of the plateau on which the temple and palace stood is honeycombed underneath with works of various kinds. Captain Warren describes thirty-four such excavations, some of which are cisterns and others passages. One of these extends about 150 feet from north to south, and nearly as much from east to west, and its roof is supported by massive rude piers, which give the place a look of elephantine strength."

17 then Zedekiah the king sent, and took him *out:* and the king asked him secretly in his house, and said, Is there *any* word from the Lord? And Jeremiah said, There is: for, said he, thou shalt be delivered into the hand of the king of 18 Babylon. Moreover Jeremiah said unto king Zedekiah, What have I offended against thee, or against thy servants, 19 or against this people, that ye have put me in prison? Where *are* now your prophets which prophesied unto you, saying, The king of Babylon shall not come against you, nor against 20 this land? Therefore hear now, I pray thee, O my lord the king: let my supplication, I pray thee, be accepted before thee, that thou cause me not to return *to* the house of Jona- 21 than the scribe, lest I die there. Then Zedekiah the king commanded that they should commit Jeremiah into the court of the prison, and that *they* should give him daily a piece of bread out of the bakers' street, until all the bread in the

many days] during which time the Chaldaeans resumed the siege and the danger became so pressing that Zedekiah was induced to send for the prophet, and ask him for some intimation of the future.

17. *asked him secretly*] This shews us that the prophet was as unpopular as ever. It also points to Zedekiah's moral weakness, as dreading the interference of the princes in the matter.

thou shalt be delivered...] coinciding with the prophecies delivered at greater length and in writing *about* the same time. See chaps. xxxii. 3, 4, xxxiv. 2, 3.

19. *Where are now your prophets which prophesied unto you*] Jeremiah in this verse addresses the whole people through their king ('your ...you') as opposed to his address in the singular number before and after. The question is equivalent to a challenge to them to come forward and defend their prediction or acknowledge their falsehood.

20. *let my supplication...be accepted before thee*] See note on xxxvi. 7.

21. *court of the prison*] court of the **guard**. See note on xxxii. 2.

a piece of bread] a round cake of bread. The dough was divided into round cakes not unlike flat stones in shape and appearance (Matt. vii. 9, comp. iv. 3) about a span in diameter and a finger's breadth in thickness: three of these were required for the meal of a single person (Luke xi. 5), and consequently one was barely sufficient to sustain life (1 Sam. ii. 36 "morsel" Eng. Vers.) *Sm. Bibl. Dict.* Art. *Bread.*

out of the bakers' street] This is the only case in which even the name of a Jerusalem street is preserved to us. The baking of a household was done from primitive times by the women of the family. But "baking as a profession was carried on by men (Hos. vii. 4, 6). In Jerusalem the bakers congregated in one quarter of the town, as we may infer from the name 'bakers' street,' and *tower of the ovens* (Neh. iii. 11, xii. 38 'furnaces' A. V.)." *Ibid.*

city were spent. Thus Jeremiah remained in the court of the prison.

CHAP. XXXVIII. 1—6. *Zedekiah allows the princes to put Jeremiah again into the dungeon.*

Then Shephatiah the son of Mattan, and Gedaliah the 38 son of Pashur, and Jucal the son of Shelemiah, and Pashur the son of Malchiah, heard the words that Jeremiah had spoken unto all the people, saying, Thus saith the LORD, 2 He that remaineth in this city shall die by the sword, by the famine, and by the pestilence: but he that goeth forth to the Chaldeans shall live; for he shall have his life for a prey, and shall live. Thus saith the LORD, This city shall 3 surely be given into the hand of the king of Babylon's army, which shall take it. Therefore the princes said unto the 4 king, We beseech thee, let this man be put to death: for thus he weakeneth the hands of the men of war that remain in this city, and the hands of all the people, in speaking such words unto them: for this man seeketh not the welfare of this people, but the hurt. Then Zedekiah the king said, 5

until all the bread in the city were spent] Compare chap. lii. 6.

CHAP. XXXVIII. 1—6. ZEDEKIAH ALLOWS THE PRINCES TO PUT JEREMIAH AGAIN INTO THE DUNGEON.

1. *Then Shephatiah*] The removal of Jeremiah from prison to the court of the guard was of course favourable to the publication of his message. Hence the princes take alarm and apply to the king for permission to put him to death. There was no doubt truth in their assertion that Jeremiah's words were 'weakening the hands of the men of war,' but the fact, that the words which he spoke were not his but the Divine message with which he was charged, made all the difference in the case.

Gedaliah] He was probably a son of the Pashur who put Jeremiah in the stocks (chap. xx. 1, 2).

Jucal]=Jehucal of chap. xxxvii. 3.

Pashur the son of Malchiah] the same who is mentioned chap. xxi. 1.

2. *He that remaineth*...] This and the following verse occur substantially in the reply of the prophet to the messengers (including Pashur) of chap. xxi. (See verses 8, 9 and notes).

4. *for thus*] rather, **Because.**

the men of war that remain] shewing that a good many had gone over to the Chaldeans, a fact which is implied also in ver. 19.

Behold, he *is* in your hand: for the king *is* not *he that* can
6 do *any* thing against you. Then took they Jeremiah, and
cast him into the dungeon of Malchiah the son of Hammelech, that *was* in the court of the prison: and they let down
Jeremiah with cords. And in the dungeon *there was* no
water, but mire: so Jeremiah sunk in the mire.

7—13. *He is rescued by Ebed-Melech.*

7 Now when Ebed-melech the Ethiopian, one of the eunuchs
which *was* in the king's house, heard that they had put
Jeremiah in the dungeon; the king then sitting in the gate
8 of Benjamin; Ebed-melech went forth out of the king's
9 house, and spake to the king, saying, My lord the king,
these men have done evil in all that they have done to Jeremiah the prophet, whom they have cast into the dungeon;
and he is like to die for hunger in the place where he is:
10 for *there is* no more bread in the city. Then the king com-

5. *the king is not he...*] The literal rendering is, *The king cannot as to you (do) a thing.* Zedekiah, aware of his own moral weakness, here acknowledges himself powerless in the hands of the princes. If they united in urging anything as requisite for the safety of the state, he declined even to argue the point, but confessed at once that he was but a cypher in the matter.

6. *the dungeon of Malchiah*] probably meaning that he was in charge of it. We might rather render **cistern**. See chap. vi. 7 with note. The depth and consequent wretchedness of this place of confinement is shewn by the means employed to place Jeremiah in it.

the son of Hammelech] See note on xxxvi. 26.

7—13. HE IS RESCUED BY EBED-MELECH.

7. *Ebed-melech the Ethiopian*] a negro eunuch, attached to the court or harem after the Eastern custom. See note on xiii. 23.

the gate of Benjamin] See note on chap xxxvii. 13.

9. *he is like to die for hunger in the place where he is*] literally, *he is dead of hunger on the spot.* The words are uttered impulsively, and when taken strictly are inconsistent, death by hunger and a speedy death ('on the spot') being incompatible. Ebed-melech's meaning however is clear, viz. that Jeremiah was probably at death's door already, as suffering at once from hunger and from confinement in so dismal a dungeon. The Heb. for 'on the spot' is still more literally *under him.* The same expression is used of Asahel ("in the same place" Eng. Vers.) 2 Sam. ii. 23.

for there is no more bread in the city] This again is an exaggeration shewing the eagerness of the speaker, and pardonable, as certain to be

manded Ebed-melech the Ethiopian, saying, Take from hence thirty men with thee, and take up Jeremiah the prophet out of the dungeon, before he die. So Ebed-melech took the men with him, and went *into* the house of the king under the treasury, and took thence old cast clouts and old rotten rags, and let them down by cords into the dungeon to Jeremiah. And Ebed-melech the Ethiopian said unto Jeremiah, Put now *these* old cast clouts and rotten rags under thine armholes under the cords. And Jeremiah did so. So they drew up Jeremiah with cords, and took him up out of the dungeon: and Jeremiah remained in the court of the prison.

14—23. *Zedekiah again seeks his counsel.*

Then Zedekiah the king sent, and took Jeremiah the prophet unto him into the third entry that *is* in the house of the LORD: and the king said unto Jeremiah, I *will* ask thee a thing; hide nothing from me. Then Jeremiah said

understood by the king. If it had been absolutely true, there could have been no object in freeing Jeremiah. As it was, the sense was only that there was so scanty a supply of provision that there was little or no chance of any reaching Jeremiah in the place where he was then confined.

10. *thirty men*] This large number seems to have been intended to preclude any attempt at interference on the part of the princes. Zedekiah knew enough of them to see that a strong force would be necessary under such circumstances.

before he die] The words of the king shew that he understood the real sense of Ebed-melech's remark *he is dead on the spot* of ver. 9.

11. *under the treasury*] more fully *to* (the place) *under the treasury*.

old cast clouts and old rotten rags] *rags of torn garments and rags of worn out garments.*

13. *court of the prison*] *court of the* guard. See note on xxxii. 2.

14—23. ZEDEKIAH AGAIN SEEKS HIS COUNSEL.

14. *the third entry*] The Eng. margin has *principal*, which however is not likely to be the sense. It was probably a chamber, retired from public observation, and connected with a passage leading from the palace to the Temple, and may have been identical with that which in 2 Kings xvi. 18 is called "the king's entry."

I will ask thee a thing; hide nothing from me] literally, *I am asking thee a thing* (or *word*); *thou shalt not hide from me a thing* (or *word*). Zedekiah's anxiety as to the future led him to take the same course as previously (chap. xxxvii. 17).

unto Zedekiah, If I declare *it* unto thee, wilt thou not surely put me to death? and if I give thee counsel, wilt thou not hearken unto me? So Zedekiah the king sware secretly unto Jeremiah, saying, *As* the LORD liveth, that made us this soul, I will not put thee to death, neither will I give thee into the hand of these men that seek thy life. Then said Jeremiah unto Zedekiah, Thus saith the LORD, the God of hosts, the God of Israel; If thou wilt assuredly go forth unto the king of Babylon's princes, then thy soul shall live, and this city shall not be burnt with fire; and thou shalt live, and thine house: but if thou wilt not go forth to the king of Babylon's princes, then shall this city be given into the hand of the Chaldeans, and they shall burn it with fire, and thou shalt not escape out of their hand. And Zedekiah the king said unto Jeremiah, I am afraid of the Jews that are fallen to the Chaldeans, lest they deliver me into their hand, and they mock me. But Jeremiah said, They shall not deliver *thee*. Obey, I beseech thee, the voice of the LORD, which I speak unto thee: so it shall be well unto thee, and thy soul shall live. But if thou refuse to go forth, this *is* the word that the LORD hath shewed me: and behold, all

15. *wilt thou not hearken unto me?*] **thou wilt not hearken unto me.** This clause is not an interrogative one in the Hebrew. Jeremiah knew too well from his experience of the king's recent conduct that he could not be depended upon to carry out even those commands which he might believe to come from God. That Zedekiah was simply swayed by the person in whose presence he happened to be at the moment and had no fixity of purpose or resolution is well illustrated by his words in the next verse, when compared with those he had addressed to the princes a short time before (ver. 5).

16. *that made us this soul*] an unusual form of oath. The soul or life being God's creation is also in His power to take away, if the speaker should prove false to this his promise.

17. *go forth*] surrender thyself.

the king of Babylon's princes] an intimation that Nebuchadnezzar was not himself at this time in command of the besieging forces. While the tedious blockade continued, he had no doubt taken up his position at Riblah, where we find him somewhat later (xxxix. 5).

19. *I am afraid of the Jews that are fallen to the Chaldeans*] See note on ver. 4. These, the king fears, would be severe upon him for not doing himself as they had done at an earlier period, and so sparing the city the miseries of a siege.

the women that are left in the king of Judah's house *shall be* brought forth to the king of Babylon's princes, and those *women shall* say, Thy friends have set thee on, and have prevailed against thee: thy feet are sunk in the mire, *and* they are turned away back. So they *shall* bring out all thy 23 wives and thy children to the Chaldeans: and thou shalt not escape out of their hand, but shalt be taken by the hand of the king of Babylon: and thou shalt cause this city to be burnt with fire.

24—28. *Result of the conference.*

Then said Zedekiah unto Jeremiah, Let no man know of 24 these words, and thou shalt not die. But if the princes hear 25 that I have talked with thee, and they come unto thee, and say unto thee: Declare unto us now what thou hast said unto the king, hide *it* not from us, and we will not put thee to death; also what the king said unto thee: then thou shalt say 26

22. *all the women that are left*] the women of the harem generally, concubines and their attendants. If Zedekiah prove obstinate, these also shall join in the reproaches that shall be heaped upon him.

Thy friends have set thee on, and have prevailed against thee] This is so like a part of Obad. 7 that either it is adapted from that passage, or both are due to the same original, in the shape perhaps of an ordinary proverb.

friends] The same expression in the Heb. is rendered "familiars" in chap. xx. 10, where see note.

have set thee on] The Heb. in the Obadiah passage is somewhat similar in sound, but there means "deceived." The sense however here comes nearly to this. Thy friends have persuaded thee against thy better judgment, and as soon as thou hast through following their advice become involved in difficulties, they turn back and leave thee.

23. *So they*] **And** *they*, etc. Not only shalt thou be mocked, but those whom thou holdest most dear shall be placed in the enemy's hands.

thou shalt cause this city to be burnt] literally, *thou shalt burn this city*. Zedekiah through his obstinacy shall be as much the cause, as if he had set fire to Jerusalem with his own hands.

24—28. RESULT OF THE CONFERENCE.

24. *Let no man know*] Zedekiah's feebleness is again conspicuous in this and the two following verses.

26. *then thou shalt say unto them*] Jeremiah is to mention but one of the subjects of his conversation with the king. This he was quite justified in doing, as the princes had no right to insist on hearing the whole purport of the conversation or even a part of it.

unto them, I presented my supplication before the king, that *he* would not cause me to return *to* Jonathan's house, to die
27 there. Then came all the princes unto Jeremiah, and asked him: and he told them according to all these words that the king had commanded. So they left off speaking
28 with him; for the matter was not perceived. So Jeremiah abode in the court of the prison until the day that Jerusalem was taken: and he was *there* when Jerusalem was taken.

I presented my supplication] For the more literal rendering of the words see note on xxxvi. 7.

to Jonathan's house] See xxxvii. 15.

28. *of the prison*] *of the* **guard.** See xxxii. 2.

and he was there when Jerusalem was taken] This, which is an inadmissible rendering of the Heb., has only arisen in connexion with an erroneous division of the chapters. These words belong to chapter xxxix., and are to be translated *And it came to pass, when Jerusalem was taken* (*in the ninth year of Zedekiah...the city was broken up*) *then all the princes of the king of Babylon*, etc.

CHAP. XXXIX. 1—7. CAPTURE OF THE CITY. FATE OF ZEDEKIAH.

There at once arises a question as to the genuineness of the greater part of this chapter. (i) Verses 4—13 (inclusive) are omitted in the Septuagint, and (ii) the narrative coincides in the main with that of chap. lii. and of 2 Kings xxv. while it yet presents certain difficulties in matters of detail, when compared with these and with other parts of the narrative. To (i) we may reply, as in earlier cases, that the Septuagint presents throughout this book far too much appearance of arbitrariness to make its testimony on such a point to be of any considerable weight, unless supported by important evidence from other sources. As regards (ii) it is not easy to give any plausible conjecture as to the reason for the repetition of so much of this chapter in the narrative contained in lii. further than to suggest that it may very possibly be connected in some way with the fact of the hiatus in the Septuagint here, and with the difference of authorship in lii. See note on ver. 1 of that chap. The difficulties of detail are (*a*) in xxxix. 2 the ninth day of the fourth month is mentioned as that on which the city was captured, but in lii. 6 as that on which provisions failed, and (*b*) Nebuzar-adan, who did not reach Jerusalem till a month after its capture (lii. 12), was commissioned to call Jeremiah from prison (xxxix. 11, 12), whereas according to xxxviii. 28 Jeremiah was freed on the day of the capture of the city. To this may be added (*c*) that the princes of Babylon on freeing Jeremiah committed him to Gedaliah (xxxix. 14), while (xl. 1) he seems to have nevertheless been made to walk in chains with the other captives, and in no wise distinguished from them till freed by Nebuzar-adan in person. All these however admit of fairly easy replies, viz. to (*a*) that the total failure of provisions would naturally coincide with the end of the siege, to (*b*) that

vv. 1—3.]   JEREMIAH, XXXIX.   257

CHAP. XXXIX. 1—7. *Capture of the city. Fate of Zedekiah.*

In the ninth year of Zedekiah king of Judah, in the tenth 39 month, came Nebuchadrezzar king of Babylon and all his army against Jerusalem, and they besieged it. *And* in the 2 eleventh year of Zedekiah, in the fourth month, the ninth *day* of the month, the city was broken up. And all the 3 princes of the king of Babylon came in, and sat in the middle gate, *even* Nergal-sharezer, Samgar-nebo, Sarsechim,

the purport of chap. xxxviii. 28, is merely to account for Jeremiah up to the date of the capture of the city without making any assertion beyond that date, to (*c*) that Gedaliah after receiving Jeremiah into his charge had gone off without him to Mizpeh (xl. 6), in which case it was by no means unnatural that in the absence of this protector Jeremiah should not receive any special favour till his meeting with "the captain of the guard" (xl. 1).

1. *In the ninth year*] This and ver. 2 give us the dates of the beginning and end of the siege. We have the former still more particularly in chap. lii. 4, where occur the words "in the tenth day of the month," as also in 2 Kings xxv. 1, and Ezek. xxiv. 1. In this last passage, which introduces a description of the crimes and consequent sufferings of Jerusalem, the date of the commencement of the siege is further emphasized thus (ver. 2) "Son of man, write thee the name of the day, even of this same day; the king of Babylon set himself against Jerusalem this same day."

2. *And in the eleventh year*...] We gather from this verse that the siege lasted one day short of eighteen months.

3. *in the middle gate*] not mentioned elsewhere, but probably between the upper and lower divisions of the city, and thus connecting Mount Zion with the rest.

Nergal-sharezer...] From the Eng. it would appear that there are six princes mentioned by name. In fact however there are but four at the most, (*a*) Nergal-sharezer (*may Nirgal protect the king*), (*b*) Samgar-nebo (*be gracious, O Nebo*), (*c*) Sarsechim, of whose name the meaning is still unknown, (*d*) another Nergal-sharezer. Rab-saris (*chief of the eunuchs*) and Rab-mag (*chief of the magi*) are the *titles* of those whose names they follow. It has been proposed to reduce the number still further by getting rid of Samgar-nebo as a proper name. Samgar will then be rendered *a cup-bearer* and attached as title to the preceding name, while the second part of the compound is rejected as a later addition on the ground that in all other cases of proper names compounded with *nebo* this part comes at the *beginning* of the word, e.g. Nebuchadnezzar, Nebuzar-adan, Nebopolassar, etc. The second Nergal-sharezer is a son-in-law of Nebuchadnezzar, and the same who murdered Evil-Merodach and after four years' reign was slain by Cyrus. In the cuneiform (arrow-headed) inscriptions he is called Raba-Emga (Rab-mag). This is the first passage of the

JEREMIAH   17

JEREMIAH, XXXIX. [vv. 4—7.

Rab-saris, Nergal-sharezer, Rab-mag, with all the residue of
4 the princes of the king of Babylon. And it came to pass,
that when Zedekiah the king of Judah saw them, and all
the men of war, then they fled, and went forth out of the
city by night, *by* the way of the king's garden, by the gate
betwixt the two walls: and he went out the way of the
5 plain. But the Chaldeans' army pursued after them, and
overtook Zedekiah in the plains of Jericho: and when they
had taken him, they brought him up to Nebuchadnezzar
king of Babylon to Riblah in the land of Hamath, where he
6 gave judgment upon him. Then the king of Babylon slew
the sons of Zedekiah in Riblah before his eyes: also the
7 king of Babylon slew all the nobles of Judah. Moreover he

Bible in which one of the magi is mentioned by this title. We find them again Dan. ii. 2, iv. 7, and in the Greek of Matt. ii. 1, etc.

It has been objected against the genuineness of this verse that the chief of the eunuchs (Rab-saris) mentioned in ver. 13 is Nebushasban, while Nebuzar-adan appears there and not here. The explanation of both these differences however is probably the same, i.e. that ver. 3 gives us those who were in command at the actual capture of the city, while, as is brought out more clearly in chap. lii. 12, Nebuzar-adan did not arrive till a month later, to which date therefore verses 13, 14 of this chapter really refer.

4. *saw them*] It was night, so that the sense may be, *learned* that they were in possession of the gate of the citadel of Zion.

by the way of the king's garden] Probably on the slope of the hill Zion.

by the gate betwixt the two walls] We are reduced to conjecture for the position not only of this gate but of the walls spoken of. Either the gate was in a double wall between Zion and Ophel which lay beneath it (but in this case we should expect a double gate also) or it pierced a wall connecting the two here spoken of.

the way of the plain] The direction in which he fled shews that his aim was to escape to the eastern bank of the Jordan.

5. *Riblah*] probably not the same as that mentioned in Numb. xxxiv. 11 as on the eastern boundary of the land. This Riblah was the place whither Pharaoh-Necho proceeded after the battle of Carchemish and summoned Jehoahaz to appear before him (2 Kings xxiii. 33). From the use which the king of Babylon made of this place it was evidently on the high road between Babylon and Palestine. "It has been discovered in modern times, and retains its name. It lies on the banks of a mountain stream in the midst of a vast and fertile plain yielding the most abundant supplies of forage." Robinson's *Bible Researches*, III. 545.

gave judgment upon him] See note on chap. i. 16.

6. *nobles*] The word here used in the Heb. differs from the word

put out Zedekiah's eyes, and bound him with chains to carry him to Babylon.

8—10. *Treatment of the city and inhabitants.*

And the Chaldeans burnt the king's house, and the 8 houses of the people, with fire, and brake down the walls of Jerusalem. Then Nebuzar-adan the captain of the 9 guard carried away captive *into* Babylon the remnant of the people that remained in the city, and those that fell away, that fell to him, with the rest of the people that remained. But Nebuzar-adan the captain of the guard left of the poor 10 of the people, which had nothing, in the land of Judah, and gave them vineyards and fields at the same time.

11—14. *Nebuchadnezzar's care for Jeremiah.*

Now Nebuchadrezzar king of Babylon gave charge con- 11

in the corresponding passage in chap. lii. ("princes," ver. 10) while the former, although not occurring in many books of the Bible, is used elsewhere by Jeremiah (xxvii. 20). This is an additional argument in favour of the genuineness of this narrative of the capture of the city.

7. *Moreover he put out Zedekiah's eyes*] See note on xxxiv. 3. "Putting out the eyes has been at all times a common Oriental punishment...The frequency of the punishment in the time of the younger Cyrus is indicated by a passage in Xenophon, where it is said that men deprived of sight for their crimes were a common spectacle along the highways within his government." Rawlinson's *Herod.* vol. IV. p. 16. Compare Jud. xvi. 21.

8—10. TREATMENT OF THE CITY AND INHABITANTS.

This section by way of introduction to the brief account of the treatment of Jeremiah, gives a sketch of the fate of the inhabitants generally. If we had only this summary, we might suppose that Nebuzar-adan was present at the time in person. We find from the two other forms of the account (chap. lii; 2 Kings xxv.) that he did not arrive till a month after the taking of Jerusalem.

9. *captain of the guard*] literally, *chief of the executioners*, i.e., of the king's body guard, to whom such duties fell.

that fell to him] i.e. that went over to the Chaldaeans, and so were under Nebuzar-adan from such time as he appeared in command.

10 *gave them vineyards and fields*] The parallel accounts (lii. 16; 2 Kings xxv. 12) say that they were left as vinedressers and husbandmen Combining the accounts then we see precisely how the matter was. They were put in charge of this kind of property, which in a sense was given to them as their own, but might be resumed at any moment by the conqueror.

cerning Jeremiah to Nebuzar-adan the captain of the guard,
12 saying, Take him, and look well to him, and do him no
harm; but do unto him even as he shall say unto thee.
13 So Nebuzar-adan the captain of the guard sent, and Nebushasban, Rab-saris, and Nergal-sharezer, Rab-mag, and
14 all the king of Babylon's princes; even they sent, and took
Jeremiah out of the court of the prison, and committed him
unto Gedaliah the son of Ahikam the son of Shaphan, that
he should carry him home: so he dwelt among the people.

15—18. *Message to Ebed-melech.*

15 Now the word of the LORD came unto Jeremiah, while
16 he was shut up in the court of the prison, saying, Go and
speak to Ebed-melech the Ethiopian, saying, Thus saith
the LORD of hosts, the God of Israel; Behold, I *will* bring
my words upon this city for evil, and not for good; and
17 they shall be *accomplished* in that day before thee. But I
will deliver thee in that day, saith the LORD: and thou
shalt not be given into the hand of the men of whom thou
18 *art* afraid. For I will surely deliver thee, and thou shalt

11—14. NEBUCHADNEZZAR'S CARE FOR JEREMIAH.

12. *Take him, and look well to him*] This favour shewn by Nebuchadnezzar was due to the fact that Jeremiah had consistently throughout counselled submission to him on the part of the Jews. A practical instance of the favour was that Jeremiah was freed from his chains at Ramah (xl. 1) instead of being compelled to proceed to Riblah under the same circumstances as the other captives.

13. For the names, see remarks on ver. 3.

14. For the apparent contradiction between this and xl. 1—4, see note at beginning of this chap.

Gedaliah] See note on xxvi. 24.

home] **to the house.** This has been taken as (*a*) Gedaliah's house, (*b*) *the* (chief) house, in the immediate neighbourhood of "the court of the guard," in other words, the king's palace, (*c*) (best, as most in agreement with the last words of the verse) Jeremiah's own house.

15—18. MESSAGE TO EBED-MELECH.

15. *came*] rather, **had come**, for this incident should in point of time be connected with the events of chap. xxxviii. It probably was postponed till now in order that there might be no break in the narrative of Jeremiah's imprisonment and the capture of the city.

17. *the men of whom thou art afraid*] meaning, not the princes, who were hostile to Jeremiah and so would punish Ebed-melech for helping

not fall by the sword, but thy life shall be for a prey unto thee: because thou hast put thy trust in me, saith the LORD.

CHAP. XL. 1—6. *Jeremiah is released and returns to Gedaliah.*

The word which came to Jeremiah from the LORD, after 40 that Nebuzar-adan the captain of the guard had let him go from Ramah, when he had taken him being bound in chains among all that were carried away captive of Jerusalem and Judah, which were carried away captive unto Babylon. And the captain of the guard took Jeremiah, 2 and said unto him, The LORD thy God hath pronounced this evil upon this place. Now the LORD hath brought *it*, 3 and done according as he hath said: because ye have sinned against the LORD, and have not obeyed his voice, therefore this thing is come upon you. And now behold, 4 I loose thee *this* day from the chains which *were* upon thine hand. If it seem good unto thee to come with me *into*

him out of the dungeon, but, as we see from the next verse, the conquering army in the day of the capture of the city.

18. *thy life shall be for a prey unto thee*] See for the same phrase xxi. 9, xxxviii. 2, xlv. 5, with note on the first of these.

CH. XL. 1—6. JEREMIAH IS RELEASED AND RETURNS TO GEDALIAH.

1. *The word which came*] The mode of introduction leads us to expect a prophetic utterance to follow. In fact, however, none such occurs until chap. xlii. 9, etc. We must take the expression then in a wider sense, including history as well as prophecy. This would present no difficulty to a Jew, as the two things were intimately connected in his mind. This is shewn by the including of Historical Books of the Bible under the title of the Prophets. This introduction then serves for both history and prophecy contained in chaps. xl.—xliv.

after that Nebuzar-adan...had let him go from Ramah] See note on xxxix. 14, and for Ramah, note on xxxi. 15.

chains] manacles, confining the hands only. This appears from ver. 4.

2. The language of this and the following verse, although spoken by Nebuzar-adan, is in Jeremiah's style throughout. We must therefore suppose either that the former had acquired a very accurate acquaintance with the prophet's teaching, or that we have here but the substance of his words.

Babylon, come; and I will look well unto thee: but if it seem ill unto thee to come with me *into* Babylon, forbear: behold, all the land *is* before thee: whither it seemeth ⁵good and convenient for thee to go, thither go. Now while he was not yet gone back, *he said*, Go back also to Gedaliah the son of Ahikam the son of Shaphan, whom the king of Babylon hath made governor over the cities of Judah, and dwell with him among the people: or go wheresoever it seemeth convenient unto thee to go. So the captain of the guard gave him victuals and a reward, and let him go. ⁶Then went Jeremiah unto Gedaliah the son of Ahikam to Mizpah; and dwelt with him among the people that were left in the land.

7—12. *Gedaliah seeks to restore quiet and prosperity to the remaining inhabitants of the country.*

⁷ Now when all the captains of the forces which *were* in

4. *I will look well unto thee*] The margin is more literal, *I will set mine eye upon thee.* Compare the phrases, to have an eye to, to keep an eye upon.

5. *Now while he was not yet gone back*] This is perhaps the most satisfactory explanation of the Heb., which is obscure. It has also been rendered, *And while he yet answered nothing.*

victuals] implying enough for a meal. The same word is rendered "dinner," Prov. xv. 17.

a reward] rather, **a present**. The Heb. word was used in older times for a mess of food sent from the table (Gen. xliii. 34; 2 Sam. xi. 8), and afterwards for a present in general (2 Chron. xxiv. 6 "collection"; Esther ii. 18 "gifts").

6. *Mizpah*] not the city in Gilead, mentioned from time to time in the history of the Judges, but a city of Benjamin, a short distance southwest of Ramah and north-west of Jerusalem. It was there that Samuel assembled the people, when sorely troubled by Philistine incursions, to confess their sins and seek deliverance (1 Sam. vii. 5), and there too Saul was publicly named King of Israel (1 Sam. x. 17). Asa, King of Judah, had fortified it against the attacks of the northern kingdom (1 Kings xv. 22), and now it became the chief scene of the incidents described in this and the next succeeding chapters. It was probably chosen as standing on a ridge commanding a view of Jerusalem. It seems to be identical with "Nob" (Is. x. 32), from which Sennacherib looked down threateningly on the holy city.

7—12. GEDALIAH SEEKS TO RESTORE QUIET AND PROSPERITY TO THE REMAINING INHABITANTS OF THE COUNTRY.

7. *all the captains of the forces*] the various leaders of bands among the Jews, who would keep out of the way during the presence of the

the fields, *even* they and their men, heard that the king of Babylon had made Gedaliah the son of Ahikam governor in the land, and had committed unto him men, and women, and children, and of the poor of the land, of *them* that were not carried away captive to Babylon; then they came to 8 Gedaliah to Mizpah, even Ishmael the son of Nethaniah, and Johanan and Jonathan the sons of Kareah, and Seraiah the son of Tanhumeth, and the sons of Ephai the Netophathite, and Jezaniah the son of a Maachathite, they and their men. And Gedaliah the son of Ahikam the son of 9 Shaphan sware unto them and to their men, saying, Fear not to serve the Chaldeans: dwell in the land and serve the king of Babylon, and it shall be well with you. As for me, 10 behold, I *will* dwell at Mizpah to serve the Chaldeans, which will come unto us: but ye, gather ye wine, and summer fruits, and oil, and put *them* in your vessels, and dwell in your cities that ye have taken. Likewise when all 11 Babylonian forces and until they found what was likely to be the condition of the country and the nature of the new government.

which were in the fields] *which were in the* **field**. See notes on iv. 17, xxxii. 43, and compare ver. 13 below.

8. *Ishmael the son of Nethaniah*] His full designation (xli. 1, where see further in note) is "Ishmael the son of Nethaniah, the son of Elishama, of the seed royal." The last words may mean (*a*) that he was a son of Zedekiah or of one of the other later kings of Judah, or (*b*) that he was a descendant of some king of the Jews, perhaps through Elishama the son of David (2 Sam. v. 16), not so probably Elishama of chap. xxxvi. 12, or (*c*) that, as he took refuge (xli. 10) at the court of Baalis king of the children of Ammon, he may have been on his mother's side related to that royal house.

the Netophathite] Netophah was a village near Bethlehem. See Neh. vii. 26.

Jezaniah the son of a Maachathite] probably not the "Jezaniah" of chap. xlii. 1, where see note.

10. *to serve the Chaldeans*] The verb is not the same as that translated *serve* in ver. 9, but is literally *stand before*, and means to be the minister of another and look after his interests. See xv. 19 and xxxv. 19, with notes.

wine, and summer fruits, and oil] Although, owing to the national troubles, no corn had been sown, yet the fruits here spoken of would be produced as usual, and as Jerusalem was taken about July ("the fourth month," xxxix. 2), they would now be ripening.

taken] **seized**. There is implied in the verb what was no doubt the case, viz. that these captains had not scrupled to take possession of such walled towns or fortresses of any kind as best suited their purposes.

the Jews that *were* in Moab, and among the Ammonites, and in Edom, and that *were* in all the countries, heard that the king of Babylon had left a remnant of Judah, and that he had set over them Gedaliah the son of Ahikam the son
12 of Shaphan; even all the Jews returned out of all places whither they were driven, and came *to* the land of Judah, to Gedaliah, unto Mizpah, and gathered wine and summer fruits very much.

13—16. *Gedaliah is in vain warned of Ishmael's intended treachery.*

13 Moreover Johanan the son of Kareah, and all the captains of the forces that *were* in the fields, came to Gedaliah to
14 Mizpah, and said unto him, Dost thou certainly know that Baalis the king of the Ammonites hath sent Ishmael the son of Nethaniah to slay thee? But Gedaliah the son of
15 Ahikam believed them not. Then Johanan the son of Kareah spake to Gedaliah in Mizpah secretly, saying, Let me go, I pray thee, and I will slay Ishmael the son of Nethaniah, and no man shall know *it*: wherefore should he slay thee, that all the Jews which are gathered unto thee

12. *the Jews returned out of all places*] The fact that a governor of their own nation had been set over such as were left in the land, gave an assurance to those Jews who were waiting in neighbouring nations to see what would be the issue, that they might return and dwell at peace.

13—16. GEDALIAH IS IN VAIN WARNED OF ISHMAEL'S INTENDED TREACHERY.

13. *fields*] See note on ver. 7.
14. *Baalis the king of the Ammonites*] It is easier to see the motives of Ishmael than those of his instigator Baalis. The former no doubt felt aggrieved that he, although of royal birth, should be set aside in favour of Gedaliah, and at once determined to get rid of him and take his place. Baalis may have had a spite against Gedaliah and his family as friends of Jeremiah, and as having probably taken the side of that prophet openly, when (chap. xxvii.) he sent back the messengers of Ammon and the other neighbouring nations, refusing the alliance against the Chaldaeans which they had desired; or it may have been only a design against Palestine generally which influenced him on this occasion, and the belief that, if he were to get rid of Gedaliah and the firm and peaceful rule which he seemed to be inaugurating, there would be more chance for himself in carrying out his plans of conquest.

should be scattered, and the remnant in Judah perish? But Gedaliah the son of Ahikam said unto Johanan the son of Kareah, Thou shalt not do this thing: for thou speakest falsely of Ishmael. 16

CHAP. XLI. 1—3. *Ishmael murders Gedaliah and others.*

Now it came to pass in the seventh month, *that* Ishmael the son of Nethaniah the son of Elishama, of the seed royal, and the princes of the king, even ten men with him, came unto Gedaliah the son of Ahikam to Mizpah; and there they did eat bread together in Mizpah. Then arose Ishmael the son of Nethaniah, and the ten men that were with him, and smote Gedaliah the son of Ahikam the son of Shaphan with the sword, and slew him, whom the king of Babylon had made governor over the land. Ishmael also slew all the Jews that were with him, *even* with Gedaliah 41 2 3

15. *the remnant in Judah perish*] Johanan no doubt hoped to influence a high-minded man like Gedaliah by this argument that on his life depended the welfare of those who remained yet in the country.

CHAP. XLI. 1—3. ISHMAEL MURDERS GEDALIAH AND OTHERS.

1. *in the seventh month*] three months after the capture and two after the burning of the city.

and the princes of the king] The Septuagint omits these words. It is objected (*a*) that if these princes, as well as Ishmael, had come to Gedaliah, the visit from so many prominent personages would have awakened in his mind a suspicion, from which we see that he was in fact wholly free; (*b*) that these princes are never again mentioned in the narrative. It is therefore proposed to render the Heb. (*of the seed royal*) *and* of *the princes of the king;* and thus to make the whole to be a description of Ishmael, and to signify that he was not merely of royal blood, but was also one of those who had counselled and assisted the king in affairs of state. In this case we shall render, **and** *ten men with him*.

and there they did eat bread together in Mizpah] Josephus (*Antiq.* X. 9) speaks of Gedaliah's defenceless state as arising from intoxication.

2. *Then arose Ishmael...and the ten men*] That eleven men should be able to overpower and murder so large a number, including men skilled in war, shews that from some cause these last must have been wholly off their guard.

3. *all the Jews that were with him*] meaning, all that were in the house with him. On their return from the exile the Jews used to keep the third day of the seventh month (Tisri) as a fast in memory of Ishmael's deed (Zech. vii. 5, viii. 19).

at Mizpah, and the Chaldeans that were found there, *and the men of war*.

4—10. *He commits further massacres and carries off captives.*

4 And it came to pass the second day after *he* had slain
5 Gedaliah, and no man knew *it*, that there came certain from Shechem, from Shiloh, and from Samaria, *even* fourscore men, having their beards shaven, and their clothes rent, and having cut themselves, with offerings and incense in their
6 hand, to bring *them to* the house of the LORD. And Ishmael the son of Nethaniah went forth from Mizpah to meet them, weeping all along as he went: and it came to pass, as he met them, he said unto them, Come to Gedaliah the
7 son of Ahikam. And it was *so*, when they came into the midst of the city, that Ishmael the son of Nethaniah slew them, *and cast them* into the midst of the pit, he, and the

4—10. HE COMMITS FURTHER MASSACRES AND CARRIES OFF CAPTIVES.

4. *the second day…and no man knew it*] The long concealment of the murder shews what precautions Ishmael must have taken, even though we suppose, which is quite possible, that the fortress inhabited by Gedaliah was not inside the town.

5. *from Shechem, from Shiloh, and from Samaria*] These three towns are in Ephraim. Shechem (the Sychar of John iv. 5), now *Náblus*, is beautifully situated in a valley between the mountains Gerizim and Ebal. For Shiloh, see note on chap. vii. 12. It lay 18 miles south of Shechem, which however is no objection to its occurrence in the present narrative. One MS. of the Septuagint however, apparently for this reason, reads Salem, a town which appears to have been close to Shechem.

having their beards shaven, and their clothes rent] in sign of mourning for the destruction of the Temple.

having cut themselves] See note on chap. xvi. 6.

offerings and incense] a **meat offering** *and incense*. For the former see note on chap. xvii. 26. Unbloody sacrifices were all that could now be offered, as the only place at which others were permitted (Deut. xii. 13, 14, 17, 18) had been destroyed.

6. *weeping all along*] so as to feign equal concern with them for the fate of the Temple, and thus put them off their guard.

Come to Gedaliah] probably as governor, to whom therefore they should shew respect and offer greeting.

7. *Ishmael the son of Nethaniah slew them*] His object probably was twofold; plunder, including captives, and to keep the land in a state of unrest, so as to help out Baalis's ambitious wishes.

the pit] the **cistern**.

men that *were* with him. But ten men were found among 8 them that said unto Ishmael, Slay us not: for we have treasures in the field, *of* wheat, and *of* barley, and *of* oil, and *of* honey. So he forbare, and slew them not among their brethren. Now the pit wherein Ishmael had cast all the 9 dead bodies of the men, whom he had slain because of Gedaliah, *was* it which Asa the king had made for fear of Baasha king of Israel: *and* Ishmael the son of Nethaniah filled it *with them that were* slain. Then Ishmael carried 10 away captive all the residue of the people that *were* in Mizpah, *even* the king's daughters, and all the people that remained in Mizpah, whom Nebuzar-adan the captain of the guard had committed to Gedaliah the son of Ahikam: and Ishmael the son of Nethaniah carried them away captive, and departed to go over to the Ammonites.

11—18. *The captives are rescued by Johanan, and they prepare to flee into Egypt.*

But when Johanan the son of Kareah, and all the cap- 11

8. *we have treasures*] we have **hidden stores.** In the East it is to this day a common custom to use "wells or cisterns for grain. In them the farmers store their crops of all kinds after the grain is threshed and winnowed. These cisterns are cool, perfectly dry, and tight. The top is hermetically sealed with plaster, and covered with a deep bed of earth. …The custom extended through the Carthaginians of North Africa into Spain.…These ten men had doubtless thus hid their treasures to avoid being plundered in that time of utter lawlessness; and in a similar time I found people storing away grain in cisterns far out in the open country, between Aleppo and Hamath, and they told me it was to hide it from the government tax-gatherers.…They would not answer in a wet country, but in these dry climates stores have been found quite fresh and sound many years after they were thus buried." Thomson (*The Land and the Book*, pp. 509, 510).

9. *the pit*] *the* **cistern.**

because of Gedaliah] **by the side of** *Gedaliah*, i.e. their corpses placed beside his.

Asa the king had made] This pit is not mentioned in the Historical Books. However, we are told (1 Kings xv. 22 and 2 Chron. xvi. 6) that Asa caused the materials of Ramah, which Baasha had just built, to be removed and used for fortifying Geba and Mizpah.

filled it with them that were slain] like the well of Cawnpore in the Indian mutiny of 1857.

10. *all the residue of the people that were in Mizpah*] It would appear from the fulness with which the previous particulars are given that Jeremiah (and probably Baruch also) belonged to this number.

tains of the forces that *were* with him, heard of all the evil
12 that Ishmael the son of Nethaniah had done, then they took all the men, and went to fight with Ishmael the son of Nethaniah, and found him by the great waters that *are*
13 in Gibeon. Now it came to pass, *that* when all the people which *were* with Ishmael saw Johanan the son of Kareah, and all the captains of the forces that *were* with him, then
14 they were glad. So all the people that Ishmael had carried away captive from Mizpah cast about and returned, and
15 went unto Johanan the son of Kareah. But Ishmael the son of Nethaniah escaped from Johanan with eight men,
16 and went to the Ammonites. Then took Johanan the son of Kareah, and all the captains of the forces that *were* with him, all the remnant of the people whom he had recovered from Ishmael the son of Nethaniah, from Mizpah, after *that* he had slain Gedaliah the son of Ahikam, *even* mighty men of war, and the women, and the children, and the eunuchs,
17 whom he had brought again from Gibeon: and they departed, and dwelt in the habitation of Chimham, which *is*

11—18. THE CAPTIVES ARE RESCUED BY JOHANAN, AND THEY PREPARE TO FLEE INTO EGYPT.

12. *the great waters that are in Gibeon*] Gibeon (the modern *El Jib*), a city of the priests (Josh. xviii. 25, xxi. 17) in the tribe of Benjamin. It stands on one of the hills which abound there. On the east of it "is a copious spring...In the trees further down are the remains of a pool or tank of considerable size. This is doubtless the pool of Gibeon at which Abner and Joab met (2 Sam. ii. 13)...Here, or at the spring, were the great waters (or the *many* waters) at which Johanan the son of Kareah found the traitor Ishmael." *Sm. Bibl. Dict.* Art. *Gibeon*.

14. *cast about*] turned round. The old English phrase may be illustrated from the writings of John Gower (1325—1408 nearly). "Then *cast* I all the world *about*." *Confessio Amantis;* and Sir Philip Sidney (1554—1586) "Musidorus could doe no more but perswade the mariners to *cast about* againe." *Arcadia*.

15. Ishmael, we see from this verse, lost eight men in the encounter.
went to the Ammonites] Compare xl. 14. It is probable that the connection of Baalis with these acts of treachery was in part at any rate the cause of the misfortunes predicted for Ammon by Jeremiah (xlix. 1—6) and Ezekiel (xxv. 1—7).

16. *mighty men of war*] Hence we learn that there were soldiers at Mizpah who, either from the sudden panic, or from disaffection towards Gedaliah, had made no stand against Ishmael and his small force.

17. *the habitation of Chimham, which is by Beth-lehem*] For Chim-

by Beth-lehem, to go to enter *into* Egypt, because of the 18
Chaldeans: for they were afraid of them, because Ishmael
the son of Nethaniah had slain Gedaliah the son of Ahikam,
whom the king of Babylon made governor in the land.

CHAP. XLII. 1—6. *Johanan and the others seek through
Jeremiah a declaration of God's will.*

Then all the captains of the forces, and Johanan the son 42
of Kareah, and Jezaniah the son of Hoshaiah, and all the
people from the least even unto the greatest, came near,
and said unto Jeremiah the prophet, Let, we beseech thee, 2
our supplication be accepted before thee, and pray for us
unto the LORD thy God, *even* for all this remnant; (for we

ham (for which however there is also another reading in the Heb.
Chemoham), the son of Barzillai, see 2 Sam. xix. 37, 38. It was natural
that David as a mark of gratitude should have given him, as appears
from this passage, a portion of land which, being in the neighbourhood
of Bethlehem the king's birth-place, may be supposed to have belonged
to him. The Heb. for habitation (*geruth*) occurs here only. The sense
however is pretty clear, viz. Khan, or Caravanserai. "The need of
shelter led very early to the erection of rude and simple buildings of
varying size, known as khans, which offered the wayfarer the protection
of walls and a roof, and water, but little more....From immemorial
antiquity it has been a favourite mode of benevolence to raise such
places of shelter." The special utility of this Khan lay in its being on
the great caravan route to Egypt. Such was the inn, and in that very
neighbourhood too, in which "there was no room" for the mother of
our Lord and Joseph just before the Nativity (Luke ii. 7).

to go to enter into Egypt] to prepare for the journey into Egypt, a
journey which, according to the first words of the next verse, was undertaken from fear of the Chaldaeans. It seemed likely that the outbreak
which had taken place in connexion with the overthrow and death of
the governor appointed by the king of Babylon, might be revenged
without much discrimination by that monarch.

CHAP. XLII. 1—6. JOHANAN AND THE OTHERS SEEK THROUGH
JEREMIAH A DECLARATION OF GOD'S WILL.

1. *Jezaniah, the son of Hoshaiah*] probably not the Jezaniah of
chap. xl. 8. In xliii. 2 he is called Azariah, a name which the
Septuagint here also has instead of Jezaniah. It is thus possible that
the latter name in this place may be due to a copyist, who thought that
the names of captains here must correspond as closely as might be with
the list in chap. xl.

from the least even unto the greatest] i.e. all, without exception.

2. *be accepted*] literally, *fall*. See note on xxxvi. 7.

3 are left *but* a few of many, as thine eyes do behold us:) that the LORD thy God may shew us the way wherein we may
4 walk, and the thing that we may do. Then Jeremiah the prophet said unto them, I have heard *you;* behold, I *will* pray unto the LORD your God according to your words; and it shall come to pass, *that* whatsoever thing the LORD shall answer you, I will declare *it* unto you; I will keep
5 nothing back from you. Then they said to Jeremiah, The LORD be a true and faithful witness between us, if we do not even according to all things *for* the which the LORD thy
6 God shall send thee to us. Whether *it be* good, or whether *it be* evil, we will obey the voice of the LORD our God, to whom we send thee; that it may be well with us, when we obey the voice of the LORD our God.

7—22. *God's will is that they should remain in their own land.*

7 And it came to pass after ten days, that the word of the
8 LORD came unto Jeremiah. Then called he Johanan the son of Kareah, and all the captains of the forces which *were* with him, and all the people from the least even to the greatest,
9 and said unto them, Thus saith the LORD, the God of Israel, unto whom ye sent me to present your supplication before
10 him: if ye will still abide in this land, then will I build you,

3. *that the Lord thy God may shew us*] The desire to ascertain God's will expressed here, even when compared with their disobedience to that will when declared (chap. xliii. 4), need not imply hypocrisy. They may have made up their minds that it was necessary to flee into Egypt, and, assuming that this resolution would be confirmed by the divine response, desired only to know what particular course they should adopt in accordance with it.

4. *I have heard you*] See note on xxxiv. 10.

5. *between us*] **against** *us*, i.e. to bear witness and punish us if we fail to do our part as we now promise.

7—22. GOD'S WILL IS THAT THEY SHOULD REMAIN IN THEIR OWN LAND.

7. *after ten days*] Generally the reply seems to have come at once. We can easily see however in the present case a reason for delay, viz. that the panic consequent upon the late disasters might be over before the command not to flee into Egypt was given.

9. *to present*] literally, *to make to fall.* See note on ver. 2.

10. *then will I build you...*] Compare i. 10 and xxiv. 6 for these figures of speech.

and not pull *you* down, and I will plant you, and not pluck *you* up: for I repent me of the evil that I have done unto you. Be not afraid of the king of Babylon, of whom ye *are* afraid; be not afraid of him, saith the LORD: for I *am* with you to save you, and to deliver you from his hand. And I will shew mercies unto you, that he may have mercy upon you, and cause you to return to your own land. But if ye say, We will not dwell in this land, neither obey the voice of the LORD your God, saying, No; but we will go *into* the land of Egypt, where we shall see no war, nor hear the sound of the trumpet, nor have hunger of bread; and there will we dwell: and now therefore hear the word of the LORD, ye remnant of Judah; Thus saith the LORD of hosts, the God of Israel; If ye wholly set your faces to enter *into* Egypt, and go to sojourn there; then it shall come to pass, *that* the sword, which ye feared, shall overtake you there in the land of Egypt, and the famine, whereof ye were afraid, shall follow close after you there *in* Egypt; and there ye shall die. So shall it be with all the men that set their faces to go *into* Egypt to sojourn there; they shall die by the sword, by the famine, and by the pestilence: and none of them shall remain or escape from the evil that I *will* bring upon them. For thus saith the LORD of hosts, the God of Israel; As mine anger and my fury hath been poured forth

I repent me] a figure of speech. I change my *conduct* towards you, which with *men* is commonly caused by change of *purpose*.

12. *I will shew mercies unto you*] **I will grant you compassion**, i.e. from Nebuchadnezzar. The Heb. phrase in the text occurs also in the same sense in Gen. xliii. 14; 1 Kings viii. 50.

cause you to return] or, with the difference of a vowel only in the original, *cause you to dwell*. The latter is perhaps preferable, not only as according more literally with the condition of the persons addressed, but also as agreeing better with the following verse ('We will not dwell,' etc.).

14. *we shall see no war*] We shall be in a land further from Babylon, and therefore not liable to invasion.

15. *and now therefore*] **now therefore**. This is the second or answering part of the sentence (*apodosis*), the first part (*protasis*) consisting of the two previous verses.

to enter into Egypt and go] **to go *into* Egypt and go**. The verbs are the same in the Heb.

17. *none of them shall remain or escape*] See note on vi. 9.

upon the inhabitants of Jerusalem; so shall my fury be poured forth upon you, when ye shall enter *into* Egypt: and ye shall be an execration, and an astonishment, and a curse, and a reproach; and ye shall see this place no
19 more. The LORD hath said concerning you, O ye remnant of Judah; Go ye not *into* Egypt: know certainly that I have
20 admonished you *this* day. For ye dissembled in your hearts, when ye sent me unto the LORD your God, saying, Pray for us unto the LORD our God; and according unto all that the LORD our God shall say, so declare unto us, and we
21 will do *it*. And *now* I have *this* day declared *it* to you; but ye have not obeyed the voice of the LORD your God, nor
22 any *thing* for the which he hath sent me unto you. Now therefore know certainly that ye shall die by the sword, by the famine, and by the pestilence, in the place whither ye desire to go *and* to sojourn.

CHAP. XLIII. 1—7. *They disobey and go down to Egypt.*

43 And it came to pass, *that* when Jeremiah had made an end of speaking unto all the people all the words of the LORD their God, *for* which the LORD their God had sent
2 him to them, *even* all these words; then spake Azariah the son of Hoshaiah, and Johanan the son of Kareah, and all

19. The Lord's reply has ended, and Jeremiah is now adding a brief and emphatic address.
The Lord hath said concerning you] the Lord hath **spoken concerning you**.
admonished] *become a witness against* is the more literal rendering.

20. *ye dissembled in your hearts*] either, (*a*) *ye err at the risk of your souls*, or (*b*) *ye have deceived yourselves*, i.e. ye believed that ye were asking of God in absolute good faith, but all the while nothing but your own way would content you.

22. *to go and to sojourn*] **to go to sojourn**, the latter verb expressing the object of the former.

CHAP. XLIII. 1—7. THEY DISOBEY AND GO DOWN TO EGYPT.

2. *then spake Azariah*] See note on chap. xlii. 1. The attack upon Baruch, and only indirectly and through him upon the prophet, may have arisen from their being reluctantly compelled to acknowledge that Jeremiah himself at any rate was possessed of integrity of purpose. This he had shewn by his refusal to seek protection and honourable treatment from the Chaldaeans, whose favour the worse section of his countrymen always suspected him of seeking.

the proud men, saying unto Jeremiah, Thou speakest falsely: the LORD our God hath not sent thee to say, Go not *into* Egypt to sojourn there: but Baruch the son of Neriah 3 setteth thee on against us, for to deliver us into the hand of the Chaldeans, that *they* might put us to death, and carry us away captives *into* Babylon. So Johanan the son of 4 Kareah, and all the captains of the forces, and all the people, obeyed not the voice of the LORD, to dwell in the land of Judah. But Johanan the son of Kareah, and all the 5 captains of the forces, took all the remnant of Judah, that were returned from all nations, whither they had been driven, to dwell in the land of Judah: *Even* men, and 6 women, and children, and the king's daughters, and every person that Nebuzar-adan the captain of the guard had left with Gedaliah the son of Ahikam the son of Shaphan, and Jeremiah the prophet, and Baruch the son of Neriah. So 7 they came *into* the land of Egypt: for they obeyed not the voice of the LORD: thus came they *even* to Tahpanhes.

8—13. *Prophecy of the fall of Egypt.*

Then came the word of the LORD unto Jeremiah in Tah- 8 panhes, saying, Take great stones in thine hand, and hide 9 them in the clay in the brickkiln, which *is* at the entry of Pharaoh's house in Tahpanhes, in the sight of the men of Judah; and say unto them, Thus saith the LORD of hosts, 10

5. *that were returned from all nations*] See note on chap. xl. 12.
7. *Tahpanhes*] See note on chap. ii. 16.

8—13. PROPHECY OF THE FALL OF EGYPT.

8. *in Tahpanhes*] The exiles would be compelled to halt here in order to secure permission to sojourn in the country and obtain if possible such recognition from the king as would help to supply them with means of subsistence.

9. *hide them in the clay*] i.e. cover them over with mortar.

in the brickkiln] The Heb. word occurs in but three (or, since 2 Sam. xii. 31 has a various reading, possibly in but two) passages in the Bible. See Nah. iii. 14. Beyond the fact that it means a place connected with bricks the form of the word in the original does not help us. Brick pavement, or wall, or building, have all been suggested as the sense here, so as to avoid the objection that a brickkiln would not be likely to be set up close to a royal palace. Such a thing however is far from impossible in that country and at that time.

the God of Israel; Behold, I *will* send and take Nebuchadrezzar the king of Babylon, my servant, and will set his throne upon these stones that I have hid; and he shall spread his royal pavilion over them. And when he cometh, he shall smite the land of Egypt, *and deliver* such *as are* for death to death; and such *as are* for captivity to captivity; and such *as are* for the sword to the sword. And I will kindle a fire in the houses of the gods of Egypt; and he shall burn them, and carry them away captives: and he shall array himself with the land of Egypt, as a shepherd putteth on his garment; and he shall go forth from thence in peace. He shall break also the images of Beth-shemesh,

10. *my servant*] See note on xxv. 9.

upon these stones that I have hid] The action of Jeremiah would naturally excite much attention and enquiry among the people, although we must not suppose, arguing from our Western and precise manners, that he would be at all necessarily interfered with. In fact he would have a twofold security, as a prophet of God to those who acknowledged him as such, and in the opinion of others as insane, and according to Eastern ideas thus specially under Divine promptings in his acts. To the crowd collected by these symbolic acts Jeremiah would proclaim the meaning of the sign which he was commanded thus to shew.

his royal pavilion] rather, **his canopy shall be stretched** (literally, *one shall stretch*). The covering, however, is probably not a fixed one, like an awning or tent, but borne by an attendant. "It had a tall and thick pole, which the bearer grasped with both his hands, and in the early times a somewhat small circular top. Under the later kings the size of the head was considerably enlarged, and at the same time a curtain or flap was attached, which, falling from the edge of the parasol, more effectually protected the monarch from the sun's rays." Rawl. *Anc. Mon.* I. 496.

11. *and deliver*] These words may be omitted. Under the name of 'the land' its inhabitants are apportioned out among the various forms of ill that follow.

for the sword] the sword of the executioner: 'death' in the earlier part of the verse referring therefore to other forms of fate such as famine or deadly wound in battle.

12. *I will kindle*] a sudden change of person, but nothing beyond what is frequent with Jeremiah. He immediately returns to the third person, 'he shall burn them,' etc.

as a shepherd putteth on his garment] Nebuchadnezzar shall have no more difficulty in carrying off the spoil of Egypt than the shepherd has in wrapping his outer garment about him at the end of his ordinary day's labour.

13. *the images*] The same word is rendered *pillar* in Is. xix. 19, and there as well as here in all probability means obelisk (see next note).

that *is* in the land of Egypt; and the houses of the gods of the Egyptians shall he burn with fire.

CHAP. XLIV. 1—10. *Rebuke addressed to the Egyptian Jews.*

The word that came to Jeremiah concerning all the Jews **44** which dwell in the land of Egypt, which dwell at Migdol, and at Tahpanhes, and at Noph, and in the country of Pathros, saying, Thus saith the LORD of hosts, the God of **2**

This announcement of the destruction of such splendid contributions to the favourite Egyptian sun worship shewed the extent to which the devastation of the land by Nebuchadnezzar should go. For the fulfilment of this prophecy against Egypt, see note on xliv. 30.

Beth-shemesh] *house of the sun* (Greek *Heliopolis*, Egyptian *On*, which last is altered by a play on the word to *Aven* = iniquity, Ezek. xxx. 17). It is near the southern point of the Delta and about ten miles north-east of Cairo. An ancient sycamore hard by is pointed out according to a local tradition as that beneath which the Holy Family rested (Matt. ii. 14). At On there was a spring which was believed by the credulous to have been salt until the Virgin's coming. It was a city of obelisks, two of which stood before the entrance to the Temple of the Sun. "When Strabo visited the city twenty years before Christ it was already a heap of ruins. Nothing now remains of Heliopolis but some traces of the massive walls, fragments of sphinxes, and an obelisk of red granite sixty-eight feet high. It is, with the exception of a small obelisk which Lepsius discovered in the Acropolis of Memphis, the oldest obelisk extant." Schaff's *Through Bible Lands*. Obelisks were brought from Heliopolis to Rome by Augustus and Caligula and still stand there. The shape of such monuments has been rendered yet more familiar to many of late by the erection on the Thames embankment of "Cleopatra's Needle."

CHAP. XLIV. 1—10. REBUKE ADDRESSED TO THE EGYPTIAN JEWS.

1. *The word that came to Jeremiah*] This is the last prophecy of Jeremiah in respect of time. The occasion we see to have been the unabated idolatry which characterised the people even in the midst of the punishment which they were undergoing in exile. It may have been uttered at any time between the arrival in Egypt (about 585 B.C.) and the fulfilment (not earlier than 572 B.C.).

at Migdol] twelve miles from Pelusium, on the northern boundary. See Exod. xiv. 2.

at Tahpanhes, and at Noph] See note on ii. 16 (*Tahapanes*). Authorities are divided as to the exact position of Pathros, some passages where it is mentioned suggesting Lower (northern) and some Upper (southern) Egypt. We have no distinct intimation that Jeremiah ever went into Upper Egypt, yet in that direction on the whole the preponderance of opinion seems to incline.

Israel; Ye have seen all the evil that I have brought upon Jerusalem, and upon all the cities of Judah; and behold, this day they *are* a desolation, and no man dwelleth therein, 3 because of their wickedness which they have committed to provoke me to anger, in that *they* went to burn incense, *and* to serve other gods, whom they knew not, *neither* they, you, 4 nor your fathers. Howbeit I sent unto you all my servants the prophets, rising early and sending *them*, saying, Oh, do 5 not this abominable thing that I hate. But they hearkened not, nor inclined their ear to turn from their wickedness, to 6 burn no incense unto other gods. Wherefore my fury and mine anger was poured forth, and was kindled in the cities of Judah and in the streets of Jerusalem; and they are 7 wasted *and* desolate, as *at* this day. Therefore now thus saith the LORD, the God of hosts, the God of Israel; Wherefore commit ye *this* great evil against your souls, to cut off from you man and woman, child and suckling, out of Judah, 8 to leave you none to remain; in that *ye* provoke me unto wrath with the works of your hands, burning incense unto other gods in the land of Egypt, whither ye be gone to dwell, that ye might cut yourselves off, and that *ye* might be a curse and a reproach among all the nations of the 9 earth? Have ye forgotten the wickedness of your fathers, and the wickedness of the kings of Judah, and the wickedness of their wives, and your own wickedness, and the wick-

---

3. *and to serve*] In the Heb. there is no *and*, and the infinitive may therefore very well depend upon 'to burn incense.'
4. *Howbeit*] literally, **And**.
7. *Therefore now*] in the face of all the warnings that ye have had. *against your souls*] against *yourselves*.
8. *the works of your hands*] your idols.
that ye might cut yourselves off] The Heb. is exactly the same as that rendered in the previous verse 'to cut off from you.' Hence, as there seems no authority for the use of the reflexive rendering, we may best consider the object of the verb in that verse ('man etc.') as understood with it here.
9. *their wives*] The Heb. has *his wives*. The Septuagint has *your princes* (compare verses 17, 21), taking thus quite a different word, for which there is no authority in any Heb. text which has come down to us. Our present reading, however, may spring from an error on the part of a Heb. copyist, arising from the word *wives* which follows in the verse. If on the other hand we are to take it as the genuine reading, the

edness of your wives, which they have committed in the land of Judah, and in the streets of Jerusalem? They are not humbled *even* unto this day, neither have they feared, nor walked in my law, nor in my statutes, that I set before you and before your fathers.

11—14. *The punishment that shall overtake them.*

Therefore thus saith the LORD of hosts, the God of Israel; Behold, I will set my face against you for evil, and to cut off all Judah. And I will take the remnant of Judah, that have set their faces to go *into* the land of Egypt to sojourn there, and they shall all be consumed, *and* fall in the land of Egypt; they shall *even* be consumed by the sword, *and* by the famine: they shall die, from the least even unto the greatest, by the sword and by the famine: and they shall be an execration, *and* an astonishment, and a curse, and a reproach. For I will punish them that dwell in the land of Egypt, as I have punished Jerusalem, by the sword, by the famine, and by the pestilence: so that none of the remnant of Judah, which are gone into the land of Egypt to sojourn there, shall escape or remain, that *they*

singular pronoun will refer either (*a*) to the nation (kings and people alike), where, however, we should have expected the feminine, or (*b*) to the *individual* kings of Judah.

10. *humbled*] literally, *bruised*, contrite and penitent for sin. The word is used of the vicarious bearing of the sins of the guilty by the innocent in Is. liii. 5, "he was *bruised* for our iniquities." The prophet changes to the third person, as including in his remark the previous generations also.

11—14. THE PUNISHMENT THAT SHALL OVERTAKE THEM.

11. *I will set my face*] See note on xxi. 10.

all Judah] all that are in Egypt, i.e. of those now going to sojourn there and with the exceptions mentioned afterwards (verses 14, 28).

12. The emphatic way in which the prediction of Judah's misfortunes in Egypt is repeated again is very remarkable. We gather at least one of the reasons from the subsequent verses. They still cling to idolatry in the face of warnings and facts.

14. *which are gone*] *which are* **going**. The prophet is not speaking of any who may be permanent residents in Egypt. Naturally those might better escape the coming troubles, as being (*a*) dispersed through the country, (*b*) acquainted with the Egyptian language and customs, (*c*) possessed of private means gathered during their previous residence.

should return *into* the land of Judah, to the which they have a desire to return to dwell there: for none shall return but such as shall escape.

15—19. *The people's reply to the prophet. They refuse to give up idolatry.*

15 Then all the men which knew that their wives had burnt incense unto other gods, and all the women that stood *by*, a great multitude, even all the people that dwelt in the land of 16 Egypt, in Pathros, answered Jeremiah, saying, As for the word that thou hast spoken unto us in the name of the 17 Lord, we will not hearken unto thee. But we will certainly do whatsoever thing goeth forth out of our own mouth, to burn incense unto the queen of heaven, and to pour out drink offerings unto her, as we have done, we, and our fathers, our kings, and our princes, in the cities of Judah, and in the streets of Jerusalem: for *then* had we plenty of

---

they have a desire] they lift up their soul. Compare xxii. 27.

15—19. THE PEOPLE'S REPLY TO THE PROPHET. THEY REFUSE TO GIVE UP IDOLATRY.

15. *had burnt*] burned. Their idolatry was still going on.

and all the women] This suggests to us, as do the words 'a great multitude,' that it was on the occasion of an idolatrous festival, in which the women took a leading part, that Jeremiah had rebuked the people. Otherwise the women at any rate would not be thus assembled.

all the people that dwelt in the land of Egypt] not of course intended to be understood literally, but that they were very numerous and represented the whole. Any difficulty connected with the statements in the Pentateuch that *all* the people were assembled before Moses at the door of the tabernacle, and addressed by him, is removed by such a passage as this.

17. *whatsoever thing goeth forth out of our own mouth*] It is not, as the Eng. Vers. implies, that the people declare in general their intention of following their own will rather than God's. For *whatsoever thing goeth forth* we should rather render **all the thing** (or, **every word**) **that is gone forth**, i.e. the particular vow that we have vowed to the queen of heaven we will perform to the uttermost. For this phrase as employed of vows, see Numb. xxx. 2, 12; Deut. xxiii. 23; Ps. lxvi. 13, 14. The people rely on the argument that this is no new worship of theirs, and that their experience shews that it was for their national advantage that it should be kept up. The queen of heaven has done more for them than the God whose prophet now addresses them.

the queen of heaven] See note on chap. vii. 18.

victuals, and were well, and saw no evil. But since we left 18 off to burn incense to the queen of heaven, and to pour out drink offerings unto her, we have wanted all *things*, and have been consumed by the sword and by the famine. And when 19 we burnt incense to the queen of heaven, and poured out drink offerings unto her, did we make her cakes to worship her, and pour out drink offerings unto her, without our men?

20—23. *Jeremiah declares that idolatry is the cause of their present troubles as a nation.*

Then Jeremiah said unto all the people, to the men, and 20 to the women, and to all the people which had given him *that* answer, saying, The incense that ye burnt in the cities 21 of Judah, and in the streets of Jerusalem, ye, and your fathers, your kings, and your princes, and the people of the land, did not the LORD remember them, and came it *not* into his mind? So that the LORD could no longer bear, 22

then had we plenty of victuals] They perversely attribute the misfortunes which had befallen their country from the battle of Megiddo and death of Josiah onwards to the attack made upon idolatry by that king; and not to the gradual degradation of the people though the medium of that idolatry during the reigns of Manasseh and Amon and the earlier part of that of Josiah.

18. *since we left off to burn incense*] Although practised, as we have seen, in the times of kings of Judah subsequent to Josiah with more or less openness, idolatry was probably always by way of being discountenanced in the time of those kings.

19. *cakes to worship her*] rather, **cakes to make an image of her**, referring to the image of the full moon either formed by the cake or stamped upon it. See note on "cakes" vii. 18.

without our men] *without our* **husbands.** The consent of the husband was necessary before the wife's vow could be binding (Numb. xxx. 6, 7). Hence the women plead that they have their husbands' approval in this worship and that therefore Jeremiah has no right to interfere.

20—23. JEREMIAH DECLARES THAT IDOLATRY IS THE CAUSE OF THEIR PRESENT TROUBLES AS A NATION.

21. *came it not into his mind?*] See note on chap. iii. 16.

22. *could no longer bear*] This contains the pith of the answer to the people's argument that they had been more prosperous while openly practising idolatry than afterwards. Jeremiah points out that even though their national misfortunes were subsequent to Josiah's reforma-

because of the evil of your doings, *and* because of the abominations which ye have committed; therefore is your land a desolation, and an astonishment, and a curse, without an inhabitant, as *at* this day. Because you have burnt incense, and because ye have sinned against the Lord, and have not obeyed the voice of the Lord, nor walked in his law, nor in his statutes, nor in his testimonies; therefore this evil is happened unto you, as *at* this day.

24—30. *With the solemn forecast of further punishment Jeremiah concludes his prophecy.*

24 Moreover Jeremiah said unto all the people, and to all the women, Hear the word of the Lord, all Judah that *are* 25 in the land of Egypt: Thus saith the Lord of hosts, the God of Israel, saying; Ye and your wives have both spoken with your mouths, and fulfilled with your hand, saying, We will surely perform our vows that we have vowed, to burn incense to the queen of heaven, and to pour out drink offerings unto her: ye will surely accomplish your vows, 26 and surely perform your vows. Therefore hear ye the word of the Lord, all Judah that dwell in the land of Egypt; Behold, I have sworn by my great name, saith the Lord, that my name shall no more be named in the mouth of any man

---

tion, and therefore after what they might have called the golden age of idolatry had ceased, yet it was owing to the idolatry so long rampant, and even afterwards cherished and practised as far as its votaries dared, that the overthrow came. The long suffering of God was at last exhausted.

24—30. With the solemn forecast of further punishment Jeremiah concludes his prophecy.

24. *Moreover Jeremiah said*] The people in all likelihood obstinately pressed forward to carry out their idolatrous intentions. Jeremiah therefore declares the consequences of this persistence, and with the announcement that in their ruin shall be involved that of the Egyptian king Pharaoh-Hophra, closes, as far as we know, the whole series of his prophecies.

25. *with your hand*] *with your* **hands.** Jeremiah no doubt points to the cakes which they were at the very moment carrying.

ye will surely accomplish] rather, **accomplish ye by all means,** the future used as imperative in an ironical sense. If ye will persist in spite of all my warnings, then be it so.

26. *my name shall no more be named*] meaning either that the Jews

of Judah in all the land of Egypt, saying, The Lord GOD liveth. Behold, I *will* watch over them for evil, and not ²⁷ for good: and all the men of Judah that *are* in the land of Egypt shall be consumed by the sword and by the famine, until there be an end of them. Yet a small number that ²⁸ escape the sword shall return out of the land of Egypt *into* the land of Judah, and all the remnant of Judah, that are gone into the land of Egypt to sojourn there, shall know whose words shall stand, mine, or theirs. And this *shall be* ²⁹ a sign unto you, saith the LORD, that I will punish you in this place, that ye may know that my words shall surely

in Egypt shall be exterminated (this however in its literal sense, as we see, was not to happen), or that the Lord would no longer reckon Himself as their covenant God, and thus they should lose the right of calling upon His name as such. See note on *shall bless themselves in him*, chap. iv. 2.

27. *I will watch*] or, *I am watching*. The verb is the same as that rendered "hasten" in chap. i. 12, and "watch" in chap. v. 6, where see notes.

28. *Yet a small number that escape the sword shall...land of Judah*] more literally, *Yet those that escape the sword shall...land of Judah*, *men of number*, i.e. easily to be numbered on account of their fewness.

whose words] rather, *whose* **word**. The reference is to the particular threat of punishment and the people's refusal to give credit to it.

As in ver. 14 above, the assertion that all the Egyptian Jews shall perish is here immediately qualified. A remnant shall escape. The many Jewish colonists afterwards living in Egypt were probably attracted thither in times subsequent to this, partly through the fertility of the country watered by the Nile, and partly through the liberality of Ptolemy Lagi, the successor of Alexander the Great. Ptolemy, after his capture of Jerusalem (B.C. 320), brought many Jews into Egypt as settlers, and gave those at Alexandria equal rights with the Macedonians (Josephus, *Ant.* XII. 1). This coupled with the mercantile advantages of Alexandria soon made the Jews to be a very important element of the population.

29. *And this shall be a sign*] It has been inferred from the fact that the overthrow of Pharaoh-Hophra (the sign referred to), uncertain as is its date (see next verse), was much later than the time of the above prophecy, that these two verses are therefore an interpolation made after the event. There is no need however of our assuming that such a sign of the truth of the rest of Jeremiah's words would not be given by the prophet. The fulfilment of it, postponed for seven years, would be all the more striking to those Jews who survived to behold it. Besides, there are various other instances in the Bible of a sign which was not to take place till many years after that of which it was to be the proof. See e.g. Ex. iii. 12; 2 Kings xix. 29.

30 stand against you for evil: Thus saith the LORD; Behold, I *will* give Pharaoh-hophra king of Egypt into the hand of his enemies, and into the hand of them that seek his life; as I gave Zedekiah king of Judah into the hand of Nebuchadrezzar king of Babylon, his enemy, and that sought his life.

CHAP. XLV. 1—5. *A supplementary notice on the part of Baruch.*

45 The word that Jeremiah the prophet spake unto Baruch

30. *into the hand of his enemies*] This clearly points to an invasion of Egypt by the Babylonish power, but by no means implies that the king shall lose his life at their hand. The parallel case of Zedekiah as adduced in the verse shews this, and thus removes the difficulty which has been raised in the fact that history makes Pharaoh-Hophra (the Apries of Herodotus) to have become intensely unpopular after a defeat from the people of Cyrene, to have been in consequence overthrown and imprisoned by Amasis (about six years after this time), and after about ten years of captivity strangled by him (Herod. II. 161, 169). We have here indeed no account of a Babylonian invasion, but the Egyptian priests, from whom Herodotus derived the above information, would be careful to omit such, if it resulted in disgrace to their own country, just as the defeat of Necho at Carchemish was passed over by them for the same reason. It is quite possible, although in the obscurity in which the dates of this period are involved, it is not easy to shew with any certainty, that a successful invasion of Egypt by Nebuchadnezzar may have had much to do with the unpopularity of Hophra and the setting up of Amasis. See also note on xlvi. 13.

CHAP. XLV. 1—5. A SUPPLEMENTARY NOTICE ON THE PART OF BARUCH.

1. *unto Baruch*] This address to an individual following upon words spoken to a nation has been compared to the Epistles addressed by St Paul to individuals (Timothy, Titus, Philemon), which in like manner are placed after those which he indites to churches. Baruch was a man of high birth, grandson of Maaseiah (chap. xxxii. 12), who was governor of the city in the time of Josiah (2 Chron. xxxiv. 8). He seems to have expected to have either important office in the state or more probably the gift of prophecy bestowed upon him. His ambition is destined not to be gratified, and the prophet here warns him of the fact. In addition to the burden of the sins and sorrows of his country which afflict him sorely, he must learn to repress the desire to be anything more than the attendant upon him whose gift of prophecy he may not hope to share. "To play a prominent part in the impending crisis, to be the hero of a national revival, to gain the favour of the conqueror whose coming he announced, this, or

the son of Neriah, when he had written these words in a book at the mouth of Jeremiah, in the fourth year of Jehoiakim the son of Josiah king of Judah, saying, Thus saith 2 the LORD, the God of Israel, unto thee, O Baruch; Thou 3 didst say, Woe is me now! for the LORD hath added grief to my sorrow; I fainted in my sighing, and I find no rest. Thus shalt thou say unto him, The LORD saith thus; Be- 4 hold, *that* which I have built *will* I break down, and *that* which I have planted I *will* pluck up, even this whole land. And seekest thou great *things* for thyself? seek *them* not: for 5 behold, I *will* bring evil upon all flesh, saith the LORD: but thy life will I give unto thee for a prey in all places whither thou goest.

CHAP. XLVI. 1, 2. *Introduction to the prophecies against the Gentiles.*

The word of the LORD which came to Jeremiah the pro- 46

something like this had been the vision that had come before him, and when this passed away he sank into despair at the seeming fruitlessness of his efforts." *Sm. Bibl. Dict.* Art. *Jeremiah.* See also Keble's *Christian Year*, 11th Sunday after Trinity, "Is this a time to plant and build, etc." Baruch is thus a signal illustration for us how far that gift of prophecy was from depending upon individuals, and how completely it was acknowledged to be for God alone to bestow or withhold. See further in Introd. III. § 6.

these words] the Roll of chap. xxxvi. as is shewn us by the addition of the date 'in the fourth year of Jehoiakim'.

3. *grief to my sorrow*] The 'sorrow' was pain at the sins of his fellow-countrymen, the 'grief' that which was caused by the impending judgments.

I fainted in my sighing] a quotation from Ps. vi. 6 ("I am weary with my groaning").

4. *Behold, that which I have built...*] the same language as in chap. i. 10, and thus forming the general burden of Jeremiah's prophecy.

even this whole land] literally, *and as regards* **the whole earth,** *it is* (*so*). According to the present text however the last words are, *it is mine.* The reference is to the scourge inflicted upon the known world by the rise and aggressions of the power of Babylon.

5. *seek them not*] do not hope to be more than thou now art. See note above.

thy life will I give unto thee for a prey] See note on xxi. 9.

CHAP. XLVI. 1, 2. INTRODUCTION TO THE PROPHECIES AGAINST THE GENTILES.

1. *The word of the Lord...against the Gentiles*] The custom of

2 phet against the Gentiles; against Egypt, against the army of Pharaoh-necho king of Egypt, which was by the river Euphrates in Carchemish, which Nebuchadrezzar king of

placing in a group as here prophecies against heathen nations is illustrated by Isaiah (chaps xiii.—xxiii.); Ezekiel (chaps. xxv.—xxxii.), and Amos (chaps. i. 3—ii. 3). It has been sought to draw significance from the division into seven nations which may be made in the case of Ezekiel and Amos, and even here, but it requires some forcing of the parts of the prophecy to carry this out. Here for instance the division into *eight* or even *nine* parts is more natural, viz. Egypt (in two parts, xlvi. 3—12, 14—28), Philistia (xlvii.), Moab (xlviii.), Ammon (xlix. 1—6), Edom (xlix. 7—22), Damascus (xlix. 23—27), Kedar and Hazor (xlix. 28—33), Elam (xlix. 34—39), and Babylon (l. li.). The order of these in the Heb. is by no means the same as that of the Septuagint, who place Babylon immediately after Egypt, with other differences. The former, however, is more likely to be correct, even judging the matter only from internal considerations. It is more natural, taking Egypt first, as the nation whose overthrow by Nebuchadnezzar would be the signal to the rest of a similar fate, to go thence to Philistia (including Tyre and Sidon), then (passing round to the East of Palestine) Moab, Ammon, and Edom, then Damascus, as representing the kingdoms of the north, Kedar and Hazor as indicating the kings mentioned in the summary of chap. xxv. (ver. 24), while lastly the nations of the East are included under Elam. The prophecies against Egypt and Babylon agree in containing a promise of restoration to Israel (xlvi. 27, 28, l. 19, 20). As each represented the great power of evil, hostile to the people of God, it is quite natural that these last should reap benefit from such an overthrow.

2. *against Egypt*] **concerning** *Egypt*. The two parts into which this prophecy is divided (see above) were probably written at different times, the new heading at ver. 13 suggesting this. As regards subject matter however the second follow naturally upon the first, the declaration of further subjugation of Egypt upon the proclamation of the enemy's signal success at Carchemish. See further in notes on verses 13, 14.

Pharaoh-necho] This monarch had defeated and slain Josiah at Megiddo, and set Jehoahaz on the throne. In three months he had deposed and imprisoned him at Riblah, and set up Jehoiakim. He was extending his conquests in the Asiatic direction when in the fourth year of Jehoiakim's reign he was overthrown at Carchemish.

Carchemish] probably not Cercesium at the junction of the rivers Chebar and Euphrates, but considerably higher up the latter stream and some distance to the north of lat. 36°. Professor Rawlinson (*Anc. Mon.* ii. 475) describes it as the key of Syria on the east and as commanding the ordinary passage of the Euphrates. It was, he adds, the only great city in that quarter. It is nearly identical in situation

Babylon smote in the fourth year of Jehoiakim the son of Josiah king of Judah.

3—12. *The first prophecy regarding Egypt.*

Order ye the buckler and shield, and draw near to battle. 3
Harness the horses; and get up, ye horsemen, 4
And stand forth with *your* helmets;
Furbish the spears, *and* put on the brigandines.
Wherefore have I seen them dismayed *and* turned away 5 back?
And their mighty ones are beaten down,

with Mabog, or Hierapolis. The word means *the fort of Chemosh* the god of the Moabites (2 Kings xxiii. 13).

3—12. THE FIRST PROPHECY REGARDING EGYPT.

3—6. These verses give us a lively description of the preparation and the advance, which were followed by the disastrous defeat at Carchemish.

3. *Order ye*] rather, **Prepare ye.**
buckler and shield] The former of these was a small round target which the light armed troops carried, the latter covered the whole body and was borne accordingly by the heavy-armed.

4. *Harness the horses*] Bring into operation the chariots which formed a very important feature of Egyptian armies.

get up, ye horsemen] probably, **mount the steeds,** although the Heb. substantive is used in both senses.

stand forth with your helmets] literally, *place yourselves with helmets* (*on*), i.e. put yourselves in battle array. Helmets were not worn except actually in battle, and hence this command was equivalent to an order instantly to engage.

brigandines] coats of mail. The word is connected with brigade (a division of an army), and brigadier (the commander of such a division); also with brigands. The sense of robber, which we now attach to this last word, is modern. *Brigandine* then, as occurring here and in li. 3, was "a kind of scale armour or coat of mail, so called from being worn by the light troops called *brigands*, the name given to light armed skirmishers (Wedgwood)....In the course of time the Italian *brigante* came to mean a robber, pirate, and hence *brigandine* denoted a light pinnace used for piracy...Of this word the modern 'brig' is an abbreviation." *Bible Word Book.*

5. *Wherefore have I seen them dismayed*] literally, *Why do I see* (*it*)? *they are dismayed.* The Heb. thus expresses the inexplicable character of the sight. That so brilliant a host should be defeated! It is beyond comprehension.

And are fled apace, and look not back:
For fear *was* round about, saith the LORD.
6 Let not the swift flee away, nor the mighty *man* escape;
They shall stumble, and fall toward the north by the river Euphrates.
7 Who *is* this *that* cometh up as a flood,
Whose waters are moved as the rivers?
8 Egypt riseth up like a flood,
And *his* waters are moved like the rivers;
And he saith, I will go up, *and* will cover the earth;
I will destroy the city and the inhabitants thereof.
9 Come up, ye horses; and rage, ye chariots;
And let the mighty *men* come forth;
The Ethiopians and the Libyans, that handle the shield;
And the Lydians, that handle *and* bend the bow.

look not back] **turn *not back*.**
fear was round about] Jeremiah's favourite expression once more and in circumstances which could not be more appropriate. See note on chap. vi. 25.
6. *Let not the swift*] rather, **The swift shall not.** Even the most active and heroic of the Egyptian army shall not gain their homes, but shall perish in a distant land.
toward the north] "Carchemish in lat. 36° would be four degrees north of Jerusalem in lat. 32°." *Sp. Comm.*
7. We are now to be told the name of the nation, the defeat of whose army we have been witnessing.
as a flood] *as* **the Nile.** The advance of the Egyptian host is likened to the annual overflow of their own sacred river.
whose waters are moved] **his waters toss themselves.**
as the rivers] like the branches of the Nile in the Delta of Lower Egypt. The same Heb. word is used in Ex. vii. 19 (rendered *streams* in the Eng. Vers.) in precisely the same application as here and in ver. 8.
9. *Come up*] **Go** *up.* The summons is to cavalry chariots and infantry that they should set forth from Egypt.
rage] **drive furiously.**
come forth] **go** *forth.*
the Ethiopians and the Libyans...and the Lydians] the mercenary troops, who formed from the days of Psammetichus the chief part of the Egyptian armies. The Ethiopians (Cush) and the Libyans (Phut) were children of Ham (Gen. x. 6). They formed the heavy-armed troops. The Lydians (the "Ludim" of Gen. x. 13) were also Africans, and not to be confused with the Lydians of the coast of Asia Minor, who were Shemites (Lud, Gen. x. 22). We have the three peoples here mentioned spoken of again as Egyptian mercenaries in Ezek. xxx. 5. In Isaiah on the other hand (lxvi. 19) Lud is connected with Asiatic

For this *is* the day of the Lord GOD of hosts, 10
A day of vengeance, that *he* may avenge him of his adversaries:
And the sword shall devour, and it shall be satiate and made drunk with their blood:
For the Lord GOD of hosts hath a sacrifice
In the north country by the river Euphrates.
Go up *into* Gilead, and take balm, 11
O virgin, the daughter of Egypt:
In vain shalt thou use many medicines;
For thou shalt not be cured.
The nations have heard *of* thy shame, 12
And thy cry hath filled the land:

and European tribes. These Lydians, as we see, formed the light-armed portion of the army.

bend] literally, *tread*, string.

10. *For this is the day of*] **But that day belongeth to.** There is a contrast between the alacrity with which the army goes forth and the fate that awaits them at Carchemish, described as 'the north country'. The joy at this disaster as rightfully inflicted on Egypt the enemy of God's people arises not only from the undying memory of the bondage of old times, but from later troubles, such as that of Rehoboam's time (1 Kings xiv. 25, 26) and those in much more recent days. See note on ver. 2.

11. *balm*] See note on viii. 22.

O virgin, the daughter of Egypt] used of the Egyptians generally, with the additional notion however of their having hitherto been kept free from hurt, like a virgin safe in her father's house.

shalt thou use] **hast thou used.**

thou shalt not be cured] **healing plaister thou hast none.** See note on xxx. 13.

"Not only was the study of medicine of very early date in Egypt, but medical men there were in such repute, that they were sent for at various times from other countries. Their knowledge of medicine is celebrated by Homer (Od. iv. 229), who describes Polydamna, the wife of Thonis, as giving medicinal plants 'to Helen in Egypt, a country possessing an infinite number of drugs...where each physician possesses knowledge above all other men.'...Cyrus and Darius both sent to Egypt for medical men (Herod. iii. 1, 132); and Pliny (xix. 5) says *post mortem* examinations were made in order to discover the nature of maladies....It is to the Arabs, who derived it from Egypt and India, that Europe is indebted for its first acquaintance with the science of medicine." (Note [G. W.] in Rawl. *Herod.* ii. 116.)

12. *the land*] *the* **earth.** See xlv. 4. The mention of 'the nations' in the parallel clause shews that the Eng. is to be thus emended.

For the mighty *man* hath stumbled against the mighty,
And they are fallen both together.

13. *Introduction to the second prophecy.*

13   The word that the LORD spake to Jeremiah the prophet, how Nebuchadrezzar king of Babylon should come and smite the land of Egypt.

14—28. *The second prophecy regarding Egypt.*

14   Declare ye in Egypt, and publish in Migdol,
And publish in Noph and in Tahpanhes:
Say ye, Stand fast, and prepare thee;
For the sword shall devour round about thee.

the mighty man hath stumbled against the mighty] The heroes fighting on the Egyptian side have in their flight and confusion got in each other's way.

13. INTRODUCTION TO THE SECOND PROPHECY.

13. *The word that the Lord spake*] In the absence of any definite statement like that prefixed to the earlier prophecy as to the date of its delivery, we are led by the general tone, which seems to point to a later time (see ver. 14) and a more intimate acquaintance with Egypt (see ver. 25), to conjecture that this one is to be ascribed to the time of the prophet's residence in that country. Compare xliii. 8—13, and xliv. 29, 30, with notes. It therefore would not be included in the Roll read before Jehoiakim, as the former prophecy probably was. The actual coming of Nebuchadnezzar at any rate was long subsequent to the battle of Carchemish. Nevertheless that victory opened the way to his advance into the country, whose army he had there defeated.

how Nebuchadrezzar...should come and smite] **of** (concerning) **the coming of Nebuchadrezzar and his smiting.**

14—28. THE SECOND PROPHECY REGARDING EGYPT.

14. *Declare ye in Egypt*] If we place the prophecy soon after the defeat at Carchemish, and therefore many years before its fulfilment, the meaning of these words will be, Announce the defeat and desolation that is in store. If on the other hand, as seems preferable, we make the words to be uttered on the eve, or almost on the eve, of their accomplishment, the sense will be, Declare that the enemy has already reached the borders.

Migdol] See note on xliv. 1. For Noph and Tahpanhes, see notes on ii. 16.

shall devour] **hath devoured.** The neighbouring nations had been subdued, perhaps including Tyre, after the capture of which Nebuchadnezzar probably advanced into Egypt.

Why are thy valiant *men* swept away? 15
They stood not, because the LORD did drive them.
He made many to fall, 16
Yea, one fell upon another:
And they said, Arise, and let us go again to our own people,
And to the land of our nativity,
From the oppressing sword.
They did cry there, Pharaoh king of Egypt *is but* a 17
noise;
He hath passed the time appointed.
As I live, saith the King, 18
Whose name *is* the LORD of hosts,
Surely as Tabor *is* among the mountains,

15. *valiant men*] The adjective in the Heb. is plural, while both the verb connected with it and the pronouns that follow are in the sing. Hence it seems probable that the singular is the right reading, and that the reference is, as the Septuagint makes it to be, to the sacred bull Apis, worshipped at Memphis, and called *the mighty one*, i.e. the deity of Egypt, just as God is named the Mighty One of Jacob or of Israel in Gen. xlix. 24; Is. i. 24; xlix. 26, etc. A failure to understand this application of the word may have early induced a Heb. copyist to alter it to the plural (which was effected by the insertion of the smallest Heb. letter). If the plural be the right reading, we must render as does the Eng. Vers.

16. *to fall*] *to* **stumble.**

to our own people] The mercenary troops, as belonging to various nations, propose among themselves to return to their several countries.

the oppressing sword] See note on xxv. 38.

17. *They did cry there*] The Septuagint, Syriac, and (Latin) Vulgate are agreed in reading for *there*, (by a mere change of vowel in the Heb.) *the name of.* This is strong evidence in itself, although there is no difficulty in understanding *there*, meaning their respective countries, in which they should report the ruin of Egypt.

a noise] **a ruin.** This sense is necessary here, and is borne out by Ps. xl. 2, where the same change must be made in the Eng. Vers. ("a pit of *noise*" marginal for "an horrible pit"), and by the sense of other words from the same Heb. root, e.g. that rendered *desolation* Lam. iii. 47 (where see note) and *destruction* Is. xxiv. 12.

he hath passed the time appointed] He hath let the time elapse within which he was called upon by God to reform. The period of grace is over, and consequently ruin can no longer be averted.

18. *as Tabor is*] The *is* should be omitted. The sense is not that his coming is as certain as is the existence of the mountains Tabor and Carmel in their respective positions, but that he, Nebuchadnezzar,

And as Carmel by the sea, *so* shall he come.
19 O thou daughter dwelling in Egypt,
Furnish thyself to go into captivity:
For Noph shall be waste
And desolate without an inhabitant.
20 Egypt *is like* a very fair heifer,
But destruction cometh; it cometh out of the north.
21 Also her hired men *are* in the midst of her like fatted bullocks;

shall resemble them as standing out conspicuous above all neighbouring rulers. Tabor (1805 feet above the sea-level) is not indeed the highest mountain of the whole region, but as standing in the midst of an extensive plain, is more striking than even loftier ones, which have not its advantages in the way of position. Carmel again (about 500 feet above the sea) stretches for about three miles as a long bold promontory into the Mediterranean.

19. *O thou daughter dwelling in Egypt*] a circumlocution for *inhabitants of Egypt*.
furnish thyself to go into captivity] The marginal "make thee instruments of captivity" is more literal, supply thyself with all that thou wilt need as thy outfit for exile.
Noph] See note on ii. 16.
desolate] the same word in the Heb. as that rendered "burnt" in chap. ii. 15, which may very well be its sense here also.

20. *is like*] **is.** This is more literal, and probably points to Apis the bull god, as that to which the country was as it were espoused.
but destruction cometh; it cometh out of the north] **a gadfly from the north is come upon her.** The least possible change in the Heb. produces the latter part of this rendering, which is supported by the early Versions. The existing Heb. text is far from untranslateable, the two verbs however being placed together at the end of the sentence and not in the middle with a considerable pause between, as in the Eng. Vers. We may compare for such a repetition, Ps. xcvi. 13, "For he cometh, for he cometh," etc. The Heb. word translated *destruction*, occurs here only. There is good authority for correcting it as above. It has also been rendered *a goad*, *an army*, and (apparently without much meaning) by the Septuagint, *a torn off shred*.

21. *her hired men*] her mercenary troops.
are in the midst of her] **in the midst of her are.**
like fatted bullocks] or, *like calves of the stall*. The mercenaries were no longer Africans, as in the days of Pharaoh-Necho (ver. 9), but Ionian and Carian soldiers, who (*Herod.* II. 163) numbered 30000 and were placed in a fertile district on the Pelusiac branch of the Nile, where they came to merit the description given of them in the text. Hophra had not ventured to send them on his expedition against Cyrene (see note on xliv. 30) but was defeated at their head by Amasis and the troops of the Cyrene expedition, who had mutinied.

> For they also are turned back, *and* are fled away together;
> they did not stand,
> Because the day of their calamity was come upon them,
> *and* the time of their visitation.
> The voice thereof shall go like a serpent;   22
> For they shall march with an army,
> And come against her with axes, as hewers of wood.
> They shall cut down her forest, saith the LORD,   23
> Though it cannot be searched;
> Because they are more than the grasshoppers,
> And *are* innumerable.
> The daughter of Egypt shall be confounded;   24
> She shall be delivered into the hand of the people of the north.
> The LORD of hosts, the God of Israel, saith;   25

they did not stand...was come] It is better to continue the present tense in Eng. *they do not stand...is come.*

and the time] **the time.** It is only a further explanation of 'the day of their calamity.'

22. *The voice thereof shall go like a serpent*] The sound of Egypt fleeing away from the enemy shall be like the rustling of a serpent escaping from danger through the thick underwood.

they shall march with an army] The enemy shall advance *with might,* as the last word may also be translated.

as hewers of wood] The fact of the Chaldaeans bearing axes would make a deep impression upon the mind of nations like the Jews, who had no such custom. "The battle-axe was a weapon but rarely employed by the Assyrians. It is only in the very latest sculptures, and in a very few instances, that we find axes represented as used by the warriors for any other purpose besides the felling of trees. Where they are seen in use against the enemy, the handle is short, the head somewhat large, and the weapon wielded with one hand." Rawlinson, *Anc. Mon.* I. 459.

23. *her forest*] or, *her* **beauty.** For this use of the word see note on xxi. 14.

though it cannot be searched] We may either with the Eng. Vers. refer these words to the 'forest,' and render in that case, *because it is impenetrable,* or to the number of the invaders, *because it is unsearchable.*

the grasshoppers] **locusts**: so rendered in Joel i. 4, where four stages of that animal's existence are represented by as many distinct words in the original. This one seems to denote the second stage of its being. The enemy shall come in like a plague, in a form but too familiar to the people of those countries.

24. *shall be confounded*] **is disgraced.**

Behold, I will punish the multitude of No,
And Pharaoh, and Egypt, with their gods, and their kings;
Even Pharaoh, and *all* them that trust in him:
26 And I will deliver them into the hand of those that seek their lives,
And into the hand of Nebuchadrezzar king of Babylon,
And into the hand of his servants:
And afterwards it shall be inhabited,
As *in* the days of old, saith the LORD.
27 But fear not thou, O my servant Jacob,
And be not dismayed, O Israel:
For behold, I *will* save thee from afar off,
And thy seed from the land of their captivity;
And Jacob shall return, and be in rest and at ease,
And none shall make *him* afraid.
28 Fear thou not, O Jacob my servant,
Saith the LORD: for I *am* with thee;
For I will make a full end of all the nations whither I have driven thee:

25. *the multitude of No*] **Amon of No**, i.e. the chief god worshipped in No (called also No Amon, margin of Nah. iii. 8). The name Amon signified *invisible*, and hence he was connected with the most spiritual form of Egyptian worship. The Greeks and Romans compared him to Zeus and Jupiter, and hence his name, familiar to us, of Jupiter Ammon.

their gods, and their kings] **her** *gods and* **her** *kings*. After the mention of the chief god, the ruler of the country, and the country itself, the inferior gods and rulers are included collectively in the coming disaster. 'Kings' however may perhaps better be taken of the predecessors of Hophra.

all them that trust in him] those Jews who had put their trust in Egypt as a support against Babylon.

26. *afterwards it shall be inhabited*] The calamity shall after all be but temporary. Peace and prosperity shall come at last. Compare the closing words of the prophecies against Moab (xlviii. 47), Ammon (xlix. 6), Elam (xlix. 39). The words have also, but not with such probability, been rendered *shall rest as in the days of old*, i.e. shall not be an aggressive power, as in its later days. History does not however justify us in believing that there was any difference between the earlier and the later days of Egypt in this respect.

27, 28. See notes on chap. xxx. 10, 11, where these verses have already occurred in substance; also for the word 'correct' (ver. 28)

But I will not make a full end of thee,
But correct thee in measure;
Yet will I not leave thee wholly unpunished.

CHAP. XLVII. 1. *Introduction to the Prophecy regarding Philistia.*

47 The word of the LORD that came to Jeremiah the prophet against the Philistines, before that Pharaoh smote Gaza.

2—7. *The Prophecy regarding Philistia.*

2 Thus saith the LORD;
Behold, waters rise up out of the north,
And shall be an overflowing flood,
And shall overflow the land, and all that is therein;
The city, and them that dwell therein:

note on ii. 19. They have probably been introduced here by the prophet as a quotation from the earlier passage, which is one prophetic of the return from exile, in order to shew that if Egypt's troubles were to be but temporary, much more should those of Judah and even of Israel also pass away.

CHAP. XLVII. 1. INTRODUCTION TO THE PROPHECY REGARDING PHILISTIA.

1. *against the Philistines*] concerning *the Philistines.*
before that Pharaoh smote Gaza] With the small amount of accurate historical information which we have relating to those times, this statement is but small help towards determining the date of the prophecy. The main views are, (i) that the Pharaoh is Necho, and that he captured Gaza about the same time that he conquered Josiah at Megiddo; (ii) that the reference is to the same king, as having taken Gaza on his way back from the defeat at Carchemish; (iii) that the Pharaoh is Hophra, and that the capture of Gaza was in his expedition against Tyre and Sidon.

2—7. THE PROPHECY REGARDING PHILISTIA.

2. *waters rise up*] In xlvi. 8 the same figure was used for an army. Compare Is. viii. 7, where the Assyrian army is likened to the floods of the Euphrates.
out of the north] the direction in which the Chaldaeans are to be looked for. Compare i. 13, 14.
an overflowing flood] a river suddenly swelling up through the effect of the winter rains.

Then the men shall cry,
And all the inhabitants of the land shall howl.
3 At the noise of the stamping of the hoofs of his strong *horses*,
At the rushing of his chariots,
And at the rumbling of his wheels,
The fathers shall not look back to *their* children
For feebleness of hands;
4 Because of the day that cometh to spoil all the Philistines,
And to cut off from Tyrus and Zidon every helper that remaineth:
For the LORD *will* spoil the Philistines,
The remnant of the country of Caphtor.
5 Baldness is come upon Gaza;
Ashkelon is cut off *with* the remnant of their valley:
How long wilt thou cut thyself?
6 O thou sword of the LORD, how long *will it be* ere thou be quiet?
Put up thyself into thy scabbard, rest, and be still.

3. *strong horses*] See note on viii. 16.
rushing] **rattling**, or **din**.
the fathers shall not look back to their children] their terror in the flight shall be so great that a father will not care for his son's safety.
4. *every helper that remaineth*] in other words the Philistines, the other helpers having been already cut off.
the remnant of the country of Caphtor] the few of the Philistine nation that still survive after the wars with Egypt and Assyria, which they had long undergone. Caphtor is spoken of also in Deut. ii. 23; Amos ix. 7, as the origin of the Philistines. Its position is somewhat doubtful. Some identify it with Crete, but more probably it was the Delta of Egypt. 'The country' is literally *the isle*, or *the sea-coast*.
5. *Baldness*] in token of mourning. See note on xvi. 6.
is cut off] or *is dumb*. Either sense belongs to the verb in the Heb.
with the remnant of their valley] It is better to omit the *with*, the remaining words being in apposition to Ashkelon, or possibly, but not so probably, in the vocative and so connected with the words that follow (*O remnant of their valley, how long, etc.*). The Septuagint reads *the remnant of the Anakim* (Numb. xiii. 33; Deut. ii. 10) the old giants, so many of whom belonged to Gath (1 Sam. xvii. 4; 1 Chron. xx. 5—8), that this town may possibly be here meant by that Version. The reading, which has not much in its favour, is got by a slight variation of the Heb. text, as it now stands.

How can it be quiet, seeing the LORD hath given it a 7
charge
Against Ashkelon, and against the sea shore? there hath
he appointed it.

CHAP. XLVIII. 1—10. *Opening of the Prophecy regarding
Moab.*

Against Moab thus saith the LORD of hosts, the God of 48
Israel;
Woe unto Nebo! for it is spoiled:
Kiriathaim is confounded *and* taken:

7. *How can it be quiet*] The Heb. verb would admit better of the rendering *How canst* thou *rest?* but probably the Eng. Vers. is right, and the original word is not pure Heb. but a dialectic form.

CHAP. XLVIII. 1—10. OPENING OF THE PROPHECY REGARDING MOAB.

1. *Against Moab*] **Concerning** *Moab.* See note on xlvi. 1. Just as chap. xlix. 7, etc. (concerning *Edom*) is closely allied to the prophecy of Obadiah (see notes on that verse), so here Jeremiah uses sometimes the substance, sometimes the actual words, of Is. xv., xvi.; Amos ii. 1—3; Zeph. ii. 8—10, together with the earlier warnings uttered by Balaam against Moab (Numb. xxiv. 17). It is however quite likely that Isaiah, Amos, and Jeremiah may have all borrowed the language of other prophets on the same subject. We have no clue to the determination of the date of the prophecy, except that in all probability it was contained in the Roll of chap. xxxvi. As to its fulfilment also the scanty records of the time give us but little information. The Moabites succeeded the Emims on the eastern side of the Dead Sea (Deut. ii. 10). Having been dispossessed of the northern part of this territory down to the river Arnon (Numb. xxi. 13) by the Amorites, Israel conquered these latter, and the tribe of Reuben obtained the district (Numb. xxi. 24, etc.). Hence arose the constant hostility between Moab and Israel shewn from the time of Balak onwards (see Judg. iii. 12 etc.; 1 Sam. xiv. 47; 2 Sam. viii. 2; 2 Kings i. 1, iii. 4, 5, xiii. 20, xiv. 25; 2 Chron. xx. 20—25). For particulars lately brought to light as to the relations between Moab and Israel see Dr Ginsburg's account of the "Moabite Stone."

Nebo] not the mountain (Deut. xxxii. 49, xxxiv. 1), but the city in the territory of Reuben (Numb. xxxii. 38). It is spoken of here and in Is. xv. 2 as a Moabite town, having been taken by Mesha king of Moab about 895 B.C. according to the records of the "Moabite stone."

Kiriathaim] either the modern *Et Teim* three miles south of

Misgab is confounded and dismayed.
2 *There shall be* no more praise of Moab:
In Heshbon they have devised evil against it;
Come, and let us cut it off from *being* a nation.
Also thou shalt be cut down, O Madmen;
The sword shall pursue thee.
3 A voice of crying *shall be* from Horonaim,
Spoiling and great destruction.
4 Moab is destroyed;
Her little ones have caused a cry to be heard.

Heshbon, or *Kureiyat*. This latter however is less likely as being in the territory belonging to Gad not Reuben.

Misgab] rather, **the height**, or, **the citadel**, meaning probably some particular fortress called by this name, and not, as it has also been taken to mean, the high lands in general.

dismayed] literally, *broken, crushed*. The same Heb. root (*châthath*) is rendered "broken down" in verses 20, 39. It has been conjectured that *Ghetto*, the word for the quarter at Rome in which the Jews used to be confined and often barbarously treated, is a derivative from it.

2. *There shall be no more praise of Moab*] **The glory of Moab is no more.**

in Heshbon they have devised] There is a play on the two Heb. words thus rendered (*b'Cheshbon hash'vu*) which cannot be reproduced in English. Heshbon was a border town between Reuben and Gad, given up to the latter tribe and made a Levitical city (Josh. xxi. 39). It was seized by the Ammonites in Jeremiah's time (see xlix. 3 with note), and was on the border of Moab. Hence it was the place where the Chaldaean enemy would lay their final plans for the attack upon the latter nation.

be cut down] or, as the Eng. margin, *be brought to silence*.

O Madmen] a town not mentioned elsewhere, but obviously distinct from Madmenah in Benjamin (Is. x. 31), Madmannah in Judah (Josh. xv. 31), and Dimnah in Zebulon (Josh. xxi. 35). Here again there is a play on the sound in the Heb. which is, *Madmên, tiddômi*.

3. *shall be from Horonaim*] 'shall be' should be omitted, and the following words 'spoiling and great destruction' taken as themselves the cry that is raised.

4. *Moab*] Some would explain this not of the country at large but of the city called Ar of Moab (Numb. xxi. 28; Is. xv. 1) and simply Ar (Numb. xxi. 15; Deut. ii. 9) in the valley of the Arnon. But this is unlikely.

her little ones] See xiv. 3. Here however, though the meaning is not *children*, the sense is slightly different from that passage, and is *her abject ones*, those reduced to an extremity of distress. There is

> For *in* the going up of Luhith 5
> Continual weeping shall go up;
> For in the going down of Horonaim
> The enemies have heard a cry of destruction.
> Flee, save your lives, 6
> And be like the heath in the wilderness.
> For because thou hast trusted in thy works and in thy 7
>   treasures,
> Thou shalt also be taken:
> And Chemosh shall go forth into captivity
> *With* his priests and his princes together.
> And the spoiler shall come upon every city, 8
> And no city shall escape:
> The valley also shall perish,
> And the plain shall be destroyed,
> As the LORD hath spoken.

but little to be said for the Septuagint rendering, *Declare ye unto Zoar*, except that Zoar occurs in Isaiah (xv. 5) in the same connexion.

5. *the going up of Luhith...the going down of Horonaim*] We thus gather that the one was situated on a hill, the other on low ground. For *Luhith* there is another reading *luhoth, planks*. The sense, if this (less likely) reading is adopted, will be that weeping mounts up upon weeping, as boards are placed one upon another in a house.

continual weeping shall go up] literally, *with weeping shall go up weeping*, i.e. there shall be successive bands of weeping fugitives.

the enemies have heard a cry of destruction] The construction in the Heb. is difficult. The most probable rendering however is, *the distress* (literally, *distresses*) *of the cry of destruction* (literally, *breaking*) *they have heard*.

6. *the heath*] **the destitute man.** See note on xvii. 6. The word here however is not precisely the same as in that passage, but similar to it, and identical, as it happens, with the proper name of a city Aroer, of which there were several in Palestine. See note on ver. 19. It is possible therefore that a play on this name may be meant as well as the literal meaning which is given above.

7. *works*] perhaps meaning *results of work, gains*. This is suggested by the word 'treasures' which follows. Compare chap. xx. 5, where however the Heb. (translated "labours") is not the same.

Chemosh] the object of Moab's national worship. The oldest Heb. form of the word in this passage seems to be Chemish, and although it is not elsewhere found, yet probability is given to its existence by such compounds as Car-chemish (see note on xlvi. 2). If the *god* is powerless to prevent his own captivity, what chance is there for the *people?*

8. *the valley*] the valley of Jordan which bounded part of Moab on the west.

9   Give wings unto Moab,
    That it may flee and get away:
    For the cities thereof shall be desolate,
    Without any to dwell therein.
10 Cursed *be* he that doeth the work of the LORD deceitfully,
    And cursed *be* he that keepeth back his sword from blood.

   11—25. *Continuance of threatening and further detail.*

11 Moab hath been at ease from his youth,
    And he *hath* settled on his lees,
    And hath not been emptied from vessel to vessel,
    Neither hath he gone into captivity:
    Therefore his taste remained in him,
    And his sent is not changed.
12 Therefore behold, the days come, saith the LORD,
    That I will send unto him wanderers, that shall cause him to wander,

the plain] the level country which stretched from the Arnon in the south to Rabbath Ammon.

9. *wings*] The word elsewhere in pure Heb. means *a flower* but in later Heb. and in Chaldee has frequently the sense which it here bears. The sense is that nothing short of wings would enable the Moabites to escape before their enemies.

10. *deceitfully*] **negligently.** The commission to Moab's foe comes from the Lord, and consequently he must not be slack in executing His command.

11—25. CONTINUANCE OF THREATENING AND FURTHER DETAIL.

11. *Moab hath been at ease from his youth*] He hath not been driven from his land hitherto. We gather from the inscription on the "Moabite stone" that the Moabites were by no means driven out of Reuben's lot, but maintained their position there more or less successfully alongside the Jewish inhabitants. The feeling of horror at suffering expatriation, as compared with the consequences of a more ordinary defeat in battle such as the nation had often suffered in past time, is well exhibited by these verses.

settled on his lees] Wine improved by being allowed to rest upon its sediment (Is. xxv. 6). If emptied from vessel to vessel it would become vapid, without fragrance and tasteless. Something like this was now to happen to the nation by being taken captives.

12. *wanderers*] literally, **lifters.** The figure of earthenware jars of wine is continued. They are emptied by being tilted on one side,

And shall empty his vessels, and break their bottles.
And Moab shall be ashamed of Chemosh, 13
As the house of Israel was ashamed of Beth-el their confidence.
How say ye, We *are* mighty and strong men for the war? 14
Moab is spoiled, and gone up *out of* her cities, 15
And his chosen young men are gone down to the slaughter,
Saith the King, whose name *is* the LORD of hosts.
The calamity of Moab *is* near to come, 16
And his affliction hasteth fast.
All ye that are about him, bemoan him; 17
And all ye that know his name,
Say, How is the strong staff broken,
And the beautiful rod!
Thou daughter that dost inhabit Dibon, 18

an operation which was performed slowly and carefully, that the jars might be safe and the wine run off clear while the sediment was left. This work however in the case of Moab shall be done roughly.

shall cause him to wander] **shall lift him.**

bottles] literally, *skins*, but used elsewhere also for earthenware bottles.

13. *shall be ashamed of Chemosh*] because he could not help them.

was ashamed of Beth-el their confidence] Bethel was the southern seat of Jeroboam's idolatrous worship. But they found their confidence in the worship there misplaced, when Shalmaneser carried them away.

15. *and gone up out of her cities*] The Heb. is difficult. The sense is either (i) *people* (i.e. the enemy) *have gone up to her cities;* or (ii) *her cities have gone up* (*in smoke and flame*). The latter way of rendering is the best. The difficulty which it presents in the original is that the verb is singular, but this is not in the Heb. an insuperable difficulty, and may here be caused by the prophet's mind dwelling upon the image of the cities all vanishing in *smoke*. By a change in the vowels of one word we might read, *The waster of Moab and of her towns is coming up* (to the attack), which gives an easy sense, and is held to be the right meaning by Ewald.

16. The language of this verse is based upon Deut. xxxii. 35.

17. *All ye that are about him...all ye that know his name*] the near and more remote nations respectively.

the strong staff...the beautiful rod] For these expressions, as implying national glory and power over others, compare Ps. cx. 2; Is. xiv. 29; Ezek. xix. 11, 12, 14.

18. *Thou daughter that dost inhabit Dibon*] literally, Thou inhabitress daughter of Dibon, a longer way of saying, Inhabitants of Dibon.

Come down from *thy* glory, and sit in thirst;
For the spoiler of Moab shall come upon thee,
And he shall destroy thy strong holds.
19 O inhabitant of Aroer,
Stand by the way and espy;
Ask him that fleeth, and her that escapeth,
And say, What is done?
20 Moab is confounded; for it is broken down:
Howl and cry;
Tell ye *it* in Arnon, that Moab is spoiled,
21 And judgment is come upon the plain country;
Upon Holon, and upon Jahazah, and upon Mephaath,

Dibon] now *Dhiban* (the "Moabite stone" was found there) stands on two hills. Hence the expression 'come down' in the text. The language here is intensified in both clauses from the corresponding passage relating to the daughter of Babylon in Is. xlvii. 1. For "come down" we have *come down from thy glory*, and for "sit in the dust" *sit in thirst*. The picture is of the inhabitants driven forth from the city and about to be led away, but obliged meanwhile to sit on the ground hungry and thirsty and await their captors' pleasure.

thy strong holds] the fortifications of the place are said to be still visible.

19. *inhabitant*] used collectively, as so constantly.

Aroer] not to be confounded with the Aroer of Numb. xxxii. 34, a Gadite city, or with an Aroer belonging to Judah (1 Sam. xxx. 28). This was the southernmost city in the tribe of Reuben, and hence was that which would be mentioned next after Dibon in tracing the progress of the Chaldaean enemy from north to south. Mesha records on the "Moabite stone" that he "built (i.e. restored) the city and made the road over the Arnon." The city stood on the north side of the river.

20. *Moab is confounded; for it is broken down*] In the original the first verb is mas. the second fem. The probable sense is, *Moab* **is ashamed**, *for it* (*Dibon*) *is overthrown.*

in Arnon] rather, **on** *Arnon*, i.e. in Aroer on its banks.

21. *the plain country*] the word rendered "the plain" in ver. 8, where see note. Then follows an enumeration of the several towns involved in the overthrow, in order that by particularizing these the coming disaster might be the more thoroughly realized. They were mostly towns enumerated in Joshua as within the portion allotted to the tribe of Reuben and were afterwards reconquered by the Moabites.

Jahazah] one of the Levitical cities (Josh. xxi. 36). There Moses defeated Sihon (Numb. xxi. 23, 24).

Mephaath] also a Levitical city (Josh. xxi. 37). It was afterwards a Roman military post established to keep in check the desert tribes, and hence we learn that it must have been in the eastern part of the country.

And upon Dibon, and upon Nebo, and upon Beth- 22
diblathaim,
And upon Kiriathaim, and upon Beth-gamul, and upon 23
Beth-meon,
And upon Kerioth, and upon Bozrah, 24
And upon all the cities of the land of Moab, far or near.
The horn of Moab is cut off, 25
And his arm is broken, saith the LORD.

26—47. *Conclusion of the lament over Moab.*

Make ye him drunken: for he magnified *himself* against 26
the LORD:
Moab also shall wallow in his vomit,
And he also shall be in derision.
For was not Israel a derision unto thee? 27

22. *Dibon*] See note on ver. 18.
Nebo] See note on ver. 1.
Beth-diblathaim] literally, *house of two figs*. Some identify it with Almon-diblathaim of Numb. xxxiii. 46, but this is doubtful.
23. *Kiriathaim*] See note on ver. 1.
Beth-gamul] not elsewhere mentioned.
Beth-meon] called also (Numb. xxxii. 38) Baal-meon, and (Josh. xiii. 17) Beth-baal-meon.
24. *Kerioth*] It is thought with much probability that this is another name for Ar, the old capital of Moab (Numb. xxi. 28), for in the lists where either is mentioned the other name does not occur, while each evidently denotes a place of importance. The place may have grown to be a union of two or more towns, and hence the name Kerioth (towns).
Bozrah] not the Bozrah of chap. xlix. 13; Is. lxiii. 1, which belonged to Edom, but either the Bezer of Deut. iv. 43, or better the Bosora of Maccab. v. 26. "As the word means *sheepfolds*, it was no doubt a common name for places in this upland region, fit only for pasturage."
far or near] the latter denoting nearer the borders of the country.
25. The *horn* is an emblem of strength, the *arm* of authority. For the former see Ps. lxxv. 4, 5, 10, for the latter chap. xvii. 5.

26—47. CONCLUSION OF THE LAMENT OVER MOAB.

26. *Make ye him drunken*] The comparison of the exhibition of God's wrath upon a nation to an intoxicating draught is illustrated by chap. xxv. 15, where see note.
he magnified himself against the Lord] He resisted Reuben in his occupation of the territory which the Lord had assigned him.
wallow] more literally, *splash into.*
he also shall be in derision] just as Israel has been. See next verse.

> Was he found among thieves?
> For since thou spakest of him, thou skippedst for joy.
>
> 28 O ye that dwell in Moab, leave the cities, and dwell in the rock,
> And be like the dove *that* maketh her nest in the sides of the hole's mouth.
>
> 29 We have heard the pride of Moab; *he is* exceeding proud:
> His loftiness, and his arrogancy, and his pride, and the haughtiness of his heart.
>
> 30 I know his wrath, saith the LORD; but *it shall* not *be* so;
> His lies shall not so effect *it*.
>
> 31 Therefore will I howl for Moab,

27. *was he found among thieves?*] i.e. Thou couldst not, O Moab, have treated him with more contempt, hadst thou caught him in the act of stealing.

skippedst for joy] **waggedst thy head**, in scorn. Compare Matt. xxvii. 39.

28. *dwell in the rock*] seek the most secret or inaccessible hiding places. See note on iv. 29.

in the sides of the hole's mouth] *in the* **further side** *of the mouth* **of the pit**.

29. *We*] the prophet and his fellow countrymen. The character of Moab for haughtiness is brought out forcibly by the accumulation of synonyms that succeed. This and the following verse are in substance the same as Is. xvi. 6.

30. *I know his wrath*] The Lord corroborates the assertion of the prophet in the former verse.

but it shall not be so; his lies shall not so effect it] **and the unreality of his lies; they have wrought what is unreal**. The passage in Isaiah shews us that the stop should be after and not before the word rendered *lies*, which is also found in the senses *staves, princes*. It is in this latter sense that those who added the stops in the Heb. Bible seem to have understood it, and hence the division of the clauses. The words rendered *not so* here are those which appear as "not aright," "not right" in chaps. viii. 6, xxiii. 10. See note on the former of those two passages.

31. *Therefore*] not immediately connected with the two preceding verses, but rather going back to the thought of the judgment that was coming.

will I howl] In the corresponding passage in Isaiah it is first the country that mourns itself, and only later the prophet also expresses grief. The greater tenderness of Jeremiah's sorrow is shewn not only by his personal lamentation in this verse, but in the later part by the substitution of the word 'men' for the 'foundations' of the

And I will cry out for all Moab;
Mine heart shall mourn for the men of Kir-heres.
O vine of Sibmah, I will weep for thee with the weeping 32
of Jazer:
Thy plants are gone over the sea,
They reach *even* to the sea of Jazer:
The spoiler is fallen upon thy summer fruits and upon
thy vintage.
And joy and gladness is taken from the plentiful field, 33
and from the land of Moab;
And I have caused wine to fail from the wine presses:

Isaiah passage. The two words in the original resemble each other in sound.

mine heart shall mourn] The insertion of the words 'mine heart' in the Eng. Vers. here is hardly justified by their occurrence in the Heb. of the Isaiah passage (xv. 5). Rather it is, *one* (*they*, indefinitely) *shall mourn*.

Kir-heres] the chief stronghold of Moab, the Kir-hareseth and Kir-haresh of Is. xvi. 7, 11.

32. *O vine of Sibmah*] Sibmah according to St Jerome was only five hundred paces from Heshbon, while Jazer was fifteen miles north of the latter city. The grapes of the region of Heshbon are even now excellent.

with the weeping of Jazer] **more than** *the weeping of Jazer* over its ruins, and wasted vineyards.

thy plants] *thy* **tendrils.**

over the sea] to the western shore of the Dead Sea, a poetical way of saying that the influence of this part of the Moabite nation had made itself felt to that distance.

the sea of Jazer] Nothing like a sea is found now-a-days in the high valley in which the town lies. It would seem however that a considerable body of water was found there then, now represented by some ponds. We must also remember that the word *sea* may easily convey to our ears a very erroneous idea of the dimensions intended by the corresponding Heb. word. Compare for this 1 Kings vii. 23.

the spoiler] Isaiah has "a shouting."

thy vintage] Isaiah, whose word differs only by a single letter, has "thy harvest."

33. This verse corresponds closely to Is. xvi. 10.

the plentiful field] The Heb. is *Carmel*, but of course without any particular reference to the promontory of that name on the west coast of Palestine.

winepresses] *wine*-**vats**, the receptacles in which the wine was stored, not made.

> None shall tread *with* shouting;
> *Their* shouting *shall be* no shouting.
>
> 34 From the cry of Heshbon *even* unto Elealeh,
> *And even* unto Jahaz, have they uttered their voice,
> From Zoar *even* unto Horonaim,
> *As* a heifer of three years old:
> For the waters also of Nimrim shall be desolate.
>
> 35 Moreover I will cause to cease in Moab, saith the LORD,
>   him that offereth *in* the high places,
> And him that burneth incense to his gods.
>
> 36 Therefore mine heart shall sound for Moab like pipes,
> And mine heart shall sound like pipes for the men of Kir-heres:
> Because the riches *that* he hath gotten are perished.
>
> 37 For every head *shall be* bald,
> And every beard clipt:

with shouting] For the shout of the wine treaders, see note on xxv. 30. The clause which here follows means that the vintage shout shall be transformed into the battle cry.

34. This verse resembles Is. xv. 4. The sense is that the cry uttered from Heshbon (see note on ver. 2) is heard at Elealeh (about two miles distant) and is even carried on to Jahaz, a considerable distance south-west. Again, the wail uttered from Zoar is borne to Horonaim, both in the south of the land. Thus the lamentation shall be caught by one from another and be universal.

a heifer of three years old] The corresponding Heb. is in the Isaiah passage appended to Zoar. The sense is difficult in each place. The probable rendering is either, *the third Eglath*, or, *Eglath with the other two* (cities), and the sense either that there were three cities of that name, numbered thus by way of distinction, or that Zoar, Horonaim, and Eglath formed a group or league of cities corresponding to the three cities named earlier in the verse.

Nimrim] not the place ("Beth-nimrah") mentioned in Numb. xxxii. 36; Josh. xiii. 27, which is much too far north, but probably the modern *Wady en-Nemeirah* at the south-eastern end of the Dead Sea.

36. *shall sound for Moab like pipes*] Their use was connected with funerals, so that the word is appropriate as expressing mourning. Isaiah's word is "an harp" (xvi. 11).

the riches] literally, *the superfluity*. His substance was much more than a mere competency.

are perished] There are but two cases in which the word riches (French *richesse*) is treated as singular in the Eng. Vers. (Wisdom v. 8; Rev. xviii. 17), although this seems merely to have arisen from the word's happening to end in letters commonly used to denote the plural.

Upon all the hands *shall be* cuttings,
And upon the loins sackcloth.
There shall be lamentation generally upon all the house- 38
tops of Moab, and in the streets thereof:
For I have broken Moab like a vessel wherein *is* no plea-
sure, saith the LORD.
They shall howl, *saying*, How is it broken down! 39
How hath Moab turned the back with shame!
So shall Moab be a derision and a dismaying to all them
about him.
For thus saith the LORD; 40
Behold, he shall fly as an eagle,
And shall spread his wings over Moab.
Kerioth is taken, and the strong holds are surprised, 41
And the mighty *men*'s hearts in Moab at that day
shall be
As the heart of a woman in her pangs.
And Moab shall be destroyed from *being* a people, 42
Because he hath magnified *himself* against the LORD.
Fear, and the pit, and the snare, *shall be* upon thee, 43
O inhabitant of Moab, saith the LORD.

37. All shall have the usual emblem of mourning. See notes on chap. xvi. 6.

38. *generally*] **wholly.**

a vessel] the same word as that rendered idol in xxii. 28, where see note.

39. *They shall howl, saying, How is it broken down!*] **How is it broken! they howl.**

40. *he shall fly as an eagle*] See note on iv. 13. The simile seems taken from Deut. xxviii. 49, but is used elsewhere (see chap. xlix. 22; Is. xlvi. 11; Ezek. xvii. 3). It well represented the Babylonian empire, which "seemed to those who witnessed it like the rising of a mighty eagle, spreading out his vast wings, feathered with the innumerable colours of the variegated masses which composed the Chaldaean host, sweeping over the different countries, and striking fear in his rapid flight." Stanley, *J. Ch.* II. 451.

41. *Kerioth*] See note on ver. 24. The double sense (both a proper name, and *towns*) gives rise to a play upon the word, which we cannot translate.

are surprised] **are seized.**

43, 44. Substantially the same as Is. xxiv. 17, 18, and very probably a proverb in frequent use. See note on Lam. iii. 47.

44   He that fleeth from the fear shall fall into the pit;
And he that getteth up out of the pit shall be taken in the snare:
For I will bring upon it, *even* upon Moab, the year of their visitation, saith the Lord.

45   They that fled stood under the shadow of Heshbon because of the force:
But a fire shall come forth out of Heshbon,
And a flame from the midst of Sihon,
And shall devour the corner of Moab,
And the crown of the head of the tumultuous ones.

46   Woe be unto thee, O Moab!
The people of Chemosh perisheth:
For thy sons are taken captives,
And thy daughters captives.

47   Yet will I bring again the captivity of Moab
In the latter days, saith the Lord.
Thus far *is* the judgment of Moab.

Chap. XLIX. 1—6. *The Prophecy regarding Ammon.*

49   Concerning the Ammonites, thus saith the Lord;

44. *He that fleeth*] or, *He fleeth*, but the former is the better reading.

45. *They that fled stood under the shadow of Heshbon because of the force*] **In the shadow of Heshbon stand fugitives powerless.** The sense of the whole verse is that the fugitives of Moab shall take refuge under the walls of the neighbouring city of the Ammonites, but as they stand there in hopes of aid, there bursts forth from the city on which their only hopes rest a flame kindled by the Chaldaean foe, but like that which was in old days kindled in the same place by Sihon the Amorite conqueror. Thus the passage Numb. xxi. 28 is quoted with a new application.

the corner] either (*a*) *the side, the region,* or (*b*) *the corner of the beard*. If the latter be the sense, as seems more likely, then this and the last words of the verse together mean that Nebuchadnezzar shall destroy all that is capable of destruction.

the tumultuous ones] the proud Moabites. See ver. 29.

47. *Yet will I bring again*] Compare xlvi. 26, xlix. 6, 39.

Thus far is the judgment of Moab] probably not the words of Jeremiah himself, but of Baruch, and inserted in editing the book.

Chap. XLIX. 1—6. The Prophecy regarding Ammon.

1. *Concerning the Ammonites*] This people's territory was north of the Moabites, with whom they were closely connected by descent.

Hath Israel no sons? Hath he no heir?
Why *then* doth their king inherit Gad,
And his people dwell in his cities?
Therefore behold, the days come, saith the LORD, 2
That I will cause an alarm of war to be heard in Rabbah
   of the Ammonites;
And it shall be a desolate heap,
And her daughters shall be burnt with fire:
Then shall Israel be heir unto them that were his heirs,
   saith the LORD.
Howl, O Heshbon, for Ai is spoiled: 3
Cry, ye daughters of Rabbah, gird ye with sackcloth;
Lament, and run to and fro by the hedges;
For their king shall go into captivity,
And his priests and his princes together.
Wherefore gloriest thou in the valleys, 4

They seem to have originally possessed the country in which the tribe of Gad was placed after the conquest of Sihon, who had probably wrested it from Ammon, and no doubt their extirpation was never wholly effected even in Jewish times. They were a more wandering people than the Moabites, and had but one city of importance, Rabbah. The carrying away of the tribes on the east of Jordan by Tiglath-pileser king of Assyria (2 Kings xv. 29) strengthened their hands, and it is the occupation of the portion of Gad on that occasion which forms the crime dwelt on in this prophecy.

Hath Israel no sons?] He has been carried captive, it is true, but is he destitute of children, who will in due time return to claim the land which Ammon has wrongfully seized? See note on xli. 15.

their king] *Milcom*, the god of Ammon, and so in ver. 3. See 1 Kings xi. 5. Compare Chemosh (xlviii. 7) used as equivalent to Moab.

inherit] **take possession of.** See note on viii. 10.

2. *Rabbah*] See above on ver. 1.

a desolate heap] See note on xxx. 18. The eminence on which it stands shall be laid waste.

her daughters] the minor cities depending on her. Compare "daughters of Rabbah" in ver. 3, and the margin of Numb. xxi. 25.

3. *Howl, O Heshbon*] Recognise that thy time is at hand, now that Ai has been captured and sacked by the enemy.

Ai] not the well-known city on the west of Jordan (Josh. vii. 2), but one in the Ammonite territory, and not elsewhere mentioned.

hedges] **inclosures** of the vineyards. Hedges in our sense of the word did not exist in those days.

their king shall go] See note on ver. 1. This part of the verse is taken with some modification from Amos i. 15.

Thy flowing valley, O backsliding daughter?
That trusted in her treasures, *saying*, Who shall come unto me?

5 Behold, I will bring a fear upon thee, saith the Lord God of hosts,
From all those that be about thee;
And ye shall be driven out every man right forth;
And none shall gather up him that wandereth.

6 And afterward I will bring again the captivity of the children of Ammon, saith the Lord.

7—22. *The Prophecy regarding Edom.*

7 Concerning Edom, thus saith the Lord of hosts;

4. *Thy flowing valley*] This has been variously explained *thy valley* (i) *flows* (with abundance), (ii) *flows away*, i.e. the inhabitants are carried off. The Septuagint render, *in the valleys of the Anakim*. See note on xlvii. 5.

5. *every man right forth*] Compare Josh. vi. 5, *every man straight before him*. The sense here is that each without thought of his neighbour shall flee the shortest way.

none shall gather up him that wandereth] No one shall collect or rally the fugitives.

6. *And afterward*] Compare xlviii. 47.

7—22. The Prophecy regarding Edom.

7. *Concerning Edom*] Much of the earlier part of this section (viz. verses 7—16) is almost verbally the same as Obadiah 1—8. The latter prophet seems to have written (ver. 11) after the destruction of Jerusalem, and yet the verses, which are by no means in the same order in both, appear to come in more natural sequence in Obadiah. To meet the difficulty hence arising it has been suggested (*a*) that the earlier part of Obadiah was written before Nebuchadnezzar's destruction of Jerusalem, the later part after that event, (*b*) that both prophets embodied in their writings an earlier prediction. It has also been conjectured by some that Obadiah refers not to the overthrow under Zedekiah, but to that of Jehoram's time (2 Chron. xxi. 17). The bitterness of the tone in which Edom is addressed finds parallels in Lam. iv. 21, as also in Ps. cxxxvii. 7; Ezek. xxv. 12—14, xxxv. 15; Obad. 10—16, and is no doubt based upon a sense of the closeness of the tie of kinship between Edom and Israel. On the principle 'corruptio optimi pessima' the affinity which existed made the unnatural exultation of Edom over the fallen fortunes of the Jews most offensive. See, in addition to the above passages, Amos i. 11, and for an apparent reference to the fulfilment of this prophecy against Edom, Mal. i. 3.

Is wisdom no more in Teman?
Is counsel perished from the prudent?
Is their wisdom vanished?
Flee ye, turn back, 8
Dwell deep, O inhabitants of Dedan;
For I will bring the calamity of Esau upon him,
The time *that* I will visit him.
If grapegatherers come to thee, would they not leave 9
some gleaning grapes?
If thieves by night, they will destroy till they have enough.
But I have made Esau bare, 10
I have uncovered his secret places,
And he shall not be able to hide himself:
His seed is spoiled, and his brethren, and his neighbours, and he *is* not.

Is wisdom no more in Teman?] Teman seems to have been renowned for this quality. See ver. 20. This and the succeeding questions are a pointed way of calling attention to the stupefying suddenness and completeness of the calamity. Is it really so that the wisest of the nation are astonied, and incapable of tendering advice?

Teman] in the northern part of Edom, the birthplace of Eliphaz (Job ii. 11).

vanished] literally, *poured out*. The figure seems to be much the same as in chap. xix. 7 (see note), where however a different verb is used in the Hebrew.

8. *Dwell deep, O inhabitants of Dedan*] For the position, etc. of the Dedanites, see note on chap. xxv. 23. They are here warned to retire from their accustomed intercourse with Edom, and keep well out of the way in the deserts, lest they should be involved in its ruin.

9. *would they not leave some gleaning grapes?*] **they will not leave gleanings**. The Eng. Vers. makes the passage interrogative in order to bring it into closer correspondence with that in Obadiah. But there thieves and grape-gatherers are only introduced by way of illustration, whereas in this case the enemy are absolutely called such. Thus Jeremiah, while adopting the language in Obadiah (if it be really so; see above), changes the whole form of the thought.

till they have enough] more literally, *their fill*.

10. *But*] **For**. The success of the enemy is to be attributed to the fact that they have God on their side.

his secret places] the retreats and fastnesses of Edom.

he shall not be able to hide himself] literally, *he hides* (i.e. tries to hide) *himself, he is not able*.

his brethren] those who shared his country, e.g. the Amalekites (Amalek being a grandson of Esau, Gen. xxxvi. 12).

11 Leave thy fatherless children, I will preserve *them* alive;
And let thy widows trust in me.
12 For thus saith the LORD;
Behold, they whose judgment *was* not to drink of the cup have assuredly drunken;
And *art* thou he *that* shall altogether go unpunished?
Thou shalt not go unpunished, but thou shalt surely drink *of it*.
13 For I have sworn by myself, saith the LORD,
That Bozrah shall become a desolation,
A reproach, a waste, and a curse;
And all the cities thereof shall be perpetual wastes.
14 I have heard a rumour from the LORD,
And an ambassador *is* sent unto the heathen, *saying*,
Gather ye together,
And come against her, and rise up to the battle.
15 For lo, I will make thee small among the heathen,
And despised among men.

his neighbours] those mentioned in xxv. 23.

11. *Leave thy fatherless children*] The apparent abruptness of this verse has given rise to much questioning among commentators. The most natural way of explaining it in connexion with the context is this. All that bear arms shall be cut off, none but their widows and orphans shall remain. Bereft however as these are, they may yet look to me for protection.

12. *they whose judgment was not to drink*] For the metaphor, see note on xiii. 12. The reference is to Israel. If the chosen people of God shall not escape, how should Edom? 'Judgment' may either mean *the Divine decree*, or perhaps better, *rule, custom*. For an illustration of the latter sense, compare chap. viii. 7, with note.

have assuredly drunken] **shall** *assuredly* **drink**.

13. *Bozrah* (*el-Busaireh*)]'half way between Petra and the Dead Sea. Considerable ruins remain to this day. See note on chap. xlviii. 24.

14—18. These verses form the second part of the prophecy, and describe further the source and completeness of Edom's overthrow.

14. This and the following verse are in substance identical with the beginning of Obadiah.

a rumour] literally, *a hearing*, news.

ambassador] rather, **messenger**, since no negotiations but only a command was in question.

15. *the heathen*] *the* **nations**. The Heb. would bear either rendering, but the latter is better suited to the clause which follows.

Thy terribleness hath deceived thee, *and* the pride of
thine heart,
O thou that dwellest in the clefts of the rock,
That holdest the height of the hill :
Though thou shouldest make thy nest as high as the
eagle,
I will bring thee down from thence, saith the LORD.
Also Edom shall be a desolation : 17
Every one that goeth by it shall be astonished,
And shall hiss at all the plagues thereof.
As *in* the overthrow of Sodom and Gomorrah 18
And the neighbour *cities* thereof, saith the LORD,
No man shall abide there,
Neither shall a son of man dwell in it.
Behold, he shall come up like a lion from the swelling of 19
Jordan

16. *Thy terribleness*] This is in all probability right, though the word does not occur elsewhere in the Bible, not even in the corresponding passage (ver. 4) of Obadiah. The sense is that Edom had duped herself into believing that the strongholds and mountain fastnesses of the country, which were a source of such alarm to an invader, made her impregnable.

the clefts of the rock] The Heb. rendered *rock* is *Selah*, and may therefore well be at least an allusion to the town of that name (2 Kings xiv. 7; Is. xvi. 1) in the territory of Edom, whose position was as here described. It was probably the same as Petra, and "lay, though at a high level, in a hollow shut in by mountain-cliffs, and approached only by a narrow ravine" (Sm. *Bible Dict.*, Art. 'Selah'). Similarly, the next clause 'the height of the hill' will contain an allusion to the position of Bozrah (ver. 13).

17. *a desolation...shall be astonished*] The substantive and verb are from the same root in the Heb., a fact which should be marked in the translation, *an astonishment...shall be astonished*, or, *a dismay...shall be dismayed*. For these as well as for the words which follow, see note on xviii. 16.

18. *Sodom and Gomorrah*] The comparison appears to be taken from Deut. xxix. 23, where the neighbour cities are mentioned by name (*Admah* and *Zeboim*). It is repeated by Jeremiah in the next chapter (ver. 40). It may contain an allusion to Is. xiii. 19.

a son of man] an amplification of the preceding 'man' for greater force.

19. *he shall come up*] viz. the enemy who is to prevail over Edom.
like a lion] The same comparison was used in chap. iv. 7.
the swelling of Jordan] See note on chap. xii. 5.

Against the habitation of the strong:
But I will suddenly make him run away from her:
And who *is* a chosen *man*, *that* I may appoint over her?
For who *is* like me? and who will appoint me the time?
And who *is* that shepherd that will stand before me?
20 Therefore hear the counsel of the LORD,
That he hath taken against Edom;
And his purposes, that he hath purposed against the inhabitants of Teman:
Surely the least of the flock shall draw them out:
Surely he shall make their habitations desolate with them.

Against the habitation of the strong] The word here translated *strong*, rather means permanent, lasting (see note on *mighty*, chap. v. 15), while *habitation* may as well be rendered *pasturage* (see note on chap. ix. 10). Accordingly a preferable sense here is, **to the perennial pasturage**. As that is the spot in which a lion searching for the flock would most naturally find his prey, so the enemy shall advance to the quarter where the Edomites are most thickly gathered, and vanquish them. In the following clause the masc. pronoun refers to Edom, the fem. to the *habitation* or *pasturage*.

who is a chosen man, that I may appoint] rather, *I will appoint him who is* (my) *chosen*.

appoint me the time] rightly explained in the Eng. margin, *convent* (i.e. convene) *me in judgment*, in other words, by naming, as the plaintiff in a suit had a right to do, the time of trial, claim the power of protesting against God's decision.

20. *that he hath purposed against the inhabitants of Teman*] Even the wisdom of the Temanites shall not protect them. That this was a feature of the place we gather both from ver. 7 above and from Obad. 8, 9.

Surely the least of the flock shall draw them out] or, *Surely they will drag them about, the little ones of the flock*, the last words being in this case, in apposition to 'them' not to 'they.' With the latter rendering the sense will be, The enemy will do violence to the feeble Edomites crowding for shelter like sheep; with the former, The feeblest among the Israelites shall suffice for the rooting out of Edom. The verb is used elsewhere in Jeremiah (xv. 3, "the dogs *to tear*," and xxii. 19, "*drawn* and cast forth." Compare 2 Sam. xvii. 13) of dragging about. In adopting the Eng. Vers. thus modified, there is a certain amount of difficulty in speaking of the enemies of Edom as a flock, inasmuch as that nation has just been likened itself to one, but in the mouth of Jeremiah such a sudden change of figure is not after all very surprising, while this certainly appears the more natural mode of understanding the Heb., which however is confessedly obscure. For a repetition of the passage, see l. 45.

he shall make their habitations desolate with them] better, **their habitation (pasturage) shall be dismayed on account of them.** The

The earth is moved at the noise of their fall, 21
At the cry, the noise thereof was heard in the Red sea.
Behold, he shall come up and fly as the eagle, 22
And spread his wings over Bozrah:
And at that day shall the heart of the mighty *men* of Edom
Be as the heart of a woman in her pangs.

23—27. *The Prophecy regarding Damascus.*

Concerning Damascus. 23
Hamath is confounded, and Arpad:
For they have heard evil tidings: they are fainthearted;
There is sorrow on the sea; it cannot be quiet.

very dwelling-place of these dispirited fugitives shall be confounded at their fall.

21. *is moved*] *quakes, trembles.*

At the cry...] The Heb. is purposely less smooth. *A cry—at the Red Sea is heard its noise.* Edom in its prosperity extended thither, as we gather from 1 Kings ix. 26.

22. *he*] the enemy. As he is strong as a lion, so also he is swift as an eagle. See note on xlviii. 40.

23—27. The Prophecy regarding Damascus.

23. *Concerning Damascus*] In Syria, as it existed in the time of David, there were at least three cities of importance, Hamath, Zobah, and Damascus. The kingdom, of which the second of these was the capital, soon disappeared, and Damascus came to be held by a powerful dynasty of kings, who reduced the other cities under their own sway. It is not known however what was the political condition of Syria at the time that Jeremiah wrote, but it is clear that it was to be no more exempt than other countries from the tread of the conqueror. The tidings of his approach reach one city after another, and fill them with dismay.

Hamath] in the northern part of Syria, now *Hamah*. It was more than once subjected to Israel (2 Chron. viii. 4; 2 Kings xiv. 25).

Arpad] Its position is not known with certainty. However, as being invariably mentioned along with Hamath (2 Kings xviii. 34, xix. 13; Is. x. 9, xxxvi. 19, xxxvii. 13), it must have been situated near it.

they are fainthearted] literally, *they waste (melt) away*. The same word is used of the Canaanites, Exod. xv. 15.

There is sorrow on the sea] If we keep this reading, which is much the better supported of the two, the sense will be, the trouble extends to the very shore, i.e. throughout the country. It is objected that a certain number of Heb. MSS. read *as the sea*, thus agreeing with the accepted reading in Is. lvii. 20, from which the next clause seems taken. It is unlikely that the change from *as* to *on*, although involving

24 Damascus is waxed feeble, *and* turneth herself to flee,
And fear hath seized on *her:*
Anguish and sorrows have taken her as a woman in travail.

25 How is the city of praise not left,
The city of my joy!

26 Therefore her young men shall fall in her streets,
And all the men of war shall be cut off in that day,
Saith the LORD of hosts.

27 And I will kindle a fire in the wall of Damascus,
And it shall consume the palaces of Ben-hadad.

28—33. *The Prophecy regarding Kedar and Hazor.*

28 Concerning Kedar, and concerning the kingdoms of

but a slight alteration in the shape of one Heb. letter, would have been made in this place. If, in consideration of the borrowing of the last clause from Is., we seek the same sense for the word 'sea' here as holds in that passage, we must explain it of the trouble-tossed, anxious hearts, saddened by the ill news.

24. *is waxed feeble*] literally, *has become slack, discouraged.*
and turneth] The *and* is best omitted: **she turneth.**
25. These, which are clearly still the words of the prophet lamenting over the fortunes of so fair a city as Damascus, have been understood as meaning, either, How sad that the city has not been left untouched, or (and much better), How sad that she has not been forsaken by her inhabitants before her fall. This agrees both with the preceding verse, describing the paralysis that has taken possession of the people, and prevented them from saving themselves by flight, and also with the following words, which tell of the destruction to be wrought in the streets of the town.
26. *shall be cut off*] Some would render *shall be silent* (the Heb. being somewhat ambiguous in sense). See, however, note on viii. 14, in which verse the same word is rendered twice in the latter sense (*silent, silence*).
27. *I will kindle a fire*] This verse is made up of Amos i. 4, 14. The expression, kindle a fire, denotes elsewhere also the ravages of war, e.g. Numb. xxi. 28; Deut. xxxii. 22. Benhadad (son of Hadad) was the name, possibly rather the title, of several kings of Syria.

28—33. THE PROPHECY REGARDING KEDAR AND HAZOR.

28. *Concerning Kedar, and concerning the kingdoms of Hazor*] This section may be divided into two sub-sections, which closely correspond in length, sense and structure. Each consists of three verses, and the three consecutive thoughts in each are (i) a summons of the enemy

Hazor, which Nebuchadrezzar king of Babylon shall smite, thus saith the LORD;
Arise ye, go up to Kedar,
And spoil the men of the east.
Their tents and their flocks shall they take *away*: 29
They shall take to themselves their curtains,
And all their vessels, and their camels;
And they shall cry unto them, Fear *is* on every side.
Flee, get you far off, dwell deep, O ye inhabitants of 30
Hazor,
Saith the LORD;
For Nebuchadrezzar king of Babylon hath taken counsel against you,
And hath conceived a purpose against you.
Arise, get you up unto the wealthy nation, 31
That dwelleth without care, saith the LORD,

to the attack, (ii) a promise of booty, (iii) an intimation that safety would be sought only in flight.

For Kedar, see note on chap. ii. 10. As regards Hazor, in all its other occurrences it denotes some town in Palestine, a sense which cannot belong to it here. It is generally agreed, that as Kedar means the nomad Arabs, so Hazor, from the Heb. *hazêr*, an unwalled town, refers to that part of the nation which used fixed dwellings, and this fits in with the fact that "the stationary Arabs...are still called *Hadariye*. ...*hadar* is a fixed abode." Clark's *Delitzsch's Isaiah*, Vol. II. p. 182.

shall smite] literally, *hath smitten*. It is therefore probable, that this clause was subsequently inserted, as perhaps that of chap. xlvii. 1 ("before that Pharaoh smote Gaza"), where see note.

29. *curtains*] See note on chap. iv. 20.

Fear is on every side] See note on chap. vi. 25.

30. *dwell deep*] See ver. 8, with note.

against you (2º)] *against them*, which is the other reading in the Heb., is much the more probable one. The pronouns *you* and *them* will both indeed refer to the people of Hazor, but as in the clause following (ver. 31) that people are spoken of in the third person, while the Chaldaeans have begun to be addressed as 'you,' this reading in ver. 30 will supply a transition. The people of Hazor are no longer addressed with eagerness, but are spoken of as at a greater distance from the speaker's point of view.

31. *Arise*] Addressed to the Chaldaeans.

wealthy] rather, **tranquil**, dwelling at ease. Three grounds of encouragement are given to the invading army, (*a*) the people have felt hitherto secure against attack, (*b*) they have no walled towns, (*c*) they have no powerful neighbours, from whom to seek aid.

Which have neither gates nor bars, *which* dwell alone.
32 And their camels shall be a booty,
And the multitude of their cattle a spoil:
And I will scatter into all winds them *that are* in the utmost corners;
And I will bring their calamity from all sides thereof, saith the LORD.
33 And Hazor shall be a dwelling for dragons,
And a desolation for ever:
There shall no man abide there,
Nor *any* son of man dwell in it.

34—39. *The Prophecy regarding Elam.*

34 The word of the LORD that came to Jeremiah the prophet against Elam in the beginning of the reign of Zedekiah king of Judah, saying,
35 Thus saith the LORD of hosts;
Behold, I *will* break the bow of Elam,
The chief of their might.

32. *them that are in the utmost corners*] See note on chap. ix. 26.
33. *dragons*] jackals. See note on chap. ix. 11.

34—39. THE PROPHECY REGARDING ELAM.

34. The LXX., who place this prophecy as chap. xxv. 14, etc., headed simply by the words τὰ Αἰλάμ, the Elam, subsequently have the substance of the present verse as chap. xxvi. 1, followed however by the prophecy against Egypt (our xlvi. 2, etc.), thus shewing some confusion in their manuscripts, or in those from which their translation was derived. According to the Heb. order, Jeremiah proceeds from the nations bordering on Palestine to the more remote.

Elam] now *Chuzistan*, a country west of the Tigris, which river separated it from Chaldaea. We see from Ezra iv. 9, that Elam once was subject to Assyria. As in the case of so many others, we are without materials for determining anything as to the date or manner of fulfilment of this prophecy, and are thus quite uncertain whether it points to an overthrow on the part of the Babylonian power (which however the prophecy itself in no way even suggests) or on the part of any other.

in the beginning of the reign of Zedekiah] thus about seven years later (chap. xlvi. 2) than the preceding prophecies of this group, but somewhat earlier than the long prophecy against Babylon that follows. See chap. li. 59.

35. *the bow of Elam*] the weapon on which the nation chiefly relied. Compare Is. xxii. 6.

And upon Elam will I bring the four winds	36
From the four quarters of heaven,	
And will scatter them towards all those winds;	
And there shall be no nation	
Whither the outcasts of Elam shall not come.	
For I will cause Elam to be dismayed before their enemies,	37
And before them that seek their life:	
And I will bring evil upon them,	
Even my fierce anger, saith the LORD;	
And I will send the sword after them,	
Till I have consumed them:	
And I will set my throne in Elam,	38
And will destroy from thence the king and the princes,	
Saith the LORD.	
But it shall come to pass in the latter days,	39
That I will bring again the captivity of Elam,	
Saith the LORD.	

36. *the four winds*] invaders from all sides.
38. *set my throne in*] sit in judgment upon.
the king and the princes] **king and princes.** No *particular* persons are meant.

CHAP. L. THE PROPHECY REGARDING BABYLON.

This and the following chapter have been held by some commentators not to be a genuine part of Jeremiah's writings, but to have been written by Baruch or some other at a time considerably later than that assigned to them in li. 59, perhaps about the middle of the exile. The chief reasons for the above view are these:—

(*a*) Jeremiah elsewhere speaks in friendly terms of the Chaldaeans; here he predicts their overthrow.

(*b*) Style and words betray a writer other than the prophet.

(*c*) There is a greater knowledge of Babylonian customs, of topography, etc. than could be expected from Jeremiah.

To (*a*) we may reply: Jeremiah elsewhere is pointing out the Chaldaeans as the ministers of God's vengeance, and urging upon his countrymen the necessity of yielding to them. Thus he could not help appearing as though on the Chaldaean side, being opposed to the transgressions of his countrymen, which were bringing punishment in this form. Already however, viz. in chap. xxv. 12, 26, we have the thoughts of which these chapters are the natural development.

To (*b*), The style, to say the least of it, so closely resembles Jeremiah's, that we cannot suppose it to be the product of an imitator, working in accordance with the theory above-mentioned at a distance from Jerusalem. This is shewn by such a passage as chap. l. 5, "They shall ask

Chap. L. *The Prophecy regarding Babylon.*

1—7. *Babylon shall fall and Israel return.*

50 The word that the LORD spake against Babylon *and against the land of the Chaldeans by Jeremiah the prophet.*

2 Declare ye among the nations, and publish, and set up a standard;

the way to Zion with their faces *hitherward*." "How certainly any one not living at Jerusalem would have said *thitherward* is shewn by our translators having actually so rendered it in the Eng. Vers. One little undesigned touch like this is more convincing than elaborate arguments" (*Sp. Comm.*). As regards the words quoted as of later date than Zedekiah's time, the contrary can be conclusively shewn in the case of each.

To (*c*), The knowledge here referred to is nothing but what might naturally be expected in the case of a prophet living in frequent intercourse with the Chaldaeans, and who may very possibly have already spent some time in Babylon. (See note on xiii. 1.)

In general we may add that the words of li. 51 are much more in accordance with the time after Nebuchadnezzar's *plundering* of the Temple in Jehoiakim's reign than with the period which followed its *destruction*, and further that the mention of the "kings of the *Medes*" (li. 11, 28) and not the Persians, as the conquerors of Babylon, points to a time when the former power was still in the ascendant, and consequently precludes the supposition entertained by those who would maintain that the prediction was made only just before its fulfilment. By the time of the actual capture of Babylon the Persians had acquired the ascendancy, and the Medes, though sharing with them in the attack and thus fulfilling what is here predicted, played but a subordinate part.

This prophecy against Babylon forms an appropriate conclusion to the series. The nations immediately bordering upon Palestine have had their fate foretold, and then the more remote, but none the less is that Empire, which is to execute God's vengeance upon them, destined in its turn to fall. And this, the climax of the prophecies against foreign nations, is marked by the grandeur of the images employed by the prophet.

Babylon is a golden cup, from which all the nations have been forced to drink the wine of God's wrath (li. 7); God brings forth from His armoury the weapons of His indignation for her destruction (l. 25); Babylon is a volcano which has poured out flames upon all the nations round, and now shall itself be consumed, while Israel the people of God shall at length be delivered from her oppressors and restored to her land.

1—7. BABYLON SHALL FALL AND ISRAEL RETURN.

2. *set up a standard*] lift *up a standard*, as the speediest way of calling attention to the news.

Publish, *and* conceal not:
Say, Babylon is taken, Bel is confounded, Merodach is broken in pieces;
Her idols are confounded, her images are broken in pieces.
For out of the north there cometh up a nation against her, 3
Which shall make her land desolate,
And none shall dwell therein:
They shall remove, they shall depart, both man and beast.
In those days, and in that time, saith the LORD, 4
The children of Israel shall come,
They and the children of Judah together,
Going and weeping: they shall go,
And seek the LORD their God.
They shall ask the way *to* Zion with their faces thither- 5
ward, *saying*,

Bel...Merodach] If the first of these was the sun-god, he was no doubt the same as Baal. It is more likely however that he is to be identified with Jupiter, and that Merodach is not a distinct deity, but only another name (perhaps originally a title) of Bel. He was the guardian divinity of Babylon, but under the name Merodach (Marduk of the cuneiform inscriptions) does not seem to have been worshipped till the time of Pul and onwards. The inscriptions of Nebuchadnezzar's time speak of him as "the great lord, the senior of the gods, the most ancient." His name is contained in that of two Babylonian kings, Evil-Merodach, son of Nebuchadnezzar (lii. 31; 2 Kings xxv. 27), and Merodach-Baladan (margin of 2 Kings xx. 12; Is. xxxix. 1).

is confounded...are confounded] *is* **ashamed**...*are* **ashamed**. The words 'idols' and 'images' would be better transposed in the Eng. Vers. The Heb. for the latter is a term of contempt, meaning literally, what may be rolled about, senseless logs or lumps.

3. *out of the north*] The Medo-Persian Empire is meant. Media was north-west of Babylon.

cometh up] This and the last two verbs of the verse ('shall remove ...shall depart') will be more forcibly as well as literally rendered by the (prophetic) past (*hath come up...have fled...are gone*).

Which shall make] It shall make.

4. The overthrow of Babylon shall be the signal for the deliverance and return of the people of God.

They and the children of Judah together] See ch. iii. 18 with note.

Going and weeping: they shall go] The colon should be placed before *going*. **They shall go up weeping as they go.**

5. *They shall ask the way to Zion with their faces thitherward*] more

Come, and let us join ourselves to the LORD
In a perpetual covenant *that* shall not be forgotten.
6 My people hath been lost sheep:
Their shepherds have caused them to go astray, they have turned them away *on* the mountains:
They have gone from mountain to hill,
They have forgotten their resting place.
7 All that found them have devoured them:
And their adversaries said, We offend not,
Because they have sinned against the LORD, the habitation of justice,
Even the LORD, the hope of their fathers.

8—16. *Chaldaea's Exultation over Israel shall be punished.*

8 Remove out of the midst of Babylon,
And go forth out of the land of the Chaldeans,
And be as the he goats before the flocks.
9 For lo, I *will* raise and cause to come up against Babylon

literally, *They shall enquire about Zion; to the way hitherward are their faces turned.* For **hitherward** see introductory note to this chapter.

6. *they have turned them away on the mountains*] If we take the present (Massoretic) text in the Heb., where however the reading is very doubtful, we should rather render **on seducing mountains**, to be connected immediately with 'have caused them to go astray.' The reference is to the mountains as the favourite seats for idolatry, and to their enticing influence as such upon the people.

They have gone from mountain to hill] they have simply passed from one idolatrous pleasure to another.

resting place] literally, *crouching place*, the fold in which they should lie.

7. *We offend not*] For this word see note on ii. 3. The enemy's plea is, Israel is no longer holy to the Lord, and thus it is no sacrilege, though we devour her.

the habitation of justice] The same expression is used of Jerusalem in xxxi. 23.

8—16. CHALDAEA'S EXULTATION OVER ISRAEL SHALL BE PUNISHED.

8. Having told of the repentance of Israel, and of their sufferings in the land of exile, he now calls upon them to set out upon their return.

Babylon] See note on ver. 16.

be as the he goats] strive each to outstrip his neighbour in your alacrity and joy. A better reading perhaps is, *let them go forth...and let them be...*

9. *raise*] **awaken.**

An assembly of great nations from the north country:
And they shall set *themselves* in array against her;
From thence she shall be taken:
Their arrows *shall be* as of a mighty expert *man*;
None shall return in vain.
And Chaldea shall be a spoil: 10
All that spoil her shall be satisfied, saith the LORD.
Because ye were glad, because ye rejoicèd, 11
O ye destroyers of mine heritage,
Because ye are grown fat as the heifer at grass,
And bellow as bulls;
Your mother shall be sore confounded; 12
She that bare you shall be ashamed:
Behold, the hindermost of the nations
Shall be a wilderness, a dry land, and a desert.

an assembly of great nations] the Medo-Persian Empire. See the names of individual nations who helped to compose it in li. 27, 28.

expert man] This is much better than the reading in the Eng. margin, viz. *destroyer*. In the Heb. the two differ by the position of a dot.

none shall return] Arrows do not in any case return, as does *e.g.* a sword. Therefore we may not on the analogy of the expression contained in 2 Sam. i. 22 understand *none* of the arrows, but rather of the warriors.

11. This verse is probably to be connected with the preceding, and thus gives the reason why Chaldaea is to be spoiled. We should therefore make ver. 12 begin a new sentence, and not form part of this one, as in the Eng. Vers. If on the other hand we retain the punctuation adopted in our Vers., we had best render not *Because* but *Although*. The verbs in the Heb. are in the fem. sing., but have been altered to the plural through a failure to perceive that the former might be used of the nation. In the English however we must keep the plural on account of the word 'destroyers.'

destroyers] **plunderers.**
are grown fat] **leap.**
at grass] better, **threshing.** The command not to muzzle the mouth of the ox that trode out the corn (Deut. xxv. 4) would bring about special playfulness on the part of the animals thus unusually well fed.
bellow as bulls] **neigh as steeds.** For the last word see note on viii. 16.

12. *confounded*] **ashamed**, a word closely akin to that used twice in ver. 2.
shall be ashamed] *shall* **blush.**
the hindermost of the nations shall be...] rather, **she shall be** *the hindermost of the nations, a wilderness, a desert, and a waste.* Babylon,

13 Because of the wrath of the LORD it shall not be inhabited,
But it shall be wholly desolate: every one that goeth by Babylon shall be astonished,
And hiss at all her plagues.
14 Put *yourselves* in array against Babylon round about:
All ye that bend the bow, shoot at her, spare no arrows:
For she hath sinned against the LORD.
15 Shout against her round about:
She hath given her hand:
Her foundations are fallen, her walls are thrown down:
For it *is* the vengeance of the LORD: take vengeance upon her;
As she hath done, do unto her.
16 Cut off the sower from Babylon,

which was as Amalek of old (Numb. xxiv. 20) "the first of the nations," shall now take the lowest place.

13. For the language of this verse see chaps xviii. 16, xix. 8, xlix. 17, with notes.

14. Babylon's enemies are called upon to begin the siege, and that the picture may be the more graphic, the archers in particular are addressed.

15. *Shout*] Raise the battle cry.

she hath given her hand] This expression denotes *to make an agreement, bargain*, and hence *to submit oneself*. Its application is illustrated by the following passages: Gen. xxiv. 2, xlvii. 29; 2 Kings x. 15; 1 Chron. xxix. 24 (margin); 2 Chron. xxx. 8 (margin); Ezra x. 19; Lam. v. 6. Compare the Latin phrase *manus dare*.

foundations] rather, *supports*, **battlements**, that on which the city rests her strength: so the Septuagint.

her walls are thrown down] This was not done by Cyrus, who entered the city beneath the walls by the river bed, after diverting the stream. It therefore points on to the later capture of Babylon by Darius, who "having become master of the place, destroyed the wall, and tore down all the gates; for Cyrus had done neither the one nor the other when he took Babylon." Herod. Bk. iii. 159 (Rawl.). See however Rawlinson's note, shewing that breaches in the wall are all that can have been here meant.

it is the vengeance of the Lord] because Babylon has afflicted His people.

16. *Cut off the sower from Babylon*] As the word used is Babylon, not Chaldaea, it has been thought that the reference is to the large spaces which we know were reserved within the city for agricultural and pastoral purposes in case of siege. It is better however to take *Babylon* (as probably in ver. 8 above) to be equivalent to Babylonia,

And him that handleth the sickle in the time of harvest;
For fear of the oppressing sword
They shall turn every one to his people,
And they shall flee every one to his own land.

17—20. *While punishment is decreed for Babylon, Restoration and Forgiveness shall be the Lot of Israel.*

Israel *is* a scattered sheep; 17
The lions have driven *him* away:
First the king of Assyria hath devoured him;
And last this Nebuchadrezzar king of Babylon hath broken his bones.
Therefore thus saith the Lord of hosts, the God of 18 Israel;
Behold, I *will* punish the king of Babylon and his land,
As I have punished the king of Assyria.
And I will bring Israel again to his habitation, 19

whose fertility is thus described by Herod. Bk. i. 193 (Rawl.), "in grain it is so fruitful as to yield commonly two hundred-fold, and when the production is the greatest, even three hundred-fold." As Cyrus was careful to spare the country about Babylon, this feature of the attack may also point to a subsequent siege (see ver. 15).

sickle] better than the marginal *scythe*, as a small instrument is meant, such as was used for cutting grapes (Joel iii. 13).

they shall turn...] taken from Is. xiii. 14. The members of different conquered nations, whom Nebuchadnezzar had brought together to servitude in Babylon, shall be freed.

17—20. While punishment is decreed for Babylon, Restoration and Forgiveness shall be the Lot of Israel.

17. The people of God are like a stray sheep, driven hither and thither and preyed upon by savage beasts.

the lions] lions.

first the king of Assyria hath devoured him] **the first (lion) devoured him, (even) the king of Assyria.**

and last...bones] **and this one, the last, hath...(even) Nebuchadrezzar king of Babylon.** The people, thoroughly weakened by the wars with Assyria, and by the captivity of the Ten Tribes, have afterwards had the feeble remnant of their strength crushed at the hands of Babylon. Assyria was a mighty Empire, but it has already paid the penalty for its cruelty towards the people of God. Such too shall be the fate of Babylon.

19. *habitation*] **pasture-ground.** This, while an equally accurate rendering of the Heb., accords better with the figure of speech found in

And he shall feed on Carmel and Bashan,
And his soul shall be satisfied upon mount Ephraim and Gilead.

20 In those days, and in that time, saith the LORD,
The iniquity of Israel shall be sought for, and *there shall be* none;
And the sins of Judah, and they shall not be found:
For I will pardon them whom I reserve.

21—32. *Babylon, both city and country, is hopelessly doomed.*

21 Go up against the land of Merethaim, *even* against it,
And against the inhabitants of Pekod:
Waste and utterly destroy after them, saith the LORD,
And do according to all that I have commanded thee.

22 A sound of battle *is* in the land,
And of great destruction.

23 How is the hammer of the whole earth cut asunder and broken!

the remainder of the verse. The parts of the land which follow are chosen as those which were most productive.

20. *In those days and in that time*] the formula for introducing a prophecy which has to do with the times of the Messiah. Compare note on chap. xxiii. 5. Thus we see that the return of the people from Babylon is to be itself typical of the great and glorious period to follow for the Church of God.

whom I reserve] literally, *whom I cause to remain*, the remnant, who come forth at the end out of the long tribulation.

21—32. BABYLON, BOTH CITY AND COUNTRY, IS HOPELESSLY DOOMED.

21. *Merethaim...Pekod*] Modern investigations have ascertained the existence of the latter name as that of a place in Babylonia; it is therefore at least possible that the former may also have existed. Whether however Jeremiah intended to play upon the names of actually existent places or not, he doubtless meant to emphasize the senses of these two names, viz. *double rebellion...punishment*. The former, which has the Heb. termination of the dual number, is formed on the analogy of such words as Mizraim, Aram-Naharaim, etc., and *double* seems not to have reference to any two distinct acts of rebellion, but rather to mean *intense*, that which exceeds the rebellion of other nations. Compare ver. 31. See also note on xvii. 18.

waste] better, **slay**, as the context in ver. 27 shews that the same verb is there to be rendered.

23. *the hammer*] For the figure itself compare xxiii. 29. The title,

How is Babylon become a desolation among the nations!
I have laid a snare for thee, and thou art also taken, O 24
  Babylon,
And thou wast not aware:
Thou art found, and also caught,
Because thou hast striven against the LORD.
  ₄e LORD hath opened his armoury, 25
And hath brought forth the weapons of his indignation:
For this ⁺he work of the Lord GOD of hosts
In the land of the Chaldeans.
Come against her from the utmost border, 26
Open her storehouses:
Cast her up as heaps, and destroy her utterly:
Let nothing of her be left.
Slay all her bullocks; let them go down to the slaughter: 27

here given to Babylon, has been applied in other times to individuals, to Judas *Maccabaeus* (Heb. *Makkâbh*=a hammer, though this derivation for the name is but dubious), for his victories over Syria, to Charles *Martel* (French), who was grandfather of Charles the Great, and conquered the Saracens in a decisive battle at Tours in 732 A.D., and to Edward I. of England, on whose tomb at Westminster Abbey are inscribed the words "Scotorum *Malleus*."

24. *I have laid a snare for thee*] If this refer to the capture by Cyrus, see note on ver. 15 above for the manner in which it was effected. Whether however it applies to that occasion, or to Darius's later capture by Zopyrus's stratagem, the following words "thou wast not aware" will have equal point, as Herodotus speaks in each case of the amazement of the inhabitants (Bk. i. 191, iii. 158).

25. *armoury*] literally, *store-house*.

the weapons of his indignation] used also in Is. xiii. 5 of the nations who unconsciously discharge God's bidding in war.

for this is the work of the Lord God of hosts] **for the Lord, the Lord of hosts, hath a work.**

26. *from the utmost border*] The Heb. is 'from the end,' which may mean either as in Eng. Vers., or, all from every quarter, *every one from first to last*.

store-houses] quite a different word from that so rendered in ver. 25, and meaning **granaries**.

cast her up as heaps] pile up the treasures of grain which are contained in her and consume them in her midst.

27. *Slay*] See note on ver. 21.

her bullocks] her choice youths, the flower of her army. For the expression 'go down to the slaughter' compare xlviii. 15, and for 'the time of their visitation' xlvi. 21.

Woe unto them! for their day is come,
The time of their visitation.

28 The voice of them that flee and escape out of the land of Babylon,
To declare in Zion the vengeance of the Lord our God,
The vengeance of his temple.

29 Call together the archers against Babylon:
All ye that bend the bow, camp against it round about;
Let none thereof escape:
Recompense her according to her work;
According to all that she hath done, do unto her:
For she hath been proud against the Lord, against the Holy One of Israel.

30 Therefore shall her young men fall in the streets,
And all her men of war shall be cut off in that day, saith the Lord.

31 Behold, I *am* against thee, *O thou* most proud,
Saith the Lord God of hosts:
For thy day is come, the time *that* I will visit thee.

32 And the most proud shall stumble and fall,
And none shall raise him up:
And I will kindle a fire in his cities,
And it shall devour all round about him.

28. *them that flee*] the liberated Jews.
the vengeance of his temple] the requital for having burned it in their final capture of Jerusalem.

29. *the archers*] This is no doubt right, as is shewn by the context, although the old rendering of the word was *many*.

against it] against **her**, so as to agree with the subsequent pronouns, which have the same reference.

proud] **presumptuous**.

30. This verse has occurred in words almost absolutely the same with regard to Damascus (xlix. 26, where see note).

31. *O thou most proud*] literally, O (thou who art) *Presumption* (itself); so also in next verse. Compare ver. 21.

32. *raise him*] *raise* **her**, the reference being to Babylon as before. In the Heb. indeed the pronoun is masc., but only because that is the gender of the noun by which Babylon is here called (Presumption).

and I will kindle...] The latter part of the verse is almost a transcript of xxi. 14*b*, except that for *in his cities* that passage has "in the forest thereof."

33—40. *The Prophet enlarges upon the thoroughness with which Babylon shall be destroyed.*

Thus saith the LORD of hosts; 33
The children of Israel and the children of Judah *were* oppressed together:
And all that took them captives held them fast;
They refused to let them go.
Their redeemer *is* strong; 34
The LORD of hosts *is* his name:
He shall thoroughly plead their cause,
That he may give rest to the land,
And disquiet the inhabitants of Babylon.
A sword *is* upon the Chaldeans, saith the LORD, 35
And upon the inhabitants of Babylon,
And upon her princes, and upon her wise *men*.
A sword *is* upon the liars; and they shall dote: 36

33—40. THE PROPHET ENLARGES UPON THE THOROUGHNESS WITH WHICH BABYLON SHALL BE DESTROYED.

33. *were oppressed*] **are** *oppressed*.
held...refused] **have** *held...***have** *refused*. The Babylonian oppressors are acting like Pharaoh of old.

34. *redeemer*] The Heb. is *Goel*, the title of the near kinsman, to whom according to Jewish law belonged the duty of revenging a murder, as well as that of advocate and general protector. In like manner the Lord is about to rescue His people and take vengeance upon their foe.

he shall thoroughly plead their cause] literally, *pleading he will plead their plea*.

may give rest] It is all one word in the Heb., and some would on the contrary render *may trouble*, a sense which another part of the same Heb. verb is found to bear. This however neither fits the requirements of the passage here so well, nor is it in harmony with Is. xiv. 7, 16, where, as here, the overthrow of Babylon is the subject.

land] **earth**. All known nations had been more or less troubled by Babylon.

35. *upon her princes, and upon her wise men*] The former were the rulers in civil the latter in religious matters. Astrology was much practised in Chaldaea.

36. *liars*] more literally, *babblers*, utterers of random prophecies.

dote] *be mad, foolish*. So 1 Tim. vi. 4. The derived sense, to be foolishly *fond*, occurs in Ezek. xxiii. 5, etc. Compare, as illustrating the sense in the present passage:

> Unless the fear of death doth make me *dote*,
> I see my son Antipholus and Dromio.
> Shakespeare, *Com. of Err.*, v. 1. *Bible Word Book.*

A sword *is* upon her mighty *men;* and they shall be dismayed.

37 A sword *is* upon their horses, and upon their chariots,
And upon all the mingled people that *are* in the midst of her;
And they shall become as women:
A sword *is* upon her treasures; and they shall be robbed.

38 A drought *is* upon her waters; and they shall be dried up:
For it *is* the land of graven images,
And they are mad upon *their* idols.

39 Therefore the wild beasts of the desert
With the wild beasts of the islands shall dwell *there*,
And the owls shall dwell therein:
And it shall be no more inhabited for ever;
Neither shall it be dwelt in from generation to generation.

40 As God overthrew Sodom and Gomorrah

    37. *their…their*] literally, *his…his*, referring either to the king of Babylon, or to Babylon itself. See note on ver. 32.

the mingled people] See note on xxv. 20.

    38. *A drought*] The words for *drought* and *sword* (differing by one vowel only) are sufficiently like to make it quite possible that here as at the beginning of the two previous verses the latter should be read. In that case *sword* will be equivalent to *war*, and the reference will be to the stratagem by which Cyrus captured the city. *Drought* on the contrary will more naturally refer to the drying up of the many canals by which the water of the Euphrates was distributed throughout the whole country for drainage and irrigation as well as for commercial purposes. Compare li. 13.

the land] a *land*.

their idols] idols, literally, *terrors*, as meaning probably the grotesque objects by which the heathen often represent their gods.

    39. *the wild beasts of the desert*] The whole is expressed by one word in the Heb., and means those who dwell in the desert, either men as in Ps. lxxii. 9, or beasts, as here.

the wild beasts of the islands] **the jackals**, literally, *the shriekers*. The word here used probably denotes the whole class, Tannin on the other hand (see chap. ix. 11 with note) being a particular species.

owls] **ostriches**. It appears however that the former animals are also found there. "Shapeless heaps of rubbish cover for many an acre the face of the land. The lofty banks of ancient canals fret the country like natural ridges of hills…Owls" (which are of a large grey kind, and often found in flocks of nearly a hundred) "start from the scanty thickets, and the foul jackal skulks through the furrows." (Layard's *Nineveh and Babylon*, p. 484, quoted by Rawln., Herod. vol. i. p. 434).

    40. See xlix. 18.

And the neighbour *cities* thereof, saith the LORD;
So shall no man abide there,
Neither shall any son of man dwell therein.

41—43. *Picture of the enemy's approach.*

Behold, a people shall come from the north,   41
And a great nation, and many kings
Shall be raised up from the coasts of the earth.
They shall hold the bow and the lance: 42
They *are* cruel, and will not shew mercy:
Their voice shall roar like the sea,
And they shall ride upon horses,
Every one put in array, like a man to the battle,
Against thee, O daughter of Babylon.
The king of Babylon hath heard the report of them,   43
And his hands waxed feeble:
Anguish took hold of him,
And pangs as of a woman in travail.

44—46. *It is the Lord's decree and therefore inevitable and terrible.*

Behold, he shall come up like a lion from the swelling of   44
    Jordan
Unto the habitation of the strong:
But I will make them suddenly run away from her:
And who *is* a chosen *man, that* I may appoint over her?
For who *is* like me? and who will appoint me the time?
And who *is* that shepherd that will stand before me?
Therefore hear ye the counsel of the LORD,   45

41—43. PICTURE OF THE ENEMY'S APPROACH.

41—43. A repetition, with the necessary changes, of vi. 22—24, where Jerusalem is the object of the threat. See notes on that passage. Here 'and many kings' (ver. 41) is added to suit the present application.

44—46. IT IS THE LORD'S DECREE AND THEREFORE INEVITABLE AND TERRIBLE.

44—46. This passage also is adapted from a preceding one, viz. that concerning Edom (xlix. 19—21, where see notes), the difference in the comparative importance of the two being well marked by the fact that now the cry is no longer heard "in the Red Sea" only, but in general *among the nations.*

> That he hath taken against Babylon;
> And his purposes, that he hath purposed against the land
>   of the Chaldeans:
> Surely the least of the flock shall draw them out:
> Surely he shall make *their* habitation desolate with them.

46 At the noise of the taking of Babylon the earth is moved,
And the cry is heard among the nations.

CHAP. LI. 1—14. *It only remains for Israel to depart and leave Babylon to its fate.*

51 Thus saith the LORD;
Behold, I *will* raise up against Babylon,
And against them that dwell in the midst of them that
    rise up against me,
A destroying wind;

2 And will send unto Babylon fanners, that shall fan her,
And shall empty her land:
For in the day of trouble they shall be against her round
    about.

3 Against *him that* bendeth let the archer bend his bow,

CHAP. LI. 1—14. IT ONLY REMAINS FOR ISRAEL TO DEPART AND LEAVE BABYLON TO ITS FATE.

1. *in the midst of them that rise up against me*] For the figure of *Atbash*, by which the expression in the text is equivalent to *Chaldaeans*, see note on xxv. 26. Another proof that Jeremiah was a sharer in the love which his countrymen had for artificial arrangement of the letters of the alphabet is given by the fact that the greater part of the Lamentations (chaps. i—iv) is alphabetical. See Introduction to Lamentations, Chap. I. § 4.

a destroying wind] or, *the spirit of a destroyer*, but the former reading is better suited to the subsequent context.

2. *fanners*] The Heb., as it stands, is *strangers*, but by a very slight change can be rendered as in the Eng. Vers., so as to correspond to the verb that follows.

empty] the same verb as that which is translated "make void" in xix. 7, where see note.

3. Although the Babylonians post themselves on the walls with their weapons and arrayed in armour, yet the archer is to attack them from without, and not one of the fighting men is to be spared. Some grammatical difficulty is presented by the first words of the verse in the original: and it is somewhat tempting to alter them (as we easily may) thus, *Let not the archer bend his bow, and let none lift*, etc. The words which follow however shew that it is not the attacked but the attacking host that are addressed. The Eng. Vers. is therefore to be preferred.

And against *him that* lifteth himself up in his brigandine:
And spare ye not her young men;
Destroy ye utterly all her host.
Thus the slain shall fall in the land of the Chaldeans, 4
And *they that are* thrust through in her streets.
For Israel *hath* not *been* forsaken, 5
Nor Judah of his God, of the LORD of hosts;
Though their land was filled *with* sin
Against the Holy One of Israel.
Flee out of the midst of Babylon, 6
And deliver every man his soul:
Be not cut off in her iniquity;
For this *is* the time of the LORD'S vengeance;
He *will* render unto her a recompence.
Babylon *hath been* a golden cup in the LORD'S hand, 7
That made all the earth drunken:
The nations have drunken of her wine;
Therefore the nations are mad.
Babylon is suddenly fallen and destroyed: 8
Howl for her;

brigandine] see note on xlvi. 4.
4. *Thus the slain shall fall...and they that are thrust through*] rather, **And they shall fall slain...and thrust through.**
5. *For*] The reason of the overthrow of the Chaldaeans is that God remembers Israel, and again the reason of His remembering Israel is the wickedness of Chaldaea. This is the connexion of thought and consequently *though* of the Eng. Vers. should also be **for**, *their* referring to the Chaldaeans. *Forsaken* is literally *widowed*.
sin] rather, **guiltiness.**
the Holy One] The Septuagint here, as elsewhere also, render *holy ones*, without any authority.
6. *soul*] **life.**
be not cut off] See note on xlix. 26.
7. *a golden cup*] In chap. xxv. 15, 16 it was Jeremiah himself who was commanded to make the nations drink of the wine of God's wrath. Inasmuch however as Babylon was the means which God employed for their overthrow, she is here spoken of under the same figure, as having made all the nations drunk. She is called a golden cup from the splendour and glory which belonged to her as an empire. For the New Test. application of the figure to the spiritual Babylon see Rev. xvii. 4, 5.
8. *howl for her*] This is addressed to the Jews and other nations, held captive in Babylon. The terrible character of her fall is most

> Take balm for her pain,
> If so be she may be healed.
>
> 9 We would have healed Babylon, but she is not healed:
> Forsake her, and let us go every one into his own country:
> For her judgment reacheth unto heaven,
> And is lifted up *even* to the skies.
>
> 10 The LORD hath brought forth our righteousness:
> Come, and let us declare in Zion
> The work of the LORD our God.
>
> 11 Make bright the arrows: gather the shields:
> The LORD hath raised up the spirit of the kings of the Medes:
> For his device *is* against Babylon, to destroy it;
> Because it *is* the vengeance of the LORD,
> The vengeance of his temple.
>
> 12 Set up the standard upon the walls of Babylon,

skilfully suggested by the prophet when he thus calls upon those who had suffered most grievously at her hands to have compassion upon the ills of their former oppressor.

take balm] compare xlvi. 11.

9. *We would have healed*] literally, *We have healed*, i.e. We have tried to heal. The Jews speak in the name of all the exiles in Babylon.

her judgment] her guilt.

skies] literally, *clouds*.

10. *hath brought forth our righteousness*] hath made known the justice of our cause (by thus delivering our enemy over to the sword). God has at length judged that the idolatry of the people has been sufficiently punished, and thus they are again to be treated as righteous.

11. *Make bright*] or, *sharpen*.

gather] literally, *fill*, i.e. place your arms within, or your bodies behind, them. Compare the expression in margin of 2 Kings ix. 24, "filled his hand with a bow," i.e. grasped it.

shields] The Septuagint, who vary much in their rendering of the Heb. word, here and in Ezek. xxvii. 11 have *quivers*, and they are followed by the Vulgate, but this rendering seems to have been adopted merely as being apparently most suited to the present context. Both here and in the other passages where the Hebrew word occurs, it is best taken to mean *shields*.

the kings of the Medes] Media was a country lying north-west of Persia. It consisted in early times of a number of small tribes, whose leaders are here called 'kings.' It was the Medo-Persian empire that succeeded by conquest to the dominions of Babylon. For the last words of this verse compare l. 28 with note.

12. *upon*] **against.** Although the Heb. preposition is not free from

Make the watch strong, set up the watchmen,
Prepare the ambushes:
For the LORD hath both devised and done
That which he spake against the inhabitants of Babylon.
O thou that dwellest upon many waters, abundant in 13
  treasures,
Thine end is come, *and* the measure of thy covetousness.
The LORD of hosts hath sworn by himself, *saying*, 14
Surely I will fill thee *with* men, as *with* caterpillars;
And they shall lift up a shout against thee.

15—19. *The Creator of the Universe alone is God.*

He hath made the earth by his power, 15
He hath established the world by his wisdom,
And hath stretched out the heaven by his understanding.
When he uttereth *his* voice, *there is* a multitude of waters 16
  in the heavens;
And he causeth the vapours to ascend from the ends of
  the earth:

ambiguity, yet the words 'prepare the ambushes' that follow, seem to decide that throughout the verse the besiegers and not the besieged are addressed.

the ambushes] to attack any of the besieged that ventured beyond the walls.

13. *upon many waters*] See note on l. 38.

abundant in treasures] conveyed to Babylon from the conquered provinces.

the measure of thy covetousness] *the measure of thy* **gain.** Some would render the last word *cutting off*, i.e. in the web of thy destiny the limit has been reached, at which the thread is to be cut. Although the Heb. root may in itself bear this sense, it is best to render it in its more usual sense, as above, which is also better adapted to the mention of treasures immediately preceding.

14. *I will fill*] literally, **I have filled**, the thing is viewed as though it had already taken place. Babylon shall swarm with the hostile armies. They shall effect an entrance.

caterpillars] **locusts.**

a shout] **the vintage song,** see note on xxv. 30.

15—19. THE CREATOR OF THE UNIVERSE ALONE IS GOD.

15—19. These verses are all but identical with x. 12—16. This need not the least surprise us in the case of a writer like Jeremiah. It is obvious however, that the other, and not this, is the original place for the words. There they form a natural sequence with that

He maketh lightnings with rain,
And bringeth forth the wind out of his treasures.
17 Every man is brutish by *his* knowledge;
Every founder is confounded by the graven image:
For his molten image *is* falsehood, and *there is* no breath in them.
18 They *are* vanity, the work of errors:
In the time of their visitation they shall perish.
19 The portion of Jacob *is* not like them;
For he *is* the former of all *things:*
And *Israel is* the rod of his inheritance:
The LORD of hosts *is* his name.

20—58. *Amplification of the description of Babylon's doom.*

20 Thou *art* my battle axe *and* weapons of war:
For with thee will I break in pieces the nations,

which precedes, assuring the Israelites that they need not fear the power of false gods, while here they are quoted by the prophet as a solemn declaration to the Chaldaeans that their idols will prove worthless in the day of their calamity. The omission of the word Israel in the Heb. of ver. 19 here, and one or two minor differences in the original, are the only points of distinction between the two passages.

Pascal gives verse 18 an application which shews that he understands it, not of the idols, but apparently of their worshippers. "Thus you see, fathers, that ridicule is in some cases a very appropriate means of reclaiming men from their errors, and that it is accordingly an act of justice, because, as Jeremiah says, 'the actions of those that err are worthy of derision, because of their vanity'." (*Provincial Letters*, XI.)

20—58. AMPLIFICATION OF THE DESCRIPTION OF BABYLON'S DOOM.

20. *Thou art my battle axe*] Although Cyrus, and again Israel have been suggested by some, there can be little doubt that Babylon is the subject of the address in this and the succeeding verse. Compare chap. l. 23, where she is likened to a hammer. It is clear from the tense of the oft repeated verb in the original that she is thought of as still in the height of her power and in the midst of her oppressive treatment of the nations of the earth.

battle axe] **mace.** "The Assyrian mace was a short thin weapon, and must either have been made of a very tough wood, or—and this is more probable—of metal. It had an ornamented head, which was sometimes very beautifully modelled, and generally a strap or string at the lower end, by which it could be grasped with greater firmness." (Rawlinson's *Anc. Mon.* I. p. 458.)

for] **and.**

And with thee will I destroy kingdoms:
And with thee will I break in pieces the horse and his 21
  rider;
And with thee will I break in pieces the chariot and his
  rider;
With thee also will I break in pieces man and woman; 22
And with thee will I break in pieces old and young;
And with thee will I break in pieces the young man and
  the maid;
I will also break in pieces with thee the shepherd and his 23
  flock;
And with thee will I break in pieces the husbandman and
  his yoke of oxen;
And with thee will I break in pieces captains and rulers.
And I will render unto Babylon 24
And to all the inhabitants of Chaldea
All their evil that they have done in Zion
In your sight, saith the LORD.
Behold, I *am* against thee, O destroying mountain, saith 25
  the LORD,

22. *old and young*] literally, *old man and boy*.

23. *captains and rulers*] The two original words are uncertain in their origin and exact sense. They both occur again in ver. 28 and the second (*sâgân*) also in ver. 57. The former (*pekhâh*) seems a title given to provincial governors below the first rank. It is applied to Tatnai (Ezra v. 6), Nehemiah (Neh. v. 14), and Zerubbabel (Hag. i. 1). It may possibly be identical in root with the word *pasha*, but almost all that can be ascertained about the word is that it is probably Assyrian. Thus Babylon carried her severity even to the extent of ill-treating her own subordinate governors.

24. *I will render...in your sight*] These words are to be joined in sense. The Jews are to have the satisfaction of seeing the requital of their enemy. For this thought compare Ps. xci. 8.

25. *O destroying mountain*] The same phrase is used in 2 Kings xxiii. 13 (Eng. Vers. "the mount of corruption") of the Mount of Olives the scene of pernicious idolatry. Here Babylon receives the title, as at once hurtful and conspicuous. It is not quite clear whether the figure of a volcano is meant throughout the verse, with rocks mingled with burning lava rolling down its sides. At any rate the last words mean that it will be reduced, as it were, to a cinder, its power for evil exhausted. "Such was Babylon. Its destructive energy under Nebuchadnezzar was like the first outbreak of volcanic fires, its rapid collapse under his successors was as the same volcano when its flames have burnt out, and its crater is falling in upon itself." (*Sp. Comm.*)

Which destroyest all the earth:
And I will stretch out mine hand upon thee,
And roll thee down from the rocks,
And will make thee a burnt mountain.

26 And they shall not take of thee a stone for a corner,
Nor a stone for foundations;
But thou shalt be desolate for ever, saith the LORD.

27 Set ye up a standard in the land,
Blow the trumpet among the nations,
Prepare the nations against her,
Call together against her the kingdoms of Ararat, Minni, and Ashchenaz;
Appoint a captain against her;
Cause the horses to come up as the rough caterpillars.

28 Prepare against her the nations with the kings of the Medes,

26. The figure of stones, which by the action of fire have been rendered unfit for use in building, is continued in this verse. No empire shall again have Babylon for its centre. Its position as a capital city is for ever shattered, and its glory burnt out.

27. *in the land*] **on the earth.**

prepare] **sanctify.** See notes on vi. 4, xxii. 7.

Ararat, Minni] These were respectively the central or southern, and the western portions of Armenia, which word is possibly = Har-Minni = the mountainous country of Minni. Armenia was by this time under Median sway, and so would contribute to the force of that army, when marching against Babylon.

Ashchenaz] Its position we can only gather from this passage to have been near the former two places. Rawlinson (Herod. vol. IV. 204) suspects a wrong reading in the Heb. text.

captain] The Heb. word is rare, occurring only once besides, Nah. iii. 17. There also the context concerns locusts, and the "captains" are likened to grasshoppers. Even in the time of the Septuagint the meaning of the word seems to have been doubtful, and it probably denotes some particular kind of troops, as this will best suit the Nahum passage.

as the rough caterpillars] *as the rough* **locusts.** If we retain this rendering, we are to understand it of the "locusts in their third stage, when their wings are still enveloped in rough horny cases, which stick up upon their backs. It is in this stage that they are so destructive." (*Sp. Comm.*). The *rough* of the Eng. Vers. however may mean, according to another sense of the verb, *causing terror, destruction*. In any case the enemy's horsemen are to advance to the attack in numbers which shall suggest a plague only too familiar to Eastern countries.

28. *Prepare*] See note on previous verse.

> The captains thereof, and all the rulers thereof,
> And all the land of his dominion.
> And the land shall tremble and sorrow: 29
> For every purpose of the LORD shall be performed against Babylon,
> To make the land of Babylon a desolation,
> Without an inhabitant.
> The mighty *men* of Babylon have forborn to fight, 30
> They have remained in *their* holds:
> Their might hath failed; they became as women:
> They have burnt her dwelling places;
> Her bars are broken.
> One post shall run to meet another, 31
> And one messenger to meet another,
> To shew the king of Babylon
> That his city is taken at *one* end,
> And *that* the passages are stopped, 32
> And the reeds they have burnt with fire,

captains...rulers] the same words as in verse 23.

his dominion] The pronoun refers to the king of Media, who is to gather together the various tribes over which he rules, with their governors.

29. *shall tremble*] **trembles**, and so for the other verbs of the verse.

30. *forborn*] **ceased**.

they have burnt] i.e. the enemy.

bars] defences generally.

31. *post*] The word is not used in modern English in this sense, except in the expression *post-haste*. For the sense, running messenger, compare

"Your native town you entered like a *post*."

Shakespeare, *Coriolanus*, Act V. sc. 5.

First denoting that which is placed (*positum*), it came to denote a fixed spot, e.g. a military post, or a place where horses are kept for travellers, then the person so travelling, and then any one travelling quickly. See *Bible Word-book*.

shall run to meet another] Bearing the tidings from opposite quarters, they shall meet at the king's castle in the heart of the city.

at one end] better, **from all sides**. See note on l. 26.

32. *passages*] not shallow places, fords, for such did not, as far as we know, exist in the Euphrates at Babylon, but probably *ferries*. There was but one bridge within the city.

reeds] **pools**. The word *reeds* has been substituted to avoid the difficulty of declaring that pools of water are to be burned. It is only

And the men of war are affrighted.

33 For thus saith the LORD of hosts, the God of Israel;
The daughter of Babylon *is* like a threshingfloor,
It is time to thresh her:
Yet a little while, and the time of her harvest shall come.

34 Nebuchadrezzar the king of Babylon hath devoured me,
he hath crushed me,
He hath made me an empty vessel,
He hath swallowed me up like a dragon,
He hath filled his belly with my delicates,
He hath cast me out.

35 The violence done to me and *to* my flesh *be* upon Babylon,

in a figure however that this is said of them, and the meaning of the statement is, that the reservoirs and pools round Babylon, made to contain the overflow of the river, and so to prevent inundations, shall, like all the other adornments of Babylon, disappear as completely as that which is inflammable does by the action of fire.

33. *it is time to thresh her*] **at the time that it is trodden.** "The most common mode of threshing is with the ordinary slab called *mowrej*, which is drawn over the floor by a horse, or yoke of oxen, until not only the grain is shelled out, but the straw itself is ground into chaff. To facilitate this operation, bits of rough lava are fastened into the bottom of the *mowrej*, and the driver sits or stands upon it.... The intention of the farmer is to beat and grind down his hills of grain to chaff, and much of it is reduced to fine dust, which the wind carries away." Thomson, *The Land and the Book*, p. 538. For the same figure used in reference to Babylon, see Is. xxi. 10.

the time of her harvest shall come] **the harvest time shall come to her.**

34. For 'me' we should probably read *us* throughout this verse, 'my' remaining in the singular. The speaker is of course the oppressed Israel.

hath made me] **hath pushed me aside.**

dragon] The singular noun Tannin (plural Tanninim), to be distinguished from Tannin, which is itself the plural of Tan, *a jackal* (see note on ix. 11), denotes any great monster, such as a serpent, that might naturally inhabit the plains of Babylon. In Is. li. 9, however, and elsewhere also, it is used of Pharaoh or Egypt, and hence there, and possibly here as well, means a *crocodile*. In Gen. i. 21, it is used of *sea-monsters* (Eng. Vers. *whales*).

delicates] used as a substantive here only in the Bible. Compare Shakespeare (3 *Hen. VI.* II. 5), where the king speaks of the shepherd's homely curds as 'far beyond a prince's *delicates*.' (*Bible Word Book*.)

35. *The violence done to me and to my flesh*] literally, *my violence, and my flesh*, i.e. the violence done by devouring me.

Shall the inhabitant of Zion say;
And my blood upon the inhabitants of Chaldea,
Shall Jerusalem say.
Therefore thus saith the LORD; 36
Behold, I *will* plead thy cause,
And take vengeance for thee;
And I will dry up her sea,
And make her springs dry.
And Babylon shall become heaps, 37
A dwelling place for dragons,
An astonishment, and a hissing,
Without an inhabitant.
They shall roar together like lions: 38
They shall yell as lions' whelps,
In their heat I will make their feasts, 39
And I will make them drunken, that they may rejoice,
And sleep a perpetual sleep,
And not wake, saith the LORD.
I will bring them down like lambs to the slaughter, 40
Like rams with he goats.

36. *sea*] not used metaphorically, as some have supposed, for the restless multitude of Babylon, but rather of the great lake or reservoir, four hundred and twenty furlongs in circumference, made by queen Nitocris (Herod., Bk. I. 185).

springs] The word is the same as that rendered "fountain" in the Eng. Vers. of ii. 13, where see note. The literal sense is *digging*, and the noun is in the singular. It refers to the network of canals dug throughout the country, which were necessary not only for commerce but also for irrigation. It is through the drying up of them that the country is barren to this day. See ver. 13, and l. 38.

37. *heaps*] "Vast 'heaps' or mounds, shapeless and unsightly, are scattered at intervals over the entire region where it is certain that Babylon anciently stood." (Rawl. *Anc. Mon.* II. 521.)

dragons] **jackals**, not the same word as in ver. 34 (see note there and on ix. 11), but Tannim=Tannin, plural of Tan.

hissing] See note on xviii. 16.

39. *In their heat I will make their feasts*] While they are exulting over the spoil which they have won from the conquered nations, I will allow them to carouse (*feasts* should be **drinking bouts**), and then destroy them at unawares. This found a signal fulfilment in the capture of Babylon during a feast.

40. *lambs...rams...he-goats*] all classes of the people. See Is. xxxiv. 6; Ezek. xxxix. 18.

41 How is Sheshach taken!
And *how* is the praise of the whole earth surprised!
How is Babylon become an astonishment among the nations!
42 The sea is come up upon Babylon:
She is covered with the multitude of the waves thereof.
43 Her cities are a desolation,
A dry land, and a wilderness,
A land wherein no man dwelleth,
Neither doth *any* son of man pass thereby.
44 And I will punish Bel in Babylon,
And I will bring forth out of his mouth that which he hath swallowed up:
And the nations shall not flow *together* any more unto him:
Yea, the wall of Babylon shall fall.
45 My people, go ye out of the midst of her,
And deliver ye every man his soul
From the fierce anger of the LORD.
46 And lest your heart faint,
And ye fear for the rumour that shall be heard in the land;
A rumour shall both come *one* year,
And after that in *another* year *shall come* a rumour,

41. *Sheshach*] See note on xxv. 26.
the praise] the object of praise.
surprised] seized.
42. *The sea is come up*] The approach of the hostile army is thus represented. Compare xlvi. 7, 8.
43. *a wilderness*] a desert, a place absolutely without vegetable life. See note on ii. 6.
44. *Bel*] See note on l. 2.
that which he hath swallowed up] the riches of the subjugated nations.
the wall of Babylon shall fall] and so the city shall lose that which was its main source of strength as a fortress.
45. *go ye out*] See l. 8.
46. *lest your heart faint*] **(beware) that your heart faint not.**
a rumour...a rumour] literally, *and there shall come in* (*the course of*) *the year the rumour, and afterward in* (*the course of*) *the year the rumour.* Rumour shall succeed rumour, as the years go on, and revolts and intestine disputes shall foreshadow the final break up of the Babylonian empire.

And violence in the land, ruler against ruler.
Therefore behold, the days come, 47
That I will do judgment upon the graven images of Babylon:
And her whole land shall be confounded,
And all her slain shall fall in the midst of her.
Then the heaven and the earth, and all that *is* therein, 48
shall sing for Babylon:
For the spoilers shall come unto her from the north,
saith the LORD.
As Babylon *hath caused* the slain of Israel to fall, 49
So at Babylon shall fall the slain of all the earth.
Ye that have escaped the sword, go *away*, stand not still: 50
Remember the LORD afar off,
And let Jerusalem come into your mind.
We are confounded, because we have heard reproach: 51
Shame hath covered our faces:
For strangers are come into the sanctuaries of the LORD's house.
Wherefore behold, the days come, saith the LORD, 52
That I will do judgment upon her graven images:
And through all her land the wounded shall groan.
Though Babylon should mount up *to* heaven, 53
And though she should fortify the height of her strength,

47. *confounded*] **ashamed.** See note on chap. xlviii. 20.
48. *shall sing for Babylon*] shall rejoice over her fall.
49. The Eng. Vers. is probably correct. There is a brevity and consequent obscurity about the Heb., which has made it possible to propose other renderings, e.g. that of the Eng. margin (*Both Babylon is to fall, O ye slain of Israel, and with Babylon,* etc.). The sense is, that the fact of Babylon's having caused the death of Israelites, shall be visited upon the representatives of many nations, which shall be mixed up in her overthrow.
50. This is addressed to the Israelites, who were in exile in Babylon, and had thus escaped death in the preliminary struggles between that empire and Israel.
afar off] **from afar,** from Babylon.
51. *confounded*] **ashamed.** The exiles speak, while yet in exile, and lament the reproaches that are cast in their teeth for worshipping a God who will not defend His people from misfortune, and His Temple from sacrilege.
53. *the height of her strength*] either the height of her walls, or that of the tower of Belus.

Yet from me shall spoilers come unto her, saith the LORD.
54 A sound of a cry *cometh* from Babylon,
And great destruction from the land of the Chaldeans:
55 Because the LORD *hath* spoiled Babylon,
And destroyed out of her the great voice;
When her waves do roar like great waters,
A noise of their voice is uttered:
56 Because the spoiler is come upon her, *even* upon Babylon,
And her mighty *men* are taken,
Every one of their bows is broken:
For the LORD God of recompences shall surely requite.
57 And I will make drunk her princes, and her wise *men*,
Her captains, and her rulers, and her mighty *men*:
And they shall sleep a perpetual sleep, and not wake,
Saith the King, whose name *is* the LORD of hosts.
58 Thus saith the LORD of hosts;
The broad walls of Babylon shall be utterly broken,
And her high gates shall be burnt with fire;
And the people shall labour in vain,

55. *hath spoiled*] **spoileth.**
destroyed] **will destroy.**
the great voice] the hum of the city's life.
when her waves] **and their** *waves*, the surging hosts which encompass the city.
a noise] See note on xxv. 31.
56. *every one of*] These words do not occur in the Heb., but the verb is sing. (*is* broken). This however is not as much of an obstacle in Heb. as it would be in Eng. to our rendering simply *their bows are broken*.
for the Lord God of recompences shall surely requite] *for* **a God of recompences is the Lord; he will assuredly requite.**
58. *The broad walls*] According to Herodotus, the outer wall of Babylon was 200 royal cubits (about 373 English feet) high, while it was fifty cubits wide. This, however, both from the nature of the case, and from the conflicting testimony of other writers, seems exaggerated. Probably the height was about 60 or 70 English feet. The walls may have been 30 or 40 feet wide, as they allowed of a team of four horses being driven along them. See Herod., Bk. I. 179, and Rawlinson's notes on that passage.
utterly broken] literally, *made bare*, destroyed, so that the very foundations shall be uncovered.
high gates] "In the circuit of the wall are a hundred gates, all of brass, with brazen lintels and side-posts." Herod. I. 179.
the people shall labour...] a quotation from Hab. ii. 13, transposing

And the folk in the fire, and they shall be weary.

59—64. *Appendix, containing the history of this prophecy.*

The word which Jeremiah the prophet commanded Se- 59 raiah the son of Neriah, the son of Maaseiah, when he went with Zedekiah the king of Judah *into* Babylon in the fourth year of his reign. And *this* Seraiah *was* a quiet prince. So 60 Jeremiah wrote in a book all the evil that should come upon Babylon, *even* all these words that are written against Babylon. And Jeremiah said to Seraiah, When thou comest *to* 61 Babylon, and shalt see, and shalt read all these words; then 62

however the words for 'in vain' and 'the fire'. Jeremiah throws light on Habakkuk's meaning, and at the same time gives it a more particular application. The fact that the Chaldaean conquests involve nothing in the end but exhaustion and suffering to the nations who have to do the behests of their ambitious rulers ("quicquid delirant reges, plectuntur Achivi") is by Jeremiah applied to the final overthrow of the Babylonian empire.

59—64. APPENDIX, CONTAINING THE HISTORY OF THIS PROPHECY.

59. *Seraiah*] brother of Baruch, both being sons of Neriah. See xxxii. 12.

when he went with Zedekiah] This journey to Babylon was probably made as an act of homage to Nebuchadnezzar. Possibly it was in consequence of suspicions aroused in the mind of that king by the coming of ambassadors in the same year to Zedekiah from Edom, Moab, and Ammon (xxvii. 3). (The order of these two events may however have been just the converse; see note on lii. 3.) The command to Seraiah is not actually stated till ver. 61, etc., the intermediate words being explanatory and so of the nature of a parenthesis.

a quiet prince] **a prince of the camping place**, what we should now call a quarter-master-general. It seems to have been his duty, as in attendance on the king in a journey, to ride forward each day, and arrange that matters should be in readiness at the next halting place.

60. *in a book*] literally, *in* one *book*. Although the numeral is sometimes used in Heb. simply as an indefinite article, yet it may well have its proper force here, implying that the whole prophecy of chapters l., li., was written upon one parchment, that so it might be the more conveniently sunk in the river.

61. *and shalt see and shalt read*] **then see that thou read**, not to the people of Babylon, nor even perhaps to a solemnly convoked assembly of Jews, as either course would have been at least attended with much danger, and the first of them probably impossible to carry out. The words are nevertheless to be pronounced in the presence of Jewish witnesses, who could in after days testify that thus, long before the overthrow of Babylon, these words had been read in the midst of

shalt thou say, O Lord, thou hast spoken against this place, to cut it off, that none shall remain in it, neither man nor
63 beast, but that it shall be desolate for ever. And it shall be, when thou hast made an end of reading this book, *that* thou shalt bind a stone to it, and cast it into the midst of
64 Euphrates: and thou shalt say, Thus shall Babylon sink, and shall not rise from the evil that I *will* bring upon her: and they shall be weary. Thus far *are* the words of Jeremiah.

the very city where they were to take effect, and then buried in the heart of the same.

64. *and they shall be weary*] This utterance by Seraiah of that which forms the (one) last word of the prophecy in the original, is for the solemn coupling of the symbolic act with the prophecy which has thus been read.

Thus far are the words of Jeremiah] These words are added in all probability by the writer of the concluding chapter, and shew how careful he was that he should not be identified with the prophet by future generations. See Introd., chap. iii. § 6.

CHAP. LII. HISTORICAL APPENDIX TO THE BOOK.

With respect to this concluding portion, two questions at once arise; (i) is its author Jeremiah? (ii) what relation does it bear to the two other portions of the Bible with which it has much in common, viz. chap. xxxix. of this Book, and 2 Kings xxiv. 18—xxv. 30?

As regards (i), this question seems already settled by the last words of chap. li. We find moreover a certain diversity from Jeremiah's style, the most noteworthy instance of which perhaps is the use of the name Jehoiachin (Coniah and Jeconiah being the forms always used in the early part of this Book). Moreover, verses 31—34 refer to events which in all probability Jeremiah did not live to witness, though it is just possible that he may have recorded them in extreme old age. Much of this chapter may be *in a sense* the work of Jeremiah, as we shall now see in replying to the second enquiry mentioned above.

In answer to (ii) we note that while a considerable portion of the three narratives is almost verbally identical, yet the account now before us contains, in common with that of the Kings, particulars relating to the Temple vessels, etc., which are omitted in chap. xxxix., while Nebuchadnezzar's charge concerning Jeremiah's safety (xxxix. 11—14), and the subsequent Jewish history connected with Gedaliah (2 Kings xxv. 22—26, and given also in full, Jer. xl.—xlii.), are not found in the present narrative. Practically, we have to choose between these two solutions of the question, (*a*) that the present passage was taken from the Book of the Kings, which are held by many to be the work of Jeremiah, while the modifications and additions represent independent sources of information possessed by the person who introduced it here, or (*b*), that the only connexion between the passages lies in their being both derived from some older historical record, which has been therefore made use of in a somewhat different manner and degree in each.

CHAP. LII. *Historical Appendix to the Book.*
1—11. *Capture of the City.*

Zedekiah *was* one and twenty year old when he *began* to 52 reign, and he reigned eleven years in Jerusalem. And his mother's name *was* Hamutal the daughter of Jeremiah of Libnah. And he did *that* which *was* evil in the eyes of the 2 LORD, according to all that Jehoiakim had done. For 3 through the anger of the LORD it came to pass in Jerusalem and Judah, till he had cast them out from his presence, that Zedekiah rebelled against the king of Babylon. And it 4

Other differences, as in the matter of numbers, have doubtless arisen from corruptions of the text in the hands of copyists, and are by no means peculiar to these passages, which, however, form an easy and interesting method of testing the extent (hereby shewn to be extremely slight) to which such corruptions may be considered to have affected the sacred Text. The Septuagint Version, which omits xxxix. 4—13 (see introductory notes to that chapter for further remarks), contains the whole of lii. with the exception of verses 2, 3, 15, 28—30.

CHAP. LII. 1—11. CAPTURE OF THE CITY.

1. *Zedekiah was one and twenty year old*] So 2 Chron. xxxvi. 11, but, if we compare 1 Chron. iii. 15 with 2 Kings xxiii. 31 (=2 Chron. xxxvi. 2), we find that, supposing the numbers which we now read there to be correct, Zedekiah should by this time have been thirty-four or thirty-five years of age. We must therefore assume that an error in the figures has somewhere crept into the text.

year] This and not *years* is the original reading of the Eng. Vers.: so in 2 Kings xxiii. 36 ("twenty and five year"); Dan. v. 31; Am. i. 1; Rom. iv. 19; so "mile" in marg. of John xi. 18.

his mother's name was Hamutal] Hamital is the other reading both here, and in the parallel passage in 2 Kings. So in the Heb. of 1 Sam. xxv. 18, we have Abugail, but in the rest of the chap. Abigail. Zedekiah was thus brother of Jehoahaz but half-brother of Jehoiakim (2 Kings xxiii. 31, 36).

2. *did that which was evil*] We have already noticed Zedekiah's weakness of character in xxxvii. 2, 3, xxxviii. 5, 24, etc.

3. *it came to pass*] this *came to pass*, i.e. the evil courses of the king. *that Zedekiah rebelled*] **and** *Zedekiah rebelled.* It has been suggested that as there was an impression prevalent both at Jerusalem (xxviii. 1—11) and at Babylon (xxix.), that Jehoiachin and the rest would return soon from exile, Zedekiah's personal visit to Nebuchadnezzar (li. 59) may have been in consequence of this, while his failure may possibly have been the cause of the assembling of the ambassadors of Edom, etc. (xxvii. 3), and of Zedekiah's overtures to Egypt (Ezek. xvii. 15). Then came open revolt on the part of the Jews, encouraged by the

came to pass in the ninth year of his reign, in the tenth month, in the tenth *day* of the month, *that* Nebuchadrezzar king of Babylon came, he and all his army, against Jerusalem, and pitched against it, and built forts against it round
5 about. So the city was besieged unto the eleventh year of
6 king Zedekiah. And in the fourth month, in the ninth *day* of the month, the famine was sore in the city, so that there
7 was no bread for the people of the land. Then the city was broken up, and all the men of war fled, and went forth out of the city by night *by* the way of the gate between the two walls, which *was* by the king's garden; (now the Chaldeans *were* by the city round about:) and they went *by* the
8 way of the plain. But the army of the Chaldeans pursued after the king, and overtook Zedekiah in the plains of Jeri-
9 cho; and all his army was scattered from him. Then they took the king, and carried him up unto the king of Babylon to Riblah in the land of Hamath; where he gave judgment

successful resistance of Tyre year after year (Ezek. xxix. 18), while Nebuchadnezzar was engaged in a distant part of the empire.

4. *in the tenth month*] A fast was instituted in memory of this time, Zech. viii. 19.

in the tenth day of the month] On that very day it was revealed to Ezekiel (xxiv. 2), that the siege was commencing. See note on xxxix. 1.

Nebuchadrezzar] a more accurate form than Nebuchadnezzar.

pitched] i.e. *they pitched*. In 2 Kings the verb is singular.

forts] moveable towers, sometimes with battering rams, such as Assyrian sculptures shew.

6. *in the fourth month*] In memory of this date also, a fast was appointed (Zech. viii. 19).

famine] described in detail in the Lamentations. Compare Ezek. iv. 16, 17, v. 16, 17.

the people of the land] the poorer classes, who had taken refuge in Jerusalem, or who had dwelt there.

7. *was broken up*] rather, *was broken* **into**. No doubt the north wall of the city is referred to, its most vulnerable point. For further particulars, see notes on xxxix. 3, 4.

by night] So Ezekiel foretold (xii. 12).

they went] 2 Kings, *he went*.

8. Lam. iv. 19, 20 may refer to this, in which case the circumstances probably were these, that one body of Chaldaeans followed, and another laid wait in the plain. Compare Ezek. xii. 13.

Zedekiah] 2 Kings, *him*.

9. *Riblah*] See note on xxxix. 5.

upon him. And the king of Babylon slew the sons of Zede- 10
kiah before his eyes: he slew also all the princes of Judah
in Riblah. Then he put out the eyes of Zedekiah; and the 11
king of Babylon bound him in chains, and carried him to
Babylon, and put him in prison till the day of his death.

12—27. *Severities following upon the Capture.*

Now in the fifth month, in the tenth *day* of the month, 12
which *was* the nineteenth year of Nebuchadrezzar king of
Babylon, came Nebuzar-adan, captain of the guard, *which*
served the king of Babylon, into Jerusalem, and burnt the 13

in the land of Hamath] not found in 2 Kings.
he gave judgment upon him] See note on i. 16. In 2 Kings it is *they gave*.
10. *the king of Babylon slew*] 2 Kings, *they slew*.
he slew also all the princes of Judah in Riblah] omitted in 2 Kings.
the princes] See note on *nobles*, xxxix. 6.
11. *he put out the eyes*] See note on xxxiv. 3, and on xxxix. 7.
the king of Babylon] not found in 2 Kings.
and put him in prison till the day of his death] an addition to the narrative in 2 Kings, which takes leave of Zedekiah at Riblah, since that record was probably made before anything further could be learned of him.
prison] The Septuagint render *mill*, and hence it has been inferred that they ascribed to him the same fate in his old age, as that to which the Philistines consigned Samson (Jud. xvi. 21).

12—27. SEVERITIES FOLLOWING UPON THE CAPTURE.

12. From this to ver 23, a part of the narrative which has been summarized in xxxix. 8—10, we find an almost verbal accord with 2 Kings xxv. 8—17.
in the fifth month] See Zech. vii. 3 for the commemorative fast.
tenth] 2 Kings has *seventh*. Such discrepancies in numerals are often explained by supposing that the numbers were denoted originally by letters, so that similar letters might well be mistaken one for another by copyists. Here however it is easy to allow such a margin of time between the arrival of Nebuzar-adan in the neighbourhood of Jerusalem and his actual entry upon the work which he had been sent to do. He is not mentioned in xxxix. 3 in the list of generals who entered the city at once.
the nineteenth year of Nebuchadrezzar] B.C. 586 or 587, according as we reckon his reign from the time of his father's actual decease or from the previous year.
captain of the guard] See note on xxxix. 9.
served] **stood before.** The expression implies close personal attendance on the king. (Compare note on xv. 19). The mass, even of those about the palace, would not have access to his presence. 2 Kings

house of the LORD, and the king's house; and all the houses of Jerusalem, and all the houses of the great *men*, 14 burnt he with fire: and all the army of the Chaldeans, that were with the captain of the guard, brake down all the walls 15 of Jerusalem round about. Then Nebuzar-adan the captain of the guard carried away captive *certain* of the poor of the people, and the residue of the people that remained in the city, and those that fell away, that fell to the king of 16 Babylon, and the rest of the multitude. But Nebuzar-adan the captain of the guard left *certain* of the poor of the land 17 for vinedressers and for husbandmen. Also the pillars of brass that *were* in the house of the LORD, and the bases, and the brasen sea that *was* in the house of the LORD, the Chaldeans brake, and carried all the brass of them to Babylon. 18 The caldrons also, and the shovels, and the snuffers,

has simply *a servant* of the king of Babylon. The Heb. by itself is ambiguous, and but for our knowing otherwise that Nebuchadnezzar was not at Jerusalem at this time, might mean, as the Syr. and Vulg. actually render, *stood before the king* at *Jerusalem*.

13. *all the houses of the great men*] Both here and in the parallel passage in 2 Kings xxv. 9 (where however the Heb. is slightly different), the rendering should rather be **every great house**. The words are intended to prevent a misconception arising out of those which immediately precede them. All the *houses of importance* were burned.

14. 'with' and 'all' are omitted in the Kings, the former doubtless by accident.

15. The whole verse is omitted by the Septuagint. The words 'certain of the poor of the people and' seem to have come in from the next verse through an error of sight on the part of a copyist. The three classes of persons actually spoken of in the verse appear to be (*a*) those found within the city at the time of its capture, (*b*) those who had gone out to the Chaldaeans during the siege (see note on xxxix. 9), (*c*) the country people. The word denoting this last (*the multitude*) occurs once (Prov. viii. 30) in the sense of *workman* (Eng. Vers. "one brought up with him"). From a comparison of the parallel passages however it is not likely that such is its sense here.

16. *Nebuzar-adan*] omitted in Kings.

17. This description of the fate of the Temple furniture is much fuller than in the Kings' passage, and has no parallel whatever in chap. xxxix. For the vessels here mentioned see chap. xxvii. 19 with note. They were too large to be conveniently carried as they were, and so were broken and taken to Babylon for the sake of the material. In Kings *all* is omitted before *the brass*.

18. *caldrons*] for carrying away the ashes after sacrifice, *the shovels* being for a similar purpose.

and the bowls, and the spoons, and all the vessels of brass wherewith they ministered, took they *away*. And the ba- 19 sons, and the firepans, and the bowls, and the caldrons, and the candlesticks, and the spoons, and the cups; *that* which *was of* gold *in* gold, and *that* which *was of* silver *in* silver, took the captain of the guard *away*. The two pillars, one 20 sea, and twelve brasen bulls that *were* under the bases, which king Solomon had made in the house of the LORD: the brass of all these vessels was without weight. And 21 *concerning* the pillars, the height of one pillar *was* eighteen cubits; and a fillet of twelve cubits did compass it; and the thickness thereof *was* four fingers: *it was* hollow. And a 22 chapiter of brass *was* upon it; and the height of one chapiter *was* five cubits, with network and pomegranates upon the chapiters round about, all *of* brass. The second pillar

spoons] **incense-cups**. This we gather from Numb. vii. 14, etc.
19. *fire pans*] or, *snuff-dishes*.
bowls] This word should probably stand but once (see ver. 18). In the Kings it is omitted on the earlier occasion. *Caldrons* and *spoons* also occur twice in this enumeration, while in Kings these articles as well as *candlesticks* and *cups* do not appear.
20. The repetition marks the regretful contemplation of these things by the writer, as he connects them with the golden age of the kingdom and the reign of Solomon.
twelve brasen bulls that were under] These words do not occur in the Kings' passage, and hence it is possible that they may be an erroneous addition made at some time to the sacred Text. This is however far from certain, as the figures in question were probably at Jerusalem up to this date, and so would naturally form a conspicuous feature in the spoil. There remains however a certain amount of difficulty in the description of their position. In the Temple as built by Solomon the bases were under the lavers, while the bulls supported the sea. (1 Kings vii. 25, 43.)
21. *eighteen cubits*] a cubit was about 18 inches.
fillet] literally, *thread*.
four fingers] about four inches. Thus as the diameter was something under six feet (the circumference being twelve cubits=eighteen feet), about five feet of the diameter were hollow.
22. *a chapiter*] a capital.
five cubits] From this, which agrees with 1 Kings vii. 16, we must correct the "*three* cubits" of 2 Kings xxv. 17, unless we take the smaller number to denote the actual measurement of the network of the chapiter, excluding the pomegranates.
pomegranates] a very common ornament in Assyria both for buildings and weapons.

23 also and the pomegranates *were* like unto these. And there were ninety and six pomegranates on a side; *and* all the pomegranates upon the net work *were* an hundred round 24 about. And the captain of the guard took Seraiah the chief priest, and Zephaniah the second priest, and the three 25 keepers of the door: he took also out of the city an eunuch, which had the charge of the men of war; and seven men of them that were near the king's person, which were found in the city; and the principal scribe of the host, who mustered the people of the land; and threescore men of the people 26 of the land, that were found in the midst of the city. So Nebuzar-adan the captain of the guard took them, and 27 brought them to the king of Babylon to Riblah. And the king of Babylon smote them, and put them to death in

23. There is an apparent discrepancy between the number of the pomegranates as given here and in 1 Kings vii. 20. From the latter passage we gather that each pillar had two rows, a hundred in each, the one above and the other below the ornamental network of the chapiters. It is possible that the account here may not be inconsistent with the existence of such a *double* row upon each chapiter, though it certainly does not suggest it, or again, one of the rows may have been removed before this period, leaving one hundred on each chapiter, probably twenty-four on each side, (Heb. *windward*, i.e. directly facing each wind,) and one at each corner. We should thus render *on a side*, **on the (four) sides**, in order to bring out the sense.

24—27. This passage is omitted in xxxix., but is almost identical with 2 Kings xxv. 18—21.

24. *Seraiah the chief priest*] Nebuzar-adan chose out those who were highest in authority and therefore most responsible for the prolonged resistance. His conduct in this respect has been remarked on, as shewing a very pleasing contrast with the indiscriminate vengeance so often wreaked by Eastern conquerors. This Seraiah is identified by some with him who is mentioned in Ezra vii. 1.

Zephaniah] See note on xxi. 1.

keepers of the door] See note on xxxv. 4.

25. *which had the charge of*] The Heb. is *who was Pakîd* (*lieutenant*) *over*. For remarks on the sense of Pakîd see note on xx. 1.

seven men] in the King's passage *five* men.

were near the king's person] literally, *saw the king's face*. See note on ver. 12.

principal scribe of the host] or, *scribe of the* **commander in chief**, a rendering which the words that follow make the more probable of the two.

threescore men of the people of the land] perhaps leading men whose homes were in the country parts.

Riblah in the land of Hamath. Thus Judah was carried away captive out of his own land.

28—30. *Enumeration of Nebuchadnezzar's captives.*

28 This *is* the people whom Nebuchadrezzar carried away captive: in the seventh year three thousand Jews and three and twenty: 29 in the eighteenth year of Nebuchadrezzar he carried away captive from Jerusalem eight hundred thirty and two persons: 30 in the three and twentieth year of Nebuchadrezzar Nebuzar-adan the captain of the guard carried away captive *of* the Jews seven hundred forty and five persons: all the persons *were* four thousand and six hundred.

31—34. *Last notice of Jehoiachin.*

31 And it came to pass in the seven and thirtieth year of

28—30. ENUMERATION OF NEBUCHADNEZZAR'S CAPTIVES.

28. *in the seventh year*] This passage does not occur in the Septuagint, perhaps as coming out of a separate document from the rest, and containing certain difficulties. In the *seventh year* the reference can hardly be to the captivity of Jehoiakim, as that was in the *eighth* year of Nebuchadnezzar, and the number of captives was far greater than is here specified (2 Kings xxiv. 12, 14). Probably therefore the Heb. for *tenth* has dropped out before *seventh*, and we are to read *seventeenth* year. If then we consider the document from which this is taken to have dated from Nebuchadnezzar's *formal* (one year later than his *actual*) accession (see note on ver. 12), we make the reference to be to the time when the siege was going on (his eighteenth year, according to the common reckoning). Thus this captivity would consist chiefly, at any rate, of inhabitants of the *country* parts. In the next year, his '*eighteenth*' (nineteenth), Jerusalem was taken, and the second of these three deportations took place, while five years later in his '*three and twentieth* (four and twentieth) *year*', (and therefore a considerable time after the troubles related chaps. xl.—xlii.), a third deportation occurred, of which we have no other account than this. To reconcile the total given here (ver. 30) with the much larger number who returned with Ezra (Ezra ii. 64) leaving many behind in Babylon, we have only to remember (*a*) those who were carried away with Jehoiachin before any of the three captivities here mentioned, (*b*) the probably constant emigration of Jews to Babylon, and (*c*) the lapse of time, equal to two generations, which intervened before the return.

31—34. LAST NOTICE OF JEHOIACHIN.

31. This passage occurs also with slight variations in 2 Kings xxv. 27—30.

the seven and thirtieth year] B.C. 561, as his captivity had begun B.C. 597.

the captivity of Jehoiachin king of Judah, in the twelfth
month, in the five and twentieth *day* of the month, *that*
Evil-merodach king of Babylon in the *first* year of his
reign lifted up the head of Jehoiachin king of Judah, and
32 brought him forth out of prison, and spake kindly unto him,
and set his throne above the throne of the kings that *were*
33 with him in Babylon, and changed his prison garments:
and he did continually eat bread before him all the days of
34 his life. And *for* his diet, there was a continual diet given
him of the king of Babylon, every day a portion until the
day of his death, all the days of his life.

the five and twentieth day of the month] in 2 Kings xxv. 27 *the* seven
and twentieth *day of the month*.
Evil-merodach] son of Nebuchadnezzar. He reigned two years, and
was slain by his brother-in-law Neriglissar (the Nergal-sharezer of xxxix.
3, 13) who succeeded him.
lifted up the head] For the phrase in this sense compare Gen. xl. 13,
20.
32. *set his throne above*] in general, *paid him more honour*.
the kings] captured kings were kept at the court of their conqueror as
a means of perpetuating the memory of his triumph. Compare Jud. i.
7. So Crœsus dwelt at the court of Cyrus.
33. *changed his prison garments*] Compare Gen. xli. 42; Esth.
viii. 15; Dan. v. 29; Luke xv. 22. The frequent mention of such a
circumstance shews the importance attaching in the Oriental mind
to the style of a person's dress.
did continually eat bread before him] was admitted to the king's
own table. Compare 2 Sam. ix. 7, xix. 33, etc. So this privilege was
accorded to Democêdês the Greek physician after his cure of Darius,
(Herod. iii. 132).
34. *until the day of his death, all the days of his life*] The latter òf
these clauses, as the text now stands, is probably either an addition to,
or originally a substitution for, the former, in order to avoid the in-
auspicious ending with the word *death*. The general object too of the
paragraph seems to have been somewhat similar, viz. to leave the
reader with a parting ray of comfort and encouragement in the thought
that even in exile the Lord remembered His people and softened the
heart of the heathen tyrant towards David's seed.

THE LAMENTATIONS OF JEREMIAH.

INTRODUCTION.

CHAPTER I.

NAME, POSITION, DATE AND STRUCTURE OF THE BOOK.

1. The name Lamentations corresponds to that under which this Book appears in the Latin Vulgate, and which is a translation of the Septuagint *Threni*, itself a rendering of the Heb. word *Kînôth*. This last, though not prefixed to the Book, is yet of frequent occurrence in the Hebrew Scriptures: Jeremiah uses the word three times (vii. 29, ix. 10, 20 [in the Heb. 9, 19]; each time rendered "lamentation"). It is the title of David's funeral song over Saul and Jonathan in 2 Sam. i. 17, while the corresponding verb is used in the Heb. of 2 Sam. iii. 33. This last is also used of the dirge composed by Jeremiah on the death of Josiah in battle (2 Chron. xxxv. 25). The title of the Book itself in the Heb. Canon is *Aichah*, (=*How*), the word which commences the first, second and fourth of the five songs to which the five chapters correspond. It is in accordance with Jewish custom to name a Book of the Bible by a conspicuous word at or near its beginning.

2. This book is placed in the Heb. in the last division (*C'thubhim = Psalms*, etc.) according to the threefold classification of the Jewish Scriptures (see Luke xxiv. 44). It is thus rightly reckoned by them among the poetical books of the Canon. It is now placed for synagogue use as one of the five *Megilloth*

(or *Rolls*, appointed to be read on special occasions), which stand thus, Canticles, Ruth, Lamentations, Ecclesiastes, Esther.

3. The date, as determined by Josephus, is considerably earlier than the one generally received. That writer (*Antiq.* X. 5) says, referring no doubt to this Book, that "Jeremiah composed a dirge for Josiah's funeral, *which remains unto this day.*" He was apparently misled by the statement in 2 Chron. xxxv. 25 (see § 1 above) that the dirges composed by Jeremiah and others on that occasion were "written in the *Lamentations.*" St Jerome supported this view, and in particular chap. iv. was referred to this event and not to the capture of Zedekiah. Both the earliest external testimony, however, viz. that of the Septuagint (see chap. ii. § 1), and the contents of the Book itself, point to the events of which a brief sketch is given in Jer. xxxix. and lii. That the Book could not have been written *long* after this time is clear from the graphic manner in which the horrors of the siege are portrayed. We know from the history that Jeremiah was well off in comparison with many of his countrymen after the capture of the city, and the favour shewn him by the Chaldaeans may well have allowed him the opportunity of writing this Book some time before he went down to Egypt. "In the face of a rocky hill, on the western side of the city, the local belief has placed 'the Grotto of Jeremiah.' There in that fixed attitude of grief, which Michael Angelo has immortalised, the Prophet may well be supposed to have mourned the fall of his country."—Stanley's *J. Ch.* II. 473.

4. Four out of the five poems of which this Book consists, may be divided into as many parts (viz. twenty-two) as there are letters of the Heb. alphabet, beginning with the letters consecutively, except in one case, where in the second, third and fourth chapters the order of certain two letters is reversed. More than one of the alphabetical Psalms also shews breaks in the strict order of succession of the letters. The peculiar and hitherto unexplained feature however in the present Book is that it is the *same pair* of letters in each of the three cases which are thus transposed. Further, if we take the four alphabetical poems separately, we find that in the first three each of

the twenty-two parts (or verses, but note that in chap. iii. each part = *three* Eng. verses) itself may as a rule be subdivided into three, in chapter iv. into two only, while in the third chapter each of these three subdivisions (or verses) begins with the same letter, and is itself divisible into two. In chap. v., although the number of the verses is the same, the alphabetical order is dropped. The above mentioned artificial arrangement, by which a definite rule for the beginning of verses was attained, may be compared with modern rhymed endings, as well as with the more complicated Greek and Latin metres. In such a structure of the poems we may easily discern an additional advantage here, as aiding the memory of the captives to recall them in their distant exile.

CHAPTER II.

AUTHORSHIP OF THE BOOK.

1. That the Book of the Lamentations is the work of Jeremiah the prophet has been the apparently universal belief first of the Jewish and then of the Christian Church from the earliest times until recently. The Hebrew indeed contains no direct assertion of the fact. The earliest extant translation however, that called by the name Septuagint, ascribes it to him in a note prefixed to the first chapter to the following effect, "*And it came to pass after Israel was taken captive and Jerusalem made desolate, Jeremiah sat weeping and lamented with this lamentation over Jerusalem, and said.*" This evidence brings us back to at least one or two centuries before Christ. Other early authorities also ascribe the Book to Jeremiah, while the Latin Vulgate (4th cent. A.D.) repeats the assertion of the Septuagint, as given above, amplifying however the last words into "*and in bitterness of heart sighing and crying said.*"

2. A few persons in recent times, assuming that the prophecies commonly attributed to Jeremiah are at any rate in the main rightly so ascribed, have suggested the following objections

to the received view that the Lamentations are the composition of the same author:

(*a*) Contradictions between the two Books;

(*b*) Inconsistencies in language;

(*c*) Inconsistencies in form;

(*d*) The occurrence of quotations from Ezekiel, shewing therefore that the Book in which they occur must be of a later date than that prophet.

3. Taking these objections singly (and marking the answers by the same letters), we may reply as follows:

(*a*) But one alleged contradiction is cited, viz. the teaching of Jer. xxxi. 29, 30 (that children shall not be punished for the misdeeds of their ancestors) when compared with Lam. v. 7, "we have borne their (i.e. our fathers') iniquities". And here the charge, if it were made at all, should rather have been that Jeremiah in his prophecies was inconsistent with himself, for in chap. xxxii. 18 we read "Thou...recompensest the iniquity of the fathers into the bosom of their children after them." In point of fact however all these passages are quite in harmony as well with each other as with the teaching of the second Commandment. Suffering as the consequence of sin naturally propagates itself through successive generations of sinners, but the operation of this law of God is at once, in the case of the repentant sinner, arrested by His gracious law of forgiveness and mercy towards those who love Him and keep His commandments.

(*b*) The less prominence given in the Lamentations to the sins of the people (which are however spoken of frequently, viz. chaps. i. 5, 8, 14, 18, 22, ii. 14, iii. 39, 42, iv. 6, 13, v. 7) quite falls in with the respective characters and objects of the two works. In the earlier, addressed as it was directly to the people, rebuke found naturally a prominent place. In the latter the prophet is pouring out his grief to God, and the case is thereby made materially different. It is now the language of a sufferer rather than of a teacher. In general however the peculiarities of Jeremiah which fall naturally under the head of *language*, are found in the most striking manner throughout the Lamentations. Besides the "union of strong passionate feeling and entire submission to Jehovah which characterizes both... In both we meet, once and again, with the picture of the 'Virgin daughter of Zion' sitting down in her shame and misery (Lam. i. 15, ii. 13; Jer. xiv. 17). In both there is the same vehement outpouring of sorrow. The prophet's eyes flow down with tears (Lam. i. 16, ii. 11, iii. 48, 49; Jer. ix. 1, xiii. 17, xiv. 17). There is the same haunting feeling of being *surrounded* with fears and terrors on every side (Lam. ii. 22; Jer. vi. 25, xlvi. 5). In both the worst of all the evils is the iniquity of the prophets and the priests (Lam. ii. 14, iv. 13; Jer. v. 30, 31, xiv. 13, 14). The sufferer appeals for vengeance to the righteous Judge (Lam. iii. 64—66; Jer. xi. 20). He bids the rival nation that exulted in the fall of Jerusalem prepare for a like desolation (Lam. iv. 21; Jer. xlix. 12)" (Prof. Plumptre in *Sm. Bibl. Dict.*). To this we may add the expressions concerning personal bodily sufferings on the part of the writer of Lam. iii. 52—55 as compared with Jer. xxxviii. 6—13. Besides the explanation of the differences of language as arising from the difference of character between the two Books, which has been already noticed, we may note the fact that one is the language of prose, the other of poetry, and we find moreover in both the strongly marked tendency to quote from older Books of the Bible, but, in accordance with what has just been said, in the case of the Prophecy, from Deuteronomy, in that of the Poems, from the Psalms as being a poetical Book. We find also that in both Books the writer repeats himself much.

(*c*) The principle of the reply has been already shewn under the head of (*b*). To the particular objection e. g. arising from the alphabetical structure of the poems (see last chapter) we may answer as before that as prophecy and history are essentially different from poetry, so the same writer when turning to a new kind of composition may well be allowed to adopt the peculiarities which belong to it.

(*d*) Taking the two supposed instances of quotation from Ezekiel (viz. Lam. ii. 14 compared with Ezek. xii. 24, xiii. 6, etc., and Lam. ii. 15 compared with Ezek. xxvii. 3, xxviii. 12) we may shew (i) that even though they be quotations from that prophet, this is no argument against Jeremiah's authorship; and (ii) that there is no reason in point of fact to assume that these two passages are quotations from him.

(i) There must have been frequent intercourse between the Jews taken captive with Jehoiakim and those who remained behind (see Jer. xxix 25), and nothing is more likely under such circumstances than that Jeremiah and Ezekiel were made speedily aware each of the other's utterances.

(ii) In Lam. ii. 14, "*vain* and foolish things" is literally "*unreal* and foolish things," while the word thus used is the same as Ezekiel's elsewhere, but differing from that commonly employed by Jeremiah, who uses a word expressive rather of moral obliquity than simple unreality. The aims of the two Books however, as we noticed above, differ. In the former, addressed directly to the people, the *iniquity* of their deeds would be insisted on, while the latter, addressed as an appeal to the mercy of God, would dwell upon the *folly* and *unreality* of their aims. In the second instance Jerusalem is called "the perfection of beauty," while a similar expression is applied to Tyre twice by Ezekiel. Almost the same word however occurs in Ps. l. 2 of Zion, and as the words which conclude the verse in the Lamentations are obviously a quotation from Ps. xlviii. 2 (which also refers to Zion), it seems clear that the earlier part of the verse is but supplying us with one more instance of a quotation of the kind which we have just noticed (see (*b*) above) to be so frequent in the Lamentations.

On the whole therefore we conclude that Jeremiah was beyond question the writer of this Book.

CHAPTER III.

SUBJECT-MATTER AND PURPOSE OF THE BOOK.

1. The subject, as we have seen already, is undoubtedly the capture of the city under Nebuchadnezzar, and the sorrow and suffering which were thereby entailed. Herewith is united both the confession that this has come upon the people on account of their sins, and entreaties for deliverance.

2. Taking the poems severally,

Chap. i. dwells upon the solitary condition and grief of the city;

Chap. ii. sets forth the destruction that has come upon her, and acknowledges that it is the result of sin;

Chap. iii., which although framed for the most part in the singular number, yet includes the nation throughout, complains of the bitter cup which God's people have to drink, and yet acknowledges that the trials which are come upon them are inflicted by a Father's hand;

Chap. iv. describes the reverses in fortune that have been brought about by recent events, and again acknowledges sin;

Chap. v. recapitulates the pitiful details of their condition, and ends by an earnest prayer for deliverance.

3. The Book from an historical point of view thus forms a supplement to the Book of Jeremiah. There we traced the life and thoughts of the prophet while events were gradually leading to the final catastrophe. Here we see him after that catastrophe has been reached, and mark that it is the same man still, clearly recognizing the sin of his fellows, but as full as ever of sympathy for them and of love for his country. "All feeling of exultation in which, as mere prophet of evil, he might have indulged at the fulfilment of his forebodings, was swallowed up in deep overwhelming sorrow" (Prof. Plumptre in *Sm. Bibl. Dict.*).

4. It was not in one who had faithfully warned his countrymen for so long, to keep silence now, and doubtless the very

pouring out of his heart in this form gave his sorrow a certain relief. As he had probably lamented for Josiah in some such manner (2 Chron. xxxv. 25), so now he was moved to come forward and embody in language those thoughts which an inspired prophet like him would be guided to publish and record.

5. "There are perhaps few portions of the Old Testament which appear to have done the work they were meant to do more effectually than this." It has not been connected with the theological or ecclesiastical disputes of any age, while it has supplied the earnest Christian of all times with words in which to confess his sins, and shortcomings, as well as with a picture of Him Who bore our sins and carried our sorrows, on Whom was "laid the iniquity of us all."

6. The Book is annually read among the Jews to commemorate the burning of the Temple. The following is Schaff's description (*Through Bible Lands*, pp. 250—252) of the scene at the 'Wailing Place of the Jews' at Jerusalem. "There the Jews assemble every Friday afternoon and on festivals to bewail the downfall of the holy city. I saw on Good Friday a large number, old and young, male and female, venerable rabbis with patriarchal beards and young men kissing the stone wall and watering it with their tears. They repeat from their well-worn Hebrew Bibles and Prayer-books the Lamentations of Jeremiah and suitable Psalms. . . . The key note of all these laments and prayers was struck by Jeremiah, the most pathetic and tender hearted of prophets, in the Lamentations, that funeral dirge of Jerusalem and the theocracy. This elegy, written with sighs and tears, has done its work most effectually in great public calamities, and is doing it every year on the ninth of the month Ab (July), when it is read with loud weeping in all the synagogues of the Jews and especially at Jerusalem. It keeps alive the memory of their deepest humiliation and guilt and the hope of final deliverance. The scene of the Wailing Place was to me touching and pregnant with meaning."

THE LAMENTATIONS OF JEREMIAH.

CHAP. I. 1—22. *The Miseries of Jerusalem.*

(א) How doth the city sit solitary, *that was* full of 1 people!
How is she become as a widow! she *that was* great among the nations,

CHAP. I. 1—22. THE MISERIES OF JERUSALEM.

The general subject running through this first chapter may be thus subdivided. Verses 1—11 lament the sufferings which Jerusalem is now undergoing, while twice in the course of this portion (verses 9, 11) the city itself breaks out into a wail of distress, and thus leads up to the second division of the chapter, verses 12—22, where the city itself is the speaker. In that second part also, their suffering is from time to time (ver. 14, etc.) spoken of as the consequence of sin, and thus we arrive at chap. ii., where that is the leading thought. See Introduction, chap. III. § 2.

We may compare these opening verses with Is. xlvii. 1. In both places we are reminded of the figure on the medal struck by Titus, to commemorate his capture of Jerusalem (A.D. 71), a woman weeping beneath a palm-tree with the inscription below, *Judaea capta*. The same picture is here presented to us, and we see thus personified the inhabitants shortly after the siege, while the miseries which accompanied and succeeded it were still fresh.

1. *How*] The Heb. (*Aichah*), which occurs also at the commencement of chaps. ii. and iv., as well as in ver. 2 of the latter, has supplied the Jewish name for this book, the custom of naming the books of the Bible by the first word being a common one with them.

sit solitary] as emptied by the departure of the captives, and deserted by her friends, and by God Himself.

how is she become] We must amend the Heb. (Masoretic) punctuation of the verse, by which it is divided into two main portions, the former of them ending with *widow*. The division should be threefold, the second and third parts running thus, **She is become as a widow, she that was great among the nations; a princess among the provinces, she is become tributary.** A threefold division of this kind prevails almost throughout.

And princess among the provinces, *how* is she become tributary!

2 (ב) She weepeth sore in the night, and her tears *are* on her cheeks:
Among all her lovers she hath none to comfort *her*:
All her friends have dealt treacherously with her, they are become her enemies.

3 (ג) Judah is gone into captivity because of affliction, and because of great servitude:
She dwelleth among the heathen, she findeth no rest:
All her persecutors overtook her between the straits.

4 (ד) The ways of Zion do mourn, because none come to the solemn feasts:

a widow] From Is. xlvii. 8. Some have thought the reference here to be to the loss of her king, or of great men and friends in general. When however we compare the use of the figure of widowhood in Is. liv. 4, 5, as well as such passages as Jer. ii. 2, it appears that the Lord is the husband who has been lost.

provinces] This name is once used of the peoples dependent on the king of Syria (1 Kings xx. 17), and afterwards frequently of those subject to the Persian empire (Esth. i. 1, etc.), and is used of Judah itself in Ezra ii. 1; Neh. vii. 6. Here it seems to be used of the neighbouring nations, Moab, Edom, etc., which were now falling under the Babylonian yoke, but had formerly been subject to the (undivided) kingdom of Israel.

tributary] **a vassal.** The original word implies bond-service, and it was only in later times that it was used of tribute, e.g. Esth. x. 1.

2. *in the night*] The time of natural silence and darkness is made a part of the picture in order to heighten the effect.

her lovers...her friends] the neighbouring states, with whom in the sunshine of prosperity she was on friendly terms. Such were Egypt, etc. For Edom, as having turned against her at this time, see latter part of note on *Concerning Edom*, Jer. xlix. 7, and for a similar charge against the Ammonites, Ezek. xxv. 3, 6.

3. *is gone into captivity because of affliction*] The better rendering is, *is gone into* **exile** *because of affliction*, i.e. the long sufferings of the Jews at the hands of Egypt and Chaldaea had induced many of them to go voluntarily to dwell in other lands. That there were many such persons, we gather from Jer. xl. 11. Others however would explain the passage of the Babylonish captivity, and render (*taken*) *out of affliction*, etc.

between the straits] The figure is taken from hunting. The Jews have been like animals, driven into a narrow space, that they may be the more easily attacked.

4. *The ways of Zion do mourn*] The approaches to Jerusalem are

All her gates are desolate: her priests sigh:
Her virgins *are* afflicted, and she *is* in bitterness.
(ה) Her adversaries are the chief, her enemies prosper; 5
For the LORD hath afflicted her for the multitude of her transgressions:
Her children are gone *into* captivity before the enemy.
(ו) And from the daughter of Zion all her beauty is 6 departed:
Her princes are become like harts *that* find no pasture,
And they are gone without strength before the pursuer.
(ז) Jerusalem remembered in the days of her affliction 7 and of her miseries
All her pleasant things that she had in the days of old,
When her people fell into the hand of the enemy, and none did help her:

meant. They are desolate, without the usual throng of those coming up to the feasts at the Holy City, which, since its religious aspect is here referred to, is spoken of as 'Zion'.

For the thought of inanimate objects as sympathizing with human affairs, we may compare the well-known passage (Scott's *Lay of the Last Minstrel*, canto v.), beginning

> Call it not vain—they do not err,
>   Who say, that, when the Poet dies,
> Mute Nature mourns her worshipper,
>   And celebrates his obsequies.

all her gates are desolate] Compare Jer. xiv. 2, with note.
her virgins are afflicted] They are mentioned as taking part in religious ceremonies. See Exod. xv. 20; Jud. xxi. 19, 21; Ps. lxviii. 25.

5. *are the chief*] In the Heb. the phrase is the same as that used in Deut. xxviii. 44 ("he shall *be the head*"), where this is foretold as the result of Israel's obstinacy.

prosper] literally, **are at peace**. See Jer. xii. 1, where the Eng. Vers. has "are...happy".

before the enemy] driven like a flock of cattle.

6. *beauty*] **glory**.

her princes are become like harts] The prophet is thinking of the flight and capture of Zedekiah and his princes, Jer. xxxix. 4, 5.

7. *remembered*] **has remembered**.

miseries] The original word is a rare one, and means *compulsory wanderings, persecutions*.

enemy] **adversary**. The word is the same as that which is so rendered immediately afterwards.

The adversaries saw her, *and* did mock at her sabbaths.

8 (ה) Jerusalem hath grievously sinned; therefore she is removed:
All that honoured her despise her, because they have seen her nakedness:
Yea, she sigheth, and turneth backward.

9 (ט) Her filthiness *is* in her skirts; she remembereth not her last end;
Therefore she came down wonderfully: she had no comforter.
O Lord, behold my affliction: for the enemy hath magnified *himself*.

10 (י) The adversary hath spread out his hand upon all her pleasant things:
For she hath seen *that* the heathen entered into her sanctuary,
Whom thou didst command *that* they should not enter into thy congregation.

11 (כ) All her people sigh, they seek bread;
They have given their pleasant things for meat to relieve the soul:

sabbaths] either, (i) the regularly recurring day of rest, which was, we know, a subject in regard to which other nations displayed as much ignorance as wonder, e.g. "Where kings the sabbath barefoot celebrate", Juvenal, Sat. vi. Gifford's Translation, l. 233; or, (ii) compulsory rest (*sabbatism;* compare the Greek in Heb. iv. 9), which the land now had. See Lev. xxvi. 34, 35.

8. *is removed*] *is* **become an abomination.** This and the next verse in figurative language describe the Jewish people, as having brought upon itself through sin and consequent national humiliation the contempt of all its neighbours, while it is painfully conscious of its own ignominy (compare iv. 21).

9. *she came down wonderfully*] Compare Is. xlvii. 1.

O Lord, behold] See introductory note to chapter.

10. *pleasant*] literally, *desirable, precious*.

the heathen entered into her sanctuary] Those who were forbidden, at any rate as nations, ever to enter into a religious covenant with Israel (e.g. Ammonites and Moabites, Deut. xxiii. 3, 4), now, as part of the invading host, entered the very Holy of Holies for plunder. No worse humiliation could befall a Jew than this.

11. The people have already given up their most valuable possessions, that they had hitherto hoarded, for bread. There is therefore nothing now between them and starvation.

meat] food. Compare note on *meat offerings*, Jer. xvii. 26.

See, O LORD, and consider; for I am become vile.

(ל) *Is it* nothing to you, all ye that pass by? behold, 12
and see
If there be any sorrow like unto my sorrow, which is done
unto me,
Wherewith the LORD hath afflicted *me* in the day of his
fierce anger.

(מ) From above hath he sent fire into my bones, and it 13
prevaileth against them:
He hath spread a net for my feet, he hath turned me
back;
He hath made me desolate *and* faint all the day.

(נ) The yoke of my transgressions is bound by his 14
hand:
They are wreathed, *and* come up upon my neck: he hath
made my strength to fall,
The Lord hath delivered me into *their* hands, *from whom*
I am not able to rise up.

---

to relieve the soul] literally, *to bring back the life*. Compare verses 16, 19.

see, O Lord] Compare introductory note to chapter.

12. The beginning of the second section of the chapter. See introductory note.

Is it nothing to you] This is almost certainly right, although the words have also been translated as not interrogative, either, *Look not on yourselves*, or, by a slightly different reading of the Heb., *I adjure all you*, etc. This latter seems that which was originally followed by the Septuagint, whose reading now however is obscure.

13. *From above*] i.e. from heaven.

it prevaileth against] *it* subdueth.

he hath spread a net for my feet] For the figure compare Jer. l. 24.

turned me back] The metaphor from hunting is continued (see ver. 3). The people are driven into a corner, and then the way is blocked, and they are headed back.

14. *is bound*] The Heb. verb occurs here only, and hence the sense is not quite certain. The Eng. however is probably correct. The manifold sins of the people are likened to a complication of cords, attaching a yoke on the neck of a beast of burden, and keeping it secure in its place. Compare note on "bonds and yokes" of Jer. xxvii. 2.

wreathed] twisted together.

to fall] literally, *to stumble*.

15 (ס) The Lord hath trodden under foot all my mighty *men* in the midst of me:
He hath called an assembly against me to crush my young men:
The Lord hath trodden the virgin, the daughter of Judah, *as in* a winepress.

16 (ע) For these *things* I weep; mine eye, mine eye runneth down *with* water,
Because the comforter that *should* relieve my soul is far from me:
My children are desolate, because the enemy prevailed.

17 (פ) Zion spreadeth forth her hands, *and there is* none to comfort her:
The Lord hath commanded concerning Jacob, *that* his adversaries *should be* round about him:
Jerusalem is as a menstruous *woman* among them.

15. *hath trodden under foot all my mighty men*] rather, **hath made of no account all my strong ones.** Compare Ps. cxix. 118, where the same word ("hast trodden down," Eng. Vers.), should be rendered *hast made light of*. The verb means properly to lift up, and hence that which can be easily lifted, which is easily *outweighed*, here, e.g. by the Chaldaeans when they are placed as it were in the opposite scale.

hath called an assembly] hath **summoned a solemn assembly.** This is the ordinary application of the substantive, which primarily means *an appointed time* and hence a *solemn assembly*, or *festival*. The festival is for the enemy, and that which is to be celebrated, the overthrow of the flower of the Jewish army.

hath trodden...] **hath trodden the wine press for the virgin daughter of Judah.** For *treading the winepress*, as a phrase to express the wrath of God, compare Is. lxiii. 3; Rev. xiv. 19, xix. 15, and for *the virgin daughter of Judah*, Jer. xiv. 17.

16. *For these things*] The particulars rehearsed in the last three verses open again the floodgates of tears.

mine eye, mine eye] This repetition is quite in Jeremiah's style. Compare Jer. iv. 19, vi. 14 (and again, viii. 11), xxii. 29, xxiii. 25.

mine eye runneth down with water] See iii. 48, and compare the phrase "to weep one's eyes out."

relieve my soul] Compare ver. 11.

17. *spreadeth forth her hands*] in supplication. Compare Exod. ix. 29; 1 Kings viii. 38, etc.

that his adversaries should be round about him] **those who are about him are his adversaries.** The neighbouring nations look upon Jerusalem at once with hatred, and, as the last words express, with contempt.

(צ) The LORD *is* righteous; for I have rebelled against 18
his commandment:
Hear, I pray you, all people, and behold my sorrow:
My virgins and my young men are gone into captivity.
(ק) I called for my lovers, *but* they deceived me: 19
My priests and mine elders gave up the ghost in the city,
While they sought their meat, to relieve their souls.
(ר) Behold, O LORD; for I *am* in distress: my bowels 20
are troubled;
Mine heart is turned within me; for I have grievously
rebelled:
Abroad the sword bereaveth, at home *there is* as death.
(ש) They have heard that I sigh; *there is* none to com- 21
fort me:
All mine enemies have heard of my trouble; they are
glad that thou hast done *it:*
Thou wilt bring the day *that* thou hast called, and they
shall be like unto me.
(ת) Let all their wickedness come before thee; 22
And do unto them, as thou hast done unto me for all my
transgressions:

18. *I have rebelled against his commandment*] This confession of sin is an anticipation of that which is so prominent in the next chapter. Compare, in the next verse but one, "I have grievously rebelled."
people] **peoples.**
19. *for my lovers*] to *my lovers.*
to relieve their souls] Compare ver. 11. The Septuagint add (but unnecessarily, as it is sufficiently understood from the context), *and found it not.*
20. *my bowels*] the vital parts (specially the heart), as the seat of the emotions.
are troubled] literally, *are red, inflamed* (with sorrow); a strong figure.
is turned] cannot rest, is violently agitated.
at home there is as death] As violent death is imminent for those who stir abroad, so even those who remain within are like to die of famine and pestilence. See Jer. ix. 21.
21. *thou wilt bring*] *thou* **bringest.** The day here spoken of is the day of punishment for Judah, but viewed as involving also the punishment of her enemies. This is shewn by the last words of the verse. Compare Jer. xxv. 17—26, in which passage Jerusalem and the neighbouring nations are all united in the same figure, as drinking in common of the cup of God's wrath.

For my sighs *are* many, and my heart *is* faint.

CHAP. II. 1—22. *God's judgments upon the city. Lamentation. Supplication.*

2 (א) How hath the Lord covered the daughter of Zion with a cloud in his anger,
And cast down from heaven *unto* the earth the beauty of Israel,
And remembered not his footstool in the day of his anger!

2 (ב) The Lord hath swallowed up all the habitations of Jacob, and hath not pitied:
He hath thrown down in his wrath the strong holds of the daughter of Judah;
He hath brought *them* down to the ground: he hath polluted the kingdom and the princes thereof.

22. *for my sighs are many*] The connexion is, I have had my punishment. Do thou then proceed to inflict upon them their share.

CHAP. II. 1—22. GOD'S JUDGMENTS UPON THE CITY. LAMENTATION. SUPPLICATION.

This chapter may be subdivided as follows. Verses 1—10 describe in detail the punishment sent upon Jerusalem, 11—17 bewail the same together with the cruelty of the lookers on, 18, 19 call upon the city to address herself to God, and 20—22 gives us the supplication which she accordingly offers. In this chapter we have not simply a renewed setting forth of miseries, but rather the same viewed now more in the light of a judgment sent from God, and therefore as the consequences of sin.

1. *How*] See note on chap. i. 1.
hath...covered] **doth...cover.**
the beauty of Israel] possibly the Temple, as in Is. lxiv. 11, but more naturally, Jerusalem herself.
his footstool] here again either the city or the Temple may be meant, or thirdly, the ark, which is actually called God's "footstool" in 1 Chron. xxviii. 2. In Ps. cxxxii. 7, the word seems used of the sanctuary (compare Is. lx. 13).

2. *habitations*] The word is that which is used for the dwellings and pasture grounds of shepherds, and thus refers to the country parts of Judaea, as opposed to the fortresses, 'strongholds', that follow.
hath polluted] By their fall they have been deprived of that sanctity which has hitherto been their character. Compare Ps. lxxxix. 39, where the original word ("hast profaned") is the same as here.

(ג) He hath cut off in *his* fierce anger all the horn of 3
Israel:
He hath drawn back his right hand from before the enemy,
And he burned against Jacob like a flaming fire, *which* devoureth round about.
(ד) He hath bent his bow like an enemy: *he* stood *with* 4 his right hand as an adversary,
And slew all *that were* pleasant to the eye,
In the tabernacle of the daughter of Zion: he poured out his fury like fire.
(ה) The Lord was as an enemy: he hath swallowed up 5 Israel,
He hath swallowed up all her palaces: he hath destroyed his strong holds,
And hath increased in the daughter of Judah mourning and lamentation.
(ו) And he hath violently taken away his tabernacle, as 6

3. *all the horn*] **every** *horn*, every means of defence, the horn being the symbol of power.
He hath drawn back his right hand] God has withdrawn His aid from His people.
burned against Jacob] *burned* **amidst** *Jacob*. He carries destruction into the heart of the nation.
4. *with his right hand*] that which has hitherto been the symbol of His help.
all that were pleasant] This suggests persons only, whereas inanimate things are doubtless meant as well. Therefore, we had best translate *all that* **was** *pleasant*.
in the tabernacle...] This belongs to the third division of the verse, and therefore there should be a stop after *eye*, while the colon which follows 'Zion' should be removed.
tabernacle] the city, daughter being, as is usual in such a connexion, a noun of multitude.
5. The stops do not accord with the threefold division of the verse, as rightly made in the text above. The Heb. on the other hand is correctly stopped.
her palaces...his strong holds] Jeremiah, in the former case, was thinking of the city, in the second of the people at large; hence the change in the gender of the pronouns.
mourning and lamentation] *groaning and moaning*, if we are to keep up the similarity of the original words, which are substantives from the same root, like our *tribulation* and *trouble*.
6. The comparison in the earlier part of the verse, as it stands in

if it were of a garden: he hath destroyed his places of the assembly:

The LORD hath caused the solemn feasts and sabbaths to be forgotten in Zion,

And hath despised in the indignation of his anger the king and the priest.

7 (ז) The Lord hath cast off his altar, he hath abhorred his sanctuary,

He hath given up into the hand of the enemy the walls of her palaces;

They have made a noise in the house of the LORD, as *in* the day of a solemn feast.

8 (ח) The LORD hath purposed to destroy the wall of the daughter of Zion:

He hath stretched out a line, he hath not withdrawn his hand from destroying:

Therefore he made the rampart and the wall to lament; they languished together.

9 (ט) Her gates are sunk into the ground; he hath destroyed and broken her bars:

Her king and her princes *are* among the Gentiles: the law *is* no *more;*

Her prophets also find no vision from the LORD.

the Eng. Vers., is of the Temple (called the *tabernacle*) to a pleasure booth in a garden, and this is perhaps the most natural sense of the Heb., although it leaves something to be supplied. If we take the more literal *as a garden*, we get the thought that the Temple was destroyed and broken up with as much ease as a garden that had failed to please its owner. The Septuagint, misreading the Heb., have "And he scattered his tabernacle *as a vine*".

his places of the assembly] *his* **festivals.** The same word in the Heb. as that which is immediately afterwards rendered *solemn feasts*. These were the annual, as the *sabbaths* the weekly, solemnities.

7. *her palaces*] *her high buildings*, according to the primary meaning of the word, which, as the context shews us here, refers to the Temple.

8. *He hath stretched out a line*] The Lord has used as much precision in the destruction of the place, as a builder shews in construction.

9. *are sunk into the ground*] have disappeared as completely as though actually swallowed up.

the law is no more] The overthrow of Jerusalem involved the cessation of the legal ritual, as the sacrifices could not be carried on elsewhere.

(י) The elders of the daughter of Zion sit upon the ground, *and* keep silence:
They have cast up dust upon their heads; they have girded themselves with sackcloth:
The virgins of Jerusalem hang down their heads to the ground.
(כ) Mine eyes do fail with tears, my bowels are troubled,
My liver is poured upon the earth, for the destruction of the daughter of my people;
Because the children and the sucklings swoon in the streets of the city.
(ל) They say to their mothers, Where *is* corn and wine?
When they swooned as the wounded in the streets of the city,
When their soul was poured out into their mothers' bosom.
(מ) What *thing* shall I take to witness for thee? what *thing* shall I liken to thee, O daughter of Jerusalem?
What shall I equal to thee, that I may comfort thee, O virgin daughter of Zion?
For thy breach *is* great like the sea: who can heal thee?

10. *The elders of the daughter of Zion*] Each city and district had a ruling body of this kind. See 1 Sam. xvi. 4; 2 Kings x. 1.

they have cast up dust upon their heads] Compare 2 Sam. xiii. 19; Neh. ix. 1; Job ii. 12.

11. Here begins the lamentation over Zion's condition, exposed to the mockery of her enemies.

my bowels are troubled] See notes on chap. i. 20.

my liver is poured upon the earth] The liver was looked upon in common with the rest of the vitals as the seat of the emotions, and hence the expression in the text merely denotes strong and painful excitement.

the destruction of the daughter of my people] See note on *tabernacle*, ver. 4.

12. *corn and wine*] a general designation for solid and liquid food.

13. *shall I take to witness for thee*] rather, **shall I testify to thee?** The prophet casts about for some sort of message of comfort, that he may bear to Jerusalem in her sorrow.

equal] *liken, compare.* 'Equal' is not elsewhere used in the Bible as a transitive verb.

great like the sea] without measure.

14. For the assertion that in this and the next verse the author makes use of the prophecies of Ezekiel, see Introduction, chap. ii. § 2 (*d*), and § 3 (*d*).

14 (נ) Thy prophets have seen vain and foolish things for thee:
And they have not discovered thine iniquity, to turn away thy captivity;
But have seen for thee false burdens and causes of banishment.

15 (ס) All that pass by clap *their* hands at thee;
They hiss and wag their head at the daughter of Jerusalem, *saying*,
Is this the city that *men* call The perfection of beauty,
The joy of the whole earth?

16 (פ) All thine enemies have opened their mouth against thee:
They hiss and gnash the teeth: they say, We have swallowed *her* up:
Certainly this *is* the day that we looked for; we have found, we have seen it.

17 (ע) The LORD hath done *that* which he had devised;

foolish things] virtually the same word as that which is rendered "folly" in Jer. xxiii. 13, where see note.

discovered] uncovered, revealed (to thee), a use of the word now obsolete. Compare Shakespeare:

"Go, draw aside the curtains and *discover*
The several caskets to this noble prince."
Merch. of Ven. Act. II. Sc. 7.

to turn away thy captivity] by producing in thee repentance.
false burdens] See note on Jer. xxiii. 30—33.
causes of banishment] The Heb. word is not elsewhere found, and probably here points to the consequences which, as Jeremiah has already said, will follow the teaching of the false prophets (Jer. xxvii. 10, 15).

15. *they hiss*] Since the context contains expressions which imply contempt, this word probably does the same here, as it certainly does in Job xxvii. 23.

16. For the inverted order of the initial letters in the Heb. of this and the next verse, see Introduction, chap. i. § 4.

all thine enemies...against thee] almost identical with iii. 46.
gnash the teeth] in token of rage. Compare Ps. xxxv. 16, xxxvii. 12.
we have seen it] **we have seen.** The *it* is best omitted, as also the *her* in an earlier clause of the verse. Thus the clauses are made more abrupt in consonance with the joyful emotions of those supposed to be uttering them. For a parallel to the last words of this verse, see Ps. xxxv. 21.

he hath fulfilled his word that he had commanded in the days of old:

He hath thrown down, and hath not pitied: and he hath caused *thine* enemy to rejoice over thee,

He hath set up the horn of thine adversaries.

(צ) Their heart cried unto the Lord,   18

O wall of the daughter of Zion, let tears run down like a river day and night:

Give thyself no rest; let not the apple of thine eye cease.

(ק) Arise, cry out in the night: in the beginning of the 19 watches,

Pour out thine heart like water before the face of the Lord:

Lift up thy hands toward him for the life of thy young children,

That faint for hunger in the top of every street.

17. *in the days of old*] That which had happened was merely a fulfilment of the threats, Lev. xxvi. 14 etc.; Deut. xxviii. 15 etc.

he hath set up the horn of thine adversaries] See ver. 3, and compare 1 Sam. ii. 1.

18. In this and the following verse we have the thought consequent on the main one on which the prophet has been dwelling, viz. that the calamity is from the Lord, and is the result of disobedience. The people cry to Him whom they have offended, to help them now in their hour of need.

Their heart] that of the people.

O wall] The rampart and wall have been already (ver. 8) said to lament. Here the wall, meaning those who had hitherto been sheltered by it, is called upon in its ruins to cry out for help.

river] **torrent**, a mountain stream, rushing down its rugged channel.

no rest] The verb corresponding to the Heb. substantive here used, is found in Psal. lxxvii. 2, where the reference is to the *hand* (so margin, not "sore" as in Eng. Text) *stretched out* in prayer, "*and ceased not*," literally, *and grew not cold*. Such then is the meaning of the word here also.

apple] For this word, meaning pupil (of the eye), compare Deut. xxxii. 10; Ps. xvii. 8.

19. *cry out*] in prayer.

in the beginning of the watches] i.e. of each watch. In New Testament times the Jews had adopted the Roman division of the night into four watches of three hours each (see Matt. xiv. 25; Mark xiii. 35). Up to that time the division was threefold, each consisting of four hours. Compare Exod. xiv. 24; Ps. lxiii. 6, etc.

pour out thine heart like water] Compare ver. 11.

lift up thy hands] in supplication.

20 (ר) Behold, O Lord, and consider to whom thou hast done this.
Shall the women eat their fruit, *and* children of a span long?
Shall the priest and the prophet be slain in the sanctuary of the Lord?

21 (שׁ) The young and the old lie on the ground in the streets:
My virgins and my young men are fallen by the sword;
Thou hast slain *them* in the day of thine anger; thou hast killed, *and* not pitied.

22 (ת) Thou hast called as *in* a solemn day my terrors round about,
So that in the day of the Lord's anger none escaped nor remained:
Those that I have swaddled and brought up hath mine enemy consumed.

20. Here begins the prayer made in response to the prophet's exhortation.

consider to whom thou hast done this] Remember that the people whom Thou thus afflictest are Thy chosen ones of old.

and children] **children.**

of a span long] The word properly means *stretched out*, and thus a better sense is given us by the Eng. margin, **swaddled with their hands**, the objects of their care, the thought of maternal tenderness in the forms in which it would ordinarily be displayed towards children of that age heightening the effect of the picture. See note on Jer. xix. 9.

21. *The young*] the same word as that used in Jer. i. 6 ("child"), where see note. The words in Italics in the Eng. text (*them—and*) rather weaken the passage and are best omitted.

22. *Thou hast called as in a solemn day my terrors round about*] As though proclaiming a festival Thou hast summoned aloud my terrors. Jeremiah here alludes, as is shewn by the form of the Heb. for *terrors* (wrongly translated *neighbouring villages* by the Septuagint) the word Magor-missabib, which had been so constantly in his mouth (see note on Jer. vi. 25, xx. 3), and which, though disregarded and no doubt mocked, the people had now come to recognise as but too well warranted by realities.

have swaddled] the same word as that so rendered in margin of ver. 20 (see note).

CHAP. III. 1—21. *The prophet, as representing the nation, bewails their sufferings.*

(א) I *am* the man *that* hath seen affliction by the rod of his wrath. 3

(א) He hath led me, and brought *me into* darkness, but not *into* light. 2

(א) Surely against me is he turned; he turneth his hand *against me* all the day. 3

(ב) My flesh and my skin hath he made old; he hath broken my bones. 4

(ב) He hath builded against me, and compassed *me* with gall and travail. 5

CHAP. III. 1—21. THE PROPHET, AS REPRESENTING THE NATION, BEWAILS THEIR SUFFERINGS.

1. For remarks upon the character and teaching of this chapter and upon its structure, see Introduction, chaps. i. § 4, iii. § 2.

affliction] the whole series of calamities, which had now reached their climax in the capture and burning of Jerusalem.

by the rod of his wrath] For the figure itself compare Job ix. 34, xxi. 9; Is. x. 5, and for an expansion of the thought of Babylon acting as the instrument of God's wrath see Jer. li. 20—23.

3. *is he turned; he turneth*] **he turneth again and again.** For the Heb. idiom see note on Jer. xii. 15.

4. *made old*] **wasted.** The Heb. verb means *to rub away*.

he hath broken my bones] For this phrase compare Is. xxxviii. 13. The flesh, skin, and bones are taken as comprising the whole man, the former two denoting the softer portions, the last the harder, which must be fractured, in order to destroy it.

5. *He hath builded against me, and compassed*] Here as in ver. 3 we have to deal with the idiom by which two verbs are used where we should in English have a verb and adverb. Translate therefore **He hath builded against me round about.**

gall] For the primary sense of the word see note on Jer. viii. 14. In a case like the present it had no doubt ceased to be a metaphor and come to mean simply *bitterness*, and so it illustrates, along with the words that follow, Jeremiah's custom of suddenly dismissing a figure and falling back upon the subject itself. See Introd. to Jer. chap. ii. § 8 (*d*), and compare verses 13 and 14 of the present chapter.

travail] From 1611 to the American edition of 1867 all editions of the Authorized Version had *travel* both here and in the case of Numb. xx. 14. It was probably in comparatively recent times that the two modes of spelling were definitely appropriated to distinct meanings of the word, as they now are. The Heb. word here (and in Numbers) is clear in its sense, viz. *weariness*.

6 (ב) He hath set me in dark places, as they that be dead of old.

7 (ג) He hath hedged me about, that I cannot get out: he hath made my chain heavy.

8 (ג) Also when I cry and shout, he shutteth out my prayer.

9 (ג) He hath inclosed my ways with hewn stone, he hath made my paths crooked.

10 (ד) He *was* unto me *as* a bear lying in wait, *and as* a lion in secret places.

11 (ד) He hath turned aside my ways, and pulled me in pieces: he hath made me desolate.

12 (ד) He hath bent his bow, and set me as a mark for the arrow.

13 (ה) He hath caused the arrows of his quiver to enter into my reins.

14 (ה) I was a derision to all my people; *and* their song all the day.

6. This verse is identical with the last part of Ps. cxliii. 3.
set me] **made me dwell.**
dark places] darkness is used as an equivalent for misery, as light for happiness. Compare Jer. xiii. 16.
dead of old] **for ever dead**, i.e. unable to return to the life of this world, as opposed to the state of those in a sleep or swoon.

7. *my chain*] literally, *my brass*. In Eng. we speak of *irons* in the same sense.

9. *hath inclosed*] the same verb as "hath hedged" in ver. 7.
hath made my paths crooked] The prophet, finding that the direct way was as it were blocked, tried side paths, but finds that they also fail to lead him in the direction he wishes to go. The whole figure expresses perplexity and dismay.

10. Not only is there misery, but active forms of danger too.
was] **is.**

11. *hath turned aside my ways*] hath driven me from the path, and then sprung upon me and devoured me.
desolate] **appalled**, stupified. For this sense of the word see notes on Jer. v. 30, xviii. 16.

12. The enemy is now likened not to the beast of prey, but to the hunter.

13. *arrows of his quiver*] The Heb. has the more poetical *children of his quiver*.
my reins] See note on Jer. xii. 2. The word therefore here expresses the sharpness of the prophet's grief at that which he hears and sees.

14. *a derision*] See note on Jer. xx. 8.

vv. 15—21.]   LAMENTATIONS, III.   377

(ה)   He hath filled me with bitterness, he hath made me 15
drunken *with* wormwood.
(ו)   He hath also broken my teeth with gravel stones, he 16
hath covered me with ashes.
(ו)   And thou hast removed my soul far off from peace: 17
I forgat prosperity.
(ו)   And I said, My strength and my hope is perished 18
from the LORD:
(ז)   Remembering mine affliction and my misery, the 19
wormwood and the gall.
(ז)   My soul hath *them* still in remembrance, and is 20
humbled in me.
(ז)   This I recall to my mind, therefore have I hope. 21

15. *He hath filled me*] literally, *He hath* satiated *me.*
bitterness] literally, bitternesses, i.e. bitter pains.
wormwood] See notes on Jer. ix. 15, xxiii. 15.
16. *broken my teeth with gravel stones*] The metaphor from food is continued. The prophet is like one whose teeth are worn away by the continued action of grit mixed with his bread.
covered] The Heb. word does not occur elsewhere. It may mean *made to eat* (Septuagint), but more probably denotes *pressed down*.
17. *thou hast removed my soul*] *thou hast* **rejected** *my soul.* The Heb. words are taken from Ps. lxxxviii. 14 (Heb. 15), and but for the fact that there the construction must be as above, we might well here have adopted a translation, which the original will equally bear, *my soul is rejected* (from prosperity). We should thus avoid the introduction of a direct address to God, which seems not to come earlier than ver. 19.
peace] health, prosperity.
prosperity] good, i.e. The very thought became a stranger to me.
18. *And I said*] within myself, i.e. I thought.
19. *Remembering*] **Remember.** God is now directly invoked.
my misery] See note on i. 7. This word as well as *gall* and *wormwood* are gathered into this verse, as suggesting the whole of the previous lament, in which they have taken a prominent place.
20. *My soul hath them still in remembrance, and*] This is better than the alternative rendering, *Thou wilt surely remember that my soul,* etc.
21. The previous verse and this are apparently suggested by Ps. xlii. 4, 5 (Heb. 5, 6), and, inasmuch as the words corresponding to *This I recall* of the present passage have reference to that which follows, it has been proposed to make these words also to relate to the more hopeful thoughts that come in ver. 22 and onwards. But the structure of the poem, ver. 21 being the third (and last) of its group, as well as the previous context rather point to the last words of ver. 20 as being what the prophet recalls for his comfort. The humility arising from

22—36. *Words of Submission and Hope.*

22 (ח) *It is of* the LORD's mercies that we are not consumed, because his compassions fail not.

23 (ח) *They are* new every morning: great *is* thy faithfulness.

24 (ח) The LORD *is* my portion, saith my soul; therefore will I hope in him.

25 (ט) The LORD *is* good unto them that wait for him, to the soul *that* seeketh him.

26 (ט) *It is* good *that a man should* both hope and quietly wait for the salvation of the LORD.

27 (ט) *It is* good for a man that he bear the yoke in his youth.

28 (י) He sitteth alone and keepeth silence, because he hath borne *it* upon him.

29 (י) He putteth his mouth in the dust; if so be there may be hope.

sin dwelt upon and acknowledged produces in due course a sense that contrition will be accepted and deliverance granted. Hence arises the change of tone in the section which follows.

22—36. WORDS OF SUBMISSION AND HOPE.

24. *The Lord is my portion*] For the expression, which is a frequent one, we may compare Ps. xvi. 5. Its origin is probably to be looked for in the Lord's words to Aaron (Num. xviii. 20).

25. *good* is the leading word of this group (25—27). The knowledge of the Lord's goodness is that which makes it good that man should be hopeful and submissive.

26. *should both hope and quietly wait*] should wait, and that in silence.

27. *in his youth*] in the time when his passions are strongest and therefore most need the discipline, which, if established in its seat then, will hold sway throughout his life. The words by no means imply that the writer was young at the time he used them. Rather he is looking back through a long life of trouble and the experience which he has gained in the course of it.

28. In this verse and the rest of the group the verbs should be translated by the hortative form, *Let him sit alone—let him keep—let him put, etc.* The connexion is, if suffering is really attended with benefit to the sufferer, then let him submit readily to it.

hath borne] hath laid. The subject is God.

29. *He putteth his mouth in the dust*] the Eastern way of expressing absolute submission.

(ן) He giveth *his* cheek to him that smiteth him : he is 30
filled full with reproach.
(כ) For the Lord will not cast off for ever : 31
(כ) But though he cause grief, yet will he have compas- 32
sion according to the multitude of his mercies.
(כ) For he doth not afflict willingly nor grieve the 33
children of men.
(ל) To crush under his feet all the prisoners of the 34
earth,
(ל) To turn aside the right of a man before the face of 35
the most High,
(ל) To subvert a man in his cause, the Lord approveth 36
not.

37—54. *Renewed expressions of suffering joined with appeal
to God for help.*

(מ) Who *is* he *that* saith, and it cometh to pass, *when* 37
the Lord commandeth *it* not?

30. *He giveth his cheek*] Here we have the climax, the exhortation of ver. 29 being more difficult to obey than that in the first of the group, and this the most difficult of all. Compare Matt. v. 39.

31—33. This group contains the two thoughts which produce the resignation, (*a*) because punishment will be only for a time, and will be succeeded by a renewal of mercy, (*b*) because even in punishment it is in no angry or vindictive spirit that God acts.

33. *willingly*] literally, *from His heart*.

34—36. Three species of wrong-doing are here enumerated; (*a*) To treat prisoners with cruelty: words to which the spectacles daily seen in Jerusalem at the time must have added much point, (*b*) To obtain an unrighteous decision at law: for the judges as representing God were called by His name (e.g. in the original of Exod. xxi. 6; see Ps. lxxxii. 6), and hence the expression 'before the face of the Most High,' (*c*) To defraud a man of his legal rights, which might be done without an actual trial. The sense of the whole will depend upon the view we take of the last words. They may be explained either, (i) the Lord regardeth not (i.e. turneth a deaf ear) to such things, the words being then spoken by unbelievers or those who despaired of obtaining help from God, or, (ii) as a question, *Doth not the Lord regard* (such acts), or, (iii) as the Eng. Vers. In favour of this last is the use of the same expression in 1 Sam. xvi. 7.

37—54. RENEWED EXPRESSIONS OF SUFFERING JOINED WITH APPEAL TO GOD FOR HELP.

37. The verse is no doubt suggested by Ps. xxxiii. 9. The order of thought in this group is, All events are absolutely in the hands of

38 (מ) Out of the mouth of the most High proceedeth not evil and good.
39 (מ) Wherefore doth a living man complain, a man for the punishment of his sins?
40 (נ) Let us search and try our ways, and turn again to the LORD.
41 (נ) Let us lift up our heart with *our* hands unto God in the heavens.
42 (נ) We have transgressed and have rebelled: thou hast not pardoned.
43 (ס) Thou hast covered with anger, and persecuted us: thou hast slain, thou hast not pitied.
44 (ס) Thou hast covered thyself with a cloud, that *our* prayer should not pass through.
45 (ס) Thou hast made us *as* the offscouring and refuse in the midst of the people.
46 (פ) All our enemies have opened their mouths against us.
47 (פ) Fear and a snare is come upon us, desolation and destruction.

God. Thus evil comes from Him as well as good. But it is man's sin that procures for him the former; he therefore may not complain.

39. The verse has had two interpretations proposed, (i) Why should a man all his life long complain that his sins are punished? (ii) Why should a man lament, while all the time he has more than he merits, viz. life? Let each one lament his *sins*.

40. *Let us search*] As it is through our sins that this evil is come upon us, let us seek out what has been amiss in us.

41. *with our hands*] literally, *unto our hands*. Let it not be a mere formal expression of prayer, but let our hearts follow the direction in which our hands point.

42. *We...thou*] The pronouns are emphatic in the original. *Thou* and *we* have been at variance.

43. *Thou hast covered*] *Thou hast covered* **thyself**, literally, Thou hast made a covering for thyself.

46. On the peculiarity of the alphabetic arrangement here see Introduction, chap. i. § 4, and for this verse compare chap. ii. 16.

47. *Fear and a snare*] See note on Jer. xlviii. 43, from which this is a quotation, fear probably meaning, if not an actual *hunting trap* (compare Latin *formido*), at any rate the cause of fear, *formidable object*, as in Gen. xxxi. 42, 53. So (*Bible Word Book*),

Or in the night, imagining some *fear*,
How easy is a bush supposed a bear!
Midsummer Night's Dream, Act v. Sc. 1.

(פ) Mine eye runneth down *with* rivers of water for the 48
destruction of the daughter of my people.
(ע) Mine eye trickleth down, and ceaseth not, without 49
any intermission,
(ע) Till the LORD look down, and behold from heaven. 50
(ע) Mine eye affecteth mine heart because of all the 51
daughters of my city.
(צ) Mine enemies chased me sore, like a bird, without 52
cause.
(צ) They have cut off my life in the dungeon, and cast 53
a stone upon me.
(צ) Waters flowed over mine head; *then* I said, I am 54
cut off.

desolation] **devastation**. The original is not any of Jeremiah's words rendered so often *desolation* in the Eng. Version, but occurs here only.

48. *runneth down with rivers of water*] a still stronger expression than that of i. 16, where see note.

49. *trickleth down*] **poureth** *down*. The Eng. Vers. is hardly strong enough.

ceaseth not] literally, *is not silent*, compare Jer. xiv. 17, where the Heb. word is the same.

51. *affecteth mine heart*] **causeth pain to my soul**. The inflammation of eyes caused by continual weeping is added to the mental suffering which already exists.

the daughters of my city] those whose untoward fate Jeremiah has already lamented (i. 4, 18, ii. 10, 21). The verse has been taken in two other ways, which commend themselves less: (i) that the daughters are the villages, daughter towns of Jerusalem, (ii) that the sense is *I weep* more than *all the daughters*, i.e. the prophet's tears exceeded those even of the most tender hearted woman.

52. This group of verses according to some has reference solely to the prophet himself, as persecuted by his countrymen. In that case verse 53 will refer to the incident of Jer. xxxviii. 6, and 'cast a stone' will mean, not probably that the princes there mentioned flung stones at Jeremiah as he lay in the dungeon, but that they covered it in with a stone, so as to increase the prophet's sufferings. The other way of understanding it is of the Israelites generally in their hour of suffering, and specially of the godly, among whom the prophet in his sufferings would be a typical instance.

Mine enemies...without cause] These words should probably go together. For the comparison to a chased bird compare Ps. xi. 1.

53. *They have cut off*] They have **destroyed**, i.e. have tried to destroy.

54. *Waters flowed over mine head*] Whether the reference be to the prophet as an individual or not, this must be merely a figure to express

55—66. *Thanksgiving and a prayer for vengeance.*

55 (ק) I called upon thy name, O Lord, out of the low dungeon.
56 (ק) Thou hast heard my voice: hide not thine ear at my breathing, at my cry.
57 (ק) Thou drewest near in the day *that* I called upon thee: thou saidst, Fear not.
58 (ר) O Lord, thou hast pleaded the causes of my soul; thou hast redeemed my life.
59 (ר) O Lord, thou hast seen my wrong: judge thou my cause.
60 (ר) Thou hast seen all their vengeance *and* all their imaginations against me.
61 (ש) Thou hast heard their reproach, O Lord, *and* all their imaginations against me;
62 (ש) The lips of those that rose up against me, and their device against me all the day.
63 (ש) Behold their sitting down, and their rising up; I *am* their musick.

intense misery. The dungeon into which Jeremiah was cast was dry (Jer. xxxviii. 6). See further in note on ver. 55.
I am cut off] an expression found in the same sense Ps. lxxxviii. 5, and Is. liii. 8, which latter serves to connect in thought the sufferings here spoken of with those undergone by Him who became sin for us.

55—66. THANKSGIVING AND A PRAYER FOR VENGEANCE.

55. *I called upon thy name*] It has been conjectured that Ps. lxix. is the composition of Jeremiah, and was uttered by him on this occasion. Compare ver. 54 with the opening verses of that Psalm.

56. *at my breathing, at my cry*] or, as the words may be translated, *at my crying for relief*, inasmuch as in the only other place where the word here rendered *breathing* occurs ("respite" Exod. viii. 15, in Heb. ver. 11) *relief* is its sense.

57. *Thou drewest near*] Compare Ps. cxlv. 18.

58. *thou hast pleaded the causes of my soul*] The enemy are likened to opponents in a suit at law. The Lord is the prophet's advocate against them.

62. *The lips*] i.e. the utterances, and hence properly governed by *Thou hast heard* of the preceding verse.

63. *musick*] **song**. Compare Job xxx. 9, where the word translated song is from the same Heb. root as here; also Ps. lxix. 12, where however the word is a different one.

(ת) Render unto them a recompence, O LORD, ac- 64
cording to the work of their hands.
(ת) Give them sorrow of heart, thy curse unto them. 65
(ת) Persecute and destroy them in anger from under 66
the heavens of the Lord.

CHAP. IV. 1—22. *The sufferings of the people are consequent on sin.*

(א) How is the gold become dim! *how* is the most fine 4
gold changed!
The stones of the sanctuary are poured out in the top of
every street.
(ב) The precious sons of Zion, comparable to fine gold, 2
How are they esteemed as earthen pitchers, the work of
the hands of the potter!
(ג) Even the sea monsters draw out the breast, they 3
give suck to their young ones:

64. For the language compare Ps. xxviii. 4, and for the general character of the prayer in this and the two following verses, note on Jer. xviii. 23.
65. *sorrow of heart*] **blindness** *of heart.* Compare 2 Cor. iii. 15.

CHAP. IV. 1—22. THE SUFFERINGS OF THE PEOPLE ARE CONSE-
QUENT ON SIN.

1. This chapter differs from the earlier ones, (*a*) in dwelling more on the sufferings of *various classes* of people, (*b*) in bringing out more clearly that these sufferings were the consequences of the national sin. Verses 1—12 set forth the miseries attendant on the siege, 13—16 point out that the prophets and priests are guilty, 17—20 the hopelessness of human aid, 21, 22 that Edom's triumph will be but short-lived.

How is the gold become dim!] In this and the rest of the verse there is no reference to the literal gold of the Temple, or, as some have thought, to the onyx stones on the shoulders of the high priest's robe (Exod. xxviii. 9—12). The next verse shews that the expressions are metaphorically used for the people themselves, similarly called elsewhere (Zech. ix. 16) "the stones of a crown".

are poured out in the top of every street] It falls in with the above interpretation, that this has been already said of the starving little ones (chap. ii. 19).

2. *work of the hands of the potter*] *They* are treated thus, who are in fact specially moulded by God's hand, the people whom He "formed for" Himself (Is. xliii. 21).

3. *the sea monsters*] **the jackals.** See notes on Jer. ix. 11, li. 34.

The daughter of my people *is* become cruel, like the ostriches in the wilderness.

4 (ד) The tongue of the sucking child cleaveth to the roof of his mouth for thirst:
The young children ask bread, *and* no man breaketh *it* unto them.

5 (ה) They that did feed delicately are desolate in the streets:
They that were brought up in scarlet embrace dunghills.

6 (ו) For the punishment of the iniquity of the daughter of my people is greater than the punishment of the sin of Sodom,

is become cruel] The italics are hardly needed in the Eng. Vers., the whole being virtually contained in the Heb.; literally, *is for a cruel one*.

like the ostriches in the wilderness] "The outer layer of eggs is generally so ill-covered that they are destroyed in quantities by jackals, wild-cats, etc., and that the natives carry them away, only taking care not to leave the marks of their footsteps, since, when the ostrich comes and finds that her nest is discovered, she crushes the whole brood and builds a nest elsewhere....To this it may be added that the female ostrich forsakes her nest at the least alarm." (Sp. Comm. on Job xxxix. 15, 16. See that passage.)

4. *the sucking child...the young children*] The Heb. expressions (*yônēk...ôlēl;* compare babes and sucklings as rendering of same Heb. in Ps. viii. 2) seem to denote respectively the second and the third stage, when the child passed beyond babyhood. "The *ôlēl* is still sucking, but it is no longer satisfied with only this nourishment and is asking bread." (Edersheim's *Sketches of Jewish Social Life*, p. 104.)

breaketh] See note on Jer. xvi. 7.

5. *delicately*] luxuriously. In the Old Testament the word occurs elsewhere only in 1 Sam. xv. 32, and Prov. xxix. 21. In the latter case the sense is the same, while the Heb. word differs from that used here; in the former the Heb. is as here, but the sense probably is *cheerfully*.

desolate] See note on chap. iii. 11.

brought up in scarlet] literally, *resting upon scarlet*, whose very swaddling clothes were rich and costly.

embrace dunghills] for want of a better couch.

6. *For the punishment of the iniquity*] **For the iniquity.**

the punishment of the sin] **the sin.** There is no assertion in this part of the verse as to the comparative amount of punishment, but from the admitted fact that the sufferings of Jerusalem exceeded those of Sodom, it is inferred that the sin must have been in like proportion. Sodom perished in a moment, there were no prolonged sufferings,

That was overthrown as in a moment, and no hands stayed on her.

(ז) Her Nazarites were purer than snow, they were whiter than milk; 7
They were more ruddy *in* body than rubies, their polishing *was of* sapphire:

(ח) Their visage is blacker than a coal; they are not known in the streets: 8
Their skin cleaveth to their bones; it is withered, it is become like a stick.

(ט) *They that be* slain with the sword are better than *they that be* slain with hunger: 9
For these pine away, stricken through for *want of* the fruits of the field.

(י) The hands of the pitiful women have sodden their own children: 10

such as are brought about or directly administered by the hand of man.

stayed on her] literally, *went round about her* (inflicting the punishment).

7. *Nazarites*] This is probably right, although it is also rendered *princes*. There is probably a reference to the Rechabites (Jer. xxxv.), who were among the most prominent examples of men following out the Nazarite rule of life in the matter of abstinence from intoxicating drinks.

rubies] **corals.** Others render *pearls*, but this involves also a substitution of *glowing* for *ruddy*, which is not permissible.

their polishing was of sapphire] **their shape was that of a sapphire.** Not only their bright, glowing appearance, but also their well-shaped figures suggested a carefully cut precious stone.

8. *Their visage is blacker than a coal*] **Their form is darker than blackness.** Here comes the contrast, shewn in their present state. Compare Job xxx. 30.

it is withered, it is become] **it is become dry.**

9. See note on Jer. xxxvii. 10. The two modes of death experienced in the siege are contrasted. From the primary sense of the word translated *pine away*, viz., *flow out*, as well as from the fact that the Heb. for *stricken through* is a verb used elsewhere only for those literally transfixed, the latter part of the verse has been by some referred to those slain with the sword, and translated, *The former pour out their lives, pierced from* (i.e. going into battle direct from the yet remaining) *fruits of the field*.

10. For the general subject of the verse see chap. ii. 20, and Jer. xix. 9.

pitiful] (hitherto) compassionate. The word is found elsewhere in the Bible only in Jam. v. 11; 1 Pet. iii. 8. Its modern use is not as

They were their meat in the destruction of the daughter of my people.

11 (כ) The LORD hath accomplished his fury; he hath poured out his fierce anger,
And hath kindled a fire in Zion, and it hath devoured the foundations thereof.

12 (ל) The kings of the earth, and all the inhabitants of the world, would not have believed
That the adversary and the enemy should have entered into the gates of Jerusalem.

13 (מ) For the sins of her prophets, *and* the iniquities of her priests,
That *have* shed the blood of the just in the midst of her,

14 (נ) They have wandered *as* blind *men* in the streets, they have polluted themselves with blood,
So that *men* could not touch their garments.

15 (ס) They cried unto them, Depart ye; *it is* unclean;

here, in the sense *full of pity*, but *much to be pitied*. For the former, compare (Latimer, *Sermons*, p. 391). "Because I speak here of orphans, I shall exhort you to be *pitiful* unto them."—*Bible Word Book*.

sodden] *boiled;* the participle of *to seethe*, for which last see 2 Kings iv. 38, and for sodden, Exod. xii. 9.

11. *hath kindled a fire in Zion*] The literal burning of Jerusalem was typical of the Lord's anger, which had blazed forth against it.

12. *all the inhabitants of the world*] an ordinary form of Eastern hyperbole, suggesting to their minds only the same notion as our *every body*, the obvious limitations being given by the sense in each case. Probably from and after the overthrow of Sennacherib (2 Kings xix. 34, 35), it came to be believed that Jerusalem was impregnable. Its fortifications had been much strengthened by Uzziah (2 Chron. xxvi. 9), Jotham (*ib.* xxvii. 3), and Manasseh (*ib.* xxxiii. 14).

13. The reason for the event which has thus amazed the world is now given, and at the beginning of the verse by way of connexion we must supply some such words as, *This has happened*.

the sins of her prophets and the iniquities of her priests] See Jer. vi. 13, xxiii. 11, xxvi. 8, etc.

14. *They*] these prophets and priests.

wandered] literally, *staggered*. The last part of the verse expresses forcibly how terribly reckless they had been of human life.

15. Those who met these blood-stained priests and prophets in the street, abhorred them, and warned them off with the leper's cry, *Unclean, unclean!* (Lev. xiii. 45). The words 'it is' need not have been inserted in the Eng. Vers. The adjective indeed is in the sing., but only as meant to correspond the more absolutely with the cry which in the case of leprosy the afflicted man was himself to raise.

depart, depart, touch not, when they fled away and wandered:
They said among the heathen, They shall no more sojourn *there*.

(מ) The anger of the LORD hath divided them; he will no more regard them: 16
They respected not the persons of the priests, they favoured not the elders.

(ע) As for us, our eyes as yet failed for our vain help: 17
In our watching we have watched for a nation *that* could not save *us*.

(צ) They hunt our steps, that *we* cannot go in our streets: 18
Our end is near, our days are fulfilled; for our end is come.

(ק) Our persecutors are swifter than the eagles of the heaven: 19
They pursued us upon the mountains, they laid wait for us in the wilderness.

when they fled away and wandered] *when they fled away*, **then they wandered.** It was the same thing when they went abroad. They travelled with step as uncertain as at home (see 'wandered' of ver. 14), and abroad also men would have none of them.

They said among the heathen] **men** said, etc. See previous note.

These two verses may well be not merely a graphic way of setting forth the horrible crimes of the prophets and priests, but an actual record of facts of which this is the only trace remaining to us.

16. *hath divided them*] hath **scattered** *them* (among the nations).

they] **men**, as in the previous verse.

17. *As for us, our eyes as yet failed for our vain help*] rather, **Our eyes still waste away (as we look) for our help in vain.** The expectation that Egypt or some other nation might come to the rescue, was cherished to the end of the year and a half of the siege, and here is set forth the heart-sickness caused by this hope deferred.

in our watching] or, according to some, *on our watch-tower*.

18. *They hunt our steps*] This expresses either the definite danger which existed in the more exposed parts of the city, from the towers advanced gradually nearer to the walls by the besiegers, in which they lay in wait and let fly at the citizens, or in general it denotes the constant dread which beset their hearts under the figure of game for which the hunter lays wait.

19. *swifter than the eagles*] a favourite simile, taken from Deut. xxviii. 49. See note on Jer. iv. 13.

They pursued us upon the mountains] See Introduction, chap. i. § 3.

20 (ר) The breath of our nostrils, the anointed of the
LORD, was taken in their pits,
Of whom we said, Under his shadow we shall live among
the heathen.
21 (שׁ) Rejoice and be glad, O daughter of Edom, that
dwellest in the land of Uz;
The cup also shall pass through unto thee: thou shalt be
drunken, and shalt make thyself naked.
22 (ת) The punishment of thine iniquity is accomplished,
O daughter of Zion; he will no more carry thee away
into captivity:
He will visit thine iniquity, O daughter of Edom; he will
discover thy sins.

This passage was supposed by those who chose the earlier date for the Lamentations to have special reference to the overthrow and death of Josiah. The real reference is no doubt either to the circumstances attendant on the capture of Zedekiah (Jer. xxxix. 4, 5; lii. 8.) who is referred to more distinctly in the following verse, or in general to the condition of the Jews at the taking of the city.

20. *The breath of our nostrils*] With this, as applied to a king, a sentence of Seneca (*ad Neronem de Clementia*, I. 4) has well been compared: "He (the Emperor) is the breath of life, which these many thousand (subjects) draw." As regards its application to Zedekiah individually we are to remember that whatever may have been his personal weaknesses (and he was weak rather than vicious), he was the one on whom the whole of the people's hopes depended for the continuance of their national life.

was taken in their pits] a metaphorical expression drawn from hunting. Compare i. 3, 13.

of whom we said...] See last note but one.

21. *Rejoice and be glad*] Enjoy thy shortlived triumph, while thou mayest. For the joy of Edom over the destruction of Jerusalem see latter part of note *Concerning Edom*, Jer. xlix. 7.

that dwellest in the land of Uz] See note on Jer. xxv. 20.

the cup] the figurative expression for God's wrath; compare Jer. xxv. 17.

thou shalt be drunken...] a figurative way of saying, thou shalt be exposed in the eyes of the world to the contempt which attends upon disaster (compare i. 8).

22. *The punishment of thine iniquity*] **Thine iniquity.** See ver. 6 above. The prophet, as he looks into the future with its Messianic hopes, sees the time when the Jews shall be delivered alike from the sinful courses which have weighed upon them for generations and from the punishment which has ensued.

he will discover thy sins] The reading of the Eng. margin (*he will*

CHAP. V. 1—18. *A sorrowful enumeration of the insults heaped on Zion because of her sins.*

Remember, O LORD, what is come upon us: Consider, and behold our reproach.
Our inheritance is turned to strangers, Our houses to aliens.
We are orphans and fatherless, Our mothers *are* as widows.
We have drunken our water for money; Our wood is sold *unto us*.
Our necks *are* under persecution: We labour, *and* have no rest.
We have given the hand *to* the Egyptians, And *to* the Assyrians, to be satisfied *with* bread.

carry thee captive for thy sins) depends upon the fact that the verb in the Heb. is the same as that so rendered earlier in the verse. It is however common in both senses, and thus the present case must rather be looked on as an untranslateable play on words. For *discover* used virtually in the sense of punish compare the converse use of *cover* in Ps. xxxii. 1, lxxxv. 2.

CHAP. V. 1—18. A SORROWFUL ENUMERATION OF THE INSULTS HEAPED ON ZION BECAUSE OF HER SINS.

1. This final poem, although its verses are equal in number with the letters of the Heb. alphabet, yet does not, like its predecessors, adhere to any rule as to the initial letters of the verses.

2. *Our inheritance*] our land.

our houses] either the houses throughout the country parts of Judaea, or those in Jerusalem as well, which had been spared. See note on Jer. lii. 13.

3. *orphans and fatherless*] not, as having lost our *king*, as some would explain, but desolate and without protectors, as the mothers of Israel are for the same reason likened in the second part of the verse to widows.

4. The bitterness of their captive state is shewn by the fact that they the rightful owners were compelled to buy from the enemy who had come into possession the commonest necessaries of life.

5. *Our necks are under persecution*] The simile of an actual pursuit is used. We are as it were hard pressed and harassed in flight by a foe who is gaining upon us.

6. The nation has been starved into willingness to submit to either of the two great powers, Egypt or Babylon. For 'we have given the hand' see note on Jer. l. 15, and for Assyria meaning Babylon, note on Jer. ii. 18.

7 Our fathers have sinned, *and are* not;
  And we have borne their iniquities.
8 Servants have ruled over us:
  There is none that doth deliver *us* out of their hand.
9 We gat our bread with *the peril of* our lives
  Because of the sword of the wilderness.
10 Our skin was black like an oven
   Because of the terrible famine.
11 They ravished the women in Zion,
   And the maids in the cities of Judah.
12 Princes are hanged up by their hand:
   The faces of elders were not honoured.
13 They took the young men to grind,
   And the children fell under the wood.
14 The elders have ceased from the gate,
   The young men from their musick.
15 The joy of our heart is ceased;
   Our dance is turned into mourning.

7. *and are not*] or, better, **they are not**.
we have borne their iniquities] See Introduction, chap. i. § 3 (*a*).
8. *Servants have ruled*] **Slaves** *have ruled*. The Chaldaeans are meant, among whom it was nothing unusual for a slave to rise through ability or favour to the highest station.
9. *We gat our bread*] *We get our bread*. The reference is to the bands of wild Arabs (Bedaween), seeking opportunities for the plunder of those who venture from the shelter of the city to reap the harvest.
10. *was black like an oven because of the terrible famine*] **glows** *like an oven because of the* **burning blast of** *famine*. The feverishness brought on by hunger is meant.
12. *Princes are hanged up by their hand*] The reference probably is not to death by crucifixion, but to subsequent impalement in order to expose to the utmost ignominy. Both death by crucifixion and impalement after death were regarded with the utmost abhorrence by the Jews. For the former see Deut. xxi. 23.
13. *They took the young men to grind*] **The young men have borne the mill**. This involves the thought of their also being employed to grind the corn, and thus the general sense of the verse is that as rank and advanced age was no safeguard, neither did tenderness of age secure against the most oppressive and menial of labours.
14. *from the gate*] the place of social enjoyment and conversation, answering to our clubs and other places of entertainment. Compare Jer. xiv. 2 with note.

The crown is fallen *from* our head: 16
Woe unto us, that we have sinned!
For this our heart is faint; 17
For these *things* our eyes are dim.
Because of the mountain of Zion, which is desolate, 18
The foxes walk upon it.

19—22. *Final appeal to God for deliverance.*

Thou, O LORD, remainest for ever; 19
Thy throne from generation to generation.
Wherefore dost thou forget us for ever, 20
And forsake us so long time?
Turn thou us unto thee, O LORD, and we shall be turned; 21
Renew our days as of old.
But thou hast utterly rejected us; 22
Thou art very wroth against us.

16. *The crown is fallen from our head*] **The crown upon** (literally of) **our head is fallen**, i.e. our honour is brought to the dust.
woe unto us, that we have sinned!] These words shew that ver. 7 is not intended to imply that the generation which utters it does not inherit the sins of its ancestors quite as much as the punishment which is their due.

18. *foxes*] **jackals**. This shews what a comparative desert it was become.

19—22. FINAL APPEAL TO GOD FOR DELIVERANCE.

19. *remainest*] literally, *sittest*. The thought is that though the sanctuary of God on earth is desolate, yet there is hope and comfort in remembering that His heavenly dwelling is and must be unshaken.

20. Since this is so, why is Israel left desolate?

21. *Turn thou us...*] taken from Jer. xxxi. 18. The appeal to God as the only source from which repentance could arise in the people has for its underlying thought the same which appears in 2 Cor. iii. 5.

22. *But*] rather, **unless**. The whole sentence is an hypothesis not to be accepted as fact, and to express this, there should be a note of interrogation after *us* in both parts of the verse and we should also insert an *unless* before *thou art*. God's anger cannot last for ever, and thus there is yet hope.

Although the Book of Lamentations, like so many even of the saddest of the Psalms, does in fact close with the language of hope, that is in the present case so little apparent on the first reading that in many Heb. manuscripts ver. 21 is repeated at the end, that so its words may rather be the last to fall upon the ear. A similar expedient is used in the case of Ecclesiastes, Isaiah, and Malachi.

APPENDIX.

NOTE I.

TRADITIONS RELATING TO JEREMIAH.

1. That Jeremiah addressed a severe rebuke to the Jews in Egypt is the last undoubted fact which we possess in connection with him (chap. xliv.; see note on ver. 1), and it has been conjectured that it was in accordance with his own desire that his faithful minister Baruch refrained from inserting in the Book of his prophecies any further particulars of his life or record of his end—so slender at the outset and even inconsistent are the traditional notices.

2. The Christian tradition was that the Jews in Egypt, provoked by his rebukes, stoned him to death "Jeremias lapidatur" Tert. *adv. Gnost.* c. 8; "Jeremias lapidatus...a populo," Hieron. *adv. Jov.* II. 37. See also beginning of § 8 below.

3. The Jewish tradition, perhaps however invented by way of hiding the truth of the charge brought against them by the Christians, was that the prophet had escaped from Egypt to Babylon, and there died.

4. In the (Apocryphal) Book of Ecclesiasticus (chap. xlix. 7), the date of which is very uncertain, Jeremiah is referred to thus:—"They entreated him evil, who nevertheless was a prophet, sanctified in his mother's womb, that he might root out, and afflict, and destroy; and that he might build up also, and plant." See Jer. i. 10.

5. In 2 Macc. ii. 1—7 we are told that Jeremiah at the exile "commanded them that were carried away to take of the fire," and that "the prophet, being warned of God, commanded the tabernacle and the ark to go with him, as he went forth into the mountain, where Moses climbed up, and saw the heritage of God. And when Jeremy came thither, he found an hollow cave, wherein he laid the tabernacle, and the ark, and the altar of incense, and so stopped the door. And some of those that followed him came to mark the way, but they could not find it. Which when Jeremy perceived, he blamed them, saying, As for that place, it shall be unknown until the time that God gather his people again together, and receive them unto mercy."

6. Judas Maccabaeus before his conflict with Nicanor sees in a vision (2 Macc. xv. 12—16) "a man with grey hairs, and exceeding glorious, who was of a wonderful and excellent majesty...a lover of the brethren,...Jeremias the prophet of God," who presents him with a sword of gold, by which to prevail.

7. The following is the form which the tradition had assumed in the time of Polyhistor (brought from the East to Rome by Sylla the Dictator). He is quoted by Eusebius (*Praepar. Evang.* IX. 39). In the time of Jehoiakim Jeremiah prophesied. He found the Jews sacrificing to a golden idol, named Baal, and announced the impending disaster. Jehoiakim was for burning him alive, but he said that they (the Jews) should as captives cook food for the Babylonians and dig canals for the Tigris and Euphrates. The historian adds that Nebuchadnezzar hearing of these prophecies came with Astibar, king of the Medes, and captured Jerusalem, removing to Babylon the treasures of the Temple, "except the Ark and the Tables which were in it; these remained with Jeremiah." On this last point, see § 4 above.

8. In our Lord's time there are traces of a popular belief that Jeremiah's work on earth was not yet done, and this was one of the phases of Messianic hope. See Matt. xvi. 14, and compare John i. 21, where "that" (rather *the*) "prophet" is by some thought to have reference to him.

For other prophecies attributed to him, see Note II.

9. The treatise *De Vitis Prophetarum* attributed to St Epiphanius (died A.D. 402) relates as follows (shewing that meanwhile the tradition had grown considerably), "Jeremiah the prophet was of Anathoth, and he was stoned to death by the people at Taphnae in Egypt. And he lies at the site of Pharaoh's house, for the Egyptians honoured him, having received benefits from him; for asps and...crocodiles were destroying them, and at the prayer of the prophet Jeremiah both the venomous asps were driven from that land, and in like manner the treacherous beasts from the river, and all the faithful to the present day pray at that spot, and taking of the dust cure the bite of asps and put the crocodiles themselves to flight. This prophet gave a sign to the Egyptian priests, saying, that all their idols must be overthrown and all the works of their hands [see note on Jer. xxv. 7] collapse, when there should set foot in Egypt a virgin about to bear a Divine Child [Matt. ii. 14]. And so it was." Epiphanius adds that the memory of this prophecy is kept up by a ceremony continued to his own time. He continues:—"This prophet before the capture of the temple seized the Ark of the Law with all its contents, and caused it to be swallowed up in a rock, and said to the priests of the people and to the elders who stood by, *The Lord departed from Sinai into the heavens, and He will come again in sacred might. And this shall be the sign of His coming, when all nations bow down before wood* (the Cross, see Matt. xxiv. 14). And he said to them, *No one of the priests or prophets shall disclose this*

APPENDIX. 395

Ark, save Moses the chosen of God. The Tables that are in it none shall open save Aaron. And in the Resurrection the Ark shall rise first, and shall go forth from the rock and be placed on the Mount Sinai, and all the saints shall be gathered together to it, there awaiting the Lord, and shunning the enemy who desires to destroy them. And with his finger he impressed upon the rock the name of the Lord, and the impression was as though it had been cut with an iron tool, and a cloud overshadowed the rock, and no one knows that spot till the end of the world. And this rock is in the wilderness, where the Ark was first made, between the two mountains where Moses and Aaron lie. And at night a cloud like fire rests upon the spot, after the likeness of those of olden time, inasmuch as the glory of God will never desert His Law."

NOTE II.

OTHER PROPHECIES ASCRIBED TO JEREMIAH.

1. The 6th chapter of the (Apocryphal) Book of Baruch purports to be an Epistle from Jeremiah to the captives in Babylon.

2. A quotation is attributed to "Jeremy the Prophet" in Matt. xxvii. 9, really found however in Zech. xi. 12, 13. Lightfoot (*Horae Hebraicae*) on this N. T. passage quotes a Talmudic treatise (*Baba Bathra*, fol. 14 a) which makes the order of O. T. Books Joshua, Judges, Samuel, Kings, Jeremiah, Ezekiel, Isaiah, giving as the reason, that since the Books of Kings end with disaster, and Jeremiah and Ezekiel also deal with disaster, while Isaiah contains comfort, the former class should go together. Lightfoot accordingly explains the passage on this principle, and takes "Jeremy" to denote the whole section of which it was the opening Book; comparing Luke xxiv. 44, where by "the psalms" are denoted all the Books not included under the two other divisions there mentioned.

3. Justin Martyr (*Dialogue with Trypho*, p. 646 § 72, Migne Edition) ascribes evidently by mistake to Jeremiah a passage resembling 1 Pet. iii. 19.

4. Eph. v. 14, "Awake, thou that, etc." Grote in his commentary on this passage remarks that certain (among whom he mentions, apparently by error, St Epiphanius) say that this is from the Apocryphal writings of Jeremiah. He adds that at any rate the word "Christ" does not agree with such a view.

5. In the works of Pseudo Abdias (about the latter part of the 6th century A.D.) these words (see Fabricius, *Codex Pseudepigr.* V. T. p. 1109) are quoted as Jeremiah's: "Behold thy redeemer shall come, Jerusalem, and this shall be his token, He shall open the eyes of the blind, he shall restore to the deaf their hearing, and with his voice shall raise the dead.

6. Other portions of scripture which have been at one time or another ascribed to Jeremiah are Deuteronomy, Kings, many of the Psalms, e.g. v., vi., xiv., xxii., xli., lii—lv., lxix.—lxxi., Isaiah., chaps. xlix.—lxvi., Zechariah, chaps. ix.—xiv.

NOTE III.

JEREMIAH AS A TYPE OF CHRIST.

St Jerome (*Commentary on Jer. xxiii.* 9) speaks of this prophet as one who (i) as leading a single life, (ii) as a prophet, (iii) as sanctified from the womb (compare Luke i. 15) and (iv) in his very name, *the Lord's exalted one*, prefigured Christ. To state the parallel more fully in the words of a modern writer: "In both there is the same early manifestation of the consciousness of a Divine mission (Luke ii. 49). The persecution which drove the prophet from Anathoth has its counterpart in that of the men of Nazareth (Luke iv. 29). His protests against the priests and prophets are the forerunners of the woes against the scribes and Pharisees (Matt. xxiii.). His lamentations over the coming miseries of his country answer to the tears that were shed over the Holy City by the Son of Man. His sufferings come nearest, of those of the whole army of martyrs, to those of the Teacher against Whom princes and priests and elders and people were gathered together. He saw more clearly than others that New Covenant, with all its gifts of spiritual life and power, which was proclaimed and ratified in the death upon the cross." (Professor Plumptre, *Sm. Bibl. Dict.*, Art. *Jeremiah*.)

NOTE IV.

APPROXIMATION TO A CHRONOLOGICAL ARRANGEMENT OF THE CONTENTS OF THE BOOK.

CHAPS.
```
1—12............Josiah.
14—20...........Jehoiakim.
26...............1st year of Jehoiakim.
25...............4th    ,,     ,,
¹46—49..........do.    ,,     ,,
35, 36...........do.    ,,     ,,
45...............do.    ,,     ,,
13...............Jehoiachin.
29...............(? 1st year of) Zedekiah.
27...............do.   ,,
50, 51...........4th year of Zedekiah.
28...............do.    ,,     ,,
²21—24..........9th    ,,     ,,
34...............do.    ,,     ,,
37...............9th (10th)    ,,
30—33..........10th   ,,     ,,
38...............10th   ,,     ,,
52...............11th   ,,     ,,
39—44.......... Period of exile.
```

¹ Except 46, 13—28................Period of exile.
       49, 34—39.................1st year of Zedekiah.
² But originally *spoken* at various times. See 21, 1.

INDEX.

₊ *Italics are used in modern names of places, the less familiar foreign words, and in cases where words or phrases, or particular senses of them there noted, are wholly or partially obsolete.*

Abarim, 156
Abdeel, 245
Abner, 268
access to God shall be direct, 215
Achbor, 184, 243
Adaiah, 102
Ahab, 196
Ahikam, 185
Ai, 307
Aichah, 353, 361
Alexandria, Jews at, 281
almond tree, see Jeremiah, visions connected with
alphabetical arrangement, 330
Amasis, 282, 290
ambassadors, 345
Ammonites, bands of, 97
Amon (Ammon), see No Amon
Anata, xii
Anathoth, xi.; Jeremiah conspired against by people of, 95; their punishment, 96, 97
Apis, 289
appendix to Jeremiah (chap. lii.), genuineness of, 244
apple (of the eye), 373
Apries, 247, 282
Ar, 301
Ararat, 336
ark, 30; see also footstool
arm, emblem of authority, 301
Armenia, 336
Arnon, 295
Aroer, 300
Arpad, 313
Asa, 267
asceticism of Rechabites, 236; of Nabathaeans, 238
Ashdod, 175
Ashkelon, 175, 295
Ashkenaz, 336
ass, the burial of, 155
Assyria = Babylon, 19; vacillation of the Jews between Egypt and, *ib.*
Assyrians, cruelty of, 59; battle axe of the, 291
Atbash, 176, 330
Athens, crowded during invasion of Attica, illustration from, 36; the plague at, 121
Aven, 275
avenger of blood, 327
Azariah, 269

Azekah, 233
Azriel, 245
Azur, 189
Azzah (=Gaza), 175

Baal, 15, 69, 224; = Bosheth, 32
Baalim, 21
Baalis, 264, 268
Baasha, 267
Babylon, presumption of, 326; date of prophecy (l. li) regarding, 317; capture of, 322, 325, 337, 339; Zedekiah's visit to, 192, 343; = Assyria, 19; = Babylonia, 322; likened to a golden cup, 331; to a battle axe, 334; called a destroying mountain, 335; a burnt mountain, 336; exiles commanded to pray for, 193; see also canals, and gates, and walls
Babylonia, fertility of, 323
baker, 250
baldness, 18, 304, 306; see mourning
balm, 76, 332
Baruch, minister to Jeremiah, 221, 241; lesson of humility taught him, xxxiii. 282; did he write chap. l. etc.? 317
Barzillai, 269
bases, 189, 348
basons, 349
battle-axe, Assyrian, 291, 334; Babylon likened to a, 334
beard, shaving the corners of, 82; cut in mourning, 122, 266, 304
beauty, figures expressive of, 385
Bedaween, 26, 390
Bel, 319, 340
Ben-hadad, 314
Benjamin, territory of, 1
Beth-aven, 39
Beth-diblathain, 301
Bethel, 39, 299
Beth-gamul, 301
Beth-haccerem (Beth-acharna), 52
Beth-lehem, 269; see also Ephrath
Beth-meon, 301
Beth-shemesh, 275
bird, the people likened to a, 100; birdcatchers, *ib.*
bondmen, house of, 234
Book of the Law, discovery of, xv. xvii
Boscath, 102
Bosheth, see Baal
bottle, 104, 299

INDEX.

bowels, 212, 367, 371
bowls, 349
bowmen, 43; of Elam, 316
Bozrah, 301, 310, 311
Branch, the, 159
brasen bulls, 349
bread, cake of, 250; scarcity of, 252
"breath of our nostrils," 388
brick-kiln, 196, 273
brigand, 285
brigandine, 285
brightness, gleams of, in Jeremiah, 193
bruit, 89
buckler, 285
built (=established), 102, 206, 270
bullocks (=choice youths), 325; mercenary troops likened to, 290
bulls, see brasen bulls
burden, 166
burial, lack of, as punishment, 112, 155
Buz, 176

cabins, 249
cage, 50
cakes (sacrificial), 65, 279
caldrons, 348, 349; see also Jeremiah, visions connected with
canals about Babylon, 328, 339
candlesticks, 349
cane, the sweet, 58
cannibalism, 140, 374
Caphtor, 294
captivities, Nebuchadnezzar's successive, 351
caravanserai, 76, 269
Carchemish, 284, 286, 297; turning point in history, 170
Carmel, 13, 290, 324
carpenters, 168, 193
Cassandra, Jeremiah likened to, xxvii
cast about, 268
caterpillars, 333, 336
cedars (=chief men), 152
celibacy, 121
ceremonial, if heartless, useless, 58, 60, 94; comes second to the moral law, 66
Chaldaean army composed of many distinct nations, 231
chapiters, 349
Chemosh, 297
childhood, stages of, 384
children bear the sins of their parents, 356; much prized by the Jews, 60, 117, 121, 153, 158, 246
children of the people, 130
Chimham, 268
Chittim, 15
Christ typified by Jeremiah, see Jeremiah
Chuzistan, 316
cistern, 16, 17, 109
cleansing (forgiveness), a distinctive feature of the new covenant, 214, 227

"Cleopatra's Needle," 275
clothes rent in mourning, 266
clouds, enemy likened to, 38
clouts, 253
cockatrice, 75
Commandment, bearing of Jeremiah's teaching on Second, 356; breach of Fourth, 131; Rabbinic view of the Fourth, *ib.*
compass, 212
Coniah, see Jehoiachin
consolation, the cup of, 122
correct, 20
counting. Heb. mode of, 234
court of law, figure taken from, 178
court of the Temple, 180
covenant, ceremonies attendant on, 235; superseding of the legal, 214; illustration of certainty of God's, 230
crane, 72
C'thubhim, 353
cunning, 80
cup, Babylon likened to a golden, 331
cups, 349
Cushi, 243
Cyaxares, xx

Damascus, 313
Dan, town of, 39, 74
Daniel, date of his captivity, xx.; his dumbness removed by touching, 4
Dante, Jeremiah likened to, xxvii.; quotation from, 46
Daphnae Pelusii, see Tahapanes
darkness, symbol of ignorance or of misery, 105, 376
days come, 159
Dedan, 175, 309
deed of purchase, 220
defaming, 145
Delaiah, 243, 245
delicately, 384
delicates, 338
desperately wicked, 128
Dhiban, 300
diamond, 125
Dibon, 299
disaster, likened to a bitter draught, 174
discovered, 372
divorce, 25
doings, see ways
door, keeper of the, 237
dote, 327
double, 130, 324
drought, 26, 50, 98, 108, 109, 140, 190, 328, 346, and often in Lamentations; joined with sword and pestilence, 111, 115, 195, 271. See also famine
dungeon, 249, 252, 381, etc.

INDEX. 399

eagle, 305
eagles, enemy swifter than, 39, 387
ears, tingling of, 138
eat, 119
Ebedmelech, 252, 260
eclipse, 117
Edom, 82, 175, 308; king of, 186
Eglath, 304
Egypt, Jewish colonists in, 281; study of medicine in, 287; mercenary troops of, 290; the Holy Family's flight into, 275, 394
Ekron, 175
Elam, 316; bowmen of, *ib.*
Elasah, 193
el-Busaireh, 310
"elders of Israel," 183
Elealeh, 304
Elishama, 245, 265
Elnathan, 184, 243, 245
Et Teim, 295
Emims, 295
ending, fear of an ill-omened, 352, 391
enemies of Israel, their punishment to be temporary, 101, 292, 306, 308, 317
enfranchisement of slaves, 233
English history, illustration from, 11
Ephai, 263
Ephraim, 65, 208; position of mount, 39
Ephrath (?Euphrates=), 103
equal, 371
Ethiopia, 107
Ethiopians, 107, 286; see also Ebedmelech
eunuch, 252
Euphrates, 103, 337
Evil-merodach, 157, 352
exiles commanded to pray for Babylon, 193
eyelid-staining, 43
Ezekiel, special revelation to, 346; alleged quotation from in Lamentations, 356

fallow ground, simile from, 34
falsehood=idolatry, 108, 112
false prophets, 189
fame, 59
familiars, 145, 255
family, 29
family feuds, 77
famine, cannibalism produced by, 140, 374; see also drought
fan, 116
fasts, 242, 265, 347
fatness, a mark of prosperity, 51
fear, 380
fear is on every side, 59, 374
ferries, 337
fet, 184
field, 219, 225
fire, a signal, 52; a part of Moloch-worship, 69, 139; a strong motive-power, 144; a punishment, 48, 118,
127, 149, 150, 152, 223, 306, 314, 326, 342, 365, 369, 366; on the hearth, 244; God's Word likened to a, 165; roast in the (as a punishment), 196
fire-pans, 349
firstfruits at Passover, 50; at Feast of Weeks, *ib.*
fishing, metaphor from, 124
flow, used of the tribes, 209
folds, 159
folly=idolatry, 161; see also vain (vanity)
footstool, 368
forest, 150, 291; forest of Lebanon, 152
forgiveness, see cleansing
former rain, 26, 50
fountain, 16, 76, 129
foxes, 391
fray, 70
fruit dedicated, 207
furnace, the iron, 91
furniture of Temple, 348
funerals, distribution of bread and wine at, 122

gadfly, 290
gall, 74, 162, 375, 377
Gamaliel, parallel to argument of, 182
Gareb, 217
gate, 116;=inhabitants of city, 109; the seat of justice, etc. 8, 109, 150, 390; gates of the Temple, 62, 142, 182; gates of the city, 138, 217, 249, 258; gates of Babylon, 342
Gath, 175, 294
Gaza, 293, see also Azzah
Gedaliah, son of Ahikam, 185, 260, etc.; = Igdaliah, 237; son of Pashur, 251
Gehenna, 22, 69; see Hinnom
Gemariah, son of Shaphan, 185, 242, 245; son of Hilkiah, 193
ghetto, 296
Gibeon, 189, 268
Gilead, 76, 152, 287, 324
gird up thy loins, 9
give glory, 105
give the hand, 322
glaziers, diamond used by, 126
Goath, 217
Goel, 327
gold, the people likened to, 383
Gomorrah, 162, 311, 328
grapes, sour, 214
grasshopper, 291
groves, 126

habitation, 228, 312, 323, 368
hadariye, 315
hair cut in mourning, 122, 266, 304; in ceremonial uncleanness, 68
Hamath, 258, 313, 346, 351
Hammelech, 245
hammer, God's Word likened to a, 165; Babylon likened to a, 324
Hamutal (Hamital), 345

Hanameel, 219
Hanan, 237
Hananeel, 217
Hananiah, son of Azur, 189; father of Zedekiah, 243; grandfather of Irijah, 249
hand (=palm), 99, 121; stretched out in prayer, 373
hanging, 390
harvest, a proverb taken from, 101
hasten, 6, 281
Hazor, 315
head covered in mourning, 109
heap, 204, 212, 339
heard, 234
heart, seat of the intellect, or of the will, 37; of the emotions, 373
hearth, 244
heath, 127, 297
heavenly bodies, worship of, 71, 140
hedges, 307
Heliopolis, 275
Heshbon, 296, 304, 306, 307
Hezekiah, quoted as a precedent, 183
Hierapolis, 285
high places (as a seat of idolatry,) 26, 110; see also mourning
Hilkiah, x., 1
hind, careful of its young, 110
Hinnom, 21, 69, 138, 139, 217, 224
hissing, 136, 139, 172, 195, 339, 372
Holon, 300
honey, flowing with milk and, 92
hope, gleams of in Jeremiah, 198
hope of Israel, a title of God, 110
Hophra, see Pharaoh-Hophra
horn, as emblem, 301, 369, 373
horns (of altar), 126
Horonaim, 296, 304
Hosannah, meaning of, 208
Hoshaiah, 269
hospice, see caravanserai
host of heaven, see heavenly bodies
houses thrown down to make room for defensive works, 227
humbled, 277
hunting, metaphor from, 124, 325, 362, 365, 380, 387, 388
husband, the word used of God, 215

Igdaliah, see Gedaliah
image and thing imaged blended, see Book of Jeremiah
imagination, 30, 67, 79, 92, 104, 123, 135, 163
Immer, see Pashur
imprecations, 137, 146
inanimate objects spoken of as sympathizing with sorrow, 363
incense, 58
incurable, 128
iniquity of fathers visited on children, 214
Innocents, slaughter of, 210
instruct, 211
interest, see usury

in those days, 30, 324
Isaiah, list of quotations from, 84
Ishmael, 263, etc.
isles, 175

Jaaziniah, 1, 236
jackals, 78, 383
Jahaz, 304
Jahazah, 300
Jazer, 303
Jeconiah, see Jehoiachin
Jedidah, 102
Jehoahaz, other name of, 153; Jeremiah's grief at his fate, 152
Jehoiachin, xxi., 157; childless, 158
Jehoiada, 197
Jehoiakim, character of, xviii, 151, 154, 156; murder of Urijah, 184; burning of the Roll, 244; his end, 155, 246; misreading for Zedekiah, 185
Jehucal (=Jucal), 247, 251
Jehudi, 243, 244
Jerahmeel, 245
jeremiad, xvi
Jeremiah, meaning of name, ix.; parentage, x.; family dwelling place, xi.; dedicated before birth, 3; distinctive features of his call, xvi.; age when called, 4; parallels in secular history, xxvii.; visions connected with, 5—7, 167; opposition to him, xxvi., 145; he advises submission to Chaldaea, xvii., 19; symbol of the potter's clay, 132; of the broken vessel, 138—140; of the linen girdle, 102; of the yoke, 186, 191; of the wine cup, 174; the prophet's Roll, 240; its burning ineffectual, illustration of this, xx.; letter to the exiles, 192; charged with desertion, 249; buys a field, xxiii., 219; rescued by Ebedmelech, 253; Nebuchadnezzar friendly, 103, 259; in Egypt, 273; traditions concerning him, 393; Grotto of, 354; a type of Christ, 396; other prophecies ascribed to him, 395; other portions of O. T. ascribed to him, *ib.*; references to him in N. T., 394; other Jeremiahs
Jeremiah, Book of, language of chap. 1—16; unlike the rest, 83; Chaldee verse, 86; parallels with Deut. xv.; with Lamentations, 357; repetitions of language, or thought or an image, xxviii., 63; examples of image and thing imaged blended, xxix.; use of cypher (Atbash), xxx., 176; analysis of contents, xxxi.; clue to their arrangement, xxxii.; prophecies chronologically arranged, 396; Septuagint, xxxiv., 173, 284, 316; differences in Heb. and Sept. order discussed, xxxvi.; Table shewing the two orders, xxxviii
Jerusalem, name of street in, 250; believed impregnable, 386; called God's throne, 30, 114; called a mountain,

126, 213; a valley and a rock, 150; "that killest the prophets," 23; the Jew's "wailing place" at, 360; see also footstool
Jezaniah, 263, 269
Joab, 268
Johanan, 263, etc.
Jonadab, 237
Jonathan, the scribe, 249, 250, 256; son of Kareah, 263
Jordan, the swelling of, 99
Josiah, reformation, x. xii., his end xvii., 353, 354, 360
journey of Zedekiah to Babylon, 192, 343
Jucal, see Jehucal
Judaea, exposed position of, xii.; its history from Hezekiah's time, xiii.; its overthrow shall not be final, 42; medal representing, 361
Justin Martyr, his quotation as though from Jeremiah, 395

Kareah, see Johanan
Kedar, 15, 314
keeper of the door, 237
Kerioth, 301, 305
Khan, see caravanserai
kiln, see brick-kiln
Kingly office, in what sense permanent, 229
Kings, kept at the court of the conqueror, 352
Kinôth, 353
Kinsman's right to redeem, 219
Kir-heres, 303
Kiriathaim, 295, 301
Kirjath-jearim, 184
know, 3, 123
Kolaiah, play on the word, 196
Kronos, legend of, 224
Kureiyat, 296

Lachish, 233
lamb, a pet, 95
Lamentations, Book of, its name, 353; position, *ib.*; date, 354; structure, *ib.*; authorship, 355; alleged inconsistencies with Book of Jeremiah, 356, etc.; parallelisms, 357, 359; subject matter and purpose, 359; use, 360; see also Ezekiel.
latter rain, 26, 50
Law, undue boasting in the, 73, 136
Lebanon, 135, 152
lees, of wine, 298
leopard, 46, 107
leper, 386
Libyans, 286
lift up the head, 352
lions, in literal sense, 46; figurative, 17, 23, 36, 99, 179, 311, 323, 329, 339
little ones = servants, 109; = abject ones, 296
liver, 371
Livy, illustration from, xxiii

JEREMIAH

locusts, 291, 333, 336
lodging place, see caravanserai
lovers = allied nations, 156
Luhith, 297
Lydians, 286
Maaseiah, father of Neriah, 221, 343; son of Shallum, 237; father of Zedekiah, 196; father of Zephaniah, 148, 197, 247
Mabog, 285
Maccabaeus, meaning of, 325
Madmen, 296
madness, 197, 274
Magor-missabib, 59, 374
Malleus Scotorum, 325; hereticorum, *ib.*
Manasseh, irreligion of, xiv. 24
Marduk = Merodach, 319
mark, 21
marriage, festivities of, 70, 172; forbidden to Jeremiah, 121
Martel, Charles, 325
Mattaniah, see Zedekiah
Mattan, 251
meat-offerings, 132, 266, 364
Medes, 176, 332, 336
medicine studied in Egypt, 287
Megiddo, xvii., 353
Megilloth, 353
Mephaath, 300
mercenary troops of Egypt, 290
Merethaim, 324
Merodach, 319
Merodach-Baladan, 319
Mesha, 295, 300
Messiah called David, 201
Messianic prophecies, 159, 210
metals, refining of, 120
Micah, quotation from, 183
Michaiah, 183, 243
Migdol, 275, 288
Milcom, 307
milk, see honey
mill, 390
mingled people, 175
Minni, 336
Misgab, 296
mixture of metaphors, 29
Mizpah, 262, 267
Moab, 82, 175, 264, 295, etc.
Moabites, bands of, 97; "Moabite stone," 295, 298, 300
Moloch, worship of, 69, 224
moon worship, 65, 71, 278, etc.; see also new moon
morning, the business time, 150
Moses, 114
mount, a besieger's, 53, 223, 227
mountain, as a hindrance, 105; title of Jerusalem or Zion, 126
mourners, hired, 80
mourning, on high places, 32; hand laid on head in, 25; head covered in, 109; dust on head in, 371; clothes rent in, 266; cutting of beard, etc. in, 122, 266,

26

INDEX.

304; odours burnt in, 232; Jeremiah to avoid the house of, 121
mouth put in the dust to shew submission, 378
mutiny, illustration from Indian, 267
Nabathaeans, 238
Náblus, 266
Nabopolassar, xx
name, change of, on accession, etc., xvii., 153; play upon names, 324; a Book named from a conspicuous word in it, 353, 361
nations, the wine cup administered to the, 174; order of prophecies against, 284
naughty, 168
Nazarites, 385
Nagid, 141
Nebo, 295, 301
Nebuchadnezzar = Nebuchadrezzar, 148
Nebuzar-adan, 260, etc., 273, 347
Nechoh, see Pharaoh Nechoh
neck, hardening of, 67
Nehelamite, 197
Nehemiah, 335
Nehushta, 102, 106
Nergal-sharezer, 257, 258, 260
net, 365
Nethaniah, 243
Netophathite, 263
new moon, signal of, 52; watchers for, 207
New Test. references to Jeremiah, 394
Nile, 286
Nimrim, 304
Nitocris, 70, 339
nitre, 21
No Amon, 292
Nob, 262
noon, 53, 116, 147
Noph, 18, 275, 290
numbers, difficulties connected with, 157; Jewish love of certain, 172; see also counting, Heb. mode of

Obadiah, 308
obelisk, 274
old paths, 57
olive, 94
On, 275
Ophir, 85
ostriches, 328, 304
owls, 328
ox, 95

pakid, 141, 350
Palestine, see Judaea
palm tree, upright as the, 84
partridge, 128
pasha, 335
Pashur, son of Immer, 133, 141, 251; son of Melchiah, 141, 148, 251
Passover, first fruits at, 50
pastors, 14, 29, 129, 136, 158

pastures (pasturage), 53, 78, 159, 177, 179, 312; see also habitation
Pathros, 275
pavilion, 274
Pekod, 324
pekhâh, 335
Pelusium, 275
pen-knife, 244
pestilence, joined with sword and famine, 111, 115, 195, 271
Petra, 311
Pharaoh, 174 (meaning of), 247, 248, 289, 293
Pharaoh-Hophra, 247, 281, 282, 290, 293
Pharaoh-Nechoh, xvii., 284, 290, 293
Phocion, Jeremiah likened to, xxvii
phrases imitated by the false prophets, 165, 190
pillory, 142
pit, see cistern
pitiful, 385
plague, 139
plaister, 202, 203, 287
play upon proper names, 52, 324
polygamy, 106
pomegranates, 349
Porte, the Sublime, 110
post, 337
potter, vessel of, wheel of, see Jeremiah
prayer, hand stretched out in, 373
present a supplication, 242
prey, thy life shall be for a, 261
priestly office, permanence of, 229
priests, not spread through country, xi
prophets, false: see false prophets; three modes of deception as practised by them, 112
prophets, schools of the, xv
prosperity of the wicked, 97, 98
proverbs, 98, 99
provinces, 362
Psammetichus, xvii
Pseudo-Abdias, Jeremiah alleged to be quoted by, 395
Ptolemy Lagi, 281

quarter-master general, 343
queen (= queen mother), 106, 193; queen of heaven, 65, 278
quiet prince, 343

Rabbah, 307
Rab-mag, 258, 260
Rab-saris, 258, 260
Rachel, 210
rain, see former rain, latter rain
Ramah, 210, 261, 267
Rechab, meaning of, 237
Rechabites, 236, 385; their reward, 239, later references to, 240
redeemer, 327
redemption of property, 219
reeds, 337

INDEX. 403

reins, seat of the affections, 96, 98, 128, 376
rent (= rend), 43
repentance, used of God, 115, 134
revenues, 101
reward, 262
Riblah, 254, 258, 346
riches, not properly a plural, 304
righteousness, the Lord our, 160
rising up early and speaking, 65
roast in the fire, a punishment, 195
rod of his inheritance, 87; rod implying strength, 299; implying wrath, 375
roll, see Jeremiah
roofs of houses, uses of, 140
rubies, 385

sabbaths, hallowing of 131; Gentile ignorance concerning, 364
sabbatical rest, the land forced to keep a, 127
sâgân, 335
Salem, 266, see also Jerusalem
Samgar-nebo, 257
Samuel, 114
sapphire, 385
Sarsechim, 257
Savonarola, 117, 144
schools of the prophets, xv
Scilun, 64
Scotorum malleus, 325
scribes, 73
Scythian invasion, xiv., 36
sea-monsters, 383
sea, sorrow on the, 313; = reservoir, 339; of brass, 189, 348
seething pot, see Jeremiah
Selah, 311
Septuagint, see Jeremiah, Book of
Seraiah, son of Azriel, 245; son of Neriah, 343; the chief priest, 350
served, 347
Shallum (king), see Jehoahaz; father of Hanameel, 219
Shaphan, 184, 193, 242
Sheba, 58
Shechem, 266
shekel, 220
Shelemiah, 243, 245, 247, 249, 251
Shemaiah, father of Urijah, 184; the Nehelamite, 197; father of Delaiah, 243
Shephatiah, 251
shepherds, 320; see also pastors
Sheshach, 176, 340
shields, 332
Shiloh, 64, 266
Shishak, 18
shout (vintage), 177, 333
shovels, 348
Sibmah, 303
sickle, 323
sides of the earth, 59
Sidon, see Zidon

sight, deprivation of, a common punishment, 259
sign sometimes *followed* the thing signified, 281
signet, 157
Sihor, 19
singular, collective sense of, 60
sirocco, 38, 108
sith, 116
slaughter, valley of, 139
slavery, 17; enfranchisement of slaves, 233; the Chaldaeans called slaves, 390
smiths, 168, 193
snow of Lebanon, 335
snuffers, 348
sodden, 386
Sodom, 162, 311, 328, 384
sope, 21
sorrow, as on the sea, 313; inanimate objects spoken of as sympathizing with, 363; figure for intense, 381
spoons, 349
staff, implying strength, 299
stand before, 64, 120. See also served
standard (standards), 36
star-worship, see heavenly bodies
steel, 118
stripes, 142
stocks, 142
stores, custom of hiding, 267
stork, 72
stubble, 108
sun worship, 71
swallow, 72
swift (a bird), 72
sword of the Lord, spoilers likened to, 101
sword, joined with famine and pestilence, 111, 115, 195, 271; the oppressing, 289
Sychar, 266
Syrians, bands of, 97

tabernacle, see tents
table, admission to the king's, a special honour, 352
Tabor, 289
tabor, tabret, 206
Tahapanes (Tahpanes), 18, 273, 275, 288
tale, 229
tank, see cistern
Taphnae, see Tahapanes
Tarshish, 85
Tatnai, 335
Tekña, 52
Tel, 204
tell, 228
Tema, 175
Teman, 309, 312
Temple, position of, 133, 181, 213; furniture of, 348; called God's throne, 114, 129; invaded by the heathen, 364; see also footstool
tents, still used in Jeremiah's time, 41, 88
terror, 130, 169, 222

Threni, 353
threshing, 338
throne, title of Jerusalem, 30, 114; of Temple, 114, 129
Tiglath-pileser, 307
timbrel, 206
Titus, medal struck by (Judaea capta), 361
Tophet, 69, 139, 140, 141
travail (travel), 375
tree, men described under figure of, 97, 127
trumpet, a signal of danger, 41, 52, 57
turtle (dove), 72
Tyrus (Tyre), 175, 186, 294

uncircumcised ears, 55
unclean (the leper's cry), 386
Uphaz, 85
Urijah, 184
usury, 117
Uz, 175

vain (vanity), used of idols, 12, 39, 75, 85, 112, 114, 125, 135; see also folly
valley of Hinnom, see Hinnom
vermilion, 154
vessel, meaning of water poured from, 139; vessels of the Lord's house, 188
vine, 20; vinedressers, 259
vineyard (=Israel), 100
vintage-songs, 177, 333
virgin, the people spoken of as a, 113, 135, 206; virgins taking part in religious ceremonies, 363
visit for good or evil, 219; Zedekiah's visit to Babylon, 192; iniquity of fathers visited on children, 214
volume, derivation of, 241
vows, obstinacy in idolatrous, 278

Wady en-Nemeirah, 304

walls, Babylon's broad, 342
war, a religious act, 53
ward, 249
watch (verb), 281; watch (subst.), 373
watchers for new moon, 207
waters, an army likened to, 293
waters, cold, 135
ways (your ways and your doings), 62
way-marks, 212
Weeks, firstfruits at Feast of, 50
weeping, excessive, 366
whirlwind, enemy's chariots likened to a, 38
widow, Judaea as a, 361
wilderness, 12; wind from the, 38, 108
wine, 298; filled with (figurative sense), 104, 301, 310, 331
winepress, 366
winter house, 244
works of the hands, 8, 171; also 84, 223
wormwood, 79, 162, 377
writing on earth or sand, 129; the prophecies committed to, 199, 241, 343

year (for years), 345
yoke, symbol of the, see Jeremiah; Babylon's dominion called a, 200

Zedekiah (king) xxii., his capture, 258, 346, 363, 388; his end, 347; conflicting prophecies connected with, 232; see also breath of our nostrils; son of Maaseiah, 196; son of Hananiah, 243
Zephaniah, 148
Zerubbabel, 335
Zidon (Sidon), 175
Zimri, 176
Zion, 29, 36, 113, 183, 203, 207, 209, 258, 319, 339; a mountain, 126; see Jerusalem and Temple
Zoar, 304
Zobah, 313

The CAMBRIDGE BIBLE for SCHOOLS
Opinions of the Press.

"The books are edited on the same general plan, but by different men. The critical apparatus is scholarly, but adapted to meet the wants of intelligent boys and girls who know no Greek nor Hebrew. The introduction to each book gives a clear, simple statement of our present knowledge of its authorship, authenticity, and design. The student is encouraged to study the book as a whole. The notes do not enter into abstruse questions of dogmatic theology. They aim to give a plain, rational answer to the question, What is the meaning of these words, of this sentence, of this paragraph, of this section, of this book? I have found them exceedingly suggestive and helpful. I find it more convenient for private study than any other edition of the Bible."—Prof. A. B. Stark, *Southern Methodist Quarterly Review*, U. S. A.

"We were quite prepared to find in Canon Farrar's St Luke a masterpiece of Biblical criticism and comment, and we are not disappointed by our examination of the volume before us. It reflects very faithfully the learning and critical insight of the Canon's greatest works, his 'Life of Christ' and his 'Life of St Paul,' but differs widely from both in the terseness and condensation of its style. What Canon Farrar has evidently aimed at is to place before students as much information as possible within the limits of the smallest possible space, and in this aim he has hit the mark to perfection. The introduction deals with the Gospels generally, and with St Luke's in particular. It gives an excellent biographical sketch of St Luke, points out the evidences for the authenticity of St Luke's Gospel, gives in detail the characteristics of the Gospel, furnishes an analysis of its contents, states the chief ancient manuscripts of the Gospels, and presents us with a brief account of the Herods as mentioned in the Gospels and the Acts. It is only fair to say that as a series the 'Cambridge Bible for Schools' has no equal in point of excellence and usefulness, and that Canon Farrar's work is quite the best of the series."—*The Examiner.*

"*Canon Farrar's* contribution to THE CAMBRIDGE SCHOOL BIBLE is one of the most valuable yet made. His annotations on *The Gospel according to St. Luke*, while they display a scholarship at least as sound, and an erudition at least as wide and varied as those of the editors of St. Matthew and St. Mark, are rendered telling and attractive by a more lively imagination, a keener intellectual and spiritual insight, a more incisive and picturesque style. They are marked, in short, by the very qualities most requisite to interest and instruct the class for which this work is designed. His *St. Luke* is worthy to be ranked with Professor Plumptre's *St James*, than which no higher commendation can well be given."—*The Expositor.*

"Dr Farrar, in the Cambridge *St Luke*, has laid us all under great obligation by his masterly marshalling before us of all that is necessary to know concerning the Gospel itself, and in regard to its relation to others. His notes on the verses are critical and full of information, yet concise withal; but his introductory matter is invaluable. In his fourth chapter on "*Characteristics of the Gospel*," we seem to get into the very heart of the evangelist's purpose, and, after perusal, one sees more clearly than before how wise and beneficent was the Divine plan that gave us the Gospel from more pens than one."—*The Sunday School Chronicle.*

"*The Cambridge Bible for Schools. St Luke.* Edited by Canon Farrar, D.D. We have received with pleasure this edition of the Gospel by St Luke, by Canon Farrar. It is another instalment of the best school commentary of the Bible we possess. In its general features it does not differ from the previous volumes of the series. Of the expository part of the work we cannot speak too highly. It is admirable in every way, and contains just the sort of information needed for Students of the English text unable to make use of the original Greek for themselves."—*The Nonconformist and Independent.*

"Another instalment of the *Cambridge Bible for Schools* appears in the Gospel according to St Luke, edited by Canon Farrar. Dr Farrar has written a brief introduction at once lucid and scholarly, in which he summarises what is known as to the origin, and points out the distinctive features of all the four Gospels, presents a sketch of the life of St Luke, discusses the authenticity of his Gospel, describes its characteristics, and furnishes an analysis of it. The chief value of the book to students, however, will consist in the notes, which are exceedingly numerous, and constitute a commentary at once minute, informative, and pervaded by a spirit of true Christian culture. No volume of the series is likely to command more general appreciation than this."—*The Scotsman.*

"No one who has seen Canon Farrar's 'Life of Christ' and 'St Paul,' will doubt us when we say that every page of his 'St Luke' contains useful and suggestive comments. It is intended to issue the whole of the Bible in similar style. We strongly advise our readers to obtain a prospectus of this publication."—*The Lay Preacher.*

"As a handbook to the third gospel, this small work is invaluable. The author has compressed into little space a vast mass of scholarly information. . . The notes are pithy, vigorous, and suggestive, abounding in pertinent illustrations from general literature, and aiding the youngest reader to an intelligent appreciation of the text. A finer contribution to 'The Cambridge Bible for Schools' has not yet been made."—*Baptist Magazine.*

"Canon Farrar has supplied students of the Gospel with an admirable manual in this volume. It has all that copious variety of illustration, ingenuity of suggestion, and general soundness of interpretation which readers are accustomed to expect from the learned and eloquent editor. Any one who has been accustomed to associate the idea of 'dryness' with a commentary, should go to Canon Farrar's *St Luke* for a more correct impression. He will find that a commentary may be made interesting in the highest degree, and that without losing anything of its solid value. . . . But, so to speak, it is *too good* for some of the readers for whom it is intended. An immediate demand for it will come from classes preparing for the Cambridge Local Examination. . . The more advanced the student, the more useful to him this manual."—*The Spectator.*

"*St Mark*, with Notes by the Rev. G. F. Maclear, D.D. Into this small volume Dr Maclear, besides a clear and able Introduction to the Gospel, and the text of St Mark, has compressed many hundreds of valuable and helpful notes. In short, he has given us a capital manual of the kind required—containing all that is needed to illustrate the text, i.e. all that can be drawn from the history, geography, customs, and manners of the time. But as a handbook, giving in a clear and succinct form the information which a lad requires in order to stand an examination in the Gospel, it is admirable... I can very heartily commend it, not only to the senior boys and girls in our High Schools, but also to Sunday-school teachers, who may get from it the very kind of knowledge they often find it hardest to get."—*Expositor*.

"The scheme is well started in the little book before us. Dr Maclear has formed a sound conception of the kind of book needed for school purposes, and has made his contribution thoroughly serviceable, ...With the help of a book like this, an intelligent teacher may make 'Divinity' as interesting a lesson as any in the school course. The notes are of a kind that will be, for the most part, intelligible to boys of the lower forms of our public schools; but they may be read with greater profit by the fifth and sixth, in conjunction with the original text."—*The Academy*.

"St Mark is edited by Dr Maclear, Head Master of King's College School. It is a very business-like little book. The text is given in paragraphs, and each paragraph has a title, which reappears as a division of the notes. The introduction, which occupies twenty pages, is clear and good, and concludes with an analysis of the book. There are maps and an index. The notes are pointed and instructive, and constantly give words and phrases from Wicliff's version, and quotations from classical and modern authors, which add greatly to the interest of the work and to its usefulness for schools. There is a good list of writers who have undertaken other parts of this edition of the Bible, including the editor and his distinguished brothers, Professor Plumptre, Canon Farrar, Dr Moulton, and Mr Sanday."—*Contemporary Review*.

"We welcome with enthusiasm this first fruit of the banding together of eminent divinity students of our Universities under the editorship of Dr Perowne, and are not sorry that it represents the labours of so experienced a scholar and teacher as Dr Maclear, upon the Gospel of St Mark. We gather from it an earnest of the handy and compact arrangement to be looked for in the contents of the volumes to follow, the ordering of the requisite introductory matter, the conciseness yet sufficiency of the notes to the text, the fullness of the *general* index, and the discreet choice of that of special words and phrases."—*English Churchman*.

"*The Gospel according to St Matthew*, by the Rev. A. Carr. This valuable series of school books is under the editorship of Professor Perowne, and is doing a great and thorough educational work in our schools. The volume before us condenses in the smallest possible space the best results of the best commentators on St Matthew's Gospel. The introduction is able, scholarly, and eminently practical, as it bears on the authorship and contents of the Gospel, and the original form in which it is supposed to have been written. It is well illustrated by two excellent maps of the Holy Land and of the Sea of Galilee."—*English Churchman*.

"*The Book of Joshua*. Edited by G. F. Maclear, D.D. We have the first instalment of what we have long desiderated, a School Commentary on the books of Scripture. If we may judge of the work contemplated by the sample before us it has our heartiest commendation. With Dr J. J. S. Perowne for General Editor and an eminent list of well-known Biblical scholars as contributors, we have the highest guarantee that the work will be completed in a scholarly, useful, and reliable form. The introductory chapter of the present volume on the life, character, and work of Joshua is ably and attractively written.... The 'notes' will be found brief, terse, pointed, and suggestive. The historical illustrations are apposite and felicitous. The maps and geographical explanations are accurate and valuable. The book ought to be in the hands of every teacher, and even clergymen will find it a valuable accession to their list of commentaries. We await the issue of the remaining volumes with interest."—*Weekly Review*.

"A very important work in the nature of a Scriptural text-book for the use of students has been undertaken by the Syndics of the Cambridge University Press—namely, the separate issue of the several books of the Bible, each edited and annotated by some Biblical scholar of high reputation....The value of the work as an aid to Biblical study, not merely in schools but among people of all classes who are desirous to have intelligent knowledge of the Scriptures, cannot easily be overestimated."—*The Scotsman*.

"Among the Commentaries which are in course of publication, the *Cambridge Bible for Schools* (Cambridge University Press) deserves mention. It is issued in conveniently-sized volumes, each containing a Book of the Old or New Testament. We have just received two of these volumes—one, on *The Book of Joshua*, prepared by Dr Maclear, of the King's College School; the other, by Professor Plumptre, on *The Epistle of St James*. That they are designed for the use of schools sufficiently indicates the scope of the annotations which accompany the text of each of these books. That on the Book of Joshua is enriched with notices of the most recent discoveries in Biblical archæology and geography. The volume on the Epistle of St James is, independently of a sufficient commentary, enriched with a useful introduction, in which the authorship of the Epistle and the time when written are discussed with the fulness which we had a right to expect from Dr Plumptre. The series will be valuable to schools; but it will by no means exhaust its usefulness there. More advanced readers of Holy Scripture than are to be found in our public schools will derive assistance from these handy volumes, which, when completed —if completed as those already published give us reason to expect— will be a welcome addition to our commentaries on Holy Scripture."—*John Bull*.

"*St Matthew*, edited by A. Carr, M.A. *The Book of Joshua*, edited by G. F. Maclear, D.D. *The General Epistle of St James*, edited by E. H. Plumptre, D.D. (Cambridge University Press). These volumes are constructed upon the same plan, and exhibit the same features as that on 'St Mark's Gospel,' of which we gave a full account on its issue. The introductions and notes are scholarly, and generally such as young readers need and can appreciate. The maps in both Joshua and Matthew are very good, and all matters of editing are faultless. Professor Plumptre's notes on 'The Epistle of St James' are models of terse, exact, and elegant renderings of the original, which is too often obscured in the authorised version."—*Nonconformist*.

"*The General Epistle of St James*, with Notes and Introduction By Professor Plumptre, D.D. (University Press, Cambridge). This is only a part of the Cambridge Bible for Schools, and may be bought for a few pence. Nevertheless it is, so far as I know, by far the best exposition of the Epistle of St James in the English language. Not Schoolboys or Students going in for an examination alone, but Ministers and Preachers of the Word, may get more real help from it than from the most costly and elaborate commentaries."—*Expositor*.

"With Mr Carr's well-edited apparatus to St Matthew's Gospel, where the text is that of Dr Scrivener's Cambridge Paragraph Bible, we are sure the young student will need nothing but a good Greek text.... We should doubt whether any volume of like dimensions could be found so sufficient for the needs of a student of the first Gospel, from whatever point of view he may approach it."—*Saturday Review*.

"THE CAMBRIDGE BIBLE FOR SCHOOLS: St Matthew, Joshua, Jonah, Corinthians, and James. We have on a former occasion drawn the attention of our readers to the first volume of this excellent series—St Mark. The volumes indicated above have now been published, and fully maintain the high standard won by the first. They furnish valuable and precise information in a most convenient form, and will be highly esteemed by students preparing for examinations, and also by Sunday-school teachers and others. They are particularly valuable in furnishing information concerning history, geography, manners and customs, in illustration of the sacred text."—*The Baptist*.

"THE CAMBRIDGE BIBLE FOR SCHOOLS:—*The First Epistle to the Corinthians*. Edited by Professor Lias. *Jonah*. Edited by Archdeacon Perowne. (Cambridge University Press.) Every fresh instalment of this annotated edition of the Bible for schools confirms the favourable opinion we formed of its value from the examination of its first number. The origin and plan of the Epistle are discussed with its character and genuineness. The analysis of its contents is very full and clear, and will be found of great service to the teachers of the more advanced classes in Sunday-schools and to the leaders of Bible-classes. The notes at the foot of the text are brief, but suggestive. We should recommend the committee of the City Missions, and all who have charge of rural evangelization societies, to put this book into the hands of their agents....The moral teaching of the book is so valuable, and the light it sheds upon the growth of religion amongst the Jews so interesting, that these elements ought to receive the largest share of an editor's attention."—*The Nonconformist*.

"Dr Maclear's commentary for Schools on *The Book of Joshua* is, as may be anticipated from him, clear and compendious. The historical books of the Old Testament are especially adapted for such an exegesis, elucidating many minute points, which might escape the observation of a less careful student. Another volume of the same series, *The Gospel of St Matthew*, with Mr Carr's annotations, deserves equally high praise. The commentary is terse and scholarly, without losing its interest for ordinary readers. The maps, the index, and the tabulated information in the Appendix all enhance the usefulness of this handy little volume. The name of the editor, Dr Plumptre, is in itself enough to recommend the edition of *The General Epistle of St James*, in the same series. More copious than the companion volumes, it contains some lengthy notes in the form of an excursus—*e.g.* on the personal relation of St Paul and St James the Less."—*Guardian*

"The last part, the Book of Jonah, is from the hand of (The Ven. T. T.) Perowne, Archdeacon of Norwich. The little work is well done, written in a graceful, lucid, and cheerful style, which will be attractive to young readers. The notes contain information and reflection in a very just proportion, the great preponderance being given to information."—*The British and Foreign Evangelical Review.*

"*The Book of Joshua.* By the Rev. G. F. Maclear, D.D. *Jonah.* By the Ven. T. T. Perowne, B.D. *The Gospel according to St Matthew.* By the Rev. A. Carr, M.A. *The Gospel according to St Mark.* By the Rev. G. F. Maclear, D.D. *The Acts of the Apostles* (i—xiv). By J. Rawson Lumby, D.D. We cannot have a healthier intellectual exercise than an impartial examination of the structure and contents of Scripture, and there are no books more likely to aid such an examination than the Manuals issued by the Syndics of the University Press. Works of more solid worth have not been published. The text adopted throughout is that of Scrivener's Cambridge Paragraph Bible. Each part contains a careful and scholarly introduction on the authorship, the date, the sources, &c., of the book. The notes are terse and suggestive, giving in few words the gist of elaborate researches. They abound in fine textual criticism, no less than in valuable doctrinal and ethical comments. Dr Maclear is thoroughly at home in such an historical book as *Joshua*. He draws illustrations from all quarters, especially from old English literature, and writes in a style of great elegance. The volume on *Jonah* is a literary gem, both on apologetic and hermeneutical grounds. In Mr Carr's *Matthew* there is, in addition to keen verbal criticism and archæological research, a determined effort to trace the course of thought in the inspired text, to point out the *nexus* between the various sections and verses of the Gospel. Mr Carr has all the qualifications which vigorous and refined scholarship can give, and possesses what is of far higher value, clear spiritual insight. Mr Lumby's manner of work is known to most of our readers from his papers in the *Expositor.* His notes on the *Acts* will certainly enhance his reputation, and form a valuable commentary on one of the most important books of the New Testament....All these books are, in fact, a valuable addition to our Biblical expositions, original contributions to a subject of transcendant importance; and while they cannot fail to be valued by those for whom they are expressly designed, we have a shrewd suspicion that they will be still more highly appreciated by minds of a riper order. The maps which most of the manuals contain are beautifully executed, and will be a great aid to the intelligent study of the Scriptures. Canon Perowne, to whom the general editorship of the series has been entrusted, may be congratulated on the success which the scheme has so far achieved. 'The Cambridge Bible for Schools' is one of the most popular and useful literary enterprises of the nineteenth century."—*Baptist Magazine.*

"THE CAMBRIDGE BIBLE FOR SCHOOLS—*The Second Epistle to the Corinthians.* By Professor LIAS. *The General Epistles of St Peter and St Jude.* By E. H. PLUMPTRE, D.D. We welcome these additions to the valuable series of the Cambridge Bible. We have nothing to add to the commendation which we have from the first publication given to this edition of the Bible. It is enough to say that Professor Lias has completed his work on the two Epistles to the Corinthians in the same admirable manner as at first. Dr Plumptre has also completed the Catholic Epistles."—*Nonconformist.*

"(1) *The Acts of the Apostles.* By J. RAWSON LUMBY, D.D. (2) *The Second Epistle of the Corinthians,* edited by Professor LIAS.

The introduction is pithy, and contains a mass of carefully-selected information on the authorship of the Acts, its designs, and its sources. ......The Second Epistle of the Corinthians is a manual beyond all praise, for the excellence of its pithy and pointed annotations, its analysis of the contents, and the fulness and value of its introduction."—*Examiner.*

"THE CAMBRIDGE BIBLE FOR SCHOOLS.—The Cambridge University Press has not made of late years a more valuable contribution to the literature of the age than this series of books of the Bible, which has been prepared specially for schools....We have been most careful to examine *St Matthew*, edited by Rev. A. Carr, M.A., as our thoughts are directed in the line of the International Lessons for the first six months of the next year, and we are very pleased to direct our readers' attention to a work which is calculated to be so helpful to them. The introductory portion is very able, so full of interesting matter, and yet so concisely put. This quality of conciseness characterises the notes throughout, and as they appear on the same page as the letter press to which they relate, facility of reference is thus obtained."—*The Sunday School Chronicle.*

"THE CAMBRIDGE BIBLE FOR SCHOOLS.—The 2nd Epistle to the Corinthians, with Notes, Map, and Introduction. By the Rev. J. J. Lias, M.A. We have here a noteworthy sample of the thoroughness of the editing of the various books of the English Bible under the superintendence of Dean Perowne, and a trustworthy earnest of his choice of the best coadjutors for each particular volume. We have examined the notes, and can only say that their soundness and orthodoxy are such as to give a comfortable assurance that Cambridge and Lampeter undergraduates are fortunate in being guided by such sound and sage divines as Professor Lias."—*The English Churchman and Clerical Journal.*

"*The Epistle to the Romans.* By H. C. G. Moule, M.A. This admirable school series continues its work. Mr Moule treats in this new volume of one of the profoundest of the New Testament Books. His work is scholarly, clear, full, and devout, and we are thankful that such volumes find their way into our schools....... The volumes, taken as a whole, are admirable."—*The Freeman.*

"The Rev. H. C. G. Moule, M.A., has made a valuable addition to THE CAMBRIDGE BIBLE FOR SCHOOLS in his brief commentary on the EPISTLE TO THE ROMANS. The "Notes" are very good, and lean, as the notes of a School Bible should, to the most commonly accepted and orthodox view of the inspired author's meaning; while the Introduction, and especially the Sketch of the Life of St Paul, is a model of condensation. It is as lively and pleasant to read as if two or three facts had not been crowded into well-nigh every sentence."—*Expositor.*

"*The Epistle to the Romans.* It is seldom we have met with a work so remarkable for the compression and condensation of all that is valuable in the smallest possible space as in the volume before us. Within its limited pages we have 'a sketch of the Life of St Paul,' which really amounts to a full and excellent biography; we have further a critical account of the date of the Epistle to the Romans, of its language, and of its genuineness. The notes are numerous, full of matter, to the point, and leave no real difficulty or obscurity unexplained."—*The Examiner.*

"*The Epistle to the Romans.* To the mature reader, the book may be most confidently recommended. He will have his reserve about the theology, but he will find it an admirably careful and complete commentary, avoiding no difficulties, tracing out distinctly the sequences of thought, and expressing in perspicuous language what St Paul meant, or, at least, what a learned and intelligent critic believed him to have meant."—*The Spectator.*

"This is a volume of that very useful series, 'The Cambridge Bible for Schools,' edited by Dean Perowne. Mr Moule's work, we need hardly say, bears marks of close, conscientious study; the exposition is clear, suggestive, and thoroughly sound. There is not the slightest parade of scholarship, and yet this Commentary will bear comparison with any even of the highest rank for ability and erudition. . . Mr Moule has evidently read much, and pondered carefully; but he gives, in small compass, the conclusion at which he has arrived. We are greatly pleased with this book."—*The Churchman.*

"We heartily commend to the notice of our readers the volume containing the notes of Mr Moule on the Epistle to the Romans, which appears as one of the series of 'The Cambridge Bible for Schools.' Added to his refined scholarship, Mr Moule appears to us to have executed his task with accuracy and sound judgment. The sketch of St Paul's life is sufficiently complete for the purpose for which it is designed. So is the introduction generally."—*Clergyman's Magazine.*

"This handy little volume is one of the "The Cambridge Bible for Schools" series now being published under the superintendence of Dean Perowne. It thoroughly well merits the praise, *multum in parvo.* Mr Moule has evidently read much, and pondered carefully; but he does not overload his exposition with details, and he has judged it best in a work "for schools" to give simply on orthodox lines his conclusions. Hence, the well-packed notes are interesting, and although there is nowhere the slightest parade of scholarship the work has unmistakably the flavour and the value of sound scholarly divinity. It is hardly necessary to add that the exposition is Evangelical. Many Bible students who have long ago left school will find Mr Moule's work a really valuable help."—*The Record.*

The First Book of Samuel, by A. F. Kirkpatrick, M.A. "This forms an additional volume of the Cambridge Bible for Schools, and is well worthy to take its place beside those which have already appeared . . . The text is enriched with ample notes, both critical and literary, which give every assistance to the better understanding and appreciation of the book which the student can desire."—*Cambridge Independent Press.*

"To the valuable series of Scriptural expositions and elementary commentaries which is being issued at the Cambridge University Press, under the title "The Cambridge Bible for Schools," has been added The First Book of Samuel by the Rev. A. F. Kirkpatrick. Like other volumes of the series, it contains a carefully written historical and critical introduction, while the text is profusely illustrated and explained by notes."—*The Scotsman.*

"To the volume on I. Samuel we give our very warm commendation. It is designed, not for teachers, but for learners, and especially for young men in schools and colleges. At the same time, it will be interesting and profitable to all who wish to read the Bible intelligently."—*Methodist Recorder.*

UNIVERSITY PRESS, CAMBRIDGE.
February, 1881.

PUBLICATIONS OF
The Cambridge University Press.

THE HOLY SCRIPTURES, &c.

The Cambridge Paragraph Bible of the Authorized English
Version, with the Text revised by a Collation of its Early and other Principal Editions, the Use of the Italic Type made uniform, the Marginal References remodelled, and a Critical Introduction prefixed, by the Rev. F. H. SCRIVENER, M.A., LL.D., one of the Revisers of the Authorized Version. Crown Quarto, cloth gilt, 21s.

THE STUDENT'S EDITION of the above, on *good writing paper*, with one column of print and wide margin to each page for MS. notes. Two Vols. Crown Quarto, cloth, gilt, 31s. 6d.

The Lectionary Bible, with Apocrypha, divided into Sections adapted to the Calendar and Tables of Lessons of 1871. Crown Octavo, cloth, 3s. 6d.

Breviarium ad usum insignis Ecclesiae Sarum. Fasciculus II.
In quo continentur PSALTERIUM, cum ordinario Officii totius hebdomadae juxta Horas Canonicas, et proprio Completorii, LITANIA, COMMUNE SANCTORUM, ORDINARIUM MISSAE CUM CANONE ET XIII MISSIS, &c. &c. juxta Editionem maximam pro CLAUDIO CHEVALLON et FRANCISCO REGNAULT A. D. MDXXXI. in Alma Parisiorum Academia impressam: labore ac studio FRANCISCI PROCTER, A.M., et CHRISTOPHORI WORDSWORTH, A.M. Demy 8vo., cloth, 12s.

Fasciculus I. *In the Press.*

The Pointed Prayer Book, being the Book of Common Prayer with the Psalter or Psalms of David, pointed as they are to be sung or said in Churches. Embossed cloth, Royal 24mo, 2s.
The same in square 32mo, cloth, 6d.

The Cambridge Psalter, for the use of Choirs and Organists. Specially adapted for Congregations in which the "Cambridge Pointed Prayer Book" is used. Demy 8vo. cloth, 3s. 6d. Cloth limp cut flush, 2s. 6d.

The Paragraph Psalter, arranged for the use of Choirs by BROOKE FOSS WESTCOTT, D D., Canon of Peterborough, and Regius Professor of Divinity, Cambridge. Fcp. 4to. 5s.

Greek and English Testament, in parallel columns on the same page. Edited by J. SCHOLEFIELD, M.A. late Regius Professor of Greek in the University. *New Edition, with the marginal references as arranged and revised by* DR SCRIVENER. Cloth, red edges. 7s. 6d.

London: Cambridge Warehouse, 17 Paternoster Row.

Greek and English Testament. THE STUDENT'S EDITION of the above on *large writing paper*. 4to. cloth. 12s.

Greek Testament, ex editione Stephani tertia, 1550. Small Octavo. 3s. 6d.

The Gospel according to St Matthew in Anglo-Saxon and Northumbrian Versions, synoptically arranged: with Collations of the best Manuscripts. By J. M. KEMBLE, M.A. and Archdeacon HARDWICK. Demy Quarto. 10s.

The Gospel according to St Mark in Anglo-Saxon and Northumbrian Versions, synoptically arranged, with Collations exhibiting all the Readings of all the MSS. Edited by the Rev. Professor SKEAT, M.A. Demy Quarto. 10s.

The Gospel according to St Luke, uniform with the preceding, edited by the Rev. Professor SKEAT. Demy Quarto. 10s.

The Gospel according to St John, uniform with the preceding, edited by the Rev. Professor SKEAT. Demy Quarto. 10s.

The Missing Fragment of the Latin Translation of the Fourth Book of Ezra, discovered, and edited with an Introduction and Notes, and a facsimile of the MS., by R. L. BENSLY, M.A., Fellow of Gonville and Caius College. Cloth, 10s.

THEOLOGY—(ANCIENT).

Sayings of the Jewish Fathers, comprising Pirqe Aboth and Pereq R. Meir in Hebrew and English, with Critical and Illustrative Notes; and specimen pages of the Cambridge University Manuscript of the Mishnah 'Jerushalmith'. By C. TAYLOR, M.A., Fellow and Divinity Lecturer of St John's College. Demy Octavo. 10s.

Theodore of Mopsuestia's Commentary on the Minor Epistles of S. Paul. The Latin Version with the Greek Fragments, edited from the MSS. with Notes and an Introduction, by H. B. SWETE, D.D., Rector of Ashdon, Essex, and late Fellow of Gonville and Caius College, Cambridge. In two Volumes. Vol. I., containing the Introduction, and the Commentary upon Galatians—Colossians. Demy Octavo. 12s.
VOLUME II. *In the Press.*

Sancti Irenæi Episcopi Lugdunensis libros quinque adversus Hæreses, versione Latina cum Codicibus Claromontano ac Arundeliano denuo collata, præmissa de placitis Gnosticorum prolusione, fragmenta necnon Græce, Syriace, Armeniace, commentatione perpetua et indicibus variis edidit W. WIGAN HARVEY, S.T.B. Collegii Regalis olim Socius. 2 Vols. Demy Octavo. 18s.

London: Cambridge Warehouse, 17 Paternoster Row.

M. Minucii Felicis Octavius. The text newly revised from the original MS. with an English Commentary, Analysis, Introduction, and Copious Indices. Edited by H. A. HOLDEN, LL.D. Head Master of Ipswich School, late Fellow of Trinity College, Cambridge. Crown Octavo. 7s. 6d.

Theophili Episcopi Antiochensis Libri Tres ad Autolycum. Edidit, Prolegomenis Versione Notulis Indicibus instruxit GULIELMUS GILSON HUMPHRY, S.T.B. Post Octavo. 5s.

Theophylacti in Evangelium S. Matthæi Commentarius. Edited by W. G. HUMPHRY, B.D. Demy Octavo. 7s. 6d.

Tertullianus de Corona Militis, de Spectaculis, de Idololatria, with Analysis and English Notes, by GEORGE CURREY, D.D. Master of the Charter House. Crown Octavo. 5s.

THEOLOGY—(ENGLISH).

Works of Isaac Barrow, compared with the original MSS., enlarged with Materials hitherto unpublished. A new Edition, by A. NAPIER, M.A. of Trinity College, Vicar of Holkham, Norfolk. Nine Vols. Demy Octavo. £3. 3s.

Treatise of the Pope's Supremacy, and a Discourse concerning the Unity of the Church, by ISAAC BARROW. Demy Octavo. 7s. 6d.

Pearson's Exposition of the Creed, edited by TEMPLE CHEVALLIER, B.D., late Professor of Mathematics in the University of Durham, and Fellow and Tutor of St Catharine's College, Cambridge. Second Edition. Demy Octavo. 7s. 6d.

An Analysis of the Exposition of the Creed, written by the Right Rev. Father in God, JOHN PEARSON, D.D., late Lord Bishop of Chester. Compiled for the use of the Students of Bishop's College, Calcutta, by W. H. MILL, D.D. late Regius Professor of Hebrew in the University of Cambridge. Demy Octavo, cloth. 5s.

Wheatly on the Common Prayer, edited by G. E. CORRIE, D.D. Master of Jesus College, Examining Chaplain to the late Lord Bishop of Ely. Demy Octavo. 7s. 6d.

The Homilies, with Various Readings, and the Quotations from the Fathers given at length in the Original Languages. Edited by G. E. CORRIE, D.D. Master of Jesus College. Demy Octavo. 7s. 6d.

London: Cambridge Warehouse, 17 Paternoster Row.

Two Forms of Prayer of the time of Queen Elizabeth. Now First Reprinted. Demy Octavo. 6*d*.

Select Discourses, by JOHN SMITH, late Fellow of Queens' College, Cambridge. Edited by H. G. WILLIAMS, B.D. late Professor of Arabic. Royal Octavo. 7*s.* 6*d*.

Cæsar Morgan's Investigation of the Trinity of Plato, and of Philo Judæus, and of the effects which an attachment to their writings had upon the principles and reasonings of the Fathers of the Christian Church. Revised by H. A. HOLDEN, LL.D. Head Master of Ipswich School, late Fellow of Trinity College, Cambridge. Crown Octavo. 4*s.*

De Obligatione Conscientiæ Prælectiones decem Oxonii in Schola Theologica habitæ a ROBERTO SANDERSON, SS. Theologiæ ibidem Professore Regio. With English Notes, including an abridged Translation, by W. WHEWELL, D.D. late Master of Trinity College. Demy Octavo. 7*s.* 6*d*.

Archbishop Usher's Answer to a Jesuit, with other Tracts on Popery. Edited by J. SCHOLEFIELD, M.A. late Regius Professor of Greek in the University. Demy Octavo. 7*s.* 6*d*.

Wilson's Illustration of the Method of explaining the New Testament, by the early opinions of Jews and Christians concerning Christ. Edited by T. TURTON, D.D. late Lord Bishop of Ely. Demy Octavo. 5*s.*

Lectures on Divinity delivered in the University of Cambridge. By JOHN HEY, D.D. Third Edition, by T. TURTON, D.D. late Lord Bishop of Ely. 2 vols. Demy Octavo. 15*s.*

GREEK AND LATIN CLASSICS, &c.
(*See also* pp. 12, 13.)

The Bacchae of Euripides, with Introduction, Critical Notes, and Archæological Illustrations, by J. E. SANDYS, M.A., Fellow and Tutor of St John's College, and Public Orator. Crown Octavo, cloth. 10*s.* 6*d*.

M. T. Ciceronis de Natura Deorum Libri Tres, with Introduction and Commentary by JOSEPH B. MAYOR, M.A., Professor of Classical Literature at King's College, London, together with a new collation of several of the English MSS. by J. H. SWAINSON, M.A., formerly Fellow of Trinity College, Cambridge. Demy Octavo, cloth. 10*s.* 6*d*.

London: Cambridge Warehouse, 17 *Paternoster Row.*

The Agamemnon of Aeschylus. With a translation in English Rhythm, and Notes Critical and Explanatory. By BENJAMIN HALL KENNEDY, D.D., Regius Professor of Greek. Crown 8vo. 6s.

The Theætetus of Plato by the same Editor. [*In the Press.*

P. Vergili Maronis Opera, cum Prolegomenis et Commentario Critico pro Syndicis Preli Academici edidit BENJAMIN HALL KENNEDY, S.T.P., Graecae Linguae Professor Regius. Cloth, extra fcp. 8vo, red edges, price 5s.

A Selection of Greek Inscriptions, with Introductions and Annotations by E. S. ROBERTS, M.A., Fellow and Tutor of Caius College. [*Preparing.*

Select Private Orations of Demosthenes with Introductions and English Notes, by F. A. PALEY, M.A., Editor of Aeschylus, etc. and J. E. SANDYS, M.A., Fellow and Tutor of St John's College, and Public Orator in the University of Cambridge.
Part I. containing Contra Phormionem, Lacritum, Pantaenetum, Boeotum de Nomine, Boeotum de Dote, Dionysodorum. Crown Octavo, cloth. 6s.
Part II. containing Pro Phormione, Contra Stephanum I. II.; Nicostratum, Cononem, Calliclem. Crown Octavo, cloth. 7s. 6d.

M. T. Ciceronis de Officiis Libri Tres with Marginal Analysis, an English Commentary, and Indices. Third Edition, revised, with numerous additions, by H. A. HOLDEN, LL.D., Head Master of Ipswich School. Crown Octavo, cloth. 9s.

Plato's Phædo, literally translated, by the late E. M. COPE, Fellow of Trinity College, Cambridge. Demy Octavo. 5s.

Aristotle. The Rhetoric. With a Commentary by the late E. M. COPE, Fellow of Trinity College, Cambridge, revised and edited by J. E. SANDYS, M.A., Fellow and Tutor of St John's College, and Public Orator. 3 Vols. Demy 8vo. £1 11s. 6d.

ΠΕΡΙ ΔΙΚΑΙΟΣΥΝΗΣ. The Fifth Book of the Nicomachean Ethics of Aristotle. Edited by HENRY JACKSON, M.A., Fellow of Trinity College, Cambridge. Demy 8vo, cloth. 6s.

Pindar. Olympian and Pythian Odes. With Notes Explanatory and Critical, Introductions and Introductory Essays. Edited by C. A. M. FENNELL, M.A., late Fellow of Jesus College. Crown 8vo. cloth. 9s.

The Isthmian and Nemean Odes by the same Editor.
[*Preparing.*

London: Cambridge Warehouse, 17 Paternoster Row.

SANSKRIT AND ARABIC.

Nalopákhyánam, or, The Tale of Nala; containing the Sanskrit Text in Roman Characters, followed by a Vocabulary and a sketch of Sanskrit Grammar. By the Rev. THOMAS JARRETT, M.A., Regius Professor of Hebrew. Demy Octavo. 10s.

Notes on the Tale of Nala, by J. PEILE, M.A., Fellow and Tutor of Christ's College. Demy 8vo. 12s.

The Poems of Beha ed din Zoheir of Egypt. With a Metrical Translation, Notes and Introduction, by E. H. PALMER, M.A., Lord Almoner's Professor of Arabic in the University of Cambridge. 3 vols. Crown Quarto. Vol. II. The ENGLISH TRANSLATION. Paper cover, 10s. 6d. Cloth extra, 15s. [Vol. I. The ARABIC TEXT is already published.]

MATHEMATICS, PHYSICAL SCIENCE, &c.

Mathematical and Physical Papers. By GEORGE GABRIEL STOKES, M.A., D.C.L., LL.D., F.R.S., Fellow of Pembroke College and Lucasian Professor of Mathematics. Reprinted from the Original Journals and Transactions, with additional Notes by the Author. Vol. I. Demy 8vo, cloth. 15s. Vol. II. *In the Press.*

Mathematical and Physical Papers. By Sir W. THOMSON, LL.D., D.C.L., F.R.S., Professor of Natural Philosophy, in the University of Glasgow. Collected from different Scientific Periodicals from May, 1841, to the present time. [*In the Press.*

A Treatise on Natural Philosophy. Volume I. Part I. By Sir W. THOMSON, LL.D., D.C.L., F.R.S., Professor of Natural Philosophy in the University of Glasgow, and P. G. TAIT, M.A., Professor of Natural Philosophy in the University of Edinburgh. Demy 8vo. cloth, 16s.

Part II. *In the Press.*

Elements of Natural Philosophy. By Professors Sir W. THOMSON and P. G. TAIT. Part I. *Second Edition.* 8vo. cloth, 9s.

An Elementary Treatise on Quaternions. By P. G. TAIT, M.A., Professor of Natural Philosophy in the University of Edinburgh. *Second Edition.* Demy 8vo. 14s.

A Treatise on the Theory of Determinants and their Applications in Analysis and Geometry. By ROBERT FORSYTH SCOTT, M.A., of Lincoln's Inn; Fellow of St John's College, Cambridge. Demy 8vo. 12s.

Counterpoint. A practical course of study. By Professor G. A. MACFARREN, Mus. Doc. Second Edition, revised. Demy 4to. cloth. 7s. 6d.

The Analytical Theory of Heat. By JOSEPH FOURIER. Translated, with Notes, by A. FREEMAN, M.A., Fellow of St John's College, Cambridge. Demy 8vo. 16s.

London: Cambridge Warehouse, 17 *Paternoster Row.*

The Electrical Researches of the Honourable Henry Cavendish, F.R.S. Written between 1771 and 1781, Edited from the original manuscripts in the possession of the Duke of Devonshire, K.G., by J. CLERK MAXWELL, F.R.S. Demy 8vo. cloth, 18s.

Hydrodynamics, a Treatise on the Mathematical Theory of Fluid Motion, by HORACE LAMB, M.A., formerly Fellow of Trinity College, Cambridge; Professor of Mathematics in the University of Adelaide. Demy 8vo. cloth, 12s.

The Mathematical Works of Isaac Barrow, D.D. Edited by W. WHEWELL, D.D. Demy Octavo. 7s. 6d.

Illustrations of Comparative Anatomy, Vertebrate and Invertebrate, for the Use of Students in the Museum of Zoology and Comparative Anatomy. Second Edition. Demy 8vo. cloth, 2s. 6d.

A Catalogue of Australian Fossils (including Tasmania and the Island of Timor), by R. ETHERIDGE, Jun., F.G.S., Acting Palæontologist, H.M. Geol. Survey of Scotland. Demy 8vo. 10s. 6d.

A Synopsis of the Classification of the British Palæozoic Rocks, by the Rev. ADAM SEDGWICK, M.A., F.R.S., with a systematic description of the British Palæozoic Fossils in the Geological Museum of the University of Cambridge, by FREDERICK McCOY, F.G.S. One vol., Royal Quarto, cloth, Plates, £1. 1s.

A Catalogue of the Collection of Cambrian and Silurian Fossils contained in the Geological Museum of the University of Cambridge, by J. W. SALTER, F.G.S. With a Preface by the Rev. ADAM SEDGWICK, F.R.S. With a Portrait of PROFESSOR SEDGWICK. Royal Quarto, cloth, 7s. 6d.

Catalogue of Osteological Specimens contained in the Anatomical Museum of the University of Cambridge. Demy 8vo. 2s. 6d.

Astronomical Observations made at the Observatory of Cambridge by the Rev. JAMES CHALLIS, M.A., F.R.S., F.R.A.S., Plumian Professor of Astronomy from 1846 to 1860.

Astronomical Observations from 1861 to 1865. Vol. XXI. Royal Quarto, cloth, 15s.

LAW.

An Analysis of Criminal Liability. By E. C. CLARK, LL.D., Regius Professor of Civil Law in the University of Cambridge, also of Lincoln's Inn, Barrister at Law. Crown 8vo. cloth, 7s. 6d.

London: Cambridge Warehouse, 17 Paternoster Row.

A Selection of the State Trials. By J. W. WILLIS-BUND, M.A., LL.B., Barrister-at-Law, Professor of Constitutional Law and History, University College, London. Vol. I. Trials for Treason (1327—1660). Crown 8vo., cloth. 18s. Vol. II. [*In the Press.*

The Fragments of the Perpetual Edict of Salvius Julianus, Collected, Arranged, and Annotated by BRYAN WALKER, MA., LL.D., Law Lecturer of St John's College, and late Fellow of Corpus Christi College, Cambridge. Crown 8vo., cloth. *Price* 6s.

The Commentaries of Gaius and Rules of Ulpian. (*New Edition.*) Translated and Annotated, by J. T. ABDY, LL.D., late Regius Professor of Laws, and BRYAN WALKER, M.A., LL.D., Law Lecturer of St John's College. Crown Octavo, 16s.

The Institutes of Justinian, translated with Notes by J. T. ABDY, LL.D., and BRYAN WALKER, M.A., LLD., St John's College, Cambridge. Crown Octavo, 16s.

Selected Titles from the Digest, annotated by BRYAN WALKER, M.A., LL.D. Part I. Mandati vel Contra. Digest xvii. 1. Crown Octavo, 5s.

Part II. De Adquirendo rerum dominio, and **De Adquirenda** vel amittenda Possessione, Digest XLI. 1 and 2. Crown 8vo. 6s.

Part III. **De Condictionibus,** Digest XII. 1 and 4—7 and Digest XII. 1—3. Crown 8vo. 6s.

Grotius de Jure Belli et Pacis, with the Notes of Barbeyrac and others; accompanied by an abridged Translation of the Text, by W. WHEWELL, D.D. late Master of Trinity College. 3 Vols. Demy Octavo, 12s. The translation separate, 6s.

HISTORICAL WORKS.

Life and Times of Stein, or Germany and Prussia in the Napoleonic Age, by J. R. SEELEY, M.A., Regius Professor of Modern History in the University of Cambridge. With Portraits and Maps. 3 vols. Demy 8vo. 48s.

Scholae Academicae; some Account of the Studies at the English Universities in the Eighteenth Century. By CHRISTOPHER WORDSWORTH, M.A., Fellow of Peterhouse; Author of "Social Life at the English Universities in the Eighteenth Century." Demy Octavo, cloth, 15s.

History of Nepāl, translated from the Original by MUNSHI SHEW SHUNKER SINGH and Pandit SHRĪ GUNĀNAND; edited with an Introductory Sketch of the Country and People by Dr D. WRIGHT, late Residency Surgeon at Kāthmāndū, and with numerous Illustrations and portraits of Sir JUNG BAHĀDUR, the King of Nepāl, and other natives. Super-Royal Octavo, 21s.

London: Cambridge Warehouse, 17 *Paternoster Row.*

The University of Cambridge from the Earliest Times to the Royal Injunctions of 1535. By JAMES BASS MULLINGER, M.A. Demy 8vo. cloth (734 pp.), 12s.

History of the College of St John the Evangelist, by THOMAS BAKER, B.D., Ejected Fellow. Edited by JOHN E. B. MAYOR, M.A., Fellow of St John's. Two Vols. Demy 8vo. 24s.

The Architectural History of the University and Colleges of Cambridge, by the late Professor WILLIS, M.A. With numerous Maps, Plans, and Illustrations. Continued to the present time, and edited by JOHN WILLIS CLARK, M.A., formerly Fellow of Trinity College, Cambridge. [*In the Press.*

CATALOGUES.

Catalogue of the Hebrew Manuscripts preserved in the University Library, Cambridge. By Dr S. M. SCHILLER-SZINESSY. Volume I. containing Section I. *The Holy Scriptures;* Section II. *Commentaries on the Bible.* Demy 8vo. 9s.

A Catalogue of the Manuscripts preserved in the Library of the University of Cambridge. Demy 8vo. 5 Vols. 10s. each.

Index to the Catalogue. Demy 8vo. 10s.

A Catalogue of Adversaria and printed books containing MS. notes, preserved in the Library of the University of Cambridge. 3s. 6d.

The Illuminated Manuscripts in the Library of the Fitzwilliam Museum, Cambridge, Catalogued with Descriptions, and an Introduction, by WILLIAM GEORGE SEARLE, M.A., late Fellow of Queens' College, and Vicar of Hockington, Cambridgeshire. 7s. 6d.

A Chronological List of the Graces, Documents, and other Papers in the University Registry which concern the University Library. Demy 8vo. 2s. 6d.

Catalogus Bibliothecæ Burckhardtianæ. Demy Quarto. 5s.

MISCELLANEOUS.

Lectures on Education, delivered in the University of Cambridge in the Lent Term, 1880. By J. G. FITCH, Her Majesty's Inspector of Schools. Crown 8vo. 6s.

Statuta Academiæ Cantabrigiensis. Demy 8vo. 2s.

Ordinationes Academiæ Cantabrigiensis. New Edition. Demy 8vo., cloth. 3s. 6d.

Trusts, Statutes and Directions affecting (1) The Professorships of the University. (2) The Scholarships and Prizes. (3) Other Gifts and Endowments. Demy 8vo. 5s.

A Compendium of University Regulations, for the use of persons in Statu Pupillari. Demy 8vo. 6d.

London: Cambridge Warehouse, 17 *Paternoster Row.*

The Cambridge Bible for Schools.

GENERAL EDITOR: J. J. S. PEROWNE, D.D., DEAN OF PETERBOROUGH.

THE want of an Annotated Edition of the BIBLE, in handy portions, suitable for school use, has long been felt.

In order to provide Text-books for School and Examination purposes, the CAMBRIDGE UNIVERSITY PRESS has arranged to publish the several books of the BIBLE in separate portions, at a moderate price, with introductions and explanatory notes.

Some of the books have already been undertaken by the following gentlemen:

Rev. A. CARR, M.A., *Assistant Master at Wellington College.*
Rev. T. K. CHEYNE, M.A., *Fellow of Balliol College, Oxford.*
Rev. S. COX, *Nottingham.*
Rev. A. B. DAVIDSON, D.D., *Prof. of Hebrew, Free Church Coll. Edinb.*
Rev. F. W. FARRAR, D.D., *Canon of Westminster.*
Rev. A. E. HUMPHREYS, M.A., *Fellow of Trinity College, Cambridge.*
Rev. A. F. KIRKPATRICK, M.A., *Fellow and Lecturer of Trinity College.*
Rev. J. J. LIAS, M.A., *late Professor at St David's College, Lampeter.*
Rev. J. R. LUMBY, D.D., *Norrisian Professor of Divinity.*
Rev. G. F. MACLEAR, D.D., *Warden of St Augustine's Coll. Canterbury.*
Rev. H. C. G. MOULE, M.A., *Fellow of Trinity College, Cambridge.*
Rev. W. F. MOULTON, D.D., *Head Master of the Leys School, Cambridge.*
Rev. E. H. PEROWNE, D.D., *Master of Corpus Christi College, Cambridge, Examining Chaplain to the Bishop of St Asaph.*
The Ven. T. T. PEROWNE, B.D., *Archdeacon of Norwich.*
Rev. A. PLUMMER, M.A., *Master of University College, Durham.*
Rev. E. H. PLUMPTRE, D.D., *Professor of Biblical Exegesis, King's College, London.*
Rev. W. SANDAY, D.D., *Principal of Bishop Hatfield Hall, Durham.*
Rev. W. SIMCOX, M.A., *Rector of Weyhill, Hants.*
Rev. ROBERTSON SMITH, M.A., *Professor of Hebrew, Aberdeen.*
Rev. A. W. STREANE, M.A., *Fellow of Corpus Christi College.*
The Ven. H. W. WATKINS, M.A., *Archdeacon of Northumberland.*
Rev. G. H. WHITAKER, M.A., *Fellow of St John's College, Cambridge.*
Rev. C. WORDSWORTH, M.A., *Rector of Glaston, Rutland.*

Now Ready. Cloth, Extra Fcap. 8vo.

THE BOOK OF JOSHUA. By the Rev. G. F. MACLEAR, D.D. With Two Maps. Cloth. 2s. 6d.

THE FIRST BOOK OF SAMUEL. By the Rev. A. F. KIRKPATRICK, M.A. Cloth. 3s. 6d.

London: Cambridge Warehouse, 17 Paternoster Row.

THE BOOK OF JEREMIAH. By the Rev. A. W. STREANE, M.A. Cloth. 4s. 6d.

THE BOOK OF JONAH. By Archdeacon PEROWNE. With Two Maps. Cloth. 1s. 6d.

THE GOSPEL ACCORDING TO ST MATTHEW. By the Rev. A. CARR, M.A. With Two Maps. Cloth. 2s. 6d.

THE GOSPEL ACCORDING TO ST MARK. By the Rev. G. F. MACLEAR, D.D. With Two Maps. Cloth. 2s. 6d.

THE GOSPEL ACCORDING TO ST LUKE. By the Rev. F. W. FARRAR, D.D. With Four Maps. Cloth. 4s. 6d.

THE GOSPEL ACCORDING TO ST JOHN. By the Rev. A. PLUMMER, M.A. With Four Maps. Cloth. 4s. 6d.

THE ACTS OF THE APOSTLES. Part I., Chaps. I.—XIV. By the Rev. Professor LUMBY, D.D. Cloth. 2s. 6d.

THE EPISTLE TO THE ROMANS. By the Rev. H. C. G. MOULE, M.A. Cloth. 3s. 6d.

THE FIRST EPISTLE TO THE CORINTHIANS. By the Rev. J. J. LIAS, M.A. With a Plan and Map. Cloth. 2s.

THE SECOND EPISTLE TO THE CORINTHIANS. By the Rev. J. J. LIAS, M.A. With a Plan and Map. Cloth. 2s.

THE GENERAL EPISTLE OF ST JAMES. By the Rev. E. H. PLUMPTRE, D.D. Cloth. 1s. 6d.

THE EPISTLES OF ST PETER AND ST JUDE. By the Rev. E. H. PLUMPTRE, D.D. Cloth. 2s. 6d.

Preparing.

THE SECOND BOOK OF SAMUEL. By the Rev. A. F. KIRKPATRICK, M.A.

THE BOOK OF ECCLESIASTES. By the Rev. E. H. PLUMPTRE, D.D. [*Immediately.*

THE BOOKS OF HAGGAI AND ZECHARIAH. By Archdeacon PEROWNE.

In Preparation.

THE CAMBRIDGE GREEK TESTAMENT
FOR SCHOOLS AND COLLEGES,

with a Revised Text, based on the most recent critical authorities, and English Notes, prepared under the direction of the General Editor,

THE VERY REVEREND J. J. S. PEROWNE, D.D.,
DEAN OF PETERBOROUGH.

THE GOSPEL ACCORDING TO ST MATTHEW. By the Rev. A. CARR, M.A. [*Nearly ready.*

The books will be published separately, as in the Cambridge Bible for Schools.

London: *Cambridge Warehouse*, 17 *Paternoster Row.*

PUBLICATIONS OF

THE PITT PRESS SERIES.

ADAPTED TO THE USE OF STUDENTS PREPARING FOR THE
UNIVERSITY LOCAL EXAMINATIONS,
AND THE HIGHER CLASSES OF SCHOOLS.

I. GREEK.

The Anabasis of Xenophon, Book VII. With a Map and English Notes by ALFRED PRETOR, M.A., Fellow of St Catharine's College, Editor of Sophocles (Trachiniæ) and Persius. *Price 2s. 6d.*

────── **Books I. III. IV. and V.** By the same Editor. *Price 2s. each.* **Books II. and VI.** *Price 2s. 6d. each.*

Luciani Somnium Charon Piscator et De Luctu. (*New Edition with Appendix.*) With English Notes, by W. E. HEITLAND, M.A., Fellow of St John's College, Cambridge. *Price 3s. 6d.*

Agesilaus of Xenophon. The Text revised with Critical and Explanatory Notes, Introduction, Analysis, and Indices. By H. HAILSTONE, M.A., late Scholar of Peterhouse, Cambridge, Editor of Xenophon's Hellenics, etc. *Price 2s. 6d.*

Aristophanes—Ranae. With English Notes and Introduction by W. C. GREEN, M.A., Assistant Master at Rugby School. Cloth. *3s. 6d.*

Aristophanes—Aves. By the same Editor. *New Edition.* Cloth. *3s. 6d.*

Euripides. Hercules Furens. With Introduction, Notes and Analysis. By J. T. HUTCHINSON, M.A., Christ's College, and A. GRAY, M.A., Fellow of Jesus College, Cambridge. *Price 2s.*

The Heracleidæ of Euripides, with Introduction and Critical Notes by E. A. BECK, M.A., Fellow of Trinity Hall. [*In the Press.*

II. LATIN.

P. Vergili Maronis Aeneidos Liber VIII. Edited with Notes by A. SIDGWICK, M.A., Tutor of Corpus Christi College, Oxford. *Price 1s. 6d.*

────── **Books VI. VII. X. XI. XII.** By the same Editor. *Price 1s. 6d. each.*

────── **Books VII. VIII.** bound in one volume. *Price 3s.*

────── **Books X. XI. XII.** bound in one volume. *Price 3s. 6d.*

M. T. Ciceronis de Amicitia. Edited by J. S. REID, M.L., Fellow of Gonville and Caius College, Cambridge. *Price 3s.*

M. T. Ciceronis de Senectute. Edited by J. S. REID, M.L., *Price 3s. 6d.*

London: Cambridge Warehouse, 17 *Paternoster Row.*

PITT PRESS SERIES (*continued*).

Gai Iuli Caesaris de Bello Gallico Comment. VII. New Edition, revised. With Maps and Notes by A. G. PESKETT, M.A. Fellow of Magdalene College, Cambridge. *Price* 2s.

Gai Iuli Caesaris de Bello Gallico Comment. I. II. With Maps and Notes by the same Editor. *Price* 2s. 6d.

Gai Iuli Caesaris de Bello Gallico Comment. IV., V. By the same Editor. *Price* 2s.

Quintus Curtius. A Portion of the History (Alexander in India). By W. E. HEITLAND, M.A., Fellow and Lecturer of St John's College, Cambridge, and T. E. RAVEN, B.A., Assistant Master in Sherborne School. With Two Maps. *Price* 3s. 6d.

P. Ovidii Nasonis Fastorum Liber VI. With Notes by A. SIDGWICK, M.A. Tutor of Corpus Christi College, Oxford. *Price* 1s. 6d.

M. T. Ciceronis Oratio pro Archia Poeta. By J. S. REID, M.L., Fellow of Gonville and Caius College, Cambridge. *Price* 1s. 6d.

M. T. Ciceronis pro L. Cornelio Balbo Oratio. By J. S. REID, M.L., Fellow of Gonville and Caius College. *Price* 1s. 6d.

Beda's Ecclesiastical History, Books III., IV., printed from the MS. in the Cambridge University Library. Edited, with a life, Notes, Glossary, Onomasticon, and Index, by J. E. B. MAYOR, M.A., Professor of Latin, and J. R. LUMBY, D.D., Norrisian Professor of Divinity. *Price* 7s. 6d.

M. T. Ciceronis in Q. Caecilium Divinatio et in C. Verrem Actio. With Notes by W. E. HEITLAND, M.A., and H. COWIE, M.A., Fellows of St John's Coll., Cambridge. *Price* 3s.

M. T. Ciceronis in Gaium Verrem Actio Prima. With Notes by H. COWIE, M.A., Fellow of St John's Coll. *Price* 1s. 6d.

M. T. Ciceronis Oratio pro L. Murena, with English Introduction and Notes. By W. E. HEITLAND, M.A., Fellow of St John's College, Cambridge. Second Edition. *Price* 3s.

M. T. Ciceronis Oratio pro Tito Annio Milone, with English Notes, &c., by the Rev. JOHN SMYTH PURTON, B.D., late Tutor of St Catharine's College. *Price* 2s. 6d.

M. T. Ciceronis pro Cn. Plancio oratio by H. A. HOLDEN, LL.D., Head Master of Ipswich School. *Price* 4s. 6d.

M. Annaei Lucani Pharsaliae Liber Primus, with English Introduction and Notes by W. E. HEITLAND, M.A., and C. E. HASKINS, M.A., Fellows of St John's Coll., Cambridge. 1s. 6d.

London: Cambridge Warehouse, 17 Paternoster Row.

PITT PRESS SERIES (*continued*).
III. FRENCH.

Lazare Hoche—Par ÉMILE DE BONNECHOSE. With Three Maps, Introduction and Commentary, by C. COLBECK, M.A., late Fellow of Trinity College, Cambridge; Assistant Master at Harrow School. *Price 2s.*

Histoire du Siècle de Louis XIV. par Voltaire. Chaps. I.—XIII. Edited with Notes Philological and Historical, Biographical and Geographical Indices, etc. by GUSTAVE MASSON, B.A. Univ. Gallic., Assistant Master of Harrow School. and G. W. PROTHERO, M.A., Fellow and Lecturer of King's College, Cambridge, Examiner for the Historical Tripos. *Price 2s. 6d.*

—— Part II. Chaps. XIV.—XXIV. By the same Editors. With Three Maps. *Price 2s. 6d.*

Le Verre D'Eau. A Comedy, by SCRIBE. With a Biographical Memoir, and Grammatical, Literary and Historical Notes, by C. COLBECK, M.A., late Fellow of Trinity College, Cambridge; Assistant Master at Harrow School. *Price 2s.*

M. Daru. par M. C. A. SAINTE-BEUVE (Causeries du Lundi, Vol. IX.). With Biographical Sketch of the Author, and Notes Philological and Historical. By GUSTAVE MASSON, B.A. Univ. Gallic., Assistant Master and Librarian, Harrow School. *Price 2s.*

La Suite du Menteur. A Comedy by P. CORNEILLE. With Notes Philological and Historical by the same. *Price 2s.*

La Jeune Sibérienne. Le Lépreux de la Cité D'Aoste. Tales by COUNT XAVIER DE MAISTRE. With Biographical Notices, Critical Appreciations, and Notes, by the same. *Price 2s.*

Le Directoire. (Considérations sur la Révolution Française. Troisième et quatrième parties.) Par MADAME LA BARONNE DE STAËL-HOLSTEIN. With Notes by the same. *Price 2s.*

Frédégonde et Brunehaut. A Tragedy in Five Acts, by N. LEMERCIER. With Notes by the same. *Price 2s.*

Dix Années d'Exil. Livre II. Chapitres 1—8. Par MADAME LA BARONNE DE STAËL-HOLSTEIN. With Notes Historical and Philological. By the same. *Price 2s.*

Le Vieux Célibataire. A Comedy, by COLLIN D'HARLEVILLE. With Notes, by the same. *Price 2s.*

La Métromanie, A Comedy, by PIRON, with Notes, by the same. *Price 2s.*

Lascaris, ou Les Grecs du XVᴱ Siècle, Nouvelle Historique, par A. F. VILLEMAIN, with a Selection of Poems on Greece, and Notes, by the same. *Price 2s.*

London: Cambridge Warehouse, 17 *Paternoster Row.*

PITT PRESS SERIES (*continued*).
IV. GERMAN.

Zopf und Schwert. Lustspiel in fünf Aufzügen von KARL GUTZKOW. With a Biographical and Historical Introduction, English Notes, and an Index. By H. J. WOLSTENHOLME. B.A. (Lond.), Lecturer in German at Bedford College, London, and Newnham College, Cambridge. *Price* 3s. 6d.

Goethe's Knabenjahre. (1749—1759.) Goethe's Boyhood: being the First Three Books of his Autobiography. Arranged and Annotated by WILLIAM WAGNER, Ph. D., late Professor at the Johanneum, Hamburg. *Price* 2s.

Hauff, Das Wirthshaus im Spessart. By A. SCHLOTTMANN, Ph.D., Assistant Master at Uppingham School. *Price* 3s. 6d.

Der Oberhof. A Tale of Westphalian Life, by KARL IMMERMANN. With a Life of Immermann and English Notes, by WILHELM WAGNER, Ph.D., late Professor at the Johanneum, Hamburg. *Price* 3s.

A Book of German Dactylic Poetry. Arranged and Annotated by WILHELM WAGNER, Ph.D. *Price* 3s.

Der erste Kreuzzug (1095—1099) nach FRIEDRICH VON RAUMER. THE FIRST CRUSADE. Arranged and Annotated by WILHELM WAGNER, Ph. D. *Price* 2s.

A Book of Ballads on German History. Arranged and Annotated by WILHELM WAGNER, PH. D. *Price* 2s.

Der Staat Friedrichs des Grossen. By G. FREYTAG. With Notes. By WILHELM WAGNER, PH. D. *Price* 2s.

Goethe's Hermann and Dorothea. With an Introduction and Notes. By the same Editor. *Price* 3s.

Das Jahr 1813 (THE YEAR 1813), by F. KOHLRAUSCH. With English Notes by the same Editor. *Price* 2s.

V. ENGLISH.

The Two Noble Kinsmen, edited with Introduction and Notes by the Rev. Professor SKEAT, M.A., formerly Fellow of Christ's College, Cambridge. Cloth, extra fcap. 8vo. *Price* 3s. 6d.

Bacon's History of the Reign of King Henry VII. With Notes by the Rev. Professor LUMBY, D.D., Fellow of St Catharine's College. Cambridge. Cloth, extra fcap. 8vo. *Price* 3s.

Sir Thomas More's Utopia. With Notes by the Rev. Professor LUMBY, D.D. *Price* 3s. 6d.

Locke on Education. With Introduction and Notes by the Rev. R. H. QUICK, M.A. *Price* 3s. 6d.

Sir Thomas More's Life of Richard III. With Notes, &c., by Professor LUMBY. [*Nearly ready.*]

Other Volumes are in preparation.

London: Cambridge Warehouse, 17 Paternoster Row.

University of Cambridge.

LOCAL EXAMINATIONS.

Examination Papers, for various years, with the *Regulations for the Examination*. Demy Octavo. 2s. each, or by Post 2s. 2d. (*The Regulations for the Examination in* 1881 *are now ready.*)

Class Lists for Various Years. 6d. each, by Post 7d. After 1877, Boys 1s. Girls 6d.

Annual Reports of the Syndicate, with Supplementary Tables showing the success and failure of the Candidates. 2s. each, by Post 2s. 2d.

HIGHER LOCAL EXAMINATIONS.

Examination Papers for 1880, *to which are added the Regulations for* 1881. Demy Octavo. 2s. each, by Post 2s. 2d.

Reports of the Syndicate. Demy Octavo. 1s., by Post 1s. 1d.

TEACHERS' TRAINING SYNDICATE.

Examination Papers for 1880, *to which are added the Regulations for* 1881. Demy Octavo. 6d., by Post 7d.

CAMBRIDGE UNIVERSITY REPORTER.

Published by Authority.

Containing all the Official Notices of the University, Reports of Discussions in the Schools, and Proceedings of the Cambridge Philosophical, Antiquarian, and Philological Societies. 3d. weekly.

CAMBRIDGE UNIVERSITY EXAMINATION PAPERS.

These Papers are published in occasional numbers every Term, and in volumes for the Academical year.

Vol. VIII. Parts 87 to 104. Papers for the Year 1878—9, 12s. cloth.
Vol. IX. ,, 105 to 119. ,, ,, 1879—80, 12s. cloth.

London:
CAMBRIDGE WAREHOUSE, 17 PATERNOSTER ROW.
Cambridge: DEIGHTON, BELL AND CO.
Leipzig: F. A. BROCKHAUS.

CAMBRIDGE: PRINTED BY C. J. CLAY, M.A. AT THE UNIVERSITY PRESS.

www.ingramcontent.com/pod-product-compliance
Lightning Source LLC
Chambersburg PA
CBHW022115300426
44117CB00007B/722